Macroeconomics in Emerging Markets

This book is a rigorous yet nonmathematical analysis of key macro-economic issues faced by emerging economies. In the book's first part, Peter Montiel develops an analytical framework that can be used as a workhorse model to study short-run macroeconomic issues of stabiliza-tion and adjustment in such economies, comparable to the IS-LM frame-work widely used in intermediate-level macroeconomics textbooks for industrial countries. The remainder of the book consists of three parts – the consideration of fiscal issues, financial sector issues, and issues con-cerning exchange-rate regimes and policies. In the fiscal area, the focus is on the formulation of intertemporal policies, that is, fiscal sustainability, seignorage, and the roles of central bank independence and privatiza-tion of public enterprises in the achievement of fiscal credibility. In his analysis of the financial sector, the author examines its role in promoting welfare and growth, as well as in generating crises. Finally, he explores recent developments in the theory of appropriate exchange-rate regimes and management and provides an overview of recent currency crises in emerging markets.

Peter J. Montiel is Professor of Economics at Williams College, Massachusetts. He formerly served as Senior Policy Advisor at the Inter-national Monetary Fund and as Chief of the Macroeconomics and Growth Division of the Policy Research Department of the World Bank, both in Washington, DC. Professor Montiel's other recent books include *Devel-opment Macroeconomics* (2000), coauthored with Pierre-Richard Agenor, and *Exchange Rate Misalignment* (1999), coedited with Lawrence Hinkle. He has published extensively in leading professional journals such as the *Journal of International Economics*, the *Journal of International Money and Finance*, and the *Journal of Development Economics*. Professor Montiel has also served as a consultant at various times to the IMF, World Bank, Inter-American Development Bank, and the Asian Development Bank.

To my wife Susan

Macroeconomics in Emerging Markets

PETER J. MONTIEL

Williams College, Massachusetts

CAMBRIDGE
UNIVERSITY PRESS

PUBLISHED BY THE PRESS SYNDICATE OF THE UNIVERSITY OF CAMBRIDGE
The Pitt Building, Trumpington Street, Cambridge, United Kingdom

CAMBRIDGE UNIVERSITY PRESS
The Edinburgh Building, Cambridge CB2 2RU, UK
40 West 20th Street, New York, NY 10011-4211, USA
477 Williamstown Road, Port Melbourne, VIC 3207, Australia
Ruiz de Alarcón 13, 28014 Madrid, Spain
Dock House, The Waterfront, Cape Town 8001, South Africa

http://www.cambridge.org

First published 2003

Printed in the United Kingdom at the University Press, Cambridge

Typeface Minion 11/13.5 pt.   *System* LaTeX 2_ε [TB]

A catalog record for this book is available from the British Library.

Library of Congress Cataloging in Publication data
Montiel, Peter.
Macroeconomics in emerging markets / Peter J. Montiel.
p.   cm.
Includes bibliographical references and index.
ISBN 0-521-78060-8 – ISBN 0-521-78551-0 (pb.)
1. Developing countries – Economic conditions.
2. Macroeconomics.   I. Title.
HC59.7 .M5763   2002
339–dc21   2002023391

ISBN 0 521 78060 8 hardback
ISBN 0 521 78551 0 paperback

Contents

Preface

My motivation for writing this book stems from my experiences teaching a Master's level macroeconomics course at the Center for Development Economics at Williams College, as well as from delivering lectures on various topics in macroeconomics to audiences of policymakers from emerging economies in a variety of settings. In both contexts the audiences have often been very bright, very knowledgeable about the problems of their countries, and not very interested in sophisticated mathematics. These experiences convinced me that there is a need for a book on macroeconomic policy in emerging economies that treats the most important issues facing these countries in a way that is conceptually sound but that does not place excessive technical demands on the reader, thus making it accessible to students and policymakers who are less mathematically inclined than the typical graduate student in economics. This book is my attempt to meet that need. It is intended to be accessible to upper-level undergraduates (i.e., undergraduates who have taken a course in intermediate macroeconomics), to students in policy-oriented master's degree programs in economics or in public policy, and to policymakers.

Why a book on macroeconomics in emerging economies instead of a more general macroeconomics text that could be applied to emerging economies? This is an important question, and I think that there are essentially two answers to it. The first is that, in thinking about developing-country macroeconomic issues, it is often necessary to modify the conceptual frameworks that are generally available in macroeconomics texts written with industrial countries in mind. All macroeconomic models are based on stylized descriptions of the environment in which economic agents interact, and this environment often differs in important ways in emerging economies from that in industrial countries. The second reason is probably more important. It is that, precisely because of the "emergent" nature of these economies, the most significant policy issues that economists and policymakers in developing countries face are often quite different from those that typically occupy center stage in industrial-country texts.

While macroeconomists who work on industrial countries do not always concur on the appropriate way to model the economies they study, the models they use have certain important features in common, at least in their textbook forms and in the forms most commonly used for policy analysis. For example, the governments in these models are usually assumed to be solvent, and are thus expected to service their debts on schedule. Indeed, the rate of return on short-term government debt is usually taken to represent the "safe" rate of interest in these models. The financial system is usually described as highly developed, with few if any credit market imperfections present. Domestic financial markets are well integrated among themselves. In this setting, banks are "special" as financial institutions only to the extent that their liabilities serve as means of payment, and bank loans are equivalent to securities traded in open markets. Banks themselves are solvent, and while potentially vulnerable to "runs," they are protected from such events by well-functioning deposit insurance schemes. Not only are financial markets well integrated internally, but they are also well integrated with world capital markets, and financial parity conditions link domestic interest rates with international ones. The exchange rate regime is typically taken to consist of a clean float, in which the exchange rate is fully market-determined. Unfortunately, these conditions do not hold in a typical "emerging economy."

Moreover, even the very focus of macroeconomic analysis is different in the emerging-economy context. Among industrial countries, short-run macroeconomics is typically concerned with business cycle phenomena, a name that connotes a fairly regular and mild rhythm of economic activity. Among emerging economies, by contrast, the concern is instead macroeconomic "instability," as well as "crises." These are of concern not only for their short-run costs, but also for their implications for the pace of economic growth and development that represents the main concern of macroeconomic policymakers in these economies. The words "instability" and "crises" refer to macroeconomic events that are both more irregular and more severe than those that usually concern industrial-country policymakers.

This book, then, has dual aims. The first is to provide students with a relatively simple analytical framework for thinking about macroeconomic issues in emerging economies. The second is to analyze in some detail several specific areas of macroeconomic policy that have recently been – and, I believe, will continue to be – important in these economies.

The content of the book is based on the course I have been teaching at the Williams College Center for Development Economics, and as such, it reflects my particular views regarding key macroeconomic challenges that face developing countries as they become increasingly financially integrated with the world economy. These consist of the management of the public sector's budget, of the domestic financial system, and of the exchange rate. These three areas are mutually interdependent, and the analytical framework developed in the first part of the book is subsequently used to shed light on all of them.

While the central importance of the budget in developing-country macroeconomic performance has come to be widely acknowledged over the past decade or so, it has not yet received pride of place in textbooks. The similarly important roles of the financial system and of exchange rate management, by contrast, have only recently begun to receive increased attention in the wake of the 1994 Mexican and 1997 Asian financial crises. My view is that the major macroeconomic crisis that afflicted many developing countries during the decade of the eighties – the international debt crisis – was at bottom a fiscal phenomenon, while the major emerging-economy crises of the nineties – the Mexican and Asian ones – arose from interactions between inappropriate financial sector and exchange rate policies in a context of increased financial integration. Thus, the analytical portion of the book (the model) focuses heavily on the macroeconomic implications of financial integration, while the more policy-oriented portions focus on the dimensions of policy failure that I feel have been critical for developing countries over the past two decades. I believe that this structure will continue to make the book relevant to students of developing-country macroeconomics for the foreseeable future.

This text is divided into four parts. Part 1 consists of a single overview chapter that examines the links between short-run macroeconomic performance and economic development (defined in a narrow way in terms of the growth of an economy's productive capacity). The analytical framework is presented in Part 2. The four chapters in Part 2 develop a model, essentially at the intermediate macroeconomics level of rigor (i.e., relying primarily on simple behavioral relationships and described with graphs rather than equations), that can serve as an organizing principle for thinking about emerging-economy macroeconomic policy issues. The model differs from the standard versions found in intermediate-level industrial-country textbooks in several ways. First, it describes a small economy that is open to trade in goods and financial assets with the rest of the world. Second, the exchange rate regime is one in which the nominal exchange rate is officially determined, rather than floating. Third, the aggregate supply side of this economy incorporates flexible wages and prices, ruling out Keynesian unemployment disequilibria which, though obviously not unknown in emerging economies, do not tend to be as central in policy debates as they are in the United States and other industrial countries. Fourth, in describing financial links with the rest of the world, the model assumes that domestic and foreign interest-bearing assets are imperfect substitutes and describes short-run financial market equilibrium as a *stock* equilibrium rather than the flow equilibrium that, while long discarded in research, continues to figure prominently in many macroeconomic textbooks. This specification permits the analysis of financial autarky and perfect capital mobility as special cases. Finally, the model incorporates current account dynamics. To do so, it is developed in two stages: the first stage describes a short-run equilibrium conditioned on a given level of the country's net international creditor position, and the second traces the implications of the transition to a medium-term equilibrium in which the country's net international creditor position reaches a sustainable level.

Part 3 is devoted to issues related to the management of the public sector's budget. The central concept is the public sector's intertemporal budget constraint. The key points made in this part of the book are that the requirements of fiscal solvency create trade-offs between spending (and/or tax cuts) today and tomorrow, and that prospective fiscal insolvency can have severe macroeconomic implications, in the form of high inflation or the creation of a "debt overhang" problem, both of which can create crises and retard long-run growth. This portion of the book also analyzes the fiscal requirements for inflation stabilization and considers two ways in which the government can make an announced fiscal adjustment more credible – through granting independence to the central bank and by privatizing public enterprises.

In Part 4, the book turns to the management of the domestic financial system. The links between financial sector performance and growth of productive capacity are taken up first. This is followed by an analysis of financial repression and a discussion of appropriate methods for achieving reform of a previously repressed financial system. The role of capital account convertibility in the process of financial reform is considered separately, since financial openness has become the single most controversial aspect in the process of financial reform. Lastly, this part of the book concludes with a treatment of the macroeconomic problems posed by the capital inflows that have often accompanied capital account liberalization in emerging economies.

The final part of the book, Part 5, considers management of the exchange rate. While this is an old topic, it has received increased attention of late because of the implications for exchange rate management of opening up the capital account of the balance of payments in the process of reforming the financial system. Part 5 opens with a chapter on the meaning and measurement of equilibrium real exchange rates, before turning to issues of nominal exchange rate management. Many observers have recently claimed that with an open capital account, countries will be forced to adopt extreme exchange rate regimes. Accordingly, the next chapter considers the characteristics of extreme exchange rate regimes recently adopted in developing countries, notably currency boards and floating rates. The following chapter considers how to manage an officially determined exchange rate, taking into account specifically interactions with fiscal policy as well as with the condition of the domestic financial sector. These issues are illustrated in Chapter 19, with an analysis of the Mexican and Asian crises. The final chapter expands on these themes by exploring the lessons that can be drawn from these and other emerging-economy financial crises of the 1990s for domestic macroeconomic management in such economies, drawing on material from the preceding portions of the book.

PART 1

Overview

Macroeconomics and Development

Why should someone who is primarily concerned with long-term growth and development in emerging-market economies concern themselves with short-run macroeconomic performance? The answer to this question is that short-run macroeconomic stability has increasingly been recognized as an important determinant of long-term growth performance in such economies. Indeed, over the past two decades a significant consensus has emerged among professional economists and policymakers in developing countries that providing a stable and predictable macroeconomic policy environment and getting key macroeconomic relative prices "right" help to induce the accumulation of physical and human capital as well as the improvements in productivity that are the basic ingredients of long-term economic growth. A wide array of evidence is consistent with this proposition, derived from cross-country experience as well as from case studies of both successful and unsuccessful developing economies. The growing attention paid to macroeconomic issues by development-oriented institutions such as the World Bank is one consequence of this new perception.

What do we mean, however, by macroeconomic stability, and by "key macroeconomic relative prices"? In the emerging-market context, "stability" has come to mean the avoidance of high and variable rates of inflation, as well as of "financial" crises – a term that covers a variety of sins, including the public sector's inability to service its debts, domestic banks' inability to fulfill their obligations to their depositors, and the central bank's inability to sustain the value of the currency. The key macroeconomic relative prices are those that guide the allocation of production and consumption between present and future goods, as well as between domestic and foreign ones. Those relative prices are the real interest rate and real exchange rate, respectively.

The most important policies that influence macroeconomic performance in each of these areas are the management of the public sector's budget and its financing (fiscal and monetary policies), policies directed at the domestic financial sector, and exchange rate management. This book is concerned with the effects that the quality of domestic policies in each of these areas can have on domestic macroeconomic stability and the behavior of key macroeconomic relative prices.

What are the links between fiscal management, financial sector policies, and exchange rate management, on the one hand, and long-run growth, on the other? That is the question we will address in this chapter. By way of motivating the issues that will concern us throughout the rest of the book, in this first chapter we will briefly review the theory and evidence linking macroeconomic stability to long-term growth. We will begin by reviewing the basic factors that underlie long-term economic growth, as summarized in aggregate production functions, before turning to a theoretical consideration of how such factors may be affected by short-run macroeconomic performance. Then we will briefly discuss some recent empirical research that investigates the importance of these links in practice.

I. THE AGGREGATE PRODUCTION FUNCTION

At the heart of the link between short-run macroeconomic performance and long-term economic growth is the concept of the "production function", a technological relationship that summarizes how the feasible level of output of a particular good is influenced by the state of technology and the efficiency of resource allocation, as well as by the amounts used of whatever inputs are relevant for the production of the particular good. Because production functions specify the factors that determine the level of real output that an economy is potentially capable of producing, they help us identify the channels through which short-run macroeconomic performance is capable of influencing the rate of growth of an economy's productive capacity.

a. Complete Specialization and the Aggregate Production Function

The first step in describing how goods are produced in a given economy is to specify how many distinct types of goods we must consider. For simplicity, it is convenient to assume that only one type of good is produced in the domestic economy (economists refer to this as *complete specialization in production*).[1] We will let the symbol Y denote the amount of this good produced during a given period of time. Notice that Y is a *real* quantity, since it is measured in units of goods, not of currency, and that it has the characteristics of a *flow* magnitude – that is, it is measured per unit of time. In the real world, Y would represent a country's *real GDP*. To produce the good, we will suppose that firms in the economy employ the services of labor and capital. The maximum amount of the good that can be produced with a given quantity of

[1] We can think of this single good as a composite, possibly consisting of many individual goods. Our assumption of complete specialization just means that we will not be analyzing changes in relative prices among goods produced domestically.

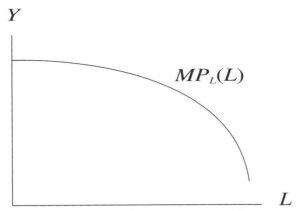

Figure 1.1. The Marginal Product of Labor

labor and capital services is determined by the *aggregate production function*, which we will write in the form:

$$Y = AF(L, K), \qquad (1.1)$$

where A is a parameter that serves as an index of the productivity of the resources employed, L denotes the level of employment, and K is the capital stock, which determines the level of capital services employed in production each period.[2] An increase in A means that the economy becomes more productive, in the sense that more output can be produced with the same amounts of labor and capital services. Because changes in A correspond to changes in the productivity of both factors of production, A is usually referred to as an indicator of *total factor productivity*.

In order to use this production function, we will need to say something about its properties. We will assume that this function has three properties that are typical of *neoclassical* production functions. First, the function will be assumed to be *continuously differentiable*. This just means that each of the factors of production can be varied continuously, and that such variations will produce continuous changes in the level of output. The change in the level of output corresponding to a small increase in one of the factors, holding the other constant, is the *marginal product* of that factor. A second property is that these marginal products are positive and decreasing (the familiar property of diminishing marginal returns) for both labor and capital. This means that we can draw the marginal products of labor and capital as negatively sloped curves in the positive quadrant. For example, the marginal product of labor can be depicted as in Figure 1.1. A similar picture could be drawn for the marginal product of capital. This property turns out to be important in short-run macroeconomic models such as one we will be building in the next chapter. Finally, the function will be assumed to exhibit *constant returns to scale (CRTS)*,

---

[2] An appendix to this chapter contains a very brief review of mathematical functions.

which implies that if both of the factors of production are multiplied by a positive constant (i.e., if they are both changed by the same proportion), the level of output will change by a factor equal to that same constant (e.g., doubling the amounts of capital and labor used in production doubles the amount of output produced).

b. Short Run and Long Run in Macroeconomics

In the next three chapters, we will build a simple macroeconomic model that can be used to study the economy's short-run equilibrium. The macroeconomic "short run" is usually defined as a period of time over which the capital stock and technology are fixed. The basic intuition is that stocks of capital and knowledge tend to change very slowly compared to the pace at which several other important macroeconomic phenomena play themselves out.[3]

Given the capital stock and technology, the level of output that the economy can produce depends on how much labor is employed. Heuristically, "full employment" refers to a situation in which everyone who wants a job can get one. When total employment L is at its full-employment level, say L_P, the resulting level of output is variously referred to as the *potential*, *capacity*, or *full-employment* level of GDP. Thus, potential GDP is given by:

$$Y_P = AF(L_P, K). \tag{1.2}$$

Short-run macroeconomics is typically concerned with stabilization of employment around its full-employment level, the determination of the average price level, and the behavior of various items in the economy's balance of payments. The "long run," by contrast, is a period of time long enough that the capital stock and technology can change. Long-run macroeconomics is primarily concerned with what determines how the level of the economy's productive capacity (potential GDP) changes over time. Increases in economic capacity are what we refer to when we use the phrase "economic growth."

Notice that this means that growth does not just refer to an increase in real GDP, but to an increase in productive "capacity," whether that capacity is used or not. It is useful to clarify the distinction algebraically. Using the aggregate production function, we can approximate the change in (actual) output during any given period

---

[3] To get a sense for this, consider the following example illustrating "typical" annual changes in a country's capital stock. Suppose the ratio of the capital stock to annual output (the capital-output ratio) is 3, and that 7 percent of the capital stock wears out each year. Under these circumstances, gross domestic investment of 21 percent of GDP would be required to keep the capital stock from changing. If an economy invests 30 percent of GDP (a high figure), then the net addition to the capital stock each year would be 9 percent of GDP. But this is only a 3 percent change in the capital stock. In many countries, this would barely be enough to keep up with the expansion of the "effective" labor force (that is, labor force growth augmented by the change in worker productivity), so that the ratio of the capital stock to effective labor would remain unchanged. Thus, achieving large changes in the capital stock relative to the size of the economy would tend to be a slow process.

of time as the sum of contributions made by each of the three arguments in the production function, where the contribution of each is the change in that argument multiplied by its marginal product:

$$\Delta Y = MP_A \Delta A + MP_L \Delta L + MP_K \Delta K.$$

Dividing through by Y:

$$\Delta Y/Y = MP_A(A/Y)\Delta A/A + MP_L(L/Y)\Delta L/L + MP_K(K/Y)\Delta K/K$$
$$= \Delta A/A + MP_L(L/Y)\Delta L/L + MP_K(K/Y)\Delta K/K, \qquad (1.3)$$

since MP_A, the marginal product of A, is just F, and $AF/Y = 1$. Recalling that $\Delta X/X$ is the *rate of growth of X*, this states that the growth of Y depends on the rates of growth of technology (alternatively, of total factor productivity), of the labor force, and of the capital stock.

Recall that under competitive conditions, the services of factors of production are remunerated at a rate equal to their marginal products. Thus, the quantities $MP_L L/Y$ and $MP_K K/Y$ are respectively the shares of the aggregate income generated in the economy that are received by labor and capital. Under constant returns to scale, these shares must sum to unity. To simplify matters further, let's assume that these shares are constant, and let the symbol θ denote the share of labor – that is, $\theta = MP_L(L/Y)$.[4] Then we can write equation (1.3) as:

$$\Delta Y/Y = \Delta A/A + \theta \Delta L/L + (1 - \theta)\Delta K/K. \qquad (1.4)$$

Now, doing the same thing for potential GDP:

$$\Delta Y_P/Y_P = \Delta A/A + \theta \Delta L_P/L_P + (1 - \theta)\Delta K/K. \qquad (1.5)$$

Subtracting the second of these equations from the first and reorganizing:

$$\Delta Y/Y = \theta(\Delta L/L - \Delta L_P/L_P) + \Delta Y_P/Y_P. \qquad (1.5')$$

This equation explains how the economy's actual growth (in the form of year-to-year changes in output) can differ from the growth in its productive capacity. Growth of actual real GDP and growth of productive capacity (given by the last term on the right) are not the same thing. They differ whenever the rate of growth of employment differs from that of the labor force.

II. MACROECONOMIC STABILITY AND LONG-RUN GROWTH: THEORY

The actual rate of growth of employment $\Delta L/L$ cannot permanently exceed or fall short of the average growth rate of the labor force $\Delta L_P/L_P$. A basic tenet of

---

[4] This means that the aggregate production function takes the Cobb-Douglas form $Y = AL^\theta K^{1-\theta}$.

modern macroeconomics is that the economy contains a number of mechanisms that tend to drive it back sooner or later to a position of full employment after a shock that drives L away from L_P. Thus, when averaged over enough time periods, the first term on the right-hand side of equation $(1.5')$ must be approximately zero, and the economy's average growth rate must approximate the rate of growth of its productive capacity. An important question, however, is whether it makes any difference for the growth rate of productive capacity $\Delta Y_P/Y_P$ how stable or unstable actual year-to-year economic performance (that is, $\Delta Y/Y$) tends to be around its long-run average. In other words, how – if at all – does short-run macroeconomic management affect the rate of growth of the economy's productive capacity?

Equation (1.5) indicates that if it does so at all, it must do so through one or more of three potential channels of influence:

a. The rate of growth of total factor productivity $\Delta A/A$.
b. The rate of growth of the labor force $\Delta L_P/L_P$.
c. The rate of growth of the capital stock (net investment) $\Delta K/K$.

Macroeconomists typically assume that the growth of the size of the labor force is affected primarily by longer-term demographic factors, rather than by short-run macroeconomic events. If this is true, we are left with two channels through which short-run macroeconomic events can affect the rate of growth in long-run productive capacity: growth in total factor productivity and investment in the physical capital stock.

a. Macroeconomic Instability, Total Factor Productivity, and Capital Accumulation

Why might these be influenced by short-run macroeconomic performance? The key reason is that in a market economy, resource allocation is guided by intratemporal and intertemporal relative prices. Intratemporal relative prices such as the real exchange rate provide the incentives that guide the allocation of resources between broad sectors of the economy, such as those that produce traded and nontraded goods. If relative prices such as these are not "right" – that is, do not reflect true social scarcities – then resources such as capital will be guided into uses that are not as productive as they might otherwise have been, reducing the rate of growth of total factor productivity in the economy. On the other hand, intertemporal relative prices (the real interest rate) convey information to the economy about the relative value to society of goods that are available at different points in time. They thus provide the incentives to shift resources between the production of present or future goods – that is, to defer consumption and accumulate capital. If an economy that has access to highly productive technologies cannot signal the need to defer consumption through a high real interest rate – meaning it cannot get the real interest rate "right" – the capital accumulation required to implement these technologies will not take place, and the economy's growth rate will be lower than it would otherwise have been.

But getting the key relative prices "right" on average is not enough. It is also important that economic agents be able to respond to these relative prices. The stability of the domestic macroeconomic environment is important in allowing these relative prices to convey their information efficiently.

Macroeconomic instability tends to generate uncertainty, and in particular, uncertainty about whether the relative prices observed in the present will prove to be permanent or transitory. This is important because the reallocation of resources from one type of economic activity to another often involves incurring a fixed cost – such as the costs of acquiring irreversible physical capital (meaning capital that, once invested, cannot be converted to other uses). In the presence of such costs, the relative prices that determine the allocation of resources are "normal" or "permanent" relative prices, not necessarily the relative prices that are observed at any given time. The problem is, of course, that when there is uncertainty about the future, the relevant "permanent" prices cannot be observed directly. Instead, they must be inferred. This situation has important implications both for growth of total factor productivity as well as for the accumulation of productive factors.

Effects on the growth of total factor productivity arise from two sources:

a. The inference problem involved in generating estimates of "permanent" relative prices itself absorbs resources. This has a direct effect on total factor productivity, because the resources absorbed in generating and processing information are not available to be used in the production of goods and services.

b. Moreover, even under the best of circumstances, the expenditure of resources in solving this inference problem will be unable to resolve all uncertainty about future relative prices. In the presence of risk aversion (that is, when economic agents have to be compensated for bearing risk), the remaining uncertainty will cause economic agents to demand a risk premium in order to undertake activities – such as resource reallocations in the presence of fixed costs – that have highly uncertain payoffs. Such risk premia act as the equivalent of a tax on such activities, reducing the efficiency with which resources are allocated and thus the level of total factor productivity.

These considerations, which adversely affect the efficiency of the economy's intratemporal allocation of resources, also discourage the accumulation of productive factors – that is, the *intertemporal* efficiency of resource allocation. The reasons are similar. Uncertainty has negative effects on investment due to the irreversible character of much fixed capital. When capital is irreversible, a potential investor in effect owns a valuable option before he or she makes the commitment to invest, the option being not to undertake the investment. The value of this option is higher when there is uncertainty, because the potential gains from not investing (in the form of losses avoided) are larger the greater the degree of uncertainty in the economic environment. When capital is irreversible, making the decision to invest means surrendering this option, which thus represents an important opportunity cost of investment. By increasing the degree of uncertainty in the environment, short-run macroeconomic instability thus increases the value of the option to wait rather than invest, and thereby discourages the accumulation of physical capital.

b. Symptoms of Macroeconomic Instability

But what precisely do we mean by macroeconomic instability? At a heuristic level the answer is obvious: it refers to a situation in which the future evolution of key macroeconomic variables is difficult to predict. But how might this situation arise? The symptoms of macroeconomic instability can take many forms, but in the context of emerging market economies, certain specific manifestations have been of particular importance over the past two decades:

1. Prospective Fiscal Insolvency
When a country's government is prospectively insolvent, something has to change. Either the government will have to make a fiscal adjustment, which may involve reducing expenditures that benefit some economic activities or raising taxes on others; it may increase its reliance on the inflation tax, thereby triggering high inflation; or it may simply *de jure* or *de facto* repudiate its debt. Debt repudiation, in turn, may generate a variety of macroeconomic dislocations through the actions of the government's creditors. We will discuss this in detail in Chapter 7.

2. High Inflation
As we shall see in Chapter 5, the government can seek to remain solvent by relying on monetary financing of fiscal deficits, which has the effect of increasing the domestic rate of inflation. If the government opts for high inflation to maintain its financial solvency, one form of uncertainty (the nature of the government's response to its prospective insolvency) will be replaced by another – that associated directly with high inflation. High inflation creates uncertainty both because high inflation tends to be unstable inflation, increasing the uncertainty associated with intertemporal relative prices, as well as because different speeds of nominal price adjustment imply that high and unstable inflation is associated with instability in intratemporal relative prices. The consequences of this type of macroeconomic instability for long-term growth are explored in Chapter 6.

3. Financial Sector Fragility
Similarly, weaknesses in the financial sector, in the form of low net worth of banks coupled with poor financial regulation and supervision, affect growth directly by impairing the sector's ability to allocate investment resources efficiently across alternative uses as well as by sending inappropriate signals about intertemporal relative

prices. In addition, however, financial fragility tends to magnify macroeconomic boom-bust cycles, both by generating such cycles as well as by amplifying them when they originate outside the financial sector itself. Extreme swings in economic activity are likely to be associated with greater uncertainty for both intra- and intertemporal relative prices. Moreover, generalized insolvency in the financial sector is likely to be associated with potential fiscal insolvency as well, through the government's backing of the liabilities of the financial system. Financial fragility is the subject of Chapter 12.

4. Exchange Rate Misalignment

Finally, large and persistent real exchange rate misalignment also increases the uncertainty associated with intratemporal as well as intertemporal relative prices. When the real exchange rate is known to be far from its equilibrium value, that equilibrium value becomes unobservable and therefore uncertain. Moreover, when the country's capital account is open, the expectation of a real exchange rate adjustment will affect the level of the country's equilibrium real interest rate through international financial parity conditions, as well as the potential dispersion around the expected real interest rate. We will return to this subject in Chapter 15.

As mentioned before, these are not the only conceivable symptoms of macroeconomic instability, but they seem to have been the most important ones in emerging economies during the past two decades. The major macroeconomic crisis that afflicted many developing countries during the eighties – the international debt crisis – was at bottom a fiscal phenomenon, while the major crises of the nineties – the Mexican and Asian crises – arose from interactions between inappropriate financial sector and exchange rate policies in a context of increased financial integration.

III. MACROECONOMIC STABILITY AND LONG-RUN GROWTH: EVIDENCE

The previous section described some analytical links between short-run macroeconomic performance and the rate of growth of the economy's productive capacity, highlighting the potential role of macroeconomic instability in impairing growth of total factor productivity and the accumulation of productive factors through its effects on uncertainty and the information content of relative prices. It also identified some specific phenomena that can be interpreted as symptoms of this macroeconomic uncertainty. But is there any evidence that such phenomena have indeed been associated with slower growth of productive capacity?

To answer this question we first face a methodological issue: how would we determine empirically whether these theoretical arguments are right? They basically claim that there is a cause-and-effect relationship between macroeconomic uncertainty and growth. This suggests an association between these two variables in the data. How do we find out if this is true?

a. Cross-Country Evidence

Consider, for example, the link between high inflation and the rate of growth of productive capacity. A naïve way to test whether a negative association indeed exists between these two variables is to see whether changes in real GDP and changes in the price level are correlated in some sample, either for a single country over time (a time series) or across countries (a cross-section). Notice, however, that the arguments we discussed above refer to links between long-run (capacity) growth and inflation. Thus, year-to-year correlations may be meaningless as evidence. The first step, therefore, is to make sure we have an appropriate operational definition of the variables.

Inflation can be observed directly, but growth of productive capacity cannot. It must be estimated. One way to get an empirical handle on it is to exploit the observation made above that the *actual* growth rate of GDP in a country during a given year tends to fluctuate around the growth of capacity, either because the production function is subject to random shocks or because random demand shocks cause temporary deviations from capacity output that are gradually eliminated through nominal wage flexibility (this mechanism is discussed more fully in the next chapter). From a statistical perspective, these fluctuations can be taken to be mean-zero serially correlated random shocks. With such a statistical model in mind, we could estimate the growth of productive capacity by taking the average of several years' growth rates during which we believe the statistical model to be valid. In other words, for a given country, the mean of several years' actual growth rates is taken to be a good estimate of capacity growth during those years in that country.

Thus, with an appropriately chosen sample, our best bet is to look at correlations between long-run average growth rates and long-run average inflation rates. This cannot generally be done for a single country, unless we have enough data to generate periods that are long enough for meaningful averages to be calculated. Thus, a natural approach is to look at cross-country experience – to use *cross-section* evidence.

To illustrate some of the methodological issues involved, consider as an example a well-known recent study by Fischer (1993) on the relationship between macroeconomic performance and long-run growth. Fischer describes various ways to examine empirically the links between macroeconomic stability and growth. One way to do it is to look at correlations across regions and for the same region over time between average rates of economic growth and various macro variables that serve as indicators of stability (Table 1 in Fischer 1993). Using Asia, Latin America, and Africa as the regions, and observations averaged for 1960–73, 1973–80, and 1980–88, he finds:

- Negative correlations between growth and inflation, as well as between growth and government budget deficits.

- Positive correlations between growth and the current account balance of the country's balance of payments, as well as between output growth and export growth.

But just how strong is evidence of this type? One problem with such evidence is that these correlations could simply reflect accidental outcomes. By using regions as our basic unit of observation, we do not have enough data to be statistically sure that this is not so – or at least, to form some idea of the likelihood that the outcome is purely accidental. Suppose, for example, that countries' long-run growth experience is unrelated to their inflation rates, contrary to the hypothesis above. In particular assume that, while countries differ with respect to their long-run growth rates, their "normal" inflation rates are all the same, but their actual inflation rate during any sample period is purely random. Then how could we be sure that the association we observe between growth rates and observed inflation rate does not simply reflect a lucky draw for the high-growth countries and an unlucky one for the low-growth countries?

The answer is, of course, that we cannot be sure. However, we can use statistical methods to quantify the extent of our uncertainty about the role of random factors. For example, since the hypothesis concerning the link between growth and macroeconomic stability is about countries in any event, suppose we use countries rather than regions as our unit of observations, and pose the question whether the normal inflation rate for high-growth countries is lower than that for low-growth countries. To address this question, we can classify countries according to their growth experience, and examine the differences between the average inflation rates of the high-growth and low-growth country groups. The more countries are in each group, the more precise the average inflation rate of each group will be as an estimate of the normal inflation rate in that group. The question, then, is what the likelihood would be that any observed difference between the average inflation rates of the two groups could emerge purely as the result of random factors if indeed there were no difference between the normal inflation rates of the two groups. This is precisely the kind of question that can be addressed through statistical "difference of means" tests.

For example, Fischer cites the work of Levine and Renelt (1992), who ranked countries by average growth rates and found statistically significant differences between fast (56 countries with growth above the mean) and slow growers in their sample of 109 countries (1960–89) with regard to the ratio of investment to GDP, the ratio of government consumption to GDP, the rate of inflation, and the black market premium (the percentage difference between the exchange rate in the unregulated foreign exchange market and that in the official market) as indicators of macroeconomic stability.

What can we learn from tests of this sort? These tests tell us whether long-run growth tends to be correlated with several indicators of macroeconomic stability, taken one at a time, in the cross-country evidence. However, the well-known adage that correlation does not establish causation should give us pause about taking such evidence too seriously. To address the question of whether macroeconomic stability fosters long-run growth, we need to investigate whether the variables that we use as indicators of macroeconomic stability have a causal association with growth. A systematic (non-random) negative correlation between growth and inflation could have arisen in any of three ways:

i. Greater instability reduces growth (the hypothesis we are considering).
ii. Some third factor causes high growth and lower instability and/or slow growth and high instability.
iii. Higher growth reduces instability (reverse causation).

We need to eliminate (ii) and (iii) if we are to believe (i). How can we do this?

Conceptually, think of running an experiment. Countries would be assigned randomly to control and treatment groups, and a dose of "instability" would be administered to the treatment group, allowing us to see what happens to growth in those countries as a result. The random assignment would ensure that third factors would be expected to behave similarly between the control and treatment groups, and would simultaneously ensure that the treatment was exogenous (i.e., not influenced by the country's growth performance). Thus, running a controlled experiment would allow us to eliminate the possibility that any correlation we observe in the data arises from the effects of third factors or from reverse causation.

But running such an experiment is obviously impossible. Since we cannot do so, to try to identify the *independent* (partial) correlation between each factor and the growth rate, we have to deal with the factors that complicate inference through statistical rather than experimental methods. The most commonly used tool by economists for this purpose is regression analysis.

b. Cross-Country Growth Regressions

Regression analysis is important in empirical economics because it provides a statistical means of controlling for the effects of "third factors" that may affect a particular economic relationship under study. In the context of this chapter, and in many other places in this book, we will be making reference to a particular application of regression analysis that has become common in the empirical study of growth determinants, usually referred to as "cross-country growth regressions."

These are typically multivariate cross-section regressions. The dependent variable in such regressions generally consists of the average growth rate recorded by individual countries over some extended period of time which, as we have seen, serves as a measure of capacity growth in the country during that time. Explanatory variables are specified to control for determinants of growth other than the one(s) that the investigator happens to be interested in. The variables that are taken to be "standard" growth determinants differ slightly across applications, but they typically include the country's initial level of real per capita GDP, a human capital measure such as the secondary school enrollment rate, the rate of growth of population, and a measure of political stability. Regional dummy variables, usually for Latin America and Sub-Saharan Africa, are often included as well to capture unmeasured region-specific influences on growth. The effects of particular policy variables on the long-run growth rate are then tested by adding the relevant variable to this "core" regression, to see whether the variable exhibits a significant partial correlation with the average growth rate – that is, whether its coefficient in the estimated regression has the theoretically expected sign and is measured with sufficient statistical precision.

If it does, then further investigation can shed light on whether the relevant variable affects the growth rate primarily by inducing greater accumulation of productive resources or by enhancing the efficiency of resource use in the economy. This is tested by adding the investment rate to the growth equation and determining whether the coefficient on the relevant variable retains its sign and statistical significance. If so, then an efficiency effect is detected, since any influences operating through investment are already accounted for by the inclusion of that variable in the regression. If not, and if the variable is statistically significant in an equation similar to the "core" regression but with the investment rate as the dependent variable, then its association with growth is attributed to a resource-accumulation effect.

Fischer adopted this approach as his third cut at investigating the effects of macroeconomic stability on long-term growth. As indicated above, the first step in implementing the method is to identify the full set of potential third factors that could influence the growth rate. Fischer thus began by specifying cross-section regressions of the type:

$$\Delta Y / Y = a_0 + a_1 Y_0 + a_2 (I / Y) + a_3 (\Delta N / N) + \sum a_j X_j.$$

The first four terms on the right-hand side of this equation capture the influence of standard growth determinants. Levine and Renelt (1992), for example, estimated cross-section growth regressions with a sample of 101 countries and data over 1960–89. They found that initial GDP, the level of secondary school enrollment in 1960, and the rate of population growth were all independently related to growth, as was the rate of investment. Fischer built on this by adding other variables, captured in the last term on the right-hand side (the Xs). Using a sample of 73 countries with data averaged from 1970 to 1985, he found that, in addition to the Levine–Renelt variables, high growth was associated with low inflation and high budget surpluses. Other variables, such as the country's level of debt in 1980, while potentially (theoretically) important, were not statistically significant in the regression, though dummy variables for Sub-Saharan African and Latin American countries proved to have negative coefficients that were statistically significant, suggesting that some potential growth determinants had been omitted from the regression.

These results suggest that, if macroeconomic stability in the form of low inflation and responsible budgetary policies has independent effects on growth, these effects must operate at least partly through their influence on total factor productivity, since the regression already controls for the effect of investment on growth. To investigate whether the effects might also operate through influences on investment, Fischer replaced real output growth with the rate of growth of the capital stock as the dependent variable, and found that capital accumulation was negatively linked with inflation and the black market premium, though not with the other macro variables.

c. Evaluating the Evidence

What can we learn from studies such as the one just described?[5] Unfortunately, because they suffer from several methodological problems, probably the best we can hope for is to extract a set of suggestive empirical regularities from the data, and we will use studies of this type in that spirit throughout this book.

The most obvious problem with cross-country growth regressions is that heterogeneity among countries is likely to be very important. Because countries are different, what can emerge from cross-country regressions at best is an average relationship, not particularly applicable to any single country. One implication of heterogeneity, both across countries and over time, is that this empirical methodology suffers from a lack of robustness. That is, the variables of interest may cease to enter the regression with coefficients that bear the theoretically expected sign and are statistically significant when the sample changes, or once other "reasonable" variables are added to the growth regression.[6] Unfortunately, few of the variables typically included in such regressions fail to exhibit this property.

A second problem is one that is endemic in the use of statistical procedures to control for the possible influence of "third" factors in studying a hypothesized relationship between two economic variables. Specifically, note that while Fischer controlled for a variety of such factors that may affect growth, it is hard to ever establish that relevant ones have not been omitted. For example, as mentioned before, the fact that Sub-Saharan African and Latin American countries had systematically lower growth than the others, even after accounting for all of the variables included in the regression, suggests that systematic growth determinants have been omitted.

Third, even if the estimates can be shown to be robust, unless the reverse causation problem (interpretation (iii) above) is explicitly dealt with, all that the parameters may really indicate is the strength of a partial correlation.[7] That is, the finding of a statistically significant coefficient just indicates that there is a reasonably tight

[5] A systematic analysis of the problems associated with the application of cross-country regressions to learn about the effects of policies on growth is given by Levine and Renelt (1992).
[6] See Levine and Renelt (1992).
[7] Notice that Fischer did not attempt to deal with the problem of potential reverse causation.

relationship in the data between the explanatory variable of interest and the portion of the dependent variable not accounted for by other independent variables. It does not necessarily indicate a causal relationship running from the relevant independent to the dependent variable.

Finally, even if one can establish the direction of causation, the explanatory variable typically included to study the effects of policy is often not itself a policy variable, but a performance indicator that is endogenous to policy. Thus, the coefficient cannot be interpreted as revealing the long-run growth effect of a given change in policy.

There are ways to deal with each of these statistical problems, and some of the existing cross-country empirical growth work has implemented them. Heterogeneity, for example, has been tested by including slope and/or shift dummies for regions, and robustness has been investigated through sensitivity analyses, in which different sets of explanatory variables are included in the regression to detect whether the coefficients on the variables of interest are affected by the inclusion or exclusion of other variables in the regression. Statistical techniques are also available to attempt to deal with the problem of reverse causation – for example, by using initial values of explanatory variables, rather than average values during the sample period, or by using special statistical techniques designed for the purpose. Some of these are described in Chapter 5. Finally, alternative proxies for policies have been tried to examine the sensitivity of results to different ways of measuring the explanatory variables of interest.

We will review more of the evidence generated by cross-country growth regressions about the links between macroeconomic policies and long-run growth – keeping in mind these methodological concerns – later in this book. For now, however, we conclude that, while the evidence cannot be regarded as definitive, it is certainly suggestive of a positive relationship between macroeconomic stability and long-term economic growth.

IV. SUMMARY

This chapter has examined the basic proposition underlying this book: that good short-run macroeconomic performance, in the form of appropriate values of key macroeconomic relative prices as well as a predictable domestic macroeconomic environment, is conducive to long-term growth in emerging economies. We have examined the analytical channels through which appropriate relative prices, as well as a stable macroeconomic environment, could foster growth in an economy's total factor productivity as well as factor accumulation, and have reviewed some important and widely cited empirical evidence on the topic. We concluded that theory supports the presence of a link between short-run macroeconomic performance and growth of productive capacity, while the evidence we reviewed in this chapter is at least consistent with the existence of such a link.

Given this link between short-run macroeconomic performance and long-run growth, we next want to address the issue of how short-run macroeconomic performance in emerging economies is influenced by domestic macroeconomic policies. The first step in doing so is to develop an analytical framework linking macroeconomic policies to macroeconomic outcomes. That is the task that we will undertake in the next three chapters.

APPENDIX 1.1: A BRIEF REVIEW OF FUNCTIONS

Before moving to the construction of our model in the next chapter, it is useful to briefly review an analytical tool that will be employed repeatedly in the rest of the book: the concept of *functions*.

a. Functional Notation

A function is simply a relationship between two variables. When we want to say that the variable X affects the variable Y, we can use functional notation to do so by writing:

$$Y = F(X),$$

or Y is a function of X. This just says that Y depends on X in some way. If Y depends on variables other than X as well, say on Z, we can write the function as:

$$Y = F(X, Z, \ldots),$$

where the dots indicate that Y may depend things other than X and Z as well.

We will also be interested in the *way* that X or Z affect Y. That is, if X or Z increase, for example, we will want to know what will happen to Y. Will it increase or decrease? Suppose that an increase in X tends to increase Y, while an increase in Z tends to decrease Y. We can indicate this as follows:

$$Y = F(\underset{+}{X}, \underset{-}{Z}, \ldots),$$

where the symbols indicate the direction of influence running from X and Z respectively to Y.

b. Graphing Functions

Suppose we wanted to illustrate these relationships on a graph. If we want to show the relationship between X and Y holding Z constant, we can simply draw a pair of coordinate axes along which we measure the quantities of Y and X, as in Figure 1.2. If the influence of X on Y is positive, the curve depicting this relationship will have

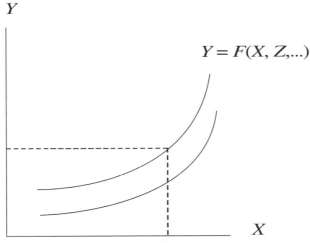

Figure 1.2. Graphing Functions

a positive slope. If the influence is negative, it would have a negative slope, and if there were no relationship, the curve would be a horizontal straight line.

How would we show the relationship between Z and Y? We can't simply plot a negatively sloped curve in the same picture, because Z is not on either axis. One option would be to draw another picture with Y and Z on the axes. But we can do it in the same picture that we used to show the relationship between X and Y by remembering that changing Z to see what happens to Y means holding X constant. Thus, we can show that if Z goes up, the value of Y *associated with a given X* would fall – that is, there would be a new Y, one not on the original curve, but below it. Since this would be true for any arbitrarily chosen X, the effect of increasing Z must be to shift the whole curve downward, as shown in the graph. If the function F also depended on some other variable, say W, which has a *positive* influence on Y, then an increase in W would have been reflected in an *upward* displacement of the curve.

Finally, consider holding Y constant, and asking what the set of combinations of X and Z, or X and W, looks like that are consistent with a given value of Y. Since X and W have positive partial effects on Y, while Z has negative partial effects, it is easy to show that, in X-Z space (that is, in a graph with X and Z on the axes), the set of combinations of X and Z associated with a given value of Y would have a *positive* slope, while in X-W space the set of combinations of X and W associated with a given value of Y would have a *negative* slope. This is because Z must *rise* to offset the effects on Y of an increase in X, while W would have to *fall* to offset the effects on Y of an increase in X.

These tools will prove very useful to us in analyzing macro models in the chapters that follow.

PART 2

A Benchmark Macroeconomic Model for an Emerging Economy

2

Equilibrium in the Domestic Labor and Goods Markets

This chapter and the next will develop an analytical framework (a "model") that can be used to study short-run macroeconomic issues in a "representative" emerging-market economy. This model will differ from standard textbook treatments of short-run industrial-country macroeconomics in a variety of ways. First, the model will feature "real" as well as financial openness to trade with the rest of the world. "Real" openness – openness to the exchange of goods and services with the rest of the world – is an important feature of the vast majority of developing economies, and the effects of financial openness on domestic macroeconomic performance in emerging economies will be one of our main concerns throughout this book. Second, in contrast to what is typically done in the industrial-country context, the model will assume that the economy under study maintains an officially determined exchange rate regime, which again is true of many emerging markets. In this context, we will examine the use of the exchange rate as a policy instrument. Finally, the allocation of emphasis between fiscal and monetary policies will be somewhat different from what is typical in industrial-country applications. Because the key player in the formulation of countercyclical policies in emerging economies tends to be the central bank, rather than the government, the model developed in this part of the book will focus heavily on the effects of monetary instruments of stabilization, including central bank intervention in foreign exchange markets as well as in domestic securities markets.

Our strategy in building the model will be the following: we will begin by examining what determines the supply of domestic goods – in other words, the level of production in the economy. Because in the short run this will depend on the level of employment, we'll begin by studying supply and demand in the labor market. Then we will use the labor market to derive the supply side of the market for domestic goods. From there we will move to the demand side of the goods market, and conclude this chapter with an analysis of the properties of goods market equilibrium. Equilibrium in markets for financial assets will be the subject of Chapter 3, and in Chapter 4 we will put both markets together.

I. AGGREGATE SUPPLY

To describe the supply side of the goods market, we need two components. The first is the *aggregate production function* that was introduced in the previous chapter. Recall that this describes the technology that determines what firms have to do in order to produce goods and services. From the aggregate production function we can determine how much output the economy can produce from given levels of employment of the services of labor and capital. As we have already seen, the answer to this question is given by the function:

$$Y = AF(L, K). \tag{2.1}$$

We are going to be concerned for now only with *short-run* variations in the level of output Y. As we saw in the previous chapter, this means that, since both the stock of capital K and the technology A can be taken as effectively fixed over the time frame that will concern us, the only way that real output Y can change is when the level of employment L changes. Thus, our first task is to examine what determines the equilibrium level of employment in our economy. This means that we must begin the construction of our model by examining the determination of equilibrium in the labor market.

a. The Labor Market

1. The Demand for Labor

How much labor do firms want to hire, given their technology and capital stock? A familiar result from introductory economics is that to maximize profits, firms must choose the level of employment for which the marginal product of labor is equal to the real product wage (i.e., the real value of the wage paid, measured in units of the good or service that the firm produces). Equivalently, they must choose the level of employment that sets the marginal revenue of labor equal to the nominal wage:

$$PMP_L(L^D, \ldots) = W.^{[1]} \tag{2.2}$$

This behavioral equation describes the demand side of the labor market. To see why this is so, notice that for any given W, the solution of this equation for L^D tells us how much labor firms would like to hire. At the price level P_0 in Figure 2.1, for example, firms would like to hire L_0 workers at the wage rate W_0. Similarly, desired employment at any other value of W could be determined by solving equation (2.2) for L^D using that value of W.

What happens to the demand for labor at a given wage when the price of output changes? The answer is given in Figure 2.2. When the price level changes, the labor

---

[1] The ellipsis dots in the function $MP_L(L^D, \ldots)$ remind us that the marginal product of labor depends not just on the level of employment, but also on the capital stock as well as on the level of total factor productivity in the economy.

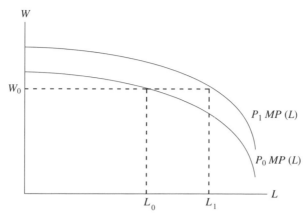

Figure 2.1. The Demand for Labor

demand curve shifts vertically in the same proportion as the change in price. Thus, when P increases by $(P_1 - P_0)/P_0$ percent, the labor demand curve shifts by $(P_1 - P_0)/P_0$ percent. For a given value of W_0 the effect, as shown in the figure, is to increase employment from L_0 to L_1.

2. The Supply of Labor

We will assume in our model that labor is nontraded – that is, domestic workers cannot work abroad and foreign workers cannot work in the domestic economy. In this case, the supply of labor depends only on the behavior of *domestic* households. Based on the standard analysis of the labor-leisure choice made by consumers, the supply of labor is typically taken to be an increasing function of the real wage, measured in terms of the typical worker's consumption basket. The dependence on

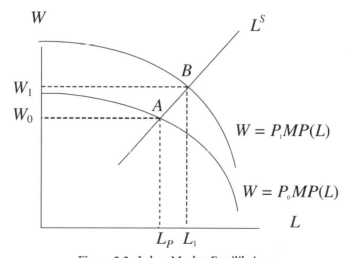

Figure 2.2. Labor Market Equilibrium

the *real*, rather than nominal, wage reflects the assumption that workers care about the purchasing power of their wages.

Notice that firms care about the real wage measured in units of *their own output* (the *product* wage), while workers care about the real wage measured in units of their consumption basket. This asymmetry has an important implication. While firms can continuously observe the price of what they sell, workers cannot necessarily continuously observe the prices of the goods that they consume, since they typically consume a wide variety of things, some of which they buy infrequently. Consequently, at any given moment in time they may not be perfectly informed about all of the prices of goods and services that are relevant to them. This means that workers may have to make their labor supply decisions *before* they know the prices of the goods that they intend to buy with their wages. Under these conditions, the price level relevant for their labor supply decision is the one that they *expect* to prevail during the term of their employment at the agreed wage, which we can denote P^e. Thus, the labor supply function can be written as:

$$L^S = L(W/P^e); \quad L' > 0.$$

This labor supply function can equivalently be expressed in terms of the expected real wage that workers must be offered in order for them to supply a given amount of labor. That is:

$$W/P^e = w(L^S); \quad w' > 0,$$

or as the *nominal* wage that workers must be paid for a given amount of labor:

$$W = P^e w(L^S). \tag{2.3}$$

Graphically, this relationship can be depicted as a curve with a positive slope in W-L space, drawn holding the expected price level constant. You should be able to show that, if the expected price level changes, the curve will shift vertically in the same proportion as the change in the expected price level.

3. Labor Market Equilibrium

Finally, we need to describe what happens when the labor market is out of equilibrium. This is one of the more contentious areas in modern macroeconomics, and has been since the time of Keynes. The assumption we will make in this book is that nominal wages adjust very quickly to clear the labor market. Notice that this is the polar opposite of what we assumed about the speed of adjustment of the capital stock and technology. Changes in these variables were taken to be so slow that over the time frame of the analysis they could essentially be considered to be fixed. In contrast, wages are assumed to change so fast that we cannot see it happening over time. Under these conditions, continuous changes in W would ensure that the equilibrium condition:

$$PMP_L(L, \ldots) = P^e w(L, \ldots) \tag{2.4}$$

holds at every moment. This equation states that the equilibrium level of employment L is that at which the wage that firms are willing to offer (the demand wage, given by 2.2) is equal to the wage that workers require to be paid (given by 2.3). Our labor market model consists of equations (2.2)–(2.4). Given the equilibrium level of employment determined by (2.4), the equilibrium wage can be determined from equation (2.2) or (2.3).

The model is depicted graphically in Figure 2.2. Equilibrium is initially at the point A, where equation (2.4) holds. To see how the model works, suppose that at the point A workers' price level expectations are correct, so $P = P^e$, and that employment is initially equal to L_P. Now consider three exercises:

a. What happens when the price level changes, holding the expected price level constant? As we have already shown, the labor demand curve shifts in the same proportion as the change in the price level, but in this case the labor supply curve is unchanged. The labor market will move to a new equilibrium, say at B in Figure 2.2, and employment will increase. The reason this happens is that the nominal wage increases *less than in proportion to the price level*. Workers believe they will be receiving a higher real wage, so they agree to provide more labor, while firms know they are paying a lower real wage, so they hire more labor.

b. Now suppose instead that workers expect a price level increase, but the actual price level stays unchanged – in other words, that P^e increases with an unchanged value of P. In this, the labor supply curve shifts vertically upward in proportion to the increase in P^e, while the labor demand curve stays where it is. Again, the nominal wage rises, but this time less than in proportion to P^e. Employment falls because workers believe they are receiving a lower real wage, so they supply less labor, while firms know they are paying a higher real wage, so they hire less labor.

c. Finally, suppose that P and P^e both increase by the same amount. In this case, both labor demand and supply curves shift upward by the same amount, and employment remains unchanged.

The labor market equilibrium that prevails in case (c), when workers' price level expectations are correct, is an important one, since it is the only one that does not call for a subsequent revision in expectations, and thus the only one that would tend to be sustained. Its sustainability makes it natural to refer to the level of employment that prevails under these circumstances as the *full employment* level of employment, which we previously denoted L_P. Note that this full employment level of employment depends on the positions of the labor demand and supply curves when $P = P^e$. Thus, we can write it as:

$$L_P = L_P(A, K, \ldots),$$

where the ellipsis dots leave room for other factors that may affect full-employment labor supply. Finally, the *actual* level of employment differs from L_P only when workers' price level expectations are incorrect, so we can write:

$$L = L(P/P^e)L_P, \qquad (2.5)$$
$$+$$

with $L(1) = 1$. That is, if $P = P^e$, then $L = L_P$.

b. Output of Domestic Goods

It is now easy to see what determines the level of output in this economy. Substituting the level of employment given by (2.5) into the aggregate production function (2.1), we have:

$$Y = AF[L(P/P^e)L_P, K]. \qquad (2.6)$$

This relationship is the economy's *aggregate supply function*. Notice that, since L is an increasing function of P/P^e, Y will be so as well. This means that *aggregate supply is an increasing function of the domestic price level*. It is easy to see that the elasticity of aggregate supply with respect to P must be directly related to the elasticity of labor supply with respect to the nominal wage: the flatter is the labor supply curve, the flatter the aggregate supply curve (drawn with P on the vertical and Y on the horizontal axis) be. Finally, it is also easy to see from (2.6) that equal changes in P and P^e must leave aggregate supply unchanged. When $P = P^e$, the economy's output is given by:

$$Y_P = AF[L_P, K], \qquad (2.6')$$

which is independent of the value of P.

The economy's aggregate supply relationship can be graphed as in Figure 2.3. The curve AS is drawn for a given value of the expected price level, say P^e_0. It has a positive slope, because an increase in P for a given value of P^e causes the labor demand curve to shift up along an unchanged labor supply curve, thus increasing the level of employment and output, as we have already seen. This means that the AS curve will be flatter the flatter the labor supply curve. Notice also that, since equations (2.6) and (2.6') indicate that when $P = P^e$, we must have $Y = Y_P$, the AS curve must pass through the point (P^e, Y_P). The implication is that the *height* of the AS curve above the point Y_P is given by the level of expected prices P^e. Thus, when P^e changes, the AS curve will shift vertically by the same amount. For example, when P^e increases from P^e_0 to P^e_1 in Figure 2.3, the AS curve must shift upward from AS to AS', passing through the point B.

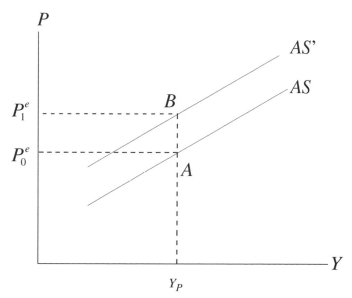

Figure 2.3. The Aggregate Supply Curve

II. AGGREGATE DEMAND

Now that we have seen what determines the supply of goods produced in the domestic economy, we can examine what determines the total demand for those goods. Recall that we have assumed that the goods market is open to trade with the rest of the world, and that the domestic economy is completely specialized in the production of a single good. We will assume that the domestically produced good is an *imperfect substitute* for the single (possibly composite) good produced by the rest of the world. A production structure in which the domestic economy is completely specialized in the production of a single good which is an imperfect substitute for the rest of the world's output is the defining characteristic of the *Mundell-Fleming* model. We will begin describing aggregate demand for the domestic good by examining what determines aggregate expenditure by domestic residents.

a. Aggregate Expenditure

The good produced in this economy is purchased by domestic households, firms, and government, as well as by foreigners. Aggregate expenditure by domestic agents (sometimes called "absorption") is thus given by:

$$A = C + I + G,$$

where C denotes total consumption spending by domestic households, I is desired investment spending by domestic firms, and G is total spending on goods and services by all levels of domestic government. All of these quantities are measured in *real* units – that is, in units of the domestic good. To simplify things, we will draw a basic distinction between *private* absorption $C + I$, which we will denote A_P, and *public* absorption G. We will assume that spending by the government on current goods and services is an exogenously determined policy variable. On the other hand, private absorption is given by:

$$A_P = A_P \underset{+\ -\ -}{(Y,\ T,\ i)}.$$

That is, private absorption is an increasing function of income, but a decreasing function of taxes paid to the government by the private sector (T), as well as of the domestic interest rate i.[2] Finally, we will make the traditional assumption that the private sector's marginal "propensity" to spend out of current income is less than unity, so a one-unit increase in Y increases private absorption by less than one unit. With these assumptions, aggregate expenditure becomes:

$$A = A_P \underset{+\ -\ -}{(Y,\ T,\ i)} + G.$$

b. Aggregate Demand for Domestic Goods

Aggregate demand for domestic goods differs from aggregate expenditure by domestic agents both because not all spending by domestic agents is on domestic goods (some is on foreign goods, in the form of imports) as well as because foreigners also buy domestic goods (in the form of exports). Taking these two facts into account, we can write the aggregate demand for domestic goods as:

$$AD = (A_P + G - eZ) + X, \tag{2.7}$$
$$= A_P + G + (X - eZ),$$

where X denotes foreign demand for exports from the domestic economy, measured in units of the domestic good, and Z is the domestic demand for foreign goods, measured in units of the *foreign* good. Because Z is measured in units of the foreign good, we need to convert it into the equivalent number of domestic goods in order to compare it with the other magnitudes in equation (2.7). We make this conversion by multiplying Z by the relative price of foreign goods in terms of domestic goods, called the "real exchange rate" and denoted e. The first term on the right-hand side of the first line in (2.7) is the domestic demand for domestic goods (total domestic spending minus the portion devoted to the purchase of foreign goods), while the second term captures the foreign demand for domestic goods. This is rewritten in the second line as the sum of domestic expenditure and net exports, equal to exports minus imports.

---

[2] The level of tax revenues will be taken to be an exogenous policy variable, while the determination of the domestic interest rate will occupy us for all of the next chapter.

What determines the real exchange rate e? As the relative price of two goods, the real exchange rate is just the ratio of the nominal prices of the two goods, expressed in the same currency. Recall that the price of a domestic good in terms of domestic currency is P, and suppose that the price of the foreign good in terms of foreign currency is P^*. Let s denote the *nominal* exchange rate (the units of domestic currency that must be given up per unit of the foreign currency). Then e must be given by:

$$e = sP^*/P. \tag{2.8}$$

Assuming that the domestic economy is small, the domestic economy cannot influence foreign variables such as P^*. Thus, P^* will be taken to be exogenous in our model. The determination of s, on the other hand, depends on the country's *foreign exchange regime* (the rules that govern the central bank's behavior in the foreign exchange market). We will be assuming that s is *officially determined*. This means that the central bank determines its value by announcing its willingness to exchange the domestic currency for foreign exchange in unlimited amounts at the announced price s. In textbook parlance, this is referred to as a "fixed exchange rate." For our purposes, the importance of the assumption is that it makes s an exogenous policy variable. With s and P^* exogenous, the conclusion is that e is determined by P, with P and e being inversely related.

c. Net Exports

Since we have already explained the determinants of aggregate expenditure, all we have left to do to complete the explanation of the determination of aggregate demand is to discuss what drives net exports $X - eZ$. Exports from the domestic economy reflect foreigners' demand for domestic goods, while imports by domestic residents reflect their demand for foreign goods. We will assume that the domestic government only buys domestically produced goods, while the share of the domestic private sector's aggregate expenditure devoted to demand for domestic goods depends positively on the relative price of foreign goods (the price of foreign goods in terms of domestic goods, or the real exchange rate). Thus, demand for domestic goods by the domestic private sector is given by $\phi(e)A_P$, where ϕ is an increasing function of e.[3] This means that spending on imports is given by:

$$eZ = (1 - \phi(e))A_P. \tag{2.9}$$
$$\underset{+}{}$$

---

[3] Notice that, since this means that total spending on imports must be a *decreasing* function of the real exchange rate, the demand for imports must implicitly be assumed to be elastic with respect to the real exchange rate. This is a stronger assumption than the more familiar Marshall-Lerner condition, which only requires the sum of export and import demand elasticities to exceed unity.

On the other hand, we will suppose that exports respond positively to the real exchange rate. The reason is, of course, that an increase in the real exchange rate represents an *increase* in the relative price of foreign goods (thus reducing domestic demand for such goods in the form of imports), but a *decrease* in the relative price of domestic goods (thus increasing foreign demand for them in the form of exports). We will also suppose that exports depend as well as on a "shift" parameter θ, which is just a catch-all variable that can represent a host of other exogenous influences on the domestic economy's exports, such as partner-country incomes, terms-of-trade changes, weather effects, etc. Thus, exports are given by:

$$X = X(e, \theta). \tag{2.10}$$
$${+\ \ +}$$

Since θ is a catch-all variable, its positive influence on X is arbitrarily assumed for convenience. When we are interested in the effects of shocks to export revenues, we will have to specify how these translate into changes in θ.

Using equations (2.9) and (2.10), we can write net exports as:

$$X - eZ = X(e, \theta) - (1 - \phi(e))A_P. \tag{2.11}$$

The assumptions made so far imply that net exports are an increasing function of the real exchange rate.

d. The Aggregate Demand Curve

Substituting (2.11) into (2.7) we now have our final expression for aggregate demand for domestic goods:

$$AD = \phi(sP^*/P)A_P(Y, T, i) + G + X(sP^*/P, \theta). \tag{2.12}$$

Since aggregate demand is measured in units of the domestic good, we can plot it in P-Y space, as we did the aggregate supply curve. The aggregate demand curve is shown in Figure 2.4. The curve has a negative slope, because a decrease in the domestic price level will cause the real exchange rate to depreciate, which will cause both domestic and foreign residents to switch away from buying foreign goods and into buying domestic goods, thus increasing the aggregate demand for domestic goods. The stronger this expenditure-switching effect, the greater the effect of price changes on aggregate demand, and the flatter the AD curve.

The position of the AD curve depends on all of the factors that influence the demand for domestic goods other than the domestic price level. Changes in any of these factors will cause the curve to shift. For example, an increase in government spending, a reduction in taxes, or an exogenous increase in exports (through an increase in θ) would all increase the demand for domestic goods at any given value of the domestic price level, from a point such as A at the price level P_0 in Figure 2.5

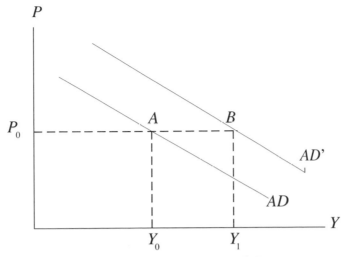

Figure 2.4. The Aggregate Demand Curve

to a point such as *B*. Consequently, each of these shocks would cause the *AD* curve to shift to the right, to a position such as *AD'* in Figure 2.4.

An increase in the domestic-currency price of the foreign good sP^*, brought about by changes in S or in P^*, would have a similar effect, because the resulting depreciation of the real exchange rate at any given initial value of the domestic price level would stimulate demand for the domestic good. In this case, however, it is useful to consider the magnitude of the *vertical* shift in *AD*. To do so, suppose that at some initial level of domestic real output Y_0, the real exchange rate $sP^*/P = e_0$ satisfies equation (2.12). Then, if there is a change in sP^*, say to $(sP^*)'$, the new price level $P' = (sP^*)'/e_0$ must continue to satisfy (2.12) at the level of output

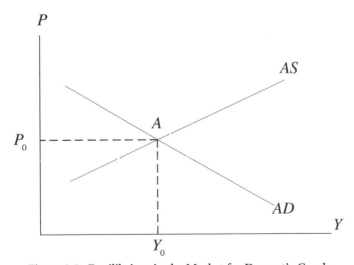

Figure 2.5. Equilibrium in the Market for Domestic Goods

Y_0, because it would produce the same real exchange rate that prevailed before the change in sP^*. That means that the price level that satisfies (2.12) at $Y = Y_0$ must increase *in proportion* to the increase in sP^* – that is, the AD curve must shift upward in proportion to the increase in sP^*. We will make use of this result later on.

III. EQUILIBRIUM IN THE MARKET FOR DOMESTIC GOODS

We can now put together the aggregate supply story from Section I and the aggregate demand story of Section II. Setting supply equal to demand ($Y = AD$), and using the supply relationship (2.6) together with the demand relationship (2.12), yields the goods-market equilibrium condition:

$$Y(P/P^e, \ldots) = \phi(sP^*/P)A_P[Y(P/P^e, \ldots), T, i] + G + X(sP^*/P, \theta). \quad (2.13)$$
$$ + + + - - + +$$

Equilibrium in the market for domestic goods can also be depicted graphically, as in Figure 2.5. Putting together the aggregate supply and demand curves, the market will be in equilibrium at the combination of P and Y that lies on both curves – that is, at the point of intersection of AS and AD. In this section we will explore the properties of equilibrium in the goods market. This could be done directly from equation (2.13), but instead we will proceed graphically using Figure 2.5.

A good place to start is to identify the economic variables that affect the equilibrium in the goods market. On the demand side of the market, as we have seen, G and T are exogenous fiscal policy variables, while under our assumption that the central bank maintains an officially determined exchange rate s is also a policy variable, determined by the bank. P^* and θ are also exogenous, the former being a characteristic of the international economy not subject to influence by the small domestic economy, and the latter being exogenous by construction, as a variable intended to capture exogenous influences operating on the country's exports. The expectations-driven variable P^e plays an important role in goods-market equilibrium, as we will see in the next section. When shocks to the economy are unanticipated by workers, however, they have no reason to alter their expectations about the price level, and P^e is not affected by shocks, meaning that we can treat it as constant.

This leaves the domestic interest rate i. The domestic interest rate will be an endogenous variable in our model, but for now we can treat it "as if" it were an exogenous variable. That is, we can hold it constant when we change some of the exogenous variables in the model, and we can consider the effects of changes in i on the equilibrium in the goods market. We will come back to the endogeneity of i in the last section of this chapter.

Consider, then, the effects on the goods market of an unanticipated shock to the economy that has the effect of shifting the aggregate demand curve to the right. This

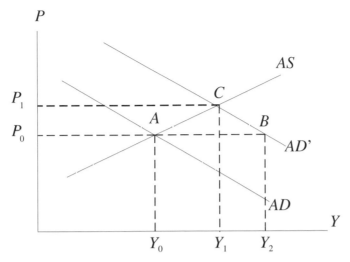

Figure 2.6. An Unanticipated Shock to Aggregate Demand

could take the form of a change in the government's budget (an increase in spending or reduction in taxes), an increase in the domestic-currency price of foreign goods (perhaps as the result of a devaluation of the currency), a favorable shock to the demand for exports, or a reduction in the domestic interest rate. The implications of such a shock for the goods market are shown in Figure 2.6. Since the aggregate demand shock increases the demand for domestic goods at any given value of the domestic price level, it causes the *AD* curve to shift to the right, to a position such as *AD'*. At the original value of the domestic price level, this would result in an excess demand for domestic goods (in the amount $Y_2 - Y_0$), so the domestic price level rises. The higher price level induces additional output, since the labor demand curve shifts upward and nominal wages rise. Workers interpret this as an increase in the real wage, though the real wage has actually fallen, since the increase in the nominal wage is less than proportional to the increase in the domestic price level. Thus, employment and output expand as prices rise, and the economy moves to the northeast along the aggregate supply curve. At the same time, the higher price of domestic goods causes both domestic and foreign residents to switch into foreign goods, so the aggregate demand for domestic goods contracts, and the economy moves to the northwest along *AD'*. The supply expansion and demand contraction continue until the equilibrium between supply and demand is restored at the point *B*. This point is associated with the following macroeconomic outcomes:

a. As we have seen, it results in a higher level of domestic prices, output, and employment, as well as a *lower* real wage.
b. Because domestic prices are higher, if the shock takes any form other than an increase in the domestic-currency price of foreign goods (sP^*), the real exchange rate will have appreciated. However, if the shift in *AD* is the result of an increase

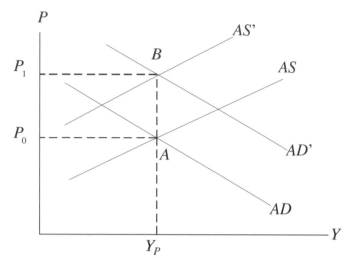

Figure 2.7. Anticipated Aggregate Demand Shocks

in sP^*, the end result is a *depreciation* of the real exchange rate. The reason is that, as we saw in the last section, when sP^* increases, AD shifts vertically by an amount that is proportional to that increase. But, as can be seen from Figure 2.7, the increase in the domestic price level from P_0 to P_1 is smaller than the vertical shift in AD. Since P rises less than in proportion to the increase in sP^*, $e = sP^*/P$ must increase.

c. Unless the shock takes the form of an increase in sP^* or an increase in θ, net exports must fall. The reason is that the real exchange rate has appreciated and domestic income has increased, both of which contribute to a reduction in net exports. However, if the shock consists of increases in either sP^* or θ, then net exports must increase. The reason is that in both of these cases the expansionary impulse to aggregate demand is transmitted precisely through an increase in net exports, and an increase in net exports is required to sustain the higher level of domestic real output.

All of these results would, of course, be reversed in the event of an unanticipated *contractionary* aggregate demand shock.

IV. ANTICIPATED SHOCKS

When shocks to the economy come as a complete surprise to workers, there is no reason for the arrival of such shocks to have any effect on the price level that workers had expected to prevail when they formulated their labor supply decisions. However, when newly arrived shocks had previously been anticipated by workers, we have to consider how that anticipation would have affected the price level expectations built into the labor supply function. In other words, the case of anticipated shocks forces us to confront the question of how workers formulate their price level expectations.

We will assume that the expectations formation mechanism they use is one that economists refer to as "rational expectations." This means that when workers attempt to determine how an anticipated shock will affect the aggregate price level, *they actually use the same model that we are using to analyze the behavior of the economy.* Under these circumstances, workers' price level expectations must be *model-consistent:* the price level that they expect to prevail must be the equilibrium price level predicted by the model, so that $P^e = P$. An implication of this assumption about expectations formation is that P^e becomes an endogenous variable. We will see in this section how this affects equilibrium in the goods market.

Note first that when shocks are anticipated, we will have $P^e = P$. Thus, our goods market model will contain this condition as well as the aggregate supply and demand equations (2.6 and 2.12). This means that for anticipated shocks we can simply replace P^e by P in equation (2.13). In that case (2.13) becomes:

$$Y_P = \phi(s\,P^*/P)A_P[Y_P,\ T,\ i] + G + X(s\,P^*/P, \theta). \qquad (2.13')$$
$$++\ \ -\ -+\ \ +$$

It is easy to see from (2.13′) that in the case of anticipated shocks, real output will not deviate from its full-employment (capacity) level and that, since the effectiveness of changes in the domestic price level in eliminating excess in the goods market is weakened by the inability of such changes to call forth supply responses, price changes will in general have to be larger to maintain equilibrium in the goods market.

These results can be confirmed graphically. Figure 2.7 illustrates the goods-market effects of expansionary aggregate demand shocks the arrival of which had previously been anticipated. In Figure 2.7, the rightward shift in *AD* is exactly as before, except that in this case workers are presumed to have anticipated the shock. Because their price level expectations now adjust to the shock and because, as we saw in Section II, the position of the *AS* curve depends on P^e, the position of the *AS* curve will also change in response to the shock. In what direction and by how much will the *AS* curve shift? Recalling that the height of the *AS* curve above Y_P must be equal to the expected price level P^e, it is easy to see that workers' expectations can be consistent with the model's prediction for the price level (i.e., $P = P^e$) only if *AS* shifts upward so as to intersect the new *AD* curve directly above the level of full-capacity output Y_P, at a point such as *B*.

This has several macroeconomic implications:

a. In contrast to what happens when expansionary shocks are *not* anticipated, anticipated expansionary shocks result in a higher level of domestic prices, with unchanged levels of real output, employment, and the real wage.
b. Just as before, because domestic prices are higher, if the shock takes any form other than an increase in the domestic-currency price of foreign goods (sP^*),

the real exchange rate must appreciate. However, the appreciation in the real exchange rate must be larger in this case than in the previous one, because in the absence of a domestic supply response, real exchange rate adjustments bear the full brunt of maintaining equilibrium in the goods market. If the shift in AD is the result of an increase in sP^*, on the other hand, the end result is an *unchanged* value of the real exchange rate. The reason is that, since AD shifts vertically by an amount that is proportional to the increase in sP^* and since AS shifts up by exactly the same amount, the proportional change in the domestic price level must be the same as that in sP^*, leaving the real exchange rate unchanged.

c. As in the case of unanticipated shocks, unless the shock takes the form of an increase in sP^* or an increase in θ, net exports must fall. The reason is that real exchange rate appreciation provides the mechanism for maintaining equilibrium in the market, and this means that a shock-induced expansion in other components of aggregate demand must be exactly offset by a deterioration in net exports, given an unchanged supply of domestic goods. On the other hand, if the shock consists of increases in either sP^* or θ, then net exports must remain unchanged. In the case of increases in sP^*, this is because the shock leaves all of the determinants of both exports and imports unchanged. In the case of an increase in θ, exports must rise, but the appreciation of the real exchange rate moderates the expansion in exports and offsets their effects on *net* exports by inducing an expansion of imports.

V. THE *GM* CURVE

The preceding analysis provisionally treated the domestic interest rate as just another exogenous variable. But as previously indicated, this variable will actually be endogenous in our model. It is now time to consider the implications of the endogeneity of the domestic interest rate.

The endogeneity of the domestic interest rate means that we are not in fact free to vary it independently, or to hold it constant when exogenous variables change, as we have been doing up to now. The reason for the latter is that when equilibrium conditions such as (2.13) or (2.13′) are subjected to a shock, in principle the adjustment to the shock in the market could come about through changes in P or i. Without knowing how the adjustment is to be allocated between these two variables we cannot pin down the value of either of them. What we have been doing up until now is to ask how P would respond to shocks *if* it were to bear the full brunt of adjustment, but we have no reason to believe that this would actually be so.

Our dilemma can be illustrated graphically. While we may not know the individual values of i and P determined by goods-market equilibrium conditions such as (2.13) and (2.13′), we can investigate the set of all possible *combinations* of i and P that are consistent with equilibrium in the goods market, for given configurations of the exogenous variables. To identify such combinations, we can ask what values of P would be required to maintain equilibrium in the goods market for different values of i.

Based on the analysis of the last two sections in which we considered the effects of expansionary shocks on the goods market, it is easy to see that to maintain the goods market in equilibrium for given values of all of the exogenous variables, the lower the domestic interest rate is, the higher the domestic price level must be. This is true whether we assume that the values taken on by at least some of the exogenous variables may have been unanticipated by workers, as in Section III, or whether we assume that workers could accurately predict the current state of the economy, as in Section IV. It is useful to review the economics involved in the specific case of a lowering of the domestic interest rate.

Consider first the case of an unanticipated interest rate movement. A reduction in the domestic interest rate tends to increase private absorption A_P, and thus gives rise to an excess demand for domestic goods at the initial value of the domestic price level P. To maintain equilibrium in the domestic goods market, P therefore has to adjust. The adjustment in P must be such as to increase the net supply of domestic goods so as to meet the additional demand caused by the lower domestic interest rate. This requires an *increase* in P, which restores equilibrium through two separate mechanisms: first, when the reduction in i is unanticipated, an increase in P relative to P^e increases the supply of domestic goods. Though this stimulates additional absorption of domestic goods, under our assumption that the marginal propensity to spend is less than unity there is a net increase in the supply of domestic goods. Second, an increase in P reduces the demand for domestic goods. It does so by causing the real exchange rate to appreciate (i.e., by decreasing $e = s P^*/P$), which causes both domestic and foreign residents to switch demand from domestic to foreign goods. These two effects together create the additional supply of domestic goods required to sustain equilibrium in the market in response to a decrease in the domestic interest rate.

This equilibrium relationship between the two endogenous variables i and P is illustrated in the form of the curve GM (for "goods market") in Figure 2.8. The GM curve depicts the set of all combinations of i and P that are consistent with equilibrium in the domestic goods market. This curve has a negative slope to reflect the fact that reductions in the domestic interest rate must be accompanied by increases in the domestic price level for goods-market equilibrium to be sustained. The properties of the GM curve are as follows:

a. Its slope depends on the sensitivity of private absorption to the domestic interest rate, as well as on the effectiveness of changes in domestic price level in restoring market equilibrium after that equilibrium is disturbed. Price level adjustments will be more effective the more sensitive aggregate supply is to changes in P, the smaller the private sector's marginal propensity to spend, and the greater the

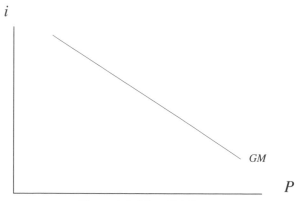

Figure 2.8. The *GM* Curve

elasticity of demand for domestic goods by both domestic and foreign residents with respect to changes in the real exchange rate. The weaker the effect of the domestic interest rate on private absorption, and the more effective are domestic price level adjustments in equilibrating the market, the steeper the *GM* curve will be.

b. The position of the curve depends on the stance of fiscal policy, given by G and T, on variables determining the level of external demand for domestic goods (proxied by the parameter θ), and on the domestic-currency price of foreign goods sP^*. As we saw in the two previous sections, increases in G or θ, and/or reductions in T, create an excess demand for domestic goods and, given the domestic interest rate, require an increase in the price of domestic goods to maintain equilibrium in the goods market. Since this means that the equilibrium value of P is higher for a given value of i, the *GM* curve must shift to the right. An increase in the domestic-currency price of the foreign good, such as would be brought about by a devaluation of the nominal exchange rate, must have the same effect, because it also increases the demand for domestic goods.

The derivation of the *GM* curve can be repeated for the case in which workers correctly anticipate movements in the interest rate. In comparison with the previous case, it is easy to see that the slope of the *GM* curve would be *flatter*, and changes in its position in response to changes in exogenous variables would be *larger*, than when price level changes are unanticipated. The reason is essentially that under these circumstances changes in the price level become less effective in restoring market equilibrium than in the previous case, because anticipated price level changes cannot affect the level of domestic real output. This means that price level adjustments can affect the goods-market equilibrium only through their effects on the composition of domestic and foreign demand. Because the price level has weaker effects on the market, larger price level adjustments are required to restore market equilibrium in response to shocks.

In the case of a change in the domestic-currency price of the foreign good, we can be more specific about the magnitude of the shift in the *GM* curve. We saw in the previous section that a correctly anticipated increase in sP^* would shift both *AS* and *AD* upward in the same proportion, leaving the economy's real equilibrium unchanged. Translated into the *i-P* space of Figure 2.8, this means that an anticipated change in sP^* must shift the *GM* curve to the right in the same proportion as the change in sP^*.

VI. SUMMARY

In this chapter, we have constructed the "real" (goods-market) side of our model. We adopted a Mundell-Fleming production structure and derived an aggregate supply mechanism that related the determination of the level of domestic output to price level misperceptions among workers.

For the demand side of the model we adopted standard textbook descriptions of the determinants of the various components of aggregate demand for domestic goods, and putting supply and demand together we derived a goods-market equilibrium condition that could be summarized in the form of the *GM* curve – a curve drawn in a diagram with coordinate axes measuring the domestic interest rate and price level. Because any combination of interest rate and price level on this curve is consistent with equilibrium in the market for domestic goods, this curve illustrates our inability to determine the equilibrium value of the domestic price level without knowing the value of the domestic interest rate.

How do we pin down the domestic interest rate? The answer is that we have to look at the requirements for equilibrium in the economy's financial markets. That is the subject of the next chapter.

3

Equilibrium in Financial Markets

Our next task is to explain what determines the domestic interest rate. We will address that issue in this chapter by examining equilibrium in domestic financial markets. We will see that the domestic interest rate is influenced by a variety of exogenous factors, as well as by the domestic price level. In the next chapter we will put together the labor market, goods market, and financial markets to show how the domestic price level and interest rate are simultaneously determined.

So far, we have not identified the financial asset with which the domestic interest rate is associated. We will assume that there are a total of three financial assets in our model: domestic money, domestic bonds, and foreign bonds. Money (the quantity of which in existence at any moment will be denominated M) will be taken to consist of currency issued by the central bank, since we assume that there are no commercial banks in this economy (and therefore no demand deposits, or checking accounts, which are usually part of the definition of money). Domestic bonds are debts issued by the domestic government, denominated in domestic currency. They are one-period bonds – that is, they have a one-period maturity and pay the variable interest rate i. Foreign bonds are similarly one-period bonds, but are denominated in foreign currency. Both types of bonds trade in well-organized secondary markets, and except when explicitly stated, we will suppose that domestic residents can hold foreign bonds, and foreign residents can hold domestic bonds. It should be acknowledged at the outset that this set of assumptions about the domestic financial structure does not represent very accurately the situation that prevails in many emerging markets, where banks play important roles as financial intermediaries and secondary markets for securities are often limited in scope. The justification for proceeding without banks, as we will do in this chapter, is that it simplifies the analysis of the short-run macroeconomic role of financial markets. We will return to all of these issues in Part 4 of the book.

In this chapter we will focus on two key characteristics of the financial side of the economy that play a large role in determining its short-run macroeconomic

42

behavior: the links between domestic and foreign financial markets, and the type of monetary policy regime implemented by the central bank. As we will see throughout the rest of this book, these are vitally important factors that influence many of the key policy issues that have confronted emerging economies in recent years. This focus will lead us to consider as the standard case that of imperfect substitutability between domestic and foreign financial assets, rather than the more extreme cases of financial autarky or perfect capital mobility. This framework has two advantages for our purposes: first, the degree of substitutability between domestic and foreign financial assets can be treated as a measure of the strength of links between domestic and foreign financial markets, and second, the central bank retains the option under fixed exchange rates of targeting the domestic money supply or the domestic interest rate. This imperfect-substitutes approach represents a departure from the standard industrial-country textbook models of asset markets for open economies, and it introduces some complexities into the analysis.

I. BALANCE SHEETS AND ASSET DEMANDS

To describe the financial structure of our model and explore how the interest rate on domestic bonds (which we'll continue to refer to as the domestic interest rate) is determined, we need to say something about who holds each of the assets in our model. We will assume that:

i. Domestic money is a nontraded asset (i.e., one that is held only by domestic residents), while all bonds are traded (i.e., held by both domestic and foreign residents). The foreign-currency value of foreign bonds held by the domestic private sector will be denoted F_P^*, while the domestic-currency value of domestic bonds held by foreign residents will be called B_F.

ii. The domestic economy is small in the market for foreign bonds, so it can have no influence over the interest rate paid on those bonds, denoted i^*.

With these assumptions in place, we can proceed to write down the *balance sheet constraints* faced by all the agents in our model, as well as their *asset demand functions*. These essentially describe what financial assets are held by each type of agent in the model, and how each type of agent chooses to allocate his or her net financial wealth, or net worth, among these assets.

a. The Domestic Private Sector's Balance Sheet and Asset Demand Functions

The domestic private sector holds domestic money, domestic bonds, and foreign bonds. The sum of all of these assets held by all the agents in this sector is the financial wealth of the domestic private sector (W_P):

$$W_P = M + B_P + sF_P^*, \tag{3.1}$$

where B_P is the value of the domestic bonds held by domestic private agents. The financial wealth of the domestic private sector represents a stock of assets the total value of which is fixed at any moment of time and can be varied over time only by accumulating new assets – that is, by saving (a flow variable). At any moment of time, therefore, W_P can be taken as fixed, so we will refer to it as a *predetermined* variable. The only exception to this statement occurs in the event of exchange rate changes, which will give rise to capital gains or losses on the foreign bonds held by domestic households, as we will see later.

While the private sector cannot change its total wealth in the short run, it can change the form in which it holds its wealth – in other words, it can alter the composition of its financial *portfolio* – instantaneously. The desired amounts of the various assets that private agents want to hold, given their wealth, are referred to as the *asset demand functions* of those agents. We need to specify such functions for each of the three assets in the domestic private sector's portfolio in order to describe how the private sector allocates its financial portfolio among competing assets. We will assume that the domestic private sector essentially makes two decisions. First, it decides how much of its wealth to hold in the form of money. In determining its *real* demand for money M/P, it is influenced in the usual manner by transactions needs (captured by Y) and opportunity costs (given by i).[1] Because money is held strictly for transactions purposes, the demand for money does not increase if the private sector has more wealth to allocate to asset holdings (that is, it does not depend on W_P). Thus, the *nominal* demand for money is given by:

$$M = PL(i, Y). \tag{3.2}$$
$$\underset{-\ +}{}$$

Once they have decided how much of their wealth to hold as money, private agents split the rest of it between domestic and foreign bonds, allocating a fraction b of their nonmonetary financial wealth $W_P - M$ to the former and a fraction f to the latter (so it must be the case that $b + f = 1$).[2] These fractions depend on the relative rates of return on the two bonds, expressed in a common currency. The domestic-currency return on one unit of domestic currency invested in domestic bonds is, of course, just given by $(1 + i)$. The domestic-currency return on the foreign bond is somewhat more complicated, however. One unit of the domestic currency can be used to purchase $1/s$ units of the foreign currency, each of which yields a return (principal plus interest) of $(1 + i^*)$ units of foreign currency, where i^* is the interest rate on foreign bonds. Thus the *foreign* currency return on one unit of the domestic currency invested in foreign bonds is $(1 + i^*)/s$. This can be converted back into foreign currency by selling it at the expected future exchange

---

[1] Notice that $L(\ )$ is not taken to depend on i^*. This is conventional, but is not strictly right. It will make a difference when i^* changes, as we will see below.

[2] Notice that $f(\ )$ thus determines the *domestic-currency* value of households' demand for foreign bonds.

rate s_{+1}^e, making the expected domestic-currency return on the foreign bond equal to $(1 + i^*)s_{+1}^e/s$. Thus, the relevant comparison is between the rate of return i on domestic bonds and $(1 + i^*)s_{+1}^e/s - 1$ on the foreign bond. However, if the exchange rate is fixed *and expected to remain so*, then $s_{+1}^e/s = 1$, and the expected domestic-currency rate of return on the foreign bond is just equal to the foreign-currency rate of return i^*. Assuming for simplicity that this is the case, we can write the domestic private sector's bond demand functions as:

$$B_P = b(i, i^*)(W_P - M).$$ $$(3.3)$$
$$+ -$$

$$sF_P^* = f(i, i^*)(W_P - M).$$ $$(3.4)$$
$$- +$$

The basic assumption is that holding more bonds of either type exposes people to higher levels of the particular risks associated with such bonds, so it takes a higher interest rate to induce them to do so. The assumption that domestic and foreign bonds are inherently different in this manner is referred to as *imperfect substitutability*. We will also examine the implications of alternative extreme assumptions in our model: that domestic and foreign residents do not hold each other's bonds at all (*financial autarky*), and that domestic and foreign bonds are held by all agents and are considered to be identical to each other (*perfect substitutability*).

Financial autarky could arise if the domestic authorities place very strong restrictions on capital movements into or out of the domestic economy. Suppose that the presence of such restrictions forces domestic residents to hold fewer foreign assets than they would have done if their ability to do so were unfettered by official impediments. Then their "effective" demand for foreign assets could be written as:

$$sF_P^* = \lambda_1 \, f(i, i^*)(W_P - M),$$ $$(3.4a)$$

where λ_1 is an index of the severity of capital-outflow restrictions, with $\lambda_1 = 0$ if the holding of foreign assets by domestic residents is strictly prohibited, and $\lambda_1 = 1$ if there are no restrictions in place. Notice that, since the sum of the domestic and foreign bonds in the portfolio of the domestic private sector must add up to its nonmonetary wealth, in the presence of restrictions on capital outflows we must have $b = (1 - \lambda_1 f)$. In the extreme case of financial autarky ($\lambda_1 = 0$), this implies that $b = 1$, because the domestic private sector must devote all of its nonmonetary wealth to the accumulation of domestic bonds.

Perfect substitutability would arise in the absence of capital account restrictions and if either of two conditions prevail: domestic and foreign bonds have the same risk characteristics or private portfolio managers do not care about risk, but only about expected return. In either case, domestic and foreign bonds would be identical with respect to all of the characteristics that matter to portfolio managers. Thus, under perfect substitutability it becomes meaningless to distinguish between B_P

and sF_P, since they refer to what is essentially the same asset. In this case, the total demand for bonds by the domestic private sector is given by:

$$B_P + sF_P = (W_P - M).$$

b. Public Sector Balance Sheets

Just as the domestic private sector has a financial balance sheet that determines its financial wealth, so do the other agents in the model. The government (nonfinancial public sector) has financial wealth W_G given by:

$$W_G = -B, \tag{3.5}$$

where B is the government's net cumulative borrowing over all of its past history. Thus, its net wealth is *negative*, equal to the outstanding stock of government debt. Since the government only issues one type of financial liability and holds no financial assets in our model, unlike the private sector it has no portfolio allocation decisions to make. Its contribution to the financial side of the model is in the form of the inherited stock of domestic bonds outstanding, a legacy of the government's *past* budgetary policies, which makes W_G a predetermined variable.

The central bank holds assets in the form of foreign exchange reserves (i.e., foreign bonds) with foreign currency value R^*, and government bonds in the amount DC (for domestic credit).[3] Its liabilities consist of domestic money (currency) M. Its balance sheet is therefore given by:

$$W_C = sR^* + DC - M, \tag{3.6}$$

where W_C is the central bank's net financial wealth, a predetermined variable that is the result of the central bank's past interest earnings on the assets it holds, net of any transfers that it has made to the government. Like the private sector, the central bank has to make decisions concerning the composition of its financial portfolio. But these are taken to be *policy*, not portfolio allocation, decisions. The central bank has two policy roles in our model: it conducts exchange rate policy and monetary policy.

To conduct exchange rate policy, the central bank intervenes in the foreign exchange market by using domestic currency that it prints for the purpose of buying or selling foreign bonds. These transactions show up in its balance sheet in the form of changes in R^*, offset by changes in M, leaving the bank's financial net wealth unaffected. The general rules that govern the central bank's behavior in the foreign exchange market are referred to as the country's "foreign exchange regime." We have already indicated how the central bank will be behaving in the foreign exchange market in our model. Specifically, we will be assuming that the central bank will be operating an *officially determined exchange rate regime*, in which it will determine

---

[3] The central bank effectively extends credit to the government by buying its bonds.

the value of the exchange rate that prevails in the foreign exchange market – that is, the exchange rate that it "fixes" in the market – by announcing its willingness to buy or sell unlimited amounts of foreign exchange at a given price in terms of domestic currency (this price, of course, represents the official exchange rate). Its behaving in this way will make the value of foreign exchange reserves R^* an endogenous variable in our model, with changes in R^* determined by the balance of payments, since that will determine the excess demand for foreign exchange from the central bank or excess supply of foreign exchange to the central bank.

The bank also intervenes in the domestic bond market, when it uses domestic currency to buy or sell domestic bonds. This is called "monetary policy," and shows up in the balance sheet in the form of changes in DC that are offset by changes in M, again leaving its financial net wealth unchanged. Alternative *monetary policy regimes* are identified by whether the central bank uses its monetary policy instrument to fix a specific value of the domestic money supply, the stock of domestic credit, or the domestic interest rate. Which of DC, M, or the domestic interest rate are endogenous or exogenous in the model will depend on the monetary policy regime that is pursued by the central bank, as we will discuss in detail below.

c. Aggregate Domestic Financial Wealth

To determine the net financial wealth of the country as a whole, we can add together the wealth of all of the domestic agents. The result is:

$$
\begin{aligned}
W_P + W_G + W_C &= (M + B_P + sF_P^*) - B + (sR^* + DC - M) \\
&= s(R^* + F_P^*) - B_F \\
&= NICP,
\end{aligned}
\tag{3.7}
$$

since the M's cancel out and since $B_F = B - B_P - DC$, where B_F is the stock of domestic bonds held by foreigners (note that any domestic bonds not held by domestic residents must be held by foreigners). The home country's aggregate financial wealth is referred to as its "net international creditor position" (NICP). It consists of the domestic economy's financial claims against the rest of the world minus the claims by the rest of the world against the domestic economy. Notice that, since $NICP = W_H + W_G + W_C$, it is the sum of three predetermined variables. Thus, $NICP$ must be predetermined as well. This has a useful implication that we will exploit below.

d. Balance Sheet and Asset Demands of the Rest of the World

Finally, consider the financial wealth of the rest of the world. The rest of the world holds financial claims on the domestic economy in the form of domestic government bonds held by foreigners, which we have labeled B_F. But as we have seen, the domestic economy also holds financial claims on the rest of the world in the form of foreign bonds held by domestic households, denoted F_P^*, and by the central bank, R^*. Thus, the domestic-currency value of the financial net worth of the rest of the world, denoted $NICP_F$, is the mirror image of the financial wealth of the domestic economy. For the world as a whole, net financial claims, given by $NICP + NICP_F$ (where $NICP_F = B_F - s(R^* + F_P^*)$ is the net international creditor position of the rest of the world), must sum to zero.

We now turn to foreigners' asset demand functions. The agents in the foreign private sector are assumed to behave just like domestic ones. Thus, their aggregate demand for the foreign country's own money is given by:

$$M^* = P^*L^*(i^*, Y^*),$$ (3.8)
$$\underset{-\quad\;+}{}$$

where M^* is the money stock of the rest of the world, and i^* is the foreign interest rate. We will assume that, since the domestic economy is small, the foreign central bank does not hold any of its foreign exchange reserves in the form of claims issued by agents in the domestic economy. This being so, foreigners' total demand for domestic bonds emanates only from the foreign private sector. The rest of the world's demand for domestic bonds, expressed in *foreign currency* terms, can therefore be expressed as:

$$B_F/s = b^*(i, i^*)(W_F^* - M^*),$$ (3.9)
$$\underset{+\;-}{}$$

where W_F^* is the financial wealth of the foreign private sector, measured in units of the foreign currency. Notice that because B_F is the *domestic* currency value of the domestic bonds demanded by the rest of the world, it has to be divided by s to make it commensurate with the foreign currency values W_F^* and M^*.

Just as we discussed the potential role that restrictions on capital outflows could play in determining the "effective" demand for foreign assets by the domestic private sector, we can now consider how restrictions on capital *inflows* could affect the effective demand for domestic bonds by foreign private agents. By analogy with what we did before, in the presence of such restrictions we can rewrite (3.9) as:

$$B_F/s = \lambda_2 b^*(i, i^*)(W_F^* - M^*),$$ (3.9a)

where λ_2 is a measure of the intensity of restrictions on capital *inflows* in the domestic economy. Again, financial autarky would correspond to $\lambda_2 = 0$, while the absence of restrictions implies $\lambda_2 = 1$.

II. ASSET SUPPLIES

Now consider the determination of the supply of assets. Recall that there are three assets, consisting of domestic and foreign bonds, as well as domestic money.

a. Bond Supplies

Consider first the supply of domestic and foreign bonds. Since the outstanding stock of government bonds depends on the past history of fiscal deficits, the supply of domestic bonds is predetermined (the supply curve is vertical at any moment of time), and equal to the outstanding stock of government debt B. Thus, the supply curve for domestic bonds is:

$$B^S = B. \tag{3.10}$$

In the case of foreign bonds, because of the small country assumption, the domestic economy faces a perfectly elastic supply of foreign bonds at the world interest rate i^*bar. Thus, the supply curve for foreign bonds is:

$$i^* = i^*bar. \tag{3.11}$$

b. The Supply of Money

What about the supply of domestic money? Unfortunately, this is a little more complicated. There are essentially five options, depending on the degree of capital mobility that characterizes the economy and the monetary policy being pursued by the central bank. We'll consider each of them in this section before restricting attention to three representative possibilities in the rest of the chapter.

Before exploring the various options, note first that, from the central bank's balance sheet, and assuming for the present that the central bank has no financial net worth ($W_C = 0$), we can derive the *monetary identity*:

$$M = sR^* + DC.$$

Now recall that, according to equation (3.7), $NICP$ can be written as $NICP = sNICP^* = s(R^* + F_p^* - B_F/s)$. Solving this for sR^*, we can write:

$$sR^* = s(NICP^* + B_F/s - F_p^*).$$

Substituting this into the monetary identity, we get the money supply relationship:

$$M = s(NICP^* + B_F/s - F_p^*) + DC. \tag{3.12}$$

This relationship forms the basis for the money supply discussion in the rest of this section. It has some important implications about the determination of the domestic money supply. Notice in particular that, since $NICP^*$ is predetermined, discrete changes in R^* can occur only as the result of portfolio reallocations between domestic and foreign bonds by domestic and foreign residents (capital flows), which affect the quantity $(B_F/s - F_p^*)$ in equation (3.12). Other balance of payments transactions (i.e., the current account) will affect the stock of foreign exchange reserves through *NICP*, but this effect will only happen slowly over time. Thus, the key implication of (3.12) is that short-run changes in the money supply can result from two sources: capital inflows and outflows and changes in domestic monetary policy operating through *DC*. In the remainder of this section, we will consider how these factors interact to determine the supply of money.

1. Financial Autarky

Under financial autarky ($\lambda_1 = \lambda_2 = 0$), domestic residents do not hold foreign bonds and foreign residents do not hold domestic bonds, so $B_F = F_P^* = 0$. From equation (3.12), therefore, the monetary identity becomes:

$$M = sNICP^* + DC. \tag{3.13a}$$

Since *NICP** is predetermined, the money supply becomes a policy variable determined at any given moment by the stock of domestic credit.

2. Monetary Targeting

On the other hand, when imperfect capital mobility prevails, the determination of the money supply depends on the monetary policy being pursued by the central bank. Under *monetary targeting*, the central bank fixes the money supply as an exogenous (policy) variable, and the domestic money supply is just given by:

$$M = Mbar, \tag{3.13b}$$

where *Mbar* is the value of the money supply target chosen by the authorities. To enforce this target, the central bank has to offset any effects that its foreign exchange operations have on the domestic money supply by expanding or contracting domestic credit. Thus, the domestic credit stock becomes an endogenous variable. Using equations (3.12) and (3.13b), and solving for *DC*, its value is given by:

$$DC = Mbar - s\{NICP^* + b^*(i, i^*)(W_F^* - P^*L^*(i^*, Y^*)) - f(i, i^*)(W_P - PL(i, Y))/s\}.$$

Setting the stock of domestic credit in this way is referred to as "sterilizing" the effects of foreign exchange market intervention. We will use the terms "monetary targeting" and "sterilization" interchangeably.

Comparing equations (3.13a) and (3.13b), we note that in both cases the money supply is a policy-determined variable and is independent of the domestic interest rate. When plotted in i-M space, as in Figure 3.1, the money supply curves implied by equations (3.13a) and (3.13b), denoted M_A (for autarky) and M_S (for sterilization) can therefore be represented as vertical straight lines.

3. Domestic Credit Targeting

On the other hand, under imperfect capital mobility and *domestic credit* targeting, the exogenous variable is the stock of domestic credit, rather than the money supply.

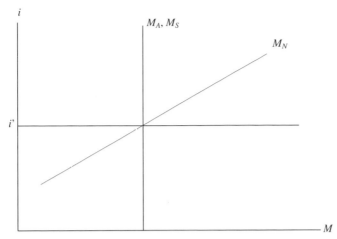

Figure 3.1. The Domestic Money Supply

In that case the supply of money is given by equation (3.12), with DC becoming an exogenous policy-determined variable and M an endogenous variable. Interpreted in this way, this equation states that when the central bank fixes the exchange rate and maintains a domestic credit target, the domestic money supply can change discretely as the result of capital inflows (in the form of higher B_F and/or lower F_P^*) or outflows (lower B_F and/or higher F_P^*). To see what these capital inflows and outflows themselves depend on, we can use the asset demand functions for B_F and F_P^*. The result is:

$$M = s[NICP^* + b^*(i, i^*)(W_F^* - P^*L^*(i^*, Y^*))$$
$$- f(i, i^*)(W_P - PL(i, Y))/s] + DC. \qquad (3.13c)$$

Since under a domestic credit target the central bank does not offset the monetary impact of its foreign exchange market operations by altering the stock of credit, under this policy its foreign exchange operations are said to be *unsterilized*.

The term in square brackets in equation (3.13c) represents the foreign-currency value of the stock of foreign exchange reserves. This term captures the dependence of the supply of money on the domestic interest rate, as well as on other macroeconomic variables, through the effects of capital flows when the capital account is open and the central bank pursues a domestic credit target. To see how the domestic interest rate affects the supply of money, consider what happens to the domestic money supply when the domestic interest rate rises.

As the domestic interest rate increases, foreigners switch away from their own bonds into domestic bonds. Thus B_F increases. How do domestic residents react? The higher domestic interest rate causes them to reduce their holdings of domestic money, increasing the share of their portfolios held in the form of bonds, both domestic and foreign. At the same time, however, the increase in the domestic interest rate induces them to switch from foreign into domestic bonds. As a result of these two effects together, their demand for domestic bonds will certainly rise, but their holdings of foreign bonds may increase or decrease. They will *decrease* as long as domestic and foreign bonds are "gross substitutes" in the portfolios of the domestic private sector – that is, as long as the negative effect on the demand for foreign bonds by domestic residents arising from the lower relative return on such bonds dominates the positive effect on their demand for foreign bonds that arises from their desire to hold more bonds in total, rather than money.

Under this assumption, the domestic money supply increases because higher domestic interest rates attract capital inflows both from foreigners who want to buy domestic bonds as well as from domestic residents who want to repatriate their capital from abroad. These capital inflows arrive in the form of foreign exchange, which has to be purchased by the central bank in order to maintain the value of the official exchange rate. The higher money supply reflects the emission of domestic currency by the central bank in order to purchase the foreign exchange.

In sum, this analysis implies that – if the central bank's monetary policy consists of setting a domestic credit target (fixing the value of DC exogenously) and capital mobility is imperfect – the domestic interest rate will have a *positive* relationship with the money supply. This relationship can be shown in i-M space in the form of a money supply curve (relating the domestic interest to the supply of money) with a positive slope. This curve is called M_N in Figure 3.1.

We have already seen that the positive slope of the M_N curve arises from the monetary effects of the capital inflows induced by higher domestic interest rates. What determines how steep or flat the curve is, however? Under domestic credit targeting, the slope of this curve depends on the *degree of international capital mobility* that characterizes this country, which encompasses both the degree of substitutability between domestic and foreign assets as well as the intensity of any capital account restrictions that may be in place. As shown previously, the MM curve has a positive slope because an increase in i causes foreign residents to increase their demand for domestic bonds and causes domestic residents to repatriate capital. MM will be *shallower* the stronger both of these responses are, because when these responses are strong a given change in the domestic interest rate induces larger capital movements and thus larger changes in the domestic money supply.[4] In turn, these responses will be strong when domestic and foreign assets are close substitutes and when restrictions on capital movements are weak or nonexistent – in other words, when the degree of capital mobility is high.

---

[4] Thus, the intensification of capital account restrictions (capital controls) that weaken the response of foreign and domestic portfolios to changes in interest rates would tend to make this curve steeper.

4. Interest Rate Targeting

Under conditions of financial autarky or imperfect capital mobility, the domestic central bank can alternatively conduct monetary policy so as to target a specific value of the domestic interest rate, say i'. To sustain the domestic interest rate at this value, the domestic money supply has to become endogenous, adjusting to changes in the demand for money. The money supply is given by:

$$M = PL(i', Y). \tag{3.13d}$$

The money supply is kept at this value in the face of changes in P and Y through suitable changes in the stock of domestic credit, which means that DC is also endogenous in this case, and is given by:

$$DC = PL(i', Y) - s\{NICP^* + b^*(i', i^*)(W_F^* - P^*L^*(i^*, Y^*)) \\ - f(i', i^*)(W_P - PL(i', Y))/s\}.$$

In terms of Figure 3.1, the case of interest rate targeting can be depicted as a horizontal straight line at height i' in i-M space.

5. Perfect Capital Mobility

We saw in the case of domestic credit targeting that the more sensitive capital flows are to interest rate differentials, the flatter the M_N curve would be in Figure 3.1. In the limit, if these flows are sufficiently sensitive, the M_N curve would be flat (a slight change in the domestic interest rate would trigger effectively infinite capital flows), and money market equilibrium could occur only when the domestic interest rate equals the foreign interest rate i^*. This situation arises when restrictions on capital flows are absent or ineffective and when domestic and foreign assets are *perfect substitutes*, and is known as *perfect capital mobility*. In this case, the money supply is given by:

$$M = PL(i^*, Y), \tag{3.13e}$$

with i^* exogenous. Because i^* is exogenous, the supply of money is once again – as when the central bank targets the domestic interest rate – a horizontal straight line in Figure 3.1. The difference between this case and that of interest rate targeting is, of course, that the value of the domestic interest rate is exogenously determined by international financial conditions, rather than reflecting a policy decision of the central bank.

In this case, monetary policy can have no effect on the domestic money supply or the domestic interest rate. Instead, from (3.12) we have:

$$B_F - sF_P^* = PL(i^*, Y) - sNICP^* - DC.$$

For given values of Y and P, the money supply is determined from the demand side of the market, and policy-induced change in domestic credit serves only to alter $B_F - sF_P^*$ on a one-for-one basis.[5]

6. Summary

We can thus summarize the factors determining the slope of the money supply curve as follows:

i. When the domestic economy is completely closed off to asset transactions with the rest of the world (i.e., in a situation of financial autarky), capital movements cannot take place regardless of the level of the domestic interest rate, and money supply must be vertical. This is the situation that would prevail under very severe capital controls that prevent foreign residents from buying domestic assets and domestic residents from buying foreign assets.

ii. The money supply curve could also be vertical with an open capital account, if the central bank pursues a policy of monetary targeting, since under such a policy any capital flows that arise in response to changes in the domestic interest rate would be sterilized by the central bank, leaving the domestic money supply unchanged.

iii. Under domestic credit targeting and imperfect capital mobility (i.e., when domestic and foreign bonds are imperfect substitutes, the money supply curve has a positive slope, and becomes flatter the weaker are restrictions on capital flows and the greater the degree of substitutability between domestic and foreign assets).

iv. When capital mobility is imperfect, the central bank can choose the domestic interest rate as its intermediate target for monetary policy. In that case, the money supply curve would be a horizontal straight line with height given by the targeted value of the domestic interest rate.

v. Finally, the money supply curve is also flat when capital mobility is perfect, but in that case the central bank has no monetary policy discretion over either the domestic interest rate or money supply.

Notice that the two extreme capital mobility assumptions – financial autarky and perfect capital mobility – generate money supply curves that resemble those that would result respectively from monetary targeting and interest rate targeting under imperfect capital mobility. To simplify things in the rest of this chapter, therefore, we will work under the assumption that capital mobility is *imperfect*, and consider alternative intermediate targets of monetary policy in the form of the money supply, the stock of domestic credit, and the domestic interest rate, being mindful that the first and last of these can also be used to describe the economy's behavior under the extreme assumptions of financial autarky and perfect capital mobility.

---

[5] The coefficient of DC in this equation is often referred to as the "offset coefficient" on domestic credit. Under perfect capital mobility, this coefficient must be unity.

III. ASSET MARKET EQUILIBRIUM

Generally, with three assets in our model, balance sheet constraints would imply that the model would contain two independent asset market equilibrium conditions. However, since the domestic economy is small in the market for foreign bonds, it can have no impact on the price of these bonds, so the domestic demand for such bonds is *identically* equal to the (perfectly elastic) world supply of them.[6] That means that our model really only contains *one* independent asset market equilibrium condition. In other words, any value of the domestic interest rate that clears the domestic bond market must also clear the domestic money market, and vice versa. The implication is that we can express asset market equilibrium in terms of either market.[7]

a. Bond Market Equilibrium

In terms of the domestic bond market, the equilibrium condition can be expressed in the most general case (that of imperfect capital mobility and domestic credit targeting) as follows:

$$B - DC = b(i, i^*)[W_P - PL(i, Y)] + sb^*(i, i^*)(W_F^* - P^*L^*(i^*, Y^*)),$$

where $B - DC$ is the portion of the outstanding stock of domestic bonds available for sale to the private sector (the existing stock B minus the portion purchased by the central bank DC), and $b(W_P - PL)$ and $sb^*(W_F^* - P^*L^*)$ respectively represent the demand for domestic bonds by domestic and foreign residents.

b. Money Market Equilibrium

But since the interest rate that clears the bond market must simultaneously clear the money market, we can replace the bond market equilibrium condition above by the money market equilibrium condition:

$$M = PL(i, Y). \tag{3.14}$$

We can think of our model's money market equilibrium as consisting of a money supply equation, a money demand equation, and an equilibrium condition that sets money supply equal to money demand. Equation (3.14) essentially represents the result of substituting the money demand equation into the equilibrium condition. What remains for us to do is to substitute the money supply equation into the left-hand side of (3.14). But since, as we have seen, the determination of the money supply depends both on the nature of the economy's financial links with the rest of

---

[6] "Identically" in this case means that the supply of foreign bonds equals the demand for foreign bonds for *all* possible values of the endogenous variables in the model, so the need to clear this market does not impose any restrictions on the values that these variables can take.

[7] These statements are explained and demonstrated formally in Appendix 3.1.

the world as well as on the monetary policy followed by the central bank, the actual form that this equilibrium condition takes will depend on these conditions as well.

Under monetary targeting, we substitute equation (3.13b) into (3.14), which produces the money market equilibrium condition:

$$Mbar = PL(i, Y). \tag{3.15a}$$

Under imperfect capital mobility and domestic credit targeting, we substitute for M from equation (3.13c) to derive:

$$s[NICP^* + b^*(i, i^*)(W_F^* - P^*L^*(i^*, Y^*))$$
$$- f(i, i^*)(W_P - PL(i, Y))/s] + DC = PL(i, Y). \tag{3.15b}$$

The left-hand side is the supply of money which, as we have seen, depends positively on the domestic interest rate (through capital inflows), while the right-hand side is the demand for money. The money market equilibrium conditions (3.15a) and (3.15b) can be used to determine the domestic interest rate, for a given value of the domestic price level P. To determine the domestic money supply in each case, we can just substitute the solution for the interest rate into equation (3.14).

Finally, under domestic interest rate targeting, the money market equilibrium condition becomes:

$$M = L(i', Y). \tag{3.15c}$$

In this case, of course, the domestic interest rate is determined exogenously, and equation (3.15c) determines the money supply.

c. The Effects of Shocks in the Money Market

To demonstrate the determination of the domestic interest rate graphically, we can now introduce a money demand curve into Figure 3.1. Since nominal money demand is given by $PL[i, Y(P/P^e)]$, this curve must have a negative slope for a given value of P^e (recall from Chapter 2 that Y is increasing in P/P^e), as in Figure 3.2. The equilibrium value of the domestic interest rate is determined by the intersection of the money supply and demand curves at a point such as A in this figure. We can now explore the properties of the domestic money market equilibrium depicted above by seeing how it would be affected by a variety of macroeconomic shocks.

1. A Change in the Domestic Price Level
The money-market effects of changes in the domestic price level depend on whether those changes are anticipated by workers. Since the demand for money is given by $PL[i, Y(P/P^e)]$, the demand for money will increase in proportion to the increase in the price level when the increase is anticipated (because in this case $P = P^e$ and Y remains unchanged), and *more* than in proportion to the increase in the

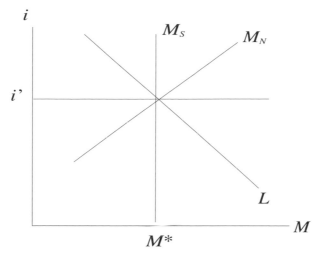

Figure 3.2. Equilibrium in the Domestic Money Market

price level (because the induced increase in Y would further increase the demand for money) when the price level change is unanticipated. This difference will affect the *magnitude* of the effects of price level changes on money market variables (i.e., the interest rate and the money supply), but not the *qualitative* properties of these effects. In what follows, therefore, we will restrict our attention to the more general case of unanticipated changes in the price level.

Suppose, then, that the economy experiences an increase in the domestic price level that was not previously anticipated. Then, since the nominal demand for money increases more than in proportion to the increase in the domestic price level, an increase in P shifts the money-demand curve L to the right by an amount that is more than proportional to the increase in P. The effects on the domestic money market are shown in Figure 3.3. They depend on the domestic economy's financial links with the rest of the world as well as on the way that the central bank conducts its monetary policy.

Under monetary targeting (or financial autarky), as can be verified from equation (3.15a), the money supply is unaffected by a change in P, and the increase in P simply increases the domestic market-clearing interest rate, moving the economy from point A to B in Figure 3.3, with the money supply unchanged and the domestic interest rate rising to i_1.

Under domestic credit targeting, the rightward shift in the demand for money is accompanied by a rightward shift in money supply as well, because higher prices at home cause domestic residents to repatriate capital to satisfy their demand for money (this is captured in the term $f(\ )(W_P - PL)$ in the money supply function), and the resulting capital inflow triggers a monetary emission when the central bank absorbs the foreign exchange. However, as shown in Figure 3.3, the rightward shift of the money supply curve must be smaller than that of the demand curve, because

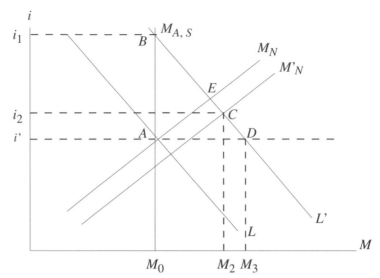

Figure 3.3. **Effects on the Money Market of an Increase in the Domestic Price Level**

$f < 1$ – that is, some of the increased demand for money is met by selling domestic bonds, rather than repatriating capital. Thus, the money market equilibrium moves from A to C in Figure 3.3, and the increase in the domestic price level raises both i and M. Notice, however, that the increase in the domestic interest rate at C is smaller than at B. In other words, an increase in the domestic price level has a smaller impact on the domestic interest rate under credit targeting than under monetary targeting.

Finally, when the central bank targets the domestic interest rate, the money demand curve simply moves along the horizontal money supply curve $i = i'$ to the point D. In this case, the increase in the domestic price level has no effect on the domestic interest rate and acts only to increase the domestic money supply.[8]

One way to think intuitively about what is happening in Figure 3.3 is as follows: as we have seen, the money supply curve under monetary targeting is the same as that which would be observed under financial autarky. M_A thus indicates what the domestic money supply would be in the absence of endogenous capital flows – with foreign exchange reserves given only by their initial value R_0^*. We can think of this vertical curve as shifting to the right or the left when reserves are augmented or diminished by capital flows that are allowed to affect the money supply (i.e., that are not sterilized by the central bank).

---

[8] When the increase in the domestic price level is unanticipated, the demand for money increases *more* than in proportion with the increase in the price level. This means that the shifts of the curves in Figure 3.3 are larger than in the case considered above. Under monetary and domestic credit targeting, changes in domestic interest rates and the money supply will therefore both be larger in this case for a given-size change in the domestic price level. Under domestic interest rate targeting, the increase in the money supply will be larger, but the domestic interest rate will, of course, remain unchanged.

When capital mobility is imperfect and the central bank targets domestic credit, the increase in the domestic price level itself causes this curve to shift to the right, because the increase in the demand for money caused by the higher level of domestic prices induces capital repatriation by domestic residents, even at an unchanged domestic interest rate. With the domestic money supply augmented by this repatriated capital, and no additional capital flows, the vertical money supply curve would shift to the right to pass through a point such as E, and domestic money market equilibrium would yield an interest rate higher than i^*. But at this point, the domestic interest rate is higher than would be consistent with domestic portfolio equilibrium, because the point E lies above the equilibrium point D corresponding to the new money supply curve M'_N. At the interest rate passing through E there is an excess supply of domestic money, and thus an excess demand for domestic bonds. This excess demand attracts capital inflows into the domestic economy, increasing the money supply and shifting the vertical money supply curve further to the right until it intersects the M'_N curve at C.

The same process is at work under interest rate targeting, except that in this case the capital inflows must be supplemented by an expansion of domestic credit until the domestic interest rate is driven back to its original level i'.

2. Expansionary Monetary Policy

The form that expansionary policy takes in this model depends on the variable that the central bank is designating as its intermediate policy instrument: the stock of domestic credit, the money supply, or the domestic interest rate.

When domestic credit is the intermediate target of policy, an increase in the central bank's stock of domestic credit shifts the money supply curve to the right by the same absolute amount as the increase in the stock of credit, as long as capital mobility is less than perfect. This follows because DC enters the money supply function (3.12) additively.

Under financial autarky this rightward shift represents the total change in the domestic money supply. The effect of the increase in the money supply is to lower the domestic interest rate so as to generate the additional demand for money required to maintain equilibrium in the money market. When the capital account is open, however, this reduction in the domestic interest rate triggers capital outflows. Under monetary targeting, these induced capital outflows must be sterilized – the initial credit boost must be followed by whatever additional increases in credit prove necessary to keep the money supply at its targeted higher value. Essentially what is going on here is that the lower domestic interest rate caused by the initial credit expansion lowers the demand for domestic bonds, and the excess supply of bonds available at this interest rate is in effect purchased by the central bank through its sterilization operations.

Now suppose that the central bank targets the stock of domestic credit as its intermediate policy instrument, instead of the money supply. Under domestic credit targeting, the central bank does not sterilize capital outflows, so the central bank's reserve losses have the effect of reducing the money supply. The upshot is that the final increase in the money supply at the new money market equilibrium must be *smaller* than the initial increase in *DC*. It is easy to see that this offset effect must be larger the flatter the M_N curve, because when the curve is flatter its rightward horizontal displacement in response to an increase in *DC* would be the same as when it is steeper, but it would intersect *PL* closer to the original equilibrium. The implication is that the impact of the expansionary credit policy on the domestic money supply is smaller the higher the degree of capital mobility. In fact, as we have seen, when capital mobility is perfect the money supply curve is horizontal. In that case the supply of money does not depend on the stock of domestic credit. The economic interpretation is that under perfect capital mobility the credit expansion is completely offset by reserve losses, leaving no impact on the money market equilibrium.

3. A Change in the Country's Net Creditor Position

Consider next the money market effects of a change in the country's net international creditor position, $NICP^*$. To make things interesting, suppose that the central bank targets domestic credit. From equation (3.15b), $NICP^*$ enters the money supply equation additively, as does the stock of domestic credit, *DC*. It might thus seem as though a change in $NICP^*$, say in the amount $\triangle NICP^*$, would change the money supply in the first instance by the amount $s\triangle NICP^*$, and from then on we could analyze the money market effects of this change very much as we did the effects of a change in the stock of credit.

Unfortunately, matters are not quite so simple. The problem is that domestic and foreign private wealth, which enter (3.15b) as W_P and W_F^* respectively, must themselves change when $NICP^*$ does. To see why, recall that the country's net financial wealth (its net international creditor position) is the sum of the net financial wealth of the three types of domestic agents: the private sector, the central bank, and the government. Thus:

$$sNICP^* = W_P + W_C + W_G.$$

But since $W_G = -B$, and since we have been assuming that $W_C = 0$, it follows that $sNICP^* = W_P - B$, or in other words, that:

$$W_P = sNICP^* + B.$$

Moreover, since the same relationship must hold for the rest of the world, we also have:

$$W_F^* = NICP_F^* + F^*,$$

where W_F^* and F^* respectively denote the financial net worth of the foreign private sector and the stock of foreign government bonds outstanding, both measured in foreign-currency terms. Furthermore, since the rest of the world's net creditor position is simply the negative of the net creditor position of the home country – that is, $NICP_F^* = -NICP^*$, we can write this last expression as:

$$W_F^* = F^* - NICP^*.$$

That means that we can replace W_P by $sNICP^* + B$, and W_F^* by $F^* - NICP^*$ in equation (3.15b). Making these substitutions in (3.15b), we can write it as:

$$M = s[NICP^* + b^*(F^* - NICP^* - P^*L^*) \\ - f(sNICP^* + B - PL)/s] + DC.^9$$

Combining the terms in $NICP^*$ this becomes:

$$M = s[(1 - (b^* + f))NICP^* + b^*(F^* - P^*L^*) - f(B - PL)/s] + DC.$$

$$(3.16)$$

The advantage of this formulation is that it enables us to see the full effect of changes in $NICP^*$ on the domestic money supply. Notice that, holding F^* and B constant, an increase in $NICP^*$ represents a transfer of wealth from the foreign to the domestic private sector.[10] Conversion of this new wealth from foreign into domestic currency by the private sector would tend to increase the central bank's stock of foreign exchange reserves and the domestic money supply. But as the domestic private sector gets richer, it will tend to devote a share f of its new wealth to holding foreign bonds. Similarly, as the foreign private sector gets poorer, it will reduce its holdings of domestic bonds by a fraction b^* of its reduced wealth. These two effects result in capital outflows of $(b^* + f)$ times the change in wealth, and these capital outflows reduce the central bank's stock of foreign exchange reserves as well as the domestic money supply. The net impact of the wealth transfer on the domestic money supply is thus $[1 - (b^* + f)]$ times the change in wealth.

From equation (3.16) it is easy to see that an increase in $NICP^*$ has effects on the domestic interest rate and money supply that are qualitatively – if not quantitatively – the same as those of an increase in DC of the same magnitude, since this variable enters the money supply function in the same additive way that DC does. When $NICP^*$ increases under conditions of less than perfect capital mobility, the domestic interest rate falls and the domestic money supply increases. Under credit targeting, this increase is less than the initial impact $[1 - (b^* + f)]s\triangle NICP^*$. Again, the effects on the money supply and domestic interest rate are smaller the higher the degree of capital mobility, and under perfect capital mobility there is no change either in the domestic interest rate or the domestic money supply.

---

[9] Recall that b^* and f are positive fractions that depend on domestic and foreign interest rates.

[10] We will see in Chapter 5 that this would in fact tend to happen gradually over time through surpluses in the current account of the domestic country's balance of payments.

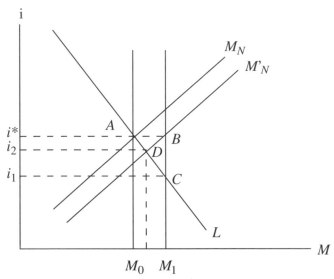

Figure 3.4. Effects of a Reduction in the Foreign Interest Rate under Credit Targeting

4. A Change in the Foreign Interest Rate

Changes in foreign interest rates have no effect on the money market equilibrium under financial autarky, because by assumption such changes have no effect on the domestic demand for money, and the domestic money supply is effectively insulated from any capital flows that such changes would induce.

Under monetary targeting, the money market equilibrium is also undisturbed. However, in this case the change in the foreign interest rate will trigger capital inflows or outflows that will have to be sterilized by the central bank, so the effects will be felt in the form of changes in the composition of the central bank's balance sheet. Under the "gross substitutes" assumption that we made above, a decrease in the foreign interest rate causes both domestic and foreign residents to seek to shift out of foreign and into domestic bonds. This shock will give rise to an excess demand for domestic bonds. To keep the domestic money supply unchanged, the central bank will have to sterilize the resulting capital inflows. In effect, it will have to provide to the market the extra domestic bonds it desires in view of the lower return on foreign bonds.

With domestic credit targeting, a reduction in the foreign interest rate shifts M_N to the right by an amount that depends on the degree of capital mobility – that is, on the sensitivity of b^* and f to i^* – while leaving the money demand curve L unaffected, as in Figure 3.4. Consequently, its effect is to lower the domestic interest rate and increase the domestic money supply M, as at point D.

Just as in the case of the price level shock, we can decompose the market's response into two parts. The reduction in the foreign interest rate gives rise to a capital inflow as both domestic and foreign residents adjust the composition of their bond portfolios to the new foreign interest rate. This increases the domestic money supply at any given value of the domestic interest rate, say from M_0 to M_1, accounting for the rightward shift in M_N, to a point such as B. But the higher money supply M_1 would not be willingly held at the original value of the domestic interest rate, since the domestic demand for money is unchanged. Thus, for M_1 to be willingly held, the domestic interest rate would have to fall to a value such as i_1. But at the interest rate i_1, the original portfolio reallocation would no longer be optimal. Indeed, at i_1 there would be an excess supply of domestic bonds, and this triggers capital outflows that partially – but only partially – offset the initial inflows, leaving the domestic money supply higher, and the domestic interest rate lower, than before the shock.[11]

A useful question to ask in this context is whether the reduction in the domestic interest rate is larger or smaller than that in the foreign interest rate under credit targeting. The answer is that it must be *smaller*. To see why, suppose that the domestic interest rate fell to a level equal to the new lower foreign rate. At this lower domestic interest rate the domestic demand for money would be higher, while the preferences of both domestic and foreign residents between domestic and foreign bonds would be roughly unchanged. Thus, the only source of additional money supply available to satisfy the increased demand for money would be capital inflows associated with domestic residents' desire to reduce the nonmonetary component of their portfolios. Since these capital inflows are by assumption smaller than the increase in the demand for money itself ($f < 1$), at this interest rate there must be an excess demand for money. Thus, the domestic interest rate must be higher than this – it must be above the new level of the foreign rate.

Under interest rate targeting, a change in the foreign interest rate would give rise to capital inflows or outflows that would tend to affect the domestic money supply and thus the domestic interest rate. To sustain the desired value of the domestic interest rate, the central bank would thus have to respond through changes in domestic credit. The situation is exactly the same as under monetary targeting, since sustaining the original value of the domestic interest rate is equivalent to sustaining the original money supply in response to this type of shock.

Under conditions of perfect capital mobility, by contrast, the central bank cannot maintain the original value of the domestic interest rate. If i^* falls, for example, the economy moves down along the money demand curve L. The domestic interest rate falls by exactly the same amount as the foreign interest rate, and capital inflows cause an increase in the domestic money supply.

---

[11] If the domestic demand for money depends (negatively) on the interest rate on foreign bonds, this conclusion would not necessarily hold. In this case, a reduction in the foreign interest rate would also shift the LL curve to the right, and could potentially shift it by *more* than the M_N curve. This is an unlikely scenario, since it would require the demand for money to be very sensitive to the foreign interest rate, while domestic and foreign bonds are not very close substitutes for each other. Nevertheless, if these conditions materialize, the reduction in the foreign interest rate could result in an increase in the domestic money supply and a *higher* domestic interest rate.

5. *A Change in the Nominal Exchange Rate*

Next, consider the effects on the market of a change in the nominal exchange rate, such as a nominal devaluation. Changes in s have no direct effect on the demand for money. Thus, the money demand curve is unaffected by a nominal devaluation. It is easy to see that devaluation also has no direct effects on the supply of money under either monetary targeting or interest rate targeting. Thus, in both of these cases a devaluation would leave the money market equilibrium undisturbed.

Under domestic credit targeting, however, the effect of a nominal devaluation turns out to be somewhat more complicated. In this case, the component of the money supply arising from domestic credit would be unchanged. But what about the component of the money supply backed by foreign exchange reserves (sR^*)? This component may indeed respond to a devaluation of the exchange rate. To see how, notice that the change in this component can be approximated by:

$$\Delta M = \Delta s R^* + s \Delta R^*,$$

where the symbol "Δ" denotes a change, as in the last chapter. The first term on the right-hand side corresponds to the capital gain on the existing stock of reserves caused by a devaluation, while the second term captures any change in reserves directly induced by the devaluation, valued at the original (pre-devaluation) exchange rate.

Consider the second term first. How might a devaluation directly induce a change in reserves? Recall that domestic and foreign households both hold bonds denominated in the currency of the other country. Because a change in the nominal exchange rate will change the value of these bonds measured in the households' own currency, both the composition and level of household wealth will be affected in both countries. Domestic residents who hold foreign-currency assets will gain wealth and find themselves with an *excess* of foreign assets in their portfolios, due to the increase in the domestic-currency value of these assets, while foreign residents who hold domestic-currency assets will lose wealth and find themselves *deficient* in domestic-currency assets due to a decrease in their value when measured in foreign currency.

The resulting change in nonmonetary wealth will give rise to capital flows as households in both countries readjust their portfolios. Domestic residents sell some of their excess holdings of foreign currency assets, while foreign residents buy more domestic currency assets in order to replenish the foreign-currency value of their holdings of domestic bonds. The effect of the capital inflows arising from both sources is to increase the home country's reserves. While this mechanism may be empirically important in some cases, it will simplify matters if we initially abstract away from it. We can do this by assuming that initially $B_F = F_P^* = 0$. That is, *initial* holdings of foreign bonds by households are set equal to zero both at home and abroad. This does not mean that bond holdings cannot change (i.e., they need not *always* be zero), just that we will be analyzing changes from an *initial* *position* of zero. This assumption eliminates the second term above, since there are now no capital gains or losses to directly trigger capital flows as a result of devaluation.

Turning to the first term, its relevance depends on whether the central bank "monetizes" the capital gains on reserves. A devaluation will increase the domestic-currency value of the foreign exchange reserves held by the central bank, by the amount ΔsR^*. What happens to these gains? Suppose that they are transferred to the government. The central bank can do so by simply extinguishing an equal amount of its claims on the government – that is, of domestic credit. If that is all that happens, the central bank's balance sheet changes in composition. The domestic-currency value of its foreign exchange reserves rises and the value of its claims on the government (domestic credit) falls by an equal amount, with the amount of money remaining unchanged. The government's wealth increases because the central bank now holds fewer of its liabilities, but the assets held by the private sector, both money and bonds, remain unchanged, so the financial equilibrium of the economy is undisturbed.

But what if the central bank "monetizes" the government's gains by extending *new* credit to the government in an amount that is just sufficient to keep its claims on the government unchanged? Consider what the government would do with these resources. Since all of the components of the government's budget are being held constant in this exercise, the government must use them to retire debt. As we have just seen, if it uses all of the proceeds to retire debt held by the central bank, then DC falls by ΔsR^*, and the money supply remains unchanged, leaving the M_N curve undisturbed. But if it retires debt held by the public, M_N must shift to the right by the amount ΔsR^* as the central bank issues the currency for the government to buy back the debt from the public. In this case the central bank's balance sheet initially shows an increase in sR^* offset by an increase in M, with unchanged DC. In the new equilibrium, the domestic money supply would increase and the domestic interest rate must fall, as in the case of an increase in domestic credit.[12]

IV. SUMMARY

In this chapter we have investigated how the domestic interest rate is determined by exploring the properties of financial market equilibrium in our model. We have found that the shape of the money supply curve and the effects of a variety of shocks on the equilibrium outcome in domestic financial markets depend on the nature of the domestic economy's financial links with the rest of the world as well as the monetary policy regime followed by the central bank.

---

[12] If the capital gains on reserves were not transferred to the government, there would be no effect of devaluation in Figure 3.4 under domestic credit targeting. In this case, capital gains on reserves associated with the increase in their domestic-currency value would directly increase the central bank's net worth.

Among the financial links with the rest of the world, we considered the cases of financial autarky, imperfect capital mobility, and perfect capital mobility. Financial autarky arises when the domestic economy maintains an effective prohibition against the holding of foreign assets by domestic residents or of domestic assets by foreign residents. Imperfect capital mobility exists when restrictions on capital movements are less severe, and domestic and foreign assets are imperfect substitutes in the portfolios of private agents. Perfect capital mobility represents the extreme case in which there are no restrictions on capital movements (or those that exist are ineffective) and either domestic and foreign assets share the same risk characteristics or portfolio managers don't care about risk.

In a situation of imperfect capital mobility, the domestic central bank has three options of intermediate targets for monetary policy: it can target the money supply, the stock of domestic credit, or the domestic interest rate. If it seeks to target the domestic money supply, it is obliged to sterilize fully the effects of capital flows on the domestic money supply. If it targets the stock of domestic credit, on the other hand, it does not sterilize at all. Finally, if it instead targets the domestic interest rate, whether it sterilizes or reinforces the effects of capital flows depends on the source of shocks to the money market. The ultimate effects of shocks on domestic financial markets depend on which strategy the central bank chooses to pursue.

In the next chapter we will put goods and asset market together to explore how the general macroeconomic equilibrium of the domestic economy responds to a variety of macroeconomic shocks under the various financial conditions introduced in this chapter.

APPENDIX 3.1: BALANCE SHEET CONSTRAINTS AND ASSET MARKET EQUILIBRIUM CONDITIONS

Balance sheet constraints imply that in a model with n assets, there can be at most $n - 1$ independent asset market equilibrium conditions. To see this in the specific context of our model, we can proceed as follows. First, notice that total asset demands by each agent are constrained by their financial wealth plus the supply financial liabilities that they are willing to issue to other agents. This is what we mean by the term "balance sheet constraints." For the four types of agents in our model, we can express these balance sheet constraints as:

$$M^D + B_P^D + sF_P^{*D} = W_P \qquad \text{(private sector)}$$
$$-B^S = W_G \qquad \text{(government)}$$
$$sR^{*D} + DC^D - M^S = W_C \qquad \text{(central bank)}$$
$$B_F^D - s(R^{*S} + F^{*S}) = NICP_F \qquad \text{(rest of the world)}$$

Adding these balance sheet constraints together, we have:

$$(M^D - M^S) + \left(B_P^D + DC^D + B_F^D - B^S\right) + s\left[\left(R^{*D} + F_P^{*D}\right) \right.$$
$$\left. -(R^{*S} + F^{*S})\right] = W_P + W_G + W_C + NICP_F = 0,$$

since we have already seen (page 61) that the right-hand side of this expression is equal to zero. This equation states that the sum of the values of the excess demands for all of the assets in our model must equal zero. Thus, if for some combination of values of endogenous variables two of these markets clear (i.e., have excess demands equal to zero), the third must clear as well. That means that the third market does not impose an *independent* constraint on the values that endogenous variables can take – there are two independent asset market equilibrium conditions.

But in our model, the home country is small in the market for the foreign asset, so it faces an infinitely elastic supply of those assets. In other words, the rest of the world will satisfy *any* demand for the foreign asset generated by the domestic economy. The implication is that the supply of foreign bonds will be equal to the demand for foreign bonds by the domestic economy no matter what that demand is. In other words, supply and demand for foreign bonds are *identically* equal (equal under all conditions). Thus, the third term on the left-hand side of the equation above drops out, and we are left with:

$$(M^D - M^S) + \left(B_P^D + DC^D + B_F^D - B^S\right) = 0.$$

Thus, our model contains only *two* independent asset market equilibrium conditions. If for some set of values of the endogenous variables the market for domestic bonds clears, the market for domestic money must clear as well. The equilibrium can be analyzed in terms of either market.

APPENDIX 3.2: MONETIZATION AND REVALUATION ACCOUNTS

Recall equation (3.6) describing the balance sheet of the central bank:

$$W_C = sR^* + DC - M.$$

What happens to W_C when the exchange rate is devalued? Suppose that initially W_C was zero, so:

$$W_{C0} = 0 = s_0 R_0^* + DC_0 - M_0.$$

After the devaluation, we have:

$$W_{C1} = s_1 R_0^* + DC_0 - M_0.$$
$$= (s_1 - s_0) R_0^* + s_0 R_0^* + DC_0 - M_0.$$
$$= (s_1 - s_0) R_0^*.$$

What happens to the money supply after the devaluation depends on what the central bank does with this capital gain, and what domestic credit policy it pursues at the same time. Consider three options:

a. No Monetization

If the central bank keeps the capital gain on its foreign exchange reserves $(s_1 - s_0) R_0^*$ in its own accounts, the above is the end of the story. The quantity $(s_1 - s_0) R_0^*$ is kept in a "revaluation account" which simply records the increase in the central bank's net worth. M_0 does not change, and there is no change in the money supply or the M_N curve.

b. Monetization

Now suppose the central bank transfers these gains to the government. Since the central bank simply credits the government's account at the central bank by the amount $(s_1 - s_0) R_0^*$, the initial effect is simply to reduce the amount that the government owes the central bank – that is, the stock of domestic credit – by $(s_1 - s_0) R_0^*$. Now the central bank's balance sheet becomes:

$$W_{C1} = s_1 R_0^* + DC_1 - M_0 = 0, \quad \text{where } DC_1 = DC_0 - (s_1 - s_0) R_0^*.$$

The central bank's net worth is zero, because the amount $(s_1 - s_0) R_0^*$ is added to $s_0 R_0^*$ and subtracted from DC_0. Notice that the money supply still hasn't changed. The government is the one that experiences an increase in its net worth in this case. Its net worth becomes:

$$W_G = -(B - (s_1 - s_0) R_0^*) = -B + (s_1 - s_0) R_0^*,$$

so the government is richer.

What if the government uses its new wealth to retire debt held by the private sector? It can do so by using its credit line at the central bank, thereby restoring its debt to the central bank to the original level DC_0 and using the proceeds in the form of $(s_1 - s_0) R_0^*$ of new money to buy back debt from the private sector. The government's balance sheet is now unchanged from the one immediately above, but the central bank's balance sheet becomes:

$$W_{C1} = s_1 R_0^* + DC_0 - M_1 = 0, \quad \text{where } M_1 = M_0 + (s_1 - s_0) R_0^*.$$

The central bank's net worth is still zero, because the amount $(s_1 - s_0) R_0^*$ has been added to $s_0 R_0^*$ as well as to M_0.

What's happened to the money supply? The percentage increase in M is given by $(M_1 - M_0)/M_0$, or:

$$(M_1 - M_0)/M_0 = [(s_1 - s_0)/s_0](s_0 R_0^*/M_0) < (s_1 - s_0)/s_0, \text{ because } s_0 R_0^*/M_0 < 1.$$

c. Monetization with Credit Expansion

If the central bank were also to expand DC by $(s_1 - s_0)/s_0$ at the same time, however, then the change in the money supply would be:

$$(M_1 - M_0)/M_0 = [(s_1 - s_0)/s_0](s_0 R_0^* + DC_0)/M_0 = (s_1 - s_0)/s_0.$$

That is, the money supply would expand in the same proportion as the rate of devaluation.

4

Short-Run Macroeconomic Equilibrium

In Chapter 2, we described how simultaneous short-run equilibrium in the labor and goods markets could be summarized in the form of the *GM* curve, a relationship between the domestic price level and the domestic interest rate. To find the value of the domestic price level – and thus of the real exchange rate – that cleared the market for domestic goods, we needed to know the value of the domestic interest rate. In Chapter 3, we saw that in general, the short-run equilibrium value of the domestic interest rate itself depends on the domestic price level, through the effects of the latter on financial market equilibrium in the economy.

In this chapter we will put these two pieces of the story together to see how the domestic price level and interest rate are simultaneously determined in a general equilibrium involving the labor market, the goods market, and the financial markets. We will then explore how this short-run general macroeconomic equilibrium is affected when the economy is subjected to a variety of policy and exogenous shocks originating in various domestic markets as well as abroad. This short-run model will link the determination of intertemporal and intratemporal relative prices with domestic macroeconomic policies, as well as with the various types of exogenous shocks to which emerging economies are typically vulnerable. In the chapter that follows, we will see how the configuration of domestic macroeconomic prices evolves over time as the economy moves from a short-run to a medium-term equilibrium.

I. THE *FM* CURVE

The first step in analyzing the economy's short-run equilibrium is to construct a graphical representation of the relationship between the domestic price level and the interest rate on domestic bonds that is consistent with equilibrium in domestic asset markets. In effect, we already derived this relationship in Chapter 3 when we examined the impact of a change in the price level on the value of the domestic interest rate that cleared the money market. We saw that, except when the central

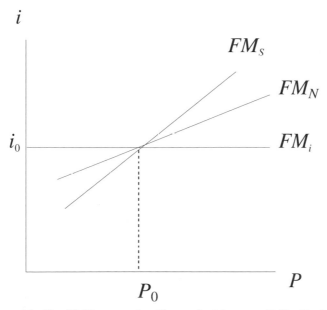

Figure 4.1. The *FM* Curve under Alternative Monetary Policy Regimes

bank is targeting the domestic interest rate, an increase in the domestic price level required an increase in the domestic bond interest rate in order for the money market to return to equilibrium, and that this increase was larger under monetary targeting than under credit targeting. Under domestic interest rate targeting, the only value of the domestic interest rate consistent with equilibrium in the domestic money market was, of course, the one targeted by the central bank. All that remains is to plot these relationships in i-P space.

We do so in Figure 4.1. The resulting curve tells us what interest rate is required to clear the domestic money market for given values of the domestic price level.[1] As shown in Appendix 3.1, the set of combinations of i and P that clear the domestic money market must clear the domestic bond market as well. We will refer to this curve as the *FM* (for "financial market") curve. Three such curves are depicted in the figure, corresponding to the three monetary policy regimes just mentioned.

The steepest *FM* curve in the figure is that corresponding to monetary targeting (FM_S). Its positive slope summarizes the relationship just mentioned: an increase in the domestic price level requires an increase in the domestic interest rate to clear the money market. Intuitively, the reason for the positive relationship is that in this case the money supply is fixed, so an increase in the domestic price level increases the nominal demand for money, with no effect on its nominal supply. The

---

[1] We will be deriving the equilibrium relationship between i and P for the general case of *unanticipated* price level changes in this chapter. The extension to the special case of anticipated changes is straightforward. We will discuss it briefly at the end of this section, and will come back to it in the next chapter.

resulting excess demand for money can be eliminated only through an increase in the domestic interest rate. The higher domestic interest rates attract capital inflows that the domestic central bank is obligated to purchase so as to maintain the official value of the exchange rate, but the central bank sterilizes the monetary effects of these purchases by selling domestic bonds in the open market.

The next steepest curve is M_N, which depicts all the combinations of i and P consistent with money market equilibrium when the central bank does *not* sterilize the effects of capital flows on the money supply. In this case the domestic interest rate does not have to rise as much as in the previous one when the increase in P increases the demand for money, for two reasons:

a. As we saw in the last chapter, the higher domestic price level causes domestic residents who want to hold more money to repatriate capital from abroad. Since these capital inflows are monetized, they increase the supply of money, meaning that the initial excess demand for money created by an increase in P is smaller in this case than in the previous one. In other words, the effects of changes in P on the *supply* of money through capital flows tend to (partially) offset the effects of changes in P on the demand for money, thus weakening the effects of changes in P on the excess demand for money relative to the case of full sterilization.
b. As the domestic interest rate rises, not only does the demand for money fall, but its supply increases as well, due to the capital inflows that are attracted by a higher domestic interest rate. This means that the effects of changes in i on the supply of money tend to reinforce the effects of changes in i on the demand for money, thus strengthening the effects of changes in i on the excess demand for money relative to the case of full sterilization.

In short, changes in P have weaker effects on the excess demand for money, and changes in i have stronger effects, when the central bank does not sterilize the monetary effects of capital flows than when it does. Putting these two factors together, a given change in P requires a smaller change in i to maintain money market equilibrium when the central bank does not sterilize than when it does – that is, the FM_N curve is flatter than FM_S.

Finally, under interest rate targeting the domestic money market can only clear if the domestic interest rate is equal to the policy-determined rate, so the FM curve in this case, labeled FM_i in Figure 4.1, is flat. In this case, the increase in the demand for money created by an increase in P generates an increase in the supply of money of exactly equal magnitude as the result of a combination of capital inflows attracted by the increased demand for domestic money as well as a credit expansion sufficient to satisfy the remaining excess demand for money at an unchanged value of the domestic interest rate.

Because the FM curve summarizes the conditions under which domestic financial markets are in equilibrium, its properties can be derived from the money market equilibrium diagram of Chapter 3. The most important ones are as follows:

a. As we have just seen, except in the case of interest rate targeting the *FM* curve has a positive slope. The reason is because an increase in the domestic price level increases the demand for money more than its supply, while an increase in the domestic interest rate increases supply relative to demand. This means that a higher value of the domestic interest rate is required to clear the money market when domestic prices are higher.

b. Since, under domestic credit targeting, the slope of the money supply curve depends on how strongly capital flows respond to changes in the domestic interest rate, so does the slope of the *FM* curve in this case. The FM_N curve is flatter (and capital flows are larger) the stronger this response is. In the limiting case of zero capital mobility the curve will have a relatively steep positive slope, coinciding with the FM_S curve. With perfect capital mobility, it will be flat at the height $i = i^{*}$.[2]

c. When capital is mobile and sterilization is not complete, movements to the northeast along the *FM* curve are associated with an increase in the domestic money supply. The reason is that, as we saw in the previous chapter, the money supply is increased both by increases in the domestic price level as well as by increases in domestic interest rates, in both cases through induced capital inflows.

d. Variables analyzed above other than the domestic price level that affect the equilibrium interest rate tend to shift the *FM* curve. Because the *FM* curve shows the value of the domestic interest rate required to achieve equilibrium in the domestic money market for given values of the domestic price level, when any of these variables change, the size of the vertical shift in the *FM* curve must be exactly the same as the magnitude of the change in the domestic interest rate required to restore equilibrium in the money market diagram in the previous chapter.

Before moving on to the determination of short-run macroeconomic equilibrium, it is worth pausing to note how these results would be affected by a switch to circumstances in which price level changes were previously anticipated. We saw in the previous chapter that if changes in *P* are anticipated, the demand for money changes in proportion to changes in *P*, rather than *more* than in proportion to such changes, as is the case for unanticipated price level changes. This means, as pointed out in Chapter 3, that effects of price level changes on the excess demand for money will tend to be smaller when those changes are anticipated. Thus, for a given change in the domestic price level the change in the equilibrium interest rate will be smaller when the price level change is anticipated. The implication is that the FM_S and FM_N curves are flatter when price level changes are anticipated

---

[2] Note that, since the slope of the *FM* curve depends on how strongly portfolio allocations respond to interest rate changes, an intensification of capital account restrictions would tend to make it steeper.

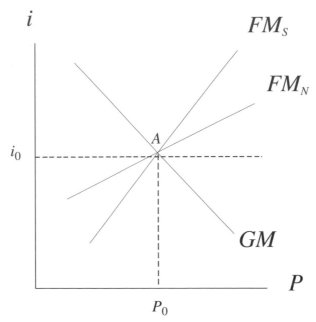

Figure 4.2. Short-Run Macroeconomic Equilibrium

than when they are not. Moreover, since price level changes have weaker effects on money market equilibrium in this case, horizontal shifts of these curves associated with money supply shocks will tend to be larger in the anticipated case.[3]

II. SHORT-RUN MACROECONOMIC EQUILIBRIUM

We can now assemble all the parts of our model to describe the economy's *short-run equilibrium*. In doing so, we will focus on the case of imperfect capital mobility, comparing what happens with full sterilization of foreign exchange market intervention by the central bank, with no sterilization, and with interest rate targeting. In considering the effects of shocks on the economy, it is straightforward to extend the analysis to the more extreme assumptions of financial autarky and perfect capital mobility. For concreteness, we will continue to focus on the case in which changes in the economy have *not* previously been anticipated by workers. Extension to the case of anticipated shocks is straightforward based on what has already been said about the properties of the *GM* and *FM* curves.

Putting the *GM* and *FM* curves together, as in Figure 4.2, the economy's short-run equilibrium corresponds to the point where the two curves intersect, labeled *A* in Figure 4.2. This will represent our point of departure to study what happens to the economy in the short run when shocks arrive, so both the *FM$_S$* and *FM$_N$* curves are drawn passing through *A*.

---

[3] Under interest rate targeting, the *FM* curve retains its horizontal shape when price level changes are anticipated, and shifts (vertically) only when the interest rate target is modified by the central bank.

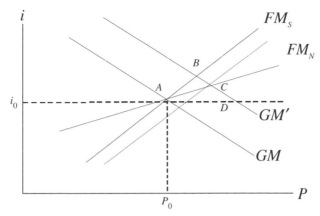

Figure 4.3. Effects of Expansionary Fiscal Policy

The point where the two curves intersect corresponds to a situation in which equilibrium prevails in both the domestic labor and goods markets, on the one hand, as well as in the domestic money and bond markets, on the other. Consequently, the point of intersection of the GM and FM curves determines the short-run equilibrium values of the domestic price level and the domestic interest rate. The equilibrium is short run in the sense that it holds for given values not only of the capital stock and technology, but also of the country's net international creditor position ($NICP^*$) and stock of government bonds outstanding (B) as well, since all of these slowly evolving variables were held constant in deriving the equilibrium conditions on which the curves are based.

To see how the model works, we can trace the effects on the economy of a variety of policy and exogenous shocks. The shocks that we will consider cover changes in domestic fiscal, monetary, and exchange rate policies as well as aggregate supply shocks and both foreign financial as well as real shocks.

a. Expansionary Fiscal Policy

An (unanticipated) increase in government spending affects only the goods market directly. Since an increase in government spending represents an increase in demand for domestic goods, this shock creates an incipient excess demand for domestic goods. This excess demand can be eliminated, and goods-market equilibrium restored, through some combination of higher domestic prices (to increase production and shift demand away from domestic toward foreign goods) and higher domestic interest rates (to reduce total spending by domestic residents, including spending on domestic goods). Because maintaining goods market equilibrium after the increase in government spending requires a higher level of domestic prices and/or a higher domestic interest rate than it did before the shock, the shock must shift the GM curve to the right, say from GM to GM' in Figure 4.3. At the original price level, a higher domestic interest rate is required to maintain goods-market equilibrium, and at the original interest rate a higher price level is required. The question is where the economy will wind up on the new GM' curve.

Suppose, for example, that the central bank sterilizes its intervention in the foreign exchange market, leaving the domestic money supply unaffected by such intervention. Then the relevant FM curve is FM_S, and the economy's new equilibrium is at B, with a relatively large increase in the domestic interest rate and only a relatively small increase in the domestic price level. Notice that, since both the increase in the domestic price level as well as in the domestic interest rate attract capital inflows from abroad, to maintain the domestic money supply constant at point B the central bank must sterilize heavily. If the central bank did not sterilize at all, then the supply of money would be increased by the capital inflows attracted by the higher domestic interest rates and prices that prevail at point B. This would cause the FM_S curve, which is drawn for a *given* money supply, to shift to the right along the new GM curve, until it reaches the point where the "no sterilization" FM curve, FM_N, intersects the new GM curve (i.e., at the point C). Thus, in the absence of sterilization, the new equilibrium is associated with a higher domestic price level and lower interest rate than when the central bank sterilizes the monetary effects of capital flows.[4] When the central bank targets the domestic interest rate, on the other hand, the increase in government spending results only in an increase in domestic prices, with no changes in interest rates.

We can say quite a bit about the domestic macroeconomic effects of this policy. To be concrete, suppose that we focus on the case of domestic credit targeting. We have already seen that the domestic price level and interest rate both rise in this case. Because the shock is unanticipated, the higher domestic price level represents an increase in P relative to P^e, and thus real GDP increases as well. Moreover, since the economy moves to the northeast along the FM_N curve, the domestic money supply must have increased at C. Since domestic credit is unchanged, this must be the result of reserve accumulation caused by capital inflows. In addition, because of the higher domestic price level, the real exchange rate must appreciate.

What happens to the country's trade balance in this case? To answer this question, based on Chapter 2 we can write the trade balance as:

$$N = X - eZ$$
$$= X(sP^*/P, \theta) - [1 - \phi(sP^*/P)] A_P[Y(P/P^e), T, i].$$
$$\quad + \quad + \quad \quad \quad \quad + \quad \quad - -$$

---

[4] There is another way to see why this must be so. Recall from Chapter 3 that increases in domestic prices have relatively weaker positive effects on the excess demand for money, and increases in domestic interest rates have relatively stronger negative ones, when the central bank does not sterilize than when it does. Thus, relatively larger increases in the domestic price level and smaller increases in the domestic interest rate are required to clear the money market when the central bank does not sterilize capital flows than when it does.

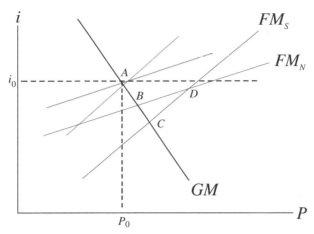

Figure 4.4. Effects of Expansionary Monetary Policy

The appreciation of the real exchange rate associated with the increase in P tends to cause the trade balance to deteriorate, but the increase in the domestic interest rate causes it to improve, by reducing private absorption and thus the domestic demand for imports. In principle, the net result is ambiguous. The trade balance will deteriorate if the composition of domestic and foreign demand for goods is very sensitive to the real exchange rate, and if domestic private absorption is not very sensitive to the interest rate. It will improve if these conditions are reversed.

b. Expansionary Monetary Policy

Next, consider the effects of an increase in domestic credit. As we saw in the last chapter, at a given value of the domestic price level, with or without sterilization, restoring money market equilibrium after such a policy would require a lower domestic interest rate. More generally, some combination of higher domestic prices and/or lower domestic interest rates would be required to restore equilibrium in the domestic money market – that is, with or without sterilization, the FM curve shifts to the right, as in Figure 4.4. At the new short-run equilibrium, the money and goods markets are simultaneously cleared by a combination of lower domestic interest rates and higher domestic prices along the GM curve. Together these have the effect of increasing the demand for money to accommodate the higher money supply caused by the domestic credit expansion, but they have opposing effects in the goods market, thus permitting the aggregate demand for domestic goods to remain equal to aggregate supply.

But again, where the new equilibrium lies depends on whether or not the central bank sterilizes the effects of capital inflows. In particular, one interesting question that arises in this context is whether the credit expansion has a larger impact on the price level and real output when the central bank pursues a policy of monetary targeting or one of domestic credit targeting.

To answer this question, recall from Chapter 3 that the effects of a change in P on the excess demand for money are weaker, and those of a change in i are stronger, when the central bank targets credit than when it targets the money supply. This means that the *horizontal* displacement of the FM_N curve must be larger than that of the FM_S curve in response to a domestic monetary expansion (since the effects of a change in P on the excess demand for money are weaker, a larger change in P is required to restore money market equilibrium), while its *vertical* displacement must be smaller (since the effects of a change in i on the excess demand for money are stronger, a *smaller* change in i is required to restore money market equilibrium). Thus, the two curves must cross at a point like D. It follows that whether the monetary expansion will have stronger effects on the domestic price level and real output with sterilization or without it depends on the slope of the GM curve.

When the GM curve is relatively steep, as in Figure 4.4, a relatively large share of adjustment in the *money* market will have to be borne by interest rates and less by prices. Because interest rate changes have weak effects on the excess demand for money and price level changes strong ones under sterilization, placing more of the burden of adjustment on the variable with relatively weak effects means that the movements in domestic prices and interest rates required to absorb the higher money supply will have to be larger when the central bank sterilizes than when it does not. Conversely, when the GM curve is flat, more of the burden of adjustment in the money market is placed on the price level and less on interest rates. Since changes in the price level are the relatively weak equilibrating variable in the money market when the central bank does not sterilize, placing more of the burden of adjustment on this variable means that movements in domestic prices will have to be larger under these circumstances without sterilization than with it.

Note that the domestic money supply must be higher in the new equilibrium whether the central bank targets the money supply or the stock of credit. In the former case, this result is trivially true, because a higher desired value for the money supply must have motivated the credit expansion in the first place. This is not true in the case of domestic credit targeting, but we can see that the money supply must be larger in this case as well, because with higher prices and lower domestic interest rates, the demand for money must have risen.

A second interesting question that arises in the context of this shock, however, is whether when the central bank targets money, it needs to follow up the initial expansion of credit with a secondary expansion in order to meet its money supply target, or with a secondary contraction. Alternatively, we can ask whether when the central bank targets credit, the final increase in the money supply after any induced capital flows are taken into account will be larger or smaller than the original credit expansion. These are two sides of the same coin, because whenever the money supply would increase by *more* than the original credit expansion because of induced capital *inflows* under domestic credit targeting, the central bank would be forced to contract credit under money supply targeting, while whenever the money supply would increase by *less* than the original credit expansion under credit targeting because of induced capital *outflows*, the central bank would be forced to expand credit under money supply targeting.

Whether the initial credit expansion gives rise to capital inflows or outflows is not obvious. To absorb the higher stock of money associated with the credit expansion while maintaining equilibrium in the goods market under financial autarky would require some combination of lower domestic interest rates and higher domestic prices, as at point *C* in Figure 4.4. But the lower domestic interest rate that prevails at a point such as this will tend to induce capital outflows, while the higher domestic prices induce inflows. It can be shown, however, that if the *GM* curve passes to the northeast of the point *D* in Figure 4.4, the initial increase in domestic credit must induce a capital inflow, while if it passes to the southwest, it must induce a capital outflow. Thus, when the *GM* curve is flat, the central bank must contract credit to sterilize capital inflows induced by its original credit expansion when it is targeting the money supply, while when it is targeting the stock of domestic credit, induced capital inflows will cause the final increase in the money supply to exceed the size of the initial credit expansion. On the other hand, when the *GM* curve is steep, the central bank must expand credit to sterilize capital outflows induced by its original credit expansion when it is targeting the money supply, while when it is targeting the stock of domestic credit, induced capital outflows will cause the final increase in the money supply to fall short of the size of the initial credit expansion. The reason is easy to see. When the *GM* curve passes to the northeast of *D*, the goods market must be cleared with a relatively large increase in the domestic price level and small decline in the domestic interest rate, so factors tending to attract capital dominate factors tending to repel it. On the other hand, if the *GM* curve passes to the southwest of *D*, the increase in domestic prices will be small relative to the decline in domestic interest rates. Thus, factors that repel capital dominate those that attract it. The critical point *D* is identified by where the FM_S and FM_N curves cross, because at that point the money supply must be the same whether the central bank targets the money supply or the stock of credit, implying that induced capital flows must be zero – that is, the change in the interest rate and the price level are such that the effects of interest rate and price level changes on capital flows exactly offset each other.

The higher equilibrium price level that emerges from the credit expansion, whether sterilized or not, means that the real exchange rate must appreciate, as in the case of the fiscal expansion. However, in this case the domestic interest rate falls and private absorption increases, so the trade balance must deteriorate.

c. Nominal Devaluation

Consider now the effects on the economy of a nominal exchange rate devaluation that is *not* monetized by the central bank. Since this shock has no effect on the money market, its only effect is to shift GM to the right somewhat less than in proportion to the change in the exchange rate, as we saw in Chapter 2. Since a nonmonetized devaluation would leave the *FM* curve unchanged, the new equilibrium would look very similar to that in Figure 4.3, with a higher domestic price level and higher domestic interest rate.

Because both the domestic interest rate and the domestic price level have risen, the devaluation triggers a capital inflow that increases the stock of foreign exchange reserves immediately. If the central bank sterilizes this inflow fully, the capital inflow shows up in the form of a change in the composition of the central bank's balance sheet, with an increase in the central bank's foreign exchange reserves and a reduction in its stock of domestic credit. If it does not do so, then the capital inflow increases both the central bank's foreign exchange reserves and the domestic money supply. In that case, the increase in domestic interest rates is smaller, and that in the domestic price level is larger, than when the central bank sterilizes.

Since the increase in the domestic price level is smaller than the rightward shift in the *GM* curve, which itself is smaller in magnitude than the change in the exchange rate, the percentage increase in the domestic price level is smaller than that in the nominal exchange rate, which means that the real exchange rate must depreciate, albeit because of the price offset, by less than the nominal devaluation. Just as in the case of the fiscal expansion, however, effects on the trade balance are ambiguous in principle, because the increase in the domestic interest rate will tend to curtail private absorption and with it the demand for imports. A trade balance improvement will result if import and export demand elasticities are sufficiently high and the interest rate elasticity of private spending sufficiently low.

If the nominal devaluation is monetized, we saw in the last chapter that the money supply will increase, but by less than in proportion to the nominal devaluation. The *FM* curve will shift to the right, once again with the rightward shift in FM_N larger than that in FM_S. Relative to what happens when the devaluation is not monetized, there will be a smaller increase in the domestic interest rate, but a larger one in the domestic price level. However, as long as the stock of domestic credit is not increased, or is increased by less than in proportion to the rate of devaluation, the real exchange rate will depreciate, because the increase in the domestic price level will be proportionately smaller than the change in the exchange rate.

d. A Domestic Supply Shock

The three shocks we have considered so far have affected the demand side of the goods market. Consider next how the economy's short-run equilibrium would respond to a supply shock. For concreteness, we can think of this as a discrete increase in the parameter A that measures total factor productivity in the aggregate production function. In the real world this could correspond, for example, to an exceptionally favorable harvest or an important technological innovation. Its effect is to increase the level of real output Y corresponding to any given value of P/P^e.

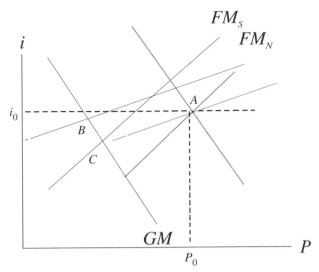

Figure 4.5. Short-Run Effects of a Favorable Aggregate Supply Shock

This shock affects both the financial and goods markets. The increase in domestic output creates an excess supply of domestic goods, requiring a reduction in their relative price (a decrease in P) to restore goods-market equilibrium. Thus, the GM curve shifts to the left in Figure 4.5. At the same time, the increase in domestic income increases the demand for money, requiring an increase in the domestic interest rate to restore equilibrium in the domestic money market, and thus causing both FM_S and FM_N to shift upward. Because the increase in domestic income causes domestic residents to repatriate some capital, the initial excess demand for money is smaller when the central bank does not sterilize than when it does. Together with the fact that changes in domestic interest rates are more effective in eliminating excess demand in the money market in the absence of sterilization than in its presence, this means that the vertical shift in FM_N is smaller than that in FM_S. At the same time, and for reasons similar to those we discussed previously, the *horizontal* shift in FM_N is larger than that in FM_S. Thus, the two curves cross, as in Figure 4.5.

As shown in Figure 4.5, the shock must unambiguously lower the domestic price level, thus depreciating the domestic economy's real exchange rate. While the figure shows the domestic interest rate falling, this is not a necessary outcome. If the shift in the GM curve is smaller (that is, if substitution elasticities between domestic and foreign goods are large), the GM curve could intersect either or both FM curves above the original domestic interest rate, thus causing the domestic interest rate to be higher in the new equilibrium. It is also possible that the interest rate outcome could differ depending on the policies pursued by the central bank, with the domestic interest rate falling under full sterilization, and rising if the bank does not sterilize.

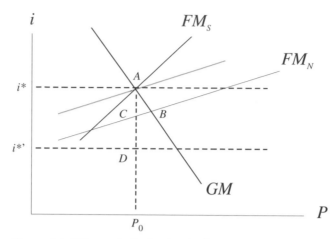

Figure 4.6. Effects of a Reduction in the Foreign Interest Rate

e. A Reduction in the Foreign Interest Rate

Next, consider the effects of external shocks. First, suppose that the relevant shock to the economy consists of a decrease in i^* (it's useful to consider a decrease instead of an increase to replicate the capital-inflow phenomenon that several developing countries experienced during the first part of the decade of the nineties, a subject that we will take up in Chapter 15). This shock has no direct effect on the GM curve, and if the central bank sterilizes, the FM curve is undisturbed as well, so there would be no effect on the domestic short-run macroeconomic equilibrium.[5] If the central bank does not sterilize, the effect of the shock would be to shift the FM_N curve to the right, as domestic residents repatriate capital and foreign residents shift funds into the domestic economy. The economy moves from A to B in Figure 4.6. The domestic interest rate falls, the price level rises, capital flows in, and because of the real exchange rate appreciation and reduction in the domestic interest rate, the trade balance deteriorates.

How large is the drop in the domestic interest rate in the absence of sterilization? The answer is that the reduction in the domestic interest rate must be smaller than that in the foreign interest rate as long as capital mobility is imperfect. To see why, recall from Chapter 3 that, at a given domestic price level, the reduction in the domestic interest rate must be smaller than that in the foreign interest rate. Thus, the downward shift in FM_N must be of a smaller magnitude that the reduction in

---

[5] What difference does it make whether the response to a reduction in i^* is sterilization or capital controls? The difference shows up in the central bank's balance sheet. If the fixed value of M arises from sterilization rather than capital controls, there will have to be a one-for-one credit contraction to sustain the original value of the money supply. Thus, R^* increases in the central bank's balance sheet and DC contracts by an equal amount. Since domestic bonds typically pay higher interest than do reserves, the central bank's interest income falls under sterilization, but not under capital controls.

the foreign interest rate, as in Figure 4.6, where the foreign interest rate drops from i^* to $i^{*\prime}$, while the interest rate required to clear the domestic money market falls only from A to C. Both because the reduction in the domestic interest rate must be less than of the foreign rate to clear the domestic money market (i.e., because the point C is above D), as well as because, in order to clear the goods market, further increases in domestic interest rates and prices are required from the point C (at which the domestic money market clears with unchanged prices), the final reduction in the domestic interest rate must be smaller than that in the foreign rate.

Another interesting question is whether capital inflows will be larger when the central bank sterilizes them or when it simply fixes DC. With sterilization there is no drop in the domestic interest rate at all, as there would be when the central bank just concentrates on fixing DC. The higher interest rate that prevails in this case tends to attract more capital into the country than when the central bank does not sterilize inflows and allows domestic interest rates to fall. On the other hand, in the case of full sterilization, domestic prices are lower, which reduces incentives for domestic residents to repatriate capital. Whether capital inflows are larger at A or at B – that is, with or without sterilization – depends on the extent to which the adjustment from A to B primarily takes the form of lower interest rates or higher prices (that is, on the shape of the GM curve), as well as on the relative sensitivity of capital flows to the domestic interest rate and the domestic price level (the shape of the FM_N curve). Capital inflows will be *smaller* in the *absence* of sterilization (i.e., smaller at B than at A) the more that adjustment takes the form of lower interest rates instead of higher prices (i.e., the *steeper* the GM curve) as well as the more sensitive capital flows are to domestic interest rates and the less to domestic prices (i.e., the *flatter* the FM_N curve).

f. An Increase in Partner-Country Incomes

As our final shock, consider the effects on the domestic economy of an exogenous increase in demand for its exports caused by an increase in partner-country incomes.[6] As in the case of the domestic aggregate supply shock that we examined above, this shock would directly affect both the domestic goods and money markets. The increase in demand for exports from the domestic economy represents an increase in aggregate demand for domestic goods (operating through the shift parameter θ), and thus causes the GM curve to shift to the right, as in Figure 4.7. At the same time, the increase in their incomes causes foreign residents to repatriate capital, in order to satisfy their increased demand for their own currency. The ensuing capital outflow from the domestic economy has no effect on the FM_S curve, which assumes that the domestic central bank sterilizes the capital outflow, but shifts the FM_N curve

---

[6] In other words, suppose that θ is a positive function of partner-country incomes, so that $\theta = \theta(Y^*, \ldots)$, where Y^* denotes the incomes of partner countries, and that Y^* increases.

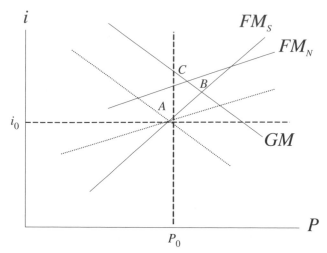

Figure 4.7. Effects of an Increase in Partner-Country Incomes

vertically upward, since the capital outflow and associated monetary contraction caused by the reduced demand for domestic bonds by the rest of the world requires an increase in the domestic interest rate to maintain equilibrium in the domestic money market.

This shock will unambiguously cause domestic interest rates to rise, but its effect on the domestic price level (and thus on the economy's real exchange rate) depends on the central bank's monetary policy. If the central bank sterilizes the capital outflows associated with capital repatriation by foreigners, domestic prices will rise together with domestic interest rates, as at the point B. On the other hand, if there is no sterilization, prices may rise or fall. The outcome depends on the relative magnitudes of the vertical shifts in the GM and FM_N curves. If the economy is very open commercially, and if domestic aggregate demand is not very sensitive to interest rate changes, the vertical shift in the GM curve will be large, and an expansionary outcome is more likely. It is also more likely if the domestic economy is financially relatively closed, or if domestic assets represent a very small share of the financial portfolios of private agents in partner countries. Under these conditions, the vertical shift in FM_N will be small, and the shock will be expansionary even if the central bank does not sterilize, as in Figure 4.7.

III. APPLICATION: MACROECONOMIC INSTABILITY IN EMERGING ECONOMIES

The model we have been exploring can be used to identify the sources of instability in intertemporal as well as intratemporal relative prices in emerging economies. Note that in analyzing our model our central focus has been on two endogenous variables: the domestic interest rate and the domestic price level. Indeed, these two variables have been on the axes in all of the diagrams we have used in this chapter. The reason for this focus is that these are precisely the two variables that determine the values of the real interest rate and real exchange rate, the two relative prices that we emphasized in Chapter 1. In an economy such as the one we have modeled, with no ongoing inflation and no anticipated future changes in the price level, the nominal and real interest rates coincide. Thus, all of the shocks we have analyzed affect both nominal and real interest rates in the domestic economy. Moreover, as we have seen throughout this chapter, changes in the domestic price level translate directly into changes in the real exchange rate in this economy, since under fixed exchange rates the domestic price level is the only endogenous variable in the real exchange rate definition $e = sP^*/P$.

It follows that instability in the real interest rate and real exchange rate in the economy under study can result from all of the shocks we have investigated. It is useful to classify them into several categories:

a. Domestic Policy Shocks

In industrial-country macroeconomics, the potential stabilizing roles of fiscal and monetary policies are usually emphasized. In principle, at least, policymakers can make use of these policies to offset sources of instability arising elsewhere in the economy. While it is often debated whether such policies can be effective in playing this stabilizing role, little attention is usually given to the possibility that domestic policy shocks, in the form of changes in fiscal and monetary policies (i.e., G, T, and DC in our model) may themselves represent an important source of shocks. In many emerging economies they have typically done just that. Political instability, changing political coalitions, and central banks with little policy independence have often resulted in frequently changing fiscal and monetary policies, with attendant effects on instability of key macroeconomic relative prices that have disrupted the roles of such prices in the efficient allocation of resources.

b. Changes in the International Environment

Many developing economies are small, highly open to international trade, and relatively specialized in their export production. Consequently, changes in the prices of their primary export commodities, and thus in their export revenues (captured in our model by the parameter θ), have large impacts on their domestic economies. High volatility in individual commodity prices thus tends to translate into high volatility of domestic macroeconomic relative prices.

Moreover, emerging economies have been characterized by increasing financial openness, as we will discuss later on, and this has also left them exposed to volatility in international financial markets. This has manifested itself not only in the form of fluctuations in international interest rates that reflect monetary policies adopted in the industrial countries for their own domestic stabilization reasons, but perhaps even more importantly, in the form of fluctuations in the interest rate premia paid by specific countries over the international risk-free rate. These premia have proven very volatile, sometimes driven by sharp responses to domestic macroeconomic events but at other times by events happening elsewhere (a phenomenon known as "contagion"). In the context of our model, fluctuations in the interest rate at which the domestic economy can access international market show up, of course, in the form of changes in i^*.

c. Supply Shocks

Even emerging economies with exports concentrated in manufactured goods tend to have large agricultural sectors, and primary production continues to loom relatively large in these economies. Consequently, weather-related supply shocks can still represent an important source of macroeconomic instability.

d. Policy Responses to Exogenous Shocks

Finally, even in an unstable external and natural environment, macroeconomic instability can be reduced by implementing stabilizing domestic policy responses. But in many emerging economies not only do policies themselves represent an important source of shocks, as we have seen, but rather than play a stabilizing role in response to exogenous shocks, they often serve to *aggravate* the macroeconomic consequences of such shocks. For example, expansionary fiscal and monetary policies are often associated with export booms, and such policies tend to be tightened during cyclical downturns. In other words, policies tend to be *procyclical*. We shall explore in Part 3 of this book some reasons why this might be so.

IV. SUMMARY

In this chapter, we put the financial markets together with the goods and labor markets to derive the economy's short-run macroeconomic equilibrium. We also examined the ways in which this equilibrium was affected by a variety of policy and exogenous shocks that can affect emerging economies. While the list of shocks we examined was by no means exhaustive of such possibilities, most shocks that we will be interested in throughout this book can be interpreted as "real" shocks (shocks affecting the domestic goods market, in the form of exogenous changes in the demand for or supply of domestic goods), "nominal" shocks (shocks affecting the domestic money market, in the form of exogenous changes in the supply of or demand for domestic money), or foreign financial or real shocks. The shocks we have examined here provide representative examples of each of these.

We have seen that the domestic macroeconomic effects of such shocks depend in an important way on how domestic monetary policy is conducted (i.e., whether the domestic central bank sterilizes or not), as well as on the shapes of the GM and FM curves that summarize key parts of the general macroeconomic equilibrium. While we have not explicitly considered how the effects of these shocks would differ under financial autarky or perfect capital mobility, it is a straightforward exercise to extend the analysis of this chapter in order to do so.[7]

In all of these cases, the period of analysis has been the short run, during which not only the domestic capital stock and state of technology, but also the country's net international creditor position and the outstanding stock of domestic government bonds, have all been held constant. In the next chapter we will move to the medium term, and will consider how the analysis we conducted in this chapter needs to be modified when we allow time for some of these variables to adjust.

---

[7] In the case of financial autarky, the exercise is trivial, since it simply consists of re-labeling the FM_S curve.

5

Medium-Term Macroeconomic Equilibrium

In developing our benchmark model in the last three chapters, we described the macroeconomic equilibrium that we were analyzing as a short-run one, because we took the economy's stock of capital and its production technology as given during the period of the analysis. Our reason for holding these variables constant was that they tend to change very slowly over time, relative to the other variables in our model.

But these were not the only variables that we took as given when we built the model. Recall that in describing the determination of equilibrium in domestic asset markets, we introduced several variables that corresponded to financial stocks: the economy's net international creditor position, the domestic government's outstanding debt, and the net worth of the private sector. In the short-run model that we have been studying, these financial stocks were also assumed to be constant. But if the economy's short-run equilibrium results in a surplus or deficit in the current account of the country's balance of payments, its net international creditor position will actually be changing over time. Similarly, if the government runs a deficit in its budget, it will need to issue additional bonds to finance that deficit, and if it runs a surplus it will retire existing bonds. In either case, the outstanding stock of bonds would tend to change. Finally, if the private sector tends to save in excess of the amount that it chooses to devote to investment in physical capital, this will increase its financial wealth. All of these changes will tend to alter the economy's short-run macroeconomic equilibrium over time.

This chapter will extend our model to analyze these dynamic effects, and in particular will consider what the macroeconomic equilibrium looks like when all of these changes are completed, a situation that we will describe as a "medium-term" equilibrium, to distinguish it both from the short-run equilibrium that we have been studying as well as from the long-run equilibrium of growth theory.

In principle, this dynamic analysis will make it possible to consider both the short-run and medium-term effects of a variety of exogenous and policy shocks to an emerging-market economy. The specific issues that we will focus on in this chapter, however, are the roles of monetary and exchange rate policies in determining the domestic price level over the medium term. What we would like to understand is how a small open economy can sustain ongoing inflation over the medium term. This is a phenomenon that was missing from our short-run model, but that will figure prominently in the next part of the book, since high inflation has been considered an aspect of macroeconomic performance with important implications for long-run capacity growth. A key point that will emerge from the analysis is the central role that the exchange rate plays as a nominal anchor in an open economy with an officially determined exchange rate.

I. SOURCES OF MACROECONOMIC DYNAMICS

The term "short-run" as applied to the macroeconomic equilibrium that we studied in the last chapter was meant to indicate that the equilibrium in question would not last very long. Why wouldn't it? The reason is that certain financial variables that influence that short-run equilibrium themselves tend to change over time, and as they do so, the short-run equilibrium changes along with them. If these adjustments are sufficiently rapid relative to those of the capital stock and technology, then it is meaningful to talk about a *medium-term equilibrium*, in which we continue to take the capital stock and level of technology as given, but in which the relatively rapidly adjusting macroeconomic variables have reached a stable level, so that the economy's macroeconomic situation would tend to persist for some time.

To see how this happens in our model, consider the money supply relationship given by equation (3.16) of Chapter 3:

$$M = s[(1 - (b^* + f))NICP^* + b^*(F^* - P^*L^*) - f(B - PL)/s] + DC.$$

According to this relationship, the economy's money supply at any given time depends on the three predetermined variables $NICP^*$, B, and F^*. Under the small-country assumption, however, the behavior of F^* is unaffected by what happens in the domestic economy, so we can take F^* as an exogenous variable, and for the sake of simplicity assume that it is constant over time. This leaves two predetermined variables in the money supply relationship ($NICP^*$ and B). To isolate their influence on the domestic money supply, it is useful to rewrite the equation above as:

$$\begin{aligned} M &= [(1 - (b^* + f))s\,NICP^* - fB + DC] + sb^*(F^* - P^*L^*) + fPL \\ &= M_0 + sb^*(F^* - P^*L^*) + fPL, \end{aligned} \tag{5.1}$$

where $M_0 = (1 - (b^* + f))s\,NICP^* - fB + DC$.

Now we can establish the key point that motivates this chapter: since $NICP^*$ and B are predetermined variables that change gradually over time depending on the economy's short-run equilibrium, the money supply contains a component, which we have called M_0, that changes over time. Thus, the money supply itself must also be changing over time if domestic credit is held constant. If so, then the economy's short-run equilibrium must be changing as well. What this means is that to find the economy's medium-term equilibrium, we have to find the conditions under which $NICP^*$ and B, the predetermined variables in M_0, reach stable values.

To do so, we need to begin by describing what determines the evolution of $NICP^*$ and B over time. Consider $NICP^*$ first. The country acquires net claims on the rest of the world when it runs a surplus on the current account of its balance of payments, since in that case the rest of the world can pay for its excess of purchases from the home country over sales to the home country only by borrowing from the home country. Thus we can write:

$$\Delta NICP^* = CA^* = NP/s + i^*(F_P^* + R^*) - iB_F/s. \tag{5.2}$$

The home country's current account surplus CA^* (expressed in units of the foreign currency) is the surplus on its balance on goods and services NP/s plus its net receipts of interest payments from the rest of the world, consisting of its interest receipts on foreign bonds held by the private sector and the central bank $i^*(F_P^* + R^*)$ minus the domestic government's interest payments on its bonds held by foreigners, iB_F.

The corresponding relationship for B relates changes in B to the government's overall budget deficit:

$$\Delta B = P(G - T) + iB. \tag{5.3}$$

This equation, which is called the government's *budget constraint,* is expressed in units of domestic currency. It states that the government will issue bonds (ΔB will be positive) when it needs to finance an overall deficit in its budget, consisting of a *primary* (noninterest) deficit $P(G - T)$, and net interest payments on its outstanding debt iB. $NICP^*$ and B are both predetermined variables in the sense that their current values are the result of past accumulation through the relationships:

$$NICP^* = \sum CA^* \tag{5.4a}$$

$$B = \sum [P(G - T) + iB]. \tag{5.4b}$$

With these tools in hand, we can now examine what it would take for M_0 to remain unchanged – that is, for the economy to attain a *medium-term equilibrium.* Write the change in M_0 as:

$$\Delta M_0 = (1 - (b^* + f))s \Delta NICP^* - f\Delta B + \Delta DC \tag{5.5a}$$

$$= (1 - (b^* + f))s CA^* - f[P(G - T) + iB + \Delta DC. \tag{5.5b}$$

It follows that, as long as CA^* and $P(G - T) + iB$ are not equal to zero and do not have offsetting effects on the money supply, M_0 will be changing unless DC is used to offset those changes – that is, unless the impact of these *flow* changes on the money supply are sterilized.[1]

To study how the economy adjusts over time to its medium-term equilibrium, let's restrict ourselves for the present to a situation in which the government's budget is balanced and the central bank pursues a domestic credit target – that is, $P(G - T) + iB = \Delta DC = 0$. That means that for M_0 to remain unchanged, we would need $CA^* = 0$. We will now explore how the economy would adjust to its medium-term equilibrium under three alternative assumptions about its financial integration with the rest of the world: financial autarky, perfect capital mobility, and the intermediate case in which domestic and foreign bonds are imperfect substitutes.

II. MEDIUM-TERM EQUILIBRIUM UNDER FINANCIAL AUTARKY

As we have seen, under financial autarky, domestic residents do not hold foreign bonds, and foreigners do not hold domestic bonds. In that case, the current account balance can be written as:

$$\Delta NICP^* = CA^* = NP/s + i^* R^*.$$

To simplify matters further, suppose that foreign exchange reserves do not pay interest. In that case, the current account balance becomes:

$$
\begin{aligned}
\Delta NICP^* = CA^* &= NP/s \\
&= (X - eZ)P/s \\
&= \{X(e, \theta) - [1 - \phi(e)] A_P(Y, T, i)\}P/s, \qquad (5.6) \\
&\quad\;\; {}^{+\;\;+} \qquad\qquad\quad {}^{+} \qquad\;\; {}^{+\;-\;-}
\end{aligned}
$$

where the balance on goods and services N has been written in terms of its determinants. Equation (5.6) describes how $NICP^*$ evolves over time. Because in a medium-term equilibrium $NICP^*$ must have reached a stationary level, we can express the necessary condition for the economy to be in a medium-term equilibrium as:

$$\{X(sP^*/P, \theta) - [1 - \phi(sP^*/P)] A_P(Y, T, i)\}P/s = 0. \qquad (5.7)$$

A medium-term equilibrium is one in which the economy has had time to adjust to exogenous shocks. It is sensible, therefore, to require as one of the conditions of medium-term equilibrium that price level expectations be correct. Our model of medium-term equilibrium thus consists of the *GM* and *FM* curves we derived previously, with $P = P^e$ imposed, plus equation (5.7). In contrast with the

---

[1] From the preceding equation, $\Delta M_0 = 0$ requires:

$$s\,CA^* = \frac{f}{1 - (b^* + f)}[P(G - T) + iB] - \frac{\Delta DC}{1 - (b^* + f)}.$$

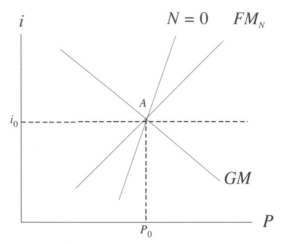

Figure 5.1. Medium-Term Equilibrium

short-term model in which $NICP^*$ was held constant, in the medium-term model it becomes an endogenous variable, so in effect we have added one equation and one endogenous variable to the model we constructed in Chapters 2–4.

What are the properties of medium-term equilibrium in this economy? This equilibrium can be analyzed with the use of Figure 5.1, which plots equation (5.7) (labeled $N = 0$) in the i-P space we previously used to analyze the economy's short-run equilibrium. Note that this equation is depicted as a curve with a positive slope. The reason is that an increase in P causes the trade balance to deteriorate (since it results in a real exchange rate appreciation), requiring a higher domestic interest rate to restore a zero trade balance. In Figure 5.1 only the FM_N curve is depicted, since we will concentrate on the case in which the monetary effects of balance of payments flows (in this case in the form of *current account* surpluses and deficits) are not sterilized.

The key observation about this figure is that, since the endogenous variable $NICP^*$ only enters the money market equilibrium condition depicted by the FM curve, the medium-term equilibrium values of i and P will be determined by the intersection of the $N = 0$ and GM curves, with $NICP^*$ adjusting so as to cause FM to pass through this point of intersection. To see how this works, note that to the right of the curve $N = 0$ the trade balance must be in deficit, since the price level is too high (the real exchange rate too appreciated) to be consistent with a zero trade balance. Conversely, to the left of the $N = 0$ curve, the trade balance must be in surplus, due to the relatively depreciated real exchange rate. This means that the right of $N = 0$, $NICP^*$ must be decreasing, while to the right of it, $NICP^*$ must be increasing. We saw in Chapter 3 that increases in $NICP^*$ would shift the FM curve to the right, while decreases in $NICP^*$ would shift it to the left. Thus, if in the short-run equilibrium FM and GM intersect to the right of $N = 0$, FM will shift left, until it passes through the intersection of $N = 0$ and GM. Similarly, if in short-run equilibrium *FM* and *GM* intersect to the left of $N = 0$, *FM* will shift to the right over time, until it passes through the intersection of $N = 0$ and *GM*.

With these observations, we can now identify some of the most important properties of the medium-term equilibrium for our present purposes:[2]

a. In the medium term, nominal exchange rate changes and changes in partner-country price levels must result in proportionate changes in the domestic price level. This must be so because when price level changes are anticipated – as we have assumed to be the case in medium-term equilibrium – Y is constant. In that case, the *GM* curve must shift horizontally in proportion to any change in sP^*. It is easy to see that $N = 0$ must do so as well, since P enters equation (5.7) only in the form of sP^*/P. It follows that proportionate changes in sP^*/P and P would leave equation (5.7) satisfied. Since $N = 0$ and *GM* both shift horizontally by the same proportion as the change in sP^*, at their new intersection the domestic price level must have changed in the same proportion.

b. On the other hand, changes in the stock of domestic credit have no effect on the domestic price level in the medium term. This must be the case, because changes in *DC* have no effect on either the $N = 0$ or the *GM* curves.

While these results follow fairly directly from what has already been said, it is useful to illustrate how the economy adjusts to the medium-term equilibrium with the properties just described.

a. An Increase in Domestic Credit

Figure 5.2 illustrates how the economy responds to an increase in the stock of domestic credit. Suppose that the economy's original equilibrium at *A* is one in which the current account is in balance (i.e., the current account surplus is zero). This means that the $N = 0$ curve must pass through *A*. In this case, there is no ongoing adjustment in *NICP** at *A*, and this short-run equilibrium is therefore also a medium-term equilibrium. Now consider the effects of a monetary expansion. Under financial autarky, the post-monetary expansion short-run equilibrium was at *C*. But if the current account was originally zero at *A*, it must be in deficit at *C*. We can see this because *C* is to the right of $N = 0$. But this means that *NICP** must be falling at the point *C*, and thus that the domestic money supply must be decreasing.

The implication is that *FM* must be shifting to the left. It must continue to do so as long as the current account deficit persists, so a stationary position

---

[2] In a similar fashion, the effects on the medium-term equilibrium of the other shocks that we studied in the last chapter can be determined by examining their implications for the positions of the $N = 0$ and *GM* curves.

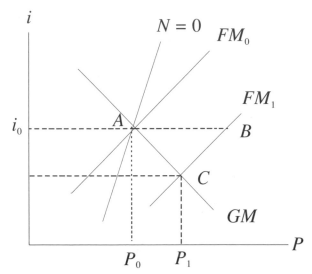

Figure 5.2. Medium-Term Effects of a Domestic Credit Expansion

for *FM* cannot occur unless the short-run equilibrium lies along $N = 0$. This means that the current account deficit persists until the *FM* curve returns to its original position and the price level and real exchange rate both return to their original values. This story has an important moral: *in an open economy with a fixed exchange rate, monetary policy cannot permanently affect the domestic price level.*

If the monetary expansion does not succeed in increasing the price level in the medium term, what macroeconomic effects does it have? The difference between the original equilibrium at A and the final one at the same point is in the composition of the central bank's balance sheet. The expansion in domestic credit simply "crowds out" an equivalent amount of foreign exchange reserves. Thus, monetary policy can affect the level of foreign exchange reserves, but not the domestic price level.

Recall that we have been analyzing a no-sterilization situation. Would the result change if, instead of targeting an increase in *DC*, the central bank had targeted an increase in M – that is, if the central bank sterilized the current account deficits induced by its initial monetary expansion? If the central bank did this, then in order to sustain the desired higher value of the money supply at the point C, it would have to continuously expand the supply of credit to offset the foreign exchange reserve losses arising from the trade deficit – that is, it would have to sterilize the reserve losses. While it does so, the *FM* curve would stay where it is, since the money supply would not be changing. But since the loss of reserves is continuous, eventually the stock of reserves would be depleted, and the central bank would no longer be able to fix the exchange rate. In other words, the policy of monetary targeting cannot be sustained in the medium term.

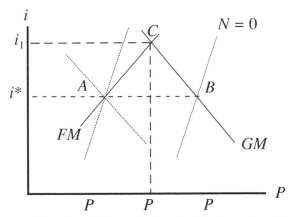

Figure 5.3. Medium-Term Effects of a Nominal Exchange Rate Devaluation

b. A Nominal Devaluation

How, then, can sustained inflation happen in this situation? The answer is: *only through continuous depreciation of the nominal exchange rate*. To see this, go back to the devaluation exercise of Chapter 4, and consider what happens in a short-run equilibrium in the case of an *anticipated* devaluation of the currency. In such a short-run equilibrium, the GM curve shifts to the right by an amount that is proportional to the exchange rate change, say from A to B in Figure 5.3. The new short-run equilibrium is at C, because the FM curve does not move unless the capital gains on reserves are monetized.

As we showed previously, the nominal devaluation must also cause the $N = 0$ curve to shift, in the same proportion as the change in s. Thus, after a devaluation $N = 0$ shifts from A to B, just like the GM curve does. Because the point C is to the *left* of the new $N = 0$ curve, it must correspond to a current account surplus. This means that reserves are being accumulated at C. Thus, given DC, the FM curve shifts to the right, until the equilibrium moves to the point B. At B the price level has increased in the same proportion as the nominal devaluation, and the domestic interest rate has returned to its original value. B is the economy's new medium-term macroeconomic equilibrium. Notice that this could be repeated period after period, sustaining an ongoing increase in the price level – which is what we mean by inflation.[3]

What has happened to the country's stock of foreign exchange reserves at the point B? Notice that, since the price level has increased in the same proportion as the rate of devaluation while the real demand for money is unchanged, the money supply must have increased in the same proportion as the rate of devaluation at

---

[3] We can now say something about what happens to the balance of payments at C. From C to B the money supply is expanding with no change in domestic credit, so the balance of payments must be in *surplus* from C to B.

B. Since the stock of domestic credit is unchanged, the domestic-currency value of the stock of foreign exchange reserves must therefore have increased *more* than in proportion to the rate of devaluation at *B*. If, as in the example just analyzed, there is no monetization, then the entire increase in reserves would come about through cumulative balance of payments surpluses as the economy adjusts from *C* to *B*.

III. MEDIUM-TERM EQUILIBRIUM UNDER PERFECT CAPITAL MOBILITY

In the previous section, we assumed that the domestic economy was completely closed off to financial trade with the rest of the world. Perfect international capital mobility reflects the imposition of the opposite assumption: not only do domestic and foreign agents freely engage in financial trade with each other, but the financial liabilities issued by domestic and foreign residents are considered by portfolio managers to be identical. In this case, we can write the current account of the balance of payments as:

$$\Delta NICP^* = CA^* = NP/s + i^*(F^* + R^*) - i B_F/s$$
$$= \{X(sP^*/P, \theta) - [1 - \phi(sP^*/P)] A_p(Y, T, i^*)\} P/s + i^* NICP^*,$$

$$(5.8)$$

since $i = i^*$ and $NICP^* = (F_P^* + R^*) - B_F/s$. Again, our medium-term model consists of equation (5.8) as well as the *GM* curve and the flat *FM* curve corresponding to the case of perfect capital mobility. However, in this case we cannot infer the properties of the medium-term equilibrium by setting $CA^* = 0$ as we did before, because the economy's short-run equilibrium is not influenced by changes in its net international creditor position $NICP^*$, and therefore it does not contain a mechanism that will impose current-account balance in the medium term.

To see why, recall from Chapter 3 that in this case the money supply curve was horizontal, since the domestic money supply would adjust endogenously (and instantaneously) to ensure that domestic financial markets clear with the domestic interest rate equal to the foreign one – that is, with $i = i^*$. Thus the domestic money supply is given by:

$$M = PL(i^*, Y).$$

The stock of foreign exchange reserves, in turn is:

$$sR^* = PL(i^*, Y) - DC,$$

and the difference between cross-border financial claims by the domestic and foreign private sectors is given by:

$$sF_P^* - B_F = s(NICP^* - R^*)$$
$$= sNICP^* - PL(i^*, Y) + DC.$$

While the difference $sF_p^* - B_F$ is determined by this expression, the individual components sF_p^* and B_F are indeterminate, since domestic and foreign bonds are by definition indistinguishable.

From this expression, it is easy to see why the country's net international creditor position has no effect on the domestic money supply. The reason is because capital inflows and outflows, in the form of $sF_p^* - B_F$, will instantaneously adjust to ensure that the domestic money supply is consistent with the condition $i = i^*$, as given by the equation above, *no matter what the level of the economy's net international creditor position*. That is, an increase in $NICP^*$, for example, in the equation above, would simply lead to an increase in $sF_p^* - B_F$ (a capital outflow) of exactly the same magnitude, leaving $PL(i^*, Y)$ (equal to the nominal money supply) unchanged. The irrelevance of the country's net creditor position for the value of the money supply means that the evolution of the country's net creditor position over time has no impact (induces no dynamics) on the economy's short-run equilibrium. That is, short-run and medium-term equilibrium are identical under the condition of perfect capital mobility.

The implications of the two shocks considered in the previous section – an expansion in domestic credit and a nominal devaluation – are, however, exactly the same as in the case of financial autarky, except that what appeared as a medium-term response under financial autarky becomes a short-run *and* medium-term response under perfect capital mobility. In particular, a domestic credit expansion is immediately offset dollar-for-dollar by a capital outflow, leaving the domestic price level unchanged and simply changing the composition of the central bank's balance sheet, while an anticipated nominal devaluation, by shifting the GM curve to the right in the same proportion as the devaluation and causing it to move along a horizontal FM curve, causes the domestic price level to change in the same proportion as the change in the exchange rate. Just as before, then, in the medium term domestic monetary policy has no effect on the domestic price level, but exchange rate changes move the domestic price level in the same proportion.

IV. MEDIUM-TERM EQUILIBRIUM UNDER IMPERFECT CAPITAL MOBILITY

The final case we will consider is that of imperfect capital mobility. Notice first that, as in the case of financial autarky, but unlike what happens under perfect capital mobility, the money supply depends in the short run on the country's net international creditor position. Thus, the economy's short-run equilibrium will indeed be changing whenever the current account balance of the balance of payments is not zero, as long as the central bank does not sterilize the effects of balance of payments surpluses or deficits on the domestic money supply. This means that a zero current account balance is once again a requirement of medium-term equilibrium. Thus we can once again try to learn about the properties of the medium-term

equilibrium by examining the conditions under which the current account balance
will be zero, as in Section II.

In this case, we can write the current account balance as:

$$\Delta NICP^* = CA^* = NP/s + i^*(sF_P^* + R^*) - iB_F/s.$$

That is, the current account consists of the balance on goods and services (written
NP/s in foreign-currency terms) plus interest receipts on foreign assets held by the
private sector and the central bank minus interest payments on foreign debts owed
by the government. Using the definition of $NICP^*$ we can write this as:

$$\begin{aligned}
\Delta NICP^* = CA^* &= NP/s + i^* NICP^* - (i - i^*)B_F/s \\
&= NP/s + i^* NICP^* - (i - i^*)b^*(i, i^*)(W_F^* - P^* L^*) \\
&= NP/s + i^* NICP^* - (i - i^*)b^*(i, i^*)(F^* - NICP^* - P^* L^*).
\end{aligned}$$

Finally, collecting the terms in $NICP^*$ we have:

$$\begin{aligned}
\Delta NICP^* = CA^* = &\{X(sP^*/P, \theta) - [1 - \phi(sP^*/P)]A_P(Y, T, i)\}P/s \\
&+ [i^* + (i - i^*)b^*(i, i^*)]NICP^* \\
&- (i - i^*)b^*(i, i^*)(B^* - P^* L^*).
\end{aligned}$$

Thus, the medium-term equilibrium condition $N = 0$ becomes:

$$\begin{aligned}
&\{X(sP^*/P, \theta) - [1 - \phi(sP^*/P)]A_P(Y, T, i)\}P/s \\
&+ [i^* + (i - i^*)b^*(i, i^*)]NICP^* \\
&- (i - i^*)b^*(i, i^*)(F^* - P^* L^*) = 0, \qquad (5.9)
\end{aligned}$$

and our medium-term model consists of equation (5.9) plus the *GM* curve and the
FM curve corresponding to the case of imperfect capital mobility.

Equation (5.9) is a little more complicated than our previous expressions for
the current account. Notice, for instance, that it contains all three of the endogenous variables in the medium-term model: that is, both of the short-run endogenous variables i and P as well as the medium-term endogenous variable $NICP^*$.
This means that the medium-term model is no longer recursive – that is, we can
no longer determine the medium-term values of i and P from the $N = 0$ and
GM curves, and then determine $NICP^*$ residually. Our medium-term model is
now fully simultaneous. We need $N = 0$ as well as both the *GM* and *FM* curves
to solve for all three variables. While we will not undertake the complete analysis of medium-term equilibrium under imperfect capital mobility in this chapter,
there are several useful things that we can say about its properties just from
equation (5.9).

a. Effects of a Domestic Credit Expansion

The most important concrete observations we can make from (5.9) alone concern the medium-term effects of changes in nominal variables. In general, changes in the stock of domestic credit will *not* leave the domestic price level undisturbed in the medium term, in contrast with the two previous cases. To see why, suppose that the economy is initially in a medium-term equilibrium in which (5.9) holds. Note that for such an equilibrium to be stable, it must be the case that when $NICP^*$ is above its equilibrium value $\Delta NICP^*$, as given by equation (5.9), must be negative, while when it is below its equilibrium value $\Delta NICP^*$ must be positive.

Now suppose there is an increase in DC. Could such a change leave the values of i and P undisturbed in the new medium-term equilibrium? For the increase in DC to leave the values of i and P undisturbed in the GM-FM diagram would require a medium-term reduction in $NICP^*$ of exactly the right magnitude so as to leave M_0 unchanged in equation (5.5a), given the increase in DC. From equation (5.5a) the required change in $NICP^*$ is given by:

$$\Delta NICP^* = -1/(1 - (b^* + f))\Delta DC.$$

For a situation in which an increase in DC has been offset by a reduction in $NICP^*$ of this magnitude, thus returning i and P to their initial values, to be a medium-term equilibrium, it would need to be consistent with equation (5.9). Could (5.9) actually continue to hold in this case? The answer must be no, because if (5.9) held with the higher initial value of $NICP^*$, it could not continue to do so with the same values of i and P but a reduced value of $NICP^*$. Such a value of $NICP^*$ would instead correspond to a current account deficit. In other words, such a value of $NICP^*$ would be still too high to be consistent with medium-term equilibrium. Since a *lower* value of $NICP^*$ is required for the economy to return to medium-term equilibrium, this means that M_0 would actually have to *fall* in order for the economy to get to its new medium-term equilibrium. But that, in turn, means that at the new medium-term equilibrium, the domestic price level would be lower, and the domestic interest rate higher, than before the credit expansion.

This should seem puzzling. Remember that an expansion of domestic credit increased the domestic price level and lowered the domestic interest rate in the short run. Yet we have just found that in the medium term these results must be reversed. Why should this be? The answer is that the increase in the domestic price level and reduction in domestic interest rate that occur in the short run cause the current account to deteriorate, to go into deficit from an initially balanced position. When this happens, $NICP^*$ begins to fall, as we have seen before. The reduction in $NICP^*$ gradually begins to undo the economic effects of the domestic credit expansion, lowering the price level and raising the domestic interest rate. But all through this process, the current account must remain in deficit and $NICP^*$ must continue to fall. The new equilibrium, therefore, must be reached with a lower value of *NICP** than the original one. But this means that the country will have larger debt service payments to make in the new equilibrium. To be able to finance such payments, it must generate a merchandise trade surplus. But that in turn requires some combination of *depreciation* of the real exchange rate and higher domestic interest rate, which can come about only if the economic contraction "overshoots" its initial equilibrium – that is, only if the price level in the new equilibrium is actually lower than that in the original one. The important implication is that not only does the domestic credit expansion not succeed in increasing the domestic price level in the medium term; in the case of imperfect capital mobility it must actually *decrease* it.

b. Effects of a Nominal Devaluation

Now consider what happens in the medium term if the country devalues its currency. The key result is that, in contrast with what happened under the more extreme capital mobility assumptions, a nominal exchange rate devaluation will not lead to an equiproportional increase in the domestic price level and an unchanged value of the domestic interest rate and *NICP**, whether or not the devaluation is monetized.

To see why, consider what would happen if the price level did increase in proportion to the devaluation and domestic interest rates remained unchanged. In this case, the goods market equilibrium condition captured in the *GM* curve would continue to be satisfied (that is, the *GM* curve would shift to the right in proportion to the size of the devaluation). However, the money market would not be in equilibrium at this point, since the demand for money would increase in proportion to the devaluation, while the supply of money would increase at best less than proportionately (under monetization) or not at all if *NICP** were unchanged. For the *FM* curve to also shift to the right and intersect the *GM* curve at a point corresponding to the original interest rate and proportionately increased price level would therefore require an increase in *NICP**. But if *NICP** is higher, the current account balance condition (5.9) could not hold. With higher *NICP** and no change either in the domestic interest rate or real exchange rate, the current account must be in surplus and *NICP** must be increasing, so this point could not constitute a medium-term equilibrium.

Since larger values of *NICP** reduce the surplus, a further increase in *NICP** is required for the economy to regain a medium-term equilibrium. Because this increase in *NICP** is expansionary, the new medium-term equilibrium will be achieved with a more appreciated real exchange rate and lower domestic interest rate than the original one. Thus, just as in the credit expansion case, the medium-term effects of the devaluation are the opposite of the short-term effects.

Why is this so? The answer is similar to that in the previous case. Since the devaluation creates a current account surplus in the short run, the economy accumulates net claims on the rest of the world all during the transition to the new medium-term equilibrium. Because this implies larger net interest receipts in the new medium-term equilibrium, the current account can only return to balance if the real exchange rate is more appreciated than originally, offsetting the larger net interest receipts with a lower trade surplus or larger deficit.

c. Credit Expansion and Devaluation Together

Finally, consider the medium-term effect of a nominal devaluation which is both monetized *and* accompanied by an increase in domestic credit in the same proportion. We saw in Chapter 3 that when it is anticipated, this combination of policies would increase the domestic price level in the same proportion as the rate of devaluation in the short term, while leaving the domestic interest rate unchanged. That is, the *GM* and *FM* curves would both shift to the right in proportion to the rate of devaluation and credit increase. What happens in the medium term? The answer is that if equation (5.9) was satisfied (i.e., the economy was in a medium-term equilibrium) before the shock, it would continue to be satisfied after the shock. Thus, the new short-run equilibrium is also a medium-term equilibrium. In other words, under conditions of imperfect capital mobility, monetized devaluations accompanied by increases in domestic credit in the same proportion result in proportionate increases in the domestic price level in both the short run and the medium term.

V. SUMMARY

It appears that the only way to create ongoing inflation in this model, then, is through continuous nominal depreciation accompanied by continuous credit expansion. Notice, specifically, that continuous credit expansion cannot do the job on its own. How can this be reconciled with Milton Friedman's famous adage that "inflation is always and everywhere a monetary phenomenon"? There are several ways:

a. First, the analysis just completed applies to an open economy. In the standard textbook closed-economy case, money growth is indeed the cause of inflation.
b. Second, even in an open economy, our analysis applies only to a fixed exchange-rate regime. When the exchange rate is allowed to float, money again becomes the nominal anchor.
c. But more importantly, consider what would happen even in our open-economy fixed exchange-rate model if domestic credit were expanded continuously. Regardless of the degree of capital mobility, this would be associated with a continuous loss of reserves. How long could this process be sustained? The answer is that it could only be sustained until reserves are exhausted. What is likely to happen before then is that the loss of reserves would trigger a devaluation since, as we have seen, devaluation tends to increase the reserve stock in the medium term. Thus, continuous credit expansion is likely to result in continuous devaluation

to preserve the reserve stock. But continuous credit expansion associated with continuous devaluation results in continuous price increases – in inflation. *The message is, then, that even in an open economy with a fixed exchange rate, continuous credit expansion would indeed result in increased inflation – not directly, but indirectly through induced devaluation to prevent reserve depletion.*

This leaves open the questions, of course, of how such a process would get started in the first place and what broader implications it might have for the domestic economy. The next part of the book turns to these issues.

PART 3

Public Finance and Macroeconomic Performance

6

The Intertemporal Budget Constraint
of the Public Sector

In the previous chapter we saw that a central bank policy of continuous credit expansion and exchange rate depreciation would result in ongoing inflation in the medium term under any of the three alternative assumptions that we have made about the economy's degree of financial integration with the rest of the world. The questions that naturally arise in this context are what would lead the central bank to undertake such a policy and what the benefits and costs associated with it might be for the economy as a whole. This chapter will take up the first of these questions, leaving the second for Chapter 7. The answer we will give to why the central bank might behave in the way we described in the last chapter is that credit expansion coupled with monetized exchange rate depreciation – monetary expansion for short – allows the central bank to finance a portion of the government's deficit.

But of course, monetary emission is not the only option available to the government to finance fiscal deficits. As we have seen in the previous chapters, the government can also borrow, both from domestic and foreign private sources. Thus, we will need to consider what determines how much the government can borrow from domestic and foreign creditors. To do so, we will analyze the government's intertemporal budget constraint, and develop the important concept of fiscal solvency, which lies at the heart of all of the issues to be discussed in the second part of this book. Other topics to be considered in this chapter include the fiscal consequences of sterilized intervention in foreign exchange markets, the issue of "unpleasant monetarist arithmetic," the budgetary consequences of postponing fiscal adjustment, and the calculation of sustainable fiscal deficits. An important policy issue to be taken up in this chapter is why the requirements of solvency often force fiscal policy to be procyclical in developing countries, in contrast to the countercyclical stance advocated in intermediate macroeconomics textbooks used in industrial countries.

I. BUDGET DEFICITS AND MONEY GROWTH

We showed in the previous chapter that the view that money growth causes inflation is compatible with the assertion that in a small open economy operating an officially determined exchange rate, inflation can only be caused by exchange rate depreciation. The logical chain was the following: domestic credit expansion causes reserve depletion, reserve depletion causes exchange rate adjustments, and exchange rate adjustments cause inflation. Ongoing inflation is the result of credit expansion accompanied by monetized exchange rate depreciation, which together result in continuous monetary expansion. Thus, so far we have learned how ongoing inflation happens in an emerging economy. In the next chapter we will see why inflation matters for long-run growth. Now, we need to determine *why* inflation happens. The answer we will give in this section is that *inflation happens because the government prints money to finance the fiscal deficit.*

a. The Budget Constraint of the Consolidated Public Sector

To show the link between fiscal deficits and money growth, we begin by reproducing the balance sheets of the government and central bank from Chapter 3:

$$W_G = -B \qquad \text{(government)}$$
$$0 = sR^* + DC - M \quad \text{(central bank)}$$

In the model we developed in Chapter 3, we assumed that the government only borrowed in domestic currency. In many developing countries, however, government borrowing from the rest of the world is primarily conducted in foreign currency. Suppose that government foreign-currency debt is called B^*. Then the government's balance sheet can be amended to:

$$W_G = -(B + sB^*).$$

We will assume that the central bank does not hold the government's foreign-currency debt, so the central bank's balance sheet remains unchanged.[1]

Recall from Chapter 3 that the change in the government's outstanding debt arises from the need to finance the government's budget deficit. Taking into account revenues from the monetization of devaluation-induced capital gains by the central bank, we can write the government's budget constraint as:

$$(\Delta B - \Delta DC) + s\Delta B^* + \Delta DC = P(G - T) + iB + i'sB^* - \Delta sR^*,$$

---

[1] What effect would the introduction of the new debt instrument have on our model? The answer is that there would now be three assets for portfolio managers to choose among: domestic government bonds denominated in domestic currency, domestic government bonds denominated in foreign currency, and foreign bonds.

where i' is the interest rate paid on the government's foreign-currency debt, and where the issue of domestic-currency debt has been separated into the portion purchased by the private sector $(\Delta B - \Delta DC)$ and the portion purchased by the central bank ΔDC. The term ΔsR^* captures the transfer of devaluation-induced capital gains from the central bank to the government (monetization revenues). The government's demand for resources from the central bank, in the form of credit and monetization revenues, can thus be expressed as:

$$\Delta DC + \Delta sR^* = P(G - T) + iB + i'sB^* - [(\Delta B - \Delta DC) + s\Delta B^*]. \quad (6.1)$$

That is, the government demands resources from the central bank to cover the excess of its deficit over its borrowing from the private sector.

Now, just as we did for the government, we can write the budget constraint for the central bank:

$$s\Delta R^* + \Delta DC = (i^* sR^* + iDC - \Delta sR^*) + \Delta M.$$

This identity states that the central bank can acquire assets by spending its current income (interest earnings net of transfers to the government) or printing money. The change in the money supply is therefore given by:

$$\Delta M = s\Delta R^* + (\Delta DC + \Delta sR^*) - (i^* sR^* + iDC). \quad (6.2)$$

That is, the central bank expands the money supply when the sum of its reserve acquisition and the resources it transfers to the government exceed its interest earnings.

An important question is how decisions are made about the resources that the central bank will make available to the government – that is, about $(\Delta DC + \Delta sR^*)$. In this chapter, we shall assume that the central bank is not independent of the finance ministry. This means that decisions about $(\Delta DC + \Delta sR^*)$ are made by the finance ministry, not by the central bank.[2] In that case, $(\Delta DC + \Delta sR^*)$ will be determined by the government's fiscal needs, a situation that is referred to as "fiscal dominance." To see the implications of this situation for the central bank's decisions about monetary emission, we can substitute from (6.1) into (6.2). This yields:

$$\Delta M = P(G - T) + i(B - DC) + i'sB^* - i^* sR^*$$
$$- [(\Delta B - \Delta DC) + s(\Delta B^* - \Delta R^*)]. \quad (6.3)$$

Since this substitution in effect consolidates the budget accounts of the government with those of the central bank, equation (6.3) is referred to as the budget constraint of the "consolidated public sector." It states that the public sector's overall deficit, consisting of the *primary (noninterest) deficit* $P(G - T)$ and net interest payments

---

[2] Central bank independence is the subject of Chapter 9.

$(iB + i'sB^* - i^*sR^*)$ must be financed by net borrowing in either domestic ($\Delta B - \Delta DC$) or foreign currency $s(\Delta B^* - \Delta R^*)$ or by printing money ΔM. Thus, the nonindependence of the central bank means that the level of monetary emission will be determined in part by the government's fiscal needs.

b. Interest Rate Differentials

So far, this has all been accounting. Here is the first bit of economic substance. Notice that there are three interest rates in the budget constraint of the consolidated public sector – the interest rate on foreign bonds and the two interest rates on bonds issued by the domestic public sector. Differences among these three interest rates mean that *public sector debt policy* – that is, changes in the composition of the public sector's financial portfolio – affect the fiscal accounts, as illustrated in Box 6.1. This raises the question: just what is the relationship among the domestic-currency rates of return for these three assets likely to be?

As a first step in answering this question, notice that, unlike the interest rate i on domestic currency-denominated bonds, the interest rates i' and i^* correspond to assets denominated in foreign currency. The *domestic-currency* rate of return from holding these assets is approximately $i' + \Delta s/s$ and $i^* + \Delta s/s$ respectively, where $\Delta s/s$ is the expected rate of depreciation of the domestic currency.[3] To make sure that we are comparing apples to apples, we should therefore ask how these three domestic-currency rates of return are likely to be related.

There are two characteristics that distinguish among the three assets to which these rates of return correspond: the identity of the borrower and the currency of denomination. The fact that the debtor is a different economic agent means that assets may carry a different probability of nonpayment (credit risk). The fact that the debt may be denominated in a different currency implies the existence of exchange rate risk – that is, the possibility that currency values may change. The existence of two different types of risk and the possibility that creditors may need to be compensated for bearing risk mean that the three assets may in principle offer very different domestic-currency rates of return. Therefore, to abstract away from some of these complications and sharpen our analysis, we will make two assumptions:

a. Future exchange rate movements are known with certainty. This means that even though $\Delta s/s$ may not be zero, there is no currency risk.
b. All assets issued by the domestic public sector bear the same credit risk. This means that neither domestic- nor foreign-currency-denominated bonds are "senior" (have a prior claim on the public sector's resources).

---

[3] Notice that this means that if it devalues, the domestic government can expect to reap a capital gain on its foreign exchange reserves, as we've discussed previously, but also to incur a capital loss on its foreign-exchange-denominated debt.

Box 6.1. Fiscal Implications of Public Sector Debt Policy

Equation (6.3) has a number of interesting applications regarding the fiscal implications of the composition of the public sector's financial portfolio – that is, of public sector debt policy.

a. Debt Versus Reserve Financing

We can ask what difference it would make, for example, if the public sector borrows in foreign currency to finance a deficit or instead uses foreign exchange reserves – in other words, if ΔB^* is positive or ΔR^* is negative. The difference depends on the relationship between i' and i^*. If the two interest rates are equal, then external borrowing and reserve depletion are equivalent – that is, from the perspective of the public sector's budget, it doesn't matter whether the public sector borrows abroad to finance a deficit or spends its foreign exchange reserves. This is so because B^* and R^* would enter the budget constraint only in the form $B^* - R^*$. But if the domestic public sector has to pay a premium above what the public sector in the rest of the world has to pay $(i' > i^*)$, then reserve depletion is a cheaper form of finance.

b. Fiscal Implications of Sterilization

Recall that when balance of payments surpluses are sterilized by the central bank, increases in foreign exchange reserves are offset by central bank sales of government bonds, so DC contracts to offset increases in sR^*. Since the offset must be dollar for-dollar in order for the money supply to remain unaffected, it is evident that if $i > i^*$, this policy will tend to increase the overall deficit of the consolidated public sector, since the assets acquired by the central bank, in the form of foreign exchange reserves, yield a lower return than the domestic-currency bonds that it has sold to the public.

   However, notice that the true effect on the fiscal accounts is not given by the difference between i and i^* only, because foreign exchange reserves increase in value in the presence of depreciation, while domestic bonds do not. Thus, the true comparison is between i and $i^* + \Delta s/s$. But since, under our assumptions, $i = i' + \Delta s/s$, sterilization of balance of payments surpluses will be fiscally costly if $i' > i^*$ – that is, if the domestic government has to pay a premium on its foreign currency borrowing, the same condition that determines whether reserve depletion is cheaper than external borrowing.

With these two assumptions, domestic- and foreign-currency-denominated bonds of the public sector must yield the same domestic-currency rate of return. In other words, we can impose the no-arbitrage condition:

$$i = i' + \Delta s/s. \qquad (6.4)$$

This leaves the relationship between the domestic-currency rate of return on the foreign bond $i^* + \Delta s/s$ and that on the domestic bond to be determined. This difference will depend on differences in credit risk. We will assume that the foreign bond carries no credit risk. That is, the domestic-currency rate of return on the foreign bond is the rate of return on a safe asset. To simplify notation, we'll call this rate of return i_D^*, so $i_D^* = i^* + \Delta s / s$. The remaining question is what determines the differential credit risk attached to lending to the domestic government. We will come back to this question below.

c. Determinants of Money Supply Growth

Returning to the thread of our argument, notice that condition (6.4) allows us to simplify equation (6.3) considerably. Let $D = (B - DC) + sB^*$ denote the domestic public sector's gross debt – in other words, its total stock of borrowing from the domestic and foreign private sectors. Noting that the change in D can be written as $\Delta D = (\Delta B - \Delta DC) + (s\Delta B^* + \Delta sB^*)$, we can use (6.4) to write (6.3) in the form:

$$\Delta D - s\Delta R^* + \Delta M = P(G - T) + iD - i^* sR^*. \qquad (6.5)$$

In what follows, we will be interested in exploring what determines the domestic public sector's ability to borrow. An important factor will be the resources available to the public sector to service debt. Since the acquisition of foreign exchange reserves will absorb some of these resources, it will be useful to define an *adjusted primary deficit*, denoted PD', which takes into account the net costs of reserve acquisition. We can express the adjusted primary deficit as:

$$PD' = P(G - T) + s\Delta R^* - i^* sR^*.$$

Using this notation, we can now write the budget constraint of the consolidated public sector in the simpler form:

$$\Delta D + \Delta M = PD' + iD$$

We are now in a position to state more concisely what determines the rate of growth of the money supply. Solving the expression above for ΔM we have:

$$\Delta M = PD' + iD - \Delta D. \qquad (6.6)$$

Thus, *monetary expansion arises from public sector deficits not financed by borrowing.* Notice that this does not rule out monetary expansion arising from central bank lending to commercial banks or from balance of payments surpluses. Though we have not included commercial banks in our model so far, it is easy to see that any domestic lending by the public sector would simply reduce its *net* borrowing from the private sector, captured by the term ΔD, and thus increase ΔM, other things equal. As we saw previously, reserve accumulation shows up in the form of a higher value of PD', which would tend to increase ΔM, unless the reserve accumulation is sterilized, which would imply an offset through an increase in ΔD. It also does not rule out monetary expansion arising from public sector external borrowing used to finance domestic spending. Suppose that the public sector borrows an amount $s \Delta B^*$ externally to finance $P \Delta G$ of domestic spending. Since the domestic currency required for such spending is acquired by depositing the proceeds of the loan at the central bank, the bank's foreign exchange reserves rise by the same amount that the public sector's external liabilities do. Thus, the adjusted primary deficit increases by $2 P \Delta G$ (the increase in spending plus the accumulation of reserves), while external borrowing increases by $P \Delta G$, leaving a net effect on monetary expansion of $\Delta M = P \Delta G$. In effect, the government has printed money to finance its increased spending.

II. THE PUBLIC SECTOR'S INTERTEMPORAL BUDGET CONSTRAINT

Equation (6.6) relates the rate of growth of the money supply to the fiscal deficit, but it does not establish the proposition that fiscal deficits cause monetary expansion, since in principle such deficits could be financed by issuing debt. In this section we will show that this option is in fact limited. This means that borrowing may not be an option to finance fiscal deficits, in which case deficits can either be eliminated or be financed through monetary expansion. It also means that a permanent reduction in the rate of monetary expansion, such as would be involved in a permanent decrease in the rate of inflation, requires a fiscal adjustment – a reduction in PD'. Why should this be so? From equation (6.6), one might think that all one needs to do in order to effect a reduction in the rate of monetary expansion is to change the composition of financing for the public sector from money to bonds. The problem, as with an increase in the deficit itself, is that creditors may not be prepared to accommodate this shift. The basic question in both instances, then, is: how do we know when creditors will be willing to extend loans to the public sector?

Creditors always have the option, instead of lending to the public sector, of lending out their funds by acquiring assets that pay the safe rate of interest. The key point, then, is that creditors will be willing to extend loans to the public sector – or to any other debtor, for that matter – if and only if they expect to receive in return a stream of future payments from the public sector that is at least equal in present value to the loans that they have extended. The need to discount such payments arises from the fact that at least some of them will be made at some point in the future. The relevant interest rate for discounting is the risk-free interest rate, since this represents the opportunity cost of funds for the public sector's potential creditors. When the public sector is expected to be able to make future payments to its creditors that are at least equal to the face value of the public sector's outstanding debt, the public sector is said to be *solvent*.

The payments made by the public sector to its creditors are typically classified into two categories: interest and amortization payments. Since amortization payments are payments that reduce the debt outstanding, we can denote total net amortization payments made by the public sector during a given period t

as $-\Delta D(t)$ – that is, the *negative* of the change in the debt over that period (if the debt is increasing, amortization payments are effectively negative, and if it decreases they must be positive). Total debt service payments made during the period t are therefore $i(t)D(t) - \Delta D(t)$. The condition for the public sector to be solvent can therefore be expressed as:

$$PV[i(t)D(t) - \Delta D(t); i_D{}^*(t)] \geq D(0),$$

where $PV[\ ]$ denotes the present value of a stream of expected future payments from the present (time zero) to infinity, with representative time-t payment of $i(t)D(t) - \Delta D(t)$, $i_D{}^*(t)$ is the risk-free rate relevant for discounting payments made at time t back to the present, and $D(0)$ is the stock of debt currently in existence.

The important point is that the solvency requirement imposes a constraint on the components of the public sector's budget. To see the implications of solvency for the government's budget, rewrite the public sector's budget constraint as:

$$PS' + \Delta M = iD - \Delta D,$$

where, for ease of notation, we have defined $PS' = -PD'$. PS' is the *adjusted primary surplus* of the public sector. The right-hand side of this expression is, as we have seen, the *flow of debt service payments* (interest plus amortization) made by the consolidated public sector each period. What this form of the identity tells us is that the resources available to service debt each period are equal to the sum of the adjusted primary surplus of the public sector (PS') and new monetary emission, called *seignorage revenue*. This identity allows us to write the solvency condition as:

$$PV[PS'(t) + \Delta M(t); i_D{}^*(t)] \geq D(0). \tag{6.7}$$

This is also referred to as the consolidated public sector's *intertemporal budget constraint*.

Notice what it means. The right-hand side of the equality (the existing stock of debt) is given at any instant, so this relationship imposes a constraint on the future path that can be followed by the sum $PS' + \Delta M$ (hence the name), in the form:

$$PV[PS'(t) + \Delta M(t); i_D{}^*(t)]_{\min} = D(0).$$

That is, at a minimum, the government must be expected to raise enough resources in the future to service its existing debt on market terms.[4]

Now let $PV[PS'(t) + \Delta M(t); i_D{}^*(t)]_{\max}$ denote the *maximum* value of the resources that the government will have available to service debt in the future. Then

---

[4] Notice that, since this condition would be satisfied by debt service payments equal to $-PD' + \Delta M = i_D{}^* D$, which would merely involve making interest payments of $i_D{}^* D$ each period, this condition does not actually require the government to *repay* its debt, just to service it on market terms. As long as it can do so, it can roll it over, if not with an existing creditor then with a new one.

the maximum amount of debt that the government can service is given by:

$$D_{max} = PV[PS'(t) + \Delta M(t); i_D^*(t)]_{max}. \qquad (6.8)$$

This permits us to address the key question: can the consolidated public sector borrow to finance a higher deficit, or to reduce the rate of monetary expansion associated with a given deficit? A necessary condition for it to be able to do so is that $D_{max} > D(0)$.[5] If this condition is satisfied, the government is at least *capable* of generating the resources required to service additional debt on market terms. If its creditors additionally believe that it will be willing to generate these required resources, then the public sector will be able to borrow to finance a larger deficit or to reduce the rate of monetary emission, given the deficit. If the condition is not satisfied, or if despite its being satisfied creditors believe that the public sector will be unwilling to raise the required resources in the future, then the public sector will be unable to borrow, since creditors would not expect it to be able to repay its debt on market terms.[6]

What determines the resources that the public sector will be able to generate to service debt in the future? It is convenient to split the relevant factors into two components, conceptually similar to the familiar decomposition of tax revenue into the product of a tax *rate* and tax *base*. First, growth in the size of the domestic economy as well as in the domestic price level are likely to be important factors. The former will affect the magnitude of real tax revenues and the demands for real government spending, and the latter will influence both the nominal value of the real primary surplus as well as the demand for money. In effect, nominal GDP is the "tax base" for the primary surplus and seignorage revenue. In other words, in an economy that is growing and in which the price level is increasing over time, there will tend to be forces causing PS' and ΔM, both of which are expressed in nominal absolute terms, to change in the future, even with unchanged fiscal efforts (i.e., with no changes in tax laws, tax administration, or in the usual procedures for determining government expenditures). A second set of factors can be considered to be those that reflect special fiscal efforts – that is, those that determine the magnitude of fiscal sources extracted from an economy of a given size, the "tax rate."

To capture this decomposition in our solvency condition, we can express the values of the variables in equation (6.7) as ratios to nominal GDP, rather than in absolute terms. Letting $ps' = PS'/PY$ and $m = M/PY$, we can rewrite equation (6.7) as:

$$PV\{[ps'(t) + (\Delta M(t)/M(t))m(t)]P(t)Y(t); i_D^*\} \geq D(0).$$

[5] Notice that this condition is equivalent to the solvency condition (6.7).

[6] At this point, we can go back to the credit risk associated with lending to the domestic public sector. This risk depends on the likelihood that the public sector will be able to service its debt on market terms, which in turn depends on the relationship between D_{max} and $D(0)$. The larger D_{max} is relative to $D(0)$, the more likely it is that the public sector will be able to service its debt successfully, and thus the lower the premium that lenders should require for lending to the sector.

Suppose, for simplicity, that these two ratios are set at their constant "permanent" values, and that the rate of growth of real GDP (denoted g), and the rate of inflation π are both constant. Notice that if m is constant, the rate of growth of the money supply $\Delta M / M$ must be equal to the rate of growth of nominal GDP, $(\pi + g)$. Dividing both sides of the equation above by the initial value of PY permits us to write:

$$PV\{[ps' + (\pi + g)m][(1 + g)(1 + \pi)]^t; i_D^*\} \geq d(0), \qquad (6.9)$$

where $d(0) = D(0)/P(0)Y(0)$ is the initial ratio of debt to nominal GDP. Notice that holding the ratios ps' and m constant means that payments to creditors in nominal absolute terms grow at the rate of growth of nominal GDP. Finally, to summarize the modified solvency condition in its most compact form, we can write equation (6.9) in the equivalent form:[7]

$$PV\{[ps' + (\pi + g)m]; r - g\} \geq d(0), \qquad (6.10)$$

where $r = i_D^* - \pi$ is the *real* interest rate. What this says is that, because debt service payments are growing at a constant rate (the rate of growth of nominal GDP), their present value is equivalent to that of a constant level of debt service payments discounted at the lower rate $r - g$, rather than i_D^*.[8]

Based on what has just been said, it is also reasonable to recast the maximum values of the adjusted primary surplus and seignorage revenue that the public sector can be expected to generate as ratios to nominal GDP, since these ratios capture the government's fiscal effort. Thus we can write:

$$
\begin{aligned}
d_{\max} = D_{\max}/P(0)Y(0) &= PV[PS'(t) + \Delta M(t); i_D^*]_{\max}/P(0)Y(0) \\
&= PV[(ps' + sgn)_{\max} P(t)Y(t); i_D^*]/P(0)Y(0) \\
&= PV[(ps' + sgn)_{\max}(1 + \pi)^t(1 + g)^t; i_D^*] \\
&= PV[(ps' + sgn)_{\max}; r - g], \qquad (6.11)
\end{aligned}
$$

where $sgn = (\pi + g)m$ denotes seignorage revenue scaled by nominal GDP. With $d_{\max}$ defined in this way, the necessary condition for public sector solvency becomes $d_{\max} > d(0)$. This completes the recasting of the solvency condition in the context of a growing and inflating economy.

---

[7] To show the equivalence, note that $(1 + y)/(1 + x)$ is approximately $1 + y - x$. This can be shown by doing the long division of $1 + x$ into $1 + y$ until the remainder consists only of second-order terms.

[8] This form of the identity can also be written as:

$$ps' + (\Delta M/M)m = [i_D^* - (g + \pi)]d(0).$$

This says that the stream of payments can be *less* than would be required to stabilize the nominal debt stock – that is, it can be less than the accrued interest, while retaining solvency. How can this be? It is because since the stream of potential payments is growing over time, it can support (have a present value equal to) a growing stock of debt over time. But the only way the latter can emerge is if the payment ratio is less than the rate of interest.

To see the implications of the solvency requirement for the relationship between fiscal deficits and money growth, suppose that $d_{max} > d(0)$, and that creditors expect the government's future fiscal plans to satisfy (6.10). Consequently, the public sector can borrow at the safe rate of interest. Notice that the original budget constraint of the public sector (equation 6.6) can be written as:

$$\Delta D(t) = -PS(t)' + i' D(t) - \Delta M(t).$$

Dividing both sides by nominal GDP and using the (constant) ratios we defined before, we can rewrite this as:

$$\Delta D(t)/P(t)Y(t) = -(ps + sgn) + i_D * d(t).$$

Using $i_D^* = r + \pi$, subtracting $g d(t)$ from both sides, and rearranging terms, leaves:

$$\Delta D(t)/P(t)Y(t) - (\pi + g)d(t) = -(ps + sgn) + (r - g)d(t).$$

Finally, since $\Delta D(t)/P(t)Y(t) - (\pi + g)d(t)$ is approximately equal to $\Delta d(t)$, we can write the budget constraint as:

$$\Delta d(t) = -(ps + sgn) + (r - g)d(t). \tag{6.12}$$

Now, the transformed solvency condition (6.10), written as an equality, can be expressed as:

$$PV(ps' + sgn; r - g) = d(0), \quad \text{or:}$$
$$(ps' \mid sgn)/(r - g) = d(0),$$

which implies:

$$ps' + sgn = (r - g)d(0). \tag{6.13}$$

The left-hand side of (6.12) is the sustainable "permanent" value of the sum of the adjusted primary surplus and seignorage revenue. According to this equation, payments each period can fall short of the accrued real interest only to the extent that economic growth allows the debt-to-GDP ratio to remain unchanged under new borrowing. What does this imply about the evolution of the debt-to-GDP ratio over time? Since following this policy makes the right-hand side of equation (6.12) equal to zero, it is equivalent to stabilizing the ratio of debt to GDP. That is, not only does debt not have to be repaid, as we showed before, but it can actually grow over time at the rate of growth of the economy, since as long as it does so the debt-to-GDP ratio will continue to fall short of d_{max}.

We can illustrate the financing choices available to the government when the fiscal deficit is increased by plotting the budget constraint (6.12) in $\Delta d - d$ space, as in Figure 6.1. It is easy to see that, assuming that $r - g > 0$, the curve depicting the budget constraint (6.12) can be depicted as a straight line in $\Delta d - d$ space, with

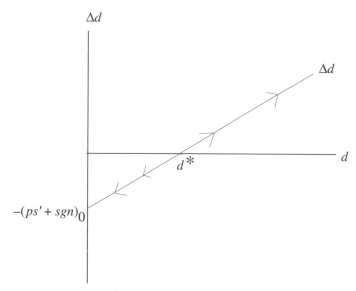

Figure 6.1. The Intertemporal Budget Constraint of the Public Sector

a positive slope equal to the effective interest rate $r - g$, and a vertical intercept at $-(ps' + sgn)$.

   This curve can be used to analyze the debt dynamics implied by the public sector's budgetary choices. The public sector's choice of ps' and sgn determines the height of the Δd curve. The initial value of the debt/GDP ratio, say $d(0)$, determines where on the horizontal axis the economy operates. Notice that the point of intersection of the Δd with the horizontal axis, labeled d^* in the figure, is where $\Delta d = 0$ – that is, the debt/GDP ratio is neither increasing nor decreasing. The dynamics of the debt stock depend on where $d(0)$ lies relative to d^*. If $d < d^*$, then $\Delta d < 0$, and the debt/GDP ratio must be falling; if $d(0) = d^*$, the debt/GDP ratio is stable; finally, if $d(0) > d^*$, the debt/GDP ratio must be rising.

   We can use this information to analyze the constraints that solvency imposes on the public sector's budget. In particular, suppose that the quantity $ps' + sgn$ is to be kept constant, so the position of the Δd line is fixed. Notice that:

a. If $d(0) = d^*$, $\Delta d = 0$. From (6.12), this implies that $ps' + sgn = (r - g)d(0)$. In this case the value of $ps' + sgn$ is exactly sufficient to service the existing debt $d(0)$ on market terms. d^* thus has the property that $(ps' + sgn)/(r - g) = d^*$. If $d(0) = d^*$, then, the necessary condition for public sector solvency is met as an equality.

b. If $d(0)$ is to the left of d^*, on the other hand, $\Delta d < 0$. This means that $ps' + sgn > (r - g)d(0)$. Thus, the public sector is making payments to creditors that are more than enough to pay the interest on the debt while keeping the debt/GDP ratio constant, so the ratio must be falling. In the case, the necessary condition for public sector solvency is met as the inequality $(ps' + sgn)/(r - g) > d(0)$.

c. Thus, given the value of $ps' + sgn$, the public sector is solvent as long as $d(0) \leq d^*$. However, for values of $d(0) > d^*$, it must be the case that $\Delta d > 0$, so $ps' + sgn < (r - g)d(0)$. In this case, given the value of $ps' + sgn$, the resources that the public sector is transferring to its creditors are not enough to service the debt on market terms. Since the shortfall in payments just adds to the debt due, if the initial ratio of debt to GDP $d(0)$ is to the right of d^*, the stock of debt must be rising faster than GDP. In this case, if $ps' + sgn$ remains unchanged, the public sector must be insolvent.

Does this mean that a government that finds itself at a position on the Δd curve where $d(0) > d^*$ is necessarily insolvent? The answer is no. The solvency condition (6.10) can be satisfied for such a government, even though its debt/GDP ratio is currently increasing, *as long as its creditors expect it to make the fiscal adjustment required to stabilize its debt-GDP ratio at some point in the future.* This is so because, as long as this adjustment is eventually made, any extra debt that the government accumulates between the present and the time when the adjustment is made will eventually be serviced on market terms.

To see what this means in terms of Δd line, recall that the position of the Δd line is determined by the vertical intercept $- (ps' + sgn)$. Thus, a fiscal adjustment that increases ps' and/or sgn would shift the curve downward, while one that reduces ps' and/or sgn would shift it upward. What this argument implies is that points on the Δd line with $d(0) > d^*$ can be sustained (i.e., the public sector will be able to borrow the amount $\Delta d(0)$ corresponding to such a point) only insofar as its creditors believe that at some point T in the future the government will make the adjustments to $ps'(T)$ and/or $sgn(T)$ required to make $d(T) = d^*$.

Notice that if $d(0) \geq d_{max}$, creditors could not have such an expectation, since no additional fiscal adjustment could be expected. Thus, for the government to be able to borrow when $d(0) > d^*$, it is necessary that $d(0) < d_{max}$. But while this condition is *necessary* for the government to be able to borrow, it is not sufficient. The additional ingredient required is that the government be able to credibly commit to stabilize its debt/GDP ratio at some point in the future.

With this apparatus in hand, we can now go back to the relationship between fiscal deficits and money growth. Suppose that, from an initial situation where the primary surplus and seignorage revenue are ps_0 and sgn_0 respectively, and the debt stock is d^*, the government *permanently* reduces its primary surplus, say to ps_1. What are its financing options? One possibility is for it to immediately print money to finance the deficit dollar for dollar. In that case the budget constraint curve Δd remains undisturbed, but with $ps_1' + sgn_1 = ps_0' + sgn_0$ and $ps_1' < ps_0'$, this means that $sgn_1 > sgn_0$, which implies a higher rate of monetary growth and inflation. Alternatively, if $d_{max} > d^*$, the government may be able to borrow to finance the higher deficit, if it is solvent in the initial situation. However, as we have just seen, it cannot *permanently* finance the deficit in this way, since if it tried to do so its debt-to-GDP ratio would expand continuously, which would violate the solvency condition (6.10). This means that at some point before d reaches d_{max}, the government would have to shift the budget constraint line back down, stabilizing the debt ratio at some value $d < d_{max}$.

How would it do this? Since by assumption the increase in the primary deficit is permanent, it would have no choice but to do so by printing money. Notice also that, once debt has begun to accumulate, the downward shift in the budget constraint line must be larger than its initial upward shift. Thus, the longer the government waits to turn to money financing, the larger its reliance on seignorage revenue will eventually have to be. The reason is, of course, that it will need to service a larger stock of debt. The upshot is that a permanently higher fiscal deficit will sooner or later have to be financed by printing money.

It is worth reemphasizing that even the initial debt financing would not be feasible unless creditors were convinced that the eventual turn to money financing would take place. If creditors believe that the government has no intention of eventually stabilizing its debt stock short of d_{max}, then they would not provide the temporary financing required for the government to avoid printing money initially, because their new loans would not be repaid on terms comparable to those they could get elsewhere.

III. MONETARY STABILIZATION AND FISCAL ADJUSTMENT

Now consider an alternative exercise, one in which the government wants to lower the rate of inflation. Suppose that the condition $d_{max} > d(0)$ is satisfied and the public sector's current fiscal plans are consistent with the intertemporal budget constraint (6.10), but with a relatively high value of *sgn*. Suppose further that, with an unchanged value of ps', the public sector decides to borrow in the present to avoid the inflationary consequences of the relatively high level of money financing (why it might want to do so is the subject of Chapter 8). Then, given the ratio of debt to GDP currently in existence $d(0)$, the requirement that the intertemporal budget constraint (6.10) must be satisfied means that lower monetary growth today must be accompanied by *faster* anticipated monetary growth in the future (because, given $d(0)$, if the present value of ps' is unchanged, that of *sgn* must be as well, so a lower *sgn* in the short run must mean a higher one later on). This "unpleasant monetarist arithmetic" thus implies that, with an unchanged adjusted primary deficit, the government can achieve lower inflation today only at the cost of higher inflation in the future.

But what if the government seeks to achieve a *permanent* reduction in monetary growth? The key point is that the government's intertemporal budget constraint (6.10) implies that any reduction in present and future monetary growth resulting in a decreased value of $PV(sgn; r - g)$, such as would be associated with a permanently

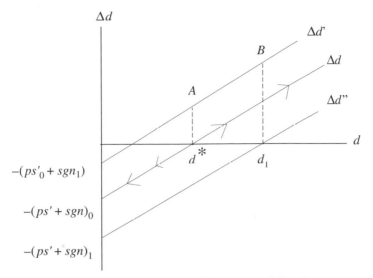

Figure 6.2. Fiscal Aspects of Monetary Stabilization

reduced rate of monetary growth intended to slow inflation, must be associated with a *higher* value of $PV(ps; r - g)$ – in other words, a permanent reduction in monetary growth requires a fiscal adjustment.

When must this fiscal adjustment take place? Suppose the solvency condition (6.10) holds, so the consolidated public sector is solvent, and that once again, $d_{max} > d(0)$, so the public sector has unused borrowing capacity. Now suppose that *sgn* is reduced. Does this mean that ps' must rise right away? The answer is no. We'll now show that, if the consolidated public sector is solvent, it can indeed borrow for a while, so no fiscal adjustment is necessary right away. But as it does so, its ratio of debt to GDP will begin to rise, and the solvency condition can continue to hold only if $PV(ps'; r - g)$ rises at the same time. What this means is that in an inflation stabilization program, *postponing fiscal adjustment now must imply a larger fiscal adjustment in the future, to service the accumulated debt.*

The analysis is described in Figure 6.2. Suppose that *sgn* falls. Since $ps' + sgn$ would decrease in this case, the Δd curve shifts up. The government now faces two choices:

a. Adjust ps' immediately to keep the debt ratio at $d(0)$. This is the immediate fiscal adjustment option.
b. Finance the reduction in monetary expansion by borrowing. In this case, the economy moves to the point A. At A, debt starts to rise.

If no adjustment in ps' is intended to ever be made, debt would rise forever, and since creditors would not be repaid on market terms under these circumstances, this path is not feasible, because the loans would not be forthcoming. On a feasible path, the public sector would have to promise to stabilize d again in the future, since

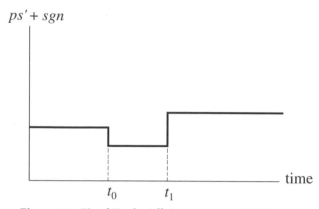

Figure 6.3. Fiscal Trade-Offs in Monetary Stabilization

only along such a path would all the debt accumulated be continually serviced on market terms.

Suppose, then, that debt has risen to $d(1)$, with the economy at the point B. To stabilize the debt at the new level, with the lower level of *sgn*, *ps′* would have to rise, so as to have the Δd line intersect the horizontal axis at $d(1)$. Notice that in this case, just as in the previous section, the adjustment in *ps′* would have to be larger than it would have been had it been undertaken immediately, because now interest on the accumulated debt has to paid as well. The path followed by *ps′* + *sgn* can be described as in Figure 6.3.

The implication of this analysis is that reducing money growth requires fiscal adjustment, either in the present or in the future. Why not just put the adjustment off? There are two reasons:

a. To postpone adjustment requires borrowing, and for borrowing to be possible, creditors have to be convinced that adjustment will indeed take place, so this may require some up-front painful changes to achieve credibility.
b. Postponing the adjustment, moreover, means that the future adjustment must be bigger.

IV. THE SIZE OF THE REQUIRED FISCAL ADJUSTMENT

So far we have shown that achieving a permanent drop in the rate of inflation requires a fiscal adjustment, either now or later. Suppose we make the adjustment today. The next question is: how big does that adjustment have to be – that is, how large is the "permanent" fiscal deficit required to achieve a given rate of inflation? Recall that the solvency condition told us the size of the "permanent" adjusted primary surplus consistent with solvency. It is given by equation (6.10), which is reproduced here for convenience:

$$PV\{[ps' + (\pi + g)m]; r - g\} \geq d(0), \tag{6.10}$$

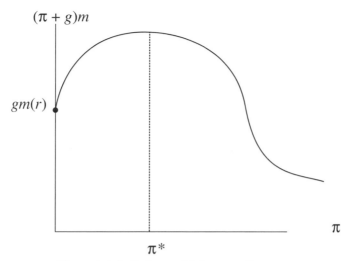

Figure 6.4. Inflation and Seignorage Revenue

But this equation does not directly yield a useful measure of how the "permanent" adjusted primary surplus is affected by a change in the long-run level of inflation. The complication is that, since the demand for money depends on the nominal interest rate, the ratio of the money stock to GDP (m, in our notation above) will itself depend on the rate of inflation. Taking this dependence into account, and using (6.10), we can express the *sustainable value of the adjusted primary surplus* as:

$$ps' = (r - g)d(0) - (\pi + g)m(\pi). \tag{6.11}$$

This equation reveals the relationship between the permanent rate of inflation and the sustainable value of the adjusted primary surplus. Consequently, it permits us to determine the magnitude of the permanent fiscal adjustment required to achieve a given permanent reduction in the rate of inflation. From (6.11), it is clear that the answer depends on what happens to $(\pi + g)m(\pi)$.

To find out what happens, we have to give a specific form to $m()$. Suppose, for example, that $m(\pi)$ takes the form:

$$m(r + \pi) = ke^{-\alpha(r+\pi)}.$$

Now let's plot $(\pi + g)m(r + \pi)$ against π. To see what shape the curve has, differentiate $(\pi + g)m(r + \pi)$ with respect to π. The result is:

$$d(\pi + g)m(r + \pi)/d\pi = ke^{-\alpha(r+\pi)} - \alpha(\pi + g)ke^{-\alpha(r+\pi)}$$
$$= ke^{-\alpha(r+\pi)}[1 - \alpha(\pi + g)].$$

This implies that the slope will be positive up to some critical value $\pi^* = 1/\alpha - g$, and then turn negative for rates of inflation above π^*, as illustrated in Figure 6.4.

What does this imply about the fiscal adjustment required to achieve a given permanent reduction in the rate of inflation? In general, there is no good reason

why an economy would be to the right of the critical point. If it is to the *left*
($\pi < \pi^*$), then it follows that reducing the rate of inflation reduces seignorage, and
the sustainable adjusted primary surplus must *increase*. Notice that an increase in g
reduces the required primary surplus, so if g responds positively to a reduction in
π, the required fiscal adjustment would be smaller than the discussion above would
indicate.

How large does seignorage revenue tend to be in practice? Easterly and Schmidt-
Hebbel (1994) estimated the average amount of annual seignorage revenue collected
by a fifty-country sample of OECD countries and emerging economies (there were
fifteen OECD countries in the sample and thirty-five emerging economies) over the
period 1970–88. They estimated annual seignorage revenue by taking the ratio to
GDP of the yearly sum of deflated monthly changes in the monetary base (i.e., they
added together the monthly values of $\Delta M / P$, and divided the sum by real GDP).
They found that the average value of seignorage revenue for the OECD countries
in their sample over the period amounted to about 1 percent of GDP, while for the
emerging economies the average was 2.1 percent of GDP. Among all of the countries
in their sample, the largest amount of seignorage collected over the period was by
Zaire (4.4 percent of GDP).

Two other observations from this study are worth noting. First, based on cross-
country data, they estimated the revenue-maximizing annual inflation rate for their
sample of countries (π^* in Figure 6.4) at about 68 percent.[9] Second, they noted that
while the inflation tax did not tend to provide large amounts of revenue for most
countries over extended periods, the ratio of seignorage revenue over GDP tended
to be highly variable in their sample, and that seignorage tended to be a large source
of revenue during times of crisis, amounting in some observations in their sample
to as much as 13 percent of GDP.

V. SUMMARY

In this chapter we have seen that the central bank policy of continuous credit
expansion-cum-devaluation may at bottom be a response to a fiscal need. In a
context in which the central bank's policies are dictated by the finance ministry, the
government is likely to raise funds in this way when it cannot borrow to finance a
large fiscal deficit, which is likely to be the case when the government's solvency is in
question – that is, when its debt obligations are already at or near the maximum that
it can reasonably expect to service on market terms, given the prospective future
resources that it will have available for debt service.

But as we saw in Chapter 5, this financing policy is likely to be associated with a
high rate of inflation in the medium term. If the government seeks to achieve a lower

---

[9] Actually, this result was sensitive to the inclusion of Argentina in the fifty-country sample. The
68 percent figure was derived when Argentina was excluded. When that country was retained in the
sample, the revenue-maximizing rate jumped to 160 percent.

rate of inflation in the near future, it will have to accept a lower rate of monetary growth. If the reduced rate of monetary growth is not accompanied by a fiscal adjustment, then the resulting debt accumulation means that the government will be faced with either accepting higher monetary growth – and thus higher inflation – in the future, or with making a larger fiscal adjustment in the future. We have also explored what determines how large the permanent fiscal adjustment has to be if the government undertakes it immediately.

The question is, of course, why the government should be so keen to reduce the rate of inflation. In addition, we may reasonably question whether all that has to be done to achieve a reduced rate of inflation is to lower the rate of monetary growth and make the requisite fiscal adjustment. These two questions will be addressed in the next chapter.

7

Consequences of Insolvency I: High Inflation

When a government is perceived by its creditors to be potentially insolvent, it is said to have a "debt overhang" – in other words, to have more debt than it can feasibly service. What will happen under these circumstances? In principle, four outcomes are possible. The most obvious one is that creditors may be prepared to forgive and (hopefully) forget the excess debt. However, as we will discuss in more detail in the next chapter, this is not an outcome that is likely to materialize spontaneously as the result of voluntary actions by the government's creditors. Failing some form of organized debt forgiveness, the government can make one of three choices: specifically, it can make a fiscal adjustment by reducing G and/or increasing T, it can accelerate the printing presses (increase $\Delta M/M$), and/or it can repudiate part or all of its debt. Deficit reduction is seldom costless or easy, so governments are frequently tempted by the two remaining options. This chapter and the next will consider the macroeconomic consequences of choosing each of these options: we will examine the macroeconomic consequences of high inflation in this chapter, and of the nonpayment of debt in Chapter 8.

Chapter 6 emphasized the fiscal origin of inflation in emerging economies. The perspective we took there was that a government in fiscal difficulties – that is, one facing prospective insolvency – would be tempted to rely on the central bank for financing, and that this type of financing would tend to be inflationary. This chapter will analyze the implications for the economy of the government's handling its prospective insolvency by printing money, and thus generating inflation.

Specifically, we will consider the implications of inflation for long-term growth, entering into much more detail than the overview of this issue presented in Chapter 1. Using as a point of departure the result of Chapter 6 that fiscal adjustment is a necessary condition for inflation stabilization, we will also analyze alternative approaches to inflation stabilization. These alternatives complement fiscal adjustment with different policies with respect to the nominal variables actually or potentially controlled by the government (money-based and exchange rate-based, orthodox and heterodox stabilization). The evidence for the effects of disinflation on growth will be reviewed, with the point being made that stabilizing from high inflation may have *positive* effects on growth even in the short run, in contrast with the "sacrifice ratio" analysis typically applied to the disinflation issue at the much lower inflation rates characteristic of industrial countries.

I. INFLATION AND LONG-RUN GROWTH: THEORY

In analyzing our benchmark model, we saw how inflation was generated in an open economy with a managed exchange rate. Subsequently, we showed that the policies that generate sustained high inflation have their origins in fiscal problems, and that fiscal adjustment, either now or later, was necessary to stabilize the domestic price level. Now we need to ask why anyone who is interested in long-run economic growth and development should care about inflation. That is, what is the relationship between economic performance and inflation?

This question can actually be posed in three separate ways:

i. What is the relationship between the *level* of the inflation rate and the *level* of output?
ii. What is the relationship between a *change* in the rate of inflation and the *level* of output?
iii. What is the relationship between the *level* of the inflation rate and the *rate of growth* of output?

The first two of these are the domain of the Phillips curve. The mainstream view in macroeconomics is that there is no relationship between the *level* of the inflation rate and the *level* of output (the long-run Phillips curve is vertical), but that a *positive* relationship may exist between changes in the rate of inflation and the level of output (the short-run Phillips curve has a negative slope). The second of these is controversial. Some have argued that the relationship depends on the rate of inflation, with a positive relationship for low inflation rates and zero or even a negative relationship for high inflation rates.

But what about (iii)? Why should there be any relationship at all between the level of inflation and the rate of growth of economic capacity? We'll consider the analytical links between these phenomena first, then turn to some empirical evidence.

Recall from Chapter 1 that the rate of economic growth is given by:

$$\Delta Y_P / Y_P = \Delta A / A + \theta \Delta L_P / L_P + (1 - \theta) \Delta K / K.$$

Thus, if inflation is going to affect the growth rate, it must do so by altering the rate of growth of productivity or the rate of accumulation of productive factors. Could it do so? Several potential channels of influence have been identified by economists. We can classify them into channels that operate through the rate of capital accumulation and those that do so through the rate of growth of total factor productivity.

Channels that operate through the level of capital accumulation include the following:

a. The Mundell-Tobin Effect

This was the effect emphasized in some of the original analyses of the relationship between inflation and growth. The basic story is as follows: if money and capital are substitute assets for domestic savers to hold, an increase in the steady-state rate of inflation lowers the real rate of return on money, which pays no interest, while leaving the real return on capital, in the form of the marginal product of capital, unchanged. The effect is to increase the share of saving devoted to capital accumulation rather than hoarding (accumulation of real money balances), thus increasing the long-run growth rate.

b. The Taxation of Capital

Because tax laws tend to be written in nominal terms, high inflation may tend to increase the effective rate of taxation on the return to physical capital. For example, in an inflationary environment, depreciation allowances that are written in nominal terms (i.e., in terms of the original nominal cost of capital) tend to understate the cost in current inflated prices of replacing capital as it wears out. This overstates profits, and consequently generates higher tax obligations than would be due with a proper accounting of the costs of depreciation. Other effects may also be important – for example, the exaggeration of capital gains on real assets.

c. Uncertainty Associated with Unstable Inflation

High inflation has empirically tended to mean unstable inflation. When inflation is unstable, future prices become difficult to predict. Since projections of future prices are an important input into investment decisions, this instability creates uncertainty for firms considering investment in physical capital. As argued in Chapter 1, when investment is irreversible, capital accumulation and growth are unlikely to be very high in such a setting.

d. High Real Interest Rates

Under officially determined exchange rates, high inflation has often resulted in real exchange rate appreciation. In a financially open economy, the resulting expectation of a future real exchange rate depreciation will tend to increase domestic real interest rates through standard open-economy financial arbitrage conditions. To see how this works, recall the uncovered interest parity condition:

$$i = i^* + \Delta s/s. \tag{7.1}$$

Now let π and π^* respectively denote the expected domestic and foreign inflation rates. Since the domestic real interest rate is defined as $r = i - \pi$, we can write:

$$r = i - \pi = (i^* - \pi^*) + (\Delta s/s + \pi^* - \pi),$$

or:

$$r = r^* + \Delta e/e,$$

where r^* is the foreign real interest rate and $\Delta e/e = \Delta s/s + \pi^* - \pi$ is the expected rate of *real* depreciation of the domestic currency. When the domestic currency is overvalued and is expected to depreciate in real terms, therefore, the domestic real interest rate will tend to be high (given the foreign real interest rate), which has the effect of discouraging real domestic investment. We will return to this in Chapter 16.

e. Capital Flight

Under a set of financial sector policies called *financial repression* (discussed in Chapter 12), deposit and lending rates of the domestic banking system are artificially kept below their market-clearing levels. Among other things, this means that banking system credit must be rationed, and is constrained by the funds flowing into the domestic banking system from domestic savers. When inflation is high and the exchange rate is depreciating, financial repression prevents bank deposit rates from adjusting to satisfy arbitrage conditions such as (7.1), which causes domestic residents to attempt to place their funds abroad, a phenomenon known as *capital flight*. The reduced flow of resources into the domestic banking system reduces the flow of credit that these institutions can make available for domestic investment, with consequent negative effects on economic growth.

f. Working Capital

Finally, it's possible that real balances and physical capital may be *complements* in domestic production, if an expansion of the stock of physical capital carries with it an increase in working capital requirements. If so, when inflation raises domestic nominal interest rates, and thus increases the costs of maintaining working capital in the form of real balances, this indirectly increases the cost of physical capital as well. When inflation causes firms to economize on real balances, the marginal productivity of physical capital may fall, and this would tend to depress domestic investment.

g. Inflation as an Indicator of Government Competence

Stanley Fischer has argued that, since economists have produced no good arguments for very high inflation (even the fiscal argument does not support very high inflation, as indicated by the seignorage "Laffer curve" of the previous chapter), a government that promises to prevent it or stop it (they all do) but nevertheless permits it to persist is one that has lost control (Fischer 1993). This creates an environment of generalized uncertainty. The same negative effects on investment and growth would be expected as discussed above.

In addition to these potential effects of the rate of accumulation of physical capital, inflation may also affect the rate of growth of *total factor productivity*. The channels through which this could happen include the following:

1. Distortions in the Information Content of Relative Prices
As we discussed in Chapter 1, high inflation typically tends to increase the variability of relative prices. This tends to reduce the information content of relative prices and interfere with the efficient allocation of resources.

2. Shoe-Leather Costs
The effect of high inflation on domestic nominal interest rates creates incentives for economic agents to economize on their holding of real cash balances. Doing so absorbs resources that could otherwise be devoted to producing goods and services, thus reducing the total output of goods and services that the economy can produce from a given level of employment of productive factors. Consequently, this absorption of resources, referred to as "shoe-leather costs," reduces the economy's total factor productivity.[1]

II. INFLATION AND LONG-RUN GROWTH: EVIDENCE

Of all the analytical links between inflation and long-run growth reviewed above, only one – the Mundell-Tobin effect – suggested that the association between inflation and long-run growth may be positive. Indeed, there is a fairly strong consensus within the economics profession that high inflation is harmful for the growth of economic capacity.[2] The consensus is based not just on the analytical arguments just discussed, but also on a substantial amount of empirical evidence. This section reviews some of that evidence.

We already saw in Chapter 1 how one could test propositions about the effect of macroeconomic factors on long-run growth. Indeed, the study by Fischer (1993)

---

[1] The (tongue-in-cheek) term "shoe-leather costs" comes from the notion that to economize on real money balances involves making many trips to the bank to withdraw currency when it is needed, rather than maintaining large stocks of currency outside the bank. All these trips would tend to wear out one's shoes.

[2] Though the consensus is not so strong on what "high" means.

discussed in Chapter 1 included the rate of inflation as one of the determinants of long-run growth performance. Fischer found, based on cross-country growth regressions, that high inflation had a negative effect on long-run growth, even after controlling for other variables – both macroeconomic and otherwise – that may affect long-run growth performance. One problem that Fischer did not resolve, however, was to rule out the possibility of reverse causation between inflation and growth. While he detected a negative partial correlation between inflation and growth, this may have arisen because low growth causes high inflation, rather than the reverse.

Robert Barro of Harvard University has conducted a number of studies on the relationship between inflation and growth that address this question explicitly. In Barro (1994), for example, he dealt with this problem by using *instrumental variables* estimation. His study was based on a sample on 100 countries, with data from 1960 to 1990. Barro's procedure, however, differed from that of Fischer in that his regression was based on *panel data*, rather than cross-section estimates. That is, rather than average his country-specific data across the entire span of time covered in his sample, he used as data points decade averages for the periods 1965–75, 1975–85, and 1985–90.[3]

The advantage of doing this is that, by first running a regression of each of the potentially endogenous variables (such as the inflation rate) on a set of lagged variables (called *instruments*), he was able to decompose each of these endogenous variables into a portion that could be predicted on the basis of lagged variables (consisting of the fitted values of this regression) and a portion that could not (the residuals of the regression). The portion that could be predicted on the basis of lagged variables could presumably not be influenced by contemporaneous inflation, so any correlation between this portion and the contemporaneous inflation rate would presumably have to arise as the result of causation running from inflation to growth, rather than the other way around. Thus, Barro was able to test whether any of the potentially endogenous variables had a causal effect on growth by including in his growth regression only the predicted component, rather than the actual value, of the variable in question. This *instrumental variable* procedure is a conventional way of attempting to eliminate reverse causation in tests of causal links among economic variables.

Barro included a large number of control variables in his regression. He found that growth within each decade was negatively affected by the initial value of the country's real GDP per capita, and positively affected by the initial value of its secondary enrollment rate, and the health of its citizens (as measured by life expectancy). Growth was positively affected by within-decade increases in a measure

---

[3] It is worth mentioning that Barro computed the standard deviation of inflation for each country within each decade, and found that high inflation was associated with more variable inflation in his sample, as claimed in Chapter 1.

of the rule of law, as well as by improvements in the terms of trade. On the other hand, within-decade increases in fertility, in the ratio of government spending to GDP, and in the premium in the parallel foreign exchange market, had adverse effects on growth. He found that even after controlling for reverse causation, within-decade inflation had a negative effect on growth, but this effect arose from the high-inflation observations in the sample, meaning from observations with annual inflation rates in excess of 40 percent.

One problem with this procedure is that lagged variables are not always reliable instruments. For example, if there is reverse causation from growth to inflation and growth tends to be persistent across decades, then a negative association between growth and *lagged* inflation could arise simply because a positive shock to growth in the last decade was associated *both* with lower inflation then as well as with higher growth in the current decade. Accordingly, in a subsequent study, Barro (1996) revisited the relationship between inflation and growth using a different instrumental variable procedure. As in the earlier study, he relied on a data set consisting of 100 countries, with annual observations from 1960 to 1990. He again used a panel data set consisting of the three periods 1965–75, 1976–85, and 1986–90. His panel regressions controlled for a large number of additional explanatory variables, including, as in the previous study, initial conditions, contemporaneous exogenous factors, and a diverse set of macroeconomic policy and outcome variables.[4]

An interesting aspect of the more recent study that lends credence to the interpretation of a negative partial correlation between inflation and growth as reflecting causation from inflation to growth was the introduction of some novel instruments for inflation. Rather than relying only on lagged values of endogenous variables as instruments, in this study Barro used prior colonial history (in the form of separate dummy variables for Spanish or Portuguese colonial background or other colonial background). These are obviously uncorrelated with innovations in recent growth experience, yet turned out to be correlated with long-term inflation performance. The key point is that using these as instruments for the inflation rate left his previous results in place, suggesting that the partial correlation between inflation and growth that Barro found in his data reflected causation from inflation to growth, rather than vice versa.

Barro's central finding regarding inflation and growth was that, other things equal, a 10 percent increase in the rate of inflation reduced long-run growth by about 0.025 percent per year. Barro found that it was the *level* of inflation, rather than its variability, that affected growth adversely. While this negative relationship between growth and inflation was again driven primarily by high-inflation countries (in the sense that when such observations were excluded the effect of inflation disappeared), he could not reject the hypothesis that the partial effect of inflation on growth was

---

[4] Barro's results are based on an instrumental variable technique using lagged values of the explanatory variables as instruments.

the same at all levels of inflation. Moreover, the results were robust with respect to the exclusion of a few high-inflation outliers.

III. INFLATION STABILIZATION: THEORY

From the previous two sections of this chapter, we have learned that there are both theoretical and empirical reasons to believe that high inflation is associated with lower long-run growth. In Chapters 5 and 6, we learned that, in a typical emerging economy, high inflation is the product of continuous exchange rate depreciation with monetary accommodation, driven by high fiscal deficits. This told us that reducing inflation requires a fiscal adjustment, either now or later, essentially because it implies a reduction in seignorage revenue. So we have strong reason to believe that high inflation is harmful, and we know what is required to bring it under control.

a. Costs of Inflation Stabilization

But does this mean that stopping high inflation is necessarily a good idea? The answer depends on what happens to an economy over time as we make the fiscal adjustment required to bring inflation down. The reason this matters is that even if inflation is bad for growth, *stopping* inflation may also be bad for growth. If the costs of stopping inflation are sufficiently high relative to the costs of continuing inflation, it may not be worth doing, even if inflation is bad for growth. To see this, consider how the path of real GDP might evolve over time in the course of an inflation stabilization episode, as shown in Figure 7.1.

This figure illustrates three possible paths for the economy's real output during an inflation stabilization episode. Suppose that the economy's real output follows the shallow low-growth path given above up to the point A in a high-inflation equilibrium (the growth rate determines the slope of the path), and that a stabilization is contemplated at time t_0. Suppose further that the transition to a low-inflation high-growth path is completed by time t_1. Then what we have learned about inflation and growth so far tells us only that the path followed by the economy after t_1 will be steeper than the path it followed before, since the economy's long-run growth rate should be expected to be higher in the post-stabilization low-inflation equilibrium than in the initial high-inflation one.

But we do not know, for example, whether the economy will start on the new path at point B or point C. This depends on what happens during the transition. Suppose we know it starts from B. Would we advise the country's authorities to undertake a stabilization? The answer depends on whether the domestic political system judges that the eventual gains (beginning where the dashed line consistent with the original growth path intersects the new growth path starting from B) are worth the transitional costs. Would we be able to give a different answer if we knew instead that the post-stabilization path starts at C? The answer is no. It depends

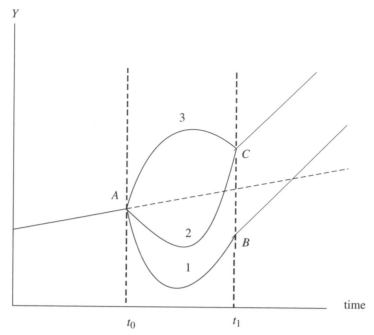

Figure 7.1. Real Output During an Inflation Stabilization Episode

on how we get there. If the path from A to C is the one labeled 2, then there is still a trade-off to face, though a more favorable one than in the previous case. However, if it happens to be the one labeled 3, then we can say that the transition is unambiguously good.

b. Modeling Inflation Stabilization

Thus, we need to worry about what happens to real output when we stabilize. A natural place to start is to see what the model that we developed in Chapters 2–5 tells us about this issue. Recall that, in the short-run version of that model, there were three key endogenous variables: the level of real GDP Y, the domestic price level P, and the domestic interest rate i. These three variables were determined by an aggregate supply relationship developed in Section I of Chapter 2, a goods-market equilibrium condition developed in Section II, and a financial-market equilibrium condition developed in Chapter 3. Since our focus in Part 2 was on determining the domestic interest rate and the real exchange rate, we eliminated Y from this three-equation system by substituting the aggregate supply relationship into the goods and financial market equilibrium conditions. This enabled us to analyze the economy's equilibrium graphically using a goods-market equilibrium curve (GM) and a financial market equilibrium curve (FM) drawn in i-P space. Since our interest is now in seeing how real output Y can be expected to behave during an inflation stabilization, we will derive an alternative graphical representation of

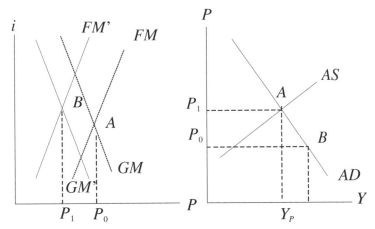

Figure 7.2. Goods and Money Market Equilibrium and the Aggregate Demand Curve

the model that instead of eliminating Y from the system eliminates the domestic interest rate, and displays the model's solution in P-Y space.

The alternative procedure can be described graphically as follows. First, since we will not be substituting the aggregate supply relationship into the goods- and financial market equilibrium conditions as we did in Chapters 2 and 3, we begin by re-drawing the original GM and FM curves of Chapters 2 and 3 for *given* values of Y. Beginning with the GM curve, from equation (2.13), holding Y constant, the goods-market equilibrium condition becomes:

$$Y = \phi(sP^*/P)A_P[Y, T, i] + G + X(sP^*/P, \theta). \qquad (7.2)$$
$$\quad + \qquad\qquad + \ - \ - \qquad\qquad\quad + \ +$$

In i-P space, this can be shown as the negatively sloped dashed curve labeled GM in the left-hand panel of Figure 7.2 (recall that the negative slope arises because a lower domestic interest rate increases aggregate demand for domestic goods, and thus requires an increase in the price of such goods to maintain equilibrium in the goods market). Next, consider the FM curve. As we saw in Chapter 3, the specification of the financial market equilibrium condition depends on the economy's degree of financial integration with the rest of the world, as well as on the monetary policy regime followed by its central bank. The analysis that follows can be reproduced for each of the cases considered in Chapter 3, but suppose that for concreteness and simplicity we consider here the case of imperfect capital mobility and monetary targeting. In that case, the FM curve is given by equation (3.15a), reproduced here for convenience:

$$\overline{M} = PL(i, Y). \qquad (7.3)$$

This equation is depicted in the left-hand panel of Figure 7.2 as the dashed curve FM. It has a positive slope (recall that an increase in the domestic interest rate reduces the demand for money; thus, given a constant money supply, a higher domestic price level is required to maintain equilibrium in the domestic money market).

Next, we want to derive the set of all combinations of P and Y that are simultaneously consistent with equilibrium in the goods and financial markets. We will call the locus of all such combinations the economy's aggregate demand curve (AD). To see what this locus must look like, we ask what happens to the equilibrium value of P determined by our *GM-FM* diagram as we consider changing the level of Y. Suppose we consider a value of Y *higher* than that used to draw the dashed *GM* and *FM* curves that intersect at the point A. Then, as long as the total marginal propensity to spend is less than one, the reduction in Y will create an excess supply of goods. To restore equilibrium in the goods market, a lower value of P would be required, since this would depreciate the real exchange rate and increase net exports, thereby increasing demand for domestic goods. The effect is to shift the *GM* curve to the left. Similarly, an increase in Y creates an excess demand for money, which implies that a reduction in P would be required to restore equilibrium in the money market – that is, the *FM* curve must shift to the left as well. The equilibrium in the left-hand panel thus moves from A to B, with a lower level of P and an indeterminate change in the domestic interest rate. In the right-hand panel, this corresponds to a movement from A to a point with higher Y and lower P, such as B. If instead we consider the effects of a *lower* value of Y, this analysis would be reversed: *GM* and *FM* would shift to the right, and the equilibrium price level would rise. Thus, the set of all combinations of Y and P that clear the goods and money markets simultaneously, which we previously called the AD curve, must have a negative slope. For any given value of Y, any shock to the economy that would tend to increase P in the *GM-FM* diagram would shift the AD curve vertically upward by the same amount, while any shock that would tend to decrease P would correspondingly shift AD downward.

It is useful to derive the properties of the AD curve a little more formally. To do so, we first solve the financial market equilibrium condition for the domestic interest rate i. From the money market equilibrium condition (7.3) the solution can be written as:

$$i = i(M/P, Y). \tag{7.3'}$$
$${-}{+}$$

That is, the interest rate consistent with money market equilibrium is lower the higher the real money supply, and higher the higher the level of real GDP. Next, substitute this expression for i into the goods-market equilibrium condition. Recall that the *GM* curve was derived as the set of all combinations of i and P that satisfied the goods-market equilibrium condition (7.2). By examination of equation (7.2), it is easy to see that the properties of this equilibrium must satisfy:

$$Y = Y(G, T, i, SP^*/P, \theta), \tag{7.2'}$$
$${+}{-}{-}{+}{+}$$

Substituting for the interest rate we have:

$$Y = Y[G, T, i(M/P, Y), SP^*/P, \theta], \qquad (7.4)$$

which represents the AD curve.

The properties of this aggregate demand curve are the following:

i. Its slope is determined by the effects of P on the real money stock and the real exchange rate. An increase in P reduces the aggregate demand for domestic goods through two channels. First, the real money supply falls, which raises the domestic interest rate and reduces aggregate expenditure, including on domestic goods (a mechanism called the "Keynes effect"). Second, as P increases, the real exchange rate appreciates. This reduces net exports (deteriorates the trade balance) and thus reduces the demand for domestic goods. This curve is relatively flat when the interest elasticity of the demand for money is small (so changes in M/P have large effects on i), when aggregate spending is highly sensitive to i, and when changes in the relative price of domestic goods have a large effect on the demand for those goods. That will be the case when the elasticities of export and import demand are large.

ii. What determines the position of the curve? The curve is shifted vertically up or down by changes in real variables such as fiscal policy and foreign output. Increases in government spending, tax cuts, and increases in the export shift parameter θ all create an excess demand for domestic goods, at a given level of output. Consequently, to restore equilibrium in the market for domestic goods, their price has to rise. This means that the AD curve is displaced vertically upward (a higher price level is required at any Y to clear the market). The curve would shift downward if any of these shocks were reversed.

iii. The AD curve is also shifted by changes in nominal variables – specifically, the exchange rate and money supply. A devaluation of the nominal exchange rate or an increase in the money supply can shift the curve vertically. More important, equal proportionate increases in s and M shift the AD upward in the same proportion, since an equiproportionate change in s, M, and P would leave both the real exchange rate and the real money supply unchanged, and thus would be consistent with equilibrium in the goods and money markets at a given level of production. This means that the process of ongoing depreciation and money growth can be illustrated in the form of continuous *upward* movements of the AD curve in proportional amounts equal to the ongoing rate of nominal exchange rate depreciation and money growth.

The final component of our model is the aggregate supply curve given by equation (2.6), reproduced here as equation (7.5):

$$Y = AF[L(P/P^e)L_P, K]. \qquad (7.5)$$

As we saw in Chapter 2, the effects of changes in the domestic price level on real output in equation (7.5) depend on whether price changes were previously anticipated

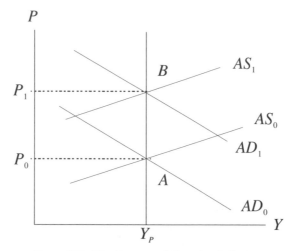

Figure 7.3. The Process of Ongoing Inflation

or not. In particular, we saw in Chapter 2 that, drawn for a *given* value of P^e, the aggregate supply curve has a positive slope in P-Y space, and that it must pass above the point on the horizontal axis corresponding to Y_P at a value of the domestic price level P that equals the price level P^e expected by workers. The latter means that when P^e changes, this new upward-sloping AS curve must shift vertically by an amount equal to the change in P^e.

Plotting the resulting aggregate supply relationship in the right-hand panel of Figure 7.2 together with the aggregate demand relationship we have just derived completes the re-casting of our model in P-Y space, and gives us the means to pin down the equilibrium values of P and Y. As drawn in Figure 7.2, the economy is initially in equilibrium at price level P_1 (which must also be the price level expected by workers – $P^e = P_1$), and with real output at its full employment level Y_P.

Anticipated ongoing inflation can be illustrated in this framework as a continuous process of upward displacements of both the AD and AS curves. The AD curve shifts upward at a rate equal to the rate of increase in the money supply and of nominal exchange rate depreciation. Since this is an ongoing process (i.e., one that repeats itself every period), workers must be aware of it. They correctly anticipate that this continuous aggregate demand expansion will cause an exactly equal rate of price increase, and this revision in their price level expectations each period causes the AS curve to shift upward by exactly the same amount as the AD curve. Each period workers' expectations are borne out by experience, because when the AD and AS curves shift vertically by equal amounts, the price level rises by that amount. The result is an equilibrium in which the price level rises continuously at a rate equal to the rate of increase in the money supply and exchange rate depreciation, with no change in the level of real output. The progression of the economy over time is illustrated in Figure 7.3.

Now suppose that the government decides to stabilize by reducing the rates of money growth and currency depreciation, and that it supports this plan by implementing a tighter fiscal policy. What happens to Y during the process of stabilization? Note first that in the period that the tighter fiscal policy is implemented, the rate of vertical displacement of the AD curve will slow down, both because the rate of depreciation and money supply expansion will decrease permanently, as well as because of the one-time change in the level of government spending or taxation associated with the adjustment of the public sector's primary surplus. In subsequent periods, the curve will shift upward at the new lower rate of depreciation and monetary expansion.

What will happen to Y during this process? The answer given by our model is that it depends on whether the slowdown in the rate of vertical displacement of the AD curve was anticipated by workers. To be more concrete, notice that nothing was said above about how workers form their expectations. Consider two options. Under *rational expectations*, which refers to a situation in which workers form their price level expectations using the "true" model of the economy, if workers can foresee the stabilization and adapt their wage demands accordingly, then their price level expectations would tend to be correct. If the stabilization is announced before it is implemented, and if this announcement is credible to the workers whose behavior is reflected in the economy's aggregate supply curve, workers will anticipate the slowdown in the rate of upward displacement of AD, and will correctly infer, using the model, what this implies for the behavior of the aggregate price level. Thus, the rate of upward displacement of AS will slow down to match that of AD, and the economy's rate of price increase will immediately slow, with Y remaining equal to Y_P all the while. In terms of the paths illustrated in Figure 7.1, the point B (or C) moves to coincide with point A. Capacity growth accelerates after the rate of inflation falls, and since Y never deviates from Y_P, the rate of growth of actual real GDP accelerates immediately as well. These are no transition problems, and stabilization is unambiguously a good thing.

Suppose, on the other hand, that the stabilization was not anticipated, either because it was not previously announced or, if announced, the announcement was not believed. The effects of a stabilization under these circumstances are shown in Figure 7.4. As we have seen, ongoing inflation at a rate of, say, x percent would imply a continuous upward adjustment in the aggregate demand curve by x percent each period, due to money growth and exchange rate devaluation of x percent. In addition, the aggregate supply curve would shift up by x percent each period as well, as workers continuously adjust their price level expectations. Now suppose that the aggregate demand curve, which in the absence of a policy change would have shifted, say, from AD_0 to AD_1, is suddenly slowed down through a fiscal adjustment coupled with a reduced rate of monetary growth and exchange rate devaluation. What would happen to the economy if workers had not expected this reduction in the rate of expansion of aggregate demand to take place?

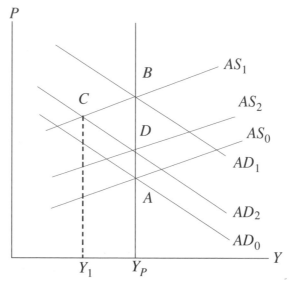

Figure 7.4. Stabilization Dynamics with Imperfect Price Level Information

The answer depends in part on how sudden the slowdown in aggregate demand is. One extreme option is to suddenly slow the pace of monetary growth all the way to a new value that is compatible with low inflation. This is referred to as a "cold turkey" approach. Alternatively, the slowdown could be more gradual, with the rate of monetary expansion only eventually reaching its desired target, a technique called "gradualism." Taking an intermediate case, suppose that as a result of the change in policies, the vertical displacement of AD is only to AD_2, rather than AD_1. If workers did not expect this adjustment – or do not believe that it will happen when it is announced – their price level expectations will remain unaffected. This means that the AS curve will continue to shift upward at the same rate as it would have if the stabilization had not taken place, say from AS_0 to AS_1, rather than to AS_2. In that case, the economy will move to a new equilibrium at C, with a substantial gap between Y and Y_P, rather than to B, where it would have been without the stabilization, or to D, where it would have been if the stabilization had been expected and credible. The conclusion is that, because of the recession created by the stabilization, the growth rate of *capacity* output may eventually accelerate, but that of *actual* output will fall short of it for some time, perhaps following a trajectory such as 1 or 2 in Figure 7.1.

A similar result would follow under *adaptive expectations*, however (a mechanism under which workers form expectations based on the last price level actually observed) or any other "backward-looking" mechanism for forming expectations. If they form their expectations in such a manner, workers would not adjust their wage demands on the basis of new information about the behavior of aggregate demand in the current period, and thus would not moderate their wage demands in response to an announced stabilization. The implication is that stabilization would move the economy to a point such as C in Figure 7.3, so that stopping inflation implies a recession in the short run. The key result of the preceding analysis, then, is that *the short-run effects of stabilization depend on the response of aggregate supply.*

c. Stabilization Strategies

We have seen that stabilization entails two necessary components: a reduction in the rate of monetary expansion and exchange rate devaluation, as well as a fiscal adjustment to adapt the public sector's budget to a lower level of seignorage revenues. These components affect the behavior of the economy's aggregate demand curve. A *stabilization strategy*, however, may supplement these components with others intended to reduce the cost of making the transition to low inflation.

Suppose, for example, that workers form their expectations rationally, but are unsure about the government's commitment to stabilization, so they cannot perfectly anticipate the behavior of the AD curve. How can a government that truly intends to stabilize – that intends to carry out the necessary monetary and fiscal components of stabilization – influence the behavior of the AS curve so as to try to avoid recession? One approach is to try to enhance the credibility of its policy intentions by taking supplementary actions which would only make sense if the government truly intended to stabilize.

For example, the government could announce a fixed exchange rate or a much slower rate of devaluation for the domestic currency. We have seen that unless domestic credit expansion is complemented with exchange rate devaluation, the central bank's reserves would tend to be depleted, which would eventually make the exchange rate policy unsustainable. This strategy is referred to as "exchange rate-based" stabilization. When no such commitment is made, the strategy is said to be "money-based", because full reliance is placed by the government on the reduction in money growth and fiscal adjustment.

In addition to making special announcements about exchange rate policy, the government may also intervene in the wage-price process directly by supplementing its monetary, fiscal, and exchange rate measures with wage and price controls intended to directly influence the position of the AS curve. Stabilization programs that feature direct intervention with the wage-price process are called *heterodox*, while those that do not are called *orthodox*.

To summarize, our model suggests that a reduction in the rate of monetary growth and exchange rate devaluation is a necessary component of inflation stabilization. We have also seen that this will need to be accompanied by a fiscal adjustment that can happen either contemporaneously with the slowdown in money growth or not, though the latter will be feasible only if the government can credibly promise its creditors to make a larger fiscal adjustment in the future. These adjustments can be either sudden ("cold turkey") or gradual, but the important thing is that the rate of displacement of the aggregate demand curve must converge to the desired lower rate of inflation. The real effects of this strategy depend on how workers' expectations respond, and the government can try to influence these expectations – or the behavior of aggregate supply more directly – through supplementary policies such as exchange rate announcements or the implementation of wage and price controls.

When all is said and done, then, whether it is worthwhile to stop inflation depends on:

i. How costly the inflation was originally (i.e., how flat and low the initial path of Y was relative to its post-stabilization path).

ii. How successful the policies mentioned above are in avoiding a long and deep recession during the transition to low inflation. This determines the *sacrifice ratio* (the ratio of cumulative lost percentage points of output to percentage-point reduction in inflation) associated with the stabilization.

iii. The society's *rate of time preference*, which determines the relative value it places on current income compared to future income. This is relevant in the event that stabilization implies a recession during the transition, because the social costs of the recession come now, while the benefits of stabilization come later, implying that trade-offs have to be made between current income losses and future income gains.

But has stabilization indeed been costly? We now review some international evidence of the experience with stabilization from high inflation to examine how successful countries have been in avoiding costs of transition.

IV. INFLATION STABILIZATION: EVIDENCE

Theory thus tells us that it may or may not be a good idea to stabilize, depending on the economy's short-run supply response. What does the evidence say about short-run costs of stabilization? The research reviewed in Section II provides fairly strong evidence that sustained low inflation is conducive to higher economic growth. However, this evidence pertains to the relationship between *sustained* low inflation and *long-run* growth rates, or growth of productive capacity. As we have just seen, this evidence is compatible with a situation in which the *transition* from high to low inflation is associated with a contemporaneous *deceleration* in economic growth. The reason is that short-run adjustment mechanisms may cause the favorable growth effects from disinflation to materialize only with a lag, so that growth may actually slow during the transition, and perhaps for some time thereafter, before achieving the higher levels suggested by the cross-country evidence described above. What, then, does the evidence say about the growth effects of the transition from high to low inflation in emerging economies?

In this section we will look at both cross-country and case study evidence. The first of these will give us an idea what the international experience has been regarding the short-run costs of inflation stabilization. The second will enable us to interpret this experience by looking at *stabilization strategies* – alternative ways to bring about stabilization.

a. Cross-Country Evidence

The effects of inflation stabilization on growth have been investigated by Bruno and Easterly (1995), who were interested in looking at the growth effects of temporary inflation crises and their stabilization aftermaths. Their procedure was to collect a sample of macro data on a large group of industrial and developing countries from the 1950s to the 1990s. They defined an *inflation crisis* as occurring in their sample whenever a country had two or more consecutive years of inflation greater than 40 percent, ending when inflation fell below 40 percent and stayed there for at least two consecutive years. They then compared the behavior of a number of macro indicators relative to the contemporaneous world average before, during, and after such inflation crises.

What did they find? First, they found that there was a strong correlation between inflation crises and fiscal deficits. Comparing crisis countries to the contemporaneous world average, they found that fiscal deficits were higher in the crisis countries before the crisis, were even larger during the crisis, and were lower after the crisis. This pattern was matched by *seignorage revenue,* which skyrocketed in the crisis countries during the inflation crisis episode. Their conclusion from this part of the study was that the international evidence is consistent with the view that high inflation is largely a *fiscal* phenomenon, as argued in Chapter 6.

Second, with regard to growth, they found that it fell by an average of 2.8 percentage points *during* the crisis (that is, up to time t_0 in Figure 7.1 above), but *rose* by an average of 3.8 percent after the crisis. This pattern was repeated for measured growth in total factor productivity, since the ratio of investment to GDP tended to be below average during the crisis, and did not rise above the world average subsequently, suggesting a temporary acceleration of growth of actual production above that of productive capacity. Their conclusion is that the sacrifice ratio may actually be *positive* when inflation is high (greater than 40 percent). In terms of Figure 7.1, therefore, their evidence is consistent with a typical path of real output during stabilization such as that labeled with the number 3. It should be stressed, however, that the Bruno-Easterly evidence applies to high inflation rates (in excess of 40 percent), and cannot be extended to inflation rates below this value. Notice that this is consistent with the evidence in Barro (1996) concerning the effects of high inflation on long-run growth. Thus, the evidence suggests that high inflation is bad for long-run capacity growth *and* that there are no short-run output costs from stabilizing high inflation.

b. Case Study Evidence: Stabilization Programs

We now turn to case studies of stabilization. These are useful because they permit us to consider stabilization *strategies*, which we defined above as the full policy package that gets implemented as part of a complete *stabilization program*. Fiscal adjustment is only part of such a program, the role of which is to stop (or at least slow down) the continuous upward shift of the aggregate demand curve. There are at least two other components, the first of which may affect both the aggregate demand and supply curves, and the second of which is directed specifically at the aggregate supply curve:

i. The choice of a *nominal anchor* during the process of stabilization (money or exchange rate). As we saw in Chapter 4, all economies must have a nominal anchor to pin down the price level. In general, the money supply, the exchange rate, or some other nominal variable must play this role. Thus, in implementing a stabilization program, the authorities must also make some decision concerning which nominal anchor to adopt during and after the stabilization process.

ii. The *orthodox-heterodox* component of stabilization. This refers to the issue of whether wage and price controls are used temporarily to support the nominal anchor. The role of expectations and credibility in determining the short-run output costs of disinflation analyzed in the previous section suggests why it might be desirable to do so – essentially direct interference with the wage-price process could be used to influence the magnitude of the shift in the short-run aggregate supply curve during the stabilization period, ensuring that aggregate supply and aggregate demand intersect at a point such as D in Figure 7.3.

Beyond these two key characteristics, the outcomes of individual stabilization programs may also depend on other accompanying policies that may be undertaken at the same time. The most important of these include the state of capital account liberalization and the state of financial reform, to be discussed in more detail in Part 4 of the book.

A very useful overview of individual country experiences in stabilizing from high inflation was provided by Vegh (1992). Vegh focused specifically on the distinction between *exchange-rate based* stabilizations (in which a predetermined exchange rate is part of the stabilization package, implying the use of the exchange rate as a nominal anchor), and *money-based* stabilization (in which the exchange rate is allowed to float and the domestic money supply is used as the economy's nominal anchor). As in Bruno and Easterly (1995), Vegh also considered threshold effects, in his case distinguishing between countries with *hyperinflation* defined in the classic Cagan sense (beginning when monthly inflation exceeds 50 percent for the first time and ending when it falls below 50 percent and stays below for at least a year) and those with only *chronic* inflation, defined in the Pazos sense (as inflation that is intermediate in intensity and lasts for a long time). To summarize Vegh's findings, we'll consider these separately.

1. Hyperinflation

The cases of hyperinflation considered by Vegh included those of central and eastern Europe in the post–World War I period (Austria from October 1921 to August 1922, Germany from August 1922 to November 1923, Hungary from March 1923 to February 1924, Poland from January 1923 to January 1924, and Russia from December 1921 to January 1924); Europe in the post–World War II period (Hungary from August 1945 to July 1946, Greece from November 1943 to December 1945), Taiwan (1945–49); and more recently, Bolivia (from April 1984 to September 1985).

The stylized facts from these stabilization experiences included the following:

a. Stabilization in these episodes tended to share common policy elements. The key elements were drastic fiscal reform, the implementation of central bank independence (which we will discuss in Chapter 9), and the restoration of currency convertibility.

b. In each of these cases, inflation stopped immediately. In other words, there was no long drawn-out period of disinflation. The explanation Vegh offers for this is that in hyperinflation, immediate price stability can be achieved by using the exchange rate as the nominal anchor, because all domestic prices tend to get quoted in foreign exchange. In terms of our model, this can be interpreted as meaning that P^e in effect gets indexed to sP^*, so that AS shifts up each period by the rate of devaluation.

c. The short-run output costs associated with stabilization was small in each of these cases. Output actually *rose* during stabilization in three episodes (Russia, Greece, and Germany) and was unchanged in two others (Taiwan and Bolivia). There was conflicting evidence regarding the short-run behavior of real output in Austria and Hungary in 1946. Real output apparently fell somewhat only in both Poland and Hungary in 1924.

The lessons drawn by Vegh from the case study experience in stabilization from hyperinflation were that credible fiscal reform is needed for success, and that in the case of hyperinflation, inflation can be stopped rapidly and without substantial output costs. The credibility of fiscal reform can be enhanced by implementing central bank independence and currency convertibility (the removal of foreign exchange controls). The former eliminates recourse to the inflation tax, and the latter signals the government's intention to pursue prudent aggregate demand policies in the future. Relatively costless stabilization is facilitated in the case of hyperinflation through the role of the exchange rate as a nominal anchor when all prices become indexed to the exchange rate. To make the fixed exchange rate credible during stabilization, the authorities in each case had recourse to large foreign exchange reserves and/or an external line of credit.

2. Chronic Inflation

Vegh classified the chronic inflation cases in his study into three categories. These included the *Latin American heterodox programs of the sixties* (Argentina in March 1967, Brazil in March 1964, and Uruguay in June 1968); the *Southern Cone* episodes (Argentina in December 1978, Chile in February 1978, and Uruguay in October 1978); and the *heterodox* programs of the mid-eighties (Argentina's "Austral" program of June 1985, Brazil's "Cruzado" program of February 1986, the Israeli program of July 1985, and the Mexican "Pacto" program of December 1987).

The early Latin American heterodox programs were populist in nature in that they did not feature strong and sustained fiscal adjustments. These programs were characterized by fixed exchange rates and the use of incomes policies. All of them achieved an initial decline in inflation, but only Brazil sustained it into the seventies.

The Southern Cone programs of the late seventies, by contrast, were orthodox, in the sense that no wage or price controls were used, though a centerpiece of each of these programs was the use of a pre-announced nominal exchange rate path, known as a *tablita*. Fiscal balance was achieved in Chile and Uruguay, but not in Argentina. All of the Southern Cone programs ended in crises featuring an appreciated real exchange rate triggering large capital outflows, as well as a collapse of the financial sector.

These experiences will turn out to be quite important for other issues that we will be discussing later in this book, and we will therefore have cause to revisit the Southern Cone episodes. For now, however, we can just summarize Vegh's assessment of where they went wrong. In his view, there were two key mistakes made in the Southern Cone stabilizations. The first consisted of leaving backward wage indexation in place, and the second of combining stabilization with opening the capital account and liberalizing the domestic financial sector. The first of these created inertia in the wage-price process, which caused the real exchange rate to appreciate, while the second permitted capital first to flow in to an underregulated financial sector, and later to rapidly flow out, resulting in a financial crisis.

Finally, the *heterodox* programs of the mid-eighties, like those of the sixties, featured both fixed exchange rates and wage-price controls. The key to success here was the role of fiscal policy. Little fiscal adjustment was achieved in Brazil, and fiscal adjustment proved to be temporary in Argentina. Only in Israel and Mexico, where large and sustained fiscal adjustment was undertaken, did stabilization prove to be successful.

Vegh summarizes experience on all three of the "chronic inflation" stabilization periods in the following way. First, in contrast to the hyperinflation cases, inflation converged slowly. Given the role of the exchange rate as a nominal anchor, a large and sustained real appreciation emerged in all of these cases, which contributed to a deterioration of the current account of the balance of payments. Economic growth rose initially in all of them, and then contracted. The key lesson drawn by Vegh is that fixing the exchange rate under chronic inflation may indeed reduce the short-run output cost of stabilization and speed the rate of convergence of inflation to its desired value, but successful stabilization under these conditions requires low capital mobility, a stable domestic financial system, and early "flexibilization" of the exchange rate.

V. SUMMARY

This chapter has covered a substantial amount of ground. We saw that there are both analytical and empirical reasons to believe that high inflation is inimical to sustained rapid growth of productive capacity in emerging economies. This does not, however, necessarily imply that the reduction of high inflation is always and everywhere justified. The reason is that the transition from high to low inflation – that is, the process of inflation stabilization – may itself involve high costs in the form of a period during which the growth rate of actual output falls below that of productive capacity. If the growth benefits of lower inflation are small, if the transition involves a prolonged period of slow growth, and if the society weighs current income very heavily relative to future income, then stabilization may not be worthwhile. However, both the cross-country and case study evidence suggests that, at least when inflation is very high (say, in excess of 40 percent per year), there may be few – if any – short-run costs associated with the process of bringing inflation down.

A credible and sustained fiscal adjustment is a necessary requirement for doing so. The role of other policies is less clear-cut. Enhanced central bank independence may increase the credibility of the fiscal adjustment, for reasons that we will explore in more detail in Chapter 9.

On the other hand, the effectiveness of the use of the exchange rate as a nominal anchor may depend on circumstances. A fixed exchange rate coupled with currency convertibility (which requires the availability of resources to defend the rate, either in the form of reserves or access to external credit) may enhance the effectiveness of stabilization when inflation is extremely high (as in hyperinflations), because domestic prices tend to be indexed to the exchange rate, and there is little inertia in the domestic wage-price process. Under chronic moderately high inflation, fixing the exchange rate may need to be supplemented with more heterodox elements such as wage and price controls if the stabilization program lacks credibility or if there is institutional inertia in the wage-price process. When the exchange rate is used as a nominal anchor and such inertia is allowed to persist, combining stabilization with domestic and external financial liberalization may provide the recipe for the failure of stabilization and a financial crash, as in the Southern Cone countries.

Thus, while stabilization from high inflation may be desirable in both the short run and the long run, it is certainly possible to do it counterproductively. A durable fiscal adjustment is a necessary condition, but exchange rate and financial sector policies also matter. As argued in Chapter 1, these lessons about the roles of exchange rate and financial sector management are of broader applicability. They apply to the attainment and preservation of macroeconomic stability in emerging economies more generally, rather than just to the issue of inflation stabilization. We will turn to them in Parts 4 and 5 of this book.

Before doing so, however, we need to consider two other fiscal issues: first, fiscal adjustment and/or reliance on seignorage revenue are not the only possible responses to a situation of prospective fiscal insolvency. Implicit or explicit debt repudiation is also an alternative, with its own consequences for macroeconomic stability and growth. That is the subject of the next chapter. Second, much has been made in both the previous chapter and this one about the credibility and sustainability of fiscal adjustment. The last two chapters of Part 3 take up two mechanisms for enhancing the credibility and sustainability of fiscal adjustment.

8

Consequences of Insolvency II: Public Sector Debt and Economic Growth

In the absence of fiscal adjustment, the alternative to printing money in order to cope with prospective fiscal insolvency is to cease servicing public debt on contractual terms, which amounts to de facto debt repudiation. Like high inflation, the nonpayment of debt is likely to have macroeconomic consequences – specifically, consequences for economic growth. This chapter will briefly examine the macroeconomic consequences of debt repudiation, in the form of "debt overhang" effects on domestic investment and capital flight. The analysis will be applied to the case of the international debt crisis, which resulted in a "lost decade" for development in Latin America.

I. THE DEBT "OVERHANG"

Our analysis in Chapter 6 indicated that there may exist a "revenue-maximizing rate of inflation," that is, a rate of inflation that maximizes the real revenue that the government can collect from the inflation tax. This maximum revenue imposes a natural limit to the extent that consolidated public sector deficits can be financed through inflation. However, Chapter 7 suggested that governments may have good reasons for stopping short of collecting the maximum feasible inflation tax – specifically because both theory and evidence indicate that high inflation is macroeconomically costly. But we also saw in Chapter 5 that if governments want to reduce their reliance on the inflation tax while retaining solvency, they have no choice but to undertake a fiscal adjustment – a reduction in spending or increase in revenue collection.

The problem is, of course, that fiscal adjustment may be politically unpopular and thus difficult to achieve. This raises the possibility of opting for a third alternative – that of sacrificing the public sector's solvency through the nonpayment of public sector debt. The attractiveness of this option, of course, depends on the costs associated with nonpayment compared with those of fiscal adjustment and/or reliance on the inflation tax. In this section, we will consider what such costs might be.

a. The Debt Overhang

As a first step in doing so, we will develop the concept of "debt overhang." This term refers to the excess of the face value of the public sector's debt over the present value of the debt service payments that the public sector is prepared to make over the indefinite future. Using the notation of Chapter 6, recall that the sustainable value of the adjusted primary surplus of the consolidated public sector could be written as:

$$ps' = (r - g)d_0 - (\pi + g)m(r + \pi)$$

where ps' denotes the adjusted primary surplus of the consolidated public sector, r is the (real) risk-free interest rate, g is the economy's sustainable growth rate, π is the desired rate of inflation, and m denotes the base of the inflation tax. Now suppose that the macroeconomic costs of inflation impose a maximum value π_{max} on the long-run rate of domestic inflation that the government is willing to tolerate, and that the social costs and/or political difficulty of fiscal adjustment places an upper limit ps_{max} on the share of the adjusted primary surplus of the public sector in GDP. Then, as in Chapter 6, we can derive the maximum sustainable value of the public sector's net debt (relative to GDP). It is given by:

$$d_{max} = [ps'_{max} + (\pi_{max} + g)m(r + \pi_{max})]/(r - g).$$

A debt overhang exists when $d_0 > d_{max}$ – that is, when the existing debt is larger than the stock of debt that the public sector is willing and able to service on market terms.

How could such a situation emerge? Clearly, for reasons described in Chapter 6, the public sector's creditors would not willingly allow an accumulation of debt in excess of d_{max}, if they could anticipate it. Thus, a debt overhang is likely to emerge as the result of an unanticipated change in circumstances. These could involve, for example, changes in economic circumstances that reduce the maximum primary surplus that the government is able to generate, or the inflation tax revenue that can be produced with the maximum tolerable rate of inflation π_{max}, a change in the time path of expected real interest rates or the country's growth rate, or even a change in political regime that alters the government's perceived willingness to produce ps_{max} or π_{max}, even under unchanged economic circumstances.

b. Macroeconomic Effects of the Debt Overhang

What happens when a debt overhang emerges? One answer is that the public sector becomes insolvent. But this, of course, is tautological. By *definition* the existence of a debt overhang is equivalent to insolvency. The interesting question is how the emergence of a debt overhang in the accounts of its consolidated public sector affects a country's macroeconomic performance.

One possibility is that the public sector's creditors simply write off the excess of d_0 over d_{max}, in effect eliminating the debt overhang by adjusting the face value of the debt to more accurately reflect the public sector's ability to pay.[1] In that case the only likely lasting consequence of the emergence of the debt overhang concerns creditors' view of the country's creditworthiness. As indicated above, creditors presumably allowed the outstanding stock of debt to exceed d_{max} in the first place because they had a more optimistic view of $ps'_{max} + (\pi_{max} + g)m(\pi_{max})$ than turned out to be justified after the fact, and the question then becomes what lessons creditors draw about the public sector's future reliability as a debtor from the need to revise their expectations. If these lessons are adverse, then the consolidated public sector may find itself restricted to a very limited supply of financing in the future.

One difficulty with arranging debt write-offs of this type is that doing so is plagued by "free rider" problems. This is so because it is in the interest of each individual creditor to have others write off their claims, thus leaving more of the public sector's limited resources available to service their own claims. Thus, in the absence of some external coordinating mechanism, individual creditors are unlikely to voluntarily agree to undertake debt write-offs. When the insolvent debtor is a firm, this coordinating mechanism is usually provided by a bankruptcy proceeding. However, when the insolvent debtor is a sovereign, as in the case of a country's consolidated public sector, matters are more complicated, because there is no overriding legal authority that can impose an orderly workout of the competing claims on the sovereign's assets. The situation is especially problematic when the debt is denominated in foreign currency and creditors have legal recourse outside the country's own political jurisdiction, as in the case of external debt.

Suppose, then, that – perhaps because of the absence of such a coordinating mechanism – the debt overhang persists. This means that creditors do not give up their claims, but nonetheless the public sector does not commit itself to servicing the debt as originally agreed.

One immediate implication of this situation is that the public sector would no longer be able to borrow on market terms. The reason is that any creditor who extended funds to an insolvent government would immediately find themselves part of the pool of claimants – on par with the existing creditors – for the fixed

---

[1] It is important to distinguish this situation, in which part of the face value of the debt is written off permanently, from *debt rescheduling*, in which creditors essentially extend new loans to tide over a borrower who is temporarily having difficulties servicing debt. Rescheduling makes sense only if the borrower is perceived as solvent – that is, as ultimately able to service the debt on market terms – and thus would not be willingly undertaken by creditors in the presence of a debt overhang.

amount of resources the government has available to service debt.[2] Since the share of the existing debt being serviced is d_{max}/d_0, the value of the new creditor's claims would immediately collapse to a proportion d_{max}/d_0 of their face value. Since the face value of these resources can be preserved at par by lending elsewhere at the riskless rate of interest, no creditor would have an incentive to willingly lend to an insolvent government. In this situation, therefore, overall deficits of the consolidated public sector could only be financed through seignorage.

But the existence of a debt overhang may also have direct effects on economic growth. To see how, note that we can measure the magnitude of the debt overhang in present-value (stock) terms as the ratio of the existing debt d_0 to the present value of the resources that the consolidated public sector can make available for future debt servicing, given by d_{max}. Alternatively, we can measure the overhang in "flow" terms as the permanent flow of resources by which the government would need to augment its debt servicing budget in order to eliminate the overhang, that is, to service the debt on market terms. Call this "flow" overhang measure τ. Then τ is given by:

$$\tau = (r - g)(d_0 - d_{max}).$$

τ measures the additional fiscal effort that would be required each period to satisfy the public sector's creditors. We can think of τ as indicating the additional tax revenue that the government would need to generate each period in order to satisfy its creditors.[3]

Notice that, as long as creditors do not relinquish their claims on the domestic public sector, τ represents a potential additional future tax burden on domestic economy activity. Any activity, such as the accumulation of physical capital, that is undertaken in the expectation of future returns, thus faces a disincentive in the form of potentially higher future taxes in the presence of a debt overhang. This disincentive would be expected to have a negative effect on domestic investment, and thus on economic growth.

But that is not all. After all, if the government were to eliminate the debt overhang by announcing its intention to make a stronger fiscal effort, that is, by somehow increasing ps_{max}, this disincentive would still be there. The fact that it appears in the form of a debt overhang (an unallocated resource shortfall, rather than one that is eliminated by allocating it) may make it more onerous as a form of prospective taxation, for two reasons.

---

[2] This assumes that new creditors are not granted "senior" status, that is, they are not paid before existing creditors. Legal covenants in syndicated loan contracts typically require existing creditors to share payments, and default clauses may be triggered if existing new creditors are paid before existing ones.

[3] For the argument to be made below, it makes no difference whether the additional fiscal effort is conceived of in the form of additional tax revenue or reduced expenditures.

First, the process of extracting resources by creditors from an unwilling government may itself be costly (e.g., through disruption of trade), potentially making the permanent flow costs of transferring the resources to the creditors exceed τ. This potential "excess burden" magnifies the disincentive effect on investment of the public sector's debt obligations when they appear in the form of a debt overhang, rather than just debt to be serviced.

Second, both the size of the total resource costs that will eventually be incurred in making the transfer to creditors, as well as the allocation of these costs among productive activities in the domestic economy, are unknown before the fact. This, of course, means that the debt overhang is associated with a significant increase in uncertainty about future tax obligations at the microeconomic level. As we have already seen, higher uncertainty tends to discourage investment by increasing the value of the option to wait until the uncertainty is resolved, and has more general disincentive effects on any activity that involves incurring a sunk cost in the expectation of future returns, such as the costly reallocation of productive resources. For these reasons, the existence of a substantial debt overhang would tend to have negative effects on economic growth, through adverse effects on factor accumulation as well as on growth of total factor productivity.

It is worth emphasizing that these negative effects on growth can be magnified through a variety of macroeconomic channels. Notice, for example, that the anticipation of potentially higher future taxes is a burden that falls on productive activities within the tax authority of the domestic government, and can therefore be evaded by moving assets abroad. This means that a debt overhang creates incentives for capital flight. But when massive amounts of capital leave the country, this imperils both the stability of the exchange rate and that of the domestic financial system.[4] If capital flight results in financial crises and/or a currency crisis, then the instability in the domestic macroeconomic environment rises to a higher order of magnitude. As we saw in Chapter 1, such instability is very harmful for long-term growth.

II. THE DEBT CRISIS OF THE EIGHTIES

How important have these debt overhang effects been empirically in emerging economies? The international debt crisis of the 1980s provides an interesting case study with which to consider this question. In this section we shall review the experience of several of the major emerging economies that were most severely affected by the international debt crisis during that decade, and interpret it in light of the mechanisms described in Section I, with a view to determining whether the events of that decade were consistent with what the analysis of the previous section would lead us to expect.

---

[4] As we will see later on, even a healthy financial system is potentially vulnerable to failure if subjected to a sudden and large withdrawal of funds.

Table 8.1. *Seven Heavily Indebted Countries: Ratios of Public Debt to GDP, 1976–1981 (percent)*

	1976	1977	1978	1979	1980	1981
Argentina	15.0	18.0	18.7	20.1	21.3	29.6
Brazil	19.8	20.9	21.3	22.2	28.5	30.1
Chile	36.1	26.5	30.1	26.8	21.5	18.8
Mexico	22.0	31.4	32.2	30.8	29.1	34.3
Nigeria	3.9	5.8	9.4	12.2	13.9	16.9
Philippines	31.0	33.8	36.8	35.5	34.6	36.3
Venezuela	11.7	17.2	28.6	35.2	36.3	40.0

Source: Guidotti and Kumar 1991.

a. Run-up to the Debt Crisis

The decade of the seventies was one during which international inflation was high, and world nominal interest rates were relatively low. Thus, the real interest rates faced by developing countries, calculated by deflating nominal interest rates either by the dollar export prices or import prices of these countries, were relatively low (and often negative), at a time when many such countries were growing rapidly. This implies that for many developing countries their perceived sustainable growth rates were in excess of the real interest rate at which they could borrow in world financial markets ($g > r$).

Under these conditions, solvency did not impose an effective constraint on the external borrowing of the public sectors in these countries, since debt servicing could be financed with new borrowing – that is, without using the countries' own resources – without approaching the constraint $d_t < d_{max}$. Not surprisingly, the governments of several large developing countries rapidly increased their stocks of debt relative to GDP over the course of the decade. Table 8.1 shows the evolution of the stock of total public debt relative to GDP for seven heavily indebted countries over the six-year period 1976–81.[5] As the table shows, ratios of public debt to GDP were particularly large in the major Latin American countries, but the phenomenon of rapid debt accumulation was not limited to countries in Latin America, as shown by the experiences of Nigeria and the Philippines.[6]

Thus, the combination of low real interest rates and high growth rates during the decade of the seventies permitted many governments in emerging economies to accumulate a sizable stock of external debt by the beginning of the decade of the eighties.

---

[5] These are the seven largest economies in the IMF's category of "heavily indebted countries," used by the Fund for analytical purposes during the 1980s.

[6] Notice that Chile is an exception within Latin America, having reduced its ratio of public debt to GDP substantially during this period. This was an outcome of the fiscal austerity imposed by the Pinochet government.

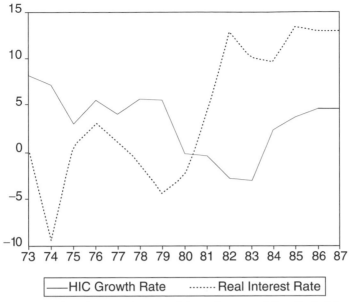

Figure 8.1. International Real Interest Rate and Growth Rates of Heavily Indebted Countries, 1973–87

b. Triggering Events

The oil price shock of 1979–80 fundamentally changed this situation. The combination of high oil prices and tight monetary policies implemented in industrial countries to combat their potentially inflationary impact resulted in two important changes in the economic environment in developing countries in 1981:

a. International real interest rates rose sharply.
b. Developing-country growth slowed substantially, due to a variety of factors. These included a growth slowdown in industrial countries, adverse changes in the developing countries' terms of trade, and poor domestic policies in those countries.

Figure 8.1 shows the sharp reversal in 1981 of the relationship that had existed during the late 1970s between international real interest rates and the average growth rate among highly indebted developing countries. International real interest rates began to rise in 1980, just as growth among heavily indebted developing countries slowed markedly. The real interest rate first exceeded the average growth rate in 1981, and the gap widened thereafter. The implication of this development was that, to retain solvency, the public sectors in highly indebted developing countries found themselves with the need to generate large fiscal adjustments.

Table 8.2. *Actual and Sustainable Primary Surpluses for*
Seven Heavily Indebted Countries 1982 (percent of GDP)

	Actual	Sustainable
Argentina	−7.6	7.3
Brazil	−5.5	1.9
Chile	1.9	6.9
México	−4.7	2.7
Nigeria	–	2.2
Philippines	−4.7	3.6
Venezuela	2.6	1.9

Source: Montiel 1992.

An indication of the magnitude of the required adjustments is provided in Table 8.2. Using the formula:

$$ps = (r - g)d_{1981} - (\pi + g)m,$$

the third column of the table estimates the sustainable value of the primary surplus required to service the debt stocks from Table 8.1 for each of the countries in that table. This can be compared to the average values of the primary surplus generated by these countries during the late seventies, given in the second column.[7] It is evident that substantial fiscal adjustments would have required in all of these cases for the heavily indebted public sectors to retain their solvency under the new circumstances.

c. Policy Responses

What most heavily indebted countries actually did was to initially implement relatively small fiscal adjustments, mainly through reduced public investment, and to rely on an increase in the inflation tax. These fiscal measures proved insufficient to enable the public sectors in these countries to continue servicing their debt on market terms. Thus, the fiscal adjustments actually undertaken were insufficient to restore public sector solvency in many of the heavily indebted countries, and developing-country debt sold at a discount in secondary markets.

Figure 8.2 illustrates what happened, using the tools we developed in Chapter 6. Recall that the (flow) budget constraint of the consolidated public sector could be expressed as:

$$\Delta d = -(ps' + (\pi + g)m) + (r - g)d.$$

As we saw in Chapter 6, taking ps', πr, and g as "permanent" values of the relevant variables, the relationship between Δd and d can be plotted as a straight line in

---

[7] For Argentina, Chile, and Mexico these are averages for 1974–82. For the Philippines the average is for 1981–82 only. For the remaining countries, the average pertains to 1976–82.

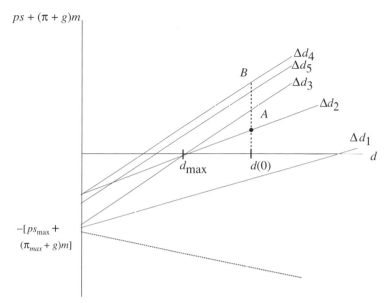

Figure 8.2. Fiscal Aspects of the International Debt Crisis

Δd-d space, with slope $(r - g)$ and vertical intercept $-(ps' + (\pi + g)m)$. Suppose that ps'_{max} and π_{max} are the maximum sustainable values of the adjusted primary surplus and domestic inflation rate, respectively, consistent with a maximum debt/GDP ratio of:

$$d_{max} = [ps'_{max} + (\pi_{max} + g)m(r + \pi_{mux})]/(r - g) \quad \text{for} \quad r - g > 0.$$

Graphically, d_{max} can be found as the horizontal intercept of a line with slope $(r - g)$ that cuts the vertical axis at $- [ps'_{max} + (\pi_{max} + g)m]$. During the 1970s, when $r - g < 0$, such a line would have had a negative slope (such as that of the dotted line in Figure 8.2), and thus would not have intersected the horizontal axis at positive values of d, implying that the public sector solvency condition did not constrain the amount of debt that governments could accumulate, as we have seen.

When $(r - g)$ turned positive in 1980, the slope of the line from $- [ps'_{max} + (\pi_{max} + g)m]$ turned positive as well, as in the line marked Δd_1 in Figure 8.2. Up to this time, the public sectors in the heavily indebted countries were incurring new debt. That is, their economies were located at a point such as A in Figure 8.2 on the line marked Δd_2, with existing debt given by $d(0)$. As long as the stock of debt in existence at that time lay to the left of the intersection of Δd_1 with the horizontal axis, the highly indebted countries remained solvent. In 1982, however, the value of $(r - g)$ increased sharply. Thus, the line from $- [ps'_{max} + (\pi_{max} + g)m]$ rotated further in a counterclockwise direction, to a position such as Δd_3 (with higher r and lower g, the intercept would also have moved up, but we can ignore this for now). At this point, $d(0) > d_{max}$, and the heavily indebted countries would have become insolvent in the absence of a fiscal adjustment. A fiscal adjustment intended to retain solvency would

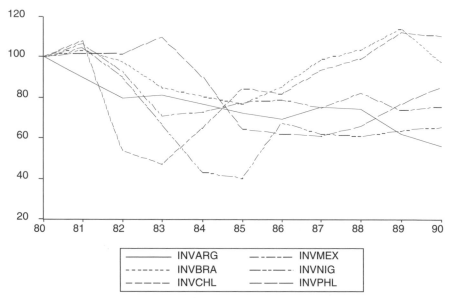

Figure 8.3. Investment Ratios for Six Heavily Indebted Countries, 1980–90

have shifted the budget line down, but such a fiscal adjustment proved not to be feasible – that is, it would have required $[ps' + (\pi + g)m] > [ps_{max} + (\pi_{max} + g)m]$. Thus, the actual fiscal adjustment turned out to be partial, from Δd_4 only to, say, line Δd_5. Since d_0 remained to the right of the horizontal intercept, the public sectors of these countries became technically insolvent. Not surprisingly, when secondary markets were created for the sovereign debt of developing countries in the mid-eighties, much of this debt sold at a substantial discount from its face value.

d. Macroeconomic Outcomes

The previous section suggested that the emergence of fiscal insolvency should have had negative effects on economic growth, through adverse effects on investment. What actually happened in these countries during the 1980s? First, as was to be expected, domestic investment contracted severely in the heavily indebted countries that faced fiscal insolvency. The data are presented for six countries in Figure 8.3. Using 1980 as a base year, Figure 8.3 shows the behavior of the investment-to-GDP ratio in six of these countries in index form. As shown in the figure, investment-to-GDP ratios fell in 1982 in all of these countries except the Philippines, where the decline did not materialize until 1984. More importantly, the ratio of investment to GDP remained below its 1980 value beyond the end of the decade in all of the countries except Brazil and Chile, where the ratio did not recover its 1980 value until 1989.

As one might expect, this investment collapse was associated with a significant reduction in the rate of growth of real GDP. The rate of growth of real GDP dropped

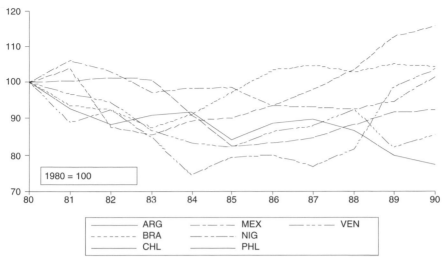

1980 = 100

ARG   MEX   VEN
BRA   NIG
CHL   PHL

Figure 8.4. GDP Per Capita in Seven Heavily Indebted Countries, 1980–90

so much in these countries that the growth rate of GDP per capita actually became *negative* for many of these countries during the 1980s, leaving them with lower incomes per capita at the end of the decade than at the beginning (Figure 8.4). This experience caused many in Latin America to refer to the decade of the 1980s as the "lost decade."

The debt crisis was ultimately resolved, at least for the major heavily indebted market borrowers, through the Brady Plan, proposed by U.S. Treasury Secretary Nicholas Brady and implemented beginning in 1989. This plan involved a partial writedown of the external debt of these governments, coordinated by the U.S. Treasury and the international financial institutions, in return for a series of policy undertakings by the indebted governments and a series of debt "enhancements" (guarantees) extended by the coordinating institutions.

This strategy for resolving the crisis can be readily interpreted in terms of the analysis in this chapter. Going back to Figure 8.2, note that the crisis arose because of the emergence of a "debt overhang" (an excess of $d(0)$ over d_{max}). Each of the three components of the Brady strategy would have contributed to eliminating this overhang by closing the gap between $d(0)$ and d_{max}. First, the "enhancements" provided by the industrial countries and the international financial organizations in effect increased the resources available to the heavily indebted countries for debt service. Thus, they can be interpreted as effectively supplementing the fiscal resources generated by those countries themselves, in other words, they were equivalent to an increase in ps'_{max}. In terms of Figure 8.2, such an increase would cause the budget constraint line Δd_5 to shift downward. Second, the growth-enhancing measures that the countries participating in the Brady plan were encouraged to adopt had the intended effect of increasing g, thus reducing $r - g$ and causing the budget constraint line to rotate in a clockwise direction. The combination of these first two measures would tend to increase d_{max} for the participating countries. Finally, the third element – the writedown of existing debt – would close the gap by reducing $d(0)$. Thus, the plan essentially attempted to close the gap between $d(0)$ and d_{max} by moving each of the two components in the direction of the other.

e. Interpreting the Evidence

The general outlines of the experience of the heavily indebted countries during the 1980s thus turn out to have been in line with what the analysis of Section I would have led us to expect. The prospective fiscal insolvency that emerged in these countries after 1981 appears to have had a severe impact on their subsequent growth performance, at least until the crisis was resolved at the end of the decade.

But while the evidence is strongly suggestive of such effects, it is not conclusive. The difficulty in interpreting the evidence is that the decade of the eighties was a period of severe macroeconomic disruption in all of these countries, featuring adverse behavior in their terms of trade and a host of poor domestic policy decisions. Thus, one can reasonably wonder whether the investment and real output collapses might not have been due to factors other than the debt overhang. Undoubtedly some of it was. How can we separate out the role of debt overhang effects?

In principle, whether the presence of debt overhang contributed to the investment collapse can be tested by estimating investment equations for this period that control for other determinants of investment in these countries. Unfortunately, in the case of the debt overhang, this procedure is not straightforward, for two reasons. First, it is difficult to obtain precise measures of the extent of the debt overhang, as opposed to the size of the stock of debt outstanding. Recall that it is prospective insolvency, rather than the debt itself, that creates uncertainty for prospective investors. Second, the effects of the debt overhang may be transmitted through a variety of domestic variables that would typically be included in empirical investment equations, for example, domestic real interest rates, changes in the stock of public capital, real exchange rate variability, and so on. Disentangling the independent effects of the debt overhang is thus a challenging task, and while the experience of these countries supports the notion that the types of mechanisms explored in this chapter can be very important empirically, the case remains to be proved.[8]

III. SUMMARY

We began this chapter by pointing out that for a prospectively insolvent government, the alternative to making a fiscal adjustment or relying on seignorage revenue

---

[8] Warner (1992), for example, finds that the behavior of the investment ratio in the heavily indebted countries can be explained entirely without debt overhang effects, while Serven and Solimano (1993) conclude that debt overhang effects are the most important single determinant of the investment-GDP ratio in these countries during the 1980s.

to service debt as scheduled is to stop servicing its debt or service it completely. The difference between the present value of the debt service payments owed by the government and the payments that it actually intends to make is its debt overhang. If creditors do not forgive the excess debt obligations, the existence of the overhang creates an unresolved future obligation of the government that represents a potentially large and highly uncertain future tax liability for the private sector, thus discouraging costly economic activities that are justified by future payoffs, like the accumulation of physical capital. The upshot is that the existence of a debt overhang can have adverse effects on growth.

We explored this issue in the context of the debt crisis of the 1980s, and found that among several countries that encountered debt servicing difficulties, events unfolded in a manner quite consistent with what theory would predict, although the magnitude of the harmful effects of the debt overhang on physical investment and economic growth among these countries during the "lost decade" of the eighties remains a matter of dispute.

Until this point we have focused on the macroeconomic implications of fiscal solvency. A recurrent issue in this analysis has been the private sector's expectations of future government budgetary policies. The credibility of government promises to make future fiscal adjustments is a key determinant of its perceived solvency and thus of its access to credit markets. Credibility of government fiscal promises also was shown to affect the macroeconomic costs of disinflation in Chapter 7. The next two chapters will explore two important types of policy actions that the government can undertake to enhance its fiscal credibility.

9

Measures for Achieving Fiscal Credibility I: Central Bank Independence

Fiscal credibility has been an important issue in previous chapters. Credibility refers to the private sector's perception that the government will follow through on its policy announcements. We have seen so far that this perception is important from the perspective of the government's actual and prospective creditors as well as from that of workers.

Credibility in the eyes of prospective creditors is of vital importance to the government in a variety of ways. We have seen that it plays the central role in determining the solvency of the public sector and thus its ability to borrow. Creditors will not lend to the government unless they perceive that it has a credible plan to service its outstanding debt on market terms in the future. Moreover, as we saw in Chapter 8, when creditors' perception of the government's ability to pay falls very far short of the outstanding stock of debt, a debt "overhang" emerges that can have serious macroeconomic consequences.

Fiscal credibility in the eyes of creditors also matters when the government is trying to change how it finances a fiscal deficit. If the government has been servicing its debt in part by relying on the seignorage revenue associated with a high rate of inflation, and the high economic costs of doing so cause it to attempt to stabilize, one of the most important determinants of its success in doing so is its fiscal credibility. We have seen that slowing inflation requires reducing the rate of money growth, and that reducing the rate of money growth requires a fiscal adjustment. But while slowing inflation requires an immediate reduction in the rate of money growth, it does not require an *immediate* fiscal adjustment. Whether the fiscal adjustment can be smoothed over time may help to influence the success of the stabilization program. In turn, the ability to postpone fiscal adjustment depends on whether creditors are willing to provide the resources required to replace the seignorage revenue that the government foregoes when it stabilizes. If creditors find the government's intention to reform its finances to be credible, then the path of fiscal adjustment can be smoothed by borrowing.

But we have also seen that it's not just the perceptions of prospective creditors that matter in determining the outcome of stabilization. The perceptions of workers are vitally important as well. If workers find the government's stabilization program to be credible, then they will moderate their wage demands in the expectation that inflation will be lower in the future. Wage moderation in turn makes it more likely that stabilization can be achieved quickly and at minimal cost in the form of foregone output, which in turn increases the probability that the stabilization will succeed.

All of this raises the question of how fiscal credibility can be achieved. This chapter and the next will consider two mechanisms for doing so. In this chapter we will explore how granting independence to the central bank can enhance the credibility of the government's commitment to future fiscal rectitude. The theory underlying the widespread movement toward central bank independence around the world will be described, as well as the evidence on whether this institutional mechanism has been conducive to inflation stabilization where it has been adopted. In the next chapter we will consider how the government can try to achieve credibility by "locking in" future fiscal adjustments through the privatization of state enterprises.

I. ACHIEVING FISCAL CREDIBILITY

How can the government convince both creditors and workers that its fiscal intentions are honorable, that is, that it means what it says? The first and most obvious question to ask in this context is why the government could not just simply announce its intentions and be believed. The answer is, of course, that the situation is complicated by the fact that the government can benefit from people's beliefs. We have seen that if creditors believe that the government will be fiscally responsible, the government will be able to borrow, and that if workers believe that the government will stabilize, they will moderate their wage demands, thus making it easier for stabilization to be achieved. What this means is that even governments that have no particularly strong intentions of following through will have strong incentives to make proclamations of future fiscal responsibility. Because both governments who mean it and those who don't will make the same policy announcements, the private sector cannot rely on the announcement itself to gauge the government's future policy intentions.

How can they do it, then? Since what is at issue is essentially a psychological mechanism concerning how people form expectations about the behavior of others, economists have no particularly distinctive insights to offer on this issue, and have found no safe and mechanical way that the credibility of government policy announcements can be assured. Instead, the basic principles governing credibility-enhancing mechanisms are the same as would apply in any other field of human activity. What is different, of course, is how they are implemented in the context of achieving fiscal credibility. Four approaches are worth mentioning:

a. Establishing a Track Record

Possibly the most reliable way for a government to achieve fiscal credibility is to establish a track record of prudent fiscal behavior. Following the maxim that actions speak louder than words, a government that wants people to believe what it says about its future policy intentions would be well advised to repeatedly do what it says – that is, to be bound in its present actions by its previous policy announcements. Repeated instances in which the public observes that the government's previous announcements bind its current behavior certainly make it more likely that the public will believe that its present announcements will constrain its future behavior.

While this is little more than common sense, it is important to note that this mechanism for establishing credibility is not always available when it is most needed. Specifically, it is impossible for the government to establish a track record when the government in question is a new government or when what is intended even for a government that is not new is a change in regime. In these cases the government's goal is precisely to convince the public that the past is not a good guide to the future. What are the options for establishing credibility under these circumstances?

b. Tying One's Hands

If it has no recourse to an established track record, then the government can try to establish credibility in several other ways. One such way is to accompany its policy announcement with actions that it would never have taken if it were not fully committed to following through on its policy announcement. Those actions would be intended to signal to the public the strength of the government's commitment, since having taken them, the costs to the government of not following through on its commitments would be much larger.

An example is the adoption of institutional mechanisms that deprive the government of access to the inflation tax. If the government accompanies its announcement of future fiscal rectitude with the implementation of such a mechanism, then if it fails to act in a fiscally responsible manner in the future its inability to avail itself of the inflation tax will force it to finance its spending in a politically more painful manner – that is, through explicit and formal taxation. Knowing this, the public is more likely to believe that the government will adhere to its announced fiscal intentions in the future, since it would never "tie its hands" (limit its options) in this way if it anticipated requiring recourse to the inflation tax in the future.

An interesting question concerns the nature of the institutional mechanisms through which the government can deprive itself of future inflation tax revenues. That is essentially what this chapter is about, and we'll turn to these mechanisms in the next section.

c. "Locking In" Future Fiscal Adjustments

The previous mechanism operated on the government's future accounts from the financing side. By depriving itself of a less painful source of financing in the future, the government can try to convince people of its intention to adjust its accounts in the future so as not to require such financing. Alternatively, the government could take actions in the present that would directly affect its future fiscal accounts, in the sense that they would be perceived as increasing the likelihood that the government would restrain its spending or increase its revenues in the future by making it easier for it to do so.

Such actions could affect either the expenditure or the revenue side of the government's budget. On the expenditure side, an important measure is the liquidation or privatization of state enterprises. Since these have often been a significant drain on the government's budget, closing them down or privatizing them could – at least in principle – "lock in" a reduction in future public sector spending. This topic is the subject of the next chapter, which will consider the conditions under which this effect would materialize. On the revenue side, the government could implement tax reform, in the form of an overhaul of the tax laws and the system of tax administration. Replacing the existing system by one that generates more revenues at given levels of economic activity, and/or generates the same revenue at less economic cost, would be intended to "lock in" improved future fiscal performance from the revenue side of the government's budget.

d. "Signaling" by Breaking Taboos

Finally, the government could attempt to signal the seriousness of its fiscal intentions to the private sector by undertaking a fiscal action that has long been perceived as politically very difficult to undertake. Even if such an action did not remedy a structural problem in the public sector's budget, and thus did not itself contribute to improving the government's future finances, actions of this type can enhance the government's credibility by demonstrating the government's willingness to make difficult decisions. The intention would be to signal the government's intention to make discretionary changes in its budget in the future when it becomes necessary to do so in the interest of fiscal rectitude, even if the political costs turn out to be high. In a sense, by breaking longstanding political "taboos" the government can indicate that it no longer intends to conduct fiscal business as usual.

The specific actions that can be taken to demonstrate such intent are likely to vary from country to country, since they depend on country-specific political circumstances. In countries with a strong and politically powerful landlord class, for example, this may involve implementing or increasing agricultural taxation, while in countries with powerful urban unions it may involve the removal of subsidies that favor urban workers at the expense of the agricultural sector. A particularly common "taboo" is the elimination of subsidies on domestic fuel prices in oil-exporting countries. Such subsidies are sometimes perceived as a birthright, and their reduction usually generates substantial political opposition. Putting the elimination of such subsidies into play can therefore be a powerful signal of the government's intention to abandon business-as-usual practices in fiscal matters.

II. TYING THE GOVERNMENT'S HANDS BY RESTRICTING ACCESS TO SEIGNORAGE

As indicated above, an important way that the government can enhance the credibility of fiscal adjustment is to undertake an action that it would not have done unless it truly intended to make a permanent fiscal adjustment. One such action is to restrict its access to the inflation tax as a residual source of finance. The euphemism is that the government "ties its hands" so it cannot avail itself of this source of revenue. It can do this in several ways. Ranging from the most to the least extreme, these include:

a. Abandoning the domestic currency, and replacing it with a foreign currency as means of payment. This is called *currency unification* if done multilaterally, and is typically referred to as *dollarization* if done unilaterally, though foreign currencies other than the U.S. dollar may be adopted as the means of exchange. In this case, seignorage revenue arising from the domestic demand for base money accrues to the foreign issuer of the currency that is newly used in the domestic economy, and the government can finance fiscal deficits only by borrowing. Panama and Liberia have long used the U.S. dollar as a means of exchange domestically, and Ecuador as well as El Salvador have begun doing so more recently.

b. Adoption of a *currency board*. This is an arrangement whereby the central bank must hold $1 of foreign exchange for every $1 of domestic currency it issues. The implication of this restriction is that the central bank is unable to issue credit, either to the government or to the domestic banking system. Unlike what happens under dollarization, the domestic public sector continues to receive seignorage under a currency board, since the right to print the country's legal tender allows it to purchase something of value, – that is, interest-bearing foreign-currency-denominated bonds that it holds as foreign exchange reserves. However, the seignorage available to the government is limited to the interest earnings on the currency board's stock of foreign exchange reserves, and most importantly, the government has no discretion over the amount of this revenue. Among the major developing countries, Hong Kong has had a currency board since 1983, Argentina adopted one in 1991, and Estonia and Bulgaria did so more recently. Currency boards have been advocated at various times in recent years for Mexico, Indonesia, and Russia in post-crisis situations.

c. A less extreme option than either of these is a *constitutional restriction on central bank lending to the government*, including possibly an absolute prohibition of such lending. In this case, the central bank may still be able to lend to the commercial banks at its discretion, or its total extension of credit may be constitutionally restricted.

d. Finally, least extreme is the granting of *legal independence* to the central bank. This means that the central bank governor does not report directly to the executive, and specifically, that the governor is not subordinate to the finance minister. Typically, this is coupled with a constitutional mandate for the central bank to seek to promote price stability, at the sacrifice of all other economic goals. This particular institutional innovation has become increasingly common among emerging economies. For example, the central bank of Chile was made independent in 1989, those of Venezuela and the Philippines in 1993, and the Mexican central bank in 1994.

We have already seen how institutional mechanisms that restrict the government's access to central bank financing would affect – or at least would be intended to affect – the government's credibility. In essence, the implementation of one of these mechanisms signals the seriousness of the government's fiscal intentions by depriving it of a source of revenue that would be valuable to it if it contemplated running large fiscal deficits in the future. That it is willing to "tie its hands" and shut itself off from the possibility of having access to such sources of revenue in the future must indicate that it means what it says when it promises to mend its fiscal ways.

Remember that the government would want to do this in order to reap the benefits of fiscal credibility – easier access to credit through enhanced perceptions of solvency and improved inflation performance. But it is not obvious that the adoption of such mechanisms will be successful in achieving the ultimate objectives sought by the government, even if the intended gain in fiscal credibility is itself attained.

Consider, for example, the effects of the government's eschewing its discretion over seignorage revenue on its perceived solvency. The reasons that such mechanisms may not enhance the government's perceived solvency is that when the government signals the seriousness of its fiscal intentions by "tying its hands" in this manner, it is simultaneously depriving itself of a discretionary source of the revenue (the inflation tax) that it can use to service its debt. Thus, while creditors may be gratified by the government's honorable fiscal intentions, they will be concerned by the implications of the loss of control over seignorage revenue for the government's ability to service its debt. It is not clear, for example, that the more extreme forms in which the government could "tie its hands" – dollarization or the adoption of a currency board – will necessarily be associated with a lower risk premium on the government's foreign-currency-denominated debt. Since this issue concerns the benefits and costs of alternative exchange rate arrangements, we will come back to it in Chapter 17.

When it comes to effects on inflation, we can distinguish between mechanisms that operate through a fixed exchange rate (points a and b above) and those that operate by creating "firewalls" between the government and the central bank (points c and d). Governments may dollarize or adopt currency boards to signal their fiscal intentions. But the government that does so cannot bind its successors to similar fiscal performance. We have seen previously that sustained inflation requires sustained devaluation of a pegged currency. This is impossible under either dollarization or a currency board, which imposes limits on the seignorage revenue that the government can hope to receive. But what happens if a future government's "demand" for seignorage revenue exceeds the "supply" that would be forthcoming under either of these arrangements? How do we know that if this happens it is the government's fiscal accounts that will adjust, rather than the exchange rate arrangement being modified to a form that provides larger seignorage revenues? The issue is whether exchange rate arrangements of this type can effectively discipline governments with a weaker commitment to fiscal rectitude than the one that implemented them. Again, because mechanisms (a) and (b) involve extreme exchange rate arrangements, we will defer discussion of such issues to Chapter 17.

This leaves for discussion the effects on the inflation rate of institutional mechanisms that create a "firewall" between the central bank and the government, without necessarily restricting the form that the country's exchange rate arrangements may take. Two questions arise in this context: first, an important difference between (c) and (d) is that a constitutional restriction on central bank lending to the government takes discretion over seignorage away from the government without giving it to the central bank. This takes flexibility away from the central bank. Is there any reason to do this, rather than simply transferring such discretion from the government to the central bank? Second, if discretion is indeed transferred to the central bank by making it independent, would such a mechanism actually be expected to produce lower inflation? These questions will occupy us for the rest of this chapter.

III. CENTRAL BANK INDEPENDENCE AND INFLATION: THEORY

At first blush, the answer to the second of these questions would appear to be straightforward. Up to now, we have been treating the rate of growth of the money supply (and the associated rate of change of the exchange rate, if any) as a policy instrument. In the hands of the government, this instrument would be used to satisfy the government's financing needs – that is, to satisfy the "demand" for seignorage. If a firewall is created that transfers control of this instrument to the central bank, then presumably the resulting equilibrium rate of inflation will be whatever the central bank decides it to be through its decisions concerning the rate of growth of the money supply: the rate of inflation will be determined by the "supply" of seignorage.

But that means that we no longer have a story about what determines the rate of inflation. Rather than the rate of growth of the money supply being determined by the government's fiscal needs, it now is determined by the central bank, and the government's fiscal needs must adjust to the resources that the central bank chooses to provide. The question is what the central bank will decide when it – and not the government – can exercise discretion over the rate of growth of the money supply and thus the rate of inflation. In this section we will build a simple model that explains how the rate of inflation chosen by the central bank may be determined, as well as why it may be desirable to deprive the central bank of the discretion to make this decision.[1]

Through its control over the exchange rate and the stock of domestic credit, a central bank that is free to act independently will be able to determine the position of the economy's aggregate demand curve, and thus the ongoing rate of inflation π. What level of π would it choose? Suppose that the bank is motivated by the desire to maximize social welfare, and assume that there are distortions present in the economy that cause the level of real output that the economy would produce at full employment (Y_P in our previous notation) to be less than its optimal level. In that case, the bank may consider inflation, on net, to have harmful effects on social welfare (it may help finance the fiscal deficit, but it reduces the rate of economic growth). But because the bank can increase real output by shifting the aggregate demand curve more than workers expected, that is, by increasing π relative to its expected value, which we can call π^e, it may consider *surprise* inflation to have positive effects, since it helps overcome the artificial restriction on output caused by the distortions. The social welfare function that the bank tries to maximize can thus be written as:

$$B = \beta(\pi - \pi^e) - (\alpha/2)\pi^2. \tag{9.1}$$

The parameters α and β reflect the weights given to the level of inflation and to increases in real output over its full employment level in determining social welfare, as perceived by the bank. The negative growth effects of inflation make α large, while the need to finance the fiscal deficit makes it small. The value of α thus depends on how these are traded off against each other. Notice that the effects of inflation on welfare are assumed to be nonlinear, in other words, inflation becomes disproportionately costly to the economy the higher it is, which is consistent with the evidence about the negative effects of inflation on growth reviewed in Chapter 7. The value of β depends on how much society is perceived to gain by overcoming the negative effects of distortions on real output.

Suppose the central bank makes an announcement about the level of inflation that it intends to achieve, based upon which the public forms its inflationary

---

[1] In general terms, the analysis follows Barro and Gordon (1983).

expectations π^e. After the public has formed its expectations, the central bank sets the rate of money growth and currency crawl required to determine the rate of inflation. What rate of inflation should the central bank announce *ex ante* (that is, before the public's expectations are formed)? If the social welfare function is as in equation (9.1), the announced inflation rate should be zero, since society cannot benefit (but can lose) by having the public expect a higher rate of inflation.[2]

If the bank announces the intention to achieve zero inflation and this is believed ($\pi^e = 0$), then it faces two choices: it can either follow through on the announcement and produce zero inflation, in which case $\pi^e = 0$, $Y = Y_P$, and $B = 0$, or it can act in a discretionary fashion, reneging on this commitment and attempting to achieve the socially optimal rate of inflation (the one that maximizes 9.1), conditional on $\pi^e = 0$. To see what the socially optimal rate of inflation must be, notice that the marginal benefit of inflation is constant at the value β, while the nonlinearity of the social costs of inflation means that the marginal cost of inflation is higher the higher the rate of inflation. With the formulation (9.1), the marginal cost of inflation is actually given by $\alpha\pi$. This means that when inflation is very low, the marginal benefit of a little more inflation will exceed its marginal cost, but as the rate of inflation is increased its marginal cost will rise, while its marginal benefit remains the same. At a sufficiently high rate of inflation, the marginal benefit of inflation will be exactly outweighed by its marginal cost ($\beta = \alpha\pi$), and beyond this point further increases in inflation would be socially harmful. Thus, the rate of inflation that maximizes B, subject to $\pi^e = 0$, is given by $\pi = \beta/\alpha$.

Notice that this is higher the more the bank cares about real output (the larger β), and the less it cares about the negative growth effects of inflation (the smaller α). The resulting benefit to society from this choice of inflation rate is $B = \beta^2/2\alpha$ which, being positive, is larger than that achieved by following the announced policy of zero inflation. The gain comes from the benefit of "surprise" inflation in raising output above its potential level. This benefit must always outweigh the cost of inflation when inflation is zero, because the quadratic form of the latter implies that these costs are zero at the margin when inflation is zero. Thus, the central bank always has an incentive to announce zero inflation, but then renege on its announcement and generate a rate of inflation that is larger the more it cares about real output, and smaller the more it cares about the social costs of inflation. In other words, the central bank has an incentive to be "time inconsistent" – to say one thing and do another.

The problem, of course, is that the public can be expected to be aware of this incentive, and thus to disbelieve the bank's policy announcement. If the public is aware of the principles governing the central bank's behavior, it will indeed expect the central bank to produce not zero inflation, but the inflation rate $\pi = \beta/\alpha$. How does this affect the bank's subsequent behavior? The answer is that it does not affect it at all.

---

[2] Technically, subject to $\pi = \pi^e$, the social welfare function (9.1) is maximized when $\pi = \pi^e = 0$.

The public's beliefs affect neither the marginal benefit nor marginal cost of inflation, so the central bank will be led to generate the same level of inflation regardless of what the public believes. This means that when the public sets $\pi^e = \beta/\alpha$, the central bank will still set $\pi = \beta/\alpha$, validating the public's beliefs. Notice that the social welfare outcome is very different in this case, however. Substituting $\pi^e = \pi = \beta/\alpha$ into the social welfare function, we get $B = -\beta^2/2\alpha$ which, being negative, is not only a worse outcome than when the central bank's announcement was believed by the public, but is even worse than what would happen if the central bank had no discretion whatsoever and was forced to set the inflation rate equal to zero. The reason for this is that there is no inflation "surprise" in either case, but a cost arising from positive inflation in the present case. Why doesn't the central bank just choose a zero inflation rate, then? The answer is that it has no means to convince the public that it will do so, so the public will continue to set $\pi^e = \beta/\alpha$, which implies a social welfare outcome of $B = -\beta^2/\alpha$, an even worse outcome than with the inflation rate $\pi = \beta/\alpha$. In the absence of a *precommitment mechanism* that forces the bank to do what it says, therefore, the inflationary outcome will be $\pi = \beta/\alpha$.

What do we learn from this analysis? First, central bank independence may indeed lower the rate of inflation. The reason is that a central bank that is *not* independent, because it reflects the Finance Ministry's preferences, may give much more weight to the positive role that inflation can play in financing the government's budget through the inflation tax. This would tend to reduce the parameter "α" since the revenue gains would tend to offset the social costs from lower growth. Lower α means higher inflation. Second, given the independence of the central bank, society may be better off directing the central bank to pursue price stability while sacrificing other objectives. This would tend to increase α and reduce β in the social welfare function maximized by the central bank, resulting in a lower rate of inflation and higher level of social welfare. Recall that the reason for this is that the central bank is unable to generate "surprise" inflation, so any mechanism that produces a lower *actual* rate of inflation generates a social gain. Finally, since policymakers are assumed to be benevolent, that is, their social welfare function would tend to reflect social preferences at least to some extent, society would be better off by removing their discretion if possible. This could be achieved by causing the central bank to set $\beta = 0$, for example, by having the central bank pursue price stability as its only objective as a constitutional mandate, perhaps by imposing a constitutional restriction on credit creation by the central bank.

We have seen, therefore, that theory can describe ways in which options (c) and (d) of the previous section may indeed result in lower inflation than would be generated under a nonindependent central bank. But what has happened in practice under central bank independence? To answer this question, we would want to determine whether central banks that have been more independent have indeed tended to produce lower inflation, other things equal. The next section will review some of the evidence that is available on this issue.

IV. CENTRAL BANK INDEPENDENCE AND INFLATION: EVIDENCE

The first requirement in testing the proposition that central bank independence tends to lower the rate of inflation is to devise a measure of central bank independence. How do we do this? Many countries have granted the central bank legal independence over recent years. One possibility would be to simply record when the legal status of the central bank changed in some sample of countries, and then test whether the behavior of the inflation rate changed in these countries after that date, controlling for other observable determinants of inflation.

But unfortunately, simply giving the central bank legal independence (i.e., ensuring that the governor of the central bank does not report to the finance minister, but directly to the parliament) is not enough to make it effectively independent, since the bank may remain influenced by the government. In other words, what is required is a measure of *de facto* independence, rather than *de jure*.

Some recent work by Cukierman, Neyapti, and Webb (1992, hereafter CNW) provides a useful illustration of how these complications can be addressed in empirical research. CNW proposed some alternative measures of de facto central bank independence in a large group of countries, and tested whether these have been associated with lower inflation. They used both formal and informal indicators of independence, noting that laws tend to be incomplete, and that actual practice often deviates from what is specified in them (for example, they noted that in Argentina the legal term of the governor is four years, but over their sample period the average tenure was one year). They used these indicators to construct measures of central bank independence for each of four decades: 1950–59, 1960–69, 1970–79, and 1980–89 for seventy-two countries, of which fifty-one were developing countries. They then examined whether these indicators were correlated with inflation performance in panel regressions, both for the full sample and for industrial and developing countries separately.

a. Formal Indicators of Independence

CNW examined four aspects of legal independence, encompassing sixteen different legal variables, each of which they coded on a scale from 0 (lowest independence) to 1 (highest). The legal variables included four variables concerned with the terms of office of the governor of the central bank, three variables concerned with policy formulation, one dealing with the legal objectives of the central bank, and eight concerning restrictions on lending to the government. They aggregated these as described below to capture the four different aspects of independence of interest to them. These aspects were:

1. Terms of Office for the Governor

The bank was judged to be more independent if the governor has long legal tenure, if his/her appointment is by the bank's directors, rather than by the executive, if he or she cannot be dismissed for reasons based on the bank's policies, and if the governor cannot hold another government office (the latter would subject the governor to government control through an alternative channel). The four different dimensions, each coded from 0 to 1, were aggregated into a single variable addressing the terms of the governor's appointment by taking the mean of the four variables.

2. Formulation of Policy

The bank was judged to be more independent if it was able to set policy without consultation with the government, if it had final authority in conflicts with the government in areas that fell within its policy mandate, and if it had a role in setting the government's budget. These three dimensions of independence in policy formulation, each ranked on a scale from 0 to 1, were aggregated into a single variable by using weights of 0.5, 0.25, and 0.25 respectively.

3. Legal Objectives

A separate variable measuring the legal objectives of the central bank was computed for inclusion in the regressions. In this regard, independence was assumed to be greater if price stability was the bank's only legal objective (only Germany and the Philippines had such a restrictive objective in their sample), and if the central bank has the final word on what this means. Independence was less if price stability was specified as one among several objectives, but the others were deemed compatible with the objective of price stability, and even less if price stability was listed as one among several potentially conflicting objectives.

4. Lending to Government

Eight total possibilities were allowed under this category. The first four variables were treated separately, while the last four were aggregated into a single variable. The variables that were treated separately included two pertaining to the extent to which advances and securitized lending to the government were legally restricted, the third to the extent to which the central bank can set the terms on such lending, and the fourth to the number of government agencies entitled to borrow from the central bank. The stricter the limitations, the more independent the central bank was judged to be. The variables that were aggregated together measured how the limits on central bank lending to the government were specified, the presence of legal restrictions on loan maturities, restrictions on loan interest rates, and the scope for the central bank to purchase government securities in the open market. These last four lending variables were aggregated into a single variable by taking their unweighted mean, for a total of five lending limitation variables.[3]

A total of eight legal variables were constructed this way for each decade for each of the countries in the sample. They were aggregated into a single legal variable using subjective weights.

b. Informal Indicators of Independence

Since the indicators just reviewed are all of a legal nature, they can at best indicate the *de jure* independence of the central bank. To complement these with measures of *de facto* independence, CNW considered two informal indicators of bank independence: the turnover of the central bank governor, and an indicator of independence based on the results of a questionnaire. They reasoned that with high turnover, the central bank governor becomes more susceptible to influence by the executive branch. Also, long tenure endows the governor with an independent reputation that may help him or her resist pressure from the government. In developing countries, this ratio tended to range above the highest level for industrial countries. CNW found that the legal term of office had little influence on the turnover rate.

The questionnaire CNW used was sent to monetary policy specialists in central banks. They received useful replies for twenty-nine countries on nine questions, which were then coded from 0.25 to 1. These questions pertained to the tenure of the governor and its overlap with the terms of politicians, limitations on lending in practice, mechanisms for the resolution of conflicts with the government, the financial independence of the bank (with regard to its budget and the salaries of top officials), whether intermediate policy targets were specified as monetary aggregates or interest rates, whether priority was given to price stability in practice, and to the role of the central bank as a development bank. The answers to these questions were aggregated with subjective weights, and large differences were found between industrial and developing countries on this measure.

c. Relationship Between Independence and Price Stability

As we have seen, in principle we might expect a relationship to exist between central bank independence and inflation performance, because independent central banks can be endowed with a built-in bias against inflation. Legal independence both strengthens their hand in pursuing that objective and can be used to strengthen the objective through legal means.

---

[3] In a separate paper (CNW 1992), the authors also included a variable measuring the central bank's financial independence, which depended on whether the bank manages its own budget and whether salaries of top officials are determined by the board of directors, rather than by the executive or legislative branch.

Is there empirical evidence that independence matters? The evidence in CNW was based on regressions of transformed decade inflation on an intercept, on central bank independence variables in the form of those measuring the tenure of the governor, policy formulation, the five variables capturing objective limitations on lending, the turnover variable, and three decade dummies. For the whole sample, none of the separate legal variables was statistically significant. Thus, the legal variables were aggregated together with subjective weights. The more parsimonious regression thus contained variables measuring legal independence and turnover of the governor, as well as decade dummies. The results were as follows:

i. For industrial countries, the aggregated legal variable had a significantly negative correlation with average decade inflation, but turnover, which was low for these countries, did not. The results were driven by the lending-limit component of the index, since the others did not enter the regression significantly when entered simultaneously.

ii. For developing countries, the turnover variable entered with a statistically significantly positive sign, while the legal variable did not. The interpretation CNW offered was that legal norms have been adhered to less strictly in developing countries.

How reliable are these results? Notice that CNW did not control for variables other than central bank independence that may affect the rate of inflation, such as the incidence of various types of economic shocks, the nature of wage bargaining institutions, the efficiency of the tax system, etc. They did, however, address the issue of reverse causality.[4] To address this problem, they used the previous decade's inflation and turnover ratios, legal independence, the legal term of office, and the decade dummies as instruments for the current turnover ratio (legal independence was taken as exogenous, since it changed infrequently). The turnover variable remained positive and statistically significant under this approach, both for the sample as a whole as well as for the subsample of developing countries.

V. SUMMARY

In this chapter we have reviewed alternative ways that the government can seek to achieve fiscal credibility, and have focused on one of them: "tying its hands" to restrict its discretionary access to the "cookie jar" of seignorage revenue. We saw that this could be achieved in a variety of ways, some of which involve the adoption of extreme exchange rate regimes. Others, however, consisting of constitutional restrictions on central bank lending to the government and of the granting of legal independence to the central bank, do not similarly restrict the country's exchange

---

[4] Granger causality tests on inflation and turnover (with a one-decade lag) suggested bidirectional causality between the two variables.

rate regime. However, institutional mechanisms of this sort may or may not enhance the government's solvency or facilitate the achievement of low inflation. The latter, in particular, depends on how the central bank uses its newfound discretion.

We saw that theory – in the form of the analysis of the "time inconsistency" problem in the formulation of monetary policy – suggests that social welfare may be enhanced if discretion is removed from *both* the government and the central bank through constitutional restrictions on central bank lending to the government that effectively limit seignorage revenue. In the absence of such restrictions, a socially superior low-inflation outcome to that achieved under "fiscal dominance" of the central bank is also possible if the central bank is made independent and directed to concentrate on the objective of price stability. Testing this proposition encounters the serious obstacle of devising an empirical measure of central bank independence. We reviewed some recent research that devised such a measure and found that indeed central bank independence was associated with superior inflation performance.

We next turn to an examination of an alternative (though not mutually exclusive) approach to the achievement of fiscal credibility: the elimination of structural problems on the expenditure side of the public sector's budget through the privatization of state enterprises.

10

Measures for Achieving Fiscal
Credibility II: Privatization

As we saw in the previous chapter, governments can seek to achieve fiscal credibility by cutting themselves off from access to certain financing sources, something that they would be unlikely to do if they anticipated requiring recourse to those sources of finance in the future. While this may help to signal the seriousness of the government's fiscal intentions, and may even help to discipline future governments not as inclined to fiscal rectitude as the one that institutes the measure (see Chapter 17), the impact of such measures on the public sector's perceived solvency is problematic, since actual and potential creditors will correctly perceive that the government has deprived itself of a source of funds with which to service debt.

An alternative mechanism for enhancing the credibility of fiscal adjustment is to "lock in" the adjustment in present value terms by undertaking measures in the present that are irreversible – or at least, that are very costly to reverse – and that can be expected to exert favorable effects on the government's budget over the indefinite future. Privatization or reform of loss-making public enterprises is one such measure that has been widely adopted in developing countries. This chapter explores how such measures can be used by the government as mechanisms to enhance the credibility of fiscal adjustment. It also describes the economic arguments for privatization, and analyzes the implications of privatization for the government's intertemporal budget constraint, emphasizing that the effects are not limited to the revenue received from the sale of such enterprises. In addition, the experience with privatization and reform of state-owned enterprises in developing countries is reviewed.

I. ECONOMIC ROLE OF STATE-OWNED ENTERPRISES

In many developing countries, state-owned enterprises (SOEs, defined as government-owned or -controlled firms that generate most of their revenue from selling goods and services) have been a significant drain on the government budget.

Divesting itself of such enterprises by liquidating them or privatizing them is thus one way that the government can achieve a credible fiscal adjustment. Credibility in this case comes from the fact that the source of the deficit was the location of such enterprises in the public sector, and re-nationalizing them would be economically and politically costly. Thus, the government can in principle "lock in" a (present and) future fiscal adjustment by divesting itself of loss-making state-owned enterprises.

Alternatively, the government can retain these enterprises in the public sector, but implement reforms in the way that they are managed that are intended to permanently improve their economic performance. However, since these measures may be less costly to reverse, or may subsequently be undermined by new developments, reform of SOEs, no matter how successful in the short run, may be less effective as a mechanism for "locking in" fiscal adjustments than divestiture.

State-owned enterprises have been a common post-independence phenomenon in many developing countries. In many such countries, the state has been the driving force behind the country's development efforts, in part because of the absence of similarly well-organized private sector institutions and in part because of the perceived productivity of public goods (such as infrastructure, health, and education) in development. Beyond the provision of public goods, a specific role of the state in *production* was perceived to be important in many such countries in their early stages of development, for a variety of reasons. These included, of course, ideological motivations favoring the public sector over the private sector, as well as production by nationals as opposed to direct foreign investment. They also included motivations of a purely political sort, since an expanded public role in production increased the scale and scope of the economic dispensations under the control of the ruling party. Beyond these, however, there were more strictly economic reasons for favoring direct public production in some spheres of economic activity. Specifically, private firms had limited access to external finance, and domestic financial underdevelopment – not to mention financial repression – limited the access of such firms to domestic sources of finance as well.

During the 1970s, the combination of favorable terms of trade in many countries and low international real interest rates gave a huge boost to debt-financed public investment in emerging economies. The accumulation of debt during that decade (which we examined in Chapter 8) was in fact associated with an increase in investment in many heavily indebted countries, and this investment often took the form of the creation or expansion of state-owned enterprises.

An interesting question is why such enterprises have widely become drains on public sector budgets. In part, the answer is simply that they represented poor investments. The collapse of international terms of trade for many emerging economies during the decade of the eighties implied that many investments made during the previous decades turned out to be poor ones *ex post*. Beyond this, however, such enterprises have widely suffered from structural problems brought on by soft budget constraints and political interference. The absence of market discipline associated with soft budget constraints resulted in mismanagement, and political interference in the form of the imposition of nonmarket objectives on the management of the public enterprises also impaired their performance.

Thus, divestiture through liquidation or privatization of such enterprises has become an attractive way to help cope with fiscal deficits. Arguments for privatization, however, are of two types:

a. Efficiency Arguments

Economic efficiency is ultimately the most important consideration in deciding whether to privatize a state-owned enterprise. Structural problems such as those mentioned above may make it better to run many firms privately, even if in principle public ownership is compatible with economic efficiency. Even if a public firm makes substantial profits, and is therefore not a drain on the public sector budget, the economy may be better off moving the enterprise to the private sector, if the latter can produce an even higher return.

b. Fiscal Arguments

The fiscal argument for privatization has already been made above. However, the fiscal effects of privatization are often measured in the popular press by the contribution that privatization proceeds make to fiscal revenues, reducing the fiscal deficit in the year that privatization takes place and revenues from sales of public enterprises are received. But this is incorrect. The fiscal effects of privatization are *not* generally equal to privatization revenues for two reasons:

i.   This measure neglects the fact that the privatization, as an asset sale, is a one-time event.
ii. Measuring the fiscal effects of privatization in this way fails to take into account the (positive or negative) effects on the government's budget of *keeping* the enterprise.

In the next section, we will examine the fiscal effects of privatization in more detail, taking both of these factors into account.

II. THE FISCAL EFFECTS OF PRIVATIZATION

As a point of departure, recall the condition that determined the sustainable value of the public sector's adjusted primary fiscal surplus:

$$ps' = (r - g)d - (\pi + g)m(\pi).$$

To identify the impact of public enterprises on the public sector's budget, we can break down the adjusted primary surplus into two components: the portion contributed by the state-owned enterprise sector and the rest of the primary surplus:

$$ps' = p + (r_G - g)k,$$

where p is the nonenterprise component of the adjusted primary surplus, k is the public sector capital stock valued at replacement cost, expressed as a ratio to GDP, and r_G is the ratio of the net income (profits minus depreciation) received from public sector enterprises to the value of the public sector capital stock. Thus $(r_G - g)$ is the net revenue that the public sector receives on a permanent basis from maintaining a public enterprise capital-output ratio k (since each period it has to plow the amount gk back into public enterprise investment, the budget receives only the excess $(r_G - g)k$). With this notation, the sustainable value of the public sector's primary surplus can be written as:

$$p + (r_G - g)k = (r - g)d - (\pi + g)m(\pi). \tag{10.1}$$

State-owned enterprises will be a net drain on the public sector's budget if $(r_G - g)k$ is negative. The drain on the budget is larger, of course, the smaller is $(r_G - g)$. We can see that, since the sustainable value of the primary surplus is given by the right-hand side of equation (10.1), this budgetary drain puts pressure on p, which has to be larger to compensate for any revenues lost through negative values of $(r_G - g)k$.

How do we know whether privatizing state enterprises provides a permanent improvement to the public sector's budget? We can answer this question by investigating in what direction p would have to change in order for the equation above to continue to hold if the government sold the public sector capital stock k off to the private sector.

As a first pass, we may want to consider what would have to happen to p if k were simply to be given away. In that case there would be no privatization revenue, but privatization would nevertheless have a fiscal effect. The reason is because the elimination of the term $(r_G - g)k$ would require an adjustment in p to maintain the solvency condition in effect. If $(r_G - g)k$ is negative (state-owned enterprises are a budgetary drain), p could afford to fall if k were set to zero through the liquidation of state enterprises, even if that liquidation brings in no revenue. It is because the sustainable value of its primary surplus can afford to be smaller under these conditions, while still retaining the public sector's solvency, that we can say that liquidation of unprofitable state-owned enterprises can enhance the government's fiscal credibility. Removing this drain on the budget simply makes it easier (less fiscal adjustment is required) for the public sector to service its debt in the future.

This exercise also makes the point that the fiscal implications of privatization are not limited to those of the privatization revenues. To address how the sale of state-owned enterprises affects the public sector's fiscal accounts, suppose the private return from operating these enterprises would be $(r_P - g)$. Then the private sector would be willing to pay an amount given by:

$$Q = (r_P - g)/(r - g)$$

for each unit of k if it is offered for sale to the private sector. Notice, by the way, that if $(r_P - g) < 0$, then no one will buy the state-owned firms, and privatization may not be feasible (this may have been the case, for example, for many public enterprises in the former Soviet Union). Now write the public sector solvency condition in "stock" terms as:

$$\frac{p + (r_G - g)k + (\pi + g)m(\pi)}{r - g} = d_0. \tag{10.2}$$

Note that if the private sector pays Q per unit of public sector capital, then the effect of the sale is to replace $(r_G - g)k/(r - g)$ (the present value of net revenues from state-owned enterprises) on the left-hand side of (10.2) by the sales revenue Qk. Thus the fiscal impact of the sale is given by:[1]

$$\frac{\Delta p}{r - g} = \frac{[Q - (r_G - g)]k}{r - g}. \tag{10.3}$$

This means that the government's fiscal position will be eased (the required adjustment in p will be *negative*) as long as $r_P > r_G$, since this will make the term inside the brackets positive.

The lessons to be drawn about the fiscal implications of privatization are the following:

a. The state-owned enterprise can be sold to the private sector only if it can make money in private hands.
b. The government may be (fiscally) better off selling a state-owned enterprise even if the enterprise is making money in public hands.
c. The fiscal benefit to the government from the sale will be:
  i. Less than the sale price if $(r_g - g) > 0$ (that is, if the enterprise was profitable in public hands).
  ii. Negative if $r_P < r_g$ (if the enterprise was more profitable in public hands than it will be in private hands).
  iii. Equal to the sale price if $(r_g - g) = 0$ (if the enterprise was neither a net drain on nor a net contributor to the public sector's resources).
  iv. More than the sale price if $(r_g - g) < 0$ (if the enterprise was a net drain on the budget, but will be profitable in private hands).

Going back to the credibility issue, then, the important point is that by selling a loss-making state-owned enterprise, the government can "lock in" a future fiscal

---

[1] Profit taxes do not affect these calculations. If the government collects taxes on the profits earned in the private sector by the enterprises sold, then this would reduce the sale price by the present value of those taxes, but the government would exactly recoup this loss in the form of higher tax revenues.

adjustment. It can increase the primary surplus in the present *and* the future at the same time, so creditors do not have to rely on promises of future fiscal actions that may not be kept by the same or a different government. That is, the public sector can generate a "permanent" fiscal adjustment (in a present value sense) *today*.

Finally, it is worth making two additional points:

i. It is important that the actual impact of privatization on the budget be measured correctly. The key question is by how much is the sustainable nonenterprise primary surplus affected by privatization. The answer was given in "stock" terms in equation (10.3). In "flow" terms it is given by:

$$\Delta p = \frac{(r - g)[Q - (r_G - g)]k}{r - g}.$$ (10.4)

That is, the present value fiscal benefit has to be amortized in order to calculate the impact of privatization on the sustainable primary surplus.

ii. Whether privatization is or is not a good idea does not depend on its fiscal implications. It depends on whether the resources involved yield a greater *social* return in public or private sector use. But wherever their return is greater, the decision to keep the resources in the public sector or transfer them to the private sector will invariably have fiscal implications, and these have to be taken into account to retain the public sector's solvency.

III. PRIVATIZATION AND REFORM OF STATE-OWNED ENTERPRISES IN PRACTICE

As a result of the wave of market-oriented reform that swept emerging economies during the last part of the decade of the 1980s and the decade of the 1990s, privatization has received a substantial amount of attention in emerging-market economies, and many such economies have privatized at least some subset of their state-owned enterprises. Consequently, a substantial amount of experience has accumulated not just with the operation of state-owned enterprises, but also with the process of reforming and privatizing them in both emerging and transition economies. A recent World Bank study (World Bank 1995) summarized both types of experiences.

a. Evidence on State-Owned Enterprise Performance

With respect to the performance of state-owned enterprises, the Bank study summarized the *a priori* arguments to expect them to perform inefficiently as follows: because no one really owns these firms, no one has a clear stake in maximizing their economic returns. Moreover, the existence of soft budget constraints means that these enterprises operate under no threat of bankruptcy to serve as a check on inefficiency. Finally, their placement in the public sector subjects them to multiple objectives and multiple constraints, which tend to increase transaction costs, distort incentives, and decrease managerial efforts.

The question, of course, is whether the evidence supports these *a priori* arguments. The World Bank study reviewed some of the literature that attempts to test these propositions. Early studies attempted to address this issue by comparing the performance of state and private firms in the same sector, across sectors, and over time. But these studies found it difficult to control for potential influences on the performance of these firms other than the type of ownership that characterized them. More recent studies looked instead at the performance of individual firms before and after divestiture. Though this type of evidence is subject to its own shortcomings (in particular, the failure to control for other changes in the economic environment in which these firms operate), this literature tends to find that privatized firms operating in competitive markets performed better than they had in the public sector.[2] Results, however, tended to be less clear-cut for firms that operated in noncompetitive markets.

The World Bank study thus concluded that state-owned firms tended to hinder economic growth both because of microeconomic inefficiencies such as those mentioned above, as well as because of the financing implications that have been emphasized in this chapter: subsidies to state-owned enterprises put pressure on nonenterprise primary fiscal surpluses, thereby crowding out more productive government spending on health and education, and to the extent that this pressure results in money financing, it leads to inflation.

b. Evidence on Privatization and Reform

1. Privatization

Turning to the process of privatization, the Bank study found that despite much discussion of privatization and much actual divestiture during 1987–93, state-owned enterprises accounted for nearly as large a share of economic activity in developing countries in the mid-1990s as they did twenty years previously, amounting to about 11 percent of GDP. In lower income developing countries, the state-owned enterprise sector was found to be even larger, accounting for about 14 percent of GDP. The shares of state-owned enterprises in total employment in these economies tended to be similar to their shares in GDP.

The Bank also found that divestiture tended to be concentrated in a few countries. Over the relatively heavy-divestiture period of 1988–93, for example, five countries (Argentina, Brazil, Hungary, Mexico, Poland) accounted for 30 percent

---

[2] The caveat that factors other than changes in ownership need to be controlled for in such comparisons is particularly germane in such circumstances, because privatization tends to occur precisely in the context of market-oriented reform that entails substantial changes in firms' operating environments, of a type that may well be associated with improvements in profitability.

of developing-country transactions and 60 percent of the value of state-owned enterprises sold.

2. Enterprise Reform

With respect to reform of firms in the state enterprise sector, the Bank study found that such attempts were not always very successful. It concluded that for reform of SOEs to be successful, it had to be politically desirable both to the leadership and to its constituency. This can happen when the government changes in such a way that those who would lose from reform are no longer a significant part of the leadership's support, or when there is an economic crisis that increases the cost of continuing to subsidize SOEs.

The Bank identified five components of successful SOE reform, referring to measures that actually tended to improve the operation of such enterprises. These components consisted of divestiture, the enhancement of competition, the imposition of hard budget constraints, the implementation of financial reform, and the introduction of changes in the institutional relationship between state-owned enterprises and governments.

Among the countries that undertook reform of the state-owned enterprise sector, the successful reformers divested more, especially when the state-owned sector was large to begin with. Also, they tended to introduce more competition for these enterprises. In noncompetitive markets, divestiture accompanied by appropriate regulation usually improved efficiency, service, and welfare in the former SOEs. For enterprises that remained in the public sector, the more successful reforming countries hardened the budget constraints facing these firms by reducing direct subsidies, putting their access to credit on a commercial footing, improving the regulation of state-owned firm monopoly prices, and reducing hidden subsidies. The measures were abetted by reform of the domestic financial sector, which tended to help impose market-related access to credit.

Where divestiture did not take place, both successful and unsuccessful reforming countries tried to improve the incentive structure of state-owned firms by changing the relationship between these firms and the government. Noting that all contracts between the government and state-owned enterprises have to deal with common problems (regarding the transmission of information between the government and enterprise managers, the system of rewards and punishments for managers, and mechanisms for ensuring commitment), and that contracts can be crafted as performance contracts (in which government employees run the firms) or management contracts (in which private firms are hired to run them), the Bank found that the greater the extent of private participation such contracts involved, the better they tended to work.

For example, in the sample of twenty state-owned enterprises on which this part of the Bank's study was based, in only three of twelve cases using performance contracts in an attempt to improve SOE performance did enterprise total factor productivity (TFP) register improvement after the contracts were implemented, six firms continued past TFP trends, and three performed worse. The Bank judged that such contracts did not improve a poor incentive structure, and did not reduce the enterprise managers' substantial information advantage. Managers were able to use this advantage to generate "soft" targets in performance contracts. Moreover, from the government side, rewards and penalties did not tend to be applied consistently, so they had little effectiveness, and governments often reneged on key promises in the context of such contracts.

By comparison, management contracts were not widely used in attempting to improve SOE performance. Yet, they improved profitability and productivity in two of the three cases in which they were used in the sample. In these cases governments used competition to reduce management's information advantage: either the SOEs operated in competitive markets, or competitive bidding was used to award contracts for monopoly enterprises. Fees were linked to firms' performance in order to create appropriate incentives. Commitment was enhanced through long contract length, the possibility of renewal, and the provision for arbitration in case of disputes.

IV. SUMMARY

The public sector can enhance its fiscal credibility by taking up-front steps that produce "permanent" adjustments in the fiscal accounts, either on the expenditure or revenue side. Such measures have the advantage, unlike measures affecting the public sector's access to seignorage, that they work directly to increase the resources available for debt service, rather than indirectly by signaling the government's commitment to undertake whatever measures may be necessary in the future to maintain the fiscal accounts in order. The key measures on the expenditure side of the budget involve the divestiture or reform of state-owned public enterprises, while on the revenue side they involve the reform of tax laws and/or tax administration.

In this chapter we have examined how divestiture and reform of SOEs can affect the public sector's budget. The key findings were that the impacts of privatization on the public sector's budget are not well captured by the privatization revenues received by the government during any given year, and that the reform of SOEs to improve their economic performance has proven to be a challenging task, in which countries have achieved mixed success.

In a present value sense, the true fiscal impact of privatization depends not just on the revenues received, but also on what would have happened had the enterprises involved remained in public hands. The impact on the "permanent" value of the public sector's primary surplus may be either greater or smaller than the privatization revenues received by the government. With respect to reform, we have reviewed "best practice" in restructuring such enterprises to improve their economic performance, and have found that the international experience suggests that mechanisms that tend to enhance the participation of the private sector in running such enterprises have tended to be most successful in improving their economic performance, with benefits for the economy at large as well as for the pressures on the public sector budget.

PART 4

The Financial Sector and Macroeconomic Performance

11

Finance, Welfare, and Growth

In Parts 2 and 3 of this book we took the domestic financial system for granted. The model of Part 2 and the analysis of public sector solvency in Part 3 assumed a domestic financial structure in which financial assets consisted of cash and securities that were traded in open markets. There were no specialized financial institutions as such, and in particular there were no banks.

But management of the domestic financial system is actually one of the key challenges facing policymakers in emerging economies. Macroeconomic performance in emerging economies depends critically on the state of the financial system. The functioning of the financial system strongly affects the economy's long-run growth performance, as well as its short-run macroeconomic stability. Distortions in the domestic financial sector can present serious obstacles to long-run growth by impairing both capital accumulation and growth in total factor productivity. On the other hand, financial sector weaknesses can themselves be the source of macroeconomic instability or can serve to propagate and magnify macroeconomic shocks arising elsewhere in the economy.

Part 4 takes up the role of the financial system, as well as of policies directed to the financial system. We will begin here by examining how the financial system can affect economic welfare and long-run growth. The perspective to be adopted is that, in a world of imperfect information, financial intermediation is an economic activity that is productive in a very real sense, that is, it uses scarce productive inputs to produce valuable outputs. We will see that a well-functioning and efficient financial sector can contribute to growth in three ways: by allocating capital to its most productive uses, by providing incentives for the accumulation of physical and human capital, and by minimizing the amount of resources that are absorbed in the process of intermediation. These links between financial sector performance and economic growth will be illustrated in the context of a simple model, and some of the existing evidence bearing on these issues will be described.

Subsequent chapters in Part 4 will consider policy issues that arise in the context of financial intermediation. The causes and consequences of financial repression are described in Chapter 12, followed by two chapters dealing respectively with domestic and external dimensions of financial reform, in the form of financial liberalization and financial openness. The final chapter in Part 4 will consider one of the implications of financial openness: the need to manage capital inflows. We will return to the financial sector in the final chapter of the book, when we consider how financial sector vulnerabilities have interacted with deficiencies in exchange rate management in producing some of the most severe episodes of macroeconomic instability experienced by emerging economies over the past two decades.

I. FINANCIAL TRANSACTIONS AND FINANCIAL MARKETS

It is useful to begin our examination of the role of financial intermediation with some definitions that will be used in this and subsequent chapters. A financial *instrument* is a contract that commits an economic agent to make a future payment under some specified conditions. Notice that the role of the *future* in this definition means that the stipulation that payments are made at different points in time is an essential feature of financial instruments. A financial *transaction* is one in which a financial instrument is traded, either in exchange for a current payment or for another financial instrument. *Financial markets* are the markets in which financial transactions are carried out.

To see why financial transactions exist, consider the following economic environment. Time passes in discrete periods, and in each period the world can exist in different "states of nature." Nobody knows ahead of time which state of nature will prevail in each period, and no one has any control over those outcomes, so the state of the world is inherently uncertain. There are many individuals, each of whom is endowed with a stochastic stream of income (i.e., a stream of income received each period that depends on the state of nature that prevails in that period). The welfare of each person depends on his or her stream of consumption (i.e., the amount the person can consume each period).

Individuals in this economy seek to maximize their economic well-being by engaging in trade with each other. How can they improve their well-being by doing so? To answer this question, suppose that each person's preferences regarding consumption are characterized by:

a. *Nonsatiation* (they regard consuming more as better than consuming less).
b. A *positive rate of time preference* (that means that they regard consuming now as better than consuming later).
c. *Risk aversion* (they prefer certainty to uncertainty).

Now assume that all the individuals in this economy are identical. Would they have any reason to engage in financial trades with each other? The answer is no, because any trade that would benefit one party would harm the other – that is, there would be no opportunity for *mutually beneficial* trades.

Now let's introduce *heterogeneity* among individuals. In particular, suppose that people can differ from each other in five ways:

a. Their distribution of income across the possible states of nature within each period.
b. Their degree of risk aversion.
c. The intertemporal profile of their income streams.
d. Their rate of time preference.
e. Their entrepreneurial talents. That is, some (but not all) individuals have the opportunity to buy new stochastic streams of income from nature.

In this case, there may be several motivations for financial transactions to take place. These include the desire to reduce risk, to reallocate consumption over time, and to finance investment opportunities. To the extent that financial markets facilitate transactions of these types, we would expect them to contribute to enhancing economic welfare, just as other markets do that facilitate mutually beneficial exchanges.

To see how each of these motives could give rise to mutually advantageous financial trades, consider each of them in turn.

a. Risk Reduction

The risk reduction motive can give rise to mutually advantageous financial trade when individuals have similar attitudes toward risk but differ with respect to their income streams, or when individuals with identical income streams differ with respect to their degree of risk aversion. For example, consider two individuals A and B with income streams illustrated in Table 11.1, Part A under states of nature 1 and 2. Suppose that individual A agrees to pay B 50 if the state of nature turns out to be 2, while B pays A 50 if it turns out to be 1. Then the situation becomes that illustrated in Table 11.1, Part B. Note that all risk has been eliminated by this financial transaction, making both parties better off (since they are both risk-averse). Thus, this transaction would be entered into voluntarily and would improve social welfare.

Alternatively, assume instead that both parties have the same stochastic distribution of income, but individual A is risk-averse while B is risk-neutral. The situation is illustrated in Table 11.2, Part A. Suppose that B promises to pay A 18 if the state of nature is 1, while A promises to pay B 22 if the state of nature is 2. Then the situation would become that illustrated in Table 11.2, Part B. Could this be a voluntary exchange? The answer is yes, if A is sufficiently risk-averse. The reason is that A has lost two units of expected income, but has succeeded in eliminating all risk from his/her income stream. This financial transaction reallocates risk from A to B, and both parties are better off. Social welfare again improves.

Table 11.1. *Risk-Averse–Risk-Averse Transaction*

Part A

| | State of nature | | |
Individual	1($p = 1/2$)	2($p = 1/2$)	Expected income
A	0	100	50
B	100	0	50

Part B

| | State of nature | | |
Individual	1($p = 1/2$)	2($p = 1/2$)	Expected income
A	50	50	50
B	50	50	50

Notice that in the first case considered above, risk was reduced for both parties, while in the second it was simply reallocated. The conclusion is the same in both cases, however. Whether risk is reduced or reallocated, social welfare can be improved through voluntary financial transactions.

b. Intertemporal Reallocation of Consumption

Now forget risk. A second motivation for financial transactions is to reallocate consumption over time. This could happen even if individuals have the same rate of time preference, if they have income streams with different patterns over time, or if they have income streams with the same pattern over time, but different rates of time preference.

Table 11.2. *Risk-Averse–Risk-Neutral Transaction*

Part A

| | State of nature | | |
Individual	1($p = 1/2$)	2($p = 1/2$)	Expected income
A	30	70	50
B	30	70	50

Part B

| | State of nature | | |
Individual	1($p = 1/2$)	2($p = 1/2$)	Expected income
A	48	48	48
B	32	72	52

For example, suppose A and B have the same rate of time preference, but A's income stream increases over time, while B's decreases over time. Because consumption in each period is subject to diminishing marginal utility, A would prefer to shift consumption from the future to the present, while B would prefer to shift it from the present to the future. Both parties could benefit by a trade in which A makes payments in the future to B in exchange for payments made by B to A in the present.

Alternatively, suppose the two have the same (say, flat) time profile of income, but A is very impatient to consume now, while B is more willing to defer consumption. Again, mutually advantageous financial trades are possible, with B making payments to A in the present and A paying B in the future.

c. Financing Investment

Finally, suppose that some individuals ("entrepreneurs") can "buy" new streams of income from nature ("projects"). If purchased today, a project entitles its owner to a stream of payments in the future that may vary across states of nature. We can describe these payments by listing some of their characteristics: their expected value in each period, their risk (how much payments vary across possible states of nature in each period), and their maturity (i.e., how far into the future these expected payments extend). What determines how attractive these projects are for the agents that have access to them? If we assume that people prefer more consumption to less, that they prefer present consumption to future consumption, and that they dislike risk, then projects will be more attractive when they have high expected returns, when these returns are close in time to the present, and when they have little risk associated with them.

If some of the projects available to entrepreneurs yield them enough income in the future, with enough certainty, and close enough in time, they may wish to undertake them. But suppose that at least some of these attractive projects are characterized by indivisibility, so that they must be undertaken at some minimum scale. In that case, the costs of the projects may exceed the current incomes of the entrepreneurs, or the amount of their current consumption that they are willing to forego. Then, they could offer to make future payments out of the proceeds of the project that would be more than sufficient to compensate other individuals for making enough payments to them in the present so as to finance the purchase of the project. If the project leaves enough left over to make the entrepreneur better off, then all parties are better off and would thus voluntarily undertake the transaction. Moreover, the economy as a whole would grow, since its stream of future income would be increased by the returns to the project. Moreover, this growth must be welfare-enhancing, since by assumption it is enough to compensate everyone for deferring present consumption.

Our conclusion is that heterogeneity among individuals can give rise to financial trades that are both welfare-enhancing and conducive to faster economic growth.

But so far, we have been talking only about the motivation for individual trades. What does the market equilibrium look like?

II. FINANCIAL MARKET EQUILIBRIUM IN AN IDEAL WORLD

We have just seen that, given heterogeneity among economic agents along the various dimensions we have explored, there may be mutually advantageous financial exchanges to be made in the economy. How do these exchanges happen?

As a point of departure, consider first how such exchanges would take place in a world characterized by perfect competition, with public information and costless contract negotiation and enforcement. The assumption that information is public means that each potential lender knows the identity of each potential borrower, as well as the potential payoff from the project of each entrepreneur in each possible future state of nature. Costless contract negotiation and enforcement means that there are no costs to reaching agreement on future payments to be made in all possible states of nature, and that once the agreement is reached, both sides will abide by the terms of the contract. In other words, under this assumption, commitments once made are automatically binding. Finally, perfect competition means that no agents have market power.

Financial markets would have two important properties under these circumstances:

a. Financial intermediation would be *costless* (would absorb no real resources), and could be *carried out by individuals.* This must be so because each potential lender knows the identity of each potential borrower, as well as all of the characteristics of the income streams available to each borrower in each possible future state of nature. Thus, in such a world, each lender could costlessly contract with any number of borrowers to provide purchasing power today in exchange for payments to be made at previously specified points in the future under previously specified states of nature.
b. Financial intermediation would be *efficient* (in the economists' Pareto sense). We know that this must be so, because if goods are identified by the time and state of nature in which they exist, all the usual Pareto conditions would hold in this case, and the competitive outcome would, by the usual economic reasoning, be Pareto efficient.

In this environment, the price of current resources in terms of future resources (the *real interest rate*) would be determined by market conditions (the total supply of funds from net lenders and demands from net borrowers). People with access to very attractive projects or with a high degree of impatience would be net borrowers, and people without very attractive projects or with a low degree of impatience would be net lenders. The amount of investment that goes on in this economy would depend on the net cost of borrowing facing entrepreneurs, while the amount of saving that goes on would depend on the net return available to savers. In short, the market would costlessly allocate income efficiently between consumption and saving, and also allocate saving efficiently among investment projects.

Now consider the pricing and allocation of risk in such a world. The total risk of each project can be decomposed into *systematic risk* (the common risk element in all projects) and *idiosyncratic* risk (the component of risk not correlated with systematic risk). In equilibrium, the price of systematic risk would depend on the degree of risk aversion among agents in the economy. The price of idiosyncratic risk would be zero, however, since it can be costlessly diversified away. Thus, only systematic risk is left to influence saving and investment. The *risk premium* (the amount of compensation that borrowers have to pay risk-averse lenders for assuming risk) paid by individual borrowers would differ across borrowers only as a function of the amount of systematic risks in their investment projects. Given the market price of risk, agents with a high tolerance for risk (low degree of risk aversion) would acquire claims on risky projects, while agents with a low tolerance for risk (high degree of risk aversion) would prefer to acquire safe income streams. Thus, risk would be borne by those most willing to do so, in other words, it would be *optimally shared.*

Notice also that in this idealized world:

- There would be no role for specialized financial institutions.
- For a potential borrower, the cost of funds would be the same whether they were internally or externally generated.
- A borrower's net worth would play no role in determining the terms on which that person can borrow.
- The financial structure of enterprises would not affect their value.
- Liquidity problems (unexpected needs for cash) would never arise, because borrowers and lenders can make fully contingent arrangements to insure against unanticipated needs for funds.
- There is no role for public policy.

III. THE REAL WORLD: IMPERFECT INFORMATION AND OPPORTUNISTIC BEHAVIOR

The real world, however, is very different from this. In the real world, information is imperfect (not everyone knows what a given individual knows), behavior is opportunistic (people can't credibly commit their future actions), and perfect competition is at best an approximation. We will focus on the first two problems. As we will see, these two features of economic life create a productive role for specialized financial institutions.

Suppose, then, that instead of public information and costless contract enforcement, the economic environment is characterized by information deficiencies and opportunistic behavior. The kind of information deficiency involved is one in which information is private, rather than public. That is, each individual knows his/her own circumstances, but not those of other individuals. This leads to two types of information problems:

i. Searching and matching: borrowers and lenders do not know where to find each other.
ii. Asymmetric information: borrowers know the properties of their projects, but lenders do not.[1] On the other hand, opportunistic behavior means that any commitments made by individuals today will not be considered by them to be binding in the future. Thus, promises about future behavior are not self-enforcing. Instead, they have to be enforced through legal sanctions.

a. Financial Intermediation as a Costly Activity

What are the implications of these phenomena for financial intermediation? The central point is that in this environment, financial intermediation – the transformation of saving into investment and allocation of risk – is not automatic or costless. In a world in which information is not free and agreements cannot be costlessly enforced, intermediation requires the expenditure of resources – that is, it becomes a form of production. To see why, notice that to strike a loan contract between saver and borrower, several costly (resource-absorbing) activities have to take place: first, lender and borrower must find each other. This means that *brokerage costs* must be incurred. For future reference, note that such costs are likely to be independent of the size of the loan that is subsequently negotiated.

Second, having found each other, lender and borrower have to strike a bargain. It turns out that this is not trivial in the context of asymmetric information.

To see why, suppose that borrowers are entrepreneurs, all of whom have access to projects with the same expected return, but with different distributions across states of nature. And suppose that borrowers and lenders are trying to agree on a *debt contract*. Debt contracts stipulate fixed payments (principal plus interest) in all states of nature in which the projects yield enough to make such payments, and maximum payments in all other states of nature (so creditors get paid before the entrepreneur does). If the lender could observe the characteristics of the individual borrowers, the lender would presumably demand higher returns from riskier projects in good states of nature to compensate for the likelihood of nonpayment in bad states of nature. Stated simply, loan contracts would be tailor-made to the circumstances of the borrowers.

But asymmetric information means that lenders cannot costlessly observe the properties of individual projects. This being so, the best the lender can do is to

---

[1] Notice that borrowers cannot credibly transmit this information costlessly, because everyone knows that it is in their interest to dissemble.

charge everyone an interest rate that would yield the desired expected return for the *average* project. But that means that riskier-than-average borrowers would face lower borrowing costs than safer-than-average borrowers (because they would expect to have to pay the interest rate demanded by the lender less often), and thus the average borrower who actually takes up the lender's offer would tend to be riskier than the population at large. But this being the case, the lender could not expect to receive the required expected return under these circumstances (because this particular group of borrowers would on average tend to pay less than that). Thus, the lender would not make these loans. This problem, known as *adverse selection*, makes it impossible for a bargain to be struck that both sides would consider advantageous. Neither raising nor lowering the interest rate demanded by the lender would help, since the same phenomenon would then repeat itself as at the original terms. Thus, markets cannot handle this problem through the price mechanism. Indeed, an important implication of adverse selection is that it causes the price mechanism to break down.

To get around this problem, the lender has to become informed about the likelihood of repayment. Since lenders cannot rely on disclosure by the borrowers, lenders would have to produce an independent evaluation of the loan. This requires obtaining general information about the type of economic activity involved, as well as specific information about characteristics of the borrower. All of this implies incurring *evaluation costs*. It is reasonable to think of this as a fixed cost per project (a given fee has to be paid by each lender for each project to which it lends) to acquire the information.

What determines the magnitude of evaluation costs? Evaluation costs are likely to be larger the more "opaque" a borrower is (i.e., the more difficult it is to obtain information about that specific borrower's activities), and smaller the more "transparent" the borrower is. The opaqueness of a borrower depends on factors such as the type of economic activity he or she is engaged in (new activities, of course, tend to be more opaque), the borrower's previous track record, the amount of publicly available information on the borrower, prevailing accounting and disclosure standards, and so on.

Third, once the loan has been struck and money has changed hands, a resource has been entrusted by one entity (the principal) to another (the agent) who will actually make the decisions on how to manage it. At this point a new problem arises in the form of the borrower's tendency to behave opportunistically. That is, given a choice, the agent will always have an incentive to make decisions that benefit him or her at the expense of the principal, a situation which is known as "moral hazard". Moral hazard is a general problem in economic interactions, and it can take many different forms. In the context of financial intermediation, the form that moral hazard takes depends on the nature of the contract between borrower and lender.

Consider, for example, a debt contract. Suppose that once money changes hands, the borrower can choose from several projects. What project characteristics will the borrower find attractive under such a contract? Assuming no risk aversion, from the standpoint of society (that is, taking the borrower and lender together), the optimal project choice would be the one with the maximum expected *social* (total) return. But the borrower, behaving opportunistically, would tend to choose the project that maximizes *private* return. Given the nature of the debt contract, this would tend to be a project that pays very high returns (which the borrower gets to keep) in some states of nature even if its expected return is low because of offsetting losses in other states of nature (since under a loan contract, these losses are borne by the principal). The upshot is that the debt contract creates incentives for opportunistic borrowers, left to their own devices, to choose very risky projects (projects with returns that vary greatly across states of nature) even if they have low expected returns. This creates the problem of how, in the absence of pre-commitment, the principal can ensure that the agent will make resource-management decisions that are in the interests of the principal. This is known as an "agency problem." It creates the need for measures to safeguard the interests of the lender (*control*), all of which involve costs, known as *agency costs*.

How can borrowers and lenders cope with agency costs? There are several possibilities:

i. *The use of collateral.* Under debt contracts, the key is ensuring that losses in bad states of nature are borne by the borrower. This can happen if the borrower offers sufficient collateral, or has sufficient "collateralizable" net worth at stake (defined as net liquid assets plus the collateral value of nonliquid assets).[2] With full collateral, lenders can be completely protected from the possibility of non-payment. In that case, no agency problems arise, because the actions of the agent do not affect the returns received by the principal. The effectiveness of this solution depends on the size of the borrower's collateralizable net worth relative to that of the loan, as well as on the efficiency of the legal system that makes it possible to seize collateral. Alternatively, if the borrower has an established reputation that would be harmed by nonpayment, then agency problems are reduced, because opportunistic behavior that harms the interests of the principal is penalized.

ii. *The imposition of restrictive covenants.* To the extent that agency problems cannot be fully resolved by ensuring that the borrower has a large stake in the project's outcome (through reputation and/or the offer of collateral), lenders could resort to formally restricting the behavior of the borrowers through the imposition of restrictive covenants on loans. These are provisions in loan contracts that reduce moral hazard by ruling out undesirable behavior and encouraging desirable behavior by borrowers. For example, they may stipulate that loans can be used only for specific activities, or may encourage behavior like keeping net worth high (i.e., low debt-equity ratios), may require the borrower to keep ownership of collateral and maintain it in good condition (examples: auto loans, home

---

[2] Note that under limited liability, not all the borrower's net worth will be at stake.

mortgages), or may impose periodic reporting by firms, or may give the lender the right to inspect and audit the firm's books. However, this involves incurring monitoring costs.

iii. *Requiring short maturity*. Restricting the maturity of the debt facilitates control, because it gives the lenders a sanction over the borrowers (withdrawing funds), but it involves incurring monitoring and enforcement costs.

iv. *Designing incentive-compatible contracts*. The principal and agent can agree to structure the contract between them so as to cause their interests to be more closely aligned. For example, a lender can become an owner by transferring resources in the form of *equity* (a share of the profits), thus encouraging managers to maximize total profits. But if opportunities exist for managers and majority shareholders (*insiders*) to dispossess minority shareholders (*outsiders*), then the latter would still have to incur monitoring costs. Costly state verification by outsiders makes it possible for managers to exploit owners, for majority owners to exploit minority owners, etc. The upshot is that, while agency costs may be reduced through these means in some circumstances, they cannot be eliminated.

Finally, since opportunistic behavior means that contracts are not self-enforcing, lenders may have to be prepared to enforce them through the legal system. *Contract enforcement costs* can be thought of as a fixed cost that has to be paid for access to the legal system to enforce agreed future payments.

b. The External Finance Premium

Thus, the activity of financial intermediation involves incurring brokerage costs, evaluation costs, agency costs, and enforcement costs. All of these costs create a wedge between the *gross* return paid by a borrower and the *net* return received by a lender. Since these costs only have to be incurred when funds are acquired externally, the same wedge applies to the difference between the cost of borrowed funds and internally generated funds. This wedge is referred to as the "external finance premium." The costs of financial intermediation are generally not likely to increase in proportion to the size of the loan, so there will be economies of scale in each of these activities. In other words, because these costs have to be incurred per loan (not per dollar loaned), the sum of brokerage, evaluation, agency, and contract enforcement costs would tend to be very high per dollar loaned for small loans. The implication is that, because each individual lender makes small loans, the external finance premium would tend to be extremely high if intermediation were to be done by individuals.

To see some of the social implications of this situation, consider the fifth motive for engaging in financial transactions that we considered previously: the financing of investment. In the absence of the external finance premium, the real interest rate would be determined by the intersection of an upward-sloped saving schedule and downward-sloped investment schedule, as at the point *A* in Figure 11.1. When the

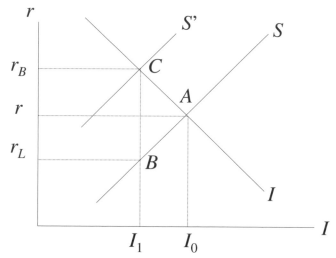

Figure 11.1. Social Implications of the External Finance Premium

external finance premium is high, lenders would have to receive a very high gross return for the use of their funds, to compensate them for these costs of intermediation. This shifts the saving schedule to S'. The wedge between the interest rate paid by borrowers r_B, and that received by lenders r_L, is determined by the magnitude of the required external finance premium. When the external finance premium is large, the resulting high costs of obtaining external funds would deter entrepreneurs from undertaking all but the most remunerative projects, reducing aggregate investment from I_0 to I_1. *The upshot is that potentially highly productive projects that involve a sacrifice of current consumption in return for higher future incomes would not be likely to be undertaken, and the rate of economic growth would thus tend to be low.*

IV. BANKS AND CAPITAL MARKETS

We can now address the question of what financial intermediaries do. Financial intermediaries are essentially a market response to the situation just described. They are specialized agents that arise to exploit the high external finance premium that would exist in their absence. Essentially, economies of scale and scope created by the implications of imperfect information and opportunistic behavior make it profitable for firms to arise that specialize in producing financial intermediation.

a. What Do Banks Do?

Banks are firms that announce their willingness to supply liquid assets with attractive features (security, return), and to make information-intensive loans. Their main activity is on the asset side of their balance sheets, consisting of identifying potential borrowers (the brokerage function), gathering information about them (the evaluation function), monitoring their loans, and enforcing the payment of loan contracts. Essentially, banks are profitable because they can carry out these functions more cheaply than individuals can. This means that, if they were to charge an external finance premium for their services comparable to that which would exist in their absence, they would make excess profits. It is the allure of these excess profits that triggers the emergence of banks as a market response to the opportunities that would exist in their absence.

How can they do all this? They can intermediate more cheaply than individuals by pooling their liabilities, pooling their assets, and exploiting economies of scale and scope.

Liability pooling permits banks to fund lumpy, high-return projects. By pooling the resources of lenders, they can overcome the indivisibility problem that we discussed earlier. Liability pooling also protects banks against liquidity risk, permitting them to offer assets of short maturity. By pooling the resources of lenders, they can take advantage of the law of large numbers to issue liquid liabilities while keeping only a small share of these resources in liquid assets. They invest the rest in financing the productive projects of entrepreneurs.

Asset pooling, on the other hand, permits diversification, which protects banks from idiosyncratic risk, leaving them exposed only to systematic risk. In other words, by financing a large number of projects they can achieve the high expected return that these projects offer at relatively low (systematic) risk. This reduces the monitoring costs that have to be borne by bank creditors, allowing the banks to raise funds at lower interest rates.

Though asset and liability pooling provide benefits to banks, they still must incur the costs of locating borrowers, evaluating them, monitoring them, and enforcing loan contracts. But because costs of information gathering, monitoring, and contract enforcement are incurred per loan (rather than per dollar lent), and because engaging in some of these activities reduces the costs of engaging in others, banks can take advantage of economics of scale and scope by making large loans, reducing such costs per dollar lent.

In short, banks can attract savings and still be profitable because asset and liability pooling, together with economies of scale and scope, permit them to offer assets with attractive combinations of expected return, risk, and liquidity that dominate cash in the portfolios of prospective lenders.

In performing these functions, banks improve the welfare of both borrowers and lenders. By decreasing the amount of productive resources, per unit of intermediation, that society has to devote to overcoming costs associated with imperfect information and opportunistic behavior, banks enhance the efficiency of intermediation and thus reduce the external finance premium. This permits an increase in the return to saving and a reduction in the cost of borrowing, improving the welfare of both borrowers and lenders. At the same time, banks promote economic growth by improving the composition of the economy's real assets and thus increasing the rate of return of the social portfolio of productive capital. They do so by allowing the economy to undertake projects that may have a high expected return, but that would not otherwise be undertaken because their riskiness, lumpiness, and/or illiquidity would not permit them to attract financing from individual savers.

But despite these important contributions, banks are not a complete answer to the problems that the real world poses for the activity of financial intermediation. By definition, banks are institutions that offer safe, liquid assets to savers. They also tend to engage in information-intensive lending. This specialization on the liability and asset sides of their balance sheets means that they do not universally dominate other forms of financial intermediation. That is, there are market niches that banks leave unfilled.

The advantages that banks possess are more important for certain types of lending and for certain types of borrowing than for others. Because banks make information-intensive loans, they will seek out borrowers who are not too opaque (e.g., that are known to bank managers or otherwise have characteristics that make information gathering about them less costly), and they will not have special advantages in competing for borrowers that are very transparent. Banks also will not have special advantages in competing for borrowers whose large stakes in their own projects (because of reputation or collateral) reduce the agency costs of lending to them. Moreover, because they issue liquid liabilities and acquire information-intensive assets, banks are likely to prefer relatively liquid assets or illiquid assets of short maturity. The latter are likely to be less costly to maintain, because the shorter the maturity of bank assets, the smaller the stock of liquid reserves that banks will be forced to keep, and the lower monitoring costs will be. Finally, banks are also likely to seek to diversify their portfolios to avoid idiosyncratic risk. This does two things for them: it reduces their need to monitor, and it reduces the need for bank creditors to monitor the banks, thus allowing banks to attract deposits at more favorable rates. The desire for diversification means that banks will be unwilling to make loans that are too large relative to the size of their portfolios.

b. Capital Markets

We have seen that the cost of bank lending is likely to rise with the maturity of the loan, and is also likely to increase as the loan becomes large relative to the bank's total portfolio. Thus, in a bank-dominated environment a relatively high demand price for long-term borrowing in large amounts will exist, set by the cost to banks of making such loans. In this situation, there is a market niche that can be filled by bond financing.

Whether this niche will be filled depends on the factors that determine the supply price of this type of lending, including:

i.   The magnitude of brokerage and evaluation costs associated with this type of lending. In turn, this will depend on the visibility and transparency of the potential borrowers, as well as the presence and efficiency of specialized firms (underwriters and credit rating agencies) to perform these functions.

ii. The magnitude of the collateralizable net worth of the potential borrowers relative to the size of the prospective loans (projects), as well as the value placed by such borrowers on their financial reputations. Borrowers with large net worth, or who place a high value on their reputations, do not present the types of agency problems that banks can address through loan evaluation and repeated monitoring.

iii. Since contract enforcement costs also have to be borne under bond financing, the supply price of this type of lending will also depend on the adequacy of legal provisions for creditor protection (bankruptcy law), as well as the quality of its enforcement.

iv. Finally, whether bond markets will arise will also depend on the existence of a class of lenders that does not place a high value on liquidity and/or on factors that affect the liquidity of bonds, such as the potential "thickness" of the bond markets.

Once again, filling this market opportunity is welfare-enhancing, because it permits certain investments (i.e., long-term investments by transparent, low-agency cost firms) to be carried out that yield returns exceeding those required by lenders to make the funds available – that is, they permit the execution of mutually advantageous trades.

Another reason that banks may not dominate as intermediaries is because firms may prefer *equity* financing. They may do so because characteristics of the firm may make the agency costs associated with equity contracts lower than those associated with debt contracts, because the size of the project for which financing is sought may be large relative to the firm's equity (thus raising the *relative* agency costs associated with debt financing), and/or because equity financing, by reducing leverage, reduces risk to the entrepreneur, by making profits less vulnerable to fluctuations in revenues and interest rates. Thus, firms that are risk-averse or that face relatively high agency costs associated with debt finance will generate a high demand price for equity financing.

As with bond markets, whether a supply of equity financing will be forthcoming depends on the attributes of equity claims, such as their access to insider information, their legal standing, and their liquidity. All of these are enhanced by well-functioning stock markets, the existence of which depends on factors such as the presence of specialized firms to provide brokerage and evaluation services (stock brokerage firms tend to do both), the legal protection provided to shareholders (corporate law) and the quality of its enforcement, as well as the potential thickness of equity markets.

Like banks and bond markets, equity markets also create a number of economic benefits that improve the welfare of borrowers and lenders. For example, by facilitating trade, stock markets make claims on long-gestation projects liquid. This makes equity claims more attractive, and thus increases the supply of equity financing. By ameliorating agency problems and reducing risk, equity financing may prevent firms from being too small because they forego large, risky investment projects that would be costly to finance with debt. The result is to foster economic growth. Moreover, large, liquid stock markets make it easier for an agent to earn money on private information, which creates an incentive for the acquisition of such information. Through effects on the cost of capital, the near-continuous valuation of firms based on all available information promotes efficiency in capital allocation. Liquid stock markets also facilitate takeovers of inefficient firms, which promote X-efficiency by imposing discipline on managers. Better stock markets can promote corporate control by allowing owners to index the salaries of managers to the value of the firm, thus reducing agency problems by aligning their incentives with the interests of the managers. Finally, stock markets facilitate the trading of risky assets, thus allocating risk to relatively less risk-averse individuals, who are better able to bear it, thereby improving economic welfare.

V. FINANCIAL MARKETS AND PUBLIC POLICY

However, the desirable welfare and growth outcomes associated with a well-functioning financial system are not automatic. The next three chapters will argue that public policy has an important role to play in ensuring that these benefits indeed materialize. As a framework for that discussion, this section will present a brief overview of the role of public policy in the financial system that follows directly from our analysis so far in this chapter of the financial system as a productive activity.

In brief, the efficiency of financial intermediation will be enhanced by public policies of three types: enabling policies, policies directed at the development of financial market infrastructure, and policies designed to deal with special problems of the financial sector. We now consider each of these in turn.

a. Policies to Promote an Enabling Environment

Enabling policies are those that improve the environment in which financial intermediaries operate, without necessarily being directed at the financial sector itself. They include policies that facilitate information gathering and contract enforcement as well as policies that reduce risk and financial institutions' ability to monitor it.[3] They also include avoiding the imposition of handicaps on the financial sector through excessive taxation of financial intermediaries or their customers.

Enabling policies have both institutional and macroeconomic dimensions. Institutional policies that would promote the development of the financial system are those that make it less costly for financial intermediaries to cope with the credit market imperfections that give rise to the external finance premium in the first place.

---

[3] This includes not just risk associated with the economic environment, but also that created for financial institutions by moral hazard problems (through low borrower net worth).

This essentially refers to policies that reduce information costs and costs of contract enforcement through the imposition of an appropriate legal framework. The components of an appropriate legal framework include well-established property rights, adequate accounting and disclosure standards, corporate and bankruptcy laws to protect shareholders and creditors respectively, and an efficient judicial system to enforce contracts and punish fraud.

Macroeconomic policies can influence the evolution of the financial system in many ways. The key to understanding the influence that macroeconomic policies can exert on financial development, however, is the recognition that the size of the external finance premium can be affected by macroeconomic policies through at least two channels:

i. Macroeconomic policies can influence the financial health of potential borrowers (their net worth), and thus their ratio of collateralizable net worth to the size of prospective loans. This is an indirect influence running from macroeconomic policies to long-term economic performance to financial development.
ii. Macroeconomic policies can influence financial development in more direct ways. Taxation of the financial sector, either explicitly or implicitly, will retard its growth and development in obvious ways.[4] Less obviously, the quality of macroeconomic management will affect the degree of uncertainty that characterizes the domestic economic environment, and thus the magnitude of loan evaluation and monitoring costs. This channel of influence may be operative at any level of income per capita and any stage of financial development.

With respect to indirect influences mediated through long-term economic performance, the role of macroeconomic stability in promoting long-run economic growth was the subject of Chapter 1, and little additional elaboration is required here. The only additional link to emphasize is that faster growth of income per capita will tend to produce more creditworthy firms, as well as to improve the institutional environment for financial intermediation (for evidence, see Easterly 2000). On both accounts, the external finance premium will fall, promoting the growth of financial intermediation, and is likely to fall differentially for arms' length intermediation through securities markets, increasing the relative role of such markets.

Given the level of income per capita (and thus the average level of net worth of potential borrowers), as well as the quality of the institutional environment, macroeconomic policies can also exert more direct effects on the prospects for financial sector growth and development. The most obvious way in which this can

---

[4] For example, as we will see in the next chapter, an important reason for the persistence of financial repression in many developing countries was that it met a fiscal need – that is, it enabled the public sector to capture resources more cheaply than it might otherwise have done. Thus, the literature on sequencing of financial reform typically recommended that fiscal adjustment precede the liberalization of the domestic financial system, in order to wean the government from reliance on the financial repression "tax."

happen – the explicit or implicit taxation of the financial system – is the subject
of the next chapter. But less obviously, the uncertainty associated with an unstable
macroeconomic environment increases the costs of financial intermediation and is
thus inimical to the process of financial development.

One can imagine a variety of ways in which macroeconomic uncertainty could
discourage the development of the domestic financial sector. For example, the emergence of a debt overhang associated with prospective fiscal insolvency, as discussed
in Chapter 8, would discourage the acquisition of assets within the taxing authority
of the domestic government, and thus would act as an implicit tax on all domestic
financial instruments. Alternatively, instability itself, in the form of the "boom-
bust" cycles that too often have afflicted emerging economies, may make it much
more difficult for financial intermediaries to evaluate and monitor the activities of
their borrowers, not only increasing the costs of doing business (the external finance
premium) but also lowering the average quality of loans and thus imperiling the
health of the financial system itself, as emphasized by Gavin and Hausmann (1996).

In short, financial development requires a conducive environment, and macroeconomic stability is an important component of such an environment. Both indirectly, through the effects of growth on the financial health of potential borrowers
and the quality of the institutional environment, as well as directly, through the
degree of uncertainty in the macroeconomic environment, poor macroeconomic
policies can undermine the growth and development of financial markets.

b. Proactive Policies Directed at the Financial Sector

Proactive policies directed at the financial sector concern the provision of a regulatory and supervisory framework that promotes competition in the financial sector
(preventing collusion) and avoids excessive risk-taking due to moral hazard problems. There are three separate functions involved:

  i. Implementing and enforcing bank licensing standards and prudential
     regulations.
 ii. Developing market infrastructure for capital (bond and stock) markets.
iii. Implementing and enforcing antitrust policies directed at the banking and
     securities industries.

These policies are the subject of Chapter 13, and we can defer further discussion of
them until then.

c. Policies to Deal with Financial Sector Instability

Finally, policies are also required to deal with special problems to which the financial sector is vulnerable. These problems include banking crises and asset market
bubbles.

We will discuss banking crises in more detail in Chapter 13, but for now we
can note that because bank assets are information-intensive, they are illiquid, and

there tends to be no secondary market for bank assets. At the same time, banks issue highly liquid liabilities. Thus they are inherently illiquid institutions. This makes them vulnerable to liquidity (confidence) crises, which can actually be self-fulfilling. The disruption of bank credit in the context of a crisis affects the real economy through a variety of channels, and governments have consequently sought to avoid banking crises by implementing a variety of financial safety nets, such as the creation of a lender of last resort or the implementation of a system of deposit insurance. The lender of last resort function protects individual banks from liquidity risk, while deposit insurance functions provide systemic protection against liquidity crises.

Asset-price bubbles arise when asset prices are driven higher solely by the expectation that such prices will be higher in the future. Bubbles can arise in markets for assets that have no maturity, and no defined face value at maturity. Thus, they tend to arise in stock and real estate markets, and not in bond markets, because stocks and real estate satisfy these criteria. The value of a stock depends on the expected present value of its dividends plus the present value of its expected price at the time of sale. This last component creates the scope for self-fulfilling expectations which, by causing the value of the stock to deviate from its fundamental determinants, can undermine the efficiency-enhancing effects of equity markets that we discussed previously. When equities loom large in household wealth, stock market bubbles and collapses can have significant real economic effects.[5]

VI. FINANCIAL INTERMEDIATION AND AGGREGATE ECONOMIC ACTIVITY

The theory we have reviewed in this chapter suggests that the premium for external finance depends inversely on borrower net worth. As we will see, this suggests that financial intermediation and aggregate economic activity will tend to be interdependent both in the long run and in the short run. The influence of borrower net worth on the size of the external finance premium will tend to create an interdependence between long-run growth and financial development. Over a shorter time horizon, shocks to the external finance premium may tend to generate business cycles, and a "financial accelerator" may operate to magnify business cycles originating outside the financial sector.

a. Effects of Growth on Financial Development

The influence of the external finance premium on financial development causes the relationship between financial development and growth to be bidirectional – high income per capita promotes financial development, and financial development promotes long-run economic growth. High income per capita affects financial

---

[5] As we will see in Chapter 16, the foreign exchange market may be vulnerable to bubbles as well, for reasons similar to those that apply to stock and real estate markets.

development for several reasons:

i. Countries with high income per capita tend to have large firms. Because large net worth of firms lowers monitoring costs (both by providing collateral and by aligning the incentives of owners more closely with those of creditors), this reduces the costs of intermediation (the premium for external finance) and thus promotes financial intermediation.
ii. The presence of large numbers of firms with substantial net worth permits the emergence of "thick" securities (bond and equity) markets that provide liquidity for savers, thus fostering the development of such markets by lowering the costs of issuing securities.
iii. High income per capita is likely to be associated with greater availability of public goods that facilitate financial intermediation, such as an established system of property rights, accounting standards, and an efficient judiciary.

This means that financial development is likely to proceed sequentially. At low levels of income, self-finance and informal finance linked to social relationships are likely to be dominant, since the external finance premium will be very large outside the context of social relationships. As incomes rise, firms' net worth will tend to increase, and the availability of public goods required to reduce the external finance premium is likely to improve. Thus, the share of total intermediation done by the formal financial system is likely to rise. While the number of large firms is relatively small and collateral remains limited, the dominant intermediary is likely to be the commercial bank, because the evaluation and monitoring functions in which banks specialize will continue to be important. Arm's length securities transactions with little or no monitoring (bond and equity markets) become possible only when net worth is high.

The evidence is consistent with this kind of evolution. For example, among the "stylized facts" about financial development and growth listed by Levine (1992) are that: (i) as real income rises, the ratio of financial institutions' assets to GDP tends to grow, and (ii) the importance of intermediaries tends to change in a common pattern as income rises. Central banks become less important, deposit banks grow in importance initially, and then other intermediaries (mutual funds, pension funds, etc.) grow in importance.

Similarly, Gertler and Rose (1991), using annual data for sixty-nine developing and twenty-one industrial countries over the period 1950–88, found a positive correlation in panel data between the log of real per capita GDP and both the log of the ratio of credit to the private sector to GDP as well as the ratio of quasi-money to GDP among developing countries. They found that these results were robust to a variety of perturbations, with little evidence of nonlinearities. They concluded that countries with higher incomes have deeper financial systems.

Box 11.1. Financial Structure in Sub-Saharan Africa

Information on the financial structure of Sub-Saharan African countries is not widely available. The overview presented here is based on country-specific information for six countries, described in Appendix 11.1. Overall, the financial system in these countries fits the paradigm outlined in this chapter rather well. The countries in the region are among the poorest in the world, and their stage of financial development is one where net worth and collateral availability among borrowers continues to be such that external finance continues to be tied to evaluating and monitoring functions on the part of lenders.

By and large the formal financial sectors of these economies are dominated by a small number of commercial banks. Nonbank intermediaries tend to be small and few in number. Stock exchanges exist in some countries, but do not account for a significant share of financing of business enterprises. In the commercial banking sector, deposits tend to be concentrated in the few largest banks, and public ownership of the most important banks is common. The regulatory structure is not always well developed and is sometimes splintered, with banks and nonbanks subject to very different regulatory environments. According to the World Bank (1994):

> Bank supervision is essentially nonexistent in countries where the banking system has been nationalized. Even in countries with nominally private banks, there may be a conflict of interest because members of the supervisory agencies often sit on the boards of the banking institutions. In most instances, prudential ratios have been ineffective in preventing the degradation of loan portfolios. The ratios sometimes were poorly designed or lacked rules for classifying credit according to risk, for defining and handling delinquent loans. (p. 114)

Moreover, directed credit is common, and the quality of bank portfolios is often poor. Banks in some countries appear to hold substantial amounts of excess reserves. An informal financial sector characterized by small-scale transactions, and often based on preexisting social and economic relationships, parallels and complements the formal one. Data on its magnitude are scarce, but the perceived wisdom is that it may be quite large in several countries.

Finally, Levine (1996), using annual data for eighty countries over the 1960–89 period, found that the ratio of liquid liabilities of intermediaries to GDP increased as income per capita rose. The ratio of bank credit to bank plus central bank assets also rose with per capita GDP. The ratio of credit to private firms to total domestic credit and the ratio of credit to private firms to GDP were both positively correlated with real per capita GDP.

To illustrate this point, Box 11.1 summarizes some features of the financial systems in six very low-income Sub-Saharan African countries, described in country-specific detail in the appendix to this chapter. The financial systems in these six very poor countries fit the general description provided above rather well.

b. Effects of Financial Development on Growth: Theory

As we saw in Chapter 1, economic growth can occur through improved total factor productivity (TFP) or through the accumulation of productive factors. From this perspective, financial intermediation can affect growth through three mechanisms:

i. The more efficiently funds are allocated among competing investment projects (including to lumpy, illiquid, high-return projects), the greater the productivity of the capital stock, and the greater is TFP.
ii. The smaller the cost of intermediation, the greater the amount of investment corresponding to a given amount of saving, since savers and investors jointly have to bear the costs of intermediation.
iii. The greater the returns to investment, and the lower the cost of intermediation, the greater the net return to saving, and thus the greater the incentive to save.

The interactions among these three mechanisms can be illustrated in a simple aggregate growth model that allows a role for the allocative functions of the financial system as well as for the resources absorbed in the process of financial intermediation. Suppose that aggregate output is produced using two kinds of capital, denoted K_1 and K_2, under conditions of constant returns to scale. Thus, the aggregate production function can be written as:

$$Y = F(K_1, K_2).^6$$ (11.1)

The total capital available to the economy is given by:

$$K_1 + K_2 = K,$$ (11.2)

which changes over time according to the amount of investment undertaken each period:

$$\Delta K = I.$$ (11.3)

Investment, in turn, is equal to "effective" saving – that is, the portion of aggregate saving not absorbed by the process of financial intermediation. Aggregate saving is proportional to the level of output:

$$I = \sigma s Y.$$ (11.4)

Here $(1 - \sigma)$ is the cost of financial intermediation per unit of saving, in the form of spreads between borrowing and lending rates, commissions, etc. In other words, $(1 - \sigma)$ refers to the resources absorbed in producing intermediation services.

---

[6] This is essentially an "AK" technology, in which aggregate output is a linear function of reproducible factors of production, implying that increases in such factors are not subject to diminishing returns. It can be justified in various ways. Diminishing returns at the firm level may disappear in the aggregate due to externalities affecting the physical capital stock, or diminishing returns may apply to physical and human capital separately, but not to their composite.

To see what this model tells us about the role of financial intermediation in the growth process, let $\theta = K_1/K_2$. Then we can write equation (11.1) as:

$$Y = F(\theta, 1)K_2 = F(\theta, 1)K/(1 + \theta) = A(\theta)K, \qquad (11.1')$$

where $A(\theta) = F(\theta, 1)/(1 + \theta)$. This means that the change in Y over time (denoted ΔY) is given by:

$$\Delta Y = A(\theta)\Delta K = A(\theta)\sigma \, sY.$$

or:

$$\Delta Y/Y = A(\theta)\sigma s. \qquad (11.5)$$

This model tells us that growth depends on the productivity of the capital stock A, the efficiency of financial intermediation σ, and the rate of saving s. Now notice that:

i. By allocating funds to their most productive uses, the financial sector can increase A. The value of θ that maximizes A satisfies:

$$f'(\theta)/(1 + \theta) - f(\theta)/(1 + \theta^2) = 0,$$

or:

$$f'(\theta) = f(\theta) - f'(\theta)\theta,$$

which is the requirement that the marginal product of the two types of capital be equalized. This outcome will emerge if financial institutions are able to identify the marginal product of capital in alternative uses, and channel funds in such as a way as to give priority to high-productivity projects.

ii. By operating efficiently (at lowest cost per dollar of funds intermediated), it can increase σ.

iii. Finally, the combination of high return on investments and low intermediation costs means a potentially large return to savers, which may increase s.

We conclude that a well-functioning financial system can foster economic growth. Moreover, these effects are interactive. In other words, the positive effects of efficient financial intermediation on growth tend to reinforce each other.

c. Effects of Financial Development on Growth: Evidence

In recent years, substantial evidence has accumulated in support of the proposition that a deep and well-functioning financial system is conducive to faster long-run growth. This evidence has taken the form of cross-country growth regressions, country case studies, industry studies, and studies of the effects of structural adjustment programs supported by the World Bank.

Several studies have examined the effect of financial development on growth using a cross-country growth framework. The methodology involves adding an indicator of the adequacy of financial intermediation either to the core growth regression mentioned in Chapter 1 or to one that includes other potential policy determinants of growth, such as openness, government size, the conduct of monetary policy, etc. A large number of variables have been used as proxies for financial development. The list includes:

i. Indicators of financial depth, such as the ratios of narrow ($M1$) and broad ($M2$) money, of quasi-money, and of liquid liabilities (currency outside banks plus demand and interest-bearing liabilities of banks and nonbank financial intermediaries) to GDP.

ii. The share of financial intermediation done by commercial banks (measured by the ratio of deposit money bank domestic assets to the domestic assets of deposit money banks and the central bank together, as in King and Levine 1992, 1993).

iii. The volume of lending to the private sector, measured by ratio of the flow of credit to the private sector to GDP, as in De Gregorio and Guidotti (1996), or by the share of total domestic banking system credit extended to the private (as opposed to the public) sector (King and Levine 1992, 1993).

The most comprehensive study of the cross-country type that addressed the robustness issue raised about such studies in Chapter 1 is that by King and Levine (1993). These authors found, in a sample of seventy-seven countries with data averaged from 1960 to 1989, that their financial indicators were closely correlated with each other as well as with measures of GDP growth, capital accumulation, and total factor productivity. In standard cross-country growth regressions applied to each of these growth indicators, they found that, when entered separately, the average value of each of the financial indicators was statistically significant at the 5 percent level. These results were confirmed with pooled cross section-time series regressions using decade averages and instrumental variables techniques to deal with the reverse causation problem. They also found that initial financial depth helped to explain subsequent growth performance, again using a variety of indicators both of growth as well as of financial depth. All of these results tended to be robust across samples of countries and time periods, as well as with respect to the set of other explanatory variables included in the regressions.

More recently, Levine (1996) used the same sample, but with data averaged over the full period, to conduct a more extensive study of the effects of financial variables on growth. He estimated three cross-country regressions of the form:

$$g(j) = \alpha_0 + \alpha_1 F(j) + \alpha_i X(ij) + \epsilon_j,$$

in which the dependent variable $g(j)$ referred successively to growth of income per capita, of the capital stock, and of total factor productivity in country j, F

was a vector of four financial indicators (used one at a time), $X(ij)$ a matrix of control variables (including initial income per capita, initial education, political stability, as well as indicators of exchange rate, trade, fiscal, and monetary policy). In each regression all financial variables were statistically significant and economically important, indicating that improved financial sector performance enhances growth both by improving total factor productivity growth as well as by inducing more factor accumulation, as suggested by our model.

d. The Financial Accelerator

Finally, the analysis of this chapter points to a mechanism through which financial variables can aggravate short-run macroeconomic instability, referred to as the "financial accelerator." Because macroeconomic cycles tended to be accompanied by swings in the net worth of firms, and because these swings in net worth cause the external finance premium to move in the opposite direction (countercyclically), balance-sheet effects on firms will cause borrowing to move procyclically. This tends to aggravate the severity of macroeconomic shocks, and thus aggravate macroeconomic instability.

Also, phenomena such as deflation or exchange rate devaluation can, when debt is unindexed, result in a contraction of net worth that sharply increases the premium on external finance. The Great Depression in the United States may have been an example of the former. As we shall see in Chapter 19, the crises that many emerging market economies experienced during the 1990s provided several examples of the latter.

VII. SUMMARY

This chapter has provided an overview of the economic role of the financial system, laying the basis for the discussion of financial sector policies to come in the following chapters. We have seen that financial transactions take place for the same reason other economic transactions do: to exploit mutually advantageous trades. While in an ideal world these transactions are costless and result in efficient market allocations, imperfect information and opportunistic behavior make financial intermediation a costly activity (i.e., one that absorbs resources) in the real world. Costs of financial intermediation include brokerage, evaluation, monitoring, and contract enforcement costs. These give rise to external finance premia. Banks and other financial intermediaries arise to exploit profit opportunities that exist in the form of external financial premia.

While financial intermediaries are in business to make profits, a well-functioning financial sector enhances economic welfare by decreasing the real resources, per unit of intermediation, that society has to devote to coping with the problems posed by imperfect information and opportunistic behavior. A well-functioning financial system can also enhance economic growth by allocating capital more efficiently, including to risky, high-return projects, by increasing the resources available for investment out of a given amount of saving, and by improving the incentives to save in the form of higher risk-adjusted rates of return for savers. But achieving these benefits depends on the stance of public policy. Public policy can help through the adoption of institutional and macroeconomic policies that create an enabling environment, through the specific development of market infrastructure for financial intermediation, as well as through specific policies to cope with special problems of the financial sector.

In the next three chapters we will analyze policies toward the financial sector more explicitly, before turning in Chapter 15 to the interaction between financial sector and macroeconomic policies that arises in the context of capital inflows.

APPENDIX 11.1: FINANCIAL STRUCTURE IN SELECTED AFRICAN COUNTRIES

The summary description of financial structure in Sub-Saharan Africa is taken from Montiel (1996). It is based on a sample for five countries for which this information was available. These countries are:

a. Ghana

The formal financial system in Ghana consists of thirteen commercial and secondary banks, some small rural banks, twenty insurance companies (not regulated by the banking law), and a small (eleven listed companies) stock exchange, which began operations in November 1990 (see Kapur et al. 1991). As of the end of 1990, the three largest banks contained 73 percent of all bank deposits, and the government and the Social Security National Insurance Trust had a majority stake in eight of the thirteen banks. A large number of nonperforming assets led to an attempt to upgrade the financial system under a financial sector reform program which got under way in early 1988. According to Nissanke (1991), the informal financial sector plays an important role in Ghana, with informal financial saving amounting to about 2 percent of GDP. The functioning of the informal sector in Ghana is described by Aryeetey (1992).

b. Gambia

The financial system in Gambia consists of four commercial banks, a postal savings bank, two insurance companies, and the Social Security and Housing Finance Corporation. The largest bank was government-owned up to 1992 (it was sold in June of that year), and controls 44 percent of deposits. As in Ghana, restructuring of the assets of the financial system got under way in 1988 (see Hadjimichael, Rumbaugh, and Verreydt 1992).

c. Kenya

Kenya has a much larger financial sector than Ghana or Gambia, consisting of eighty-eight banks, many nonbank financial institutions, and a long-established, but still small, stock exchange. The largest commercial bank is government-owned. The banks and nonbanks are regulated separately, but a Deposit Protection Fund set up in 1986 protects deposits in both types of institutions.

d. Nigeria

Nigeria has a large banking system, consisting of 109 banks. The top five banks, however, account for 47 percent of all deposits. The federal and state governments control 40 percent of the commercial banks. There is a vigorous stock exchange, but most capital is still raised through the banking system.

e. Malawi

Malawi has two commercial banks, three development finance institutions, two finance houses, the New Building Society, the Post Office Savings Bank, some insurance companies, and the Malawi Union of Savings and Credit Cooperatives, an umbrella organization for fifty-eight credit unions.[7] Both commercial banks are government-controlled, and they held sixty-eight of the total assets of the formal financial system as of 1987. Little harmonization exists in the regulatory framework among the banks and nonbanks. Nissanke (1991) reports that informal sector lending to the private sector in Malawi was at least three times as great as that of the formal sector. Supporting evidence is provided by Chipeta and Mkandawire (1992).

f. Tanzania

The formal financial sector in Tanzania consists of three commercial banks, three near-banks, two insurance companies, and several development finance companies (Hyuha, Ndanshau, and Kipokola 1993). Though estimates of the relative size of the informal financial sector are not available, survey data collected by Hyuha et al. suggest that informal finance plays an important role in the economy.

[7] As reported by Nissanke (1991).

12

Financial Repression

Despite the contributions that an efficient financial system can make to economic welfare and growth, many developing countries have traditionally applied a combination of policies toward the financial sector that has impeded the functioning of their domestic financial systems. This policy package has become known as "financial repression." This chapter will describe this set of policies, and consider how they affect the functioning of the financial system, as well as how they may impinge on each of the channels through which the financial system can promote growth. We will also review some of the evidence on the growth effects of financial repression in developing countries. As we will see, a substantial amount of evidence has accumulated in various forms during recent years suggesting that financial repression has had harmful effects on economic growth.

In part because of this evidence, the view that financial repression is harmful for growth has carried the day among policymakers in emerging markets, and most emerging economies are in the process of revamping their policies toward the financial sector, a process known as financial liberalization. But this process has not proven to be an easy one. We will examine it in detail in the next chapter. As we will see there, a key question is what conditions have to be in place in the domestic economy in order for a liberalization of the domestic financial system to have a chance of being successful.

To answer this question, we have to consider why financial repression may have existed in the first place – what economic role financial repression plays in the domestic economy. This chapter will argue that the central motivation for financial repression has at bottom been a fiscal one. In effect, governments have relied on implicit taxation of the financial sector in part because of their difficulties in raising the resources they required through more conventional means.

This fiscal role of financial repression links this part of the book with the previous one. Just as the excessive reliance on seignorage or the emergence of a debt overhang reflects fiscal difficulties, placing an excessive burden of implicit taxation on the domestic financial sector can be viewed as yet another consequence of fiscal problems in emerging economies. In this chapter we will describe the fiscal effects of financial repression as well as techniques for the empirical measurement of the fiscal revenues derived from this set of policies toward the domestic financial sector.

I. THE INGREDIENTS OF FINANCIAL REPRESSION

We saw in Chapter 11 that in the early stages of financial development, commercial banks are likely to be the dominant domestic financial institutions, because of their comparative advantage in overcoming credit market imperfections. We also saw that the role of collateral in overcoming moral hazard problems, and of a well-functioning legal system in facilitating the enforcement of contracts, make formal financial institutions such as banks heavily dependent on the legal system. This dependence on the legal system makes formal banking activity highly visible to governments, and makes banks relatively easy to tax. Historically, developing-country governments have tended to tax the banking system both directly and indirectly. Indirect taxation has been levied through the mechanism of financial repression.

The set of policies characterized as financial repression includes the following:

i. *Controls of capital inflows and outflows.* Under financial repression, domestic residents are typically not allowed to hold foreign assets, and domestic firms are not permitted to borrow abroad. The implication is that financially repressed economics are typically characterized by financial autarky, and that foreign intermediaries cannot compete with the domestic financial industry. Thus, under financial repression we can think of the domestic financial sector as operating in conditions similar to those of any other domestic productive activity that is insulated from external competition through a system of prohibitive tariffs or quantitative restrictions.

ii. *Restrictions on entry into the formal financial sector.* Under financial repression, the domestic formal financial sector is not subject to free entry and exit, and many domestic banks may be publicly owned. These two conditions imply that the domestic financial sector does not typically operate under competitive conditions. Indeed, repressed banking sectors are typically dominated by a few banks, the largest of which are government-owned.[1]

iii. *High reserve and liquidity requirements on banks.* Banks are required to keep high reserve ratios, either as vault cash or on deposit with the central banks, and such deposits typically do not earn interest. In addition, they may be required to maintain "liquidity" ratios in the form of government securities which, though they pay interest, typically yield a return much lower than would be required for banks to choose to hold them voluntarily. Through both mechanisms, banks pay

---

[1] The appendix to Chapter 10 illustrates this situation in several African countries.

an implicit tax and lose the freedom to allocate a large share of their portfolios to productive loans.

iv. *Interest rate ceilings on bank assets and liabilities.* The interest rates that banks can pay on deposits, and that they can charge for their loans, are legally controlled in repressed financial systems. This means that banks cannot compete with each other on price, and cannot raise deposit rates in order to compete with nonbank intermediaries (informal financial markets or illegal capital flight) for resources. On the other side of their balance sheets, if interest rate ceilings on loans are binding, banks cannot allocate their loans on the basis of price, and are thus forced to engage in nonprice rationing of credit.

v. *Directed-credit restrictions on the composition of bank asset portfolios.* In addition to having to set aside a substantial portion of their portfolios as required reserves and to meet liquidity requirements, banks often have limited discretion over the allocation of their remaining funds, since they are typically forced to set aside designated shares of their lending portfolios for "priority" sectors or specific classes of firms, sometimes at preferential interest rates.

vi. *The use of bank credit ceilings as instruments of monetary control.* Under the circumstances described above, monetary policy has often been conducted by setting overall targets for total credit expansion by the domestic banking system, and then allocating this total among individual banks, thus restricting the amount of total credit that can be extended by each bank.

This set of policies obviously represents a severe set of restrictions on the entire process of domestic financial intermediation. It circumscribes the behavior of domestic borrowers and lenders, the number of firms that can engage in financial intermediation, as well as the behavior of firms that are already so engaged. In view of the important role of the domestic financial system in mobilizing and allocating resources described in the last chapter, the questions raised by such policies are what their implications for the functioning of the domestic economy might be, and why such a set of policies would be adopted in the first place.

From an economist's perspective, restrictions on financial intermediation such as those included in this package of policies would seem to preclude mutually advantageous trade in a variety of ways, and would thus be presumed to have adverse effects on economic welfare. It is hard to see how, under such tight restrictions on behavior, the domestic financial sector would retain the incentive and flexibility to respond to profit opportunities created by changes in the economic environment in a way that would have the effect of lowering the external finance premium. As we saw in the last chapter, this is the mechanism that drives financial development, and that enables the process of financial development to enhance economic welfare and facilitate economic growth.

It would be inappropriate to jump to this conclusion too readily, however, because imperfections in credit markets such as those described in the previous chapter suggest that *laissez faire* is not the appropriate standard of comparison to use in evaluating policies directed at the domestic financial system. These credit market imperfections may create a valid role for some types of government interventions in the domestic financial system. However, as we also saw in the last chapter, the interventions called for are those that address those imperfections directly. That is, the fact that *some* types of intervention may be justified by market imperfections does not mean that *any* intervention is justified. In the next chapter we will look in much more detail at precisely what types of interventions may make sense in light of the credit market imperfections that we have discussed.

As it happens, however, financial repression has *not* typically been motivated by the desire to address the problems created by credit market imperfections for the process of financial intermediation, and thus there is no particular reason to believe that such policies would tend to improve the functioning of the domestic financial system in light of credit market imperfections. In Section III, we will review the arguments for the view that the policies associated with financial repression indeed do substantial economic harm, and will also examine some of the empirical evidence on this issue. Before doing so, however, we need to ask: if financial repression has not typically been directed at the amelioration of the effects of credit market imperfections, and if such policies may indeed be harmful, then why have they been adopted?

II. FISCAL ROOTS OF FINANCIAL REPRESSION

In this section we will argue that the key reasons have been *fiscal* in origin. Financial repression affects both the expenditure and financing sides of the public sector's budget. It permits the nonfinancial public sector to engage in industrial policies (i.e., to favor some economic activities over other) without the expenditure of fiscal resources, and to borrow more cheaply than it could otherwise do. How does this work?

a. Financial Repression as a Fiscal Phenomenon

One way to view the set of policies that constitute financial repression is as follows: the restrictions on the behavior of bank customers and potential competitors (capital account restrictions and restrictions on entry into the domestic financial sector) have the effect of creating monopoly rents for the existing banks. Some portion of these rents is then effectively taxed away by the government through the restrictions that repression imposes on the behavior of the "protected" banks themselves.

For example, restrictions on capital inflows and outflows insulate the domestic financial system from external competition. Restrictions on capital outflows prevent the public from taking their savings abroad, thus creating a captive demand for the liabilities of the domestic financial system, while restrictions on inflows create a captive market for domestic bank loans. In effect, they make the demand curves for bank assets and liabilities less elastic by eliminating access to close substitute sources of funds as well as substitute saving vehicles. Restrictions on entry into the domestic financial industry, on the other hand, allow domestic banks to collude, thus exploiting their collective monopoly position in domestic financial intermediation.

The result of these restrictions is to create large potential wedges between bank borrowing and lending rates. Under financial repression, however, a substantial portion of this wedge is captured by the government, rather than by the banks themselves. How does this work?

i. High reserve and liquidity requirements create an artificially high demand from domestic banks for the high-powered money issued by the public sector and for public sector securities. The former increases the base on which the public sector collects seignorage revenue, while the latter reduces the interest rate that the public sector must pay on its securities, thus lowering its borrowing costs through the issuance of securities.
ii. Interest rate ceilings on loans directly reduce the cost for the nonfinancial public sector to borrow in the form of bank credit and advances from private banks.
iii. Directed credit policies permit the government to engage in industrial policy – that is, to favor specific economic activities over others – by granting them access to credit at subsidized rates, rather than by paying them explicit subsidies that would need to be financed through the public sector's budget.

b. Financial Repression and Seignorage

To see how the first of these channels operates, we need to modify the public sector solvency analysis of Part 3 of the book to take into account the existence of banks. Recall that the analysis of seignorage issues was based on a financial structure in which the central bank issued currency that was held by the public directly, and the public sector issued securities that were sold in an open market. In that context, seignorage revenue was given by $(\pi + g)m$, where m was the stock of central bank liabilities. In Part 3, central bank liabilities were equated with the money stock. However, when banks are accounted for, the two concepts are no longer equivalent. Central bank liabilities are referred to as the *monetary base*, or *high-powered money* (call it H, so m would be replaced above by $h = H/PY$). The central bank's balance sheet thus becomes:

$$sR^* + DC = H. \qquad (12.1)$$

Money, on the other hand, consists of currency held by the public plus demand deposits (checking account balances at banks). The latter are the liabilities not of the central bank, but of the commercial banks. The conceptual basis for this definition of money is that it consists of all assets that can be used directly to make payments. It is sometimes called *narrow money*, or M1, to distinguish it from definitions that also include assets that can easily be converted into means of payment.

What is the relationship between money defined this way and the monetary base? As we have already noted, commercial banks typically have to hold some fraction (call it RR_D) of their deposits as reserves. These can be held in the form of currency (a central bank liability) or deposits at the central bank (which are, of course, also central bank liabilities). Thus, total central bank liabilities H consist of currency held by the public (call this CU) plus commercial bank reserves:

$$H = CU + RR_D DD, \qquad (12.2)$$

where DD is total demand deposits. Money, on the other hand, is given by:

$$M = CU + DD. \qquad (12.3)$$

To see what impact financial repression has on H (and thus on h and on seignorage revenue $[\pi + g]h$), we need to examine how it affects the demand for H, a simple form of which is given by equation (12.2). To inject more realism into the analysis, we need to take into account that other types of deposits are also subject to reserve requirements. Including reserve requirements on time deposits (savings accounts), for example, makes the demand for H:

$$H = CU + RR_D DD + RR_T TD, \qquad (12.4)$$

where TD is the stock of time deposits. Now all we need to do is to specify the demands for CU, DD, and TD. To be concrete, consider the following asset-demand model:[2]

$$CU/PY = f_C(\pi, i_D, i_T) \qquad (12.5a)$$
$$\underset{-\;-\;-}{}$$

$$DD/PY = f_D(\pi, i_D, i_T) \qquad (12.5b)$$
$$\underset{-\;+\;-}{}$$

$$TD/PY = f_T(\pi, i_D, i_T), \qquad (12.5c)$$
$$\underset{-\;-\;+}{}$$

where i_D and i_T are interest rates paid by banks on demand and time deposits respectively. These are standard portfolio demands similar to the ones we used earlier in the model of Part 2. Inflation is assumed to reduce the demand for all nominal financial assets. On the other hand, an increase in its own rate of return increases the demand for each asset, while an increase in the rate of return on a substitute

---

[2] The model is from Anand and Van Wijnbergen (1989).

asset reduces that demand. Substituting these asset demands into equation (12.2) we now have:

$$H = f_C(\pi, i_D, i_T)PY + RR_D\, f_D(\pi, i_D, i_T)PY + RR_T\, f_T(\pi, i_D, i_T)PY. \quad (12.6)$$

Now we can see what happens to H under financial repression. Recall that under financial repression RR_D and RR_T would both tend to be high, while i_D and i_T would both be low. Thus:

i. An increase in either reserve ratio would increase the demand for H, given the values of the other variables.

ii. A reduction in i_T would tend to *reduce* the demand for H through the last term on the right (because it reduces the demand for time deposits), but to *increase* it through the first two terms (the demands for currency and demand deposits). What is the net effect? In principle, the effect is ambiguous. It depends on whether time deposits are better substitutes for assets held inside or outside the formal financial system. What might the latter consist of? Recalling the model of Part 2, the answer is primarily foreign assets, not included in the reformulation above. But this is precisely what capital controls prevent from happening. Thus, with capital controls in place, reductions in ^iTD would be likely to go primarily into CU and DD. Given that CU has an implicit reserve requirement of unity (to hold a unit of currency one has to hold a unit of high-powered money), H would tend to rise.

iii. A reduction in i_D would reduce demand for DD and thus indirectly for H, but because demand deposits are transactions balances, these funds would likely go into the other asset that can be used as a means of payment, namely CU, which carries a higher reserve requirement. Again, the demand for H would rise if currency and demand deposits are close substitutes.

The conclusion is that high values of RR_D and RR_T, as well as low values of i_D and i_T, all of which are associated with financial repression, would be conducive to higher values of H and thus to high values of seignorage revenue $(\pi + g)h$, for a given rate of inflation π.

c. Fiscal Revenues from Financial Repression

The second mechanism through which the government receives revenues from financial repression is through a reduction in its borrowing costs, either through lower interest rates on bank credit than would prevail otherwise or through mandatory holdings of government securities by domestic financial institutions. Since these securities are not held willingly, they must pay a lower interest rate than would be required for banks to hold them voluntarily. Giovannini and de Melo (1993)

Table 12.1. *Financial Repression Tax Revenue in 24 Countries*

	Tax Revenue as Percent of GDP	Tax Revenue as Percent of Total Tax Revenue	Implicit Tax Rate
Algeria	4.30	11.42	10.6
Brazil	0.48	1.57	13.4
Colombia	0.24	2.11	22.4
Costa Rica	2.33	12.76	25.1
Greece	2.53	7.76	16.0
India	2.86	22.38	11.0
Indonesia	0.00	0.00	0.0
Jamaica	1.38	4.74	7.4
Jordan	0.60	2.40	7.2
Korea	0.25	1.36	6.0
Malaysia	0.12	0.31	0.5
Mexico	5.77	39.65	45.8
Morocco	2.31	8.89	16.1
Pakistan	3.23	20.50	25.3
Panama	0.69	2.49	4.4
Papua New Guinea	0.40	1.90	5.6
Philippines	0.45	3.88	11.9
Portugal	2.22	6.93	15.8
Sri Lanka	3.40	19.24	14.5
Thailand	0.38	2.57	4.3
Tunisia	1.49	4.79	13.4
Turkey	2.20	10.89	55.8
Zaire	0.46	2.48	54.5
Zimbabwe	5.52	19.13	19.5

Source: Giovannini and de Melo 1993.

have recently estimated the magnitude of the revenues derived from this source for a sample of twenty-four developing countries during the period 1972–87. They estimated it by taking the difference between the *ex post* cost to the government of borrowing abroad (including capital gains or losses arising from exchange rate changes) and its cost of borrowing domestically in the same period, multiplied by the average stock of domestic debt held by the private sector in that period.

The estimates of financial repression tax revenues derived by Giovannini and de Melo are presented in Table 12.1. As is evident from the fourth column of the table, the implicit financial repression tax rate (the difference between the foreign and domestic interest rates, as a percentage of the former) is very high in some countries, with the implication that, when domestic debt outstanding is also high, the financial repression tax can loom large compared to conventional sources of government revenue (shown in the third column). On the average, for the countries in this sample the financial repression tax amounted to about 2 percent of GDP and about 9 percent of tax revenue. Thus, the magnitudes involved can be quite substantial.

Chamley and Honohan (1990) estimated a broader concept of the magnitude of taxation of the financial sector, including not just the implicit tax on the interest rate on domestic government securities, but also the inflation tax, the implicit tax on required reserves imposed by the fact that these reserves are remunerated at less than market rates, the implicit tax imposed by loan interest rate ceilings, and indirect taxes on the financial sector. They calculated the inflation tax as the product of the inflation rate and the stock of currency in the hands of the public, the implicit tax on required reserves as the gap between an estimated market interest rate and the rate of remuneration on reserves (usually zero) times the stock of reserves, the implicit tax on government borrowing as the gap between market interest rate and the interest rate actually paid on government debt, and the implicit tax on lending to nongovernment borrowers as the gap between an estimated market interest rate and the controlled loan rate. They also took into account indirect taxes on financial intermediaries. Thus, they estimated the volume of resources extracted from the financial system by using the following formula:

$$TAX = (R^* - 0.01)^* CURRENCY + (R^* - RRES)^* RESERVES + (R^* - RTB)^*$$
$$GOVTBOR + (R^* - RTB + MARGIN)^* NONGOVTBOR + INDIRECT\ TAXES$$

Here R^* is an estimate of the market-clearing risk-free interest rate that would prevail without interest rate ceilings, $RRES$ is the rate of remuneration on reserves, RTB is the bank lending rate, $MARGIN$ is an assumed risk premium for private borrowers, and $GOVTBOR$ and $NONGOVTBOR$ are the stocks of loans outstanding to the government and nongovernment sectors, respectively. They used several methods for estimating "shadow" market interest rates, including the rate on foreign borrowing (as in Giovannini and de Melo) and a nominal rate calculated by adding an assumed real interest rate of 1 percent to the observed rate of inflation.

Chamley and Honohan calculated tax rates for five African countries during the decade 1978–88. Their findings were similar to those of Giovannini and de Melo. Specifically, they found that the taxes on the formal financial sector that they measured were in the range of 4–7 percent of GDP for Ghana, Nigeria, and Zambia during this period, and in the range of 2 percent of GDP for Cote D'Ivoire and Kenya, compared with explicit tax revenue in the range of 10–25 percent of GDP for most Sub-Saharan African countries. Most importantly, they found that the average tax collected was in all cases greater than the value added of the banking system, and in the case of the three high-tax countries, was a multiple of banking system value added, even after excluding seignorage on currency in the hands of the public, a portion of taxation that does not fall on banks. These findings led them to conclude that the financial sector has been very heavily taxed compared with other sectors.

These results are supported by those of Ikhide (1992), who focused only on implicit taxation in the form of unremunerated reserve requirements in eight

Sub-Saharan African countries. He found that such reserves were significantly higher in the eight countries in his sample than is typical in OECD countries, and that the implicit tax on the financial sector just from this source ranged from about 1.5 percent of GDP in Tanzania to about 7.5 percent in Ethiopia. In five of the eight countries he examined, this amounted to more than a quarter of government revenue.

III. FINANCIAL REPRESSION AND GROWTH

We saw in Chapter 11 that economic theory gives us reason to believe that an efficient domestic financial system can help to promote economic growth by improving the efficiency of resource allocation, by freeing up resources that would otherwise be used in intermediation to produce other goods and services, and by encouraging accumulation through the higher rates of return that such a system could offer to domestic savers. The empirical evidence reviewed in Chapter 11 was consistent with the proposition that financial depth is conducive to faster economic growth. In this section we will review what theory and evidence have to say about the effects of financial repression on economic growth.

a. Financial Repression and Growth: Theory

To analyze the effects of financial repression on growth suggested by economic theory, we can go back to the small growth model that we used in the last chapter. Recall that in that model, the growth rate of productive capacity could be expressed as:

$$\Delta Y/Y = A\sigma s,$$

where A was a measure of total factor productivity, σ was an indicator of the efficiency of the financial system (in the sense of resources used by the sector), and s measured the ratio of saving to GDP. How are each of these components likely to be affected by the policies associated with financial repression?

1. Effects on Efficiency of Allocation

i. *Restrictions on competition* may impair allocative efficiency because state-owned and -protected banks will not have the competitive incentives to screen and monitor borrowers closely.

ii. The appropriation of funds by the public sector through the maintenance of high reserve requirements means that a portion of household saving will be channeled into government spending. To the extent that the government consumes these resources, σ will fall. To the extent that they are invested in public capital, the associated projects may not yield returns in excess of the foregone investment in the private sector.

iii. *Interest rate ceilings* on loans prevent the system from allocating capital to the most productive uses. Whether interest rates are controlled at below-market levels or not, banks have to screen prospective credit applicants. Interest rate ceilings prevent price-based allocation of funds (i.e., the weeding out of unproductive projects because they cannot yield a rate of return high enough to service the debt accumulated in financing them), leading to credit rationing, which may result in funds being allocated according to arbitrary criteria by individual banks. Moreover, low interest rates in the formal financial system are likely to create an informal financial market. When formal and informal financial markets coexist and some firms have unlimited access to the formal market, the marginal product of capital in these "favored" firms will fall below the cost of borrowing in the informal system. Capital may thus be misallocated both among firms that have access to the formal market, and between firms that have access to that market and those that do not.

iv. *Interest rate ceilings on deposits* may also cause funds to be misallocated through disintermediation – that is, by misallocating funds between the formal financial system and other types of financial intermediation. Their effect is to channel domestic saving into relatively unproductive investment by the savers themselves, into the informal financial system, or abroad.

v. The use of *directed credit* forces institutions to lend to projects that may not meet a market test, in other words, to those that may yield lower rates of return than alternative activities.

vi. Finally, the use of *bank credit ceilings* as an instrument of monetary control also reduces the efficiency of capital allocation, by misallocating funds among banks. Ceilings on individual banks, applied uniformly, prevent lending from being reallocated to the banks that have the most productive investment opportunities available to them.

Because all of these policies would tend to allocate resources in ways that fail to maximize social returns, we would expect their presence to result in a reduced value of total factor productivity in the economy.

2. Effects on the Costs of Intermediation

i. Restrictions on *capital flows* as well as restrictions on *entry* limit the scope of competition in the formal financial system, removing an important incentive to reduce costs. This tends to divert to factors of production employed in the formal financial system resources that would otherwise have been intended for investment.

ii. Measures such as *directed credit*, or the *imposition of reserve and liquidity requirements*, in addition to distorting the allocation of funds, function like a tax on financial intermediaries. This diverts resources to the government that would otherwise have been intended for investment.

iii. Policies such as *ceilings on deposit interest rates* or *credit ceilings on individual banks*, that reduce the rates of return offered to domestic savers in the domestic formal financial system and thus reduce the *scale* of formal domestic financial intermediation, compressing the size of the domestic financial system, tend to limit the size of scale economies, as well as to channel funds through the informal sector, which may be less efficient due to smaller economies of scale and scope. Both of these thus increase the costs of operating the domestic financial system.

3. Effects Through Returns to Accumulation

Finally, with a less efficient allocation of funds and higher costs of operation, the formal financial system would be forced to offer a lower return to savers under financial repression, even if deposit interest rate ceilings were not binding. In terms of the growth model, this may show up as a reduction in s (if savers respond to the lower rates of return available to them by saving less).

Recall that these channels of influence are not independent. In the basic model described above, for example, the adverse consequences of costs of financial intermediation for the growth rate depend on the volume of resources to be intermediated (s), as well as on the productivity of the investment foregone (A).

b. Financial Repression and Growth: Evidence

There is a substantial body of evidence examining the growth effects of financial repression. One strand of this evidence takes the cross-country approach that has become familiar from previous applications in this book. The methodology essentially involves estimating the determinants of capacity growth using a cross-country sample, and testing for the independent effects of financial repression after controlling for other growth determinants. For example, Roubini and Sala-i-Martin (1992) use a real interest rate dummy, the reserve ratio, and inflation as indicators of financial repression. They control for the standard Barro-type growth determinants in cross-country regressions, and test to see whether their proxies for financial repression enter the equation with the expected sign and with precisely estimated coefficients. They find that all of their indicators of financial repression were negatively and significantly related to growth in their cross-country study.

There is also substantial case study evidence on this issue, much of it focusing on the experience of countries that have liberalized previously repressed financial systems. Unfortunately, because this research of necessity adopts a before-and-after methodology, failing to control for other determinants, it has proven to be controversial and inconclusive.

IV. FINANCIAL REPRESSION IN THE "MIRACLE" ASIAN ECONOMIES

Theory and cross-country evidence thus lead us to the conclusion that financial repression is harmful for economic growth. And indeed, the financial sectors of many low-income countries have suffered from financial repression for a long time. However, matters are not quite so straightforward, because financial repression has not just been evident in countries that have been unsuccessful in sustaining extended periods of rapid economic growth. Some of the most successful economies in the world – the "miracle" economies of East and Southeast Asia – have also pursued financial sector policies that have many of the characteristics of financial repression. A handful of dynamic economies in this region have achieved what many other developing economies have sought: rapid, equitable, and reasonably stable growth sustained for long periods of time. Before leaving the topic of financial repression, then, it is worth asking the question: if financial repression is so harmful for growth, and if these countries have indeed repressed their financial systems, how did they manage to grow so fast?

Understanding the contributions of policy to generating the "East Asia miracle" has long been a high priority for development economists. The interpretation of the experience of these countries, however, has been fraught with controversy. Among the unsettled issues, we know that these countries have attained remarkable levels of saving and investment, but do not know exactly how, and economists disagree about the contribution that gains in total factor productivity have made to East Asian growth performance. The role of the financial system is central to both phenomena since, as we have seen, it both provides the incentives for private agents to accumulate and allocates saving among competing investment opportunities. Here too, however, lessons from the experience of East Asia have not been easy to distill. Specifically, to what extent can East Asia's accumulation and productivity performances be related to the financial policies pursued by these countries? Does the experience of the East Asian countries confirm the virtues or the vices of financial repression?

a. Financial Policies in the Asian "Miracle" Economies

Japan was, of course, the first spectacularly successful economy in East Asia, followed by the "four tigers" of Korea, Taiwan, and the two city states of Hong Kong and Singapore. Because of Japan's leadership position, it is useful to briefly review the role of the financial sector during Japan's economic take-off before considering its common elements with the financial policies of other countries in the region.

The Japanese financial system was restructured in 1950–55. The goal of the restructuring was essentially to organize the system so as to support the government's industrial policies. Parts of the system were oriented to providing long-term finance so as to encourage firms' taking advantage of dynamic economies of scale and to provide industrial infrastructure, while other parts were focused on combating unemployment by lending to traditional and low-productivity sectors (such as declining industries) and to support small firms, all while safeguarding the stability of the financial system itself. An important part of the new system was policy-based lending through the Trust Bureau of the Ministry of Finance, which managed the funds raised by the postal savings system. The latter had over 20,000 branches throughout the country. The growing modern sector of the economy was financed by the private financial system, while the declining traditional system was financed through the government at regulated rates.

Japan's private financial system was dominated by banks. Limitations were placed on the development of securities issues and secondary securities markets. Bond issuance was limited to government enterprises, public utilities, and a few other selected corporations, and bonds were sold through negotiation, rather than competitive bidding. The domestic securities market was thus underdeveloped, with a limited role for direct lending. Restrictions on foreign capital inflows and outflows were in place throughout Japan's rapid growth period.

Markets for banking services in Japan were legally segmented (both functionally and geographically), since financial institutions were specialized by type and size of borrower as well as depositor. A small number of large wholesale banks were nationwide in scope, and dealt with governments as well as large corporations. None of these banks were controlled by private shareholders. Smaller banks served local and regional markets. The system contained both private and government-owned banks, and their number remained roughly stable for the subsequent forty years. Specialized institutions grew up or were created to serve small family businesses and agriculture, while governments created specialized institutions to serve exporters and priority sectors. Nationwide banks were limited as to the number of branches they could open, so markets for banking services were segmented geographically as well.

Commercial banks have also dominated the financial systems of Korea and Taiwan.[3] Bond and equity markets were thus underdeveloped in all three of these "miracle" economies. As in Japan, these markets tended to follow, rather than lead, the economic take-off in Korea and Taiwan. Also as in Japan, during most of the period of rapid economic growth in each of these countries the number of major banks was small, entry into the banking sector was restricted, and the capital account of the balance of payments was relatively closed. In all three countries the ownership of banks was widely dispersed among industrial enterprises, other domestic institutions, and individuals. In Japan they were controlled by managers, and in

---

[3] For a description of the financial systems in these economies, see Patrick and Park (1994).

Korea by the government. In Taiwan until 1991 the major banks were owned and controlled by the government, while four smaller commercial banks were owned by private individuals.

Interest rates were controlled in all of these countries, with large margins between borrowing and lending rates. Though financial repression in the form of interest rate ceilings was not as severe in these "miracle" economies as in many other developing countries, it was severe enough that all three countries at one time had (and Korea and Taiwan still have) flourishing informal markets. In Japan, the formal system displaced a previously existing informal system, while in Korea and Taiwan the informal system survived in parallel with the formal system, as a consequence of financial repression.

Directed credit was an important component of government policy in these economies. All three countries used the financial system to encourage exports and to promote specific sectors in the context of their industrial policies. However, the application of directed credit policies varied among these countries. In Korea, for example, credit policy involved much heavier subsidization than in Japan. Commercial banks had been nationalized in Korea during the early 1960s, and the central bank law was changed to make it subordinate to the government. Both commercial as well as development banks were owned by the government and were involved in the administration of directed credit, responding to government directives to channel funds to priority sectors. Though controlled interest rates were doubled in 1965, this may have served primarily to transfer funds from informal markets to the banks and thus to increase the Korean government's control over credit allocation. In the 1960s, these credit allocations were directed at promoting exports, without much sectoral bias, and the performance of supported firms was closely monitored. In the 1970s, however, policy-based lending switched to supporting the "heavy and chemical industries" industrialization drive, and in the 1980s to supporting declining industries, as in Japan. Policy loans amounted to about 60 percent of assets for deposit money banks throughout the period, and mainly went to the manufacturing sector. Unlike Japan, Korea depended heavily on central bank credit and bank deposits for mobilizing funds. In Japan, government sources of funds dominated, and foreign loans were also very important, but the latter were also allocated by the government.

As in Japan, banks were closely supervised in Korea and Taiwan. However, bank regulation tended to be concerned primarily with the safety of the system. Stability was achieved through limitations on competition, and cartel-like behavior among banks was not discouraged. Prudential supervision was inadequate by the standards of fully liberalized systems. Because public disclosure was required only of the small number of firms listed on stock exchanges and the reliability of financial data available even to insiders of private unlisted companies was questionable, banks typically required loans to be heavily collateralized by real assets, and problems of assessing creditworthiness led to the prevalence of "relationship" banking in all three countries. Though legal deposit insurance was not present during the high-growth period in any of these economies, the banking system was perceived as implicitly insured by the government. In short, all three countries have had very safe but not very competitive systems. In spite of this, portfolio allocation has traditionally been very risk-averse and, especially in the case of Taiwan, overly concerned with collateral. Bank failures were minimal until the second half of the 1990s.

b. Financial Repression and Growth in East Asia: Hypotheses

Financial repression and directed credit thus appear to have been an important part of the story in three of the most successful East Asian economies. These characteristics do not seem to suggest that the financial systems in these countries would have been a key force driving either high saving rates (by offering attractive returns) or high rates of growth of productivity (by allocating resources to dynamic sectors on the basis of market criteria). What does the evidence tell us about the role of financial sector policies in the growth experience of these countries? In particular, did the "miracle" economies of Asia grow as fast as they did *despite* or *because* of financial repression?

The argument that they did so *despite* financial repression would go as follows: though financial repression is generally harmful and was actually harmful in these economies, it was not *very* harmful. The countries did not actually have the institutional mechanisms in place to operate a liberalized financial system (what these are is discussed in Chapter 13), and given that constraint, because of the way that repression was managed in these countries, they might actually have been better off with repressed systems than with liberalized ones. The aspects of the way that financial repression was managed that reduced its costs were the following:

i. Financial repression was mild because the stable macroeconomic environment (low inflation) and competitive real exchange rate kept the gap between the controlled and market-clearing interest rates small, so savers did not face excessively distorted real interest rates. The World Bank (1993), for example, emphasized that financial repression in the "miracle" economies differed from that elsewhere in that it was moderate, without very negative real interest rates, it was undertaken in context of financial stability rather than as the unintended consequence of rapid inflation, and in that bank regulators tended to squeeze spreads, ensuring that low deposit rates were passed on to borrowers.
ii. The system emphasized security of financial institutions, which may have been as important to savers as rates of return.
iii. A relatively small share of credit was influenced by policy-based lending (except for Korea).

Moreover, directed credit policies discouraged lending for consumption (which encouraged saving) and encouraged lending based on market-friendly performance criteria (exports), which enhanced productivity. Systems in Japan, Korea, and Taiwan channeled resources into infrastructure and productive business uses, and away from housing and consumer credit. By restricting credit to households and small firms due to the extreme risk aversion of managers of financial institutions, it may have indirectly stimulated saving by such agents. In addition, by allocating credit on the basis of export performance (in response to government directives), the regime was indirectly using a market-based test which may have particularly favored the most competitive and dynamic activities.

The argument that these countries grew fast *because* of financial repression is really a variation on the previous one that places much more emphasis on the positive contribution that may have been made to economic growth by the specific industrial policies that these countries implemented through the use of directed credit. It has two parts:

i. Liberalization would have been harmful, given the domestic institutional constraints, as mentioned above, and:
ii. Industrial policy was growth-promoting, because of the role of dynamic scale economies, and policy-based lending was a superior way of implementing it.

The second point is what really distinguishes the second interpretation from the first. Since the countries grew so quickly, the question is whether the way that directed credit was managed in these economies minimized the harm it might conceivably have done, or whether it was actually a key ingredient of these economies' success.

This point has two components: that industrial policies were productive, and that directed credit was a good way to implement them. As to the first, the case for industrial policies can be (and has been) based on a variety of arguments. For example, one view holds that if complementary industrial activities exhibit increasing returns, government industrial policy can play an important coordinating role. Alternatively, some observers of the east Asian "miracle" have argued for the presence of positive externalities in some activities, such as exporting. Such externalities would justify a government role in the encouragement of exports.

But why would directed credit be a good way of implementing such industrial policies? Among the arguments that have been offered are that because of asymmetric information, banks may tend to offer funds to firms that have collateral, available internal funds, or good track records, rather than to those that have the best investment opportunities. This may create a role for the support of credit to small- and medium-sized firms. Alternatively, subsidized loans may provide the firms that benefit from them with greater incentives to perform than would outright subsidies, or loans may provide superior monitoring benefits than subsidies. Finally, the implicit "financial repression" tax used to fund such loans may be less distortionary than the relevant explicit taxes required to finance outright fiscal subsidies would have been.

c. Financial Repression and Growth in East Asia: Evidence

What light does the evidence shed on these interpretations of the role of financial repression in the growth experience of the Asian "miracle" economies? We can break the evidence down into several components.

1. Financial Deepening and Growth

First, consistent with the cross-country evidence discussed in Chapter 11, financial deepening actually accompanied real growth in Japan, Korea, and Taiwan (i.e., the ratio of financial assets such as broad money to GDP increased as incomes rose). Thus, it proved possible to achieve high rates of expansion of the financial sector without liberalization of the financial system. This certainly is consistent with the view that the initial distortions were not excessively harmful, and that these economies were successful in spite of financial repression simply because they did not overdo it.

The key question, however, is whether policy helped to ease the severity of financial repression, which fostered financial deepening and contributed to growth, or whether financial deepening was simply driven by fast growth. This is the familiar direction-of-causality problem that we have encountered before. There is some indication, however, that financial deepening was not purely the result of rapid growth, but also responded to policies. This evidence is in the form of episodes in which the severity of financial repression varied due to events that could arguably be claimed to be exogenous. For example, the Korean ratio of financial assets to GDP was flat for a long period (1972–78) when inflation was rapid and real interest rates were negative, despite the rapid growth in GDP at this time. Once policy changed to bring inflation under control and liberalize the financial sector somewhat, the ratio resumed its increase. Japan had a similar experience in 1965–70, but Taiwan, which never allowed high inflation and had consistently higher real interest rates, did not. These episodes are at least suggestive of the possibility that changes in financial depth may have been affected by factors that respond to policy in the short run – such as the level of domestic real interest rates – rather than simply responding to economic growth.

2. Financial Policy and Saving Rates

Second, as we have seen, private saving rates were very high in these countries. They actually tended to increase over time. The difficulty is linking these high saving rates with policies directed to the financial sector. For example, there is no evidence that the increase necessarily had anything to do with policy-induced changes in the behavior of real interest rates in these economies. Indeed, the high saving rates in the region may have been due to a wide variety of factors. Prime candidates are rapid growth itself, as well as demographic transitions that took place in the East and

Southeast Asian regions.[4] They may also have been directly fostered by other policies. Governments encouraged saving through the pursuit of macroeconomic stability, through the way that banks were regulated, through restrictions on consumer credit, and through forced saving schemes.

Macroeconomic stability may have encouraged saving because, as we have seen, high inflation tends to be volatile, making real interest rates often negative and unpredictable. This increases the risk associated with financial saving. Moreover, by protecting banks from competition, the "miracle" economies may have made them safer, encouraging saving in the formal financial sector. These countries also made saving through formal financial institutions more convenient to small savers. Postal saving systems not only in Japan, Korea, and Taiwan, but also in Malaysia and Singapore, were designed to attract small savers by offering greater security and lower transaction costs than the informal sector. Restrictions on consumer credit in the context of financial repression, coupled with taxes on luxury goods, may also have encouraged saving. Mandatory saving schemes undoubtedly played a role as well. In some countries (Japan, Singapore, and Malaysia) the implementation of such provident funds may have made a particularly large contribution to saving rates (however, whether these encourage total saving depends on the extent to which they replace saving that would have happened anyway). Finally, these economies tended to have high public saving rates compared to other developing countries, which increased national saving rates directly.

A different perspective on saving behavior in these economies is offered by Singh (1995), who argues that high saving rates in the "miracle" economies of Asia did not reflect particularly high levels of *household* saving, but rather of *corporate* saving. These were the results of large corporate profits plus inducements and incentives for firms to retain earnings rather than pass them on to their shareholders. Large corporate profits were achieved by restrictions on domestic competition (in Japan and Korea) and through import protection (both in those countries as well as elsewhere in the region). Governments provided fiscal and other incentives for firms not to distribute these earnings as dividends, for example by taxing dividends and not taxing retained earnings or capital gains.[5]

Some panel-data econometric evidence compiled by Dayal-Gulati and Thimann (1997) attributes high saving rates among the "miracle" economies to macroeconomic stability, public saving, the presence of mandatory saving schemes, and financial deepening. Unfortunately, it does not identify the role of policies in

---

[4] Rapid growth can increase saving either through standard life cycle arguments that emphasize the higher share of income received by young savers in a growing economy or through habit effects (Carroll and Weil 1993).

[5] However, this argument would need to establish that households did not "pierce the corporate veil" – i.e., consider the savings of the corporations they owned to be their own savings, and thus reduce their own saving as corporate saving increased. Otherwise, national saving would be unaffected by whether saving is done by corporations or by households. Singh does not address this issue.

promoting financial deepening. In an overview of the issue of the determinants of high saving rates in these economies, Patrick (1994) concludes that we do not at present know the extent to which increases in saving rates and their mobilization through the financial system were due to growth, reduced inflation, higher real interest rates, the spread of financial institution offices, or other variables.

3. Financial Policies and Investment Rates

Turning to investment, private investment was much higher in the Asian "miracle" economies than in other middle-income economies, though public investment rates have not been very different.[6] We have already seen that directed credit policies tended to favor investment rather than consumption. But does that mean that high private investment rates were driven by the supply of funds – and thus by policy-directed lending – rather than by the demand for funds? The answer is that we cannot draw this conclusion too readily, because many other aspects of the policy environment also favored investment demand. Investment was in part fostered by macroeconomic stability and high growth itself. But it was also induced by secure property rights, complementary public investment in infrastructure, and policies that tended to reduce the cost of capital, such as tax policies that favored investment and low tariffs on imported capital goods. The relative contributions of all these factors to the high investment rates in the region remain to be sorted out.

4. Financial Policies and the Efficiency of Investment

A separate issue has to do with the efficiency of investment. This is a crucial issue in interpreting the roles of financial repression and directed credit, because if directed credit policies allocated capital to relatively unproductive uses, we would expect this to show up in low rates of total factor productivity growth in the region.

Unfortunately, the relative contributions of capital accumulation and total factor productivity growth to the exceptionally high growth rates of the "miracle" economies have not proved easy to sort out. A well-known study of the "miracle" economies by the World Bank (1993) concluded that accumulation accounted for about two-thirds of growth in incomes per capita among these countries on average, and growth in total factor productivity for the remaining third. The latter was still higher than in most other economies, however, both absolutely and as a share of output growth.

Two methodologies were used to address this issue in the Bank study. First, cross-country regressions were estimated for 113 countries, with per capita growth estimated as a function of the ratio of the country's per capita income in 1960 to that of the United States, the investment/GDP ratio, the rate of primary and secondary school enrollments in 1960, and the rate of growth of the economically

---

[6] However, public investment rates actually *rose* in these countries during the 1980s, in contrast to the experience of most other LDCs.

active population. This model accounted for about two-thirds of the actual growth in individual "miracle" economies on average. Primary school enrollment accounted for most of the growth, with physical investment second and secondary enrollment third. Still, most regional differences in growth remained unexplained (the model yielded a positive regional dummy for the Asian "miracle" economies, and negative ones for Latin America and Sub-Saharan Africa). The Bank concluded from the latter that the "miracle" economies must have been more successful in allocating resources to high-productivity activities, since the growth residuals would have tended to capture this phenomenon.

The Bank study also calculated TFP growth using a production function estimated for a sample of eighty-seven countries from 1960–89. The East Asian economies were found to have had high absolute levels of TFP growth. Hong Kong, Japan, Korea, Thailand, and Taiwan were in the top decile of countries in this regard. Indonesia, Malaysia, and Singapore were closer to the TFP growth rates of the high-income countries (about 1.5 percent per year) but were in the top third of all developing countries.

To see whether the "miracle" economies were catching up to international technological best practice, the study estimated growth residuals for each country using the estimated output elasticities of capital and labor for industrial countries, as well as the average rate of TFP growth for such countries (1.5 percent) over 1960–89 (the latter was taken to be a measure of the international rate of technological advance). The residual TFP growth for all the countries in its sample was then taken as a measure of the extent to which developing countries have been catching up to international technological best practice.

It found that TFP growth was in a fairly compact range, around 1.5 percent per year for the rich countries, presumably reflecting the common international rate of technological change, so that residuals for these countries were close to zero. It also found that among the "miracle" economies, Japan, Hong Kong, Taiwan, and Thailand were catching up in TFP levels with the industrial countries, in the sense that all of these countries had positive residuals (see also Page 1994). Korea was just keeping up with rich countries in its rate of TFP growth (i.e., it had a residual of approximately zero), while the investment-driven economies of Malaysia, Indonesia, and Singapore were falling behind. Still, even these countries were doing better than developing countries in other regions. For these economies, TFP growth provided a very small share of total output growth (TFP growth contributed less than 33 percent), while the others tend to look more like industrial countries (TFP growth contributed 30–50 percent of total output growth).

The main conclusion from the Bank study, as well as a subsequent study along the same lines by Page (1994) is that, while the growth story among the miracle economies is primarily one of accumulation, these economies were also good at allocation. Based on average world TFP growth, accumulation underpredicted growth for the "miracle" economies as a group. The fact that these countries had higher rates of productivity growth than 70 percent of all countries suggests that not only were they accumulating, but they were also using resources efficiently. How did they do so? The Bank study argues that good fundamentals and limited price distortions were important. It concludes that the industrial policies adopted in many of these countries made no difference, but that the export push adopted in all of them did, interacting with high levels of human capital (which facilitated acquisition of technological know-how) in a virtuous circle.

Bosworth and Collins (1996) also addressed the TFP growth controversy in the "miracle" economies. They based their interpretation on a study of eighty-eight countries over the period 1960–94. Using growth-accounting exercises, Bosworth and Collins found that growth in the "miracle" economies was mainly due to accumulation. They estimated TFP growth for the region over the whole period to be about 1.1 percent, about the same as for industrial countries excluding the United States, and only slightly higher than South Asia. Taiwan had particularly strong TFP growth, while TFP growth in the Philippines was particularly poor. By contrast, however, TFP growth was estimated to be negative in Africa and the Middle East, and zero in Latin America.

These results were supplemented by cross-country regressions. Growth in GDP per worker was regressed on initial GDP relative to that in the United States, life expectancy in 1960, years of schooling in 1965, the change in the terms of trade, and the standard deviation in the terms of trade. In this regression, regional dummies (using East Asia as reference) proved to be statistically significant for all developing country regions, but not for industrial countries. When the dependent variable was expressed in terms of growth of capital per worker, regional dummies again proved to be significant, but not when the dependent variable was TFP growth. Bosworth and Collins concluded that East Asia was mainly an outlier with respect to accumulation, not with respect to TFP growth.

To see the channels through which policy may have affected growth, Bosworth and Collins added the budget balance relative to GDP, the standard deviation of the real exchange rate, and the Sachs-Warner measure of trade openness to this regression. They found that fiscal surpluses promoted growth through capital accumulation, and that real exchange rate stability did so through productivity growth. Surprisingly, the Sachs-Warner trade measure, though strongly correlated with growth, was correlated with capital accumulation, not productivity growth. Inclusion of the policy variables tended to reduce the regional dummies by about a third, so these policy differences explained about a third of the otherwise unexplained growth gap between East Asia and the other developing-country regions.

Rodrik (1997) showed that estimates of the contribution to growth of total factor productivity would tend to be biased *downward* when the elasticity of substitution in production is less than unity, as long as technical change is biased toward "saving" (i.e., augmenting) the factor that is becoming relatively scarce (e.g., labor, when capital deepening is occurring), as seems plausible. Moreover, the bias is proportional to the extent of capital deepening, so it would be particularly severe for high-investing economies such as those in East Asia. In interpreting the growth experience of these countries, he also pointed out that an index of bureaucratic quality, as well as the ratio of years of schooling to initial GDP per person, tend to enter cross-country growth regressions significantly, and that East Asia is superior to all other regions with regard to the latter. This implies a high initial ratio of skilled labor to the capital stock in these countries, and thus a high return to capital that would account for the high subsequent rates of capital accumulation in the region.

Finally, Sarel (1997) expressed doubts about the "contrarian" view expressed by some economists that growth in East Asia has been almost entirely accumulation-driven, because the results of such measurements depend critically on capital stock, factor share, and labor aggregation estimates that are questionable. His own estimates, using perpetual inventory methods for estimating the capital stock starting in 1900, produced high estimates of capital stock growth and labor force participation for the East Asian countries, but also estimates of TFP growth that were very high for Korea, Taiwan, and Hong Kong (indeed, higher than in Japan), and not as high, but still respectable, for Singapore. Sarel found that the proportion of growth explained by TFP growth was not different in the "four tigers" from that in the United States and Japan.

Overall, these studies seem to yield one important conclusion: whether the growth of total factor productivity was exceptional or not in the Asian "miracle" economies, there is little evidence to support the view that it was abysmally poor. Thus, directed credit appears not to have created very severe distortions in the allocation of capital. The question is why not.

5. Management of Directed Credit Policies

A recent study by Vittas and Cho (1995) asks precisely this question: they investigate why directed credit policies were apparently successful in East Asia, though they have not been so elsewhere. They cite the roles of both economic and institutional factors in the region as contributing to this outcome. The economic factors include the pursuit of macroeconomic stability as well as of the general development strategy adopted by these countries. This strategy featured an export orientation, the encouragement of domestic competition, the reliance on the private sector, and the presence of a bias toward industrialization. Institutional factors include the creation of an effective monitoring system by the banks, the use of extensive consultation arrangements, and the development and propagation of credible development visions for these economies. They argue that the combination of macroeconomic stability with intense domestic competition, export orientation, and a reliance on the private sector promoted efficiency and provided objective criteria for monitoring on the part of banks. Moreover, the goals of policy-based lending were narrowly focused (on industrialization and export promotion) and were well coordinated with other policies.

Vittas and Cho draw lessons of two types from the experience of these countries with directed credit policies. What they call "good vision" lessons are that credit policies should have a small size and focus, should be of limited duration with clear sunset provisions, and that they should involve a low level of subsidy (to minimize distortions). In addition, they should aim at activities that generate positive externalities, such as those associated with industrialization and exports and they should be based on a competitive private sector with internationally competitive operations. Finally, they should form part of a broader credible vision of economic development promoting growth with equity, and involving a long-term strategy to develop a sound financial system operating on economic criteria. They also draw "good management" lessons. These include the principle that policy-based loans should be channeled through well-capitalized, administratively capable and autonomous institutions, should be based on clear, objective, and easily identifiable criteria, should aim at good repayment records and low loan losses, and should be supported by effective mechanisms for consultation and communication between public and private sectors.

d. Financial Repression and Growth in East Asia: Lessons

What is clear from all of this is that the management of financial repression in the "miracle" economies was special. Financial repression was managed in a way that at the very least prevented financial repression from posing a serious obstacle to growth and may even have permitted it to support growth in these countries. The key points were that the macroeconomic environment was stable, controlled nominal interest rates were not kept unduly low, and policy-based lending was used to allocate funds on the basis of reasonable performance indicators. This last was determined in part by the particular development strategy that these countries had adopted. It is unclear whether the net effect of all of these components was positive or simply not very negative. The answer depends in part on whether the institutional mechanisms could have been put in place to make an alternative set of financial sector policies feasible and on the view one takes about the contribution of industrial policies to the economic success of these countries. What is clear is that the relatively benign role of financial repression in these countries reflected a special set of circumstances that would be difficult to replicate elsewhere.

V. SUMMARY

We saw in the previous chapter that a well-functioning financial system could make potentially important contributions to economic welfare and growth. The emergence of such a system, however, can be influenced in important ways by government policy. These influences can be beneficial or harmful. Because of the many imperfections from which credit markets are likely to suffer in the real world, it is unlikely that the optimal set of policies toward the financial system would be one characterized by a laissez faire stance on the part of the government. But this does not provide carte blanche for government intervention. A well-designed set of policies to promote the efficient functioning of the domestic financial system must target credit market imperfections narrowly and efficiently. When policies toward the domestic financial system are designed with other goals in mind, the net effect of such policies may turn out to be harmful.

This chapter has explored this issue in the context of financial repression, a set of policies toward the financial system that arose out of fiscal motivations and that imposed severe restrictions on the behavior of the customers of domestic banks, their potential competitors, and the banks themselves. These policies were widespread among emerging markets until relatively recent times. Theory suggests that policies of this type would tend to have harmful effects on economic welfare and growth, and we have seen that the evidence is consistent with this conclusion. While under very favorable circumstances – such as those that prevailed in the Asian "miracle" economies – these effects may be mitigated, the evidence on this is unclear and the relevant circumstances may in any case themselves be difficult to create.

The question, then, is how to make the transition from a repressed financial system to a well-functioning liberalized one – that is, how to conduct an appropriate financial reform. This involves identifying both what the residual role of the government should be in the liberalized financial system that ultimately emerges from the reform process as well as determining how to get from here to there – in other words, what is the sequence of steps required to make the transition? The next chapter turns to these questions.

13

Financial Reform, Public Policy, and Financial Crises

A natural response to the recognition of the adverse consequences that financial repression can have for growth is to attempt to undo these harmful policies. Because these policies take the form of restrictions on financial intermediation, their removal is referred to as "financial liberalization." Many emerging economies have indeed embarked on such a path over the past two decades. But if these restrictions are removed, the question arises of what – if anything – to replace them with. Should the government simply adopt a hands-off approach to the financial sector, or are there specific government policies that may enhance, rather than inhibit, the efficiency of financial intermediation?

It turns out that simply removing the harmful policies associated with financial repression overnight and adopting a *laissez faire* approach toward the financial system may do more harm than good. In particular, it may generate new kinds of resource misallocations and may result in severe financial crises with important macroeconomic implications. As we saw in Chapter 11, credit market imperfections create a role for public policy in a well-functioning financial system. The problem with financial repression is not so much the *fact* of public sector involvement in regulating the financial sector, as it is the *type* of public sector involvement. Because what is required is a redefinition of the government's role, rather than the removal of any role for the government, a better term for the process of moving from a repressed financial system to a well-functioning one is financial *reform*, rather than liberalization.

Two questions are posed by the process of financial reform. The first is what the appropriate role of public policy should be in a fully reformed system. In other words, if financial repression involves the wrong set of interventions, then what is the right set? The second question is how to progress from a repressed to a fully reformed system, in other words, how to conduct the *sequencing* of financial reform.

Sequencing may matter for several reasons. First, recall from the two previous chapters that financial repression has a fiscal dimension, and that the damage done by financial repression may depend on the macroeconomic circumstances in which the financial system operates. Thus, in formulating a strategy for reform, financial reformers will need to consider the interactions between macroeconomic conditions and the reformulation of financial sector policies. Second, financial repression has many components – both domestic and external ones – and it may make a difference in what order these are removed. Finally, if a liberalized financial system requires an alternative set of public policies to support it, then the removal of repressive restrictions may be conditional on the implementation of these alternative policies. This chapter will take up the first of these questions. It will explore the consequences of abrupt ("premature") financial liberalization, and its relationship to subsequent financial crises. In Chapter 14 we will consider how to sequence financial reform.

I. VULNERABILITY OF A LIBERALIZED BANKING SECTOR

Financial liberalization means the removal of the restrictions associated with financial repression. Accordingly, it takes the form of freeing interest rates to be determined by market forces, lowering or abolishing reserve and liquidity requirements, removing directed credit regulations, adopting indirect instruments of monetary control (instead of credit ceilings on individual banks), opening up entry into the financial sector (including privatization), and opening up the capital account of the balance of payments. A *laissez faire* approach to financial reform would have the government undertake all of these measures, and then rely on competition and market efficiency to ensure the appropriate functioning of the deregulated financial system.

The fundamental problem with this approach, however, is that, as we saw in the last chapter, the financial system essentially represents a market response to the dual problems of asymmetric information and opportunistic behavior. Under these circumstances, there is no presumption that unregulated competitive markets will be Pareto efficient. For example, information is nonrivalrous (its use by one agent does not prevent use by another) and nonexcludable (agents that have not paid for it cannot be prevented from acquiring it). Thus, it has the characteristics of a public good, which is known to be undersupplied in competitive markets. Moreover, imperfect information also makes it less likely that financial markets will be perfectly competitive. Because the acquisition of information involves incurring fixed costs, the resulting scale economies make this likely to lead to noncompetitive outcomes. From a purely microeconomic perspective, then, it is by no means obvious that a *laissez faire* approach will result in an efficient and well-functioning financial system.

But as we shall now see, a fully liberalized system would also be vulnerable to other, potentially more serious types of problems, in the form of systematic misallocation of resources as well as vulnerability to systemic breakdowns in which many financial firms go out of business, severely disrupting financial intermediation in the economy. It is useful to classify these systemic breakdowns into two categories: *banking crises*, which are *solvency* problems (typically defined as a situation of generalized insolvency in the banking industry) and *bank panics*, which are *liquidity* problems (situations in which there is wholesale withdrawal of deposits from otherwise solvent banks). As we shall see, depending on the country's institutional and policy environment, a banking crisis can be accompanied by a bank panic, but it need not be, and a bank panic may or may not trigger a banking crisis.[1]

a. Banking Crises

Just as is true for any other borrower, moral hazard problems characterize the activities of financial intermediaries such as banks. Moral hazard problems in banking are caused by the principal-agent relationship between bank depositors and bank managers, particularly in the case of banks that have low net worth. Acting on behalf of the owners of banks, bank managers have an incentive to offer high deposit rates in order to attract large quantities of funds and then invest these in risky ventures, because if such ventures are successful, bank owners get to keep the large gains that remain after paying off the bank's depositors, while if they are not, the owners of the bank lose very little of their own money. This is simply another example of the standard agency problems associated with borrowing and lending that we examined in Chapter 11.

As we saw there, one solution to this problem is for the lender to monitor the borrower and impose penalties for behavior that is not in the interest of the lender. Since the losers when risky ventures fail to pay off are the depositors, depositors have an incentive to monitor the conduct of bank managers in order to prevent such activities. They can penalize the managers by withdrawing their funds from the bank. Indeed, the liquidity of bank liabilities can be interpreted as a market-based response to moral hazard problems in banking. Liquid liabilities serve as a device through which depositors who learn of inappropriate behavior by bank managers acquire a means to penalize such activity at low cost to themselves (by withdrawing their funds) and thus are able to discourage it. This permits monitoring by depositors to discipline bank managers and, by reducing the scope of the moral hazard problem, may actually allow banks to borrow more cheaply.

But the question is how effective this disciplining device is likely to be in practice. The incentives of depositors to monitor banks are weakened by several factors. First, the private, nontraded information generated by the banks in their loan activities makes the quality of their portfolios difficult (i.e., costly) for depositors to monitor. That is, using the language of Chapter 11, bank activities tend to be inherently opaque. Second, since the monitoring of bank activities by some depositors is enough to discipline the banks, and since monitoring is a costly activity, *all* depositors benefit if *some* depositors monitor. This means that monitoring would tend

---

[1] It would not be, for example, if deposits are explicitly or implicitly – and credibly – insured.

to be discouraged by a free rider problem, in the sense that all depositors have an incentive to leave the monitoring to others. Finally, depositors may come to believe that in the event of a bank failure, the government would step in to bail them out by guaranteeing the value of their deposits. The government has an incentive to do this because, as we shall see below, bank failures may tend to spread and become systemic, which creates the potential for substantial economic harm. While the government may publicly deny its willingness to do this, time inconsistency problems such as those we studied in the context of central bank behavior in Chapter 9 may make it impossible for the government to make this commitment credible. If depositors come to believe that their assets are not at risk, they will have no incentive to monitor.

The upshot is that there are ample reasons to expect that depositors, on their own, are unlikely to provide the appropriate amount of monitoring. If that is so, moral hazard will induce banks to take excessive risks (i.e., risks larger than their creditors would choose). This has important microeconomic and macroeconomic consequences.

From a microeconomic perspective, the decisions of bank managers acting as agents will tend to misallocate resources, favoring risky activities that maximize their expected private gains, rather than the expected gains to society. These distortions in resource allocation harm the economy's growth performance just as do those arising from financial repression.

From a macroeconomic perspective, the prevalence of risky loans makes the values of bank portfolios excessively sensitive to the inherent volatility of the economic environment. The implication is that bank failures and generalized bank solvency crises will be more frequent than they would be if the influence of moral hazard were restrained. This is particularly the case if there are mechanisms that operate to spread bank failures from one bank to another. Bank panics provide just such a mechanism.

b. Bank Panics

Vulnerability to panic is inherent in banking. The reason has to do with the structure of bank portfolios. On the liability side of their balance sheets, by definition, banks offer liquid liabilities. As we have seen, the liquidity of their liabilities confers certain advantages to banks. In particular, it reduces the premium that they must pay for external finance by giving depositors greater leverage over the institution. On the other side of bank balance sheets, bank assets are not only of longer maturity than their liabilities (that is why banks are often said to engage in maturity transformation), but more importantly, their loans are not typically traded in secondary markets. The reason is that, as we have seen, these loans are information-intensive, and so are difficult to sell to others for "lemons" reasons: asymmetric information about the quality of these loans creates an adverse selection problem, in the sense that potential buyers of these loans may fear that banks trying to sell them are doing so precisely because the loans are of poor quality, and thus would be unwilling to pay enough for them to compensate the banks for disposing of them. Without secondary markets for bank assets, banks cannot liquidate them quickly and at low cost.[2] Because their assets are thus much less liquid than their liabilities, banks are inherently illiquid institutions.

Why is this a potential problem? The reason is that it makes banks vulnerable to liquidity (confidence) crises. An important feature of the liquid liabilities of banks is that their depositors have access to them on a first come–first served basis (this is called the *sequential servicing constraint*). Suppose that, though information on the health of individual banks is costly for depositors to acquire, individual depositors can observe each other's actions at low cost. Then the loss of faith in the bank's soundness by any one depositor, causing him or her to withdraw funds from the bank, is likely to spill over to the others, who will tend to suspect that the depositor withdrawing funds has superior information about the bank and who will thus have an incentive to withdraw their funds as well. The incentive arises because withdrawing funds under these circumstances can yield a high return. By definition it costs little to do so, and it may enable the depositor to avoid large losses arising from the sequential service constraint. The latter means that in the event that the bank becomes insolvent, only depositors who remove their funds early will avoid losses. The likelihood of insolvency is increased by the fact that confidence crises can actually be self-fulfilling, in the sense that they can trigger insolvency of the bank through distress sales of the bank's assets. Thus, individual depositors have to consider not just whether the actions of other depositors in withdrawing funds signal a preexisting solvency problem, but also whether such actions may trigger withdrawals by other depositors that may actually *cause* a solvency problem. In this situation, banks become highly vulnerable to confidence crises.

There are various possible solutions to this problem. First, individual banks can address it directly by holding part of their portfolios in liquid, marketable assets. But this would leave less of their portfolios for banks to devote to the information-intensive loans that are their reason for existence, so this is not a socially desirable option if superior options are available that would achieve the same protection with less asset liquidity. One such option is an interbank market for reserves, which would allow individual banks to hold fewer reserves. In the United States prior to the founding of the Federal Reserve System, for example, banks issued clearing-house loan certificates (a joint liability of all members of the clearing house) to their depositors in times of panic. Two problems with this approach are that asymmetric information may make this market dry up at times of crisis (banks may not be

---

[2] Banks' acquisition of nontraded, rather than traded, assets plays an important microeconomic role. Because it prevents others from free-riding on banks' information acquisition, it allows banks to retain the profits from this activity, and thus preserves their incentives to undertake it.

willing to lend to each other, any more than depositors are willing to lend to banks) and that it does not provide protection against a *generalized* liquidity crisis.

II. BANK VULNERABILITY AND PUBLIC POLICY

As we have just seen, a liberalized banking sector is potentially vulnerable to both banking crises and bank panics. While there are market mechanisms that can help to ameliorate these problems, these mechanisms suffer from certain shortcomings. In this section we will examine how public policy can be used to address both types of vulnerabilities.

a. The Lender of Last Resort and Deposit Insurance

The shortcomings of market-based mechanisms for protection against bank panics could be avoided if there is an informed lender that can provide a large amount of resources to banks that are affected by a panic. This is the *lender of last resort* function. The traditional prescription (articulated by Bagehot 1999) for how a lender of last resort should behave in times of crisis is that it should be prepared to lend in generous amounts, but at penalty interest rates and only on good collateral. The stipulation that lending should be in generous amounts serves to reassure depositors that the required amount of resources will be available, the imposition of a penalty interest rate is intended to restrict access to the last-resort borrowing only to times of crisis, and the restriction requiring backing by good collateral is to make sure that lender of last resort funding is used for liquidity, rather than for solvency problems.

While the lender of last resort could in principle be another bank, the possibility that bank panics can become generalized suggests that the role may best be performed by the central bank. Thus, one role of public policy in a reformed financial system is to provide the lender of last resort function.

But the lender of last resort function has its own problems. From the perspective of the individual depositor, one shortcoming is that the function is exercised with discretion by the central bank, so the depositor is not sure to recover his/her assets in the event of a panic. This may leave an incentive for depositors to still "run" from the affected bank. From the perspective of policymakers, on the other hand, placing the lender of last resort function with the central bank tends to complicate monetary policy. The reason is that a generalized panic will contract the money supply (by reducing the money multiplier), but it may also reduce the demand for money (since currency and demand deposits are imperfect substitutes, people may "run" into assets other than currency). This makes it difficult for the central bank to know how much liquidity it should inject into the economy at times of panic in order to avoid the emergence of disequilibrium in the money market.

A public policy alternative that handles both problems is the institution of *deposit insurance*, usually in the form of a guarantee by a private or public institution that the value of deposits at participating banks is insured up to a certain amount. Banks pay a premium for insuring the value of their deposits, which is typically expressed as a percentage of the deposits covered and may or may not be related to the composition of the banks' portfolio. When depositors know that their claims are insured by such a mechanism, they have no incentive to "run" from a bank whose ability to meet its obligations is suspect. Because the removal of this incentive can be expected to reduce the incidence of bank panics, the life of monetary policymakers is made simpler under deposit insurance than with only a lender of last resort in place.

But deposit insurance also has potentially harmful side effects. First, deposit insurance may aggravate the moral hazard problems in banking caused by the principal-agent relationship between bank depositors and bank managers, particularly for banks with low net worth. Once their deposits are insured, not only do depositors no longer have an incentive to "run" from potentially troubled banks, but they also have no incentive to monitor the behavior of bank managers in the first place. The presence of insurance may thus induce bank managers to undertake riskier behavior than they would have otherwise, since they will not be penalized by their depositors for doing so. Thus, the presence of deposit insurance aggravates the moral hazard problem.

Second, deposit insurance may encourage adverse selection in entry into the banking industry. Risk-loving individuals would reap the largest benefit as bank owners from the opportunity to gamble with other people's money that arises from the insurance provided to bank depositors, especially when they do not have to take large stakes in their own banks. The likely result from both effects is that financial crises in which a large number of banks find themselves with negative net worth may be more likely in the presence of deposit insurance. The upshot is that deposit insurance may provide protection against bank panics (liquidity crises) at the cost of increasing exposure to bank crises (solvency crises).

However, the properties of deposit insurance schemes may matter for this outcome. Such schemes, for example, may be explicit (announced by the government and written into law), or implicit (i.e., everyone believes that depositors will be bailed out in the event of a crisis). Explicit schemes may have several advantages over implicit ones. For one thing, they allow the costs of insurance to be met by premiums on bank deposits, rather than by taxpayers. This makes it possible to make these premiums risk-based (i.e., based on the composition of banks' portfolios), which reduces the moral hazard problem by penalizing banks with riskier portfolios. The legal framework that they provide may also make it easier to close insolvent banks by obviating the need for expensive litigation with small depositors, again ameliorating the moral hazard problem (if banks are more likely to be closed down, bank owners are more likely to incur losses). Finally, they make it possible to limit the coverage of the protection, leaving more incentives in place for larger depositors to undertake monitoring activities. Thus, an explicit scheme may create less moral hazard than an implicit one, through risk-based premia, added credibility on bank closures, and by putting limitations on the government's liabilities.[3]

However, recent cross-country empirical evidence that we shall review later in this chapter (Demigurc-Kunt and Detragiache 2000) indeed suggests that the presence of deposit insurance has tended to increase the probability of banking crises. We shall see below that the solution is appropriate bank regulation and supervision. For now, though, we can simply note that even well-run banks are inherently vulnerable to panics, and that this situation creates a role for public policy. Because the specific public policies that can address the problem of panics may themselves create (or aggravate) distortions, however, they need to be accompanied by other types of policy intervention.

b. Bank Regulation and Supervision

The additional intervention required involves bank regulation and supervision. These may be necessary to avoid solvency problems with or without deposit insurance, but they become more important if deposit insurance deters monitoring. What should bank regulation do? In principle, regulation has several objectives:

 i. *Avoid adverse selection in bank entry*, by making sure that individuals more likely to misuse banks (by taking excessive risk or engaging in related lending) do not get bank charters. This is the role of chartering regulations that require adequate capital investment, proscribe cross-ownership, and include character stipulations for bank ownership.
 ii. *Align the incentives of bank owners with those of depositors* by ensuring that bank owners stand to make substantial losses in the event of insolvency. This is the role of capital adequacy requirements and loan loss provisions.
 iii. *Prevent excessive risk-taking* more generally through asset management supervision. This means limiting bank holdings of excessively risky assets (such as stocks, real estate, or consumer credit), preventing lending to related parties, requiring diversification, and making sure that banks have appropriate loan evaluation procedures in place.[4]

In contrast with the lender of last resort function and generalized deposit insurance, such measures imply substantial intervention with bank functions at the microeconomic level. But why should the government intervene in private transactions between depositors and their banks? There are essentially two reasons. First,

---

[3] Within the set of explicit schemes, fully funded schemes that offer extensive coverage and that are run by the government may actually create more moral hazard than schemes with partial coverage of deposits run by the private sector.
[4] The supervision of bank portfolios mirrors the approach taken by insurance companies that cannot base premiums on sufficiently fine risk categories.

as previously mentioned, the problems that call for these interventions arise from market failures created by asymmetric information and opportunistic behavior. Government intervention allows mutually advantageous trades (between depositors and banks) that would not otherwise take place, in the following sense: if bank managers could commit themselves to refrain from opportunistic behavior, depositors would entrust them with their money and both would be happy. Since they cannot do so, depositors hold nonbank assets instead and both are worse off. Thus, government supervision in effect supplies a commitment mechanism for bank managers.

The other reason is because the failures of individual banks may create negative externalities, in the sense that they may affect the prospects of other banks. Since individual bank managers and depositors do not have the incentive to take these spillovers into account, there is a rationale for policy intervention. The problem is that banking crises can become systemic. While not all generalized banking crises need reflect bank-to-bank transmission – that is, they may also arise from general macroeconomic shocks that affect all banks (sometimes referred to as "monsoonal effects") – banking crises can be contagious. Channels of bank-to-bank contagion include the following:

i. *Transmission.* The failure of one bank may affect the health of other banks through cross-bank claims, or through the ability of depositors in the failed bank to service debt with other banks.

ii. *"Pure" contagion.* As we have seen, asymmetric information means that depositors are not well informed about the quality of bank loans. Suppose it becomes known that some fraction of banks are insolvent, but not which ones, and that there is no mechanism for deposit guarantees in place. Then, as we saw above, in the absence of information about the solvency of a depositor's own bank, it may make sense for that depositor to withdraw funds from his own bank when it is known that some banks are in trouble just as it does when other individuals are seen to be withdrawing funds from the depositor's bank, since converting deposits into cash is relatively costless, and the expected return from doing so may be high.

The upshot is that the information problems that characterize the banking sector call for appropriate public policy measures to address the vulnerability of a liberalized banking system to panics and solvency crises. These measures involve some combination of a lender of last resort role for the central bank and a system of deposit insurance with a system for the regulation and supervision of banks specifically designed to address the moral hazard problems inherent in this type of activity. When these measures are not implemented, or when they are inadequate, a liberalized banking system will be vulnerable to panics and solvency crises.

III. BANKING CRISES: THEORY

Unfortunately, implementing an appropriate regulatory and supervisory framework is not a trivial matter. Bank regulation may fail for many reasons. The most basic of these is that the legal framework for appropriate bank regulation may be inadequate. The legal basis of regulation must provide regulators with the means to acquire the information they need to do their jobs (this refers to the adequacy of accounting and disclosure standards) as well as the authority to compel compliance with their strictures.

But even when the legal means are in place, inadequate knowledge or resources on the part of regulators can impair the regulatory process, particularly after a transition from financial repression or during a period of rapid financial innovation (when neither banks nor regulators are well prepared for loan evaluation and risk assessment).

Even with well-informed and well-funded regulation, principal-agent problems may arise between regulators and taxpayers, since the interests of the individual regulators may differ from those of the framers of regulatory policy. This may permit regulators to be "captured" by the banks, and may encourage regulatory "forbearance" in the case of bank failure for "bureaucratic gambling" motives (hoping a problem of insolvency will go away through good luck so as not to be blamed for allowing it to happen).

Finally, regulation may be confounded by political pressures placed on regulatory agencies from politicians' constituencies.

Inappropriate regulation arising from any of these sources means that banks may become vulnerable to shocks that could wipe out their capital, resulting in solvency crises. Indeed, we can think of bank vulnerability as arising when the shocks to which a bank's balance sheet may be subjected are large relative to the size of the bank's capital. Thus, vulnerability can arise when banks have large risk exposures and/or limited capital, both of which, as we have seen, may reflect regulatory failures.

It is obvious from this, however, that vulnerability is a matter of degree. Banks, like other firms, are in the business of taking risks, and they can be more or less vulnerable to shocks in their environment. That is, even a well-functioning banking system can always be thrown into insolvency by a sufficiently large shock. What matters is the degree of sensitivity of bank balance sheets to the underlying volatility of the economic environment, and one function of regulation is to adapt prudential standards for bank lending and capital adequacy requirements to the volatility of the environment in which banks operate.

These considerations suggest that regulatory failure is only one possible source of bank vulnerability. The origins of vulnerability can be classified into three types:

i. *Bank-specific.* This essentially refers to incompetence and/or fraud at the level of individual banks. This type of problem can emerge at individual banks even under an efficient regulatory system, but in the presence of effective mechanisms to prevent the spread of bank panics, problems of this type should not have systemic repercussions.

ii. *Industry-specific.* Regulatory failure can be described as an industry-specific problem. Probably the most common and most important source of regulatory failure arises from the deregulation of bank activities without an adequate regulatory and supervisory mechanism in place, which allow the inappropriate incentives associated with moral hazard to have free rein. But in some cases, this general problem has been aggravated by the way that some aspects of the liberalization process were handled. For example, in some of the banking crises that we shall review in the next section (e.g., Chile in 1982 and Mexico in 1994), the privatization of previously nationalized banks that occurred before the crisis happened had been conducted in such a way as to allow unqualified buyers to acquire banks, or to allow inappropriate links between banks and nonfinancial firms. In other cases, previously liberalized and still weak banks were subjected to a loss of franchise value from the allowing of new entry or as the result of competition arising from capital account liberalization.

As we shall see in Chapter 19, some of the major financial crises experienced by emerging economies in recent years may have had their origins in problems of this type. The Southern Cone, Mexican, and Asian crises were all preceded by lending booms, which are a prime symptom of "premature" domestic financial liberalization – that is, financial liberalization with an inadequate regulatory structure.

iii. *Macroeconomic.* Vulnerability can also arise from macroeconomic sources. For example, it may be created by perceived guarantees (which turn out not to have been valid *ex post*) for the assets of bank owners, which in effect makes them behave as if their own resources are not at risk. This creates a moral hazard problem that encourages banks to take risks.[5] Somewhat paradoxically, macroeconomic booms may also make banks vulnerable, in the sense of reducing the average quality of the loans in their portfolios. The reason is that maturity-based monitoring devices (i.e., short-term loans that have to be repaid frequently and thus reveal information about the financial health of the borrowers) may fail to provide much information during good times, when most debtors (even bad ones) will be able to make payments on schedule.

Once vulnerability has arisen from any of these sources, a crisis can be triggered by a variety of factors, either microeconomic or macroeconomic in nature. Microeconomic factors include prospective insolvency at one or more large banks which, as we have seen above, may spread panic elsewhere in the banking system when panic-prevention policies are not effective. But even when such policies are effective, macroeconomic shocks can nevertheless trigger banking crises, because such

---

[5] This may be the most severe potential indictment of "crony capitalism" in the East Asian case.

shocks can undermine the solvency of vulnerable banks. Macroeconomic sources of banking crises may come in a variety of forms, depending on the nature of banks' exposure. These include:

i. *High interest rates.* Because they are engaged in maturity transformation, banks' liabilities are likely to be more sensitive to changes in interest rates than their assets. This means that banks are typically exposed to interest rate risk. Moreover, since higher interest rates tend to worsen adverse selection problems among bank borrowers, banks may also restrict credit expansion when interest rates rise. For both reasons, higher interest rates may impair the value of bank capital.

ii. *Exchange rate devaluation.* If either banks themselves or their customers have significant currency mismatches in their balance sheets, a large devaluation may also impair the value of bank capital, either directly or indirectly.

iii. *Asset price collapses* (stocks, real estate). The obvious channel through which such events could impair the value of bank capital is through bank ownership of such assets. But even if banks do not own stocks or real estate, a collapse in the price of these assets will lower the net worth of bank borrowers which, by worsening agency problems, increases the banks' cost of doing business (i.e., increases the external finance premium) and thus the profitability of banking activity. As we shall see, property booms and collapses featured prominently in some of the crises to be reviewed in the next section.

iv. *Recession.* The obvious channel through which a recession would hurt banks is through credit risk – the effect of reduced earnings on the capacity for bank debtors to service their debt.

v. *Terms of trade shocks.* For banks not diversified outside their home countries, adverse terms of trade shocks could trigger many of the negative events listed above, and could directly affect the banks through negative effects on the business prospects of many bank customers.

vi. *Unanticipated deflation.* A decrease in the average price level that was not anticipated at the time interest rates were set has the effect of increasing *ex post* real interest rates. This reduces the net worth of bank debtors who are highly leveraged.

This list suggests that there are many macroeconomic events that can arise to impair the value of bank capital. When any of these events are likely to happen, and when banks lack sufficient capital to allow them to withstand the losses that these events would entail, a generalized banking crisis is likely to emerge.

But why worry about this possibility? The key reason, of course, is that banking crises tend to have significant effects on the real economy. Banking crises invariably have fiscal effects, because when the government guarantees the value of deposits, the difference between banks' deposit obligations and the value of their assets that emerges when banks are insolvent has to be made up by taxpayers. These are often described as the costs of the crisis. However, this fiscal cost represents a transfer from taxpayers to depositors. While it does reflect a social cost (that in the absence of the transfer would have been borne by the depositors), it does not reflect a cost of the crisis itself, but rather of the resource misallocations that may have helped cause the crisis.

How may the crisis itself affect the real economy? There are various reasons to worry about generalized bank failures. First, generalized bank failures disrupt the economy's payments mechanism. Banking crises encourage a switch from deposits to cash that, in the absence of countervailing policies, would cause the money supply to contract. Because it economizes on transactions costs, money is socially productive, so a drastic reduction in the money supply has the effect of curtailing economic efficiency. Second, by reducing the money supply, the switch from deposits to cash that occurs in a banking crisis raises domestic interest rates, which reduces aggregate demand through the traditional channels of monetary transmission. Banking crises are thus likely to trigger recessions or even more severe macroeconomic downturns. The traditional remedy would be expansionary monetary policy, which would not tend to be inflationary, because it would simply match the supply of monetary base to the increased demand for it, but as we already noted above, fine-tuning this injection of reserves may pose a difficult challenge for the central bank. Third, monetary policy may also work through a *credit channel*, in other words, even in economies with well-developed securities markets, there may be a class of borrowers with agency costs sufficiently high that they have no access to such markets, and can only borrow from banks. If so, this will tend to magnify the negative effects on the economy operating through the traditional mechanism of monetary transmission, because the disruption of bank credit associated with generalized banking crises will curtail spending among such bank-dependent firms.[6] Finally, to the extent that banks are liquidated as the outcome of a generalized banking crisis, the economy loses the knowledge capital that the liquidated banks had accumulated, which reduces the efficiency of the financial intermediation mechanism. The cumulative impact of all of these effects can be substantial. One study has estimated the typical output loss over the course of a crisis episode (based on a sample of sixty-one such episodes during 1975–97) at about 7.3 percent of the GDP of the affected economies.

IV. BANKING CRISES: EVIDENCE

Thus, the potential stakes involved in the adoption of an appropriate policy framework for the domestic financial system are high indeed. We saw in the previous chapter that both theory and evidence suggest that the real costs of financial repression

---

[6] Even contractions of bank capital, without outright insolvency, may trigger a decline in bank lending. If there is a credit channel to monetary policy, this could slow real economic activity. A "credit crunch" of this sort, due to inadequate bank capital, has been assigned part of the blame for the recession in the United States that began in 1990.

are paid in the form of slower growth of the economy's productive capacity as resources are misallocated and dissipated, and as the incentives for accumulation are reduced. We have just seen, on the other hand, that an inappropriate liberalization of the financial system may also be costly, both by inducing misallocation of resources as a result of incentive problems, and by making the banking system vulnerable to crises with potentially severe macroeconomic impacts. But so far, the case for the harmful effects of "premature" liberalization has been based on a priori reasoning. In this section, we review some of the international evidence on the causes of banking crises. We will first examine some evidence arising from cross-country studies, and then turn to some case studies.

a. Cross-Country Evidence

1. Demigurc-Kunt and Detragiache (1998)

A recent cross-country study by Demigurc-Kunt and Detragiache (1998) was designed to explain the empirical determinants of banking crises. The authors relied on annual data drawn from samples of 45–65 countries (depending on data availability for specific equation specifications), over the period 1980–94. They determined whether each country in their sample experienced a generalized banking crisis during each year in the sample by examining whether any one of four conditions were met. These included whether the ratio of nonperforming loans to total assets in the banking system exceeded 10 percent, whether there was a bank rescue operation during the year with fiscal costs in excess of 2 percent of GDP, whether banking sector problems resulted in widespread bank nationalizations, and whether extensive banks runs, deposit freezes, or prolonged bank holidays took place in that year, or generalized deposit insurance was enacted in response to banking difficulties. If any of these things happened, the year in question was classified as characterized by a generalized banking crisis. They found 31 crisis episodes out of the 546 observations in their sample.

Next, they used a logit regression procedure designed to estimate the factors that influenced the probability that any observation in the sample would be classified as a crisis or noncrisis situation. Among the crisis determinants they considered were indicators of institutional development intended to capture the adequacy of the regulatory environment, as well as measures of macroeconomic volatility. Their empirical model performed well in explaining whether observations would be classified as crisis or noncrisis.

They found that a low value of the law and order index that they used to indicate the adequacy of the institutional environment helped predict crises, and that the presence of deposit insurance increased the probability of a crisis in their sample. There was weak evidence that rapid growth of credit to the private sector – such as would emerge in a liberalized environment with inappropriate regulation of banks – predicts subsequent crises. A high ratio of $M2$ to the central bank's stock of foreign exchange reserves increased the likelihood of a crisis. Among macroeconomic variables, slow domestic GDP growth, poor performance of the country's terms of trade, and high domestic nominal and real interest rates were associated with crisis, but exchange rate depreciation and fiscal variables were not.

2. Hutchinson and McDill (1999)

A similar study by Hutchinson and McDill (1999) supplemented a statistical study of determinants of banking crises in a large sample of countries with an examination of the "typical" time series behavior of macroeconomic variables and financial variables in crisis countries. They found that in crisis countries compared to the others, the pre-crisis period was characterized by a faster rate of currency depreciation, a higher rate of inflation, and a higher ratio of $M2$ to foreign exchange reserves. Stock prices were somewhat higher in crisis countries, but fiscal performance showed no noticeable differences. In economies that had crises, real output growth experienced a boom before a crisis, but slowed gradually prior to the crisis. It dropped sharply at the onset of the crisis, and gradually recovered. Credit growth was strong prior to the crisis, contracted during the first year, and then rebounded slowly. Exchange rate depreciation jumped significantly at the onset of the crisis, and stock prices dropped markedly.

In their examination of these time series patterns, Hutchinson and McDill thus found stronger evidence for the role of macroeconomic booms triggered by periods of rapid credit expansion in triggering subsequent banking crises than had Demigurc-Kunt and Detragiache in their formal statistical analysis. The formal statistical analysis conducted by Hutchinson and McDill confirmed these results. Among institutional variables, they found that financial liberalization, deposit insurance, and their interaction, all increased the likelihood of a subsequent crisis, while greater central bank independence reduced it. Among macroeconomic variables, slower growth of real GDP and lower stock prices helped to explain the incidence of crises.

The cross-country evidence in these two studies is thus consistent with the perspective adopted earlier in this chapter: financial liberalization in the presence of a weak domestic institutional environment for regulating and supervising banks gives free rein to moral hazard problems in the banking system, resulting in excessive expansion of risky lending. While this may trigger a macroeconomic boom in the short run, it makes banks vulnerable to an adverse turn of macroeconomic events, resulting in an increased likelihood of generalized banking crises.

b. Case Study Evidence

We now turn to some case study evidence on the same issues drawn from a wide range of country experiences.

1. Historical Case Study Evidence for the United States

Because of the prevalence in the United States of unit banks (banks with only one branch), which tended to be undiversified, banking failures have been relatively common in American economic history. According to Mishkin (1989), the typical sequence of events in American bank panics has been as follows:

i. Most of these crises started with a sharp rise in interest rates, a stock market crash, and an increase in uncertainty arising after the start of a recession.

ii. This led to increased adverse selection (more perceived risk led to higher interest rates, which squeezed out the more creditworthy borrowers) and moral hazard problems (lower firm net worth increased agency costs).

iii. Weakened bank balance sheets and higher costs of intermediation gave rise to bank panics, which in turn aggravated adverse selection and moral hazard problems due to the implied reduction in intermediation activity by informed lenders.

iv. In the most severe panics, unanticipated declines in the average price level, leading to debt deflation, aggravated this process by further reducing borrower net worth. This happened in 1873 and 1929.

The most severe banking crisis in the United States was during 1930–33. It was preceded by a credit boom during the decade of the 1920s, by a recession that began in mid-1929, and by the stock market crash in October of that year. The percentage of banks failing in each year from 1930 to 1933 was 5.6, 10.5, 7.8, and 12.9. By the end of 1933, just above half the number of banks that existed in 1929 were still in business. It ended with a bank holiday in March 1933.

2. The Nordic Crises of the Early 1990s[7]

Prior to the early 1980s, financial repression prevailed in Finland, Norway, and Sweden (interest rates were controlled, directed credit was used, capital flows were restricted, and the terms and quantities of bond issuance were restricted). Deregulation, in the form of the rapid removal of these restrictions, was carried out during the early to mid-eighties. At the time, bank capitalization was very low in all three countries, and formal deposit insurance existed in Finland and Norway, as well as implicit guarantees in Sweden. No consideration was given to adapting regulatory standards to the new environment. Bank lending practices and risk management practices received no in-depth review during the immediate post-liberalization period. No exposure limits were in place, so many banks had concentrated exposures to small groups of borrowers.

Liberalization took place in an environment of rapid economic growth. Following liberalization, nominal interest rates rose and credit boomed from the middle to the late eighties, resulting in consumption and investment booms. The household

---

[7] This description is based on Drees and Pazarbasioglu (1995).

saving rate fell sharply in all three countries. The expansion of bank lending was accompanied by more risk-taking, in the form of lending to more volatile sectors, such as real estate, construction, and services. Credit expansion was in part financed by large capital inflows at relatively low foreign interest rates, as well as through money markets. Foreign exchange-denominated lending increased sharply. The decline in interest rate spreads at this time suggested increased competition at the time of liberalization, accompanied by reduced franchise values.

The lending boom was ended in part by tighter monetary policy, as well as by reductions in the tax deductibility of interest payments. Combined with a collapse in oil prices (an important export for Norway), in paper and pulp prices (important exports for both Sweden and Norway), and in trade with the Council for Mutual Economic Assistance (CMEA) countries of the former Soviet bloc (important for Finland), the result was recession and asset price deflation, as well as exchange rate depreciation in all three countries.

Finance companies showed the effects of these developments first, as property prices collapsed. The difficulties of the finance companies spilled over to banks, initially through their involvement in lending to finance companies. Direct bank losses were initially in the real estate market, but as the recession deepened, nonperforming loans grew in activities not connected with real estate. Failed institutions tended to have lower capital ratios, and to rely more extensively on funding from the money market and from foreign loans, than those that survived. Only a few small banks were actually liquidated. The authorities mostly assumed ownership of banks or provided funds to the banks that continued to operate. In Norway, the direct fiscal impact of the crisis amounted to about 3.5 percent of GDP. By the end of 1991, the government had become the sole owner or majority shareholder of the three largest banks.

3. Seven Developing Countries

Baliño and Sundararajan (1991) compiled a set of stylized facts about the experience of banking crises in seven developing countries. These crises include the "Southern Cone" crises in Argentina during 1980–82, Chile in 1981–83, and Uruguay in 1982–85, as well as those in the Philippines during 1983–86, Thailand in 1984–86, Spain over the period 1978–83, and Malaysia in 1985–86. In all countries, generalized insolvency of banks was a problem during the crises. In all of these cases, nonperforming loans grew sharply just prior to and during the crisis (so none of these crises could be interpreted as a self-fulfilling bank panic).

All of these episodes were preceded by periods of deregulation, though the extent of deregulation and the lead time before the crisis varied widely. Lending to related parties figured prominently in Chile (where the related parties have been known as "grupos") and Spain.[8] The crises in these countries happened both with and without

---

[8] Connected lending was also important later in Mexico, during the banking crisis that began in 1994.

deposit insurance. Full deposit insurance was abandoned in Argentina in November 1979, and in the Philippines the deposit insurance agency had insufficient funds, causing the settlement of claims to be delayed. Consistent with the experience we have reviewed so far, in each country the crisis occurred after a period of rapid economic growth (a boom) with substantial variations in relative performance among sectors.

Movements in asset prices (real estate and stocks) were important elements in some cases (e.g., in the Southern Cone crises, as well as in Malaysia). As in the Nordic countries, the outbreak of these crises was associated with major external shocks and balance of payments problems. Sharp adjustments in exchange rates and interest rates occurred around the time of the crises, though in some cases the balance of payments crisis came before, and in others after, the banking crisis. In most countries, however, external imbalances were severe just before the crisis.

The effects of the crises were those that our previous discussion would lead us to expect: there was a significant shift from deposits into currency and/or a decrease in the interest elasticity of currency demand following the crises in all of these countries. There were sharp reductions in money multipliers in Argentina, the Philippines, Spain, and Uruguay, but not in Thailand and Chile (in Thailand this is because the crisis affected mainly finance companies, rather than banks). The crises were associated with strong reductions in GDP growth and initial deceleration of inflation, though the latter was subsequently reversed in some cases. Confidence was restored by last-resort lending (which was used in all of these cases), intervention of some of the troubled institutions, and reimposition of deposit insurance.

Last-resort lending, however, soon gave way to long-term lending at concessional rates, because of the generalized insolvency of financial institutions. Thus, governments wound up subsidizing failed institutions. To minimize the moral hazard implications of these actions, nonpecuniary penalties were imposed, such as replacing management, requiring the surrender of shares, or preventing dividend distribution. The losses to depositors were minimal in all cases (though Argentina and Thailand permitted some losses) and the fates of troubled banks differed across countries (they were liquidated in some cases, merged or restructured in others, and nationalized or subsidized in still others). Bank borrowers were assisted with financial support, technical assistance, and debt-equity conversions.

4. Chile (1982)

Chilean banks had been nationalized under the socialist government of Salvador Allende in the early 1970s. The government of Augusto Pinochet, which deposed the Allende government in 1973, adopted a *laissez faire* approach to the financial sector. First, banks were privatized by auctioning them off or returning them to their original owners without paying much attention to the character of the new bank owners or their connections with nonfinancial enterprises. Second, interest rate controls were lifted. Third, minimal regulations and supervisory requirements were imposed, but the government explicitly announced that deposits were not guaranteed, counting on depositors to police the banks. Fourth, reserve requirements were lowered. By 1980, they had been reduced to less than 10 percent. Finally, capital account restrictions were relaxed in 1979, at which time the exchange rate was fixed against the U.S. dollar.

The result of the policies just described toward the financial sector included an economic boom during the late 1970s, a very rapid rate of credit expansion in 1978–81, and a severe financial crash in the first half of 1982, involving the widespread failure of banks as well as an exchange rate crisis.

An interesting aspect of the Chilean experience is that it demonstrates why assertions by governments that deposits are not guaranteed may not tend to be credible, and therefore why depositors may not tend to police banks adequately, counting on the government to later bail them out. The Chilean government, which was well known for its free market orientation, expressly declared before the collapse of the domestic financial system that deposits were not guaranteed by the government, but after the financial crisis depositors were nevertheless bailed out.

5. Mexico (1994)

We will return to the Mexican case in much more detail in Chapter 19, but it is useful to examine it briefly in the current context for the sake of comparison with the international experience reviewed in this section.

Mexican banks had been nationalized in September 1982, after the Mexican government's announcement in August of its inability to service its external debts as scheduled led to the outbreak of the international debt crisis. After that time, half of the lending business of Mexican banks went to the government. Consequently, when these banks were rapidly reprivatized in the early 1990s, they had little expertise in evaluating private credit risk. Moreover, the agency in charge of supervising banks, the National Banking Commission, did not have the capability to adequately monitor banks' portfolios. As we have already seen, connected lending was one symptom of poor bank regulation and supervision in Mexico during the early 1990s.

An enormous bank lending boom was driven by capital inflows in the early 1990s, following Mexico's signing of a Brady Plan agreement to restructure its debt in 1989. This boom in lending not only depressed asset quality in banks, but also stressed the regulators. It was associated with a consumption boom and a deterioration in Mexico's current account performance. All of these phenomena are already familiar from our discussion of similar events elsewhere.

A sharp increase in U.S. interest rates beginning in February 1994, together with pressures on the peso arising from domestic political unrest, raised interest rates in Mexico in the first half of 1994 and increased adverse selection and moral hazard problems in the economy, partly because short debt maturities immediately transferred the effects of higher interest rates to the net worth of domestic firms through a financial accelerator mechanism such as that discussed in Chapter 11. Political events later in the year further increased uncertainty, and together with high interest rates and a 20 percent stock market decline in the fall, weakened the domestic banking system.

For reasons that we will examine in Chapter 19, Mexico's eventual devaluation and subsequent floating of the exchange rate in early 1995 resulted in a liquidity crisis, which raised domestic interest rates to very high levels (in excess of 100 percent), and the stock market crashed. Together with the effects of the devaluation on the balance sheets of firms, these high interest rates would have been enough to make most of the financial system insolvent and trigger a run on banks, but as in Chile, the government stepped in and guaranteed deposits. However, banks' loss of capital restricted their ability to lend, and this "credit channel" factor contributed to a sharp contraction in the real economy in the last three quarters of 1995, by nearly 10 percent.

6. Overview

There is, then, a fairly consistent story in all these different types of evidence about what causes banking crises. Moral hazard arising from financial liberalization with poor regulation and supervision results in lending booms. The poor asset quality acquired by banks in this environment makes them vulnerable to macroeconomic shocks. These macroeconomic shocks have come in a variety of forms, including the onset of recession, high interest rates, asset price collapses, and problems in the external sector. Shocks such as these provide the immediate trigger for the crisis. The crisis results in a decline in bank lending and a sharp contraction in real economic activity.

V. SUMMARY

As we have seen in previous chapters, the economy pays a high cost when the government finances itself through the domestic financial system, by relying on financial repression. Where such a regime is in place, financial reform is appropriate – there are ways to raise revenue that are less costly to the economy. However, the alternative to financial repression is not necessarily a *laissez faire* policy stance toward the financial system. As we have seen in this chapter, insufficient government involvement can also be harmful. The appropriate role of government in the financial sector has both institutional and macroeconomic dimensions. Based on theory and evidence, we can summarize this role as follows.

From an institutional perspective, the most basic requirement is for the government to create an appropriate legal framework within which the financial sector can function. This includes clear and well-established property rights, appropriate accounting and disclosure standards, and a judicial system that functions effectively to enforce contracts and punish fraud. Such a framework facilitates the use of collateral and lowers the costs of monitoring as well as those of contract negotiation and enforcement. These circumstances combine to reduce the premium for external finance and thus expand the role of financial intermediation.

Second, as we have seen in this chapter, the government needs to ensure the existence of a financial safety net to avoid liquidity crises. Even in a deregulated financial system, it may be impossible for the government to fail to operate a financial safety net in the form of an implicit deposit insurance system. The likelihood of financial panics under imperfect information, and the role of banks in the payments mechanism, probably mandate this result. Making the deposit insurance system explicit and charging banks a fee in accordance with the riskiness of their portfolio may be the best way to avoid moral hazard problems.

However, if deposit insurance is improperly priced, even a competitive financial system could malfunction after liberalization unless it is adequately supervised, due to moral hazard problems. Thus, the third responsibility of the government in the institutional realm is to provide an adequate supervisory and monitoring framework to prevent collusion as well as to avoid the excessive risk-taking associated with moral hazard problems. The supervisory function would complement the financial safety nets mentioned above, inducing liberalized institutions to behave in a prudent fashion by monitoring their portfolios, ensuring that appropriate provisions are made against suspect loans, and that bank capital is adequate.

A separate dimension to the government's regulatory function is the prohibition of collusion, not explicitly treated until the next chapter but worth mentioning here for completeness. In the absence of foreign competition (capital mobility), freeing the domestic financial system could result in noncompetitive behavior, with low deposit rates and high lending rates providing substantial profit margins to colluding institutions. This would be more likely in countries with limited access to external finance, strong domestic banking associations, and limited supervisory mechanisms.

Finally, the government's role also has a macroeconomic dimension, with a narrow budgetary component and a broader component related to macroeconomic management. The budgetary component arises because if other forms of revenue are not in place to replace those that the government was previously receiving from financial repression, inflation is the likely result. As we have seen, for a variety of reasons, the emergence of inflation may undermine the very growth process that financial liberalization is intended to promote. Thus, fiscal adjustment is an important component of financial liberalization to replace lost revenue from financial repression.

In addition to this, as we saw in Chapter 11, the government has a broader role through its macroeconomic management more generally to ensure a stable macroeconomic environment. In Chapter 11 we interpreted this as meaning an environment in which financial intermediation was not confronted with avoidable macroeconomic uncertainty, since macroeconomic volatility tends to increase the loan evaluation and monitoring costs that contribute to higher external finance premiums. Based on the results of this chapter, we see that this also involves avoiding subjecting the domestic economy to large macroeconomic shocks that could trigger a costly and disruptive banking crisis in a weak and vulnerable domestic financial system.

14

Financial Openness and the Sequencing
of Financial Reform

The previous chapter argued that there is a meaningful distinction to be drawn between financial liberalization, which means the removal of the panoply of restrictions on the financial sector that constitute financial repression, and financial reform, which combines liberalization with a more affirmative role of the government in the financial sector. We concluded that if this affirmative role is to contribute to a more efficient financial sector, then the government's policy interventions should be targeted specifically at the credit market imperfections that may impede the proper functioning of a liberalized financial system, and examined what some of those interventions might be in order to characterize the government's role in a fully reformed financial system.

The next step is to consider whether there is anything we can say about how the *process* of reforming the domestic financial system might be carried out. Though theory tells us that a well-functioning financial system can make an important contribution to fostering economic growth, the process of reforming the financial system may prove to be a difficult one. We have already seen that without the necessary institutional preconditions in place, financial liberalization can go wrong, and not only may the favorable growth outcomes expected from the process not be achieved, but the financial system may itself become a source of macroeconomic problems that undermine economic growth. More generally, since the distortions associated with different components of financial repression are likely to interact with each other as well as with the macroeconomic environment, the sequence in which financial reform measures are adopted may affect how the economy performs during the reform process. The question, then, is: what considerations determine the optimal sequence in which measures should be implemented during the process of financial reform?

Before we can address this question, however, we have to complete our analysis of the various components of reform. Up until this point, we have concentrated on the *domestic* dimension of financial reform. That is, our attention has been occupied by policies toward the domestic financial sector. Before looking at the reform process as a whole we have to complement this with a consideration of the *external* dimension of reform. As we have seen, restrictions on capital inflows and outflows are an integral part of financial repression. Thus, we have to factor into the analysis of the sequencing of reform the role of *financial opening* as well. This means that we will need to give separate consideration to the analytical case for capital account liberalization before we can turn to the sequencing of the various components of financial reform.

Consequently, this chapter will begin by exploring the arguments for and against opening up the capital account of the balance of payments. Having done so, it will consider how different steps in the process of capital account liberalization fit into the optimal sequencing of financial reform. After completing our examination of reform from the analytical perspective, we will review the experiences of various emerging economies around the world with the process of financial reform.

I. WHY LIBERALIZE THE CAPITAL ACCOUNT?

While restrictions on capital flows are an important component of financial re-pression, in principle it is conceivable that the domestic financial system could be reformed without removing restrictions on capital movements. Thus, a logical first question to ask is whether, if the domestic financial system could be fully reformed without liberalizing the capital account, there would be a separate argument for opening up the capital account as well. In other words, is there a case for full capital account liberalization in the context of a well-functioning domestic financial system?

a. The Effectiveness of Capital Controls

A possibility that we need to consider at the outset is that there may not be a meaningful choice to be made about capital account liberalization at all. It simply may not be possible to sustain effective capital account restrictions under certain circumstances. The effectiveness of controls on capital movements depends on factors that differ across countries as well as over time, and these factors can change exogenously or as the unintended result of various domestic policies. At the time that financial reform is undertaken in any given country, therefore, this combi-nation of influences may make it impossible to maintain effective capital account restrictions.

The set of factors that affect the effectiveness of controls includes some that are international in scope, others that are of a domestic "structural" (i.e., slowly changing) nature, macroeconomic factors, and factors related to the design of the restrictions themselves.

Factors that are international in scope include, for example, the state of the technology that is relevant for determining the magnitude of transactions costs in conducting financial arbitrage across international borders. Obviously, technological advances that reduce such costs make it more difficult to sustain effective restrictions on capital movements. Similarly, the international legal environment also matters. For example, the extent of international cooperation in reporting cross-border financial claims is likely to be an important determinant of the effectiveness of capital account restrictions. Capital flight will be discouraged if host countries declare the assets of the residents of capital-exporting countries to the taxing authorities in those countries. Finally, rates of return available in international capital markets affect the strength of the incentives for moving capital across international borders.

A second set of factors operates at a domestic structural level. The most obvious of these, of course, is the efficiency of the bureaucracy charged with administering capital account restrictions. Other domestic "structural" factors are of a type that may tend to change if financial reform is accompanied by market-oriented measures elsewhere in the domestic economy. Financial reform itself, for example, may alter the effectiveness of capital account restrictions, because as the domestic financial sector becomes more competitive, innovative, and diversified in a reformed system, the opportunities for evading capital controls may multiply.

Changes elsewhere in the economy may also have this effect. For example, increased trade integration (a greater share of tradable goods in total domestic production and consumption) may make controls on capital movements more difficult to enforce. The reason is that an increase in the volume of trade increases possibilities for under- and over-invoicing exports and imports, as well as for the use of payment leads and lags to effectively lend and borrow abroad. Similarly, an increase in the role of foreign direct investment in the domestic economy makes capital controls harder to enforce because they can be evaded through the use of transfer pricing by multinational enterprises.

A third set of factors affecting the effectiveness of capital account restrictions is the size of the domestic incentives (such as return differentials) motivating inflows or outflows. If effecting a capital inflow or outflow to carry out an arbitrage transaction involves incurring a fixed cost imposed by the control regime, then the deterrent effect of this fixed cost may be nullified if the prospective gains from the arbitrage operation significantly exceed it.[1] These incentives are generally the product of domestic macroeconomic phenomena, including monetary policy, perceived fiscal solvency, or perceived real exchange rate misalignment, among others.

Finally, the effectiveness of restrictions is very likely to depend on the design of the restrictions themselves. For example, the comprehensiveness of restrictions may affect their effectiveness. Controls that are not comprehensive – that apply only to

---

[1] This means in particular that the size of capital flows in the presence of controls is not a reliable indicator of the effectiveness of controls, since large flows may simply indicate large *ex ante* arbitrage opportunities.

particular types of flows – can be evaded by changing the composition of flows.[2] The types of cross-border flows targeted by restrictions may also matter – that is, for a variety of reasons, controls on capital outflows may differ in effectiveness from controls on inflows, other things equal.[3]

Although economists tend to have strong views about the potential effectiveness of capital controls, the empirical evidence on the issue is problematic. Restrictions on capital flows can be intended to restrict the size of net capital flows and/or to affect their composition. The evidence differs on their ability to attain these two objectives. We can summarize it as follows.[4]

First, with regard to effects of capital account restrictions on the *magnitude* of capital flows, the evidence indicates that countries have at times been successful in using controls to preserve short-run monetary autonomy, driving temporary wedges between domestic and foreign interest rates. But there is little evidence that they can sustain such wedges permanently – at least under industrial-country conditions. How large the attainable wedge is and how long it can be sustained is likely to depend on the factors influencing the effectiveness of controls (such as those listed above), though little systematic research appears to have been conducted to date on the role of the factors that may render controls effective or ineffective. Overall, controls appear to have been able to preserve a limited degree of monetary autonomy temporarily, even in the fairly sophisticated financial systems of many industrial countries. This suggests that generic capital account restrictions can remain effective after domestic financial reform. But the evidence from industrial countries also indicates that controls have not been able to prevent the emergence of large capital outflows and inflows when prospective arbitrage profits have been large.

In the emerging-economy context, by contrast, the large and persistent parallel exchange-market premia that have existed in the presence of the capital account restrictions associated with financial repression, as well as the reduction of such premia in response to changes in foreign exchange regulations, suggest that controls can affect cross-border capital flows under a wide variety of country circumstances. The fact that substantial inflows have followed the removal of controls in several cases (e.g., Korea in 1992), and that inflows have slowed after controls were reimposed

---

[2] Notice that, while this would make controls ineffective in preserving monetary autonomy (or limiting the total magnitude of flows), it would not necessarily make them ineffective if their purpose is to alter the composition of flows.

[3] One argument for this is that the residence of the capital-importing or -exporting agent may matter. Domestic residents may be more prepared to evade restrictions than foreign agents, making controls on outflows less effective than controls on inflows.

[4] This evidence does not necessarily speak clearly. One difficulty is that of attribution. For example, tests of monetary autonomy based on interest parity conditions in the presence of capital controls may be more informative if autonomy fails than if it holds, since in the latter case "natural" barriers (e.g., differing perceived risk characteristics of domestic and foreign assets) may be operative. Even when changes in the intensity of controls are examined to minimize such problems, it becomes necessary to control for changes in other conditions, such as in the stance of monetary policy.

(Chile in 1991 and Malaysia in 1994) suggests that controls *can* work, at least in some cases and at least temporarily. On the other hand, as in industrial countries, episodes of extensive capital flight in the presence of restrictions on the outward movement of capital indicate clearly that controls cannot prevent large capital movements when perceived arbitrage margins are large.

There has been a substantial amount of more systematic country-specific research on the effectiveness of capital account restrictions in emerging economies during recent years. Some of this evidence is described in Box 14.1. Overall, it can be described as providing weak evidence for the effects of controls on the total magnitude of inflows, but stronger evidence for effects on their composition.

In addition to this country-specific work, there is a limited amount of cross-country research on this issue. Montiel and Reinhart (1999), for example, tested for the effects of capital account restrictions in a group of emerging economies by estimating a set of fixed-effects panel regressions explaining the volume and composition of various types of capital inflows for a fifteen-country panel of such economies, using annual observations over the period 1990–96. Inflows were explained as a function of a variety of macroeconomic variables, including the intensity of sterilization in each country, the severity of capital account restrictions, the level of international interest rates (measured as the yield on three-month U.S. Treasury bills), and a "tequila effect" dummy to capture possible effects on capital inflows of the Mexican financial crisis at the end of 1994.[5]

The results were consistent with those of the country-specific studies cited above. In various specifications, the coefficients on the capital control proxy, though consistently of the theoretically predicted sign, proved to be measured with a relatively low level of precision. However, when the dependent variable measured the *composition* of capital inflows, the explanatory variable measuring the intensity of controls proved to be associated with a significantly lower share of short-term flows and portfolio flows in total capital inflows, as well as a higher share of foreign direct investment. The authors concluded that, while there was some weak evidence that explicit capital inflow restrictions, and "prudential measures" affecting capital inflows (usually limiting banks' foreign exchange transactions or foreign exchange exposure), affected the total magnitude of flows in their sample countries, such measures seemed to be more effective in altering the composition of capital inflows than in reducing their overall magnitude.

---

[5] It may be worth emphasizing that testing the effectiveness of capital account restrictions requires controlling for the changes in the degree of sterilization, because a loosening of monetary policy accompanying an intensification of capital account restrictions (the cases of Chile and Malaysia) could mistakenly attribute any changes in the volume and composition of capital flows to the change in restrictions, rather than to the change in monetary policy. Conversely, a tightening in monetary policy at the time when the taxes or controls are introduced (Brazil) could undermine the effectiveness of the controls by raising domestic interest rates to levels where either domestic assets remain attractive even on an after-tax basis or by providing an incentive to circumvent the new controls.

Box 14.1. Effectiveness of Capital Controls in Emerging Economies:
Country Studies

Brazil

Using monthly data from January 1988 to December 1995, Cardoso and Goldfajn (1997) found that changes in an index of various Brazilian capital account restrictions had short-run impacts on both the volume and composition of private capital inflows. The impact peaked after about six months, however, and died out thereafter.

Chile

Quirk and Evans (1995) and Le Fort and Budnevich (1996) found that the maturity composition of capital flows into Chile was altered in favor of longer maturities after the imposition of capital controls in the form of unremunerated reserve requirements (URR). Valdes-Prieto and Soto (1996), on the other hand, found that an implicit tax variable designed to capture the effects of the URR did not affect aggregate flows of short-term capital in Chile, though it did affect at least one important component of such flows. Finally, Edwards (1998) found that the controls may have reduced the speed of convergence of Chilean interest rates toward uncovered interest-parity levels, increasing Chile's degree of monetary autonomy.

Colombia

Cardenas and Barrera (1993) estimated capital-flow equations with interest differentials adjusted by an estimate of the implicit tax associated with the unremunerated reserve requirements on capital inflows imposed by Colombia during part of their sample period. They found that the tax term had no impact on capital flows. On the other hand, the tax term did tend to affect domestic interest rates as well as the parallel exchange market premium. They also found a substantial change in the structure of Colombia's external borrowing after these controls were implemented. They concluded that controls in the form of unremunerated reserve requirements had little effect on the total magnitude of flows, but altered their composition.

Malaysia

Quirk and Evans (1995) as well as Reinhart and Dunaway (1996) concluded on the basis of before-after comparisons that severe controls on capital inflows imposed in Malaysia in 1994 may have affected both the magnitude and composition of inflows in the short run.

Overall, then, the evidence from emerging economies on whether capital account restrictions have typically been effective in altering the total magnitude of capital flows is mixed. At best, there is weak evidence of their effectiveness. However, there appears to be much more consensus that controls may be effective in altering the composition of flows.

b. Optimality of Capital Account Restrictions

Even if capital restrictions *can* remain effective, that does not mean that they should be retained. In discussing the liberalization of the domestic financial system, we saw that a well-functioning liberalized financial system could be expected to confer certain benefits on the economy, but that *laissez faire* was unlikely to be the best policy – in other words, a role for public policy would remain. We can perform a similar analysis for the external component of liberalization, identifying the benefits of capital account openness and then considering whether there is a case to be made for any type of policy intervention in this area.

The argument for liberalizing capital flows is that the enhanced financial integration with world capital markets that would follow from removing restrictions on capital movements can yield a number of economic benefits. These include the following:

i. Enhanced financial openness can increase national wealth by allowing domestic firms to finance investment projects with rates of return greater than the costs of foreign borrowing, or by permitting domestic savers to invest in higher-yielding assets than may be available in the domestic economy.

ii. It may also permit an improved intertemporal allocation of consumption for the domestic economy. This is because international borrowing and lending allows the domestic economy to divorce the path of its consumption expenditure from that of its income, allowing it to allocate its consumption over time in ways that may better suit the preferences of domestic residents.

iii. Financial openness gives domestic residents access to gains from portfolio diversification, reducing the overall risk in their portfolios without necessarily sacrificing expected return.

iv. Financial openness can support the process of financial reform by promoting the efficiency of financial intermediation. It can do this by increasing competition for domestic financial intermediaries.

v. Finally, financial openness can impose macroeconomic discipline on governments by reducing their ability to tax the financial system through explicit or implicit taxes. As we have seen before, one motivation for retaining capital account restrictions under financial repression was precisely to avoid this discipline.[6]

Since the retention of effective controls on capital movements would imply foregoing – or least reducing – these potential benefits, the view that restrictions should be retained faces a serious burden of proof. Perhaps the best argument for restricting the scope of financial openness is as a means of counteracting distortions

---

[6] It may be worth pointing out that, to the extent that effective capital account restrictions can be difficult to reimpose once they have been removed, this means that the removal of such restrictions can be used by the government in the same way as the granting of independence to the central bank – that is, as a signal of its good future fiscal intentions.

in the domestic economy that are not taken into account in the list of benefits from liberalization enumerated above.

One argument for retaining controls over capital *inflows*, for example, is that there may be externalities associated with the act of foreign borrowing. If the risk premium faced by individual domestic borrowers in international capital markets, for example, depends on the country's *total* stock of outstanding external debt, then each individual's act of borrowing abroad imposes higher borrowing costs on other domestic residents. Since individual borrowers would not take this effect into account if external borrowing is conducted in a decentralized fashion, the country as a whole would tend to overborrow. In this situation there is a case for permanent intervention by the government to restrict external borrowing, in the form of a small Pigouvian tax on external borrowers that would cause individual domestic borrowers to take into account the effects of their own borrowing on the premium faced by other domestic agents.

Alternatively, capital controls could be justified as permanent second-best instruments to offset the effects of purely *domestic* microeconomic distortions that cannot be removed. The preferred ("first-best") policy would always be to remove the distortion, but where this is not possible, a case can be made for controls on "second-best" grounds.

For example, external overborrowing may arise from moral hazard problems, if domestic borrowers are induced to borrow more because they believe that they will be bailed out by the government in the event that they are unable to repay. Prudential restrictions on external borrowing and lending by domestic financial institutions can plausibly be warranted on these grounds. These restrictions on capital movements have a clear second-best rationale since they are directed at a specific distortion: the inability of the government to credibly commit to removing certain implicit guarantees.

Similarly, temporary restrictions on capital movements may be justified when the public is induced to borrow or lend abroad because it disbelieves a policy commitment that the government is actually determined to carry out. For example, if the public does not believe that an exchange-rate-based stabilization will be sustained, its expectation that a devaluation is forthcoming may cause it to move funds abroad. The resulting increase in domestic interest rates may actually make the stabilization harder to achieve. In this case, the distortion that motivates the capital flow is the absence of a precommitment mechanism for the authorities that could make their intentions credible. If credibility is not achievable, temporary capital account restrictions may be warranted, again on second-best grounds.

Finally, restrictions on capital flows have been defended on more general grounds of macroeconomic stabilization: to insulate the domestic economy from external financial shocks and to preserve monetary autonomy, thereby permitting the domestic monetary authorities to use the exchange rate and money supply as separate policy instruments.

The first goal, however, is questionable. Its justification requires that the government be better informed about the duration of financial shocks than the private sector, or that the transmission of such shocks to the domestic economy would tend to aggravate the effects of some previously existing distortion. Restrictions designed to achieve this purpose are hard to justify as a general proposition. With regard to the objective of preserving some degree of monetary autonomy, the benefits to be gained for macroeconomic management are large only if other stabilization instruments are not available. If fiscal policy is sufficiently flexible to be used for stabilization purposes, for example, then price stability and satisfactory current account performance can be pursued through the combined use of fiscal and exchange rate policy. The first-best solution to this problem may thus be to increase the flexibility of fiscal policy, rather than to adopt capital controls. At best, therefore, these considerations provide an argument for retaining restrictions as a transitory device, until the fiscal system can be reformed in such a way as to make fiscal policy an effective stabilization tool.

In short, there may indeed be legitimate arguments for retaining some forms of mild restrictions on capital movements for extended periods even after the domestic financial system has been reformed, or even for retaining or reimposing much stronger restrictions temporarily under special circumstances. But it is hard to come up with defensible arguments for the retention of the very severe forms of capital controls that typically accompany domestic financial repression. Thus, in analyzing reform, the general case should probably be taken to be one in which domestic financial reform is accompanied by at least some liberalization of capital movements. A general reform strategy, therefore, should include a capital account liberalization component. Next, we will consider how this component might fit into the general reform process.

II. THE SEQUENCING OF FINANCIAL REFORM

The concern with the "sequencing" of reform (a term that has come into wide usage as a verb) essentially reflects the view that the conditions under which domestic and external financial liberalization are undertaken may ultimately determine whether they yield the expected economic benefits, and that some of these conditions, at least, are under the control of the authorities conducting the reform process.

For example, some observers have argued that freeing domestic interest rates when bank supervision is weak and the domestic macroeconomic situation is unstable is a recipe for disaster, even if the capital account remains closed.[7] Macroeconomic instability increases the variance and covariance of a given set of projects in banks' portfolios, and as we have seen, weak supervision in the context of free

---

[7] See Villanueva and Mirakhor (1990).

(or underpriced) deposit insurance creates incentives for banks to endogenously increase the riskiness of the lending they choose to undertake. A strategy of paying high interest rates to attract deposits, and then investing these funds in high-risk projects with low expected returns, may maximize expected returns to the owners of the banks, though not to society as a whole. When banks fail, the combination of macroeconomic crisis and lost information capital contributes to lower and poorer-quality investment and reduced growth. The evidence reviewed in the last chapter about the causes of banking crises around the world is consistent with this view. But this would suggest that freeing domestic interest rates should await the establishment of macroeconomic stability as well as of the appropriate regulatory institutions for the banking system – in other words, that the process of financial reform should be "sequenced."

Indeed, there is a reasonably broad consensus among economists concerning the order in which the major steps in reforming the financial sector are best undertaken. In brief, this consensus takes the view that macroeconomic stabilization should precede domestic financial reform, and that domestic financial reform should precede the liberalization of the capital account of the balance of payments. Why should this be?

a. The Sequencing of the Broad Components of Reform

Recall from Chapter 12 that financial repression has a strong fiscal motivation, and that the revenue that governments collect from taxing the financial system through repression can be substantial. This means that financial liberalization without a fiscal adjustment is likely to increase the rate of inflation. Since higher inflation may be harmful for growth, financial reform undertaken to stimulate growth could be self-defeating without a previous fiscal adjustment. Moreover, as we saw in Chapter 13, safeguards against moral hazard need to be in place before the banking system is liberalized. One such safeguard is the adequate capitalization of banks, which may require a substantial injection of government funds to absorb the bad loans of the banking sector before it is liberalized. In other words, a fiscal adjustment may be needed to generate the resources with which to reform the banking sector. The implication is that, for both reasons, weaknesses in the government's budget have to be addressed before financial repression can be eliminated – that is, *stabilization should precede domestic financial reform.*

Regarding domestic financial reform itself, we saw in the last chapter that before the domestic financial system is liberalized, institutional policies should be put in place to protect against liquidity crises and moral hazard lending. This means, on the one hand, that *the lender of last resort function and/or mechanisms for deposit insurance should be clarified, and on the other hand, that adequate prudential systems need to be established, and banks well capitalized, before bank activities are liberalized.* This means in particular that if previously repressed banks have their capital reduced by nonperforming loans, these institutions need to be recapitalized before they are freed to make borrowing and lending decisions on their own.

Together, these observations suggest that the early stages of the reform process should emphasize fiscal reforms, institutional reforms to create an appropriate regulatory structure for the domestic financial system, and the recapitalization of domestic banks to the extent necessary. While these measures are implemented, restrictions on the activities of domestic banks should remain in place. Once they are completed, the domestic financial sector can be liberalized, permitting competition among financial institutions through the setting of interest rates, allocation of funds, and entry into as well as exit from the financial sector.

Where does the liberalization of the capital account fit into this sequence? In the context of the discussion of the debt overhang problem in Chapter 8, we saw that investor confidence in the sustainability of a fiscal policy regime that would safeguard the value of their assets is necessary to prevent capital flight when the capital account is (*de facto*) open. Moreover, as we will see in the next chapter (but as already mentioned in the last section), adequate flexibility of domestic macroeconomic policy instruments is required to counteract the effects of capital movements when the capital account is open. If fiscal consolidation and the credibility of the government's long-run fiscal policy stance are not achieved before this opening takes place, it may later prove impossible (because of creditor reactions) to adopt temporarily looser fiscal policy in response to contractionary shocks such as an increase in external interest rates. Thus, both to avoid debt overhang problems as well as to maximize the room for fiscal policy to maneuver, *stabilization should precede financial opening.*

Similarly, as we saw in the previous section, distortions in resource allocation through the domestic financial sector should be removed to the greatest possible extent before restrictions on capital flows are removed, so foreign resources are not misallocated by the domestic financial system (which could result in "immiserizing" capital inflows – i.e., foreign borrowing that yields a return lower than the cost of the funds). The implication is that *domestic financial reform should precede financial opening.* The upshot is that capital account liberalization should be undertaken as the last stage in the reform process.

Putting these observations together yields the prescribed sequence for the broad components of reform: macroeconomic stabilization, the implementation of prudential mechanisms, and the capitalization of banks should come first, followed by the liberalization of the domestic financial sector, followed finally by capital account liberalization. This sequence has come to command a wide consensus among economists who have studied the reform process. The appendix to this chapter provides a sample of the reasoning offered by several knowledgeable observers in support of this sequence, which has become the conventional wisdom on the subject.

b. Specific Reform Measures

While the preceding discussion provides some broad guidelines, it falls short of providing a specific sequence for the reform process, because each of the three broad areas of reform is itself comprised of several components. Not only can these themselves be sequenced in a variety of ways, but considering these components separately may cause us to reconsider the conventional sequence as it applies to the role of a specific component. As an illustration of the latter, in this section we will consider an analysis by Fischer and Reisen (1993) of the roles of specific components of the capital account of the balance of payments.

Fischer and Reisen take a somewhat more nuanced view of the role of capital account liberalization in the general sequence of financial reform than that which appears in the conventional analysis presented above. They decompose capital account liberalization into several parts and argue that different components of the capital account should be liberalized at different stages of the reform process.

According to Fischer and Reisen, liberalization of foreign direct investment (FDI) and trade finance should come early in the reform process, for two reasons. First, they argue that openness to FDI and to international trade are essential for development. The argument for the beneficial effects of these flows on development is that, on the one hand, positive spillovers emanate to the rest of the domestic economy from foreign direct investment, and on the other hand that the availability of trade finance helps the economy to reap the benefits of commercial openness. Second, since these types of resource flows are not intermediated through the domestic financial system, they are not subject to misallocation as the result of any distortions that may exist in that system.

Beyond this, Fischer and Reisen take fiscal consolidation to be the most important next step, for the reasons mentioned above (i.e., because it is needed to permit the government to do without revenues from financial repression and to provide a stabilization instrument when the capital account is opened, as well as because a strong fiscal position is needed to cope with bad loan problems in the reforming financial sector).

Next, they would implement steps to reform the domestic banking system. They argue that this should precede financial opening because otherwise financial opening will lead to high domestic interest rates for moral hazard reasons. They take this to mean the removal of excessive bad loans to increase the franchise value of banks, the strengthening of prudential regulation and supervision, the establishment of legal and accounting systems to cope with systemic risks, and the enforcement of competition to foster allocative efficiency in the financial sector. Because these measures take time to implement, they should be enacted early in the reform process.

Once macroeconomic stability is achieved, the requisite institutional mechanisms are in place for the domestic financial sector, and the bad loan problem is resolved, domestic interest rates can be freed. Under these conditions, overintermediation (i.e., moral-hazard-driven borrowing and lending) should not be a problem. At the same time, the government should take steps to foster deepened securities markets. Once high-yielding domestic instruments are in place and there is no debt overhang problem to trigger capital flight, capital *outflows* can be liberalized. When domestic financial reform has been completed (interest rates have been freed, bad loans removed, and reserve requirements lowered), the entry of foreign banks into the domestic financial system can be permitted.

The final step in the reform process for Fischer and Reisen should be the liberalization of short-term capital inflows. This should happen only after free entry has increased bank competition and enhanced credit market integration, after bad loan problems have been resolved and banks have accumulated experience exercising independent credit judgment, after prudential regulation has proven adept at preventing distress borrowing, and after stabilization has succeeded in producing low domestic interest rates.

III. COUNTRY CASE STUDIES

The preceding analysis suggests that the effects of financial reform should depend on how it is carried out. Unfortunately, it is not easy to bring evidence to bear on this issue. The study by King and Levine (1993) discussed in Chapter 11, for example, considered the effects of financial reforms from a variety of perspectives. For instance, they looked at the behavior of their financial indicators before and after financial reforms in five countries, finding that all four of their indicators of financial depth increased, and that the ratio of currency to demand deposits fell, in Argentina, Chile, Indonesia, Korea, and the Philippines. During all of the reform episodes that they examined but one, the real interest rate also rose after the reform. They did not try to link these phenomena with subsequent growth performance. King and Levine also looked at the relationship between their financial indicators and the success of World Bank adjustment lending, on the hypothesis that structural adjustment measures are more likely to promote growth under a well-functioning financial system, and that a given set of growth-enhancing measures is more likely to be successful if accompanied by a financial reform. They found that intensive-adjustment-lending countries with better initial financial depth tended to grow faster during the subsequent five years. This relationship held up after correcting for other growth determinants.

But of course, this kind of evidence has little to say about the effects of alternative reform *strategies* – that is, about the sequencing of reform. We have already seen some indirect evidence on this issue in the previous chapter, where it was suggested that financial liberalization in the context of an inappropriate domestic institutional environment tended to be associated with financial crises. More detailed evidence on the effects of financial reform strategies tends to be in the form of country case studies. The methodology is descriptive, and conclusions about the effects of reform strategies are typically based on before-and-after examination of the data, thereby failing to control for other influences on the variables of interest.

An extensive older literature of this type exists analyzing the financial liberalization experience of the Southern Cone countries in South America during the late 1970s.[8] As already indicated in the review of the experience of Chile in the last chapter, this literature's conclusions are that the liberalization effort there – comprising the removal of restrictions on the domestic financial sector as well as the opening up of the capital account – failed because the process was undertaken in an unstable macroeconomic setting and with an unsatisfactory domestic regulatory framework. In other words, financial liberalization was "premature" in the sense that it preceded other steps that should actually have been taken earlier in the reform process. Financial crises with severe macroeconomic implications soon followed in each of the three countries involved. Thus, the Southern Cone experience supports the policy prescription that the achievement of domestic macroeconomic stability (the centerpiece of which is a sustainable fiscal position, as we have seen before) and the implementation of an appropriate regulatory framework for the domestic financial system should precede the removal of restrictions on domestic financial institutions and the opening of the capital account.

Because this experience is more familiar (and because we will return to it in Chapter 19), in this section we will briefly examine the financial reform experience among emerging economies elsewhere – specifically, in Asia and Sub-Saharan Africa – at the times when they began their transitions from financial repression, that is, during the early years of their reform processes.

a. Financial Reform Among Asian Economies

Several countries in Asia, including the "miracle" economies, undertook reform of their financial systems during the decades of the seventies and eighties. The experience of these countries is less well known than the earlier ones of the Southern Cone countries.[9] In Chapter 19 we will consider the role of financial reform in the financial crisis that broke out in Southeast Asia in mid-1997. For now, we will focus on the cases of Japan, Korea, and Taiwan during an earlier period. Overall, we can summarize the main outlines of the experiences of these countries as follows:

i.   Among the three "miracle" economies reviewed in more detail in Chapter 12, Japan in the mid-1970s, as well as Korea and Taiwan in the early 1980s, decided to

---

[8] See, for example, Diaz Alejandro (1985). Indeed, economists' research interest in the optimal sequencing of reform was essentially triggered by the experience of these countries.

[9] An overview of financial liberalization in several of these countries during the decade of the eighties is provided in Tseng and Corker (1991), as well as the World Bank (1993).

liberalize what had been heavily regulated, domestically closed, and moderately repressed financial systems. Reform of the financial sector was undertaken in the context of a stable domestic macroeconomic environment. Growth was rapid, inflation was relatively low, and all of the governments involved were in relatively strong fiscal positions. All three systems moved from highly regulated, moderately repressed, states to less regulated, more competitive, market-based systems during the course of this process.

ii. The *scope* of reform tended to be broad in these countries. The easing of controls over interest rates was accompanied by measures to promote competition in the financial sector, such as increased freedom of entry by domestic banks, expanding the scope of permissible activities for different institutions, and relaxing restrictions on entry by foreign banks. The supervisory framework for the financial system was typically strengthened by centralizing supervisory responsibilities, developing and unifying the regulatory framework (as well as extending it to nonbanks), and in some cases providing explicit deposit insurance. Money markets were fostered by creating new instruments (such as central bank and government securities) with flexible interest rates.

iii. However, the *pace* of liberalization was gradual, and sometimes partial. Liberalization was slow and piecemeal in Japan, Korea, and Taiwan by comparison with the experience of the Southern Cone. All three countries tended to follow the conventional sequencing of reform, with real sector reform first, then domestic financial reform, then capital account liberalization. The partial nature of reform is evidenced, for example, by the fact that interest rates were not always fully liberalized. Sometimes (as in Korea), managed rates were simply adjusted more frequently. Also, while total credit controls were eliminated, sectoral credit allocation requirements and selective rediscounting remained in place for some time. The deregulation of deposits began in Japan in 1981, when new types of instruments were permitted for commercial banks, trust banks, long-term credit banks, and the postal savings system. These still had regulated rates, but new instruments with market-determined rates were introduced at about the same time. However, deregulation of small time and demand deposits was put off at that time. Interest rate controls were eventually lifted in Japan, and international transactions liberalized. In Taiwan, the pace and intensity of reform increased in the mid-1980s, and by 1989 deposit and loan rates were free. In 1990, sixteen new private banks were licensed and some government banks were privatized. The liberalization of capital flows started in the 1990s. Finally, in Korea interest rate deregulation began only in 1991, on a fixed schedule. The intended pace of capital account liberalization was slower in Korea than in the other two countries.

iv. The financial results of the early stages of this gradual liberalization process did not tend to be disruptive, as had occurred in the more rapid liberalizations of the Southern Cone. The gradual liberalization of interest rates tended to increase nominal rates, but not necessarily enough to establish very large positive real rates. Positive real rates were attained by changes in nominal rates and, especially in Korea, through a reduction in the rate of inflation. Yet in each of these countries positive real interest rates followed liberalization, and financial deepening occurred at the same time. Whether liberalization was accompanied by desirable growth effects is another matter entirely. The difficulty, of course, is in controlling for other factors that were influencing macroeconomic performance in the liberalizing countries at the same time.

b. Financial Reform in Sub-Saharan Africa

By and large, financial liberalization has taken place in Africa only relatively recently (since the mid-eighties). The adoption of some form of liberalization or bank restructuring measures has been fairly widespread.[10] A partial list of such measures undertaken recently is provided in Table 14.1. In addition to the countries listed in the table, interest rates had been freed by the end of 1992 in Burundi, Madagascar, Mauritania, and Zambia. Many other countries moved from setting rates to setting minimum deposit and maximum lending rates, or to regulating spreads.

However, low positive real interest rates have *not* been the rule after liberalization, as they had been in the Asian "miracle" economies even *before* liberalization. Sub-Saharan African countries have tended either to continue to have the negative interest rates that were typical under financial repression or, in the case of those with fixed exchange rates and currencies that have been overvalued, very high positive rates. In part this may reflect the incomplete nature of the liberalization. In the case of the Central Bank of the West African States (BCEAO) of the West African Monetary Union, for example, the abolition of the bank's preferential discount rate in October 1989 left interest rate controls in place. The same was true of the Central Bank of the Central African States (BECEA), which abolished its preferential discount rate in October 1990. While Nigeria removed interest rate controls in July 1987 and introduced treasury bill auctions in November 1989, the government continued to exert influence over interest rates emerging in such markets through the reservation prices set by the central bank. Some adjustments to previously fixed interest rates were recorded in Tanzania in 1991 and Uganda in 1988, but neither country moved immediately to flexible interest rate determination. Other possible explanations for the behavior of real interest rates after liberalization are lack of competition due to the small number of banks and the continued role of government-owned institutions.[11]

---

[10] The World Bank (1994) lists a total of 19 Sub-Saharan African countries that have undertaken some form of liberalization measures in the financial sector since the mid-eighties.

[11] The World Bank (1994) reports that the number of commercial banks in Sub-Saharan Africa in which the government retains a majority share fell from 108 in 1982 to 89 in 1992.

Table 14.1. *Financial Liberalization in Sub-Saharan Africa*

Gambia (September 1985)	Ceilings on interest rates were removed in September 1985, an auction system for issuing Treasury bills was introduced in July 1986, and quantitative controls on credit were removed in September 1990.
Nigeria (July 1987)	Directed credit restrictions were relaxed over the period 1983–87 by increasing the sectoral aggregation of directed credit allocations. On July 31, 1987, the Central Bank removed interest rate controls, and raised both the Treasury Bill and rediscount rates by 4 percentage points, to 15 and 14 percent. In November 1989, an auction system was instituted for Treasury Bills and certificates, but the Central Bank retained a reservation price.
Ghana (September 1987)	Ceilings on interest rates were removed, while the removal on quantitative credit controls was scheduled for 1992.
Malawi (April 1988)	Ceilings on interest rates were removed, and quantitative credit ceilings were eliminated in January 1991.
Uganda (July 1988)	On July 1, 1988, an increase of 10 percentage points was announced on most interest rates.
Benin and Cote d'Ivoire (October 1989)	The BCEAO abolished its preferential discount rate, but bank interest rate remained subject to regulation. Cote d'Ivoire is also a member of the BCEAO, so it was affected by these liberalizing measures.
Cameroon (October 1990)	The BEAC eliminated its preferential lending rates, simplified its interest rate structure, and increased its power to determine interest rate policy with the intention to move toward greater flexibility in rates.
Tanzania (July 1991)	The system of fixed interest rates and fixed differentials was replaced by a single maximum lending rate of 31 percent on July 25.
Kenya (July 1991)	

Note: Interest rate ceilings were removed.
Sources: Turtleboom 1991 and Galbis 1993.

In addition to the behavior of real interest rates, widening post-liberalization spreads between lending and deposit rates appear to have been a problem in several Sub-Saharan African countries that liberalized interest rates during the 1980s (Gambia, Ghana, Malawi, and Nigeria, according to Turtleboom 1991). Again, lack of competition is a possible explanation, as is the continued presence of nonperforming loans.

Regarding the latter, the experience with bank restructuring also appears unfortunately not to have been favorable. Recapitalization operations have tended to be expensive, recovery of nonperforming assets has been poor, and restructuring operations have had to be repeated in several cases (World Bank 1994). In Ghana, for example, nonperforming assets restructured under a plan undertaken in 1989 amounted to 41 percent of total bank credit to the non-government sector (Kapur et al. 1991).

Overall, then, the reform process has not proceeded smoothly in Sub-Saharan Africa.

IV. SUMMARY

The easing of restrictions on capital movements is an important part of the financial reform process since, just as a well-functioning domestic financial system holds the promise of substantial benefits in economic welfare and growth, a relatively open capital account does so as well. While there may be valid arguments for retaining (or imposing) some types of mild restrictions on capital movements, except in extreme (and temporary) circumstances these fall far short of the near-absolute barriers on international capital flows that tend to be associated with financial repression.

One valid argument for capital account restrictions is that they may serve as a useful second-best policy when there are important domestic distortions in the real or financial sectors. This implies that opening up the capital account is probably best deferred until domestic financial reform is complete. Given that domestic financial reform itself is more likely to be successful when domestic macroeconomic stability has been achieved, featuring specifically a sustainable fiscal stance without reliance on financial repression "taxes," this suggests a sequence of reforms led by macroeconomic stabilization, followed by domestic financial reform and including capital account liberalization only as a final step. Domestic financial reform itself needs to proceed in stages, with an appropriate regulatory framework and adequate bank capitalization in place to ameliorate moral hazard problems before restrictions on bank activities are removed. Such a sequence has indeed come to represent conventional wisdom among economists, though a more nuanced view might allow for a removal of restrictions on certain types of capital flows (e.g., foreign direct investment and trade credits) much earlier in the process. The experience of a wide range of emerging economies tends to support the conventional wisdom.

APPENDIX 14.1: OBSERVATIONS ON SEQUENCING
OF FINANCIAL REFORM

As indicated in the text, the sequence of reform in which the achievement of macroeconomic stability, the implementation of an appropriate regulatory and supervisory framework, and the capitalization of banks all precede domestic financial liberalization, which in turns precedes the opening of the capital account, has come to represent the conventional wisdom on the optimal sequencing of reform. This appendix illustrates this by describing the policy prescriptions of three knowledgeable observers.

a. Turtleboom (1991)

Turtleboom (1991), for example, proposes a four-step sequence of reform:

i. Proceed simultaneously in restoring macroeconomic equilibrium and restructuring or liquidating insolvent financial institutions. The latter process should be initiated early, because it is likely to take time.
ii. Introduce indirect instruments of monetary control with freely determined interest rates, such as treasury bills sold at auction. At the same time, establish supervisory guidelines for banks regarding loan classification, provisioning for bad debt, interest rate capitalization, capital adequacy, and limits on portfolio concentration.
iii. Increase competition among banks by granting more bank licenses, permitting the entrance of foreign banks, and privatizing government-owned banks.
iv. As a final step, remove interest rate controls and direct credit ceilings.

Notice that this sequence involves putting the institutional and macroeconomic conditions in place before liberalization proper (in the form of step iv) is attempted, but that no specific attention is paid to the role of capital account liberalization.

b. McKinnon (1992)

In a book entitled *The Order of Economic Liberalization*, Ronald McKinnon considered both the issues of domestic financial reform and capital account liberalization in the context of a broader reform sequence for the previously centrally planned economies of the former Soviet bloc.

The first step McKinnon advocates is to get the fiscal deficit under control, with an important contribution to be made by a broad-based tax system that raises revenue from both households and enterprises. He argues that macroeconomic stabilization would "open up" domestic capital markets by moving interest rates in the banking system to positive real levels. In McKinnon's view, the accumulated experience of many countries supports the key role of positive real interest rates in improving the efficiency of investment. He argues, however, that raising real interest rates to positive levels is more effective (in terms of growth promotion) if done through price level stabilization rather than through raising nominal interest rates. An increase in money demand would be an important growth-enhancing consequence of price level stabilization brought about by fiscal means. If anything, nominal interest rates should continue to be controlled, and if necessary *reduced*, during stabilization to keep real rates from becoming too high.

Once macroeconomic stability is achieved and domestic capital markets are "opened up" by the prevalence of positive real interest rates, the *current* account of the balance of payments can be liberalized and domestic prices can be freed. Exchange rates should be unified before quantitative controls are lifted on exporting and importing, but once this is done the advocated sequence of trade liberalization is a conventional one – to replace quantitative restrictions with "equivalent" tariffs, and reduce these gradually and predictably, beginning with the highest tariffs, to a low common tariff rate. McKinnon argues that the exchange rate should not be used as a nominal anchor. Instead, the authorities should set the rate of depreciation equal to the difference between domestic and foreign inflation rates, thereby pegging the real exchange rate.

McKinnon would put decentralization and privatization of the banking system fairly late in the reform process, citing the problem of moral hazard created by deposit insurance in the presence of macroeconomic risk that cannot be diversified away. Moreover, he would implement capital account convertibility as the very last step in economic liberalization. He views capital outflows as harmful because they reduce the base of the inflation tax, thereby increasing the rate of inflation required to finance a given fiscal deficit, and capital inflows as potentially harmful as well because they result in real exchange appreciation.

c. Williamson (1991)

Williamson shares the view that capital account liberalization should be undertaken at a very late stage of the reform process. He cites a variety of arguments in the reform sequencing literature for liberalizing capital inflows late:

i. As noted by McKinnon, capital inflows may result in an appreciation of the real exchange rate, which undermines competitiveness of tradable goods, impairing export-led growth.
ii. Permitting capital inflows before fiscal discipline is established may permit the maintenance of unsustainable fiscal deficits.
iii. Capital that flows in before trade is liberalized may go into the wrong industries, since its allocation will be responding to distorted relative prices.
iv. Capital that flows in before the financial system is liberalized may go into the wrong investments.

Thus, according to Williamson, a good time to liberalize inflows is when nontraditional export industries are firmly established, fiscal discipline is in place, and both the import regime and the domestic financial system have been liberalized.

With regard to capital outflows, Williamson argues that the removal of controls on outflows should not be viewed as part of a strategy for fine tuning the net flow of capital, since it is not clear that net inflows will actually decrease (we will consider this issue in the next chapter). He argues that, because of the "impossible trinity," controls should not be dismantled until a new policy instrument (presumably fiscal policy) becomes available. He also suggests that this policy should not be implemented until the country has been accepted as a member of a community of market-oriented democratic states that can be relied on to maintain the policy in the face of difficulties, and when participation in a multilateral tax information-sharing agreement becomes possible. Finally, Williamson maintains that because liberalizing the capital account essentially privatizes decisions concerning the allocation of foreign investments, a good time to liberalize is when substantial foreign assets have been accumulated. Thus, his criteria essentially involve waiting until an open capital account can be considered to be a policy regime that investors regard as permanent, until the ability to manage aggregate demand is enhanced by a measure of fiscal flexibility, and until arrangements are in place to limit the erosion of the tax base through capital outflows.

15

Coping with Capital Inflows

In recent years, many emerging economies have embarked on the road to financial reform. As indicated in the previous chapter, an important component of such reform has been the liberalization of the capital account of the balance of payments. And indeed, restrictions on capital movements have been removed or greatly weakened in many of these economies, in a process that gathered force around the world during the late 1980s and early 1990s. This process of financial reform and capital account liberalization was part of a much broader reorientation of economic policies among emerging economies toward a much more market-friendly disposition. In the international financial arena, this switch in policy regimes marked the transition from the debt crisis conditions that we reviewed in Chapter 8 to a situation in which many emerging economies became the recipients of substantial amounts of private capital from the rest of the world, surpassing in magnitude the inflows that preceded the international debt crisis of the early 1980s.

Ironically, just as the scarcity of external funding posed serious macroeconomic problems for the heavily indebted emerging economies during the 1980s, the large inflows of private capital that many of these economies began to receive during the first half of the 1990s was also viewed as a policy problem. Indeed, the capital inflow "problem" became a serious concern for economists and emerging-economy policymakers during the first half of the decade. This chapter will analyze the factors driving such capital flows. It will also consider the effects of these flows on the domestic macroeconomic equilibrium in the recipient countries, as well as the possible policy responses available to them. Country experiences with the management of capital inflows will be reviewed, focusing on comparisons of policy responses in Latin America and East and Southeast Asia to draw lessons about appropriate strategies for the macroeconomic management of capital inflows in a newly liberalized environment.

I. FACTORS DRIVING CAPITAL INFLOWS

a. Characteristics of Capital Flows to Emerging Economies in the Early 1990s

The history of capital flows to developing countries has tended to be an episodic one. As we saw in Chapter 8, the 1970s were a period of low international real interest rates and large capital flows into emerging economies. These dried up for many countries during the international debt crisis after 1982. The post-liberalization capital inflow episode dates from about 1987–88, when substantial amounts of private capital began to flow into Thailand. Inflows picked up during 1989 in Malaysia, and during 1990 in Indonesia. The surge of capital flows started slightly later in Latin America. The break in the capital inflow experience of this region came in 1990, when Chile and Mexico began to receive large amounts of capital. By 1992–93, capital inflows to emerging economies had become comparable, relative to the size of the recipient economies, to their pre-1982 levels. After a pause that coincided with a tightening of U.S. monetary policy in 1994, the magnitude of flows picked up again in 1995–96, shrugging off the Mexican crisis. Net private capital inflows peaked in 1996, before being curtailed by the Asian crisis in 1997. There was a gradual recovery in the first half of 1998, but a collapse once again after the August 1998 Russian default.

As already suggested, the timing of the return of capital flows to emerging economies during the decade of the 1990s did not tend to be uniform across countries. Initially, the surge of new capital was primarily an East Asian and Latin American phenomenon. The phenomenon subsequently became more widespread, however, reaching South Asia as well as Sub-Saharan Africa by 1993. Nonetheless, whether expressed in absolute dollar values, or scaled by exports or GDP, inflows clearly tended to head disproportionately to countries in East and Southeast Asia and South America.

Within each of these regions, flows tended to be concentrated in several large developing countries. Over the period from 1989 to mid-1993, for example, 85 percent of all portfolio flows to East Asia were accounted for by China, Indonesia, Korea, and Thailand, while in Latin America, Argentina, Brazil, Mexico, and Venezuela accounted for almost 95 percent of portfolio flows over the same period (Gooptu 1994). In all, 95 percent of all private capital inflows during 1988–95 went to twenty-one countries.

During the decade of the seventies, capital flows to emerging economies largely took the form of debt instruments. By contrast, equity instruments, both in the form of direct foreign investment as well as of portfolio investments, played an important role in the nineties. Syndicated bank loans, which had dominated flows in the seventies, were relatively unimportant in the early nineties, reflecting the fact that new types of lenders other than banks became involved in emerging economies. Institutional investors (mutual and pension funds), for example, played a major role in the nineties. As an indication of their growing impact during this period, in 1986 there were nineteen emerging-market country funds and nine regional or global emerging-market funds. By 1995, however, there were 500 country funds and nearly 800 global or regional emerging-market funds. The combined assets of all emerging-market funds rose from $1.9 billion in 1986 to $132 billion in the middle of 1996.

These trends away from commercial bank lending and in favor of portfolio and equity investment were geographically widespread. However, significant disparities in the composition of flows across regions were also apparent, at least during the early years of the inflow episode. For example, in Latin America portfolio flows accounted for the majority of the new inflows until 1996–97, while in East Asia foreign direct investment was dominant until 1995–96, when bank lending became much more important.

Not surprisingly in view of the fact that the capital-inflow episode of the nineties followed a market-friendly reorientation of policies and financial liberalization in the recipient countries, the sectoral composition of capital inflows in the nineties was markedly different from that of the seventies. In the more recent inflow episode, borrowers in the recipient economies tended to be private agents, rather than the public sector. The sectoral identity of the borrower presents a stark contrast between the current inflow episode and previous experience.

b. "Pull" Factors, "Push" Factors, and Changes in Financial Integration

Why did capital begin to flow back into emerging economies in such magnitudes? The debate on this question among economists began almost as soon as the new inflows materialized. Leading explanations typically have been classified into three categories: "push" factors, "pull" factors, and changes in the degree of financial integration. "Pull" factors are those that originate in the borrowing countries. They represent improvements in the risk-return characteristics of assets issued by emerging-economy borrowers that help to attract capital from abroad. "Push" factors, on the other hand, originate in the lending countries. They drive capital out by reducing the attractiveness of lending to industrial-country debtors.

As we saw in the model of Part 2, factors of either or both types could influence capital flows as long as the recipient economy is financially open, without any change in the degree of that economy's integration with world capital markets. The third factor that may have been at work during this period, however, was precisely a change in the degree of integration of emerging economies with international financial markets. The degree of integration reflects the costs of cross-border borrowing and lending, and these may have been falling during this time due to the removal of capital account restrictions in the emerging economies in the context of financial reform, because of changes in regulations in creditor countries that increased access to their financial markets by emerging-economy borrowers,

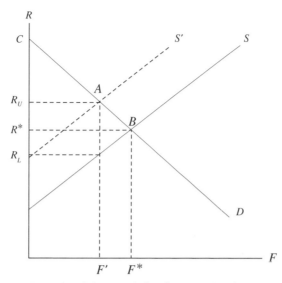

Figure 15.1. Factors Driving Capital Inflows: A Simple Decomposition

as well as because of reduced information, transportation, and communication costs.

The potential roles of these three factors are illustrated in Figure 15.1. This figure shows the supply and demand curves for external funds from an emerging economy, as a function of the interest rate on such funds R. The gap between the notional supply curve S and the "effective" supply curve S' represents the cost per dollar borrowed of moving funds from the lending to the borrowing country, a measure of the degree of financial integration. The point where the effective supply curve and the demand curve intersect represents the equilibrium value of capital inflows. This value could be increased by "pull" factors, which would be represented by rightward shifts in the demand curve for funds, by "push" factors, which would tend to shift the "notional" supply curve S to the right, bringing the "effective" supply curve S' along with it as long as the degree of financial integration is unchanged, and by a change in the degree of financial integration, which would shift the S' curve down, closer to an unchanged position of the notional supply curve S. Notice that if the cost of moving funds is sufficiently high, S' could intersect the vertical axis above C, meaning that the equilibrium value of capital inflows would be zero. This is the "capital constrained" regime that prevailed for the heavily indebted countries during the period of the international debt crisis. But a move from a constrained to an unconstrained regime could have resulted from changes in any of the three factors we have discussed.

What factors contributed to the transition from a constrained to an unconstrained regime? Unfortunately, despite the fact that a substantial amount of research has been done on this issue, no consensus has emerged on the relative roles of "push," factors, "pull" factors, and changes in the degree of financial integration.

Some of the most visible studies that have addressed this issue are reviewed in the appendix to this chapter. Much of this evidence supports the view that "push" factors – specifically, declines in asset returns in the industrial countries – played an important role in reviving capital inflows. However, differences in capital inflow levels across countries point to the importance of specific country characteristics for foreign capital absorption. While "push" factors may account for simultaneous rightward shifts in the supply curves facing many emerging economies, thus explaining the *timing* and perhaps the *overall magnitude* of capital inflows, "pull" factors that determine the position of the demand curve for funds in each country must nevertheless play an important role in explaining the *geographic distribution* of flows during this time.

II. WELFARE IMPLICATIONS OF "PUSH" VERSUS "PULL"

It may seem somewhat surprising (and perhaps paradoxical) that if capital *outflows* were perceived as a policy problem during most of the 1980s, capital *inflows* to the same countries should also be perceived that way just a few years later. So a logical question to pose in interpreting the capital inflow phenomenon from a policy perspective is the following: should the arrival of capital inflows be considered a good thing or a bad thing?

The answer is that it is hard to tell in general. Whether the arrival of capital inflows represents a positive or a negative development depends on what is driving the inflows as well as the characteristics of the economy receiving them.

It may be tempting to take the view that flows attracted to the recipient country by domestic "pull" factors do not present a policy problem, because they represent a restoration of creditworthiness – that is, the rectification of the adverse conditions that emerged in the context of the debt crisis, while flows "pushed" out of the source countries are an external shock which can easily be reversed, and thus may call for a domestic policy response. This would be incorrect, however. The distinction between "pull" and "push" factors does not necessarily have normative content. None of the problems that may be associated with the arrival of capital inflows depend in any simple way on whether those flows were "pushed" or "pulled."

What are those potential problems? The policy challenge posed by the arrival of capital inflows emerges in three independent forms:

i. Avoiding immiserizing external borrowing (making sure that funds are allocated correctly within the domestic economy).
ii. Avoiding macroeconomic overheating (destabilization associated with large inflows).
iii. Avoiding vulnerability to sudden outflows (destabilization associated with large outflows) and financial crises.

In this section we will consider the first of these, leaving the other two for the sections that follow.

Immiserizing external borrowing can arise because decisions about the amount of resources borrowed, and their allocation among competing domestic uses, are undertaken in decentralized fashion, rather than by a benevolent social planner. This means that in the presence of distortions, resources may be misallocated, yielding a social return that is lower than the cost of funds. There are two types of distortions that can result in immiserizing external borrowing:

i. *Static* distortions, which cause a given amount of external resources to be allocated inefficiently among competing domestic uses, thus causing those resources to yield a social rate of return lower than the external cost of capital.
ii. *Dynamic* distortions, which result in "overborrowing," in other words, even if resources are allocated to their most productive domestic uses, the volume of resources absorbed pushes the marginal rate of return below the cost of capital.

We have already seen examples of these in previous chapters. For instance, static distortions can arise when the state borrows externally and allocates those resources directly according to political criteria, as happened during the period leading up to the international debt crisis in the eighties (Chapter 8), or as in the case of the policy-based lending (directed credit) that arises under financial repression, where the state allocates external resources indirectly (Chapter 12). Static distortions can also arise in the real sector, for example, when the international trade regime – and thus domestic resource allocation – is distorted by excessive protection. We saw examples of dynamic distortions that encouraged excessive foreign borrowing in the last chapter. These included, for example, "incredible" domestic reforms. Some policies may create *both* types of distortions. As discussed in the last chapter, for example, "premature" financial liberalization, which may involve implicit or explicit guarantees to domestic financial intermediaries without appropriate regulatory safeguards, would have this effect by encouraging moral-hazard-driven borrowing and lending for excessively risky activities by these intermediaries.

What is the relationship between the roles of "push" or "pull" factors and immiserizing external borrowing? The answer is that there is very little connection between them. Both types of factors can be welfare-enhancing or welfare-reducing.

"Pull" factors can improve the welfare of the domestic economy if they emanate from a favorable exogenous shock in an undistorted domestic economic environment – for example, a positive domestic productivity shock or the discovery of new natural resources. If this is what attracts capital inflows, those inflows would be welfare-enhancing because their role would be to permit domestic residents to smooth over time the added consumption that their increased wealth would make possible. Alternatively, "pull" factors arising from the removal of a previously existing distortion in the domestic economy, with the effect of leaving an undistorted domestic economic environment, would also attract welfare-improving inflows. An example would be the removal of a policy-induced gap between private and social rates of return on domestic investment, such as would occur through the elimination of a debt overhang (Chapter 8) or the removal of domestic interest rate ceilings in the context of a comprehensive financial reform (Chapter 14).

But "pull" factors can also be welfare-reducing. They would have this effect if they represented the creation of a new distortion in an otherwise undistorted environment (e.g., the "incredible reforms" alluded to before), or if they emerged as the result of the aggravation of a preexisting distortion. With respect to the latter, Dooley (1994) has stressed, for example, that improved creditworthiness of the domestic public sector may make previously existing inappropriate guarantees more credible, since the government would have an increased ability to make them effective. Another example, taken from the "sequencing" analysis of the last chapter, is the removal of capital controls when the financial system has *not* been reformed.

"Push" factors can also be either welfare-enhancing or welfare-reducing. An example of a welfare-enhancing "push" factor is the arrival of a favorable external shock in the context of an undistorted domestic economic environment, for example, a permanent or transitory reduction in the world real interest rate for an economy that is a net international debtor, or a favorable terms of trade shock. Welfare-reducing "push" factors, on the other hand, would include favorable external shocks in the presence of domestic distortions – such as lower world interest rates in a financially open economy with a domestic financial system characterized by important distortions, or a favorable external shock when the domestic private sector cannot distinguish whether it is of a permanent or transitory character.

The policy implications associated with immiserizing external borrowing are clear. In each of the welfare-reducing cases just discussed, the appropriate policy response is to remove the distortions and allow the free inflow of capital. On the other hand, if the distortions are in place and cannot be removed, it *may* (but also may not) be preferable to resist financial integration until the distortions are removed. If even the suboptimal return available in the presence of domestic distortions exceeds the cost of funds, the country may be better off borrowing abroad, even in the presence of domestic distortions.

III. MACROECONOMIC OVERHEATING: DESTABILIZING INFLOWS

The arrival of capital inflows has represented a large macroeconomic shock to the host countries, in the form of an excessive expansion of aggregate demand. Digesting resources of this magnitude without macroeconomic overheating would present a policy challenge no matter what triggered the inflows. Thus, once again there is no mapping from the domestic or external origin of the triggering factor to the policy challenge. What is the nature of the policy problem in this case?

Capital inflows ↑ → *Capital account* ↑ → *Reserves* ↑ → *Monetary base* ↑ → *Money supply* ↑ →

Aggregate demand ↑→ *Domestic price level* ↑ → *Real exchange rate* ↓ → *Trade deficit* ↑

↘   ↗

Real output ↑

Figure 15.2.

a. Inflows and Overheating: The Transmission Mechanism

In the previous section we saw how capital inflows could reduce the *level* of domestic income, through immiserizing external borrowing. But the arrival of large inflows could also *destabilize* income. The specific mechanism through which they would do so depends on the exchange rate regime used by the domestic economy. Consider the fixed exchange rate model of Part 2 and assume that inflows are triggered by a "push" factor in the form of a reduction in the world rate of interest. Then, recalling the analysis in Chapter 4, it is easy to see that this change in the external financial environment represents an expansionary shock to the domestic economy. In terms of the model, the *FM* curve shifts to the right as capital inflows resulting from portfolio reallocations on the part of both foreign and domestic agents cause the domestic money supply to expand. The resulting policy challenge takes the form of macroeconomic *overheating* – that is, an expansion of aggregate demand, causing an appreciation of the real exchange rate and deterioration of the trade balance.

The mechanism through which inflows would have this effect is as follows: with a predetermined exchange rate, large capital inflows are likely to generate an overall balance of payments surplus. To avoid an appreciation of the nominal exchange rate, the central bank would have to intervene in the foreign exchange market to buy the excess supply of foreign currency at the prevailing exchange rate. *Ceteris paribus*, this would result in an expansion of the monetary base. Base expansion would lead to growth in broader monetary aggregates, which would fuel an expansion of aggregate demand. This, in turn, would put upward pressure on the domestic price level. With the nominal exchange rate fixed, rising domestic prices would imply an appreciation of the real exchange rate. Schematically, we can depict the transmission mechanism as illustrated in Figure 15.2.

b. Policy Intervention: A Menu

This causal chain can be broken at various points by policy intervention. One useful way to organize the menu of policies available to the authorities to resist the emergence of overheating is thus according to where the intervention occurs along the chain of transmission described above. Accordingly, policy interventions can be classified as follows:

i. Policies designed to restrict the net inflow of capital, either by restricting gross capital inflows or promoting gross capital outflows. Such policies include the imposition of administrative controls on capital inflows as well as the elimination of a variety of restrictions on capital outflows. They may also include the widening of exchange rate bands with the intention of increasing uncertainty.

ii. Policies that seek to restrict the net *foreign exchange* inflow (reserve accumulation) by encouraging a current account offset to a capital account surplus. Trade liberalization and nominal exchange rate appreciation would have this effect. In the limit (flexible exchange rates), the latter could avoid any foreign exchange accumulation whatsoever.

iii. Policies that accept the reserve accumulation associated with a balance of payments surplus, but attempt to ameliorate its effects on the monetary base. These amount to sterilized intervention, as well as attempts to limit recourse to the central bank's discount window.

iv. Policies that accept an increase in the base, but attempt to restrain its effects on broader monetary aggregates. Increases in reserve requirements and quantitative credit restrictions are examples of such policies.

v. Policies that accept a monetary expansion, but attempt to offset expansionary effects on aggregate demand that could result in inflation and/or real exchange rate appreciation. This refers essentially to fiscal contraction.

In the rest of this section, we will examine some of the considerations involved in framing a policy response to avoid macroeconomic overheating. We'll begin by considering the pros and cons of individual policies in the list above, and then turn to overall policy strategies.

c. Restrictions on the Magnitude of Gross Inflows

As we have already seen, the key requirement for controls on capital movements to improve welfare is the presence of a distortion that creates an excessive level of foreign borrowing. When such a distortion exists and cannot be removed, capital controls (in this case, restrictions on inflows) may represent a first-best (when the act of foreign borrowing itself creates externalities) or second-best (when the negative welfare consequences of a new or preexisting domestic distortion that cannot be removed are magnified by external borrowing) policy. Alternatively, such restrictions could be justified on macroeconomic grounds, as providing insulation from foreign financial shocks when other stabilization instruments are not available or are too costly to use, as preserving monetary autonomy, or as useful tools for liquidity management – altering the composition of external liabilities in favor of longer maturities. Recall, however, that in Chapter 14 we argued that these macroeconomic justifications for capital account restrictions were subject to important limitations.

Aside from these, the use of this instrument raises serious questions of feasibility. As we saw in the previous chapter, the evidence that restrictions on capital inflows are effective in altering the total magnitude of such flows is weak. While there is stronger evidence that restrictions on gross flows can alter their composition, this may matter for the problem of vulnerability (to be described in the next section), not for that of overheating.

d. Encouragement of Gross Outflows

The optimality and feasibility issues that arise in the context of the restriction of capital inflows also arise when the issue is the liberalization of gross outflows. Some of the benefits that can be expected from liberalizing capital outflows were discussed in Chapter 14. It is unclear, however, whether liberalizing gross outflows can help to address the macroeconomic overheating problem by reducing the volume of *net* capital inflows. The reasons are several. First, in parallel with the case of liberalizing inflows, restrictions on *outflows* may not be effective. Second, even if such restrictions are potentially effective, they may not be binding at the time they are removed – that is, residents may prefer to keep their money at home. Finally, facilitating gross outflows may not succeed in reducing *net* capital inflows.

Evidence on the effectiveness of outflow restrictions was mixed prior to the inflow episode of the nineties. Mathieson and Rojas-Suarez (1993), for instance, tested whether capital flight responded to economic fundamentals in the same manner in countries with and without strong restrictions on capital outflows, with mixed results. They found that, while fundamentals continued to influence capital outflows even in the presence of controls, responses to fiscal imbalances were slower, and those to default risk were weaker, in countries with strong capital controls. Overall, they concluded that controls on outflows tended to prove ineffective in stemming capital flight.

That restrictions on outflows would not be binding in the midst of an inflow episode would not be surprising if domestic residents respond to the same economic incentives that cause foreigners to bring capital into the country. Indeed, much of the inflow episode may represent the repatriation of capital by domestic residents.

Finally, there are various reasons to suspect that even if outflow restrictions are effective and binding, their removal may not have the desired effect of reducing net inflows, because the very act of removing such restrictions may attract additional inflows. Laban and Larrain (1993), for example, have pointed out that the presence of effective controls on outflows renders inflows irreversible. If future policies affecting the return on loans to domestic agents are uncertain, the option to keep funds abroad while the uncertainty is resolved becomes valuable, and foreign creditors may thus refrain from lending in this situation. Removing the outflow restrictions eliminates the irreversibility, and thus increases the relative return on domestic lending by eliminating the value of the option to wait. Similarly, Bartolini and

Drazen (1995) have argued that, since controls on outflows are often maintained for fiscal reasons (recall from Chapter 13 that such controls facilitate the collection of financial repression taxes), their removal is interpreted by foreign investors as a signal that future capital taxation is less likely, thereby inducing capital inflows.

What is clear from country experience is that substantial inflows followed the removal of restrictions on outflows in many countries, an experience that has also characterized industrial countries.[1] Whether the removal of outward restrictions diminished net inflows to any significant extent is impossible to say on the basis of present evidence, but it is clear that they did not represent a complete solution to the inflow problem anywhere that they were used. The observation just mentioned – that the inflow episode was often preceded by capital account liberalization, including the removal of restrictions on outflows – is certainly consistent with the view that the removal of restrictions on outflows simply attracts additional inflows.

e. Trade Liberalization

From a macroeconomic perspective, trade liberalization lowers the domestic currency price of importable goods directly, and may lower the price on nontraded goods indirectly (by depreciating the equilibrium real exchange rate). To the extent that it induces a trade deficit, it absorbs some of the foreign exchange generated by the capital inflow, easing monetary pressures as well. The most controversial issue that arises with respect to trade liberalization as a means to restrict the net inflow of foreign exchange concerns its potential efficacy.

First, trade liberalization may not produce a trade deficit. Because the trade balance is the difference between domestic saving and investment, the effect of trade liberalization on the trade balance depends on how saving and investment are affected. Both theory and evidence suggest that the effects of trade liberalization on the trade balance are ambiguous, depending on a host of structural characteristics of the domestic economy as well as on the nature of the liberalization program. The former include the importance of nontraded goods, sectoral factor intensities, the nature of accompanying fiscal policies, and the extent of labor market rigidities. The latter include the incidence of tariffs (whether they fall on intermediate or final goods) and their projected future paths.

Ostry (1991), for example, shows that if temporary tariffs on intermediate goods are reduced, and tradable goods are more intensive in both intermediate and capital goods than nontradables, then the effect of the liberalization program will be to increase saving and reduce investment, thereby unambiguously improving the trade balance. The reduction in tariffs on intermediates will result in a short-run real appreciation as the traded goods sector expands, absorbing resources from the nontraded sector. This real appreciation will cause agents to expect a larger real

---

[1] See Bartolini and Drazen (1995).

depreciation over time, since future trade policy is left unaffected. Consequently, the real interest rate rises, and consumption tilts toward the future, increasing domestic saving. In turn, the increase in future consumption causes a future real appreciation which, relative to the undisturbed equilibrium, shifts capital from the traded to the nontraded sector in the future. Because the traded sector is relatively capital-intensive, the implication is a reduction in today's aggregate investment. With saving higher and investment lower, the trade balance unambiguously improves.

While this example may appear contrived, it merely illustrates the general principle that it is indeed quite possible in theory for a trade liberalization to improve the trade balance. The experience of liberalizing countries, as summarized, for example, in Thomas et al. (1991), suggests that this result is more than a theoretical curiosity.

Second, even if trade liberalization produces a trade deficit, the associated efficiency gains may trigger new capital inflows.

f. Exchange Rate Flexibility

The potential inflationary implications of capital inflows can be completely avoided by refraining from intervention in the foreign exchange market. Permitting a (temporary) appreciation of the nominal exchange rate in response to a favorable external interest rate shock (by restricting the scale of foreign exchange intervention) will dampen and possibly reverse the expansionary effect of the foreign shock on domestic aggregate demand, by appreciating the real exchange rate. Indeed, a capital inflow arising from a reduction in external interest rates becomes a *deflationary* shock under fully flexible exchange rates. This outcome will be desirable if domestic macroeconomic conditions are such that policymakers seek to avoid stimulating aggregate demand. Thus, to the extent that capital inflows are permitted to materialize, the desirability of foreign exchange intervention depends in part on the requirements for macroeconomic stability.

The trade-off, however, concerns the implications for domestic resource allocation. If the authorities allow the nominal exchange rate to appreciate in response to capital inflows, the profitability of the traded goods sector obviously will be affected adversely. Aside from possible political economy considerations, policymakers may have two reasons to be concerned with this outcome:

First, if the capital inflow is believed to be temporary, an appreciation of the official exchange rate may tend to aggravate the effects of any previously existing domestic distortions biasing domestic resource allocation away from the traded goods sector (and causing the "shadow" value of foreign exchange to exceed its official value).

Second, with temporary capital inflows, the associated real exchange rate appreciation will also be temporary, and any costly resource reallocations induced by changes in relative sectoral profitability between the traded and nontraded goods sectors would later have to be reversed. Since such costs represent fixed costs from the perspective of private agents, the associated resource reallocations would not be undertaken unless the incentives for doing so were perceived to be long-lasting. Because private agents will find it in their best interest to avoid the costs of transitory resource reallocation, the noise introduced into relative price signals by allowing excessive nominal exchange rate variability may reduce the efficiency of resource allocation.

Third, the preceding discussion treats the exchange rate as an instrument of short-run stabilization policy. However, the exchange rate also plays another role in small open economies – that of nominal anchor. We saw the role of the exchange rate in the analytical model of Part 2, and will come back to it again in Chapter 17. Allowing the exchange rate to adjust means using money as a nominal anchor. If this is less desirable (say because money demand is unstable), then allowing the exchange rate to pick up some of this pressure has a cost.

On the other hand, *nominal* exchange rate instability may be a good thing, because it increases the uncertainty faced by potential foreign investors, and an increase in uncertainty may be desirable to discourage capital inflows that are driven at least in part by moral hazard considerations. We will discuss this in much greater detail in Chapter 17.

What was the experience with exchange rate policy during the early nineties among countries experiencing large inflows? Several countries (e.g., Chile and Colombia) undertook revaluations in response to capital inflows. A second group of countries (Chile, Colombia, Indonesia, and Mexico) adopted exchange rate bands to allow more flexible nominal exchange rates, but full flexibility has tended to be adopted only after crises (e.g., in Mexico in 1994, Southeast Asia in 1997, and Brazil in 1998). Moreover, despite the operation of the transmission mechanism described previously, many countries managed to avoid real appreciation over the course of the surge episode. This would seem puzzling if the only shock at work is the one that triggered the inflow. The role of fiscal policy responses in generating these outcomes is considered below. Finally, the link between real appreciation and the emergence of current account deficits was certainly not airtight among the countries receiving capital inflows. On the one hand, the emergence of large current account deficits during the inflow episode was not restricted to countries that experienced real appreciations (Malaysia and Thailand both had large adverse movements in the current account balance with stable real exchange rates). On the other hand, some of the countries that experienced very substantial real exchange rate appreciation in the early nineties (Argentina and Mexico, in particular) also exhibited very large current account deficits.

g. Sterilization

We saw in Part 2 that in the extreme case that domestic and foreign assets are perfect substitutes, sterilization becomes impossible. We also saw that even if it is possible, sterilization may under certain circumstances (concerning the shape of the *GM* curve) tend to magnify the size of capital inflows, since it prevents the domestic interest rate from falling to restore portfolio equilibrium. Finally, we saw that sterilized intervention has quasi-fiscal costs, since the central bank exchanges high-yielding domestic assets for low-yielding reserves. The magnitude of these costs will be greater the higher the degree of capital mobility and the larger the gap between domestic and foreign rates of return. Thus, the fiscal feasibility of this policy is an issue.

But sterilization faces other limitations in practice not completely captured in the model we developed in Part 2. Those reflect the fact that, even if sterilization succeeds in limiting domestic monetary expansion, it may not succeed in insulating the domestic economy from the effects of capital inflows. This would be true under two sets of circumstances:

i. If domestic interest-bearing assets are perfect substitutes among themselves, as assumed in the model of Part 2, insulation would fail if the shock that triggers the inflows affects domestic money demand. In this case, with shifting money demand but fixed supply, domestic interest rates would change. This can be verified in the model of Part 2.

ii. On the other hand, if domestic interest-bearing assets are *imperfect* substitutes among themselves (a feature not captured in our model), then a capital in-flow may be associated with a shift in the composition of demand for domestic interest-bearing assets, as well as with an increase in the total demand for such assets. In this case, unless the composition of domestic assets emitted in steriliza-tion operations matches that demanded by creditors, the structure of domestic asset returns would be altered.

In practice, sterilized intervention tended to be the most widely used stabiliza-tion tool in response to capital inflows, because it possessed the great advantage of flexibility. An important lesson is that sterilization proved to be possible in spite of the capital account liberalization that many of the recipient countries had previously undertaken, and of the large magnitude of inflows that they received. Indeed, many countries registered an *increase* in domestic interest rates over the period of steril-ization. Thus, the removal of capital account restrictions in the context of financial liberalization did not imply that emerging economies moved into a regime of per-fect capital mobility. It is possible, however, that "offset coefficients" associated with sterilization may have been increasing over time.

On the other hand, many countries did not sustain policies of aggressive ster-ilization consistently over the inflow period. This clearly suggests that sterilization was not a panacea, despite its widespread appeal among the countries that experi-enced inflow surges. In the absence of data on quasi-fiscal costs, the importance of fiscal rigidities that made the quasi-fiscal costs of sterilizing too burdensome can-not be dismissed as an explanation, but it is clear that shifts in domestic economic circumstances that made lower interest rates more attractive have also played a role.

Finally, the effectiveness of sterilization in insulating economies from the effects of external financial shocks during the inflow episode is open to question. By and large, sterilization does not seem to have completely insulated the recipient economies from the effects of capital inflows. Asset markets, in particular, typically recorded massive increases in value during the surge periods. This is consistent with an imperfect-substitutability story in which foreign creditors demand domestic financial assets different from those issued by the central bank in the course of its sterilization operations.

h. Policies to Influence the Money Multiplier

If for fiscal or other reasons sterilization is incomplete, the implication of a foreign exchange inflow is an expansion in the monetary base. Monetary expansion can still be avoided by a commensurate reduction in the money multiplier achieved through an increase in reserve requirements or other restrictions on credit expansion by the banking system. Measures directed at increasing the money multiplier by increasing reserve requirements may indeed avoid quasi-fiscal costs, but as we saw in Chapter 12, they do so through implicit taxation of the banking system. The economic implications of this tax will depend on how the tax burden is ultimately shared among bank shareholders, their depositors, and their loan customers. Nonetheless, as we saw previously, the likely effect of this policy is to shrink the domestic financial system, an outcome that runs counter to the financial reform that has been undertaken in most reforming economies, and which may have adverse implications for economic growth.

Moreover, such measures may be of limited effectiveness. Increases in reserve requirements may have little effect, for example, if banks are already holding excess reserves. If reserve requirements are changed selectively for different components of banks' liability portfolios, then their effects could be evaded as bank creditors shift to assets not affected by changes in reserve requirements. Finally, even if changes in reserve requirements are applied broadly across bank liabilities, domestic credit expansion could materialize through nonbank institutions (disintermediation). The scope for doing so – and thus for avoiding an increase in domestic aggregate demand – depends on the sophistication of the domestic financial system.

i. Fiscal Contraction

If domestic monetary expansion is not avoided, or if an expansionary financial stimulus is transmitted outside the banking system, the stabilization of aggregate demand will require a fiscal contraction. Feasibility and optimality issues arise in this context as well.

With respect to feasibility, fiscal policy may simply prove too inflexible to be available as a tool to respond to fluctuations in capital movements. The budgetary process in most countries may not be able to respond sufficiently quickly, and lags in response may indeed aggravate the stabilization problems created by volatile capital movements. Beyond this, political pressure may prevent fiscal contraction during the "good times" associated with inflow episodes. But even if fiscal policy can be changed, the desired effects on domestic demand (and thus on the real exchange rate) will be forthcoming – in other words, the policy will be effective – only if expenditure cuts fall on domestic goods.

Whether it is optimal for fiscal policy to respond in this way is also at issue. We have seen in Part 3 of this book that expectations of future fiscal policy have potentially important implications for macroeconomic performance. This raises the question of whether fiscal policy should be designed to anchor long-run expectations of inflation and taxation, or should be guided by countercyclical objectives. Of course, in principle these goals are not mutually exclusive, since short-run deviations from the medium-term fiscal stance can be designed to respond to transitory shocks and thus achieve stabilization objectives. The problem is, however, that if government credibility is lacking, adherence to the medium-term stance in the face of shocks may be the surest way to achieve it. In a nutshell, the issue is whether the achievement of fiscal credibility is compatible with the adoption of feedback rules for fiscal policy.[2]

A separate optimality issue is that if the stabilization objective is adopted, changes in marginal tax rates in response to temporary capital inflows should be avoided, since fluctuations in such rates would distort the intertemporal choices made by private economic agents.

In practice, fiscal policy did not prove to be a very flexible instrument in responding to inflows. After the fiscal adjustments that many emerging economies made during the late 1980s, few of them found it possible to engage in additional fiscal tightening in response to inflows, and where additional fiscal tightening took place the changes in the fiscal stance were not typically large compared with previous fiscal adjustments in the countries concerned. This may reflect a variety of factors, including "stabilization fatigue" arising from the substantial fiscal adjustment that many countries had already undertaken prior to the inflow episode, or political economy considerations that make it difficult to undertake fiscal austerity when external constraints on the economy are not perceived to be binding.

Whatever the reason for the nature of the fiscal response, however, the absence of additional fiscal tightening may have played an important role with regard to outcomes for the real exchange rate. Real appreciation was avoided, for example, in all of the East Asian countries that tightened fiscal policy in response to inflows. The frequency of real appreciation elsewhere supports the implication of theory that, in

---

[2] Notice that, if such a rule were to be applied symmetrically, it would imply that capital outflows should elicit an *expansionary* fiscal response.

the presence of capital inflows, the avoidance of real appreciation requires a fiscal contraction to free up the requisite supply of domestic goods without a relative price change.

Nonetheless, tighter fiscal policy was not sufficient to avoid a real appreciation. Real appreciation accompanied fiscal tightening in Argentina and Egypt, for example, but each of these countries was in the midst of stabilizing from high inflation, and it is likely that the behavior of the real exchange rate reflected inflation inertia. If this interpretation is correct, the implication is that real appreciation would have been more severe in these countries if fiscal policy had been looser.

j. Policy Strategies

Up to this point, we have concentrated on some of the considerations involved in implementing specific individual policies to combat the macroeconomic overheating that may be caused by the arrival of capital inflows, and have reviewed some country experience with some of these policies. Individual policies obviously have pros and cons associated with their use, and if the objective is to avoid macroeconomic overheating, then it is obvious that there are many ways to combine the policies described above in order to achieve that objective. How did the combination of policies actually chosen by emerging economies to combat overheating affect their macroeconomic performances during capital-inflow episodes? Before leaving the problem of overheating, it is useful to consider whether there are lessons to be learned from country experiences with alternative policy combinations, that is, about alternative *policy strategies.*

A recent study by the World Bank (1997) considered precisely this issue. In a sample of twenty-one countries accounting for about 90 percent of all private capital flows to developing countries during the period 1990–94, it found the following:

 i. Concerning the extent of macroeconomic overheating that actually materialized, the vast majority of the countries in the sample used by the study managed to avoid an acceleration of inflation during their inflow periods, compared to the pre-inflow period. Moreover, though increases in current-account deficits were widespread among the sample countries, they were not large, and about half of the improvement in the capital account resulted in reserve accumulation, rather than increases in current-account deficits. The study concluded that despite receiving very large capital inflows, countries had been fairly successful at avoiding overheating.
 ii. Country experience tended to differ across various dimensions:
   • As we have already seen, some countries managed to avoid real exchange rate appreciation, while others did not.
   • Countries differed as well with regard to changes in the composition of absorption (total spending by domestic residents). In some cases, the increase

in absorption relative to income was dominated by investment, and in other
cases by consumption.

iii. Countries tended to use a wide range of the policies described above, rather
than relying heavily on a small subset of them. Sterilized intervention was the
most common policy employed to resist overheating. Tighter fiscal policy was
also featured in some countries, but it was unclear whether this was a response
to the arrival of capital inflows or a continuation of previously undertaken fiscal
consolidation.

The study found strong cross-country positive correlations during the inflow
period between the extent of real exchange rate appreciation and both the increase
in the current account deficit as well as the change in the share of consumption in
absorption. It also found a weaker positive association between the increase in the
share of investment in absorption and the change in economic growth. Though in
all of these instances the correlations could be interpreted as the result of causation
operating in either direction, the study found a strong association between the
extent of fiscal contraction during the inflow period and the increase in the share
of investment in absorption. It thus concluded that a tight-fiscal loose-monetary
policy strategy to resist overheating was associated with faster growth and less real
appreciation than an alternative tight monetary–relatively loose fiscal policy strategy. Countries following such a strategy included Thailand, Indonesia, Malaysia,
and Chile.

IV. VULNERABILITY

The third potential problem associated with the arrival of capital inflows is the likelihood that such inflows will be reversed suddenly, as happened in the early eighties
at the onset of the international debt crisis. In other words, the increased financial
integration that follows financial reform, and that may initially be associated with
the arrival of capital inflows, may also make the country vulnerable to capital account crises, in the form of the sudden reversals of these capital flows. This raises
two questions: (a) What determines the probability of such capital-flow reversals?
(b) What are the macroeconomic implications of such reversals? These issues are
discussed in Chapter 19. The purpose of this section is to provide an overview of
the first of these topics, both to link it with what has been said earlier in this chapter
as well as to provide a transition to the material in Part 5 of the book.

a. Sources of Vulnerability

When is a reversal of capital inflows likely to happen? The answer is similar to
what one might say about the determinants of the likelihood of withdrawals from
banks by their depositors. Economic agents (both foreign and domestic) that have

claims on the domestic economy are likely to liquidate those claims – causing a reversal in capital inflows – when they come to believe that the value of their assets is in danger of becoming impaired. In turn, this is likely when:

i. The country's fiscal solvency comes into question.
ii. Its exchange rate is perceived to be overvalued.
iii. The domestic financial system is perceived to be fragile.
iv. The economy's public sector is highly illiquid.

The first three situations make outflows more likely, while the last makes a crisis more likely if there are outflows, and makes self-fulfilling crises more probable.

We have already seen in Chapter 8 that prospective insolvency of the public sector in the heavily indebted developing countries was the key factor behind the international debt crisis of the 1980s. It happened that at the time most of the external debt outstanding was owed by the public sectors of these countries to consortia of foreign banks in the form of syndicated loans, and was denominated in foreign exchange. However, a solvency crisis of the domestic public sector would impair the value of claims on private agents as well, if only because of the likelihood of future taxation on those claims as the public sector tries to bring its fiscal accounts into balance. This was the "debt overhang" problem that we discussed in Chapter 8. Thus, public sector solvency problems would tend to impair the value of all claims on the domestic economy, regardless of the identity of the domestic debtor or the currency of denomination.

As we shall see in the chapters that follow, an overvalued domestic real exchange rate means that a future real exchange rate adjustment is in the works, unless the domestic authorities are prepared to alter some of the real determinants of the equilibrium real exchange rate so as to make the actual real exchange rate an equilibrium one. When such an adjustment is in the offing, creditors who hold claims denominated in domestic currency face a potentially large loss of value on their assets, and have an incentive to convert them into assets denominated in other currencies. Again, such a situation would tend to lead to a reversal of capital flows, in the form of an exchange rate crisis.

Fragility in the domestic financial system (defined as in Chapter 13 as vulnerability to a loss of capital in response to even mild shocks) clearly impairs the value of claims on the financial system unless those claims are insured, and may do so even if they are insured if the insurance fund (or the government's support) is limited. Moreover, to the extent that a potential banking crisis has adverse real effects on the economy as a whole, as discussed in Chapter 13, the emergence of such a crisis would impair the value of all claims on the domestic economy, not just claims directly on the financial system. Again, wholesale withdrawal of claims on the domestic economy are likely if such a situation emerges.

As we shall see in Chapter 19, the combination of factors (ii) and (iii) together may have been behind the Chilean crisis of 1982, the Mexican crisis of 1994, and the Asian crises of 1997. Aside from the international debt crisis of the early eighties, these were the most severe episodes of capital-flow reversals among emerging economies over the past two decades.

Finally, the composition of the public sector's portfolio may also provide a trigger for a capital-flow reversal, even if the public sector is solvent. If the public sector's liabilities are liquid, but its assets are not, then the sector as a whole is in the same position as the individual banks described in Chapter 13. That is, a wholesale withdrawal of claims could make the public sector "insolvent" in the sense that it may prove unwilling to meet its obligations, since any attempt to do so by liquidating assets, cutting spending, or raising taxes could do unacceptable damage to the domestic economy. If this situation prevails, then there may be two possible equilibria: one in which the public sector creditors who hold liquid assets do not expect a crisis, and continue to renew these claims as they come due, so no crisis happens, and another in which these creditors *do* expect a crisis, so they fail to renew their claims, thereby triggering a crisis that fulfills their expectations. We will return to this analysis of multiple equilibria created by the structure of the public sector's balance sheet when we look at the Mexican crisis in more detail in Chapter 19.

b. Sources of Vulnerability: Evidence

In recent years, there has been an outpouring of research on the determinants of capital account reversals, in the form of currency crises. We will come back to this evidence after discussing exchange rate policy in the next three chapters. For now, however, it may be useful to review the findings with respect to the determinants of vulnerability to capital-flow reversals of the World Bank study (1997) discussed in the previous section.

To see what kinds of policies were associated with vulnerability, the study examined how well a sample of thirteen emerging economies had weathered the Mexican crisis during 1995. Countries were classified into two groups: those that were strongly affected by the Mexican crisis (and were thus judged to be "vulnerable"), and those that were not. The judgment was made on the basis of two criteria: whether the countries in the sample had sustained private capital inflows at previous levels during 1995, and whether equity prices in their domestic stock markets were stable in that year. On the basis of these criteria, the strongly affected group included Argentina, Brazil, India, Mexico, Pakistan, Turkey, and Venezuela. The less affected group consisted of Chile, Colombia, Indonesia, Korea, Malaysia, and Thailand.

The characteristics that distinguished the two groups were taken to be indicators of vulnerability. Over the period leading up to the Mexican crisis (1988–93), the less affected group was found to have had higher growth of real output, a higher share of investment in GDP, lower inflation, substantially less real exchange rate appreciation (20 percent on average versus 3.5 percent), much smaller fiscal deficits (a surplus of 0.6 percent of GDP on average versus a deficit of 4 percent of GDP), and a smaller debt/export ratio.[3]

The interpretation given to these results was that vulnerability to capital-flow reversals was greater when the real exchange rate was out of line, when government debt obligations were large, when fiscal adjustment was perceived as politically or administratively infeasible, and when the country's growth prospects were perceived to be weak. This interpretation is consistent with the factors listed above as being conducive to capital-flow reversals.[4]

V. SUMMARY

Whether the large capital flows to emerging economies were driven primarily by "push" factors, "pull" factors, or some combination of the two, it is likely that the market-oriented reforms undertaken by these countries in the late eighties – especially the financial reforms that resulted in more open capital accounts – left these countries much more integrated with international capital markets than they had been previously. The experience of these countries has shown that this enhanced financial integration presents both opportunities and pitfalls. In the previous chapter we saw that enhanced integration can confer many benefits on the domestic economy. In this chapter we have seen that increased integration also poses serious policy challenges, even when capital is flowing into the country, rather than out.

A possible response to this situation is for emerging economies that choose to live less dangerously to retain or reimpose restrictions on capital movements. As we have seen previously, weak restrictions on capital movements may indeed be justified on either first-best or second-best grounds. In practice, however, their effectiveness is questionable. Such restrictions may be both useful and effective in changing the composition of inflows, and if they can indeed affect total flows, may also be useful as a transitional device to preserve monetary autonomy while more fiscal flexibility is achieved. But controls on capital movements may only preserve monetary autonomy for a short time, and as financial integration proceeds in emerging economies, that time may be getting shorter.

In the alternative that enhanced financial integration is embraced by domestic policymakers, it is clear that the premium on high-quality domestic economic institutions as well as on high-quality domestic macroeconomic management increases sharply. If domestic economic institutions and the quality of domestic

---

[3] It is notable that these characteristics did *not* include the size of their current-account deficits.

[4] There is an interesting application here to the "policy mix" issue of the previous section. The Bank study concluded that a policy mix that assigns the real exchange rate to the achievement of "external balance" (an appropriate outcome for the current account) and fiscal policy to "internal balance" (full employment with low inflation) seems to be conducive to the avoidance of vulnerability.

macroeconomic management are inadequate, financial integration can lead to lower and less stable income than under financial autarky. Of particular importance are fiscal and monetary policies, financial sector policies, and exchange rate policies. In this chapter the focus of attention has been on the use of fiscal and monetary policies to avoid overheating and vulnerability to capital flow reversals.

We have seen that responsible and flexible fiscal management is a central component of good macroeconomic management under conditions of high financial integration. This can help avoid overheating, reduce vulnerability to capital flow reversals, and more generally help to cope with the volatility that capital account openness can introduce to the domestic macroeconomic environment.

In avoiding overheating in response to capital inflows, we saw in this chapter that the fiscal/monetary mix adopted in the recipient economy seems to matter. A tight fiscal/loose monetary mix of policies tends to favor domestic investment over consumption and to generate both less real appreciation and smaller current account deficits in response to capital inflows. This mix of policies also seems to have been more successful than the alternative loose fiscal/tight money mix in avoiding vulnerability to capital flow reversals during the first half of the nineties.

With regard to coping with the volatility of domestic income that can emerge with a high degree of financial integration, a prudent fiscal policy fosters the perception of public sector solvency, thus reducing country risk and avoiding having the public sector itself become a source of shocks. It also helps to generate a fiscal cushion that allows for some fiscal flexibility, providing an independent stabilization instrument and reducing incentives to restrict flows through capital controls. Where monetary sterilization is feasible, a solvent fiscal position permits the public sector to bear any fiscal costs associated with that policy, again enhancing the flexibility of an instrument of stabilization policy. Finally, a reputation for fiscal prudence allows the government to borrow long-term in domestic currency, thereby reducing its vulnerability to liquidity crises.

Turning to the conduct of monetary policy, we have seen that sterilized intervention still appeared to be possible among emerging economies in the early nineties, though it may have become more difficult to implement it over time. This stabilization tool has the strong advantage of flexibility in its use. However, many caveats are associated with relying heavily on sterilization to resist the overheating pressures triggered by capital inflows. First, sterilization may not be effective in insulating the domestic economy from external shocks. Second, its costs may weaken the fiscal accounts. Third, the creation of a large stock of domestic public debt as a result of sterilization may undermine fiscal credibility. Finally, as we have seen, an excessive reliance on sterilization to resist the macroeconomic overheating threatened by the arrival of capital inflows seems to have done less well in its effects on domestic macroeconomic performance than a mix of policies that put more weight on tighter fiscal policy.

The remaining key policy components are financial sector policies and exchange rate policies. Previous chapters have devoted a substantial amount of attention to financial sector issues, and there is nothing to add here. In the next part of the book we will turn to the third important area of macroeconomic management under financial integration: exchange rate policies.

APPENDIX 15.1: EVIDENCE ON FACTORS DRIVING CAPITAL INFLOWS IN THE NINETIES

No general consensus has emerged concerning the relative roles that various factors may have played in bringing foreign capital back to emerging economies in the early 1990s. This appendix provides an overview of the main studies that have attempted to address this issue.

a. Calvo, Leiderman, and Reinhart (1993)

In a series of papers, Calvo, Leiderman, and Reinhart (CLR) have argued that, while domestic factors such as a changed policy regime may have been important in attracting inflows, such factors cannot explain why inflows occurred in countries that had not undertaken reforms or why when reforms were started earlier, inflows did not begin to emerge in Latin America until 1990. They thus emphasized the role of external factors. Their formal analysis took the following form:

i. They used principal component analysis to establish the presence of a significant degree of co-movement among foreign reserves and real exchange rates for ten Latin American countries during 1990–91. It turned out that the first principal component explained a larger share of the variation in the ten reserve and real exchange rate series during 1990–91 than in 1988–89, suggesting that common factors exerted a stronger influence on these variables during that period.

ii. They found that the first principal components of both the reserve and real exchange rate series in the Latin American countries in their sample displayed a large bivariate correlation with several U.S. financial variables that CLR used as indicators of foreign rates of return.

iii. They conducted tests of "Granger causality." In individual countries, Granger causality tests most frequently had reserves causing real exchange rates than the reverse. This pattern also held for the first principal components of the two sets of series.

iv. Structural vector autoregressions (VARs) involving reserves, real exchange rates, and the first two principal components of the U.S. financial variables suggested that the foreign factors exerted causal influences over the domestic variables, and both variance decompositions and impulse response functions indicated that the foreign factors played a large role in accounting for reserve and real exchange rate movements.

b. Chuhan, Claessens, and Mamingi (1993)

Using monthly bond and equity flows from the United States to nine Latin American and nine Asian countries over the period January 1988 to July 1992, Chuhan, Claessens, and Mamingi (CCM) estimated separate panel regressions explaining bond and equity flows as functions of country-specific variables (country credit rating, price of debt on the secondary market, price earnings ratio in the domestic stock market, and the black market premium) as well as external variables (U.S. interest rates and U.S. industrial activity). They found that bond flows (but not equity flows) responded strongly to the country credit rating, while price-earning ratios were uniformly important. However, U.S. interest rates also entered significantly with the theoretically expected negative sign in all the regressions.

To assess the relative importance of domestic and foreign variables, they computed the sum of standardized coefficients for the two sets of variables, finding that domestic and external variables have been about equally important in Latin America, but domestic variables had sums of standardized coefficients that were three to four times larger than those of external variables in Asia for both bond and equity flows.

c. Fernandez-Arias (1994)

Fernandez-Arias (1994) argued that the attribution of variation in country-specific financial variables to domestic shocks in CCM was improper, and in particular that country creditworthiness, as indicated by the price of debt on secondary markets, is itself heavily dependent on external factors.

To assess the role of such factors, he regressed deviations in portfolio (bond and equity) inflows from their 1989 values for thirteen developing countries on corresponding deviations in the external interest rate and in the price of debt on the secondary market (based on a simple burden-sharing model that linked creditworthiness to this variable), using fixed-effect panel estimates for which the intercept term was interpreted as the change in the domestic investment climate.

For the "average" developing country in the sample, changes in international interest rates proved to be the dominant force in explaining surges in capital inflows, accounting for over 60 percent of the deviation in such flows from the 1989 level. An extra 25 percent was due to changes in creditworthiness, leaving only about 12 percent to be explained by improvements in the domestic investment climate. Moreover, when account was taken of the role of external interest rates in determining the secondary-market debt price used as the creditworthiness indicator, thereby decomposing the latter into domestic and foreign components, fully 86 percent of the surge in inflows is attributed to movements in external interest rates.

d. Dooley, Fernandez-Arias, and Kletzer (1994)

Dooley, Fernandez-Arias, and Kletzer argued that the price of emerging-economy debt to commercial banks in the secondary market is a sensitive proxy for capital inflows, because shifts in the demand for claims on developing countries, whether emanating from changes in domestic or external factors, should be reflected in these prices. Thus, rather than explaining capital inflows directly, they attempted to account for the behavior of secondary-market prices on debt since 1989 which, consistent with their interpretation of the relationship between such prices and capital flows, rose markedly at that time.

They found that essentially all of the increase in price could be accounted for by reductions in the face value of debt and international interest rates, leaving almost nothing to be explained by improvements in the domestic environment.

e. Schadler, Carkovic, Bennett, and Kahn (1993)

These findings concerning the role of foreign factors have not gone unchallenged, however. Schadler, Carkovic, Bennett, and Kahn, for example, argued that, while foreign phenomena may have been important, such influences cannot be regarded as dominant, for several reasons:

a. First, they maintained that the timing of the relevant changes in external factors did not coincide with that of the inflows.
b. Second, they noted that the timing, persistence, and intensity of inflows varied considerably across countries that received inflows, suggesting that investors responded to changes in country-specific factors over time.
c. Third, they pointed out that surges in capital inflows were not universal within regions of emerging economies, so that external creditors clearly exercised some cross-country discrimination in the allocation of funds.

f. Hernandez and Rudolf (1994)

More systematic evidence supporting a role for domestic factors in attracting capital inflows was provided by Hernandez and Rudolf. Noting that previous work tended not to provide a careful specification of domestic factors, Hernandez and Rudolf examined the extent to which standard creditworthiness indicators could explain long-term capital inflows for a sample of twenty-two developing countries over the period 1986–93. They used two methodologies:

i. First, they split their sample of countries into groups of high capital inflow recipients (HCIR) and low capital inflow recipients (LCIR). They found that the former had domestic saving rates twice as large as the latter, invested a much larger proportion of GNP, exhibited significantly lower fiscal deficits and inflation rates, had lower stocks of debt as well as larger stocks of foreign exchange reserves and faster rates of export growth. The HCIR countries were also more stable, in the sense that they both exhibited lower variability of inflation and real exchange rates and scored lower on a political risk index.

ii. Second, arranging their data into a panel of annual observations, they estimated capital-flow equations for a broad category of long-term flows as a function of lagged domestic consumption and investment rates, external interest rates, and the ratio of net external debt (gross debt minus foreign exchange reserves) to GNP, the variability of the real exchange rate, and the presence of a Brady bond deal. They found a statistically significant (albeit not very precisely estimated) role for domestic creditworthiness indicators, but no role for the external interest rate.

g. Taylor and Sarno (1997)

Taylor and Sarno tried to explain monthly portfolio flows from the United States to nine Asian and nine Latin American countries from January 1988 to September 1992. They used *Institutional Investor* credit ratings and the parallel market premium as country-specific factors, and the U.S. Treasury Bill rate and a U.S. long-term government bond rate, as well as U.S. industrial production, as global factors.

Taylor and Sarno found cointegrating relationships between capital inflows and the explanatory variables in all thirty-six cases, and based conclusions about the relative importance of the two types of variables on the relative frequency of significant coefficients in country-specific error-correction models for inflows, specified using a Hendry general-to-specific methodology. They found that "push" and "pull" factors were equally important in explaining equity flows in both Asia and Latin America, but that global factors (especially U.S. interest rates) were more important in explaining bond flows in both regions.

h. World Bank (1997)

All of the evidence cited above pertains to the early years of the capital inflow episode – 1989–93. More recent evidence provided by the World Bank (1997) suggests that the factors driving inflows may have been changing over time, and in particular that domestic factors may have played a more prominent role during 1994–95. Adopting the CLR methodology, the Bank found that quarterly portfolio flows from the United States to twelve emerging markets in East Asia and Latin

America were characterized by a substantial amount of co-movement (measured by the proportion of the variation captured by the first principal component) during 1990–93, and that the first principal component of these series was highly negatively correlated with the first principal component of a set of representative U.S. asset returns. Both of these findings are consistent with the findings of CLR for this period, as described above.

However, over the years 1993–95, co-movements among portfolio flows became much weaker (the contribution of the first principal component dropped to 45 percent, from 75 percent of the variance), and the correlation with U.S. asset returns reversed signs and became much weaker. The implication is that idiosyncratic country factors may have played a much larger role in the last part of the episode than they did in the early years.

What can we learn from all of this research? There are three things we might want to know:

i. What factors contributed to the transition from a constrained to an unconstrained capital-flow regime?
ii. How sensitive have capital flows to emerging economies been to each of their potential determining factors?
iii. Which factors have actually been driving flows during any particular sample period?

Studies that have estimated capital-flow equations (such as those by Chuhan, Claessens, and Mamingi, Hernandez and Rudolf, and Taylor and Sarno) tell us about the reduced-form coefficients of capital-flow equations, and thus address the second issue raised above. The evidence suggests that flows were responsive to *both* domestic and external factors.

The strongest evidence against the "push" view during the early years of the inflow episode is that provided by Hernandez and Rudolf (1994). However, their evidence is not necessarily inconsistent with the "push" view, despite the poor performance of the U.S. interest rate in their capital-flow regressions. Specifically, their focus on long-term capital flows and the weight given to the 1980–86 period in their data suggest that their results may primarily apply to FDI flows and are not necessarily applicable to other types of capital flows, such as portfolio or short-term flows.

Finally, the "co-movement" papers (Calvo, Leiderman, and Reinhart, as well as World Bank) tell us something about the third issue, suggesting that external factors may have accounted for most of the variation in capital inflows early in the inflow episode (until about 1993), but that country-specific factors may have played a more important role later on.

PART 5

Exchange Rate Management

16

Equilibrium Real Exchange Rates

At various places throughout this book we have discussed the role of the real exchange rate as a key macroeconomic relative price. As the relative price of foreign goods (goods produced abroad) in terms of domestic goods (goods produced at home), the real exchange rate plays an important role in guiding the broad allocation of production and spending in the domestic economy between these two types of goods. Because of this important allocative role of the real exchange rate, emerging economies are often encouraged to conduct their affairs so as to get this particular macroeconomic relative price "right" – that is, to make sure that the economy's actual real exchange rate does not stray too far from its equilibrium value, a situation that is known as exchange rate *misalignment*.

Why is the avoidance of misalignment so important? As we will discuss more fully in this chapter, there are two key reasons: when the exchange rate is misaligned, it will not provide the appropriate signal to guide the allocation of resources between domestic and foreign goods. In addition, as mentioned in the last chapter, when the real exchange rate is perceived to have become severely misaligned, the expectation will be created that it will adjust toward its equilibrium value in the future. To the extent that this adjustment is expected to take place through movements in nominal exchange rates, this will discourage domestic agents from holding assets denominated in domestic currency, which is a potential source of capital-flow reversals and exchange rate crises. Thus, large real exchange rate misalignments can have important microeconomic and macroeconomic costs.

But how do we know whether the real exchange rate is misaligned, and how do we avoid misalignment? Part 5 of this book takes up these issues, in the context of a more general discussion of *exchange rate management*. Notice that, since the actual real exchange rate can be observed, the detection and measurement of real exchange rate misalignment depends on the ability to define and estimate an *equilibrium* real exchange rate. Thus, a logical place to begin a discussion of exchange rate management is to consider what we mean by the notion of an equilibrium real exchange rate, and how we might go about measuring it. This chapter will explore the theoretical determinants of the long-run equilibrium real exchange rate and consider different approaches to its empirical measurement.

It is worth noting at the outset that this is a controversial area of research in macroeconomics. Objections to the enterprise of defining and measuring an equilibrium real exchange rate tend to take one of three forms:

i. Some economists argue that it is meaningless to distinguish between the actual real exchange rate and the equilibrium real exchange rate, because any observed real exchange rate must be an equilibrium one.
ii. Others would say that even if it is meaningful to make such a distinction, it is useless to do so, because gaps between actual and equilibrium real exchange rates have no policy implications.
iii. Finally, a third view holds that even if it is possible to make the distinction and useful to do so, measuring the equilibrium real exchange rate is impossible.

We will have to address each of these doubts during the course of this chapter.

I. THE REAL EXCHANGE RATE: DEFINITION AND MEASUREMENT

The problem of defining and measuring the equilibrium real exchange rate is complicated by a variety of factors. The most basic one is that no single definition of "the" real exchange rate is widely accepted among economists. Recall that, in broad terms, the real exchange rate is simply the relative price of foreign goods in terms of domestic ones. But what constitutes domestic and foreign goods depends on the particular analytical framework – the specific macroeconomic model – being used. Since different types of macro models are used by economists for different purposes, a variety of analytical real exchange rate definitions tend to be used, as we will see below. A second problem is that, while the notion of what are "domestic" and "foreign" goods may be relatively easy to pin down within specific theoretical models (most of which contain at most three goods), in the real world things tend to become more complicated. In particular, in a context in which there are many goods it is not always obvious how to come up with empirical counterparts to the prices of domestic and foreign goods that we are trying to measure. Different approximations result in different empirical definitions, even when the theoretical concept is unambiguous.

a. Analytical Issues

The key factor that affects the definition of the real exchange rate in analytical models is the assumed production structure of the model. Some of the most widely used modeling frameworks are the following.

1. One (Tradable) Good Model

Some models contain a single good that is assumed to be internationally traded, and arbitrage is assumed to equalize its price everywhere. Such models are useful for the analysis of purely monetary phenomena (such as inflation, as well as certain approaches to the explanation of the determinants of the balance of payments). Obviously, there can be no real exchange rate in such models, because with only a single good there is no distinction to be drawn between domestic and foreign goods.

2. Complete Specialization (Mundell-Fleming) Models

An alternative framework assumes that the domestic economy and the rest of the world are each specialized in the production of a single good, and that these goods, which are traded internationally, are imperfect substitutes for each other. This is the framework that we used in the model of Part 2 of this book. It is applicable to countries whose trade consists largely of manufactured goods, since these tend to be imperfect substitutes for what the rest of the world produces.

In this context it is easy to define the real exchange rate. It is the number of units of the domestically produced good that have to be given up for each unit of the foreign good, as indicated in Chapter 3. As we saw in Part 1, in this context the role of the real exchange rate is to determine the composition of absorption (both domestic and foreign) between goods produced at home and those produced abroad. As such, the real exchange rate determined the aggregate demand for the domestic good and was also an important determinant of the country's trade balance.

In Mundell-Fleming models, the real exchange rate happens to coincide with the (inverse of the) country's *terms of trade* (the price of exports relative to the price of imports). This is an artifact of the assumption of complete specialization in production, however, and these two concepts are in general quite different from each other in analytical frameworks that do not make this assumption, as we'll see below.

3. Dependent-Economy (Swan-Salter) Models

An alternative framework also has a production structure that contains two goods. But in this case, one is produced at home and consumed only at home (the *nontraded* good), while the other is produced and consumed both at home and abroad. Since only the latter can be bought and sold across international boundaries, it is the *traded*, or foreign, good. In this case, the definition of the real exchange rate is straightforward: it is the number of units of the nontraded good required to purchase one unit of the traded good:

$$e = P_T/P_N,$$

where P_T and P_N are respectively the domestic-currency prices of the traded and nontraded goods. This is sometimes called the *internal* real exchange rate. Notice that, since there is only one type of foreign good in this framework, there are no terms of trade in this model.[1] This model is useful to analyze issues for which the role of exogenous changes in the terms of trade are not important, in the context of economies whose terms of trade are exogenous. For example, the model is widely used to analyze the effects of domestic macroeconomic policies in small countries.

4. Three-Good (Exportable-Importable-Nontraded) Model

If changes in the terms of trade do matter, however, then a three-good model is required, consisting of *exportable* and *importable* goods (both of which may be produced and consumed at home, but one of which is exported and the other imported), as well as nontraded goods. But in this case there are two foreign goods and therefore *two* real exchange rates, as well as a separate and distinct definition of the terms of trade . Letting P_X denote the domestic-currency price of the exportable good and P_z the domestic-currency price of the importable good, we have the *exportables real exchange rate* $e_X = P_X/P_N$ and the *importables real exchange rate* $e_Z = P_Z/P_N$. In turn, the terms of trade (TOT) are defined as $TOT = P_X/P_Z$.[2] This model is useful for analyzing the macroeconomic effects of terms of trade changes, as well as of changes in commercial policies that affect the domestic relative prices of exportables and importables.

b. Measurement Issues

Given the analytical framework that is suitable for the problem at hand, the next issue in empirical applications is how to translate the relevant concept into an empirical measure of the real exchange rate. The most common way to measure the real exchange rate empirically is to take a foreign price index, express it in domestic-currency terms (by multiplying it by a nominal exchange rate index), and then dividing by a domestic price index. But this still leaves some problems. For example:

  i. What do we mean by a foreign price index when there are many foreign countries?
 ii. If there is more than one exchange rate against some foreign currency (i.e., in the case of parallel exchange rates), which one do we use?
iii. Do we use the same price index for the foreign and the domestic countries? If not, why not?
 iv. Which price index do we use (e.g., consumer prices, producer prices, GDP deflator, etc.)?

---

[1] Another, more general way of thinking about this model is that there is more than one type of foreign good, but because the home country is small, it cannot affect the relative prices among them. In particular, it cannot affect the relative price between the foreign goods that it tends to export and the foreign goods that it tends to import – that is, its terms of trade.

[2] In this case, the terms of trade are expressed as the number of importable goods that can be bought with one exportable good, which is the inverse (foreign goods per domestic good) of the way the real exchange rate was defined (domestic goods per foreign good).

The most common choice is to use the trade-weighted consumer price index in partner countries (measured in domestic currency) for the foreign price index, and the consumer price index for the domestic price index. This is called the real effective exchange rate (REER). This has several problems, however:

i. Because the denominator is a weighted average of domestic traded and non-traded goods prices, this indicator will only show changes in the internal real exchange rate in muted form (e.g., if the price of nontraded goods changes by x percent, the denominator will change in the same direction, but by less than x percent).

ii. Because the numerator contains foreign traded and nontraded goods prices, the information it contains about the incentives facing domestic agents to consume and produce traded goods or nontraded goods (captured by the internal real exchange rate) will be contaminated by changes in the foreign internal real exchange rate, which is not relevant for domestic agents. For this reason, some economists prefer to use the trade-weighted producer price index for partner countries, on the grounds that it contains a larger share of traded goods.

iii. Finally, since the numerator cannot pick up the effects of changes in commercial policies on the domestic relative prices of traded and nontraded goods, when such policies change this measure will fail to indicate the appropriate changes in the incentives facing domestic agents.

II. THE LONG-RUN EQUILIBRIUM REAL EXCHANGE RATE: CONCEPTUAL ISSUES

Notice that, whether a country operates with a fixed or floating *nominal* exchange rate, the real exchange rate is an endogenous variable.[3] If we adopt the dependent-economy framework, for example, we can define the real exchange rate as:

$$RER = P_T/P_N = SP_T^*/P_N.$$

Under a floating exchange rate regime, the nominal exchange rate s is endogenous. But even under fixed rates, P_N is an endogenous variable. In either case, then, RER is endogenous, and as such, it must therefore be determined as the outcome of the economy's macroeconomic equilibrium.

This observation has caused some economists to question the very notion of distinguishing between the actual RER and its notional equilibrium value. But this

---

[3] We have already seen this to be so in the Mundell-Fleming fixed exchange rate model of Part 2, in which the real exchange rate was endogenous both in the short run and in the medium term.

view, which was the first objection to defining and measuring the equilibrium real exchange rate mentioned in the introduction to this chapter, is fundamentally misguided. The distinction between the actual *RER* and its equilibrium value is not one between disequilibrium and equilibrium, but rather between different types of equilibria (i.e., equilibria conditioned on different values of macroeconomic variables).

a. Defining "Equilibrium"

The traditional definition of the "equilibrium" real exchange rate is that it is the value of the *RER* that is simultaneously consistent with internal and external balance, conditioned on *sustainable* values of exogenous and policy variables. The term "internal balance" in this definition refers to a situation in which the markets for nontraded goods and labor are both in equilibrium. Thus, it corresponds to what we referred to in Chapter 4 as a short-run macroeconomic equilibrium with full employment. External balance, on the other hand, refers to a situation in which the economy's current account deficit is equal to the value of the *sustainable capital inflows* that it can expect to receive. So when we refer to the equilibrium real exchange rate, we are not referring to the real exchange rate that falls out of just any arbitrary macroeconomic equilibrium, but rather from an equilibrium that is sustainable.

What does it take for a macroeconomic equilibrium to be sustainable? To answer this question, we need to formalize the dynamic structure of an economy. At any moment in time we can think of the economy's endogenous variables as being determined by three types of variables: *predetermined variables, exogenous policy variables,* and *other exogenous variables.* Predetermined variables, which we discussed in Part 2, are endogenous variables that change slowly over time. In the model of Part 2, this referred to the economy's capital stock and technology, as well as its net international creditor position. From a Keynesian perspective, it would also refer to the nominal wage. Exogenous policy variables include fiscal and monetary policies, trade policies, and other variables under the control of the domestic authorities. Other exogenous variables can usefully be classified into three types: observable variables such as the weather, the terms of trade, world interest rates, etc., unobservable variables that can be treated as random shocks, and "bubble" variables – variables that affect the economy only through their influence on expectations.

Since the real exchange rate is an endogenous variable, we can express it as determined by the reduced-form relationship:

$$RER\,(t) = F\,[\,X_1(t),\, \mathbf{X_2(t)},\, \mathbf{X_3(t)},\, B(t)\,], \qquad (16.1)$$

where X_1 represents the current values of a set of predetermined variables, $\mathbf{X_2}$ represents the current *and expected future* values of a set of real policy variables,

X'_3 corresponds to the current and expected future values of a set of exogenous (observable and unobservable) variables, and B includes any "bubble" variables that may affect the economy.[4]

At the same time that the economy determines the values of endogenous variables such as the real exchange rate, it also determines the values of all other endogenous variables. These include the *rates of change* of the predetermined variables:

$$\dot{X}_1(t) = G[X_1(t), \mathbf{X_2(t)}, \mathbf{X_3(t)}, B(t)]. \tag{16.2}$$

Notice that the actual real exchange rate observed at any moment may thus be influenced by speculative "bubble" factors, by the *actual* values of predetermined variables, and by transitory values of policy and (observable and unobservable) exogenous variables. When at least some of the variables on which the actual "equilibrium" real exchange rate depends are unsustainable, the actual real exchange rate will tend to change over time. It is possible, then, to think of alternative "equilibrium" real exchange rates, where the notion of equilibrium is defined over diffcrent time horizons.

1. The Short-Run "Fundamental" Real Exchange Rate (SRER)
Because speculative factors are transitory and are generally likely to be short-lived, we can derive a concept that we can call the "short-run" equilibrium real exchange rate (*SRER*) by setting such factors to zero. That is:

$$SRER = F(X_1, \mathbf{X_2}, \mathbf{X_3}, 0). \tag{16.3}$$

This equilibrium concept is short-run in the sense that it is conditioncd on the *current* values of X_1, $\mathbf{X_2}$, and $\mathbf{X_3}$, which can be referred to as the "short-run fundamentals."

2. The Long-Run Equilibrium Real Exchange Rate (LRER)
The short-run equilibrium real exchange rate will itself not bc sustainable, for two reasons:

i. The policy and exogenous variables that affect it can deviate from their "sustainable," or "permanent" values. Call these "permanent" values $\mathbf{X^*_2}$, and $\mathbf{X_3^*}$. Thus, *SRER* can be expected to change when the policy and exogcnous variables are themselves expected to change.
ii. Even if the policy and exogenous variables are at sustainable levels, the predetermined variables may not have completed their adjustments to sustainable positions. Endogenous changes in the predetermined variables would then cause the short-run real exchange rate to keep moving, even with no further changes in

---

[4] X_1 does not necessarily contain *all* policy variables. For example, in an economy operating with a fixed exchange rate, it would not contain the nominal exchange rate. Instead, the value of the nominal exchange rate affects the value of the predetermined variables.

the policy and predetermined variables. The predetermined variables will stop moving when they reach a "steady state," that is, when they reach a value that satisfies:

$$0 = G(X_1, \mathbf{X}_2^*, \mathbf{X}_3^*).$$

We can solve this equation for the long-run (steady-state) values of X_1 as follows:

$$X_1^* = X_1(\mathbf{X}_2^*, \mathbf{X}_3^*). \tag{16.4}$$

Substituting these values of X_1 back into (16.1), we have:

$$e^* = LRER = F[X_1(\mathbf{X}_2^*, \mathbf{X}_3^*), \mathbf{X}_2^*, \mathbf{X}_3^*]$$
$$= H(\mathbf{X}_2^*, \mathbf{X}_3^*). \tag{16.5}$$

e^* is the *long-run equilibrium real exchange rate* (*LRER*). It depends only on the sustainable values of the exogenous and policy variables that affect the real exchange rate directly or indirectly (through X_1). These are called the "long-run fundamentals."

3. The Desired Equilibrium Real Exchange Rate (DRER)

But the policy variables in $\mathbf{X}_2^*$, though sustainable, may not be desirable. Thus, $\mathbf{X}_2^*$ itself may be changing over time, as policies are adjusted in the desired direction. Suppose we call the "optimal" levels of the policy variables $\mathbf{X}_2^{**}$. In general, $\mathbf{X}_2^{**}$ will depend on the values of the exogenous variables:

$$\mathbf{X}_2^{**} = J(\mathbf{X}_3^*).$$

Substituting this in (16.5) we have:

$$e^{**} = DRER = H[J(\mathbf{X}_3^*), \mathbf{X}_3^*]. \tag{16.6}$$

We can call this the *desired equilibrium real exchange rate*.

b. Misalignment

Corresponding to each definition of the equilibrium real exchange rate offered above (that is, *SRER*, *LRER*, and *DRER*) is a corresponding measure of misalignment – defined as the difference between the actual real exchange rate and its equilibrium value. Thus, we can define the following alternative concepts of misalignment:

i. *Short-run misalignment*

$$RER - SRER$$

ii. *Long-run misalignment*

$$RER - LRER = (RER - SRER) + (SRER - LRER)$$

iii. *Ultra-long-run misalignment*

$$RER - DRER = (RER - SRER) + (SRER - LRER) + (LRER - DRER)$$

In flexible exchange rate industrial-country applications, the term "misalignment" usually refers to short-run misalignment. Long-run misalignment, on the other hand, is more often what is meant in fixed exchange rate applications, when reserves and capital flows pick up speculative factors. Ultra-long-run misalignment is what is often at issue in the context of structural reform.

Thus, depending on the definition employed, misalignment can arise from any of the following factors:

i. *Bubble factors* (accounting for the difference between *RER* and *SRER*).
ii. *Transitory policy shocks and slow adjustment of predetermined variables* (accounting for the difference between *SRER* and *LRER*).
iii. *Inappropriate policies* (accounting for the gap between *LRER* and *DRER*).

In the rest of this chapter, we will focus on long-run misalignment. There are two reasons for not emphasizing instead the more comprehensive concept of ultra-long-run misalignment. A practical reason is that the detection of ultra-long-run misalignment requires specification of an "optimal" policy framework as a benchmark. This is certainly difficult to do in general. But a more fundamental reason is that misalignment may be costly even if policies are optimal. Thus, long-run misalignment involves two types of costs: the costs of misalignment itself, and the costs of suboptimal policies.

The claim that misalignment itself may be costly, even if policies are set at their optimal levels, is a controversial one. Some economists believe that real exchange rates are always "appropriate" conditional on the fundamentals, and consequently that "inappropriate" exchange rates reflect unsustainable or otherwise undesirable macroeconomic policies. This was the second objection to the enterprise of defining and measuring equilibrium real exchange rates mentioned in the introduction to this chapter. This conclusion is implied by the view that deviations of the short-run real exchange rate from the long-run equilibrium real exchange rate are the (short-run) equilibrium outcomes of the optimizing behavior of agents operating in an undistorted environment. If so, then such deviations are optimal and cannot be improved upon by exchange rate policy.

The statement thus concerns the role of nominal rigidities in generating temporary deviations of the real exchange rate from its long-run equilibrium value, and reflects the view that nominal rigidities do not help to account for such deviations. This amounts to an application to the exchange rate arena of the broader question of the role of nominal rigidities in explaining macroeconomic fluctuations. The maintained view among those who consider the estimation of equilibrium real exchange rates a worthwhile endeavor is that nominal rigidities have an important role to play in explaining such fluctuations, and consequently that temporary deviations of the

real exchange rate from its long-run equilibrium value do indeed have implications
for nominal exchange rate policies. Specifically, the presence of nominal rigidities
implies that nominal exchange rate adjustments may often be useful in helping to
guide the real exchange rate back to its long-run equilibrium value from an initial
position of disequilibrium. The mainstream perspective, therefore, is that long-run
misalignment has costs, and the costs are greater the greater the extent of financial
integration.

What are the costs of misalignment in the presence of nominal rigidities? First,
for any given episode of misalignment, since the elimination of misalignment in the
absence of nominal exchange rate adjustments would require changes in the domestic price level, it would tend to be associated with macroeconomic instability, in the
form of a period of below-average growth (i.e., a recession) or above-average inflation, even in the absence of capital mobility. With an open capital account and high
capital mobility, on the other hand, these macroeconomically harmful events may be
magnified through capital outflows and inflows, as we saw in the last chapter. Thus,
with substantial capital mobility the emergence of substantial misalignment may be
associated with very severe macroeconomic instability. The evidence indeed suggests
both that real exchange rate misalignment helps to explain the incidence of exchange
rate crises and that such crises have substantial real output costs (see Chapter 19).

Thus, a large real exchange rate misalignment may prove very costly to reverse.
But repeated smaller episodes of misalignment may also prove to be costly. As argued in Chapter 1, for example, repeated minor episodes of misalignment would
tend to increase the "noise" component in real exchange rate movements, thereby
undermining the role of the real exchange rate as a relative price signal. This would
have harmful effects on growth, as we have seen in previous chapters, by impairing
the efficiency of resource allocation as well as by discouraging capital accumulation. The evidence from the cross-country growth literature (e.g., Corbo and Rojas
1995) indeed suggests that real exchange rate variability is negatively related to
growth. Though this does not necessarily mean that it is real exchange rate misalignment itself that has this effect (since such variability could reflect variability in the
equilibrium real exchange rate), there is more direct evidence that this is so (Razin
and Collins 1997).

Do we have evidence on the role of nominal rigidities in generating misalignment? The answer is not much, and what we have is indirect. For example, real
exchange rate variability tends to increase sharply when countries switch from fixed
to floating exchange rates, and to decrease when they revert from floating exchange
rates back to fixed (see, e.g., Mussa 1986). In addition, large episodes of overvaluation tend to end in devaluation rather than price level adjustments, suggesting
that the latter are perceived as more costly by the countries involved. Finally, the
evidence that large estimated overvaluation of the real exchange rate tends to be
associated with slower growth (as in the paper by Razin and Collins cited previously)
is consistent with the effects of nominal rigidities.

III. HOW LONG IS THE "LONG RUN"?

A tricky issue in the definition of the long-run equilibrium real exchange rate is what we mean by the "long run." In terms of the formal definition, the answer seems obvious – it is a situation when all the variables in X_1 have come to rest. But on closer inspection, this definition does not seem to be very useful. The problem is that, as we saw in Part 2, variables such as the nominal wage, the country's net international creditor position, and sectoral capital stocks may approach their long-run values at very different speeds, and some of these may be very slow. Indeed, that is how we distinguished between the short run, the medium term, and the long run in Part 2. In the short run the nominal wage had adjusted fully, but the net creditor position and the capital stock had not. In the medium term the nominal wage and net creditor position had fully adjusted, but the capital stock had not, and in the long run all three variables had completed their adjustments.

Should we require all of these to reach a stationary position in our definition of the long run, as the exposition above would seem to suggest? The problem is that if we did, the *LRER* concept derived may be of little operational usefulness, since it may be approached too slowly.

For guidance on this problem, we can consult the common definition of the *LRER* as the value of the real exchange rate that is simultaneously consistent with internal and external balance, conditioned on sustainable values of exogenous and policy variables. If this is the definition that has proven most useful for policy guidance, perhaps we can use it to help us choose where to draw the line on what meaning of "long run" is most relevant for policy purposes.

What do these have to do with the long-run equilibrium perspective adopted above, and how do we use them to determine the relevant meaning of the term "long run"? Recall that internal balance refers to a situation in which the markets for nontraded goods and labor are both in equilibrium. Thus, it corresponds to short-run macroeconomic equilibrium (full employment). External balance, on the other hand, refers to a situation in which the current account deficit is equal to the value of the sustainable capital inflow. Therefore, because it supposes a situation of full employment, "internal balance" requires that cyclical adjustment mechanisms operating through the labor market should cease to be operative. At the same time, this definition appears to reflect the view that allowing for full capital stock adjustment is too much, that the span of time required would be too long to be of much policy relevance.[5]

On the other hand, the traditional definition unfortunately doesn't help us know what to do with the country's net international creditor position. The reason is that

---

[5] Note that in such a long run there would be ongoing investment (a flow), and thus ongoing changes in the size of the capital stock. Since changes in the capital stock would in principle alter the "long-run" equilibrium real exchange rate under our definition, the implicit assumption is that ongoing investment flows have a negligible effect on the size of the capital stock, as in the short-run model of Part 2.

the term "sustainable capital inflows" is somewhat ambiguous. It can be interpreted as consistent with taking the country's net creditor position as given, and thus treating it as one of the "fundamentals," or with requiring it to have completed its adjustment. For example, if "sustainable" capital inflows are interpreted as those required to keep the country's net creditor position at its steady-state level, then "external balance" must require a steady-state net creditor position. That is, the country's net creditor position should be treated symmetrically with the nominal wage. On the other hand, if sustainable capital flows are those not driven by speculative or cyclical factors, then "external balance" does not necessarily impose the requirement that the economy's net creditor position be unchanging. In that case, the economy's net creditor position would be taken as given in the definition of the *LRER*. It would be treated as a "fundamental," symmetrically with the capital stock, and net capital inflows would just be another endogenous variable.

The key seems to be how rapidly the net creditor position is perceived as adjusting. If the country's net creditor position is perceived as adjusting quickly, the definition of the *LRER* should treat it symmetrically with the nominal wage. If not, it would treat it symmetrically with the capital stock. In practice, both approaches have been used.

IV. A MODEL OF THE LONG-RUN EQUILIBRIUM REAL EXCHANGE RATE

Recall that we defined the long-run equilibrium real exchange rate as $LRER = H(\mathbf{X}_2^*, \mathbf{X}_3^*)$, where $\mathbf{X}_2^*$ and $\mathbf{X}_3^*$ were the long-run fundamentals. Thus, before we can estimate the *LRER*, we must first identify the fundamentals. For this we need a specific model within which to investigate the factors influencing the long-run equilibrium value of the real exchange rate. In this section we will use a model that attempts to synthesize the relevant "fundamentals" that have been identified by economists.[6]

This model incorporates the three-good production structure described in Section I, but assumes for simplicity that exportable goods are not consumed in the domestic economy. It contains fixed sector-specific capital, but intersectorally mobile labor. Because the capital stock is fixed, the model does not allow for investment spending. The economy modeled is assumed to be financially open. Domestic residents pay a premium for external borrowing that depends on the country's net creditor position. Consumption decisions are assumed to be made by infinitely lived representative agents who possess perfect foresight, a standard approach in analytical research to allow the framework to handle intertemporal issues in a rigorous way. We will not analyze the model in detail here. Instead, we will summarize it in the form of two equations representing internal and external balance, on the

---

[6] The model adopted is from Montiel (1999).

assumption that external balance requires full adjustment of the country's net creditor position.

The internal balance condition for simultaneous equilibrium in the markets for labor and nontraded goods can be expressed as:

$$y_N(e, \phi) = (1 - \theta)ec + g_N, \tag{16.7}$$

where y_N and g_N are respectively the level of output of nontraded goods in the economy and the government's consumption of such goods, e is the "importables" real exchange rate, defined as the price of importable goods in terms of nontraded goods, ϕ is the relative price of exportable goods in terms of importable ones (the terms of trade), c is private absorption measured in terms of importable goods, and θ is the share of importables in private absorption. The left-hand side of this equation represents the supply of nontraded goods, while the right-hand side is the demand for such goods. Notice that a depreciation of the real exchange rate and improvement in the country's terms of trade are both assumed to reduce the supply of nontraded goods (by lowering their relative price).

The external balance condition sets the current account deficit equal to the sustainable level of capital inflows. It is given by:

$$\pi^* f^* = \phi y_X(e, \phi) + y_Z(e, \phi) + (r^* + \pi^*) f^* + t - [\tau(\pi^*) + \theta]c - g_Z, \tag{16.8}$$

where y_X and y_Z are respectively the levels of output of exportable and importable goods, r^* is the world real interest rate, π^* is the world rate of inflation, f^* is the economy's steady-state net international creditor position, t is the value of international transfers received by this economy, g_Z is the government's consumption of importable goods, and τ is the cost, per unit of consumption, of making consumption transactions. The latter is in the model to explain why people hold money. Money is held to reduce the cost of making transactions, and this cost is lower, per unit of consumption, the more money is held. Since the demand for money depends inversely on the domestic rate of inflation (equal to the world rate π^* under fixed exchange rates), transaction costs per unit of consumption are increasing in π^*. In this equation, domestic output of tradable goods is the sum of production of exportables and importables $\phi y_X + y_Z$ (measured in units of the importable good). Domestic spending on such goods is the sum of private spending $(\tau + \theta)c$ and government spending g_Z. The difference between production of tradable goods and domestic demand for them is the domestic excess supply of tradable goods $\phi y_X + y_Z - [(\tau + \theta)c + g_Z]$, which is equal to the trade balance surplus. Adding to this net interest receipts from abroad $(r^* + \pi^*)f^*$ and the receipt of net international transfers t yields the current account of the balance of payments. For external balance to hold, this must be equal to the sustainable capital inflow, which is the amount of new borrowing required to offset the inflationary erosion of the

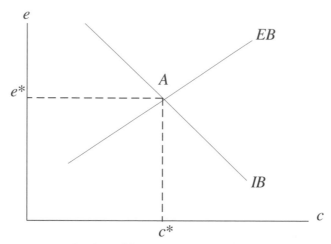

Figure 16.1. Determination of the Long-Run Equilibrium Real Exchange Rate

country's net international creditor position in the presence of world inflation. This is given by $\pi^* f^*$, the left-hand side of equation (16.8).

The solution of this model for the long-run equilibrium real exchange rate can be illustrated graphically by plotting the internal balance condition (16.7) and the external balance condition (16.8) in a diagram with real private consumption c on the horizontal axis and the real exchange rate e on the vertical axis, as in Figure 16.1. The curve traced out by the set of combinations of e and c that are consistent with internal balance (IB) must have a negative slope, because increases in consumption increase the demand for nontraded goods, and this must be offset by an increase in their relative price (a reduction in e) in order to maintain equilibrium in the market for nontraded goods. The external balance curve EB, on the other hand, must have a positive slope, because an increase in consumption of such goods increases the trade deficit, which requires a real exchange rate depreciation to shift resources into the production of traded goods so as to maintain external balance. The long-run equilibrium real exchange rate is that which is simultaneously consistent with external and internal balance in the long run. It is defined by the intersection of the two curves at point A in Figure 16.1, and is labeled e^*.

This model suggests that the long-run equilibrium real exchange rate will be affected by factors that cause changes in the positions of the curves IB and EB. A wide variety of such factors exists. Consider, for example, the effects of changes in government spending. An increase in government spending on traded goods (offset by higher lump-sum taxation) has no effect on the internal balance curve, but it shifts the external balance curve upward. The increase in government spending creates an incipient trade deficit, which requires a real depreciation in order to maintain external balance. At the new long-run equilibrium, therefore, the equilibrium real exchange rate depreciates, and private consumption of traded goods falls. On the other hand, if the increase in government spending is on nontraded goods, the affected curve is the internal balance locus *IB*. The increased demand for nontraded goods requires an increase in their relative price to maintain equilibrium in the nontraded goods market, and the *IB* schedule thus shifts downward, causing the *LRER* to appreciate. Thus, the long-run equilibrium real exchange rate is a function of the sectoral composition of government spending.

Similarly, the effect of a permanent increase in the receipt of transfer income from abroad would be to shift the external balance locus to the right – the receipt of additional transfer income permits an expansion of consumption to be consistent with external balance at an unchanged exchange rate. There are no direct effects on the internal balance locus, so the new situation involves an equilibrium real *appreciation* and an increase in private consumption. The model can be used to analyze a variety of other factors, such as changes in sectoral productivity differentials, as well as in international financial conditions, in the world rate of inflation, in the country's terms of trade, and in commercial policies. All of these factors together represent the relevant set of long-run fundamentals, and permanent changes in any of them will change the long run equilibrium real exchange rate in predictable directions.[7]

V. THE LONG-RUN EQUILIBRIUM REAL EXCHANGE RATE: ESTIMATION

Having identified the set of long-run fundamental determinants of the *LRER*, we can now turn to examining how the value of the *LRER* can be estimated in practice. In this section, we will consider four alternative approaches to estimation: the purchasing power parity (*PPP*) approach, the "trade elasticities" approach, the use of general-equilibrium model simulations, and the estimation of single-equation reduced-form models for the real exchange rate. All of these methods have been widely used by economists to estimate the equilibrium real exchange rate.

a. The Purchasing Power Parity Approach

The most venerable approach to the estimation of the *LRER* is based on the purchasing power parity (*PPP*) hypothesis. In brief, this hypothesis states that the real exchange rate is constant in the long run. Thus, using the notation of the previous section, the long-run equilibrium real exchange rate can be written as:

$$e^* = e_0,$$

where e_0 is a constant, and the actual real exchange rate e that prevails at any moment is given by:

$$\text{Log}(e) = e_0 + \epsilon, \tag{16.9}$$

[7] For further details, see Montiel (1999).

where ϵ is a mean-zero stationary random variable.[8] This would suggest estimating the long-run equilibrium real exchange rate in one of two ways: either as the value of the real exchange rate in some past period when ϵ was known to be zero, or as the average value of the real exchange rate over some number of past periods, if it is not known when ϵ may have been equal to zero. The assumption here is that, because the long-run real exchange rate is taken to be unchanged, we can use the *past* value of the real exchange rate to estimate the *current* value of the long-run equilibrium real exchange rate.

Is this a valid procedure? The answer is that it is valid only if the real exchange rate is *mean-reverting* – that is, only if ϵ is indeed stationary. Otherwise we have no reason to expect the real exchange rate to return to its mean value. How do we know whether this is so? The appropriate procedure is to apply statistical tests for stationarity to the observed real exchange series before using this method. Notice that, in terms of the theory of the previous section, for the *PPP* hypothesis to be valid, the relevant set of long-run "fundamentals" that we identified previously must on average have remained unchanged over the sample period – the "fundamentals" must themselves not have undergone permanent changes. Whether this is so for any given country over any given period of time is a purely empirical matter. Many stationarity tests have been applied to real exchange rates of emerging economies, and the vast majority of them tend to reject purchasing power parity.[9]

b. The "Trade Elasticities" Approach

The most common approach to the estimation of the *LRER* that is capable of taking account of permanent changes in the "fundamentals" is the "trade elasticities" approach. We can describe it as follows. Going back to the model of Part 1, recall that the country's trade balance was expressed as $N(e, Y, Y^*)$. Using this expression, we can write the "external balance" condition in that model in the form:

$$-K = N(e, Y, Y^*). \tag{16.10}$$

where K is the sustainable level of the "resource balance" (net capital inflows minus net interest payments on external debt), and Y and Y^* are the full-employment levels of domestic and foreign real GDP. We can use this equation to estimate the long-run equilibrium real exchange rate by implementing the following sequence of steps:

i.   First, we need to estimate the level of domestic and foreign real GDP at full employment and the sustainable level of the resource balance.

---

[8] A random variable is said to be stationary if the parameters that determine its statistical distribution are not a function of time.
[9] For references, see Hinkle and Montiel (1999).

ii. Next, we require estimates of the parameters of the function $N(\ )$ including those that determine how the trade balance responds to the real exchange rate – that is, the "trade elasticities" involved in the Marshall-Lerner condition.

iii. With an empirical estimate of the function $N(\ )$ in hand, estimating the long-run equilibrium real exchange rate amounts to substituting into equation (16.10) the estimated full-employment values of Y and Y^*, as well as the estimate of the sustainable resource balance. The long-run equilibrium real exchange rate is the value of e that solves this equation.

This method has several advantages. Notice that, unlike the *PPP* approach, the long-run equilibrium real exchange rate estimated using this method is not necessarily constant. It is affected by the "fundamentals" Y, Y^*, and K. Moreover, this approach is structural, so it has the advantage that the determination of the long-run equilibrium real exchange rate can be easily understood. Moreover, it makes use of a small set of behavioral parameters that are widely estimated and thus readily available, making it relatively simple to apply. On the other hand, the estimated trade elasticities tend to be small for most countries, and to be imprecisely estimated. This creates a large range of uncertainty for the estimated long-run equilibrium real exchange rate. A very difficult problem is how to estimate K. For small low-income countries that are not well integrated with international capital markets and rely heavily on external transfers and concessional financing from official sources, K may reasonably be taken to be exogenous. But for countries that are financially open, most procedures for estimating K will have to rely on extensions of this simple structure.

Because these shortcomings render the method of questionable reliability, it is perhaps best suited for "first-pass" back-of-the-envelope estimation of the *LRER*. However, in country applications where data limitations do not permit the implementation of the more sophisticated approaches described below, or in circumstances in which time and resource constraints on the analyst are severe, this may be the best that the analyst can do. Under these circumstances, the "trade elasticities" approach, despite its limitations, may be the method of choice.

c. General-Equilibrium Model Simulation

One way to extend this simple procedure is to embed the trade balance in a full empirical general-equilibrium model of the domestic economy that simultaneously explains the determinants of the resource balance as well as the full-employment levels of real GDP at home and abroad. Such a model could then be simulated for sustainable values of the fundamentals and solved for the steady-state value of the real exchange rate to produce an estimate of the *LRER*. Indeed, in principle, simulation of empirical general-equilibrium models should dominate other estimation methods, because the approach has several important advantages. First, it is structural, so the underlying mechanisms determining the *LRER* can be understood. Second, this approach allows the estimated *LRER* to reflect the full range of known macroeconomic interactions in the economy. Third, since the entire dynamic path of the real exchange rate from its current value to the steady-state (or semi-steady state, if conditioned on some slow-adjusting variable) *LRER* can be simulated, it provides maximum flexibility concerning dynamics.

This model-based general-equilibrium method, however, places relatively strong demands on economic theory, on the power of statistical techniques, and on the availability and quality of data. Made-to-suit models for individual developing countries with limited data and possibly unstable economic structures are vulnerable to doubts about model specification and parameter stability. Estimates derived from such models may thus fail to command much credibility, particularly when the models on which they are based have no existing track record. For the near future, it is likely that estimates of the *LRER* derived from simulations of such models would be treated as indicative, and used to supplement and inform other approaches to estimation. Model simulations may be most attractive in applications in which an existing model has demonstrated its usefulness through an established record of tracking the macroeconomic performance of a particular economy.

d. Single-Equation Reduced-Form Estimation

In the absence of a believable (multi-equation) model, single-equation estimation based on the reduced-form equation for the *LRER* becomes the alternative. One obvious possibility would be to estimate the reduced-form equation (16.5) directly. Why not do so? The answer is, of course, that neither its dependent nor any of its independent variables are observable.

However, if the real exchange rate turns out to be *nonstationary*, then the theory described in the last section suggests that at least some subset of the fundamentals must be so as well. This suggests the use of "co-integrating" equations linking the real exchange rate with the relevant set of "fundamentals," based on the observable current values of the real exchange rate and the fundamentals. Econometric theory suggests that when neither the real exchange rate nor some subset of its "fundamental" determinants is stationary, the parameters of the function $H(\ )$ in equation (16.5) linking the *LRER* to the permanent values of its nonstationary fundamentals can be estimated from these observable values. These estimated parameters would reveal the long-run relationship between the real exchange rate and its fundamental determinants – that is, the parameters of the function $H(\ )$. Coupled with a technique for estimating sustainable values of the fundamentals, this would permit us to estimate the *LRER*.

This approach obviously follows naturally from the time series tests for stationarity required to assess the applicability of the simple *PPP*-based approach. Relative to the simulation of empirical general-equilibrium models, it places fewer demands on economic theory, since the theory required is about long-run relationships, not short-run macroeconomic dynamics. Moreover, fewer data (time series) are required to implement it, since the researcher needs time series only for the variables that can be expected to appear in the reduced-form equation for the real exchange rate in short-run macroeconomic equilibrium.

To illustrate the method, consider the results of the co-integrating equation reported below for the real exchange rate in Thailand, estimated over the period 1970–96. In this application, statistical tests for stationarity suggested that the real exchange rate, the ratio of government consumption to GDP (a proxy for government spending on nontraded goods), Thailand's terms of trade, and the world rate of inflation were all nonstationary variables, and that these variables were jointly co-integrated. This means that it is possible to find a linear combination of these four variables that is stationary. This linear combination is the "co-integrating equation." If this equation is normalized so that the coefficient of the real exchange rate is unity, the coefficients of the remaining variables – the "fundamentals" – correspond to the parameters of the function $H(\ )$ in equation (16.5). The resulting equation – the co-integrating equation for the Thai real exchange rate – is given by:

$$\text{Log}(RER) = 6.113 - 0.746\ \text{Log}(CGR) - 0.581\ \text{Log}(TOT) + 0.012\ INFL,$$
$$\qquad\qquad\quad (0.028)\qquad\qquad (0.016)\qquad\qquad (0.002)$$

where CGR is the ratio of government consumption to GDP, TOT is the terms of trade, $INFL$ is the world rate of inflation, and the numbers in parentheses are standard errors of the parameter estimates. This equation suggests that the $LRER$ in Thailand appreciates when the ratio of government consumption to GDP rises and the terms of trade improve, and depreciates when external inflation increases, all of which are consistent with the theory of the previous section. When estimated "permanent" values of the fundamentals are substituted into the right-hand side of this equation, the fitted values provide an estimated time series for the $LRER$. The resulting estimates for the sample period and the actual RER are both plotted in Figure 16.2. Notice that a comparison of the actual RER with the estimated $LRER$ suggests that the Thai real exchange rate had become overvalued by 1996. We will come back to this observation when discussing the Asian financial crisis of 1997 in Chapter 19.

This technique is quite attractive, for the reasons mentioned above, and there has been a substantial amount of research in recent years on the determination of long-run equilibrium real exchange rates utilizing this method. Unfortunately, the technique has some important disadvantages. The first is that the statistical tests involved have low power in small samples, which means that they are unable to discriminate very closely between variables that are stationary and those that are not, and this is a key requirement in the implementation of this approach. Moreover, in emerging economies there are typically small numbers of annual

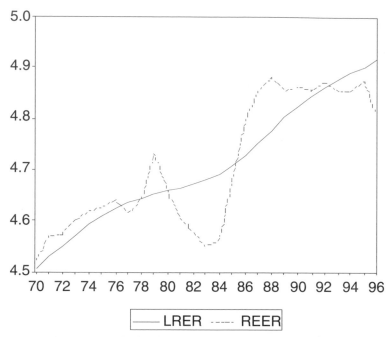

Figure 16.2. Thailand: RER and Estimated LRER, 1970–96

observations with which to work, and the prevalence of structural change reduces the number of useful observations even further. This is complicated by the fact that, as we have seen, theory can identify many potential "fundamentals." Taken together, these observations imply that there are typically few degrees of freedom available in estimation, so it is hard to extract the parameters of the co-integrating relationship from the data. Moreover, the dependent and independent variables are typically measured with error, because the available information often provides poor proxies for the theoretically correct variables, as we saw in Section I with respect to the real exchange rate itself. The former means that coefficients are measured imprecisely; the latter that they are biased toward zero. Finally, it is difficult to estimate the "permanent" component of the fundamentals, and the procedures adopted for this purpose are often arbitrary.

e. An Evaluation

How can we tell how well we are doing in estimating the *LRER*? We can't judge this either by looking at the in-sample fit of estimated regressions, or by our ability to forecast the long-run equilibrium real exchange rate, because the *LRER* is unobservable. There are three ways that we might go about answering this question:

i.   We can check to see how well estimates of misalignment based on theory and estimation of the long-run equilibrium real exchange rate fit the macroeconomic history of the country in question (e.g., do episodes of extreme estimated overvaluation correspond to poor performance in the country's external accounts)?

ii. We can test the extent to which estimated misalignment can help predict future movements in real exchange rates, holding constant changes in fundamentals and in strictly short-run influences on the real exchange rate. The relevant question in this case is: does past misalignment help predict future real exchange rate movements?

iii. We can examine the "goodness of fit" of equations designed to predict movements in *actual* real exchange rates based on estimates of misalignment. Equations that express changes in current exchange rates as functions of past misalignment, controlling for current and lagged changes in fundamentals as well as in nonfundamental influences on the real exchange rate are called error-correction models. This approach would ask: how much of the variation in real exchange rates can we explain on the basis of our theory using such equations?

The evidence from applying methods such as these is mixed (see Hinkle and Montiel 1999). The bottom line seems to be that, though we cannot estimate the *LRER* with any great precision, when there are large movements in the real exchange rate we probably know enough to say whether they can plausibly be explained by the behavior of the underlying fundamentals.

VI. SUMMARY

This chapter has emphasized that real exchange rate misalignment is costly, and it may become more so as enhanced financial integration adds to the microeconomic (resource misallocation) costs of misalignment, the potential macroeconomic costs of capital-flow reversals, and currency crises. The best way to avoid these costs, of course, is to avoid the emergence of a large misalignment in the first place. In principle, there are three ways that misalignment can be avoided:

a. Through movements in the nominal exchange rate that adjust the actual real exchange rate to the *LRER*.
b. Through movements in prices of domestic goods that achieve the same purpose.
c. Through changes in the policy components of the "fundamentals" to move the *LRER* closer to the prevailing value of the real exchange rate.

The problem with the third option, of course, is that such policies may be required to meet other objectives (e.g., should commercial policies be tightened to cope with a depreciation of the *LRER* caused by an adverse movement in the terms of trade?). The choice between the first two alternatives raises the issue of nominal exchange rate management.

There are essentially three options in this regard: allow the nominal exchange rate to achieve the adjustment endogenously by adopting a floating exchange rate system, place the burden of adjustment on the price of domestic goods by adopting an exchange rate system in which the nominal exchange rate cannot be changed, or manage the nominal exchange rate actively through adjustments in an officially determined exchange rate.

The considerations involved in choosing among these alternatives are the subject of the next two chapters. What we have done in this chapter, however, serves as an input into that discussion because, as we shall see next, being able to estimate the value of the equilibrium real exchange rate empiricially only matters for the third option, in which the exchange rate is to be managed actively. Given what has been said here about the costs of misalignment, an empirical assessment of the value of the *LRER* presumably would be an important input into the management of the nominal exchange rate. The question is, do we know enough about the empirical measurement of the *LRER* to be able to guide nominal exchange rate management?

This was the third doubt about equilibrium real exchange rate definition and estimation expressed in the introduction to this chapter. Unfortunately, this one is not as easy to dismiss as the first two. The answer to the question posed at the end of the last paragraph is that, unfortunately, we do not yet have a reliable, workhorse approach to estimation of the *LRER* in which we can place a lot of confidence. Theory is ahead of estimation in this area, since we do know at least in principle the types of economic variables that represent the fundamental determinants of the *LRER*. At present, we cannot estimate the value of the *LRER* with any great precision. However, the fact that empirical estimates of real exchange rate mis-alignment are often consistent with the episodic experience of countries, that such estimates help predict future real exchange rate movements, and that explanations of real exchange rate changes based on such estimates explain a substantial part of the variation in real exchange rates together suggest that we know enough to detect severe episodes of misalignment. We will address the implications of this state of knowledge in Chapter 18.

17

Exchange Rate Regimes

We saw in the last chapter that the avoidance of persistent real exchange rate misalignment should be an important macroeconomic objective for emerging economies. The most important policy decision that a country can make in pursuit of this objective concerns the management of the nominal exchange rate. And in managing the nominal exchange rate, the most fundamental decision that has to be made is the choice of exchange rate regime.

The considerations that govern the choice of exchange rate regime are subject to influence by the surrounding economic environment. In the context of emerging economies, an important factor influencing this choice is financial reform. As we saw in Chapter 15, capital account liberalization, in particular, is likely to interact with technological and institutional developments in industrial countries to create a much greater degree of financial integration with world capital markets among emerging economies that open up their capital accounts and have solvent public sectors under current circumstances than has been true in the past. This development has important implications for macroeconomic management in such countries, not least because the well-known "impossible trinity" of open-economy macroeconomics implies that perfect international capital mobility, monetary autonomy, and an officially determined exchange rate cannot coexist. The implication is that capital account liberalization may place restrictions on the types of exchange rate arrangements that are feasible for emerging economies.

This chapter will explore these issues, and review arguments for alternative exchange rate arrangements in emerging economies under conditions of high capital mobility. It will focus specifically on two types of arrangements that have been adopted recently among some emerging economies and advocated for others: currency boards and floating exchange rates. These represent different choices among the options offered by the "impossible trinity," and have very different implications for domestic macroeconomic management. The third choice mentioned at the end of the last chapter – the active management of an officially determined exchange rate – is the subject of the next chapter.

It is worth noting at the outset that, while the subject of exchange rate management is an old one (going back at least to Hume), it is a difficult topic, on which there has always been substantial disagreement, and on which there has been an active debate in recent years. There are probably two main reasons why this subject has proven to be so controversial. An old reason is that the exchange rate is a nominal variable (a price expressed in terms of units of domestic currency), but what we ultimately care about are its *real* effects. The latter will inevitably depend on the behavior of other nominal prices in the economy. Unfortunately, the behavior of nominal prices is the issue on which there has been the most extensive disagreement among economists since the time of Keynes.

The second reason is more recent. As we saw in Chapter 9, it turns out that well-meaning central banks may have an incentive to announce one policy and do another (the time inconsistency problem), and that the public's reaction to this situation may result in a worse macroeconomic equilibrium than what would happen if the central bank could commit itself to follow through on its policy announcements. It happens that whether central banks follow through on their policy intentions may actually depend on the kind of exchange rate policy that they announce. In other words, when analyzing exchange rate policy, we often have to consider the behavior of the monetary authorities as an *endogenous* variable. This complicates things, because the analysis of the behavior of the monetary authorities as an endogenous phenomenon is a relatively new topic that is still not well understood. In short, the issue of exchange rate policy is tied up with some very problematic areas in macroeconomics.

I. FOREIGN EXCHANGE REGIMES, EXCHANGE RATE MANAGEMENT, AND MONETARY POLICY

The most direct and obvious way that the central bank can manage the exchange rate is through its behavior in the foreign exchange market (i.e., by buying or selling foreign exchange, as in the model of Part 2). When we speak of the exchange rate *regime*, we are typically referring to the rules that govern central bank intervention in this market. However, the central bank can also influence the foreign exchange market without buying or selling foreign exchange itself, through what it does in other markets. This can happen because, as we saw in the model of Part 2, the behavior of the central bank in other markets (e.g., through the buying or selling of domestic securities in its conduct of monetary policy) can influence the behavior of private agents in the foreign exchange market.

However, the central bank does not always manage the exchange rate, either directly or indirectly. Specifically, there are two extreme cases in which it does not.

Under cleanly floating exchange rates the central bank does not intervene in the foreign exchange market in any way – it neither buys nor sells foreign exchange. Or, if it buys or sells foreign exchange because the public sector needs to acquire it or needs to convert foreign exchange earnings into domestic currency, it does so without trying to influence the exchange rate – in other words, it acts as a private bank would on behalf of the government. The extreme case of a floating exchange rate system occurs when the central bank not only does not intervene in the foreign exchange market on its own account (a clean float), but when in addition it does not allow its monetary policy to be influenced by what happens in the foreign exchange market. This can happen, for example, when monetary policy is directed at fixing the path of a monetary aggregate such as the monetary base or $M1$, or at fixing the path of the price level, without taking the exchange rate into account.

But these are not the only circumstances under which the central bank does not actively manage the exchange rate. This situation also prevails under the polar opposite fixed exchange rate regime. As we saw in the model of Part 2, a fixed exchange rate is an extreme form of intervention in the foreign exchange market, in which the central bank announces that it stands ready to buy or sell any quantity of foreign exchange that agents wish to trade at some predetermined and unchanging price. The polar case occurs when the central bank not only fixes the exchange rate unalterably, but in addition allows its monetary policy to be entirely determined by this goal, either not extending credit to domestic agents at all or tying its domestic credit policy rigidly to the behavior of its foreign exchange reserves.

This is in effect what happens under a *currency board*, as we discussed in Chapter 9. We will discuss currency boards more extensively later in this chapter. We also saw in Chapter 9 that a currency board is taken to an extreme under a *full currency union* or *dollarization*. However, the difference between currency boards and currency unions has to do with their differing fiscal consequences (the availability of seignorage revenue) and with credibility issues (the difficulty of altering the exchange rate), not with their effects on day-to-day management of the exchange rate policy or monetary policy.

This discussion, then, suggests that there is an important relationship between exchange rate policy and monetary policy. In the extreme cases:

i. The central bank does not intervene directly in the foreign exchange market, and in addition does not adjust monetary policy to influence the behavior of the exchange rate – that is, it directs monetary policy entirely to domestic objectives, or:

ii. The central bank intervenes to fix the exchange rate indefinitely, and in addition it directs monetary policy completely to this objective, which is an external one.

Note that in these extreme cases there are no day-to-day exchange rate policy decisions to be made. All decisions on exchange rate policy are taken at the time the exchange regime is chosen. But in all other possible cases, the central bank has to decide how to coordinate intervention in the foreign exchange market with monetary policy in order to influence both domestic and external policy objectives.

The implications are that when it comes to exchange rate policy, the monetary authorities have to make two independent decisions:

i. Whether or not to adopt an extreme exchange regime, in which there are no further issues of exchange rate management.
ii. If it does not, and opts for an intermediate regime, then it has to decide how to manage the exchange rate on a continuing basis.

The first decision is the subject of the sections that follow, while the second is taken up in the next chapter.

II. CONSTRAINTS ON EXCHANGE RATE MANAGEMENT

These decisions have to respect certain universal macroeconomic principles, that essentially function as constraints on the central bank's choices. We can classify these into those that operate only in the long run, and those that operate in the short run as well.

We will use these terms in a very specific way in this chapter. The distinction between an economy's long-run equilibrium and its short-run equilibrium for present purposes will be based on the assumption that the average level of wages and prices is "sticky" – it does not immediately adjust to its equilibrium value. In that case, the "long run" can be defined as a period of time that is long enough for the average level of wages and prices to have completed their adjustment, while the "short run" is the period of time before this adjustment is complete.

a. Long-Run Constraints

1. Nominal Anchors in Open Economies

The first principle is that every economy that uses a monetary unit of account must have a nominal anchor (i.e., a variable that determines the average level of domestic prices in terms of domestic currency). Since establishing a nominal anchor is a public good, it is properly a task for the government to undertake. To do so, the government has to make use of a nominal instrument. That is, it has to fix some nominal price or nominal quantity. The reason is that, because the economy's general equilibrium determines a set of *relative* prices and *real* quantities, fixing the price of any single good in terms of domestic currency, or fixing the value of any nominal quantity, would determine the prices of all other goods and services in terms of domestic currency.

This observation has two important implications for exchange rate policy:

i. The decision made with respect to the foreign exchange regime will determine the economy's nominal anchor – that is, the variable that will determine the domestic price level in the long run. If a fixed, or officially determined, exchange rate is chosen, the nominal anchor will be the nominal exchange rate, as we saw in the context of the model in Part 2 (Chapter 5). If the exchange rate is allowed to float, on the other hand, the nominal anchor must be something else. It could, for example, be the money supply, or some combination of nominal variables that could in principle vary over time.

ii. The choice of exchange rate regime and nominal anchor management will have important effects on the average price level, so exchange rate management and inflation can be expected to be closely related.

2. Monetary Neutrality

What difference does it make what is chosen as the nominal anchor? In answering this, we need to distinguish between two sub-questions:

i. How does the choice of nominal anchor affect the difference between how the government says it's going to manage the nominal anchor *ex ante* and what it subsequently actually does *ex post*?
ii. How does the actual *ex post* behavior of the variable chosen as the nominal anchor affect the economy?

As we shall see later, there is no uniformity of opinion among economists regarding the answer to the first of these sub-questions. The second macroeconomic principle that we need to discuss here concerns the second one.

In answering this question, we can break it up into two parts, corresponding to how the actual behavior of the nominal anchor affects two different characteristics of the economy: the average price level, and the economy's real equilibrium. The answers that economists give to these questions are governed by the principle of *monetary neutrality*: the economy's long-run real equilibrium is not affected either by the identity of the nominal anchor (the particular variable that is chosen as the anchor) or by the specific value that is chosen for the nominal anchor. This implies that the domestic price level must be proportional to the level of the nominal anchor in the long run. The reason behind this is that economists don't believe that people suffer from *money illusion* – that is, what they care about are relative prices and real quantities, not prices and quantities measured in nominal terms. If this is so, then the economy's equilibrium should not be affected by a change in nominal magnitudes, since neither preferences nor production opportunities are affected by the units in which goods and services are measured.

This has three important corollaries:

i. *The real exchange rate is not affected in the long run by the value of the nominal anchor.* As we have seen, the real exchange rate is the price of foreign goods and services in terms of domestic goods and services. In the model of Part 2, it was given by $e = sP^*/P$. We have seen throughout this book that this is an important relative price for the economy, because it affects production and spending decisions that determine resource allocation. What this corollary says is that the real exchange rate is an endogenous macroeconomic variable that in the long run does not depend on the exchange regime, the conduct of nominal exchange rate policy, or the specific value of the nominal exchange rate. What exchange rate policy does affect in the long run is the absolute level of prices in domestic currency, not relative prices.

ii. *Each economy can have at most one nominal anchor in the long run.* This follows directly from monetary neutrality, since fixing one nominal price or quantity determines all other prices and quantities, implying that no other price or quantity can be determined independently. It implies specifically that:

iii. *If the authorities fix the nominal exchange rate, they cannot also control the money supply in the long run.* Monetary neutrality tells us that both the real exchange rate $e(= sP^*/P)$ and the real money supply $m(= M/P)$ are independent of the nominal anchor in the long run. This means that s and M cannot be chosen independently, because a choice of s determines P, which then, through m, determines the required value of M. Similarly, if M is chosen, a required value of s is determined. It is important to emphasize that this is true regardless of the degree of capital mobility. Notice the important implication that for a fixed exchange rate to be sustainable in the long run, monetary policy must be consistent with the exchange rate target.[1]

3. Fiscal Solvency

We saw above that monetary neutrality implies that, depending on the choice of nominal anchor, exchange rate policy or monetary policy determines the domestic price level in the long run. That means that it must also determine the long-run rate of inflation. But we have seen previously (Chapter 7) that for the public sector to be solvent, the domestic rate of inflation (determined by the rate of depreciation of an officially determined exchange rate or by the rate of growth of the money supply) has to be consistent with the fiscal accounts, in the form of the government's intertemporal budget plans. What this means is that the path chosen for the nominal

---

[1] As we saw in Chapter 4, it may indeed be possible to fix s and M (or some other monetary aggregate) independently in the short run. Why can't this be done forever? Suppose that the economy operates with a fixed exchange rate. As we saw in the analysis of medium-term equilibrium for such an economy in Chapter 5, if monetary policy takes the form of fixing the stock of domestic credit (and not the money supply), then the money supply will adjust endogenously to the exchange rate through the balance of payments. But even if monetary policy tries to fix the money supply (through sterilization), the price level will nevertheless be determined by the exchange rate in the long run, not by the money supply. If the economy is not in a medium-term equilibrium with the values of the exchange rate and money supply that are chosen, the only way to keep the money supply constant is to sterilize the effects of the balance of payments on the monetary base. If there is a balance of payments deficit, this implies that the country will eventually run out of reserves. If there is a surplus, the stock of public sector debt will explode.

anchor has fiscal implications. That is, nominal anchor policy and fiscal policy are related through the government's intertemporal budget constraint.

Recall from Chapter 7 that for the consolidated public sector to be seen as solvent, actual and potential creditors have to expect that the present value of future primary surpluses plus seignorage revenue, discounted at the safe rate of interest, should be at least equal to the face value of the existing debt. Since the existing debt is predetermined at any given moment, the expected future path of the primary surplus has to be consistent with the expected future path of inflation in the long run.

We can now combine principles (1)–(3). Together they imply that there has to be consistency between the path of the primary fiscal deficit over time, the domestic rate of inflation, and the rate of change of the economy's nominal anchor. This means that if the government, for example, determines a given path for its primary deficit, it can choose either the exchange rate or the money supply as the economy's nominal anchor. But the rate of growth of whatever variable the government chooses must be consistent with the rate of inflation determined by the fiscal deficit. The other nominal variable must adjust endogenously. On the other hand, the government can choose the rate of change of the nominal anchor. This determines the rate of inflation in the long run. Then the government has to adjust its fiscal deficit to this rate of inflation, and the other nominal variable will adjust endogenously. Notice that in both cases, the real exchange rate will adjust endogenously.

b. A Short-Run Constraint: The "Impossible Trinity"

The three previous observations refer to restrictions that have to be obeyed by fiscal, exchange rate, and monetary policies in the long run. The last restriction to be discussed in this section is one that must apply even in the short run.

Recall that one consequence of monetary neutrality was that the paths followed by the money supply and the nominal exchange could not be chosen independently of each other in the long run. If one is chosen exogenously, the other is determined endogenously. However, we have previously encountered an additional constraint that must be respected even in the short run: *perfect capital mobility, a fixed exchange rate, and monetary autonomy cannot coexist, even in the short run.* As we have seen, this is known as the "impossible trinity" of open-economy macroeconomics.

Why is it true? It holds because, as we saw in Chapter 3, with perfect capital mobility the elasticity of capital flows with respect to the differential between domestic and foreign interest rates becomes infinite. Under these circumstances, if the government allows the exchange rate to float, it can control the money supply, because it is not committed to buying or selling foreign exchange. That means that changes in the monetary base can only happen at the government's own initiative. On the other hand, if the government wants to maintain a fixed exchange rate, it cannot sustain a money supply that would produce an interest rate different from the world rate, because that would produce an infinite excess demand or supply for foreign exchange reserves.

It may be worth noting that perfect capital mobility requires two conditions: that domestic and foreign interest-bearing assets are perfect substitutes, and that there are no policy-imposed barriers to capital movements. Free capital mobility just refers to the latter. Thus, the condition does *not* say that free capital mobility, fixed exchange rates, and monetary autonomy cannot coexist, since different risk characteristics between domestic and foreign interest-bearing assets may cause them to be considered imperfect substitutes even in the absence of policy-imposed barriers to capital movements.

The importance of the "impossible trinity" arises because it means that, if there are no "natural" reasons that cause assets in different currencies to be treated as imperfect substitutes, the government will only be able to choose among two of the three options: free capital mobility, monetary autonomy (control over the domestic money supply), and an officially determined exchange rate. Thus, this constraint tells us the conditions under which a country can have both an exchange rate policy and an independent monetary policy in the short run. The necessary condition is that it be imperfectly integrated with world capital markets. There is another way to put this that is also informative: the exchange rate and the money supply are only independent policy instruments in the short run when capital mobility is imperfect. When this does not hold – that is, when capital mobility is perfect – the choice of the exchange rate dictates the choice of the money supply, and the choice of the money supply determines the exchange rate (at the value that satisfies uncovered interest parity). Because the choice of one is a function of the choice of the other, they cannot be chosen independently and do not represent different policy instruments.

III. CRITERIA FOR CHOOSING AMONG EXCHANGE RATE REGIMES

Given these constraints that exchange rate regimes must respect, we can now turn to the objectives that they have been intended to achieve. These objectives can be used as criteria for evaluating alternative exchange rate regimes. In practice, three independent criteria have been widely used in the analysis of optimal exchange rate regimes. They concern the roles of different exchange rate regimes in reducing transactions costs in international commerce, promoting long-run domestic price stability, and facilitating macroeconomic adjustment to shocks. At bottom, of course, these criteria have to do with different dimensions of macroeconomic performance under the alternative regimes. Because the last two criteria raise a variety of issues, we will discuss them in some detail in subsequent sections.

a. Exchange Regimes and Transactions Costs

By contrast, the first criterion is relatively straightforward. It acknowledges that the nature of the foreign exchange regime may affect the costs of doing business across international boundaries, through the resources involved in maintaining the currency conversion mechanism as well as through the uncertainty created by possible exchange rate changes. In addition, it regards a regime as superior if it minimizes these costs, which act as a tax on international commerce. This criterion amounts to an argument for a single currency to eliminate the costs of currency conversion and exchange rate risks. The criterion has been applied most notably in the arguments for a single currency in the European Union. The real question about it is how large these costs really are and how much of a disincentive they provide to international commerce. Recent research suggests they may not be insignificant.

b. Consequences of Multiple Criteria

Before turning to the discussion of the remaining criteria, it is worth noting that considering all three criteria to be valid means that the choice of exchange rate regime must be made in light of multiple objectives, and this fact itself has implications for this choice. Specifically, it means that even if we can come to the conclusion that a single regime is best for meeting each objective, it may not be the same regime in each case. If that is so, we would face a trade-off between objectives.

To weigh the objectives in making the choice of regimes, then, we would have to ask questions such as the following:

i. How costly is high inflation to the country, and how large is the gain in lower inflation when one switches from one regime to another?[2]
ii. How large are shocks to the economy, how costly would macroeconomic adjustment without an explicit policy response be, how productive is the exchange rate regime in facilitating adjustment, and what other policies are available?

The important point is that, in light of considerations like these, countries with different preferences or facing different circumstances may choose different exchange rate regimes, and the same country may choose different regimes at different points in time as its circumstances change.[3]

We now consider the second and third criteria in more detail.

IV. EXCHANGE RATE REGIMES AND LONG-RUN INFLATION STABILIZATION

The second criterion mentioned above has to do with long-run price level performance. It concerns the effects that the exchange rate regime may have on

---

[2] We will see below that the gain may arise from differential properties of exchange rate regimes as a precommitment mechanism for the central bank. This gain may not be large, for example, if the central bank already has an independent anti-inflationary reputation.
[3] For example, we have already seen that the exchange rate may play a role during the process of stabilizing from high inflation. Once stabilization is completed, exchange-rate-based stabilization may give way to "flexibilization."

the long-run equilibrium rate of inflation, with an exchange rate regime judged superior if it results in a lower long-run rate of inflation.

As we have seen, macroeconomists agree that the long-run Phillips curve is vertical – that is, the economy's full-employment equilibrium can be associated with *any* sustained rate of inflation – and that high inflation has substantial economic costs. These two observations together imply that an important target for monetary and exchange rate policy should be to achieve a long-run macroeconomic equilibrium with a relatively low rate of inflation. But we have also seen that an economy's long-run rate of inflation is an endogenous variable that depends on the path followed by the economy's nominal anchor. Moreover, in principle the same rate of inflation could be consistent with different choices of nominal anchor (i.e., the exchange rate or the money supply), so why should we believe that the exchange rate regime should affect the long-run rate of inflation?

The reason is that, even though the same rate of inflation could be achieved with different nominal anchors, the rate of inflation actually implemented by the government with its nominal policy instrument *may depend on what instrument it chooses to use as a nominal anchor.* In particular, whether the government actually adheres to some announced low-inflation target may depend on what nominal policy it uses to achieve its inflation objective.

a. Time Inconsistency Once Again

The reason has to do with the analysis of the time inconsistency of optimal policies that we discussed in Chapter 9. Recall the general setting: a well-meaning central bank chooses the economy's optimal rate of inflation based on a social objective function in which an unanticipated increase in the rate of inflation is socially beneficial, and in which the social costs of *actual* inflation rise as a nonlinear function of the rate of inflation. The private sector forms its expectations about the rate of inflation, and acts on them by setting wages and prices, before (less often than) the central bank makes its decision about the nominal policy instrument.

We saw that under these circumstances, the central bank may find it advantageous to announce a low rate of inflation, and after the private sector has acted on these expectations, to produce an inflationary surprise in order to improve social welfare. The problem was that the private sector knew that the central bank had incentives to do this, and consequently, expected the inflation rate to be greater than that announced by the central bank. When inflation expectations were high, the central bank would no longer find it appropriate to comply with its original announcement, because this could create large social costs. The equilibrium in this situation was one in which the inflation rate had to be sufficiently high to deprive the central bank of any incentive to try to spring an inflation surprise on the economy. But the resulting social outcome was suboptimal – the economy would bear the costs of a high level of actual inflation without any of the benefits of surprise inflation.

The problem in this situation was the central bank's lack of credibility – the central bank had no way to commit itself to actually doing what it had promised to do. To solve this problem, it is necessary to find a mechanism that can commit the central bank to fulfill its promises.

Unlike what we assumed in Chapter 9, what the central bank controls in the real world is not the inflation rate directly, but a nominal variable such as the exchange rate or the money stock. As we have seen, in the long run the central bank can control only one of these variables. In the short run, it may be able to control both, if financial integration is imperfect. In principle, the central bank faces several choices in announcing its policy strategy. It can announce a future path for its nominal policy instrument – a path for the exchange rate or the stock of money – and let the public infer from that the bank's targeted path for its ultimate policy objective, the average price level. Alternatively, it could also phrase its policy announcement in terms of an intended path for the price level itself. The latter implies making no explicit commitment about the management of nominal policy instruments. The central bank would stand ready to alter the exchange rate and/or the money supply as necessary to achieve a certain price level outcome, changing the economy's nominal anchor from time to time depending on circumstances. The announcement that the central bank makes determines the exchange rate regime. The exchange rate is fixed if it announces an exchange rate path, flexible if it does not.

The key point in all this is that the exchange rate regime can be relevant for determining the economy's long-run inflation rate, because announcing a path for the exchange rate may be more or less effective as a commitment mechanism than announcing a path for the money supply. Is it?

b. Characteristics of Commitment Mechanisms

To answer this, consider first what characteristics a good commitment mechanism should have. Recall the steps in setting out the time inconsistency problem:

  i. The central bank announces a policy.
 ii. Based on this, the public forms expectations of inflation.
iii. The central bank chooses the actual policy.

This suggests that a good commitment mechanism should have the following characteristics:

  i. If the central bank acts in good faith, inflation should in fact turn out to be low. This depends on:
   • The controllability of the announced target.
   • Its effectiveness in affecting inflation. That is, if the central bank actually does what it says it will, this should produce low inflation.

- The transparency to the public of the link between the central bank's actions and the rate of inflation.

ii. If the public acts in accordance with low expected inflation, the central bank should have little incentive to deviate from its announcement.

This depends on the perceived benefits versus the perceived costs of doing so from the perspective of the central bank. The benefits depend in part on how large an impact the instrument used by the central bank can have on aggregate demand. This impact may differ for the money supply and the exchange rate, since they operate on aggregate demand in the short run through different channels. The costs depend on how easy it is for the public to detect any tendency for the central bank to renege on its commitments, and on how much damage reneging would do to the central bank.

The benefits and costs perceived by the central bank can be affected by institutional arrangements. For example, the benefits perceived to be available through surprise inflation can be reduced through the appointment of a conservative central banker who places less weight on output gains and more on the costs of inflation, while the perceived costs can be increased by tying the policy announcement to international agreements that would be costly to repudiate.

How well do the alternative nominal anchors satisfy these criteria? Consider them one at a time:

c. Exchange Rate Announcements as Commitment Mechanisms

Announcing a predetermined exchange rate path has certain advantages as a commitment mechanism:

i. It is a variable that the central bank can control directly, so it is reasonable to expect that it will move in the indicated direction if the central bank acts in good faith.

ii. The exchange rate is directly tied to the price level through the price of foreign goods and the equilibrium real exchange rate (i.e., $P = sP^*/e$).

iii. It is a simple announcement that everyone can understand.

These considerations suggest that if the central bank follows its announcement, people should indeed expect low inflation. Also:

iv. The exchange rate can be observed directly, so everyone knows whether the central bank is complying with its announcement or not.

v. It lends itself to international agreements, in the form of common exchange rate regimes adopted by groups of countries.

For these last two reasons, breaking promises with respect to the nominal exchange rate has high political costs for the central bank, and these costs may negate the benefit that the central bank may perceive from inflationary surprises.

This would leave the bank with reduced incentives to generate such surprises, and consequently may help to make policy announcements more credible.

This type of announcement also has important disadvantages as a commitment mechanism, however. These consist of the following:

i. The relationship of the nominal exchange rate to the price level may not be stable in the short run, if there are large changes in the short-run equilibrium real exchange rate.

ii. Fixing the exchange rate may be a costly promise for the central bank to keep, and that may make it less credible. This would be the case if fixing the exchange rate proves to be a markedly inferior strategy for reducing macroeconomic adjustment costs in response to the shocks that are relevant to the domestic economy (see below), or creates the possibility of larger and more severe shocks. For example, fixing the exchange rate may leave the economy vulnerable to speculative attacks that may endanger the domestic financial system if the latter is in a fragile situation. This represents an interaction between the price-stability criterion and the adjustment-cost criterion. Poor performance on the latter may undermine a regime's ability to perform well on the former.

iii. The fixed exchange rate may conceal important signals, because the loss of foreign exchange reserves that arises when policies are excessively expansionary cannot easily be detected.

iv. Finally, the instability of the equilibrium real exchange rate and vulnerability to speculative attacks makes it easier for the central bank to cheat (by claiming that it's been forced to alter the rate), and that weakens the exchange rate as a commitment device.

d. Money Supply Announcements as Commitment Mechanisms

Just as policy announcements about the future path of the nominal exchange rate have advantages and disadvantages as commitment devices, so do announcements about the future path of the money supply that leave the exchange rate to be determined by the market. The advantages include the following:

i. In principle, like the exchange rate, the money supply is a variable that the central bank can control.

ii. Monetary autonomy is retained under this option, even with high capital mobility. This may reduce macroeconomic adjustment costs, and thus make adherence to policy announcements more credible.

iii. Information about the bank's adherence to its announced targets can be known fairly quickly.

iv. Moreover, if the central bank cheats, effects on the rate of inflation cannot be hidden. They will be seen right away, in part through a depreciation of the exchange rate.

On the other hand, each of these points has qualifiers that may turn them into disadvantages. For example:

i. It is possible that the money supply measure that is being determined may not be under the complete control of the central bank. Under floating exchange rates, the central bank controls unborrowed reserves, but its control over other domestic monetary aggregates may be highly imprecise. If that is so, the signal sent by the path of the targeted aggregate is imperfect.

ii. The relationship of the money supply to the price level may not be as obvious as that of the exchange rate, since the link is not direct and immediate to any component of the average price level.

iii. When the demand for money is unstable, adhering to money supply targets may destabilize the economy. In other words, just as fixed exchange rates create the possibility of speculative attacks on the currency, monetary targeting creates the possibility of unintended policy shocks. In addition, allowing the exchange rate to float also creates scope for asset-price bubbles to affect the real exchange rate. Just as in the case of fixed exchange rates, because such shocks create incentives for deviating from the announced targets, they make those targets less credible.

iv. The money supply cannot be observed directly, but only through announcements by the central bank itself.

e. Exchange Rate Regimes and Price Stability: Evidence

Theory, then, does not provide a clear-cut verdict as to whether nominal exchange rate targeting (fixed exchange rates) or money supply targeting (flexible exchange rates) is more effective as a precommitment device and thus best promotes low long-run inflation. What does the evidence say?

Since there is substantial international experience with alternative exchange rate regimes, it would seem straightforward to examine the evidence on this matter so as to settle the issue empirically by simply running regressions on long-run average inflation rates on a set of inflation determinants as well as on the nature of the exchange rate regime. Unfortunately, this is not easy to do. Complications arise from three sources. First, it is difficult to classify many regimes as either fixed or flexible. This is because there are many intermediate regimes and also because countries often report to international institutions that maintain such data that they are observing one regime while in practice behaving in accordance to another (e.g., declaring that they maintain a freely floating regime while intervening heavily to stabilize the exchange rate). Second, the set of "third factors" that may influence inflation together with the exchange rate regime is extensive, and it is difficult to be confident that all of these have been controlled for. Finally, the exchange rate regime may be endogenous to the country's inflation performance, if countries with a preference for low inflation for other reasons choose one exchange rate regime over the other.

A recent study by Ghosh, Gulde, Ostry, and Wolfe (1997) is particularly careful about all of these issues. Using a sample of 140 countries with data for the years 1960–90, these authors found that the rate of inflation tended to be lower in countries that maintained a fixed exchange rate. On the other hand, the growth rate was lower in countries with fixed exchange rates, despite these countries having higher average rates of investment. This means that they had lower average productivity growth.[4]

The conclusion would seem to be that fixed exchange rates are probably more effective than floating rates as a commitment device for central banks, and thus that this regime tends to be more successful in promoting long-run price stability. However, because of the empirical problems just mentioned and the scarcity of studies that have addressed them, at this point the evidence is suggestive, rather than conclusive.

f. Inflation Targeting

In recent years, several central banks in both industrial countries and emerging economies have opted for a third alternative for central bank policy announcements, by targeting the rate of inflation itself. This essentially implies announcing the ultimate objective of policy, rather than the instruments designed to achieve it. Like the alternatives examined above, this has advantages and disadvantages.

Among the advantages are that this is a simple and transparent announcement, that the information on the central bank's compliance is available quickly and, most importantly, that this allows the central bank to retain substantial flexibility in its choice of instruments. This option permits the central bank to respond to changes in velocity as well as in the equilibrium real exchange rate without destabilizing the domestic economy.

The main disadvantage, on the other hand, is that the inflation rate is an endogenous variable not controlled directly by the central bank and not always easily predictable (note that because of policy lags, the central bank would have to be able to predict inflation in order to take countervailing measures to permit it to hit its target) or easily linked to the instruments controlled by the central bank (the central bank may be able to control nominal short-term money market rates, but what affects real aggregate demand is long-run real interest rates). Thus, the central bank would find it easier to evade responsibility for changes in this variable.

The experience to date among countries that have adopted inflation targets suggests that the use of inflation targets has been associated with lower inflation, but we have no careful studies that have controlled for other determinants of inflation

---

[4] The authors explain this as the result of a lower rate of growth of trade in these countries.

in evaluating the success of this strategy, or that can establish the direction of causation.

<h2 style="text-align:center">V. EXCHANGE RATE REGIMES AND THE MACROECONOMIC ADJUSTMENT PROCESS</h2>

The previous section considered the advantages and disadvantages of alternative exchange rate systems from the point of view of imposing discipline on the authorities, and thus promoting long-run inflation stabilization. But the choice of regime also has implications for the short-run adjustment process.

Economies are typically afflicted by a variety of shocks to which they need to adjust, in the sense that such shocks may call for new configurations of relative prices and real quantities. Because the reallocation of productive factors is costly, and because of the role of short-run stickiness in nominal wages and prices, moving from one equilibrium to another is not always a smooth process. The third criterion pertains to the effect that the exchange rate regime can have on the path that the economy follows to regain its long-run equilibrium after it is affected by a shock, in other words, the question is what type of exchange rate regime best promotes the adjustment process, in the sense of minimizing adjustment costs.

It is important to recognize that this could mean two things:

i. To reduce the costs associated with the adjustment process when changes have to happen, that is, when there are permanent changes in the economy's long-run equilibrium (we might refer to this as "facilitating adjustment").
ii. To prevent unnecessary real costs when shocks imply no change in the economy's long-run real equilibrium (to *avoid destabilizing* the real equilibrium).

a. An Example: Adjustment to a Permanent Real Shock

Shocks can be classified along two important dimensions: their *duration* (whether they are expected to be temporary or permanent), and their *origin*. Shocks to the domestic economy can originate in the domestic or foreign goods markets (real shocks), in domestic asset markets (nominal shocks), and in foreign asset markets (external financial shocks). To see how the exchange rate regime can play a role in the adjustment to macroeconomic shocks, consider how adjustment would work in response to a permanent real (i.e., goods-market) shock that affects the demand for domestic goods adversely (causes it to fall).

How would the domestic economy adjust to such a shock? There are several options:

i. The relative price of the domestic good could fall (price adjustment).
ii. Domestic factors of production could relocate to another country (quantity adjustment).

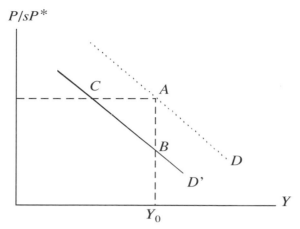

Figure 17.1. Adjustment to a Permanent Real Shock

iii. Fiscal policies (undertaken either by the domestic government or by the rest of the world) could be designed to sustain the level of demand for the domestic good (policy response).

These alternative options are illustrated in Figure 17.1. From an initial equilibrium at a point like A, the economy undergoes a reduction in the demand for its goods that is anticipated to be permanent.[5] Assuming the vertical aggregate supply curve of Part 2, adjustment through mechanism (i) above implies a new equilibrium vertically below the original one (at B), (ii) one horizontally to the left of it (at C), and (iii) a return to the original equilibrium at A through a policy-induced rightward shift of the demand curve.

If neither (ii) nor (iii) can happen (because domestic factors of production are not mobile internationally and there are no extranational institutions that can undertake the required fiscal policies), then adjustment must eventually occur through (i). This means that the long-run equilibrium real exchange rate must depreciate. The exchange rate regime determines the extent to which this happens through a change in the nominal exchange rate (an increase in s) or a change in relative price levels (a reduction in P).

What difference does it make how this adjustment in relative prices is brought about?

Notice that at A the economy's real exchange rate is misaligned. The key point about misalignment made in the last chapter was that if the price level is sticky, then bringing about a real exchange rate depreciation through adjustment in relative price levels could require a recession, which implies substantial social costs and adds an "excess burden" to the real income loss caused by the demand shift. Thus,

---

[5] Note that in Figure 17.1 the real exchange rate is expressed as the price of domestic goods in terms of foreign goods (P/sP^*), instead of its inverse, as used in the rest of the book, to permit us to draw the demand curve for the domestic good with a negative slope.

adjustment from *A* to *B* is less costly if brought about by a change in the nominal exchange rate. This advantage of nominal exchange rate adjustment is not general, however. More generally, as we shall see below, the conclusion depends on the source of the shock.

b. The General Case

More generally, exchange rate flexibility has two important consequences for the costs of adjustment to macroeconomic shocks:

i. Whether the exchange rate is free to adjust or not influences the real effects on the economy of macroeconomic shocks in the absence of a discretionary policy response. In general, whether exchange rate adjustment amplifies or reduces these real effects depends on the source of the shock.

ii. Moreover, whether the exchange rate adjusts freely or not also affects the availability of macroeconomic policy instruments that can be used in a discretionary fashion to respond to shocks.

Consider these one at a time.

1. Consequences of Macroeconomic Shocks

To see the implications of the exchange rate regime for the consequences of macroeconomic shocks, suppose initially that the authorities have a single policy objective – consisting of internal balance – and that they are constrained from undertaking a discretionary policy response when shocks arrive. Thus, the superior regime is the one that proves to be the best "automatic stabilizer" – that is, the one that is most successful in stabilizing real output automatically (that is, without explicit countervailing policy actions) in response to shocks.

The classic analysis of this situation derives the following standard results:

i. When nominal shocks dominate (i.e., shocks to the demand or supply of money), fixed exchange rates are better able to stabilize output, because the endogenous response of the money supply under fixed rates contains the adjustment in the money market, thereby protecting domestic aggregate demand and production from the effects of such shocks.

ii. When real shocks dominate (shocks that directly affect the demand or supply of domestic goods), flexible exchange rates are superior, because they allow relative prices to adjust without requiring quantity adjustments that would involve changes in domestic output, as in Figure 17.1.

iii. Foreign financial shocks tend to affect both domestic goods and financial markets. Which regime is better when shock takes this form depends on structural characteristics of the economy such as the interest elasticities of demand for money and goods.

2. Availability of Macroeconomic Instruments

Now suppose that we allow for the possibility of a policy response to shocks, and that the authorities care not only about the stability of real output (internal balance), but also about an external balance target, such as the outcome for the current account of the balance of payments. Then there may exist an important difference between the two regimes, in the sense that the instruments that are available to achieve these targets – and thus the possibility of achieving them both – may differ between the two regimes.

A basic principle of macroeconomic policy making is that to achieve n different policy targets one needs at least n independent policy instruments (independent means that they are truly different, in that they have different effects on the targets). As we have already seen, if there is high capital mobility, money and the exchange rate are not independent policy instruments, even in the short run. So we can choose one or the other.

Under these circumstances, there is an important difference between the two instruments: if the central bank chooses the money supply as a policy instrument, it can be used in a discretionary fashion, while if it chooses the exchange rate, it typically cannot. Why do these differences exist? The answer is because, as mentioned above, under conditions of high capital mobility fixed but adjustable exchange rate systems tend to be susceptible to foreign exchange rate crises.

The implications for the availability of policy instruments are the following: assuming there is fiscal flexibility, with high capital mobility and fixed exchange rates, the economy would be left with only one policy instrument (fiscal policy) to achieve two targets: internal balance and external balance. This means, for example, that if there is a recession and a current account deficit, the fiscal authorities would have to choose between one objective and the other. With money as the policy instrument, however, different mixes of monetary and fiscal policies can be used to achieve internal and external balance targets. On the other hand, if there is no fiscal flexibility, then fixing the exchange rate means being left with no policy instruments, while fixing the money supply means having one instrument to achieve two targets.

To summarize the analysis of exchange rate regimes and adjustment costs: floating exchange rates have the advantage in facilitating adjustment when shocks are real, because they permit the government to continue to hit targets for both internal and external balance in the face of such shocks. On the other hand, fixed rates have the advantage when shocks are nominal, because they protect both internal and external balance targets from the effects of such shocks, by confining these effects to the domestic money market. In the face of external financial shocks, neither regime is unambiguously better in the absence of a discretionary policy response, but flexible rates have the advantage that they allow policy more discretion in responding to such shocks by allowing the domestic authorities to bring two policy instruments to bear, rather than the single instrument that is available when the nominal exchange rate is fixed.

VI. EXTREME FOREIGN EXCHANGE REGIMES: ARGUMENTS PRO AND CON

In the last two sections, we considered how the two extreme exchange rate arrangements under consideration fared under each of the two main criteria that have been used to evaluate such regimes. In this section we take a different cut at the problem by briefly evaluating each of the extreme regimes independently.

a. Currency Boards

As explained in Chapter 9, a currency board is an exchange rate arrangement in which the central bank commits itself to issuing domestic currency only in exchange for foreign exchange reserves at a predetermined and unchanging rate of exchange. This means that the domestic monetary base is backed fully by foreign exchange reserves, and the central bank is unable to issue domestic credit. Currency boards have been advocated for many emerging economies. Among the larger such economies, currency boards have been put in place in Argentina (1991), Bosnia (1998), Bulgaria (1997), Estonia (1992), Hong Kong (1983), and Lithuania (1994). Currency boards have also been advocated at various times for Mexico, Indonesia, and Russia, among major economies that have recently undergone currency crises.

Advocates of this arrangement claim that they assure the convertibility of the currency (because the stock of foreign exchange reserves is more than sufficient to buy back the monetary base), impose macroeconomic discipline, thereby enhancing the credibility of inflation objectives (by denying the government discretionary access to seignorage), and provide a mechanism for automatic balance of payments adjustment (because the monetary implications of current account surpluses or deficits induce automatic offsets through the capital account of the balance of payments). For these reasons, currency boards are perceived as creating confidence in the domestic monetary system, which helps promote trade, investment, and growth.

None of these arguments is fully convincing, however. The convertibility of the domestic currency is not assured if the public perceives that the government would not allow the persistence of the very high interest rates that would be implied by an extreme contraction of the monetary base in the event of wholesale conversions into the foreign currency. The gains from macroeconomic discipline, on the other hand, may not be very important if the central bank has already established an anti-inflationary reputation. Finally, automatic balance of payments adjustment is also available through freely floating exchange rates, so the last advantage cited for currency boards above does not distinguish them from fully floating exchange rates.

The arguments against currency boards, on the other hand, emphasize the loss of monetary autonomy that they imply, the loss of control over the inflation tax as a source of revenue, and the loss of lender of last resort function for the central bank (since, as we have seen, the restriction that the monetary base be fully backed by foreign exchange reserves prevents it from extending domestic credit to commercial banks in times of crisis).

Again, however, the importance of these limitations depends on the circumstances facing the domestic economy. The loss of monetary autonomy is more important when there are no other stabilization policies available, and when the central bank is independent and competent – that is, when monetary autonomy would have been used appropriately under an alternative monetary arrangement. The loss of discretion over seignorage revenue is more important when the domestic tax system is very distortionary. And the inability of the central bank to extend credit in fulfilling its lender of last resort function is more important when the domestic financial system is weak. Moreover, it can be mitigated through changes in banks' required reserve ratios and through external lines of credit maintained by the domestic government to finance emergency lending to domestic banks.

Taking a more general perspective, it is not clear that confidence is easy to establish with a currency board, because if the economy becomes more vulnerable to shocks without monetary autonomy and a lender of last resort, it would not be easy for the government to convince the market that it will not abandon the system if it is unable to reap the credibility effects that are the system's major advantage. This may create a situation of multiple equilibria, in the following sense: the major advantage of the currency board comes through the benefits of credibility. Thus, if credibility cannot be achieved because the shortcomings of the system are too costly for the country in question, the government will be tempted to abandon it, ratifying the absence of credibility.

The difficulty of achieving credibility has been demonstrated by the two best-known currency boards during recent years, those of Argentina and Hong Kong. As we saw in Chapter 15, Argentina was one of the countries most affected by the Mexican financial crisis of late 1994. Argentina went through a severe crisis in early 1995, as markets saw Mexico-like symptoms (exchange rate appreciation, large current account deficit) in Argentina that raised doubts about the sustainability of the exchange rate peg in that country. The domestic banking sector lost 30 percent of its deposits in the first three quarters of 1995, domestic real interest rates rose, unemployment hit 18 percent, and growth slowed. Hong Kong also suffered from financial instability elsewhere. The colony was buffeted by the Asian crisis in the fall of 1997, as the sustainability of its peg came into question in view of the exchange rate devaluations undergone by the currencies of countries whose exports competed with those of Hong Kong. The stock market in Hong Kong collapsed, and very high domestic interest rates were required to defend the currency, calling the health of the domestic financial sector into question. Nonetheless, both currency boards withstood these shocks and remained in operation.

To conclude, what do these considerations suggest about the conditions under which the adoption of a currency board would make sense? The answer is that there are indeed circumstances that favor the adoption of currency boards, but these circumstances are far from universal. These circumstances include:

i. When fixed exchange rates are very useful because the country is very open and its trade is dominated by a single country with stable prices.
ii. When gaining credibility is very important.
iii. When asymmetric real shocks are *not* very important, or if they are, when the monetary authorities are not very competent and the fiscal authorities are (for example, when fiscal policy is flexible and can be used for countercyclical purposes, perhaps through fiscal transfers from a supranational authority).
iv. When domestic wages and prices are likely to become more flexible as a result of the adoption of the currency board, reducing the costs to the economy of adjusting automatically to those real shocks that do affect it.
v. When the domestic financial system is strong, or when there are external sources of liquidity (such as lines of credit) in place to handle domestic liquidity crises.

b. Floating Exchange Rates

Recall that under a floating exchange rate regime, the central bank does not intervene in the foreign exchange market, which means that the price of foreign exchange is determined completely by the behavior of private agents. In principle, this regime has several advantages. We have seen that it facilitates adjustment when domestic prices are not flexible and when real shocks are important, and that it increases the availability of policies by allowing for the preservation of monetary autonomy. Unlike currency boards, floating exchange rates permit the government to retain control over the inflation tax as a source of revenue, and permit the central bank to perform the lender of last resort function by using its own resources. Like a currency board, floating exchange rates provide an automatic mechanism for balance of payments adjustment, with the added benefit that they are not vulnerable to speculative attacks.

A disadvantage of floating rates is that long-term price level credibility depends on internal restraints (such as reputation, as in Japan, or the institution of an independent central bank with a conservative governor, as in pre-euro Germany). But as we have already seen, it is not obvious that in theory fixed rates are a superior disciplining device, and the evidence on this issue is limited. For these reasons, many economists have been supportive of the adoption of floating exchange rates in principle.

In practice, however, other issues have arisen that call the superiority of this arrangement into question. Under floating rates, the exchange rate is determined by the interaction of supply and demand in the foreign exchange market. Demand arises from the desire of domestic agents to import goods and services or to purchase foreign financial assets, while the supply arises from exports or from the sale of domestic financial assets to foreigners.

The important fact is that the demand for foreign exchange and supply of foreign exchange that arise from the buying and selling of financial assets are much larger than those that arise from the buying and selling of goods and services. The implication of this situation is that, for the exchange market to be in equilibrium, agents have to be willing to hold the existing composition of their portfolios between assets denominated in foreign exchange and assets denominated in domestic currency. The nominal exchange rate must adjust to make it so. This means that at a given moment in time the nominal exchange rate has to be consistent with equilibrium in the international market for financial assets. Thus, under floating exchange rates the nominal exchange rate must behave like what it really is: the price of a financial asset.

Why does this matter? It matters because the prices of financial assets in the present depend in an important way on what those prices are expected to be in the future. That means that if prices are expected to rise in the future they will rise in the present, because there are profits to be made in buying assets before their prices rise, and that creates demand for those assets in the present. The point is that expectations about the future have an important effect on the prices of financial assets, and since these expectations tend to be volatile, this transmits the volatility to the prices of the financial assets, among them the nominal exchange rate. The question is, is this a good thing or a bad thing?

An implication is that under floating exchange rates, the nominal exchange rate is much more volatile than relative price levels. The effect is that the real exchange rate will be much more variable under a flexible exchange rate system than under a fixed rate system. As we saw in the last chapter, there is substantial evidence that this is the case.

Why should we worry about this? One argument that this is a problem is based on the view that when the real exchange rate is unstable (that is, when it changes much more than could be justified on the basis of changes in its fundamental determinants), this creates large costs, because it is costly to reallocate resources, and if factors of production move from one sector to the other on the basis of the current real exchange rate, too many resources would be wasted in transitory factor reallocations.

But the real problem is probably exactly the opposite. Precisely because changing the allocation of resources is costly, economic agents will not respond if they are faced with real exchange rate changes that may prove to be transitory. This being so, the problem would be not that there would be too much movement of factors from one sector to another, but rather that the movement of factors between sectors would not be sufficient due to the "noise" created by transitory real exchange rate movements. As we saw in Chapter 16, there is empirical evidence that volatility in the real exchange rate has negative effects on real economic growth (Corbo and Rojas 1995), and the argument just made is one way to interpret this evidence.

But real exchange rate variability may not necessarily be a bad thing. One argument is based on the presence of distortions in the financial system such as those we studied in Part 4. When (explicit or implicit) deposit insurance is in place, prudential regulation is nonexistent or weak, and the net worth of financial institutions is small, we have seen that bank owners have an incentive to invest the institution's resources in very risky assets, because if those assets turn out to yield high returns the stockholders will reap large gains, while if they fail the stockholders can only lose the amounts that they have invested in the institution. In this case, the expected gains from the investments from the private (stockholder) viewpoint may be much larger than the expected social gains. As we saw, this means that there is a distortion in resource allocation. This may be a very serious matter if financial institutions in such conditions have the opportunity of intermediating a large volume of resources, as they would have if the economy's capital account is open.

This is where the exchange rate system comes in. From the point of view of external creditors, what they care about is the return that deposits pay in foreign exchange. If deposits are guaranteed, and in addition the government fixes the exchange rate, then investing in the domestic economy through the banking system carries very little risk for those who bring money in from outside. As we saw in Chapter 15, this has two negative consequences: it can destabilize the economy, through large capital inflows, and it may also immiserize the economy, because the existence of these distortions means that the external resources will tend to be misallocated.

In Chapter 14 we saw that there were a variety of ways to address this moral hazard problem, which is aggravated by the presence of deposit insurance. The best solution may be to keep restrictions on capital movements in place until a good system of regulation and supervision over the financial system is in working order. However, the regulatory and supervisory framework cannot be fixed from one day to the next, government announcements that it will not guarantee deposits may not be credible, and restrictions on capital movements may not be effective.

Under these circumstances, what remains as a possible way to deter moral-hazard-driven external borrowing is to remove the exchange rate guarantee for external creditors. This can be done by giving greater flexibility to the exchange rate.[6]

What, then, are the conditions under which the adoption of floating exchange rates would seem to be indicated? Several such conditions are suggested by the

---

[6] Apparently, this was an important element in the formulation of Chile's exchange rate policy during the 1990s, for example.

preceding discussion:

i. When long-run price stability is not a problem, because the country possesses an independent central bank with a well-established anti-inflationary reputation.

ii. When real shocks are important, domestic wages and prices are sticky in nominal terms, and monetary and fiscal policies can be deployed flexibly to achieve internal and external balance.

iii. When short-run real exchange rate variability is not too costly (for example, because financial instruments are available to trade such risk and allocate it efficiently).

All of this suggests that floating exchange rates would be suitable for countries with strong central banks, advanced financial systems, and with the ability to use monetary and fiscal policies in a flexible countercyclical manner. Generally these criteria are more likely to be satisfied by industrial countries or by relatively advanced emerging economies.

VII. SUMMARY

In this chapter we have taken the view that issues of nominal exchange rate management in emerging economies can be decomposed into two parts: whether or not to adopt an "extreme" exchange rate regime, in the form of a fixed exchange rate with monetary policy fully devoted to external objectives (a currency board), or a "clean" float with monetary policy fully devoted to domestic objectives and if not, how to manage the rate in the context of an intermediate regime.

This chapter was devoted to the first question. We saw that exchange rate regimes could be evaluated by the criteria of their effects on the costs of transacting internationally, on long-run domestic price stability, and on the costs of adjusting to macroeconomic shocks. Effects on transaction costs favor fixed rates (in the extreme form of currency unification), but the magnitude of these effects in practice is not clear. While the theoretical arguments are ambiguous with respect to effects on price stability, the limited careful empirical evidence on this issue favors fixed exchange rates as well. On the other hand, flexible exchange rates seem to have the advantage in reducing the costs of adjusting to macroeconomic shocks, at least when those shocks are real or originate in the external financial environment.

These considerations suggest that extreme exchange rate arrangements may indeed be appropriate for specific economies under well-defined circumstances. When credibility issues are important, domestic macroeconomic management is weak, domestic wage and price flexibility is high, and real shocks are not important, a currency board may be an attractive exchange rate arrangement. On the other hand, when the country possesses a central bank with a strong anti-inflationary reputation, domestic fiscal and monetary policies are well managed, wages and prices exhibit substantial short-run stickiness, and real shocks can be expected to be important, floating exchange rates may be preferable.

The problem is, of course, that many countries do not meet all of these conditions. For example, many emerging economies:

i. Do not have central banks with strong reputations, so would like to use the exchange rate as a nominal anchor.
ii. Want to give some predictability to the real exchange rate, but not necessarily to the nominal exchange rate.
iii. Want to retain some monetary autonomy, because fiscal policy is not very flexible.
iv. Are concerned about the adequacy of their regulatory and supervisory capabilities in the financial sector, and thus want to discourage excessive intermediation of external funds by that sector.

For such countries, intermediate exchange rate regimes might be appropriate that try to strike compromises among the various characteristics of the extreme regimes, such as between the objectives of stabilizing the price level and promoting adjustment. In the next chapter we will consider how the exchange rate might be managed under such arrangements.

18

Managing an Officially Determined Exchange Rate

In the previous chapter, we reviewed arguments for and against extreme exchange rate regimes. Under such regimes, whether they involve a currency board or a clean float with monetary targeting, the authorities have no need to make day-to-day decisions about how the exchange rate should be managed. All decisions about the exchange rate are made at the time that the regime is adopted. It may indeed be optimal for a country to adopt a regime of one of these types, and the last chapter reviewed some of the considerations involved in deciding whether to do so. But as we saw at the end of the last chapter, for many countries, the conditions that would make an extreme exchange rate regime appropriate are not likely to be met. When such a regime is not adopted, the exchange rate will have to be managed in some fashion, whether through intervention in the foreign exchange market or through using monetary policy to influence the exchange rate.

This chapter examines some basic principles of exchange rate management in such "intermediate" regimes. We will use as an organizing framework the assumption that a country maintains an exchange rate band, since all the exchange regime options available to an emerging economy can be thought of as variations on such a band. An exchange rate band essentially involves the announcement of a central parity for the domestic currency, together with fluctuation margins around that parity that commit the central bank to buy or sell the domestic currency in unlimited amounts whenever its value reaches previously specified lower or upper bounds. The decisions that have to be made in this context concern the setting of the central parity, the width of the band, and the rules that should govern intervention inside the band.

The considerations involved in managing an officially determined exchange rate are not of great interest, however, if operating an officially determined exchange rate is not a feasible option. In recent years the argument has indeed been made that this is the case for emerging economies that are characterized by high degrees of capital mobility. We will examine this argument in this chapter, and consider how empirical evidence might be brought to bear on it. A key question is whether attacks on currency pegs are primarily driven by "fundamentals" or by self-fulfilling expectations. We will review some of the evidence that is available on this issue here, before examining in the next chapter the determinants of some of the most important recent emerging-economy financial crises.

I. WHY MANAGE THE EXCHANGE RATE?

We have seen in previous chapters that the nominal exchange rate can potentially play two key macroeconomic roles. If the exchange rate is officially determined, it serves as a nominal anchor for the economy, influencing the price level in the short run and determining it in the long run. Whether officially determined or not, it affects the real exchange rate in the short run, though not in the long run. The criteria that have been adopted for evaluating exchange rate regimes – the promotion of long-run price stability and the reduction of the costs of adjustment to macroeconomic shocks – reflect these alternative roles that the nominal exchange rate can play. We have also seen that, while the theory is ambiguous and the evidence is limited, fixing the nominal exchange rate may be a superior way to promote long-term price stability than the adoption of other nominal anchors. At the same time, however, allowing the exchange rate to float appears to have advantages from the perspective of reducing the costs of adjustment to macroeconomic shocks when domestic wages and prices are sticky.

As we also saw in the previous chapter, the value placed by a country on the role that the nominal exchange rate can play in attaining these objectives depends in part on whether other means exist to achieve the same objectives, at relatively low cost. For example, a country whose central bank has independently attained a substantial amount of low-inflation credibility would place little value on the credibility gains that might be attainable by fixing the exchange rate, while a country with very flexible domestic wages and prices, or one not typically afflicted by real shocks, may not place much value on the role that the exchange rate can play in facilitating the adjustment of relative prices in response to such shocks. The problem is, of course, that many countries will find themselves in situations in which they value both objectives, because they have not independently achieved a sufficient amount of anti-inflationary credibility, have a domestic wage-price mechanism that generates a relatively sticky wage-price process in the short run, and can frequently expect to be hit by macroeconomically important real shocks.

Even in such a situation, if the price stability or adjustment objective is of over-whelming importance, it may still be optimal for a country to adopt an extreme exchange rate regime. For example, Argentina is a country with strong labor unions, and its exports are dominated by primary commodities. It is likely that the wage-price process in that country would exhibit substantial stickiness in normal times, and that real shocks, say, in the form of changes in the terms of trade, would tend to be frequent. However, it may still have made sense for Argentina to have adopted a currency board in 1991, because the government's anti-inflationary credibility had been shattered by a series of failed anti-inflation plans during the late 1980s, and hyperinflation was looming at the beginning of the 1990s.

However, when both roles that the nominal exchange rate can play have value for a country, and neither the price stability objective nor the adjustment objective is of overriding importance, the country has an incentive to seek to implement an exchange rate regime that strikes a different balance between the competing objectives than do the more extreme arrangements. This is essentially the argument for the "fixed but adjustable," or "pegged" exchange rate arrangements that have typically been maintained by developing countries. Such arrangements can be officially described as a fixed rate against one currency or a basket of currencies, with fluctuation margins of varying widths, with varying rules for adjusting the parity, and with varying amounts of intervention within the margins. Alternatively, they can be officially described as a float, but typically with heavy intervention that tends to stabilize the rate in accordance with some (typically unannounced) rule. As mentioned previously, all such arrangements can be subsumed into the general classification of exchange rate bands, and we will refer to them as "pegged" arrangements in the rest of this chapter.

II. ARE PEGGED EXCHANGE RATES FEASIBLE UNDER CONDITIONS OF HIGH CAPITAL MOBILITY?

While pegged exchange rate arrangements have been common among emerging economies, in the wake of a series of currency crises that afflicted both industrial and developing countries during the 1990s many economists have begun to argue that, in view of the high degree of integration that many emerging economies have attained with international financial markets over the past decade, the time for such exchange rate arrangements is past. In this view, emerging economies have to choose between the extreme arrangements of dollarization (or full currency union) or floating exchange rates. In other words, pegged arrangements are not feasible in the context of high capital mobility.

a. Self-Fulfilling Speculative Attacks

The argument goes as follows: a central bank's ability to defend an exchange rate peg depends on whether it can generate the resources to buy back with foreign exchange any amounts of its own currency that are presented to it at the officially determined exchange rate. Its ability to do so has often been taken to depend on a comparison of its liquid assets (its foreign exchange reserves) with its liquid liabilities (the monetary base). A central bank with a sufficiently large stock of foreign exchange reserves could in principle buy back its entire monetary base, and that is all that an officially determined exchange rate commits it to do. Indeed, that is one of the arguments that is sometimes made for why a currency board guarantees the convertibility of the currency (see Chapter 16).

However, a central bank's liquid assets and liabilities are not in practice limited to the stock of foreign exchange reserves and the monetary base. On the liability side, if the central bank maintains deposit guarantees, its liquid liabilities may extend beyond the monetary base to the entire stock of currency plus deposits (broad money). Thus, the commitment to buy back the monetary base is extended to the entire stock of broad money by the deposit guarantee. On the asset side, a public sector that is solvent should easily be able to augment its foreign currency assets through external borrowing. Indeed, since the conversion of domestic currency liabilities into foreign currency is in effect a portfolio transaction by the public sector that does not affect its net worth, a solvent public sector should in principle be able to borrow enough to convert *all* of its liquid liabilities into foreign exchange, including the stock of deposits.

The question is not, therefore, the *ability* of the central bank in a solvent public sector to defend the official exchange rate peg, but rather its *willingness* to do so. Why is this an issue? The reason is that if a substantial part of the monetary base is indeed presented to the central bank for conversion into foreign exchange, the domestic money supply will contract and domestic interest rates will rise, perhaps dramatically. High domestic real interest rates will have a number of harmful effects on the domestic economy. They can trigger or aggravate a recession, they can imperil the solvency of the domestic banking system and trigger a banking crisis (Chapter 13), or they can imperil the solvency of the domestic public sector itself by sharply escalating its domestic-currency debt servicing costs. Under these circumstances, the central bank may prefer to abandon the currency peg than to continue to defend it, simply because the country's economic welfare will be higher if it does so. If it indeed abandons the currency peg and the currency depreciates sharply, those who have converted domestic currency into foreign exchange will reap substantial gains.

The problem is that this situation could arise any time the currency comes under attack, *for whatever reasons*. In other words, even if the real exchange rate is not misaligned, and there is no other reason to believe that the nominal exchange rate would otherwise have been changed (i.e., even if the nominal exchange rate would otherwise have been sustainable), the emergence of a speculative attack on the currency might itself cause the central bank to abandon the currency peg, to avoid incurring the economic costs associated with the high interest rates that would be required to sustain it. In this case, a currency crisis could be *self-fulfilling* – that is, a currency peg that might have been sustainable for an indefinite period in the absence of a speculative attack is actually abandoned simply because an attack occurred, thereby validating the expectations of the speculators who launched the attack.

When would this be likely to happen? The answer is when agents become convinced that the central bank is indeed likely to abandon the peg when speculation against the currency drives domestic interest rates up. When it takes a relatively small increase in domestic interest rates to cause the peg to be abandoned, we say that the peg *lacks credibility*, and pegs that lack credibility will be particularly vulnerable to speculative attack. When credibility is lacking, currency pegs will be costly to maintain, because central banks will have to bear very high domestic interest rates to demonstrate their resolve. The problem is that credibility is hard to achieve, so any exchange rate peg will in principle be vulnerable to a self-fulfilling speculative attack. Countries are thus driven to the extremes of monetary unification – where a change in the peg is impossible – or a clean float, where speculative pressures show up in the form of continuous exchange rate changes that do not create the possibility of large capital gains.

What does high capital mobility have to do with this story? Notice that what puts pressure on central bank reserves are its purchases of the domestic currency in foreign exchange markets. When the capital account is closed and the domestic currency is only convertible for current transactions, economic agents who hold the domestic currency cannot collectively sell it to the central bank to acquire foreign assets (since the central bank will not buy it), making it more difficult for speculators to attack the central bank's foreign exchange reserves. On the other hand, when the capital account is open but capital mobility is limited because domestic and foreign assets are imperfect substitutes, the prospect of a speculative gain on foreign assets of a given magnitude would trigger a smaller conversion out of domestic currency assets – and thus fewer sales of domestic currency on the foreign exchange market and less pressure on the central bank's stock of foreign exchange reserves than would be the case under a higher degree of financial integration (as we saw in the context of the model of Part 2). As the degree of capital mobility increases, however, a given expected speculative gain triggers larger and larger movements out of domestic currency assets, increasing the pressure on the central bank.

b. The Role of Fundamentals

However, the logic of the argument presented above does not imply that pegged exchange rates are *universally* infeasible, because it suggests that pegged rate regimes should not be *uniformly* vulnerable to self-fulfilling speculative attacks. What matters in determining the vulnerability of a pegged regime to a speculative attack is the credibility of its exchange rate peg – that is, the likelihood that the central bank would abandon the peg if subjected to an attack of a given degree of severity. But since the decision of whether or not to abandon the peg is made by the central bank by trading off the costs and benefits of doing so, and since these costs and benefits themselves depend on the state of the domestic economy, there is a role for "fundamentals" to determine the sustainability of an exchange rate peg. In particular, if the characteristics of the domestic economy (the fundamentals) are such that the benefits of defending the peg are relatively high and the costs of doing so relatively small, then the currency should be in a strong position to resist speculative attack and the currency peg should be sustainable. This would be the case, for example, when the real exchange rate is not misaligned (so there is no benefit from a nominal depreciation), the financial sector is strong, the public sector does not have a large stock of domestic currency debt, and the economy is growing rapidly. Alternatively, if the currency appears to be overvalued, the domestic financial sector is weak, the public sector's solvency is precarious and it has a large stock of short-term domestic debt, and/or the economy is in recession, the prospects for a successful speculative attack would tend to be strong.

In theory, then, high capital mobility does not mean that pegged exchange rate regimes cannot be sustained. It merely means that the probability of a crisis when the domestic fundamentals are poor is likely to be much higher. That is, the financial markets will punish countries more quickly and more severely for "bad" fundamentals. At bottom, then, the issue of the feasibility of pegged rates boils down to two questions:

i. Do fundamentals matter in determining a country's vulnerability to speculative attack? If they do, as the theory just outlined suggests they should, then well-managed countries should find it feasible to sustain pegged exchange rates, even under conditions of high capital mobility.
ii. But even so, pegged exchange rates would not be feasible if countries cannot avoid bad fundamentals (i.e., fiscal insolvency, exchange rate misalignment, financial sector fragility, etc.). So the second question is: can countries reliably avoid "bad" fundamentals? If they cannot, then if the costs of attacks on their currencies are very high in the event that their fundamentals turn poor, they may be well advised to adopt more robust exchange rate regimes (such as one of the two extremes advocated by many economists) even if pegged rates would be feasible for them most of the time.

The first question above is an empirical one, and many studies have been conducted in recent years on the issue of the role of fundamentals in determining vulnerability to currency crises. A very simple version, for example, was described in Chapter 15, in the form of the World Bank (1997) study on the factors that determined vulnerability to capital flow reversals in the wake of the Mexican crisis in 1995. That study relied on comparing the economic characteristics of countries that were more or less affected by the Mexican crisis, and detected some interpretable differences in their characteristics, suggesting the fundamentals helped to determine susceptibility to "contagion" from the Mexican crisis.

More sophisticated studies have used econometric techniques (called probit analysis) to estimate from cross-country data the contributions made by various sets of fundamental factors to the probability that a country would undergo a currency crisis. Such techniques essentially involve expressing the probability of a crisis as a function of a set of potential fundamental variables, and then using information on the occurrence or nonoccurrence of crises in a large panel of countries to estimate the parameters of this probability distribution.

For example, a recent study by Frankel and Rose (1996) looked at the determinants of what they referred to as currency "crashes."[1] They used two methodologies: a graphical "event study" approach, in which the behavior of individual macroeconomic variables during periods surrounding currency crashes is compared with the behavior of the same variables during periods of tranquility, as well as probit analysis in which the contributions of individual fundamentals to the probability of a crash could be estimated. Their sample consisted of annual data on 105 developing countries over the period 1971–92, and it included 117 currency crashes.

Among the potential fundamentals they considered were the rate of growth of domestic credit, the ratio of the fiscal deficit to GDP, the ratio of foreign exchange reserves to imports, the ratio of the current account deficit to GDP, the rate of growth of real GDP, the degree of overvaluation of the real exchange rate (i.e., its deviation from a long-run equilibrium real exchange rate calculated using a period-average *PPP* methodology), the ratio of debt to GDP, world interest rates, the average growth rate of the OECD countries, and various debt and capital inflow composition variables (such as the share of debt from commercial banks, the share of debt that is concessional, variable-rate, public, short-term, loaned by multilaterals, and foreign direct investment (FDI) flows as a percent of the total debt stock).

The results of the graphical analysis were that, except for the current account and fiscal deficit ratios, all the fundamental variables behaved during the period surrounding currency crashes as theory predicts they should if such variables indeed help to determine the likelihood of such crashes.

But of course, such graphical analysis only considers the potential role of each fundamental one at a time, and provides no indication of the statistical confidence that can be associated with the results. Frankel and Rose complemented this with probit analysis to deal with both of these problems. The results from the probit estimation were as follows:

i. Most debt composition variables proved not to be statistically significant predictors of currency crashes, except for the FDI variable. A lower share of FDI in capital inflows tends to increase the probability of a crash (we will come back to this in the next chapter).

ii. Neither the current account nor fiscal deficit variables proved to be important contributors to the probability of currency crashes.

iii. Except for the rate of growth of OECD countries, all of the "external" variables (world interest rates, the reserve adequacy measure, the ratio of debt to

---

[1] They defined a currency crash as a nominal depreciation of more than 25 percent that was also more than 10 percent greater than that in the previous period, the latter criterion added so as to rule out high inflation episodes. To be included in their sample, such crashes had to be separated by at least three years from previous episodes.

GDP, and the extent of real exchange rate overvaluation) proved to be very important.

iv. Finally, high credit growth (associated with financial sector fragility) and a recession in the domestic economy both increased the probability of a crash.

These results were derived with the "fundamentals" entered contemporaneously with the qualitative dependent variable measuring the incidence of currency crashes. The results proved to be even stronger, however, when the explanatory variables were lagged. A low share of concessional debt, a low share of FDI in capital inflows, and a larger public share in total debt, all increased the likelihood of a crash, as did low foreign exchange reserves, real exchange rate overvaluation, high international interest rates, and high domestic credit growth.

The evidence from this study and others suggests that fundamentals indeed matter in determining susceptibility to speculative attacks and currency crises. Thus, they are consistent with the theory described above. The implication is that well-managed countries should face a reduced susceptibility to speculative attacks. Whether bad fundamentals can be consistently avoided, however, is another matter. The crisis that afflicted the previously highly successful "miracle" economies of East and Southeast Asia in 1997 certainly calls into question whether they can, even under very favorable circumstances. We will return to this when we discuss the Asian crisis in the next chapter. For now, we conclude that the evidence that fundamentals matter is at least consistent with the possibility that exchange rates can still be managed, and turn next to how this should be done.

III. HOW TO MANAGE AN OFFICIALLY DETERMINED EXCHANGE RATE: FIXING THE CENTRAL PARITY

As indicated previously, if exchange rates are to be managed, a useful way to organize the discussion of how this should be done is to consider exchange rate management within the framework of an exchange rate band. This breaks down the question of how to manage the rate into the three subsidiary questions of how to fix the central parity, how wide to set the fluctuation margins, and how to intervene within those margins. In this section, we will first take up the question of how to set the central parity, leaving the other two questions for the next two sections.

Notice that the central parity is what governs the medium-term path of the nominal exchange rate under a band. In setting it, then, a central bank has first to confront the question of why it would be preferable to announce a central parity at all in the first place, rather than simply float the exchange rate and intervene to influence it when desired. As mentioned previously, managed exchange rates include regimes that officially describe themselves as pegged and those that do not. The difference between them is that the former do, and the latter do not, announce a central parity.

a. Using the Central Parity as Nominal Anchor

There are two reasons that governments may find it desirable to announce a central parity, and both have to do with making known the medium-term path of the exchange rate. The first reason is the one that has been alluded to previously as a reason why a government might want to choose a managed exchange rate rather than a clean float in the first place: to use the exchange rate as a nominal anchor.

If this is the reason for opting for a managed rate, then the central parity should be set to depreciate at a rate equal to the difference between the desired domestic inflation rate (which, due to the requirements of fiscal solvency, would have to be determined simultaneously with the desired path of fiscal variables) and the weighted-average inflation rate of the country's trading partners. This rule, therefore, adopts a *forward-looking* domestic inflation measure (the desired *future* inflation rate) as a guide for the adjustment of the central parity. It would tend to stabilize the real exchange rate as long as the domestic inflation target is met, and it would avoid misalignment as long as the real fundamental determinants of the long-run equilibrium real exchange rate do not change. If the inflation target is not met over some time period, or if the fundamental determinants of the long-run equilibrium real exchange rate were to change, real exchange rate misalignment would emerge. Under this rule, such misalignment would be expected to be eliminated through adjustments in the domestic price level, which is what it means to use the exchange rate as nominal anchor.

b. Choosing the Peg

A separate question that arises in this context is which foreign currency (or currencies) to peg the exchange rate to. This makes a difference, of course, only when trading partners' inflation rates differ, and when their *real* exchange rates fluctuate substantially against each other. If their real exchange rates did not fluctuate against each other, then their inflation differentials would be offset by nominal exchange rate changes, and their price levels would be equalized when expressed in a common currency. The basic choices are whether to peg to a single country or to a basket of currencies weighted to reflect the shares of the country's trade with individual trading partners. Pegging to a low-inflation country would promote long-run domestic price stability, but if that country has a relatively small share of the domestic economy's external trade, that would tend to destabilize the domestic real exchange rate, because the domestic currency prices of goods produced by countries with which the home country does a substantial amount of trade would be affected by fluctuations among partner-country currencies.

If a single low-inflation country represents the dominant trading partner for the domestic economy, then of course the choice is easy: peg to that country's currency. The optimal choice will in general depend on the weights placed by the domestic economy on price stability versus real exchange rate stability, as well as on the distribution of trade weights across trading partners with different long-run inflation rates and different degrees of real exchange rate variability.

c. Targeting the Real Exchange Rate

However, using the exchange rate as a nominal anchor is not the only reason to opt for managed rates instead of a clean float. Countries whose central banks have sufficient anti-inflationary credibility so as to dispense with this role of the nominal exchange rate may nonetheless opt for managed rates out of the desire to avoid the excessive volatility in the real exchange rate that might be associated with a clean float. This motivation for managing the exchange rate does not necessarily require the announcement of a central parity. A "dirty float," in which the central bank intervenes to smooth out fluctuations in the real exchange rate without committing itself to a central parity, could achieve the desired goal. However, in this case private agents are given no assurances about the medium-term evolution of the real exchange rate. As the experience of industrial countries under floating exchange rates shows, the real exchange rate can exhibit substantial medium-term fluctuations under this system. If the motivation for adopting a managed rate rather than a clean float was to avoid excessive "noise" in the real exchange rate, this situation may not be satisfactory.

An alternative is to manage the central parity so as to stabilize the medium-term path of the *real* exchange rate. That means adopting a rule under which the rate of depreciation of the nominal exchange rate is set as the difference between the *past* domestic inflation rate and that of the country's trading partners (say, on a monthly basis). This ensures that the real exchange rate will not deviate far from its initial value, since fluctuations in the domestic rate of inflation are accommodated by changes in the rate of depreciation of the central parity to ensure that this does not happen. Notice that in this case, since the objective is to stabilize the effective real exchange rate, it makes sense to adjust the nominal rate in accordance with the trade-weighted inflation rate in partner countries, rather than that of a single country.

A difficulty with this approach is that the exchange rate can no longer play the role of the nominal anchor. While it may be thought that this simply means that the money supply would have to play the role of nominal anchor, this is not actually an option, since we are considering an *officially determined* exchange rate regime (not a floating rate regime), in which the domestic money supply is rendered endogenous by the central bank's commitment to intervene in the foreign exchange market to defend its announced parity.

The problem can be illustrated with the model of Part 2 of this book. Recall that in the short run, under nominal exchange rate targeting, the economy's price level was determined by the intersection of a positively sloped *FM* curve (under financial autarky or imperfect capital mobility) and a negatively sloped *GM* curve in i-P space. When the central bank targets the real exchange rate, by contrast, the price level drops out of the goods-market equilibrium condition (sP^*/P is replaced by the real exchange rate target, call it e^*). This turns the *GM* curve into a horizontal straight line parallel to the price axis. As long as the *FM* curve retains its positive slope (i.e., as long as capital mobility is not perfect), the price level remains determinate under these conditions in the short run. But the endogeneity of the money supply in the medium term (and, under perfect capital mobility, in the short run as well) leaves the domestic price level indeterminate in this model under real exchange rate targeting.

In a more complete model, however, such as the one we used in Chapter 16 to analyze the determination of the long-run equilibrium real exchange rate, this property does not hold. The reason is that such a model would incorporate wealth effects on private spending, which would reintroduce a negative slope to the *GM* curve as long as not all of the private sector's wealth is indexed to the price level. It can be shown that under these circumstances the domestic long-run rate of inflation actually becomes endogenous, and is determined in such a way as to eliminate the gap between the real exchange rate targeted by the authorities under this exchange rate regime and the long-run equilibrium real exchange rate implied by the economy's fundamentals.

This has an important implication for the setting of the central parity under real exchange rate targeting. If the central bank simply chooses a real exchange rate target and leaves it unchanged in the face of permanent changes in the underlying fundamental determinants of the economy's long-run equilibrium real exchange rate, the domestic rate of inflation will change whenever these fundamentals do. This means that the real exchange rate would be stabilized at the cost of destabilizing the domestic inflation rate. To avoid the latter, it would be necessary to alter the targeted real exchange rate in response to permanent changes in the real fundamentals. Thus, the central parity would have to be managed so as to avoid the emergence of real exchange rate misalignment. As shown in Chapter 16, our state of knowledge on the empirical measurement of misalignment might make this a challenging proposition.

In short, the choices to be made in setting the central parity depend on the trade-offs that the country is prepared to make in using the exchange rate as a nominal anchor and using it to stabilize the real exchange rate. If the exchange rate is to be used as a nominal anchor, the central parity implies a path for the nominal exchange rate that depends on the targeted domestic rate of inflation and the expected rate of inflation in a relatively important, low-inflation trading partner. If the nominal exchange rate is to be managed so as to stabilize the real exchange rate, then a *PPP*-based rule for the central parity is required, based on past domestic inflation rates as well as trade-weighted partner country inflation rates. In this case, to avoid destabilizing the domestic price level, the real exchange rate targeted by the central parity will have to be adjusted in accordance with permanent changes in the underlying real fundamental determinants of the country's long-run equilibrium real exchange rate.

IV. HOW TO MANAGE AN OFFICIALLY DETERMINED EXCHANGE RATE: SETTING THE WIDTH OF THE BAND

The next issue that arises in managing a pegged exchange rate is how much fluctuation to allow around the central parity, that is, using the exchange rate band framework, how wide to set the exchange rate band.

a. Announcing the Band Width

As in our discussion of the central parity, the first question that should be posed in this context is whether it makes sense to adopt and announce an explicit band width at all. An announced band width commits the central bank to unlimited intervention at the margins of the band. In the absence of an announced band width, the central bank retains discretion whether to intervene or not throughout the range of fluctuation of the nominal exchange rate.

One argument for announcing an explicit band width has been made by Krugman (1993). It is that, given the behavior of the "fundamental" determinants of the nominal exchange rate, the mere announcement of an explicit band width would tend to stabilize the nominal exchange rate automatically within the band, even in the absence of central bank intervention. Krugman models the link between the exchange rate and its "fundamental" determinants inside the band as:

$$s = f + E(ds/dt),$$

where s is the log of the nominal exchange rate, f is the log of its "fundamental" determinants, given by $f = m - v$, where m is the log of the domestic money supply and v (for velocity) is an exogenous shock, taken to be a random walk (i.e., a variable with the property that its *change* from period to period is a mean-zero random variable). In this equation, $E(ds/dt)$ is the expected change in the log of the nominal exchange rate from one period to the next.

Now suppose that the band is perfectly credible, and that intervention only takes place at the edges of the bands. Then, in the absence of an explicit band, the relationship between the exchange rate s and the fundamental f could be depicted as a 45 degree line (because with the random walk assumption, the expected future change in the exchange rate would be zero, making $E(ds/dt) = 0$, and leaving $s = f$). However, with an explicit band in place, this changes in the following ways:

i. The slope of the relationship between s and f becomes *less* than one inside the band, because the exchange rate would be more likely to appreciate on net (making $E(ds/dt)$ negative) the closer it is to the upper edge, and to depreciate the closer it is to the lower edge. This is called the "honeymoon effect," and it means that some exchange rate stability is achieved "for free," since the exchange rate becomes more stable than it would be in the absence of the band even *without* central bank intervention.

ii. The curve depicting the relationship between s and f is asymptotic to the edges (a property known as "smooth pasting"), essentially because the exchange rate must become insensitive to the fundamental at the edges. This is because there is a discontinuity in the expected change in the fundamental at the edge of the band (it can only move in one direction, due to the expected offsetting change in policy). The expected change in the fundamental is zero inside the band (recall that v is a random walk), but suddenly not zero at the band. But since there can be no discontinuity in the expected change in the exchange rate at the edge (because this would mean a discontinuity in the path of s itself, since the other determinant of s, the fundamental, is continuous in levels), this means that the exchange rate must be insensitive to the fundamental at the edge.

The main argument *against* explicitly announced bands, on the other hand, is the argument against pegged exchange rates: speculation against the currency, for example, would quickly drive its value to the upper bound of the band. At that point the situation becomes identical to that of a fixed exchange rate that is under speculative attack. Speculators face a one-way option for the exchange rate to move: they stand to make large gains if the parity is adjusted in a discrete fashion at that point, and face little likelihood of losses through a movement of the exchange rate back toward the center of the band. The central bank would face the same choices that it does under a fixed rate, and if the fundamentals are wrong, would be tempted to devalue or abandon the band. This situation would not arise if the central bank did not make an explicit commitment to defend upper and lower bounds for the value of its currency.

These arguments suggest that the desirability of announcing explicit bands for the exchange rate depends on the likelihood that such bounds can be made credible. If they can, then the "honeymoon effect" would tend to add stability to nominal exchange rate movements. If they cannot, then the announcement of such bands is simply an invitation to a speculative attack. As in the previous section, the achievement of such credibility depends on governments' ability to adequately manage their fundamentals.

b. Determining the Width of the Band

Suppose, then, that a country can achieve a sufficiently high degree of credibility so as to warrant the adoption of an explicitly announced band. How wide should it be? In principle, the width of the band should depend on several factors:

1. The Degree of Fiscal Flexibility

Inside the band, the domestic economy retains monetary autonomy, because the exchange rate can move by a maximum amount given by the width of the band, allowing domestic interest rates to differ from foreign ones by this amount at a maximum. One factor that should affect the optimal width of the band, then, is the desired degree of monetary autonomy that the domestic central bank finds it optimal to retain. In turn, this depends on the value of monetary autonomy to the domestic economy, which depends on the availability of other instruments of stabilization policy. The implication is that the less flexible fiscal policy is as a stabilization instrument, the more important is monetary autonomy, so the stronger is the case for a wide band.

2. The Degree of Financial Integration

But the degree of monetary autonomy that the country can achieve does not just depend on the width of the band. As we saw in Part 2, the higher the country's degree of financial integration, the less monetary autonomy it will have. Economies that are highly integrated with world capital markets will have very little monetary autonomy with a narrow band, so for such economies to achieve a given degree of monetary autonomy, they will require a larger band than countries that are less financially integrated with the world economy. Thus, other things equal, increased financial integration strengthens the case for a wider band.

3. The Nature and Amplitude of Macroeconomic Shocks

The width of the band should also depend on whether shocks to the economy tend to be permanent or transitory, real or nominal, and how large they tend to be. As we have seen previously, when the motivation for managing the exchange rate is to stabilize the real exchange rate, the central parity should respond to real shocks that are perceived to be permanent, but the response to transitory real shocks should occur within the band. On the other hand, the exchange rate should not respond at all to shocks that are perceived to be nominal in origin. Thus, the more susceptible the country is perceived to be to transitory real shocks, and the larger the perceived amplitude of such shocks, the wider the band should be.

4. The Cost of Maintaining Foreign Exchange Reserves

Finally, maintaining a stock of foreign exchange reserves will be required to defend the upper bound of the band. Because the costs of such reserves will depend in part on the width of the band, the optimal band width will be influenced by the costs of reserves. The costs of maintaining foreign exchange reserves depend on the total stock of reserves the central bank holds as well as on the cost of maintaining each unit of reserves. The latter depends on the opportunity cost of the resources tied up in reserves (say the domestic marginal product of capital minus the interest receipts on reserves). The required stock of reserves, in turn, is likely to depend on the credibility of the band as well as on its width. The greater the cost of maintaining reserves for other reasons (i.e., because large reserves are required due to limited confidence, or because the cost of maintaining a given stock of reserves is high), the wider should be the amplitude of the band.

V. HOW TO MANAGE AN OFFICIALLY DETERMINED EXCHANGE RATE: INTERVENTION WITHIN THE BAND

Finally, there is relatively less to say about the factors that should govern the rules for intervention within the band. Three such factors are worth mentioning.

First, the optimal extent of intervention should depend on the perceived source of specific macroeconomic shocks. As we have seen, the optimal response to permanent real macroeconomic shocks – which alter the long-run equilibrium real exchange rate – involves a change in the central parity. From the perspective of stabilizing aggregate demand, the optimal extent of intervention in foreign exchange markets in response to transitory shocks depends on the source of such shocks. We argued above that less intervention is indicated for real shocks, so that transitory fluctuations in real exchange rates can bear some of the adjustment burden, while more intervention would be optimal for shocks that are perceived to be nominal in origin, so that the adjustment burden is picked up by accommodating changes in the money supply. In the case of foreign financial shocks, the optimal degree of intervention depends on structural characteristics of the domestic economy.

This analysis, however, may need to be modified if the domestic authorities perceive a need to stabilize the real exchange rate for domestic resource allocation reasons. In response to perceived real shocks, the authorities face a choice between shifting the adjustment burden to the real exchange rate through transitory movements in the nominal exchange rate inside the band (produced by minimizing intervention inside the band) and allowing the response to be reflected in changes in aggregate demand (if they intervene to stabilize the nominal exchange rate within the band). The question is how much "noise" is introduced into the real exchange rate as a relative price signal by fluctuations that occur within the band. The answer, of course, depends on the width of the band as well as on private agents' perceptions that real exchange rate movements inside the band are indeed transitory. This confidence can be enhanced if the authorities indeed manage the central parity successfully to respond to perceived changes in the long-run equilibrium real exchange rate. If they do, then movements inside the band should be regarded as transitory, and should not have adverse implications for resource allocation. In that case, less intervention would be required inside the band in response to transitory real shocks.

The final factor to be considered is how desirable variability in the *nominal* exchange rate might be. The more desirable such variability is (for example, because there are distortions in the financial system that create incentives for capital flows into the country) the less intervention there should be inside the band to stabilize the nominal exchange rate. Indeed, when distortions in the domestic financial system are important, and have the effect of inducing "overborrowing" by domestic financial intermediaries, the authorities may choose to intervene within the band to *increase* variability in the nominal exchange rate, so as to create uncertainty in the domestic-currency returns faced by foreign agents who bring capital into the country.

VI. SUMMARY

Managed exchange rates have the attractive feature that they can combine characteristics of both of the extreme exchange rate arrangements discussed in the last chapter, allowing them to strike a different balance between the alternative objectives to which exchange rate policy can be devoted than is done by the more extreme arrangements. As we have seen, striking a balance between those objectives different from those available through extreme exchange rate arrangements may well be desirable for many emerging economies.

Depending on how the parity is administered, managed exchange rates can be designed to use the nominal exchange rate as a nominal anchor, or to stabilize the real exchange rate. In either case, they can in principle permit the exchange rate to be used for adjustment if desired (through movements in the rate within a band as well as through changes in the central parity). Moreover, by placing the parity within a band, they can allow the authorities to preserve some degree of monetary autonomy. Thus, with a managed exchange rate, by setting a nominal target for the central parity the monetary authorities can seek to combine the nominal anchor properties of a fixed exchange rate with the adjustment advantages of a flexible rate. Or if they have an independent source of price level credibility, by setting a real exchange rate target for the central parity they can attain the adjustment advantages of flexible rates without the real exchange rate instability that floating exchange rates can involve.

The obvious advantage of managed rates, then, is the flexibility that they allow to the domestic monetary authorities. But are pegged exchange rate arrangements feasible under conditions of high capital mobility? An important problem is that pegged exchange rate arrangements are potentially vulnerable to "self-fulfilling" speculative attacks. Theory and evidence give us some hope, in the sense that both indicate that such attacks are more likely to happen when the position of the economy's fundamentals is weak. Under such conditions, the authorities would be unable to resist a speculative attack, and the peg would have limited credibility. Thus, not all currency pegs are equally vulnerable. But can the domestic economy be managed so as to avoid "bad" fundamentals that would leave the peg vulnerable to speculative attacks?

This is an open question, to which we will turn in the next chapter by examining some case studies. The implications of the answer to this question are the following:

a. If the fundamentals can be managed appropriately, then managed exchange rates remain an option, even under conditions of high capital mobility. They may not necessarily be optimal for all countries and at all times, since some countries will find it preferable to adopt one of the extreme arrangements discussed in the last chapter, but they at least remain feasible without restricting the country's degree of integration with world capital markets.

b. If, however, small errors of policy or small random shocks make countries vulnerable to crises with very large costs under pegged rates and high capital mobility, then this option becomes much less attractive. The alternatives in this case are to retain a high degree of financial integration and move to one of the extreme exchange rate regimes, or to impose restrictions on capital movements and continue to manage the exchange rate.

In the next chapter we will examine what light the recent spate of emerging-economy financial crises can shed on these issues.

19

Banking Crises and Exchange Rate Crises in Emerging Economies

This chapter attempts to bring together much of the material covered in the rest of the book by analyzing the links between exchange rate crises and banking crises in developing countries both analytically as well as by conducting case studies of the 1994 Mexican and 1997 Asian crises. These recent crises are contrasted with the fiscally driven international debt crisis of the 1980s that we discussed in Chapter 8, and are compared to the 1982 Chilean financial crisis, which has been mentioned at various places earlier in the book. The objective of this chapter is to illustrate how the three general topics treated in this book – fiscal management, management of the financial system, and exchange rate management – lie at the heart of the most severe macroeconomic crises that developing countries have faced over the past two decades.

I. MACROECONOMIC POLICIES AND VULNERABILITY: THEORY

In Chapter 15, we discussed the "capital inflow problem" created by the capital account openness that accompanied financial reform in emerging economies. One reason that capital inflows were perceived as a problem was the possibility of capital-flow reversals. That is, the arrival of capital inflows was a symptom of an enhanced degree of financial integration that left countries vulnerable to capital-flow reversals and to the financial (banking and currency) crises that would accompany them.

Vulnerability to crises has two dimensions. These involve the probability that a country will experience an abrupt reduction (or reversal) in capital inflows as well as the costs to the economy if such an event comes to pass. As we have seen, the probability of a reversal depends in turn on the likelihood that creditors will come to believe that the value of their claims on domestic economic agents has become impaired. This situation could arise in obvious ways in the event of debtor insolvency, as in the international debt crisis of the 1980s, but as we have also seen in our analysis of banking crises in Chapter 13, it could also materialize when the debtor is merely illiquid – that is, when the claims that can be presented for payment within a given period exceed the debtor's capacity to make such payments.

The next section will take the perspective that, in contrast to the international debt crisis of the 1980s, the recent financial crises in Mexico and among the Asian "miracle" economies have been liquidity crises. The basic argument is that policies undertaken during the capital inflow period in these countries, especially toward the domestic financial system, but also with regard to the exchange rate and other policies, resulted in an exchange rate crisis, the (mis)handling of which left the economy vulnerable to a much more costly liquidity crisis after the exchange rate had been floated. To make this argument, we will first review some theory on liquidity crises in this section, before turning to the specific cases of Mexico and Thailand in the next two sections. Because the forms taken by the liquidity crises in Mexico and Thailand were superficially different – in the case of Mexico the liquid assets held by foreigners were liabilities of the public sector, while in that of Thailand they were liabilities of the private sector – the theoretical discussion in this section is divided into two parts, on public and private sector "debt runs" respectively.

a. Public Sector Debt Runs

Calvo (1988) argued that the existence of a large stock of nominal long-term government debt makes the public sector vulnerable to "confidence crises." Long-term, nominal (domestic-currency), fixed-interest debt is vulnerable to taxation by the government through inflation (or devaluation, in the case of debt held by foreign creditors).[1] If the government's creditors believe that inflation is a possibility, they will demand a premium in the yield on long-term nominal debt over that on short-term or indexed debt, to compensate them for expected inflation and for bearing the attendant risk.

Suppose the public comes to believe that, in the event of a loss of confidence in the government's inflation performance (and thus the emergence of large nominal interest rates), the government will be unwilling to raise taxes to service the debt, and will instead print money. In that case a confidence crisis on government debt may actually be self-fulfilling, in the sense that the high nominal interest rates caused by a lack of confidence may indeed induce the government to inflate the debt away. Thus, two equilibria could arise: a "good" equilibrium without a crisis, high taxes, or inflation, and a "bad" equilibrium with high nominal interest rates and high inflation.

Alesina, Prati, and Tabellini (1990) pointed out that vulnerability to a self-fulfilling confidence crisis could also arise in the context of short-term debt.

---

[1] It is also, of course, vulnerable to default (in the extreme case, repudiation), but no more so than short-term or indexed debt.

What creates the possibility of a "bad" equilibrium in the Calvo framework is the government's reluctance to make the fiscal adjustment required to meet a crisis-driven increase in its debt service requirements. But according to Alesina, Prati, and Tabellini, a short maturity structure of the public debt may actually increase the likelihood of a confidence crisis on the debt. Indeed, the shorter and more concentrated are the maturities, the more likely may a confidence crisis be. The reason for this in their model has to do with convexity of tax collection costs. This makes a given present value of tax revenue more costly to raise the less the government can smooth its collection over time – that is, the more front-loaded its collection. Because this increases the (utility) cost of servicing a given stock of debt the more bunched are maturities, it makes the government more likely to default if creditors become unwilling to roll over short-term debt. Thus, the unwillingness of creditors to roll over short-term debt in fear of default may actually become self-fulfilling. In this case, the crisis takes the form of a "debt run," comparable to the "bank runs" that we discussed in Chapter 13.

Giavazzi and Pagano (1990) summarize these results by noting that the likelihood of a Calvo "bad equilibrium" depends on three things: the size of the public debt, its maturity structure, and the time pattern of maturing debt. The logic is that when a substantial amount of debt has to be serviced at a point in time, if a "confidence crisis" breaks out at that moment, the government would have to refinance a large portion of its debt on unfavorable terms.[2] The utility cost of doing so would be high, and thus the likelihood that the government will repudiate is greater. This makes the confidence crisis more likely to happen. Under these circumstances, debt management, in the form of the issuance of long-term indexed debt, could push the economy to the "good" equilibrium, since such debt cannot be monetized away and does not create large short-run amortization obligations.

b. Private Sector Debt Runs

In the literature just reviewed, self-fulfilling confidence crises could afflict the public debt because of a choice made by the government in response to a loss of confidence – in other words, the costs of generating the fiscal resources to service its debt would lead the government to ratify the fears of its creditors. But what if the debt is issued by the private sector? The point of this subsection is that this difference is inessential. What matters for vulnerability is not the identity of the debtor, but the emergence of a situation in which, in the event of a run, creditors stand to lose part of the value of their claims. In the case of public sector debt, this would happen because of the government's reluctance to incur the fiscal costs of continuing to service the debt on market terms in the event of a run. In what follows

---

[2] The term "crisis" here could refer to fears either of a repudiation or a devaluation, since either would affect the return on domestic-currency debt.

we will consider a very simple and stylized model in which a "run" on private debt has similar consequences.

Consider an economy which maintains a fixed exchange rate, with the monetary base M backed by foreign exchange reserves R and central bank credit DC:

$$M = sR + DC, \tag{19.1}$$

where s is the nominal exchange rate. The demand for the base depends on the domestic nominal interest rate i, which in turn is given by uncovered interest parity:

$$M = \underset{+}{P(s)L(i)} \tag{19.2}$$

$$i = i^* + \hat{s}, \tag{19.3}$$

where P is the domestic price level, taken to be an increasing function of the nominal exchange rate, i^* is the foreign interest rate, and $\hat{s}$ is the expected (and actual) rate of depreciation of the currency. This describes financial market equilibrium in the model. At each moment in time, given the exogenous world interest rate, the policy-determined rate of depreciation determines the domestic nominal interest rate, which through (19.2) determines the money supply M, as in the perfect capital mobility model of Part 2. Equation (19.1) then determines the stock of foreign exchange reserves, given domestic monetary policy DC, through capital inflows and outflows.

The balance of payments in this economy (the change in the stock of foreign exchange reserves) is given by:

$$R = \underset{+ \quad +}{B[s/P(s), \theta]} + i^*(R - D) + (F - \gamma D), \tag{19.4}$$

where $B(\ )$ denotes the trade balance, which depends on the real exchange rate $s/P(s)$ (the foreign price level is set equal to unity) and a shift factor θ, D denotes the stock of net external debt, F is the magnitude of gross capital inflows, and γ is the ratio of amortization to the stock of debt, an index of the maturity of the outstanding stock of debt: the larger γ, the shorter the maturity of existing debt. If $\hat{s}$ is constant (for simplicity, suppose $\hat{s}$ is zero), M must be constant, and if DC is constant as well, the balance of payments must be zero. In that case, equation (19.4) determines the volume of gross capital inflows F. These flows determine the evolution of the stock of debt over time according to:

$$\dot{D} = F - \gamma D, \tag{19.5}$$

which completes the model. Notice that creditors' willingness to supply the level of capital inflows F must reflect their view that the economy is solvent – that the projected path of the trade balance (and thus implicitly of θ) is such that the existing stock of debt D will be serviced on market terms.

How can a liquidity crisis arise in this simple world? Suppose there is a threshold value of the nominal exchange rate, say s^*, above which domestic debtors are unable to service their foreign debt on market terms. This could happen, for example, because of currency mismatches in the balance sheets of domestic agents in which their assets are predominantly denominated in domestic currency, while their liabilities are in foreign currency. In this case, the economy could be vulnerable to a self-fulfilling liquidity crisis even if all external debt is private.

To see how, assume that in the event of a speculative attack on the currency that eliminates the central bank's foreign exchange reserves the country would adopt a floating exchange rate. Now suppose that a liquidity crisis materializes in which foreign creditors cease extending new loans to domestic residents, withdrawing from the country as existing debt matures. In this case, $F = 0$. If F was positive initially, the liquidity crisis could trigger a self-fulfilling speculative attack on the currency, because the floating exchange rate that would emerge after such an attack would be more depreciated than the initial fixed rate. This can be shown as follows: if the liquidity crisis triggers a successful speculative attack, the post-attack economy would be described by equations (19.1), (19.2), (19.4), and (19.5), with $R = 0$ in equation (19.1), $\dot{R} = F = 0$ in equation (19.4), and s determined endogenously. The cutoff of foreign lending means that the country is placed in a position of financial autarky, so (19.3) no longer holds. Under these conditions, s is determined by flow equilibrium in the balance of payments, given by:[3]

$$B[s/P(s), \theta + i^*(R - D) - \gamma D \tag{19.4'}$$

Thus, the post-attack exchange rate must satisfy:

$$s = s[\theta, i^*(R - D) - \gamma D] \tag{19.6}$$
$$\quad\;\; - \qquad\qquad +$$

This means that the floating exchange rate that would prevail after a successful attack, which is conventionally referred to as the "shadow" exchange rate, will be more appreciated the larger are "shift" factors that increase the trade surplus and the *smaller* are scheduled debt service payments.

The stock of external debt D is the predetermined variable in this model, so equation (19.6) is depicted in s-D space in Figure 19.1. Its positive slope reflects the fact that the larger is the stock of external debt, the larger is the value of debt service payments in the post-attack situation, and thus the more depreciated the floating exchange rate must be. In the figure, D^* is the value of D that would be consistent with balance of payments equilibrium with $F = 0$ at the original fixed exchange rate. For values of D larger than D^*, but smaller than D^{**}, the shadow exchange rate is more depreciated than the initial fixed rate, so given a liquidity crisis, a rational speculative attack on the currency is possible. However, there is no reason for a liquidity crisis to emerge in the range between D^* and D^{**}, since the floating rate that would emerge after a successful speculative attack would be below

---

[3] We implicitly assume here that F cannot be negative, which would be the case, for example, if controls on capital outflows by domestic residents are adopted in the event of a liquidity crisis.

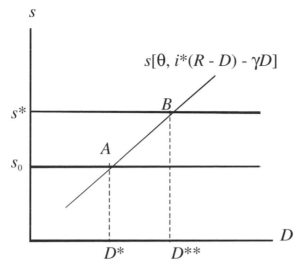

Figure 19.1. Determination of the Range of Multiple Equilibria

the critical value s^*, so foreigners would have no reason to cut off lending within this range.

Consider, however, the range $D > D^{**}$. In this range, dual equilibria can arise, because the shadow value of s is above s^*. In the absence of a liquidity crisis, debt would be serviced on schedule and the exchange rate would remain below s^* at s_0, but if a crisis-cum-speculative attack happens, individual creditors would have acted rationally *ex post*, because the exchange rate would immediately depreciate above s^*.

As is evident from equation (19.6), vulnerability to a confidence crisis (in the sense of a shadow exchange rate that is above its threshold value s^*) is increased in this model by a larger current account deficit, a larger stock of external debt, a larger share of short-term debt, and higher world interest rates.[4] All of these tend to shift the s[ ] curve upward in Figure 19.1, which increases the range of values of D for which $D > D^{**}$.[5] Since vulnerability arises at the moment when the shadow exchange rate equals the critical rate s^*, a larger current account deficit also brings vulnerability forward in time by increasing the stock of external debt.[6]

How can policy avoid vulnerability in this case? One option is for the central bank to maintain a sufficiently large stock of reserves (and/or official credit lines) to insulate itself from an attack (see footnote 6). A second option would be to adopt

---

[4] On the other hand, it would be *decreased* by a reliable flow of foreign direct investment, which would represent an additional (exogenous) additive term in equation (19.4).

[5] If F can be negative – that is, if domestic residents are able to pull capital out of the country freely in the event of a liquidity crisis – the range of values of D for which dual equilibria can exist is larger still, since negative values of F would also have the effect of shifting $s[]$ upward.

[6] Notice that in this setup the size of the stock of foreign exchange reserves (which is determined by $\hat{s}$ and C) does not affect vulnerability as long as $R/s < M$ (i.e., as long as C is positive). However, the government can insulate itself from an attack by ensuring that $R/s > M$.

policies that would have the effect of increasing s^* – for example, regulatory policies that would restrict the scope for currency mismatches in the financial system (either in the balance sheets of banks or those of their clients). Third, exchange rate and aggregate demand policies could be targeted to the achievement of a relatively low value of the trade deficit B, even if a larger trade deficit would be compatible with the country's solvency constraint. Fourth, capital account policies could be adopted to lengthen the maturity structure of external debt (i.e., to reduce γ). Finally, if none of these options are feasible, since vulnerability will be approached gradually over time when $F > \gamma D$, a country would be well advised to abandon its exchange rate peg *before $s = s^*$*.

We will now see that the recent dramatic instances of capital-flow reversals – the crises in Mexico and Thailand – followed a common pattern that culminated in the two types of liquidity crises described above. In both cases, policies followed during the inflow period resulted in an exchange rate (or balance of payments) crisis and an eventual floating of the currency. But the policy response to the balance of payments crisis left both countries vulnerable to a subsequent liquidity crisis – centered on public liabilities in the case of Mexico and private ones in the case of Thailand. The liquidity crises greatly increased the real costs of the exchange rate adjustments in both countries through their effects on fiscal policies, domestic interest rates, and the exchange rate. These real effects were in turn magnified by financial sector insolvency.

II. VULNERABILITY IN PRACTICE: MEXICO

The story of Mexico's descent into vulnerability is by now well known, but it bears reviewing in comparison with what happened in Asia $2\frac{1}{2}$ years later. Mexico in fact had two crises at the end of 1994 and beginning of 1995, a "garden variety" balance of payments crisis at the end of 1994, and a public sector debt run in early 1995. The two phenomena were, of course, closely linked.

Like Thailand in 1997 and unlike Mexico itself in 1982, Mexico did not enter 1994 with a public sector debt problem. By international standards, the stock of government debt outstanding was relatively small. Mexican public debt had been reduced from 67 percent of GDP in 1989 to a little over 30 percent in 1993. The reduction in the debt-GDP ratio was achieved in part through the use of privatization revenues to retire debt, and in part through operational surpluses on the fiscal accounts.[7] Of the total public debt, about two-thirds was external (mostly long-term, as a result of a Brady plan debt restructuring in 1989), and one-third domestic, with average maturity of about 200 days.

---

[7] Of US $20.2 billion in privatization income obtained in 1991–92, no less than 60 percent was used to retire debt (Steiner 1995), and operational surpluses of 2–3 percent of GDP were achieved from 1990 to 1993.

However, as noted by several observers at the time, Mexico did enter 1994 with an exchange rate problem. The problem consisted of a real exchange rate overvaluation caused by an exchange-rate-based stabilization undertaken in 1988 (called the Solidarity Pact; see Chapter 7). The symptoms of overvaluation included the large cumulative real exchange rate appreciation that the peso had undergone during the capital inflow period, a substantial current account deficit, with a reduction in private saving as its counterpart, and slow economic growth. All of these made devaluation a possibility. The government had, in fact, depreciated the peso substantially in the context of a widened exchange rate band that had been adopted in November 1991. Nonetheless, *ex post* estimation of the long-run equilibrium real exchange rate by several researchers, using the methods described in Chapter 16, concur that the peso had been substantially overvalued in 1994.[8]

The role of the exchange rate as a nominal anchor in the context of the Solidarity Pact, and doubts about whether the observed real appreciation may have been an equilibrium phenomenon, however, made the authorities reluctant to undertake a discrete exchange rate adjustment. Three exogenous events in the first quarter of 1994 magnified the pressures in the foreign exchange market: an uprising in Chiapas province in January, the announcement of a tighter monetary policy by the U.S. Federal Reserve Board in February, and the assassination of presidential candidate Luis Donaldo Colosio in March. These events intensified expectations of devaluation. The exchange rate moved to the top of its band in the first quarter of 1994, the central bank suffered a large reserve loss, and from March on, a large premium emerged on the domestic-currency denominated government bonds (*CETES*) over dollar-denominated ones (*Tesobonos*).

An exchange rate crisis materialized in the Mexican case through the interaction of these expectations of devaluation with the perception that the government would be unwilling to mount a high-interest rate defense of the currency – precisely through the mechanisms we discussed in the last chapter. A sustained tight money defense did not seem likely because of a combination of ongoing recession (likely due to the perceived overvaluation itself), the poor state of the domestic financial system, and upcoming elections in the fall of 1994 that appeared to pose a significant challenge to the ruling party. As we have seen, these circumstances are precisely those in which speculative attacks tend to happen, because markets do not believe the government will bear the political cost of mounting the high-interest rate defense called for by the rules of the game (see, for example, Eichengreen, Rose, and Wyplosz 1995).

---

[8] Loayza and Lopez (1997), for example, estimated a co-integrating equation for the Mexican real exchange rate using the country's stock of net foreign assets, and the relative productivity level in its traded and nontraded goods sectors, and applied the results to a calculation of real exchange rate misalignment in 1994, finding an overvaluation of 27 percent. Similarly, Warner (1997) estimated a co-integrating equation using the terms of trade and the ratio of capital inflows to GDP as fundamentals, and estimated an overvaluation of about 25 percent.

An important point of similarity with the Asian case (as well as with the case of Chile in 1982) was the fragility of the financial system. As is now well known, this fragility emerged as the result of rapid financial liberalization in Mexico in the late eighties and early nineties, in a context in which the government's capacity to regulate and supervise the domestic financial system was not well developed (see Chapter 13). Poorly supervised banks with weak capital positions, operating under the assumption of government backing of their deposit liabilities and with unconstrained access to external funds, undertook a rapid expansion of credit in the early nineties that fueled a consumption boom and left banks with a large stock of questionable assets and thus in a perilous financial situation. Given the unavoidable maturity mismatch involved in banking, and the weak position of many bank clients in the midst of the recession in Mexico, a high-interest rate defense of the currency would have imperiled the financial system and potentially severely aggravated the recession.

In the event, the government reacted to the emerging balance of payments crisis in two ways. First, it undertook sterilized intervention during the first quarter of the year, expanding the stock of credit to keep the monetary base relatively constant as foreign exchange reserves declined. Second, it shifted the composition of its debt from *CETES* to *Tesobonos*. The share of *Tesobonos* in total debt rose from less than 5 percent at the beginning of 1994 to over 55 percent by the end of the year. The share of privately held *CETES*, on the other hand, went from 60 percent of total debt in February to 20 percent by November.[9] The benefits to the government of this debt transformation consisted, of course, of lower debt servicing costs, thus protecting the public sector's operational balance, but there may also have been an element of projecting credibility to counteract devaluation expectations.

The net effect of the two policies, however, was to create a large increase in the government's net short-term (liquid) dollar liabilities and a reduction in its liquid dollar assets. As we have seen, in the presence of deposit insurance, $M2$ is backed by base money. Under officially determined exchange rates, on the other hand, base money is backed by reserves. With the two together, as in Mexico, $M2$ is backed by reserves. Thus, the loss of reserves with a fairly stable value of $M2$ implied a worsening government liquidity position. This vulnerability to a confidence crisis was clearly magnified by debt management. By converting longer-term domestic-currency liabilities into short-term dollar liabilities, the Central Bank was essentially using (net) foreign exchange reserves to pay off those liabilities. By the time of the crisis in December 1994, $M2$ in U.S. dollars amounted to $110 billion (Calvo and Mendoza 1996), and *Tesobonos* maturing in early 1995 were another $17.8 billion (Sachs, Tornell, and Velasco 1996). Foreign exchange reserves at the end of October were $17 billion, compared to a "minimum" level of $10 billion targeted by the Central Bank. Moreover, no extraordinary arrangements were in place on the part

---

[9] Werner (1995) presents evidence that the government altered its mix of instruments in response to interest rate differentials.

of external public institutions to lend to the Mexican government in the event of a private attack. At this point the government was clearly vulnerable to a liquidity crisis. An attack merely awaited a coordinating mechanism.

The first attack came in mid-November 1994, when reserves fell by $5 billion. The coordinating mechanism was clear: the new administration took office on December 1, and markets anticipated that the outgoing administration would devalue as a present to the incoming one (by removing the onus for doing so from them). The attack was halted by a public statement by President-elect Zedillo supporting the Solidarity Pact. The new administration took office with reserves of $12.5 billion. There obviously was not much room to maneuver. Clearly the exchange rate was on the new administration's agenda, and apparently a leak did them in.[10] By December 20, after only three weeks in office, the new administration effectively devalued by raising the ceiling on the exchange rate band by 15 percent. This was not perceived as enough, and the crisis was on, resulting in a float on December 21.

The interesting subsequent development for present purposes is that the immediate aftermath of the float was an increase in sovereign risk. Weekly *Tesobonos*–U.S. T-bill interest rate differentials began to climb steeply in the third week of December, rising from 1.7 percent in the second week of December to nearly 20 percent by end-January 1995. On the surface, this is a puzzle, for at least two reasons. First, given the Mexican government's low stock of debt and its fiscal track record, why should sovereign risk have been a problem? Second, why should sovereign risk *increase* after a devaluation? If an overvalued currency was the main obstacle to growth in Mexico, as Dornbusch and Werner (1994) had argued before the crisis, one would have thought sovereign risk would have fallen as growth prospects improved, especially since a renewal of growth and a reduction of domestic interest rates would have improved the prospects of the domestic financial system.

One interpretation is that the premium reflected not a *solvency* problem, but *liquidity* risk, and that the latter must be related to the balance of payments crisis. What were the links? The balance of payments crisis made the public sector more vulnerable to a "debt run" by lengthening the maturity of its assets and shortening that of its liabilities. The asset structure was made less liquid through the loss of liquid foreign exchange reserves, which were replaced on the asset side of the Central Bank balance sheet by illiquid claims on development banks as a result of sterilization. On the liability side, the endogenous change in the maturity structure of government debt also made its liabilities more liquid. A bunching of maturing short-term debt in the first half of 1995 made a run more likely. Moreover, the change in the currency composition of debt magnified the size of the peso repayment obligations after the devaluation.

---

[10] As reported in the *New York Times*, March 2, 1995.

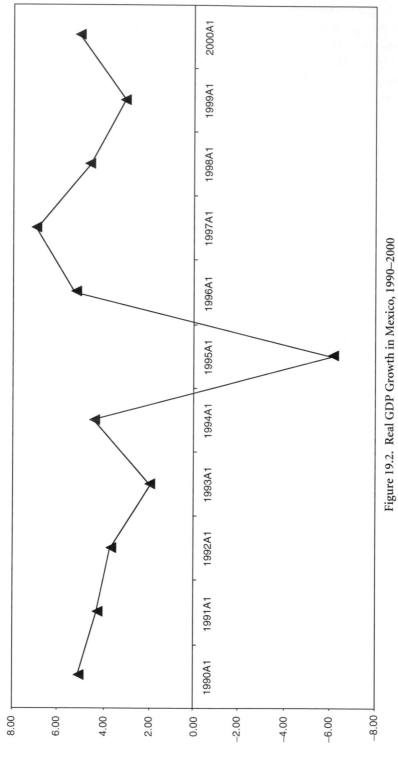

Figure 19.2. Real GDP Growth in Mexico, 1990–2000

This leaves the question, however, of why creditors may have converged on the view that in the event of a public sector debt run, default was a possibility. Faced with large short-term payment obligations, there are four things the government can do in the event of a debt run:

i. Generate a fiscal surplus of sufficient size to service the debt.
ii. Borrow from nonmarket sources (i.e., draw down reserves and/or borrow from official creditors).
iii. Print money.[11]
iv. Default (by stretching out payments, etc.).

To analyze what the government would have been likely to do, creditors would have had to look at both the feasibility and the consequences of each of these options. Since reserves were essentially depleted and official borrowing in sufficient magnitude had not been arranged as of January, (ii) was problematic. On the other hand, because the payments due were large, the distortions that would have been associated with (i) (e.g., tax distortions and an aggravated recession) as well as with (iii) (in the form of increased inflation) would have been large. This left (iv) as a realistic possibility, triggering the debt run.[12] The implications of the run were that the macroeconomic costs of the exchange rate adjustment were greatly magnified.

As shown in Figure 19.2, the combination of draconian fiscal adjustments under financial duress and very high domestic interest rates, combined with exchange rate overshooting as a result of the loss of confidence, resulted in a very severe recession in Mexico during 1995, despite the eventual resolution of the crisis through the provision of sufficient liquid official funds in March to pay off the government's liquid debt.

III. VULNERABILITY IN PRACTICE: THAILAND

The central theme of this section is that the emergence of macroeconomic vulnerability in Thailand had much in common with the Mexican experience. Three areas of similarity stand out. First, as in the case of Mexico in 1994, fiscal solvency was not an issue in Thailand in 1997. The Thai government had undertaken a sustained effort at fiscal adjustment since the mid-1980s, and by 1997 had succeeded in sharply reducing the stock of government debt relative to GDP. Second, as in Mexico, there were strong reasons to believe that the Thai real effective exchange

---

[11] Notice that, under fixed exchange rates, (ii) and (iii) are identical. Thus, (iii) is only feasible if (ii) is, and the four choices collapse to three. But by January 1995, Mexico was operating a flexible-rate system. This means that it would indeed have had four choices in the event of a debt run.

[12] Some observers have emphasized alternative coordinating mechanisms, including the way the initial currency crisis was handled (with repeated assurances that no devaluation was imminent, the emergence of leaks, a devaluation that was perceived as inadequate, and a forced float), and Mexico's financial history during the previous decade, which included debt default, bank nationalizations, and forced conversions of pesos into dollar deposits.

rate had become overvalued by 1997. While the real appreciation of the baht at the outbreak of the crisis relative to the early nineties was much smaller than that of the Mexican peso, several factors suggested that the *equilibrium* real exchange rate may have depreciated – perhaps substantially – in Thailand by that date, implying the existence of a gap between the actual and equilibrium real exchange rates. Indeed, the size of Thailand's current account deficit relative to GDP by 1997 exceeded that of Mexico in 1994. Third, as in the case of Mexico, Thailand underwent a significant financial liberalization several years before the crisis, which was followed by a domestic lending boom and a weakened financial system. Finally, Thailand's crisis, like Mexico's, played itself out over the space of about a year, during which time the authorities failed to adjust in any of the ways suggested in Part b of Section I. Like Mexico, they responded to reserve outflows by incurring short-term dollar denominated debt, thus impairing the country's liquidity position.

This being said, there were also obvious differences between Thailand's macroeconomic situation in 1997 and Mexico's in 1994. Most importantly, Thailand was growing very rapidly before its financial difficulties became apparent, in contrast to Mexico, which was experiencing a recession in 1994. In addition, Thailand's current account deficit reflected a sharp increase in domestic investment, rather than reduction in domestic saving. Finally, Thailand's outstanding stock of short-term debt was owed by the private sector, rather than the government. An important feature of this debt was that, unlike in the case of Mexico, it was quite large relative to the feasible scale of resources that could be made available to Thailand by the official international financial community. The question is, of course, whether these differences make the Thai crisis *sui generis* or whether the Thai crisis reinforced the policy lessons of the earlier Mexican one. To address this issue, it is worth reviewing the development of events in Thailand.

a. Pre-Crisis Developments

Southeast Asian countries faced two potentially important changes in their external economic environments during the early to mid-nineties. One was of a long-run nature, and the other was cyclical. The long-run change was the emergence of China as a major exporter of labor-intensive manufactured goods in the early nineties. China's share of world exports, which had grown at an average annual rate of about 6 percent during the eighties, increased at a 10 percent annual rate from 1990 to 1995. Given that Chinese exports were directly competitive with the exports of several Southeast Asian countries, this development implied that, to remain competitive, Southeast Asian countries would have had to export at lower prices. Thus, the emergence of China as a major exporter is equivalent in its effect on the long-run equilibrium real exchange rate of countries producing similar products to a terms of trade deterioration. The implication is that this development in itself would cause the long-run equilibrium real exchange rate of such countries to depreciate.

The cyclical development concerned monetary policy in Japan. The explicit adoption of an expansionary monetary policy in early 1995 to combat that country's long recession led to a rapid expansion in money growth after the second quarter of the year, which was accompanied by a sharp reduction in domestic interest rates and a strong depreciation of the yen relative to the U.S. dollar. The implications for Southeast Asia were two. First, the steep reductions in Japanese interest rates acted as a "push" factor driving capital to the region. As Figure 19.3 illustrates, the five Asian countries depicted all registered a sharp acceleration of reserve growth in 1995–96.[13] Despite countervailing domestic measures (see below), this acceleration of capital flows into the region resulted in macroeconomic overheating in the form of accelerating inflation. Second, the depreciation of the yen relative to the U.S. dollar caused the nominal effective exchange rates of the Southeast Asian countries – for which Japan was the dominant trading partner, but which tended to stabilize their exchange rates against the U.S. dollar – to appreciate after mid-1995.[14]

1. Real Exchange Rate Misalignment in Thailand

These two developments had important implications for real exchange rates in Southeast Asia. Consider specifically the case of Thailand. From 1987 to 1997, the Thai baht fluctuated in a narrow range of ±3 percent around a U.S. dollar parity of 25.4 baht per dollar. This bilateral nominal exchange rate stability against the U.S. dollar proved to be consistent with a trend real effective depreciation of the baht during the second half of the decade of the eighties, because of the secular depreciation of the dollar in nominal effective terms, and with a fairly stable real effective exchange rate from 1990 to 1994. During the latter period, the appreciation of the dollar was offset by favorable inflation performance in Thailand relative to that of the country's trading partners, making a stable real effective exchange rate consistent with a stable bilateral exchange rate against the U.S. dollar.

The monetary developments in Japan intervened to change this situation. First, the Thai economy began to overheat in response to the new surge in capital inflows. The inflation rate, which had gradually come down in the early nineties to the $2\frac{1}{2}$ percent annual range – substantially below that of the country's trading partners – began to accelerate in mid-1993, gradually ascending to the 7 percent range by early 1996. As shown in the top panel of Figure 19.4, this deterioration in relative price performance (measured by the curve *LRPI*, which depicts the (log of) the ratio of the domestic to partner-country *CPIs*) contributed to an appreciation of the real effective exchange rate.

---

[13] Kaminsky and Reinhart (1998) document the importance of interregional financial links in East and Southeast Asia, while Montiel and Reinhart (1999) provide empirical evidence of the independent role of Japanese interest rates as a "push" factor for Asian economies.

[14] See Frankel and Wei (1994).

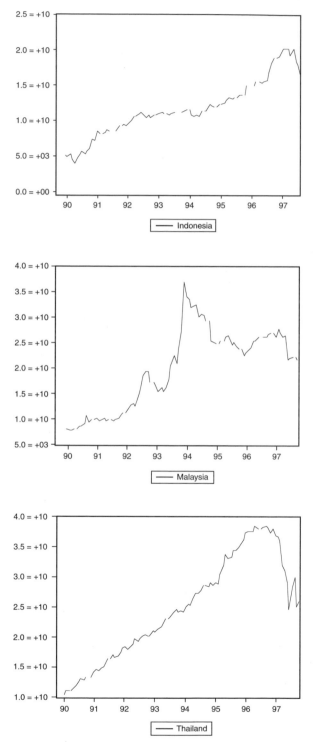

Figure 19.3. Reserve Accumulation in Five Asian Crisis Countries, 1990–98

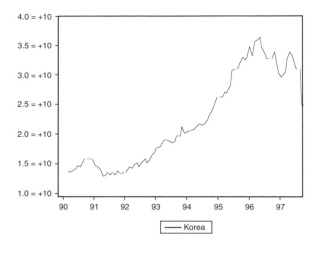

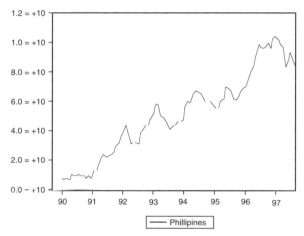

Figure 19.3. *(countined)*

Second, the depreciation of the Japanese yen in the second quarter of 1995 implied that, after depreciating sharply during the first quarter of the year, the U.S. dollar began to appreciate quite rapidly against the currencies of Thailand's other trading partners. This trend in the international value of the dollar shows up in the curve *LDOLLAR* in the bottom panel of Figure 19.4, which is an index of the value of the U.S. dollar in terms of the currencies of Thailand's trading partners, measured using Thailand's trade weights. After mid-1995, the baht depreciated in nominal terms from the bottom to the top of the range within which it had traded since 1987 (captured by the heavy dashed line in the bottom panel of Figure 19.4), but this proved to be far short of sufficient to offset the combined effects of accelerating domestic inflation and nominal effective appreciation of the U.S. dollar. As a consequence, the baht appreciated by nearly 20 percent in real effective terms over the two-year period from mid-1995 to mid-1997, a performance that represented

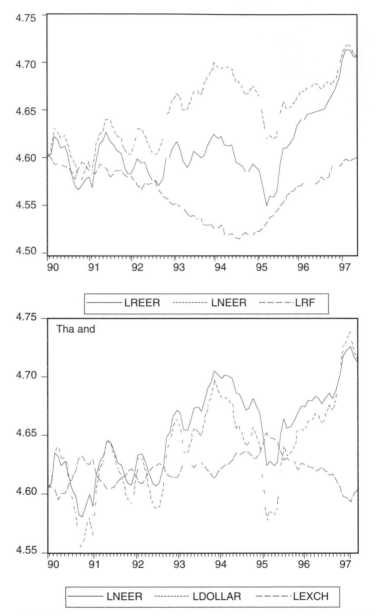

Figure 19.4. Thailand: Real Effective Exchange Rate Decompositions, 1990–97

a sharp break with experience since the mid-eighties. Even measured relative to its average value during 1990–94, the baht had appreciated in real terms by about 12 percent by mid-1997.

The significance of this change depends on what had been happening to the equilibrium real exchange rate in the meantime. As already mentioned, an important medium-term development affecting the equilibrium real exchange rate was that the countries in the region may have been losing competitiveness during the first half of the decade of the nineties due to the emergence of China as a major exporter. However, this effect has proven to be controversial. Fernald, Edison, and Loungani (1998) have argued, for example, that China's export growth during the early nineties came at the expense of Hong Kong, Korea, Singapore, and Taiwan, rather than of the Southeast Asian countries.[15]

In any case, as we saw in Chapter 16, the equilibrium real exchange rate depends on a variety of other fundamental factors as well. To assess the extent of real misalignment in Thailand on the eve of its balance of payments crisis, recall the co-integrating equation reported in Chapter 16 for the estimation of the long-run equilibrium real exchange rate in Thailand (based on annual data from 1970 to 1996):

$$\text{Log}(REER) = 6.113 - 0.746\ \text{Log}(CGR) - 0.581\ \text{Log}(TOT) + 0.012 INFL,$$
$$\quad\quad\quad\quad (0.028) \quad\quad\quad\quad\quad (0.016) \quad\quad\quad\quad\quad (0.002)$$

where REER is an index of Thailand's real effective exchange rate (with an increase representing a depreciation), CGR is the share of government consumption in GDP, TOT is an index of Thailand's terms of trade, and INFL is the world rate of inflation. Standard errors are in parentheses.[16] The theoretical rationale for the roles of these variables is described in Chapter 16. As shown in Chapter 16, an estimate of the long-run equilibrium real exchange rate for Thailand can be generated by calculating the fitted values of this equation using estimated "permanent" values of the fundamentals. The actual and estimated long-run equilibrium real exchange rates for Thailand were plotted in Figure 16.2, and are reproduced in Figure 19.5.

Notice that a gap between the actual and the estimated equilibrium real exchange rates began to emerge after 1992. By 1996 the estimated gap amounted to 11 percent of the estimated equilibrium real exchange rate.[17] How large would this gap have had to be before misalignment became a perceived problem? Recall that, by comparison, Loayza and Lopez (1997) estimated misalignment of 27 percent for Mexico in 1994. A more useful general benchmark is provided by Goldfajn and Valdes (1999) who

[15] On the other hand, in a simple bivariate regression, China's share of world exports explains about 80 percent of the variation in Thailand's terms of trade during 1970–94, suggesting that assessing China's impact on the equilibrium real exchange rates of the Southeast Asian countries may require going beyond an examination of export shares.

[16] This equation was estimated using the Johansen maximum-likelihood method. All of the variables in the co-integrating equation possessed a single unit root, according to the results of augmented Dickey-Fuller tests, and there was no evidence of more than a single co-integrating vector among them. Other potential fundamentals, including the share of public investment in GDP, the openness ratio (exports plus imports over GDP), the world real interest rate, and a time trend to capture secular Balassa-Samuelson effects, entered the co-integrating equation with theoretically inappropriate signs and/or were statistically insignificant.

[17] The range of available estimates of misalignment in Thailand before the crisis is large. Haque and Montiel (1999), using a general equilibrium simulation methodology, estimate misalignment of 17 percent. By contrast, Chinn (1998) finds the baht to have been approximately in equilibrium, while Tanboon (1998) estimates a misalignment of 30 percent.

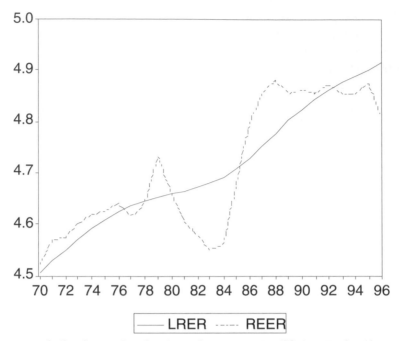

Figure 19.5. Thailand: Actual and Estimated Long-Run Equilibrium Real Exchange Rates

found, based on a large sample of countries, that the probability of a "smooth return" to the equilibrium real exchange rate from a short-lived overvaluation of 15 percent was about 16 percent in their sample for episodes that started after 1980. An even more relevant comparison might be with Thailand's own prior history. According to the methodology described above, the estimated degree of misalignment in Thailand in 1983–84, just prior to a 15 percent devaluation of the baht in November 1994, was nearly 13 percent. The implication, then, is that the prospect of a nominal devaluation had to be taken seriously in Thailand by 1996.

2. Financial Sector Vulnerability in Southeast Asia

Unlike exchange rate misalignment, which emerged rather quickly in Southeast Asia during the mid-nineties, financial fragility accumulated gradually during the inflow period. As is now well known, the late eighties and early nineties saw significant moves toward financial liberalization in several of these countries but, as in Mexico, these measures were implemented before the institutional apparatus was put in place to properly regulate and supervise these institutions. As in the case of Mexico, Southeast Asian countries, including Thailand, maintained very open capital accounts. Indeed, the establishment of the Bangkok International Banking Facility (BIBF) in Thailand in 1993 went further, by actively promoting capital inflows.

   The results were as outlined in Chapter 13: domestic lending booms, fueled in large part by external borrowing emerged in the early nineties in Indonesia, and later in Malaysia, the Philippines, and Thailand. In each of these countries, real bank and nonbank credit growth far exceeded output growth during those years. In addition, the exposure of banks to the property sector was far greater by 1997 in all four Southeast Asian countries than in Asian countries that did not experience similar lending booms, such as India and Korea. That this lending proved to be excessive is suggested by the fact that vacancy rates were much higher in the capital cities of these countries than elsewhere.[18] The upshot is that, as in Mexico earlier, exchange rate overvaluation and financial sector fragility had emerged among the Southeast Asian countries during the $2-2\frac{1}{2}$ years prior to the crisis, and particularly so in Thailand.

b. Macroeconomic Policies in 1995–96

This situation was exacerbated by the policy response to an upsurge in capital inflows during 1995–96. Capital inflows to Southeast Asia increased sharply during these years, with short-term inflows playing a much larger role than they had earlier. As mentioned above, rising inflation and increasing current account deficits increased concerns about macroeconomic overheating throughout the region during this time.

The policy response essentially took the form of tight monetary policy to sustain domestic interest rates at relatively high levels. Since, as had Mexico before, countries in the region continued to pursue nominal exchange rate targets (despite occasional official statements to the contrary), tight money essentially meant the sterilization of balance of payments surpluses, conducted through a variety of means. Indonesia, Malaysia, the Philippines, and Thailand all tended to sterilize consistently in response to large inflows. Thailand increased the intensity of sterilization in 1993, in response to an upsurge in private capital inflows associated with the establishment of the BIBF. As capital inflows continued to increase in size, domestic interest rates continued to be increased (Figure 19.6). Though Southeast Asian countries had achieved a substantial fiscal adjustment over the course of the inflow episode (which began in the region roughly in 1987–88), this fiscal adjustment was in part the product of a medium-term fiscal strategy, rather than consisting solely of a short-run countercyclical policy response to an expansionary external financial environment. Indeed, according to Alba et al. (1998), in Indonesia, Malaysia, and the Philippines the fiscal impulse moved procyclically throughout the 1991–96 period, while in Thailand fiscal policy was countercyclical in 1992–93, but had also become procyclical by 1995–96. The short-run inflexibility of fiscal policy as a stabilization instrument placed the short-run burden of stabilization on monetary policy. Consistent with the inflow experience described in Chapter 15, one implication of this policy mix was an intensification of short-term inflows intermediated through the domestic financial system.[19]

[18] Evidence on property sector exposure and vacancy rates is provided in Alba et al. (1998).
[19] For cross-country evidence on the links between sterilization and the magnitude of short-term inflows, see Montiel and Reinhart (1999).

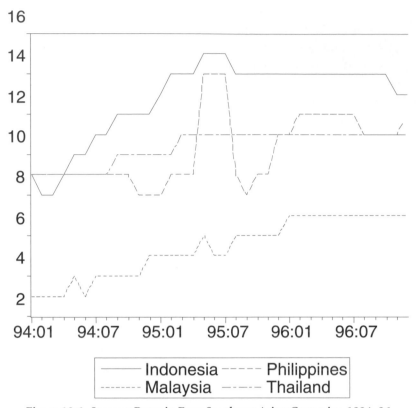

Figure 19.6. Interest Rates in Four Southeast Asian Countries, 1994–96

While it is easy to understand why funds would flow into the domestic financial system under these conditions, it is less obvious how the loan demand on which financial institutions depend to service their liabilities could have been sustained under relatively high domestic real interest rates. The answer is the emergence of asset-price inflation associated with the rapid financial expansion in the first half of the nineties described earlier. The legacy of this situation, however, was a financial system with borrowers whose creditworthiness and the value of whose collateral was heavily dependent on inflated asset values. This made the net worth of these institutions vulnerable to downward correction of domestic asset prices. Such a downward correction could come about in two ways: through a negative reassessment of the earning streams associated with these assets or an increase in the discount rates applied to these earning streams. As shown above, the second of these began to play a role by late 1995, as the sharp monetary tightening continued to raise domestic interest rates throughout the region. Indeed, due to high interest rates, stock market performance in the region turned poor in 1994–95.

In addition to premature financial liberalization and mismanagement of the exchange rate, the heavy reliance on tight money to combat overheating was a key mistake in short-run macroeconomic policy in Southeast Asia during the inflow episode prior to the events of 1997. The excessive weight placed on monetary policy put strains on domestic asset values and increased the stock of short-term external liabilities. The combination of real exchange rate appreciation, financial sector fragility, fiscal rigidity, and the accumulation of large short-term external liabilities recall the ingredients of the Mexican crisis at the end of 1994. As in Mexico, these policy mistakes did not imply the necessity of a crisis (i.e., they did not constitute sufficient conditions for a crisis), but they did create a state of heightened vulnerability centered on the financial sector. Nonetheless, in the absence of negative shocks, a crisis may have been avoidable, or at least postponable.

c. Outbreak of the Crisis in Thailand

Sufficient conditions for the crisis materialized in the form of adverse external conditions during 1996. The directly observable shock that preceded the Southeast Asian currency crisis was a collapse in export growth. Poor export performance materialized throughout the region in 1996. Asian export growth slowed markedly in the first half of 1996 (in dollar terms, 7 percent growth compared to 20 percent in 1995), and despite expectations to the contrary, failed to recover as the year wore on. The implications were the following:

i. Poor export growth implied reduced GDP growth through standard channels. This reduced the income streams expected to be associated with domestic assets, and dampened domestic asset values through this channel, which reinforced the negative impact of high domestic interest rates.
ii. Poor export growth introduced an element of noise into the medium-term competitiveness calculation. To the extent that the export slowdown reflected a loss of competitiveness, of course, it implied that the gap between the actual and equilibrium real exchange rates may have been larger than had earlier been imagined.

Why did export growth slow? Possible sources of loss of competitiveness include those already mentioned – that is, the effects of real exchange rate appreciation and growth in Chinese export capacity. Other factors included a slowdown in economic growth in Japan and a collapse in semiconductor prices (blamed by the press on worldwide overcapacity and weak personal computer market due to poor growth performance in both Japan and Western Europe). These may have been transitory real shocks, which do not in themselves affect the equilibrium real exchange rate. However, as we have seen (Chapter 17), the classic textbook response to such a shock for the objective of stabilizing aggregate demand is a temporary exchange rate depreciation. The contribution of this shock to the crisis may therefore have come in the form of increasing the perceived likelihood of a devaluation.

The upshot is that negative shocks during 1996 had two effects:

i. They may have increased the perceived likelihood of a nominal exchange rate adjustment, and:
ii. They increased the vulnerability of financial sectors in the region by depressing asset values and weakening the balance sheets of financial institutions.

In other words, these shocks reinforced the two sources of an emerging balance of payments crisis analyzed previously. The emergence of apparent misalignments implied the perception in financial markets that nominal exchange rate adjustments might be forthcoming, while fragility in the financial sector suggested that the costs of resisting such a misalignment, under pressure from speculation, would likely be perceived by the authorities in the region as prohibitively high. Because high interest rates would have impaired both the balance sheets and cash flows of domestic financial institutions, market participants would have perceived that fighting off a speculative attack through this traditional method would have been judged too costly by the authorities, particularly in light of the region's traditional commitment to the competitiveness objective. These two factors interacted, as in the case of Mexico, to make Thailand vulnerable to a crisis of confidence.

The first hints of currency problems in Thailand emerged during late July and early August 1996, triggered by worries over export competitiveness. Following a bleak report on economic prospects issued by the Bank of Thailand, the central bank was forced to spend US $1 billion to support the baht.[20,21] By the end of the month, though, the Bank still possessed US $39.4 billion in foreign exchange reserves. Nevertheless, in September Moody's downgraded Thailand's short-term foreign debt, noting financial sector problems and the rapid accumulation of foreign debt during 1995 (amounting to a 40.7 percent increase in the stock of debt outstanding over the course of the year, to a year-end value of US $41.1 billion).

While Mexico's currency crisis played itself out during a ten-month period in 1994, the crisis in Thailand took almost a full year (August 1996 to July 1997) before it culminated in the abandonment of the exchange rate parity. Over the course of that year, news on export performance, economic growth, and financial sector problems grew progressively worse, and outflow episodes became progressively more severe. As growth slowed and domestic interest rates were maintained at relatively high levels to defend the currency, the stock market fell, losing 35 percent of its value

---

[20] The Bank of Thailand revised 1996 projected real GDP growth from the 8.3 percent forecast earlier to 7.8 percent, and revised projected export growth to 10.2 percent, compared to 17.4 percent projected earlier and to 23.6 percent in 1995.
[21] Earlier blips had affected the Indonesian rupiah (but for idiosyncratic reasons – i.e., when a medical trip abroad by President Suharto fueled concerns over political instability), and the Malaysian ringgit in early January 1996, when information became available about the size of Malaysia's current account deficit.

during 1996. The government's handling of the crisis left much to be desired from
its outbreak until the final abandonment of the peg on July 2, 1997 and beyond. Key
mistakes were made in both with respect to exchange rate policy as well as policies
toward the financial sector.

In light of the analysis in Section I, the government's biggest mistake was to
attempt to hold the nominal value of the baht for almost a year. Its adherence
to the exchange rate peg in the context of devaluation expectations resulted in
large capital outflows and very high domestic interest rates which, through their
effects on the government's liquidity position and the balance sheet of the financial
system, together magnified the uncertainty and instability that resulted after the
baht was eventually floated. Despite the pressure on the currency in mid-1996 and
again in February 1997, at the end of March 1997 the Bank of Thailand continued
to report foreign exchange reserves of US $38 billion, almost unchanged from
the July 1996 level. By the time the baht was floated in July 1997, reserves had
officially fallen only to US $33 billion. It later became apparent, however, that
reserves had been maintained through large swap transactions, leaving the Bank
with a stock of future dollar liabilities in excess of US $23 billion after the flotation of
the currency.

As suggested by the model of Section I, the loss of liquidity created uncertainty
in the market after the baht was floated as to whether the country would be able
to meet its large short-term external obligations in the event that private agents
did not roll over a significant portion of these, and this perceived vulnerability to a
liquidity crisis undermined the value of the currency after the float. As the model
of that section would suggest, the perception that the exchange rate would have to
move substantially in the event of a confidence crisis may itself have accelerated the
onset of the crisis.

Given the exchange rate policy, the second key mistake was to postpone the
resolution of the problems of the financial system. The government initially (during
most of 1996) denied the vulnerability of the country's fifteen commercial banks
and ninety finance companies. However, as mentioned above, maintaining the fixed
exchange rate required very high domestic interest rates, which in turn continued
to undermine the value of assets held by the financial system that the government
was otherwise trying to support. In late February 1997, for example, depositors
engaged in a run on Thai finance companies, transferring deposits to the relatively
safer banks and moving money abroad.

Not coincidentally, renewed pressure on the baht emerged in February. The Bank
of Thailand responded by tightening monetary policy. High interest rates resulted in
a succession of financial crises triggered by falling property values. The central bank,
engaged in its lender of last resort function, extended credit to these institutions
which were later estimated to total US $15.7 billion. The effect of these policies was
to jeopardize the solvency both of finance houses and banks, which added to the
stock of nonperforming assets in the financial sector and to the eventual cost of

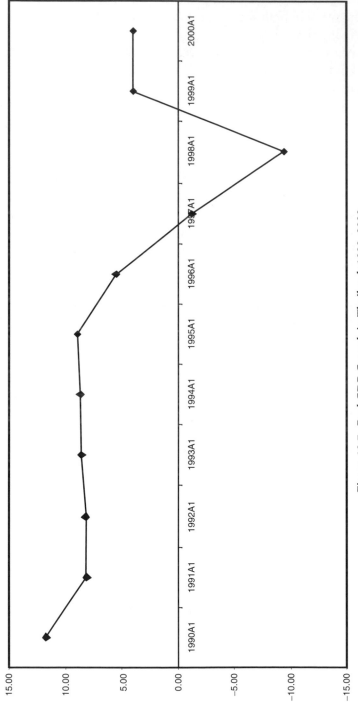

Figure 19.7. Real GDP Growth in Thailand, 1990–2000

resolving the sector's difficulties.[22] The increase in this cumulative cost impaired the government's fiscal position, and this unresolved liability overhang was a second source of uncertainty that increased instability in the period after the currency was ultimately allowed to float. It also magnified the ultimate fiscal burden associated with the crisis.

The government finally began to signal a tougher stance toward the financial sector in late June. Merger laws to accommodate the takeover of companies in difficulties were eased, and sixteen finance companies were ordered to suspend operations and seek merger partners within thirty days. The government indicated that troubled finance companies that failed to merge would be allowed to go under. This suggested for the first time that, while the government's implicit guarantee of bank deposits continued to hold, shareholders in the finance companies would not be bailed out.

Unfortunately, the measures adopted toward the financial sector in late June proved to be too little too late. The central bank announced in June that its gross foreign currency reserves had fallen to US $33.3 billion in the course of five straight months of balance of payments deficits, not including short-term foreign exchange liabilities in the form of swaps undertaken to support the baht. The baht was finally floated on July 2. In the first day, it fell by over 16 percent, and in the course of a month, it depreciated by over 25 percent. Despite the float, however, the country's problems were not over. The shortage of liquidity and the accumulation of non-performing loans in the financial sector left a significant overhang of uncertainty, and the authorities intervened to seek to avoid excessive depreciation of the baht. Rather than moving toward lower domestic interest rates, on the occasion of the float the central bank raised its discount rate by two percentage points. Despite the government's insistence as late as July 7 that it required no IMF assistance, the uncertainty surrounding the liquidity and fiscal problems led it to begin negotiations with the Fund on July 28, and a program was agreed upon one week later. As in the case of Mexico, Thailand's financial crisis resulted in a severe short-run contraction in real GDP (Figure 19.7).

IV. SUMMARY

The experience of the past decade has taught us that, whatever the macroeconomic costs associated with the overheating potential created by the arrival of large capital inflows to financially open and solvent emerging economies, they pale beside those created by the abrupt cessation and reversal of capital flows that are associated with

[22] In March 1997, Standard and Poor's rating service estimated the cost to the government of bailing out insolvent institutions at 6 percent of GDP, while by August that figure had increased to 12–15 percent of GDP.

liquidity crises in such countries. The two issues are related, however: vulnerability to such crises is the result both of policies followed during the inflow episodes, as well as of the ways that countries responded to the implications of these policies.

In both Mexico and Thailand, perceived exchange rate misalignment emerged during the inflow period as the result of policies pursued during that period – specifically, an open capital account, an inflexible exchange rate policy, and excessive reliance on monetary rather than fiscal policy to combat overheating after a premature domestic financial liberalization. Overvaluation interacted with financial sector fragility to produce the currency crisis. Thailand's higher growth rate and higher rate of investment could not protect it from this event. These features of Thailand's economy would have suggested a superior long-term debt servicing capacity, but would not have been expected to insulate it from a sharp short-run downturn as a result of a financial sector collapse brought about by a high interest rate defense of the currency. In both countries, postponing the exchange rate adjustment absorbed valuable liquid assets and left the economy in a vulnerable liquidity position. The failure of external creditors to roll over short-term debt subsequent to the flotation of the currency created a situation in which the debt was unlikely to be serviced on market terms in Mexico as well as in Thailand – albeit for different reasons, arising from the fact that the short-term external debt was public in Mexico's case and private in the case of Thailand.

What can we learn from the experiences of these two crises? There are two main lessons.

The first is that in the presence of high capital mobility – that is, once countries have become reintegrated with world financial markets – exchange rate overvaluation in a context in which the domestic economic costs of a high interest rate defense make the sustainability of such a defense problematic constitutes a recipe for a currency crisis.

Crisis avoidance can thus take several forms. The most obvious, of course, is to avoid reintegration with world financial markets in the first place. But as we saw in Chapter 14, once countries have removed long-standing capital account restrictions, there is weak evidence at best that the implementation of new market-based instruments can be effective in slowing capital movements. This does not mean, however, that countries have no choice about the pace of their reintegration with world capital markets. If they do, it may be best to postpone reintegration until the sources of vulnerability to currency crises are under control.

Where reintegration is a fact, on the other hand, escaping currency crises means avoiding overvaluation as well as the conditions that make a high interest defense of the currency less than credible. One way of achieving the first objective, of course, is allowing the exchange rate to float (and accepting the associated volatility). If the exchange rate is to be officially determined, however, it should be managed actively to avoid misalignment, perhaps with some assistance from the adjustment of policy-based fundamentals (e.g., fiscal policy), if feasible. Both Mexico and Thailand fell short on this score. A corollary of this point is that exchange-rate-based stabilization is a dangerous strategy with an open capital account. Given that stabilizing from a high (but not hyperinflationary) rate of inflation typically includes an initial period of real appreciation, the challenge is how to permit an adjustment of the real exchange rate without going through a balance of payments crisis. Chile in 1982, Mexico in 1994, and a later crisis that we have not discussed in this book – that of Brazil in 1999 – suggest that moving to the "flexibilization" stage without trauma is a challenging task. On the other hand, Israel (1987) and Poland (1990) suggest that it is not a hopeless one.

The other component is enhancement of the credibility of a high interest rate defense of the currency, were that to become necessary. The experience of the European Monetary Union in 1992–93 suggests that the achievement of complete credibility is likely to prove an elusive goal. As we have seen, credibility can be enhanced through institutional innovations such as increased central bank independence or the adoption of a currency board, but the experiences of Argentina in 1995 and Hong Kong in 1997 suggest that, even under relatively favorable circumstances (arising from Argentina's inflationary history and Hong Kong's ample foreign exchange reserves) this remains a challenge. At the very least, though, governments can avoid measures that undermine the credibility of their resolve. In both the Mexican and Thai cases, loss of credibility was greatly magnified by the fragility of the financial sector due to inappropriate liberalization during the early 1990s. Given that maturity mismatches are unavoidable in banking, policies that ensure the health of the financial system can increase the likelihood that a defense of the currency will be sustained.

The second main lesson is that, once vulnerability has arisen, in the form of perceived overvaluation and inability to mount a high interest rate defense, postponing the inevitable merely serves to aggravate its consequences, primarily by increasing vulnerability to a subsequent liquidity crisis, which involves a much more dramatic loss of confidence and larger exchange rate movements than would otherwise happen. After all, a puzzling feature of both the Mexican and Thai experiences is that, unlike the United Kingdom and Italy in 1992, the floating of the currency was followed by a severe real-sector crisis rather than an acceleration of growth. One difference, of course, was the advanced stage of financial fragility in both developing countries and the banking crises that accompanied the exchange rate crises. But one might have expected this to have been alleviated by the elimination of the misalignment, reinforcing a tendency for an acceleration of growth. The liquidity crisis that followed the float in both cases undermined this possibility.

In the Mexican case, postponement was financed by reserve losses and short-term foreign currency financing of the public debt, reducing the government's liquid dollar assets and increasing its liquid dollar liabilities. The prohibitive fiscal costs of servicing these liabilities in the event of a run made it rational for individual creditors not to roll over their claims, an event that seems to have greatly magnified the short-run costs of Mexico's real exchange rate adjustment through the requirement of draconian fiscal adjustment and loss of investor confidence, which was associated with high interest rates and an overshooting nominal exchange rate. In the case of Thailand, postponement was financed by reserve losses, and illiquidity resulted from the combination of reserve depletion and a large stock of previously existing liquid private sector external liabilities that arose in part from policies designed to combat overheating in 1995–96. The value of these claims on the private sector was impaired by the adverse effects on the solvency of private debtors of a large nominal exchange rate depreciation, again making it rational for individual creditors not to roll over their claims. The nominal exchange rate indeed moved very sharply after the currency was floated, in the context of a liquidity crisis.

The upshot is that the similarities between Mexico and Thailand mattered much more than the differences, and the policy message from the two experiences is the same: perceived exchange rate misalignment in the context of an open capital account with a fragile domestic financial sector is a reliable recipe for a currency crisis. Postponing the adjustment invites a liquidity crisis which, in the context of a vulnerable domestic financial system, creates very severe short-run real economic dislocations.

20

Domestic Macroeconomic Management in Emerging Economies: Lessons from the Crises of the Nineties

In the last chapter we examined the recent financial crises in Mexico and Thailand in some detail, because these were the two most important crises among emerging economies that entered the decade of the nineties with a policy commitment to reform domestic financial systems and integrate themselves more fully with international financial markets. But the nineties were characterized by a spate of financial crises, afflicting many other emerging economies as well. Partly this may have reflected "contagion" (spillover effects) from the crises we have studied, such as those of Argentina in 1995, or of several East and Southeast Asian economies in 1997. But partly these emerging-economy crises have also been home-grown, for example, the Brazilian crisis of 1999. Moreover, the incidence of financial crises has not been restricted to emerging economies. Crises have also occurred among industrial countries (e.g., the Nordic banking crisis that we reviewed in Chapter 13, and the ERM crisis of 1992) as well as transition economies (the Russian crisis of 1998).

What lessons can we draw from the recent spate of financial crises in emerging economies for the central topic of this book: the conduct of domestic macroeconomic policies in emerging economies? To bring together the various themes that we have explored in this book, this chapter will attempt to summarize what we may and may not have learned about this issue from the financial turbulence of the 1990s.

It is worth noting at the outset that economists are still debating the lessons to be drawn from the macroeconomic experiences of previous decades, that is, those of the thirties, sixties, and eighties, among others. Thus, it would be very surprising indeed if the profession had reached a consensus about the lessons to be learned from the financial crises that have characterized the most recent decade. Consequently, many of the "lessons" from recent crises are still in dispute. In that sense, it is still a bit premature to guess what the enduring lessons of the recent spate of financial crises around the world will turn out to be. To acknowledge this unsettled state of affairs, this chapter will classify the lessons to be discussed into two types: those on which there is widespread agreement, and those that are more problematic, with an emphasis on the first type. However, it should be pointed out that even with regard to those in the first category there are important dissidents, and what you will read below is just one economist's views on where things stand.

We will begin by discussing lessons on which there appears to be some broad agreement. These can be divided into several areas: the benefits and costs of financial integration, causes of currency crises, exchange rate policy, monetary policy, and fiscal policy. Next, we'll turn to issues that are important for macroeconomic management under current international circumstances and on which (sometimes strong) opinions have been expressed by knowledgeable observers, but on which substantial disagreement still exists. The chapter will conclude with a discussion of what all of this might mean for macroeconomic management in emerging economies.

I. LESSONS THAT WE HAVE LEARNED

The term "globalization" came into increased use during the decade of the nineties. It refers to increased mobility of goods and services across international boundaries, as well as the increased mobility of financial capital. In many countries, it has also come to mean increased international labor mobility. But globalization is not just an inevitable product of technological change. In many ways the world economy was more "globalized" – that is, more integrated – from 1890 to 1914 than it became during the last two decades of the twentieth century. Focusing just on the financial aspects of globalization, not all countries have chosen to participate equally in the integration of world financial markets – China and India are well-known examples of countries that decided to go slowly in the financial area – and some countries have decided to withdraw, at least partially, from a state of high integration. In September 1998, for example, Malaysia, which had traditionally been a financially open economy, imposed severe capital controls in response to the Asian financial crisis that had broken out during the previous year. Thus, integration reflects in part a set of domestic policy decisions. And the decision to pursue more intense integration involves trading off the benefits and costs of doing so. The first set of lessons concerns what we have learned in recent years about these benefits and costs.

a. Benefits and Costs of Financial Integration

1. Importance of External Financial Shocks
Economists believe that everything has benefits and costs, of course, and as we saw in Chapter 14, financial integration is no exception to this rule. In particular, economists have always been aware that enhanced financial integration meant exposure to external financial shocks. At the same time, increased financial integration offers, among its other benefits, to dampen the effects of certain domestic

shocks. What may not have been sufficiently appreciated prior to the experience of the nineties was how large the external financial shocks were likely to be. The first lesson, then, is the following:

> Increased financial integration, while offering significant benefits to developing countries, also comes with some important costs. The key costs involve exposure to external financial instability that, it turns out, can be quite substantial.

This is not an altogether new experience. A key lesson learned from the post–Bretton Woods era of floating exchange rates turned out to be that floating rates were much more volatile than economists had anticipated. It now appears that we also underestimated the volatility of the external financial environment facing emerging economies that become more integrated with world capital markets. In other words, the financial shocks faced by these countries have turned out to be larger and more common than was previously expected. Such shocks can arise from at least three sources:

- Monetary policy in capital-exporting countries.
- Heightened sensitivity to domestic macroeconomic developments.
- "Contagion" from shocks afflicting other capital-importing countries.

The first of these was already familiar before the crises of the nineties. Indeed, as we saw in Chapter 15, some of the early capital-inflow literature (see Calvo, Leiderman, and Reinhart 1993) worried quite a bit about this problem before any of the recent crises materialized. What the crisis experience of the nineties has suggested, however, is that:

i. In the face of domestic macroeconomic problems, the severity of the punishment inflicted by international financial markets may be far out of proportion with the magnitude of the apparent "crime" committed by the domestic macroeconomic authorities. The crisis in Mexico first made this clear (see especially Calvo 1996).

ii. Countries have to worry not just about financial developments in the capital-exporting countries and financial market reactions to macroeconomic developments at home, but also about the effects on the supply of funds facing the domestic economy of macroeconomic developments in other borrowing countries. This refers to the phenomenon of contagion, which afflicted Argentina, Brazil, and the Philippines in 1995 after the Mexican crisis in December 1994, several East and Southeast Asian countries in 1997 after the Thai crisis in July, and many countries after the Russian crisis of August 1998.

The implication of these two developments is that the external financial environment for countries that pursue increased integration with world financial markets may be much less stable than we previously thought, with attendant challenges for domestic stabilization policies.

2. Domestic Distortions and Financial Integration

A second lesson concerning financial integration has to do not with the external financial environment, but rather with domestic circumstances that may affect the benefits and costs of financial integration:

> Financial opening is particularly dangerous when the domestic financial system is heavily distorted. Not only may this result in immiserizing external borrowing, but will also increase the probability and likely severity of a domestic financial crisis.

As we saw in Chapter 14, a previously existing literature on the optimal sequencing of macroeconomic reform put financial opening at the end of the process of liberalization, after macroeconomic stabilization was achieved, commercial policy was liberalized, and domestic financial repression was removed. The fear was that the presence of financial repression would result in resource misallocation if the economy was opened up financially, largely through capital outflows.

The experience of the Southern Cone countries in the late seventies and early eighties alerted economists to a different kind of risk: that the combination of an open capital account and an improperly liberalized financial system could lead to a combination of domestic banking crisis and balance of payments crisis. As we saw in Chapter 13, the basic problem is that the combination of explicit or implicit deposit insurance, low net worth of banks, and poor prudential regulations and bank supervision creates incentives for bank managers to invest in highly risky ventures, which will cause many banks to fail, triggering a financial crisis.[1] Such crises have large fiscal costs and costs to real economic activity operating through the so-called "credit channel" of monetary policy. Because the resources absorbed by the banks can be much larger when the capital account is open, an open capital account magnifies the scale of the crisis. Moreover, under an open capital account, the fiscal costs and macroeconomic dislocations caused by a banking crisis are also likely to trigger a balance of payments crisis as both domestic residents and foreign creditors switch to foreign assets.

As we saw in the last chapter, with an open capital account and a weak financial system, not only can a domestic financial crisis trigger a balance of payments crisis, but the reverse is also true – a balance of payments crisis can trigger a domestic financial crisis. The two phenomena thus tend to be closely associated. Indeed, a recent paper by Graciela Kaminsky and Carmen Reinhart (see Kaminsky and Reinhart 1999) has documented the close association that has existed historically between crises of both types, so much so that they refer to them as "twin" crises. In the last chapter, we argued that the Mexican and Asian crises in many ways replicated the Southern Cone experience and confirmed the dangers of combining

---

[1] Recall the analysis of the Chilean experience by Diaz-Alejandro (1985). See also Andres Velasco (1987).

an open capital account with a weak domestic financial system. Indeed, the major difference between the macroeconomically destructive Mexican and Asian balance of payments crises of the nineties and the macroeconomically harmless 1992 ERM crisis was precisely the fragility of the domestic financial systems in Mexico and the Asian countries.

Because of the vulnerability it creates to "twin" crises, the combination of an open capital account and a weak financial system also has important implications for the conduct of exchange rate and monetary policies. We will discuss these implications below.

3. Factors Driving Capital Flows

As we saw in Chapter 15, during the first half of the nineties, increased financial integration was accompanied by large capital inflows into several developing countries. During the early years of this episode, many observers worried whether this new capital inflow episode would culminate a new debt crisis, just as the previous episode during 1974–81 had done. One point of view, associated with former U.K. Chancellor of the Exchequer Nigel Lawson and former IMF official Walter Robichek, was that the new capital inflows were unlikely to prove problematic, because in contrast with the inflows of the seventies, which largely reflected external borrowing by the public sector of the indebted countries, the new inflows were directed to private agents in the borrowing countries, so that each individual transaction was subject to a market test. However, an important lesson emanating from the recent crises has been the following:

> The Lawson-Robichek doctrine that capital inflows reflecting market transactions between private agents do not pose macroeconomic risks has not held up well. The sectoral identity of the agents on the borrowing side of the market is not definitive in determining whether capital inflows are likely to be followed by capital-flow reversals.

An important stylized fact is that all of the major developing-country financial crises during the decade of the nineties were preceded by periods of substantial capital inflows, and in each case the domestic borrowers were predominantly private agents. Each of these crises was accompanied by persistent capital-flow reversals in the form of a cessation of private capital inflows or actual outflows, not unlike those that characterized the outbreak of the international debt crisis during the decade of the eighties. The interpretation of this fact is a subject of dispute, with views ranging from those who emphasize the role of public sector guarantees in driving both the capital inflows and subsequent reversals that characterized the crises of the nineties (e.g., Dooley 1997) to those who blame the crises on characteristics of international capital markets (e.g., Radelet and Sachs 1998, and Calvo and Mendoza 1996). What is common to both views, however (as well as to those in between) is that, contrary to simple versions of the Lawson-Robichek doctrine, the identity of the borrower does not constitute grounds for complacency concerning the macroeconomic risks associated with large capital inflows.

b. Causes of Currency Crises

The first three lessons listed above suggest that financial integration is not a panacea, and that indeed in some circumstances it can be downright dangerous, even if the associated capital flows are strictly market-driven transactions between private agents. A natural follow-up question is what can be done to minimize these dangers – more specifically, what can countries do to avoid home-grown currency crises, as well as the adverse implications of crises elsewhere? To address this question, the next set of lessons from recent experience pertain to the causes of currency crises as well as their implications for a variety of macroeconomic policies.

1. Multiplicity of Causes
A first lesson from the recent crises in this regard is that:

> There is no single cause of currency crises. Thus there is no single cure or single policy that it is necessary to get right.

In trying to understand the causes of currency crises, the analytical literature in macroeconomics has proceeded through a succession of crisis models. "First-generation" crisis models interpreted crises as resulting from an inconsistency between exchange rate and monetary policies – specifically, as the result of a monetary policy that was excessively expansionary given the officially determined path of the nominal exchange rate. In terms of the model of Part 2, this family of crisis models involved continuous and excessive credit expansion in a situation of high capital mobility, typically presumed to be driven by the need to finance a fiscal deficit. As we saw in Part 2, the eventual result of such a policy is to deplete the country's stock of foreign exchange reserves. These models thus blamed crisis on monetary and fiscal "fundamentals," in the form of overly expansionary policies. Such models, originating with Krugman (1979), predated the international debt crisis of 1982, but that experience was interpreted as consistent with the first-generation models because of their emphasis on unsustainable fiscal policies.

"Second-generation" models originated with the ERM crisis of 1982. In these models, the government does not follow a mechanical rule of holding on to a fixed exchange rate until it runs out of reserves, but instead makes an optimal choice among competing macroeconomic objectives. A fixed exchange rate may be abandoned when the constraints that it imposes on monetary policy run counter to the government's desire to run a more expansionary monetary policy for domestic stabilization (or fiscal) reasons. Notice that, like the first-generation models, the basic conflict is between expansionary monetary policy and a fixed exchange rate.

But in second-generation models, it is not *actual*, but rather *prospective*, monetary expansion that creates the basic inconsistency. This has two implications:

i. The "fundamentals" are appropriate, in the sense that the exchange rate would be sustainable in principle.
ii. As in the examples we saw in the previous chapter, currency crises can be self-fulfilling, because the fact of an attack can alter the costs the government perceives in adhering to the fixed rate.

Both classes of models emphasize the choices facing the monetary authorities. They note that monetary policy is caught between conflicting objectives: an external one (the exchange rate) and an internal one. The models differ with regard to the internal objective. In the case of the first-generation models, it is the need to generate seignorage revenues to finance a fiscal deficit, while in the second-generation models based on the experience of Western Europe, it was the desire to combat recession or to lower public sector borrowing costs, both of which might be achieved with a more expansionary monetary policy than would be consistent with a fixed exchange rate.

The Mexican and Asian experiences reviewed in the last chapter have given rise to yet a third generation of crisis models, which emphasize a new set of objectives for monetary policy that could conflict with maintaining a fixed exchange rate – that is, to maintain low domestic interest rates to protect a fragile domestic financial system. The main point is that the potential causes of crises have been expanded gradually with experience, from macroeconomic policy inconsistencies to the existence of a recession or a large stock of public debt to a weak domestic financial system. The crises of the nineties have changed our understanding of the causes of currency crises by expanding the range of circumstances under which crises can reasonably be expected to emerge.

2. *Traditional Recipes*

This has an important implication for the rewards that countries can expect to receive from what has traditionally been understood to constitute macroeconomic "good behavior":

> Neither a strong (stock and flow) fiscal position, a relatively small current account deficit, nor a larger current account deficit accounted for by a large share of investment in GDP and accompanied by rapid growth can necessarily protect a country against a severe *home-grown* currency crisis.

As we saw in the last chapter, both Mexico and Thailand (as well as other Asian countries that were affected by the crisis of 1997) had strong fiscal positions, both in the sense of small overall deficits or actual surpluses in their overall fiscal accounts (a flow) as well as low public sector debt (a stock). Thus, fiscal prudence was not enough to insulate these countries from the outbreak of a financial crisis. One possible explanation is that, while these countries were not characterized by large *public sector* imbalances, they did have large *private sector* imbalances. As we have seen, this was true for Mexico and Thailand, which had large private-sector-led current account deficits (in the neighborhood of 8 percent of GDP) in 1994 and 1997 respectively. However, among other countries that underwent crises in the nineties, both Indonesia and Korea had relatively small current account deficits at the time of their crises, suggesting that the size of the current account deficit is not the critical variable either. That is, minimizing *both* public and private sector flow imbalances are not enough to protect an economy from a currency crisis. Finally, one lesson that at one time had been thought to have been learned from Mexico – that what mattered was the behavior of domestic saving and investment underlying the current account deficit – was proven wrong by Thailand, which registered very large rates of domestic saving and investment, together with rapid growth at the time of its crisis.

Some people have drawn from this observation the conclusions that currency attacks are whimsical (not based on fundamentals) and thus driven by pure panic. Others have concluded that they are driven by conspiracies or by the actions of a single large speculator (Malaysian Prime Minister Mahathir expressed this view at the time of the Asian financial crisis). Finally, as we saw in Chapter 18, based partly on this experience some economists have come to the conclusion that there is no combination of domestic policies that can insulate countries with officially determined rates from succumbing to speculative attacks, and thus that fixed exchange rates for national currencies are no longer feasible. We'll come back to this issue later. The point for now is that the traditional "rules of good behavior" clearly have not been enough to protect countries from the onset of currency crises.

3. The Role of Debt Composition

Note that the traditional measures of good behavior are all solvency-based macro-economic fundamentals. If these are not sufficient to explain the incidence of currency crises, there are several possibilities. The most obvious one, of course, is that the value of claims on residents of a country can become impaired through means other than general macroeconomic or fiscal insolvency. A crisis may arise not as the result of actual or prospective insolvency, but as the result of anticipated policy choices, driven by changes in circumstances, that would have the effect of shifting the burden of taxation toward agents who hold such claims. As we saw in the last chapter, a special case would be that of a liquidity crisis, in which the change in circumstances is triggered by the holders of the claims themselves in the form of a panic, as in the case of runs on solvent banks.

Models of self-fulfilling speculative attacks triggering currency crises do not exonerate the domestic authorities from responsibility for such attacks, however, since they suggest that these attacks can be successful only if the values of certain macroeconomic fundamentals (the identity of which is model-specific) fall within a specific range. One such "liquidity-based fundamental" is the stock of short-term external liabilities. Short-term external liabilities indeed appear to have played an important role in both the Mexican and Asian crises. They did so by creating a liquidity crunch when creditors refused to roll over these debts. Thus, a third lesson concerning causes of crises is the following:

> Contrary to some views expressed early in the capital-inflow experience, the maturity composition of a country's external liabilities seems to matter in determining a country's vulnerability to capital-flow reversals.

However, the consensus on this particular "lesson" from recent crises is not as strong as for the prior ones. For one thing, liquidity-based stories are not the only way to rationalize the inability of the traditional solvency-based fundamentals to explain the crises of the nineties. For any single crisis unexplained by the traditional fundamentals, it remains possible to adhere to the view that the crisis was ultimately driven by a solvency problem. This could happen if the insolvency existed before the crisis, but would not tend to be revealed by the traditional indicators, or if insolvency arises only in the event of a crisis.

The role of actual or prospective insolvency in explaining the crises of the nineties is actually an unresolved issue in some instances. As already mentioned, the leading interpretations of the 1992 ERM crises relied on domestic recession and a high stock of domestic public debt as factors undermining the fixed exchange rate by weakening the authorities' resolve to keep interest rates high in order to deter speculation against the domestic currency. Floating the exchange rate in order to pursue a more expansionary monetary policy amounts to a change in policy that has the effect of imposing a capital levy on holders of assets denominated in the depreciating currency. The flight from the domestic currency is driven by this prospective tax, not by doubts about the solvency of the government implementing the policy change. On the other hand, while one interpretation of the Mexican and Asian crises is that a fragile domestic financial system can produce the same result through a similar mechanism, some observers have offered a different interpretation. In this alternative view, these balance sheet difficulties are perceived as having undermined the fixed exchange rate by creating a large unfunded liability for the public sector that impaired its solvency. The traditional indicators would simply miss this source of insolvency.

Despite this ongoing disagreement about the roles of solvency versus liquidity in the Mexican and Asian crises, the weight of the broader econometric evidence suggests an important role for liquidity indicators such as the ratio of $M2$ to reserves and the maturity composition of debt in explaining the incidence of currency crises more generally (see, for example, Sachs, Tornell, and Velasco 1996). The weight of the evidence thus creates a strong presumption for the view that liquidity matters, and if liquidity matters, so does the maturity composition of external debt. As we shall see next, this particular lesson has important implications for a variety of policies, including monetary policy.

c. Policy Lessons

We now turn to lessons from recent crises for domestic macroeconomic policies. We will consider in turn capital account restrictions, exchange rate policies, monetary policy, and fiscal policy.

1. Capital Controls

As discussed in Chapter 14, capital controls have always been controversial among economists, because they reflect direct interference with market allocations and may thus prevent economies from reaping the gains that would otherwise be expected from intertemporal trade. However, economists have also long recognized that there may exist valid second-best reasons for the imposition (or retention) of capital account restrictions. In Chapter 14, for example, we reviewed the "sequencing" literature that advocated the retention of capital account restrictions until several other domestic problems had been addressed. On the other hand, there has always been a substantial amount of skepticism among economists that capital account restrictions could be effective, in the sense that private agents may find a way to circumvent them. The lessons from the recent crises have concerned both the motivations for adopting capital account restrictions as well as their likely effectiveness. Concerning the first:

> The recent crises have strengthened the case for capital account restrictions, for at least five reasons:
> i. As protection against instability in the international financial environment.
> ii. As a second-best measure to minimize the costs of financial sector distortions.
> iii. As a means of minimizing the risks of speculative attack by increasing the costs of speculating against the currency.
> iv. As a way of attempting to preserve some monetary autonomy.
> v. As a way of attempting to lengthen the maturity of the country's external liabilities.

We have already noted that two lessons from the crises of the nineties are that the external financial environment is likely to be less stable than we may previously have thought, and that capital account liberalization may greatly increase the costs associated with problems in the domestic financial sector. We have also noted that recent experience suggests that currency crises can be caused by a wide variety of factors, and that avoiding vulnerability to such crises is not a simple matter of following the traditional rules of good behavior. We will also suggest below that monetary policy may have very little room to maneuver under fixed exchange rates when capital mobility is high, especially when the domestic financial sector is weak. Finally, we have noted that the maturity of a country's external liabilities has come to be seen as an important factor in determining its vulnerability to currency crises. All these reasons have tended to strengthen arguments for capital account restrictions.

However, we should be clear about what this does and does not mean. These factors tend to strengthen the case for restrictions, relative to what may have been thought before experiencing the crises of the nineties. They do not clinch the case that countries should necessarily intervene in their capital accounts. They suggest that the benefits of intervening may be higher than we may have thought, but there remain costs (i.e., benefits of liberalizing), and the issue of effectiveness remains important. Regarding the latter, the lessons from recent crises can be interpreted as follows:

> Though the evidence that they can affect the total quantity of capital flows remains weak, there is substantial evidence that they can affect the composition of inflows.

It may make a difference for the effectiveness of controls whether a country has previously liberalized its capital account, whether controls are intended to apply to inflows or outflows, and whether they are applied in normal times or in the midst of a crisis. Several developing countries that had previously liberalized their capital accounts imposed controls on capital inflows before the Mexican crisis. As we saw in Chapter 14 these episodes, particularly the one in Chile, have received a substantial amount of attention. The evidence we reviewed there indicated that there is weak support for the view that these controls have succeeded in affecting the volume of total capital inflows, but stronger evidence that they have affected the composition of inflows. Whether the reimposition of controls in the midst of a crisis (as in Malaysia in 1998) can effectively restrict capital outflows, however, remains problematic.

2. Exchange Rate Policy

i. Misalignment. We have emphasized previously that the combination of an open capital account and a fragile financial system is a dangerous one. It is dangerous because in the event of a speculative attack, the government is unlikely to tolerate the high interest rates necessary to defend the currency, and thus the attack is more likely to be successful. But a weak financial sector does not *in itself* mean that the exchange rate peg is unsustainable. Thus, the peg would collapse only if the attack happened. That is, the currency becomes vulnerable to a *self-fulfilling* attack. But why should an attack happen at all? For an attack to happen, something has to coordinate the expectations of speculators.

A likely candidate is overvaluation of the domestic currency. If the currency is overvalued, then a real depreciation must happen. The only question is whether it will be brought about through a nominal devaluation or through an adjustment in relative prices. But as we saw in Chapter 16, with sticky prices an adjustment in relative prices typically requires a domestic recession. Because this would undermine the viability of the domestic financial sector, the authorities are unlikely to tolerate this mode of adjustment when the domestic financial sector is fragile. Thus, currency overvaluation is likely to be corrected through a nominal devaluation under these circumstances, and the knowledge that this is so will help to trigger speculation against the currency. The implication is:

> The costs of exchange rate misalignment can be very high when the capital account is open and the domestic financial sector is fragile.

This was indeed probably the central lesson of the Southern Cone policy experience, and the most recent crises in Mexico and Thailand have served to confirm it. As we saw, in both cases, the domestic financial sector was weak as a result of inappropriate previous liberalization in the context of an open capital account, and the currency was overvalued, though for different reasons. When speculation against the domestic currency materialized, the authorities found themselves unable to mount the traditional high-interest defense, and the currency collapsed.

ii. Credibility. Exchange rate misalignment and a fragile financial system increase the costs to the authorities of maintaining a fixed exchange rate. Thus, they make it more likely that a fixed exchange rate will be abandoned if attacked, and the increased likelihood that an attack will be successful makes it more likely that an attack will happen. One way that the monetary authorities can try to prevent attacks is to signal their commitment to the fixed exchange rate. If this signal is credible, it makes it less likely that an attack will be successful, and thus less likely that an attack will happen. The authorities can signal commitment by willingly imposing costs on themselves for changing the exchange rate. Unfortunately, one lesson of the recent crises is that successful "precommitment mechanisms" are hard to come by. Two such precommitment mechanisms, the adoption of currency boards and the issuance of foreign-currency-denominated debt, have been tried recently, and neither one managed to insulate the countries that tried them from speculative attacks. The lessons are the following:

> Exchange rate credibility cannot be achieved automatically through the adoption of a currency board.

As we have seen previously, Hong Kong implemented a currency board in 1984, and Argentina did so in 1991, the latter as part of an exchange-rate-based stabilization plan. Because the adoption of a currency board precludes a country from orienting monetary policy to domestic objectives, it sends a strong signal that the authorities are prepared to sacrifice domestic for external objectives. Moreover, because the currency board arrangement, including the prevailing exchange rate, is typically enshrined in the constitution of the country, it is costly to change. Nonetheless, it is not *impossible* to change, and recent experience suggests that this seems to make all the difference.

Despite its currency board, the Argentine peso came under heavy speculative attack in the first quarter of 1995, in the wake of the Mexican crisis. This loss of credibility of the Argentine currency board shows up in the form of large increases in the peso-dollar interest rate differential in the first quarter of 1995. The collapse of the monetary base nearly destroyed the Argentine banking system, which lost nearly a third of its deposits during this time. As a result, domestic interest rates increased sharply and the economy went into a severe recession, sending the unemployment rate to 18 percent. Similarly, Hong Kong failed to escape the Asian "flu," having been hit by a very strong speculative attack in October 1997. As in the case of Argentina, domestic interest rates rose, asset values fell, and the real economy fell into recession.

It is worth noting that in both cases there were forces at work that would have tended to increase the credibility of the currency board – specifically, the popularity of the inflation stabilization that Argentina achieved through the currency board arrangement, and the large foreign exchange reserves and sound banking system in Hong Kong. These advantages were clearly not sufficient to convince speculators that these countries would necessarily adhere to their currency board arrangements.[2] It is notable, moreover, that both speculative attacks in fact failed, implying that the authorities' true resolve was underestimated by speculators. Thus, in these cases the currency board arrangement proved inadequate as a means for communicating the authorities' true commitment.

A less drastic commitment device is for the government to issue indexed debt. This is a "poison pill" strategy for achieving credibility in which the authorities would actually impose a large fiscal cost on themselves by devaluing. This helps address the time consistency problem that may underlie expectations of devaluation, since it reduces the net benefits that the government can reap from devaluation. As we saw in the last chapter, this was the strategy pursued by Mexico in response to reserve outflows and expectations of devaluation triggered by the assassination of presidential candidate Luis Donaldo Colosio in March 1994.[3] Mexico's subsequent currency crisis suggests the following lesson:

> Exchange rate credibility cannot be bought by converting domestic-currency government debt to foreign-currency debt.

The problem with this strategy is that, while issuing indexed debt may reduce the net benefits of devaluation to the government, this may not be enough to tip the scales in favor of retaining the exchange rate peg, either in actuality or in the eyes

---

[2] To be fair, there were also disadvantages that may have made both currency boards appear fragile, specifically, the weaknesses of Argentina's banking system and the fairly recent (summer of 1997) change in Hong Kong's political status.

[3] Recall that the share of indexed *Tesobonos* in total public debt increased from less than 5 percent at the beginning of 1994 to over 55 percent by the end of the year, while the share of privately held (nonindexed) *CETES* fell from 60 percent of total public debt in February to 20 percent by November 1994.

of speculators. Moreover, if the strategy does not succeed in sustaining the peg, then the costs of devaluation could be greatly magnified. It is at least arguable, for example, that the costs of the Mexican crisis arose largely because of the liquidity crisis (the refusal of creditors to roll over maturing *Tesobonos*) that followed the December 20 devaluation, and that this crisis in turn was brought on by the fiscal implications of the devaluation in the presence of a large stock of indexed debt.

3. Monetary Policy

The most obvious lesson from the recent crises for monetary policy is a familiar one:

> Maintaining an officially determined exchange rate, without following the gold-standard "rules of the game" (i.e., sterilizing) has always been and continues to be a dangerous strategy.

This is indeed an old lesson, learned under the Bretton Woods system, which was brought down by the refusal of the United States to devote its monetary policy to the maintenance of the dollar gold parity, and by that of the European countries to accept the monetary growth rates that would have been implied by the gold standard "rules of the game," given the expansionary monetary policy in the United States. It has only been confirmed by recent events:

i. In 1992, the ERM crisis was triggered by the conflict between, on the one hand, the high interest rates required in Italy and the United Kingdom in order to maintain their parity to the Deutschmark, and on the other hand, the low interest rates required to combat recession in both countries.
ii. The December 1994 Mexican crisis was the product of the decision to resist the domestic deflationary effects of an increase in foreign interest rates and in the country risk premium by sterilizing reserve losses and borrowing short-term in foreign exchange. The result was to undermine the exchange rate and, as already indicated, to weaken the government's fiscal position when the inevitable devaluation eventually came.
iii. The Asian countries did the same thing under the opposite circumstances in 1995–96. They sterilized capital inflows, increasing their burden of short-term external debt. Thailand also sterilized when capital began to flow out in 1996–97.

In all of these cases, countries were unwilling to give up domestic objectives for external ones, and the result was the sudden collapse of the currency.

Since it will always be impossible for monetary policy, which is only one instrument, to achieve two objectives, this implies the need to abandon an objective or complement monetary policy with another instrument. We'll come back to this below.

The lesson for monetary policy has to do with the effectiveness of the gold-standard "rules of the game" in achieving the objective of protecting the currency:

> It may generally be possible to create a crisis with excessively expansionary monetary policy, but under certain circumstances, it may not be possible to prevent one with restrictive monetary policy.

The circumstance in question is one in which the financial sector is extremely fragile. When the domestic financial system is weak, restrictive monetary policy may be unable to save the currency. The reason is that the rules of the game call for the central bank to adopt a restrictive monetary policy in response to a loss of reserves triggered by a capital outflow. When this happens, the government has two choices:

i. If it is unwilling to sacrifice the domestic financial system by allowing domestic interest rates to rise, then it will be unable to defend the currency. That just means that it's unwilling to play by the rules of the game because the costs to the domestic economy of doing so when the rues call for a monetary contraction are very steep.
ii. But even if it is willing to let domestic interest rates rise, that may not save the currency. High domestic interest rates may cause the domestic financial system to fail. Depositors may switch into foreign currency in the expectation that the government may have to inflate to pay the costs of a bailout.

In other words, the attempt to protect the currency may bring about a financial crisis that leads to a balance of payments crisis, which in turn causes the fixed exchange rate to be abandoned anyway. Under these circumstances the currency peg is doomed.

In the previous case, the central bank may be unable to achieve its external objective, even if it is willing to abandon any concern it may have for domestic objectives in order to do so. While this is bad enough, a third lesson from recent crises is that things can actually get worse: there is an alternative set of circumstances under which the central bank may be unable to achieve *neither* domestic nor external objectives:

> When currency mismatches are important and the financial sector is fragile, monetary policy may be left with no desirable options.

This appears to be the central lesson of the Asian financial crises for monetary policy. When the financial sector is weak and currency mismatches are absent, the central bank may not be able to safeguard the currency, but it can at least protect the domestic economy by allowing the exchange rate to float. A depreciation of the currency in this case would imperil the financial system much less than would an increase in domestic interest rates, so abandoning the currency and allowing it to depreciate would at least prevent a domestic economic contraction. But when currency mismatches are substantial, either in the balance sheets of their banks or in those of their customers, allowing the currency to depreciate would undermine the net worth of the banks, either directly or indirectly through that of their customers, and thus bring on a financial crisis and economic contraction.

In this case, monetary policy is simply left with no desirable options. There are in fact three ways to respond to an attack on the currency under these circumstances:

i. Attempt to defend the currency with tight monetary policy. This policy would reflect the view that the currency mismatch makes currency depreciation a greater danger to the solvency of banks and their customers than are high domestic interest rates. This was the controversial policy that the International Monetary Fund initially pursued in the Asian countries, until currency markets appeared to stabilize. As mentioned above, it is a dangerous policy if the credit channel for monetary policy is strong (so many domestic firms do not have access to borrowing outside the domestic banking system) and banks are weak, since a credit crunch may cause both firms and banks to fail, thereby driving capital out of the country and perhaps even failing to sustain the currency.

ii. Abandon the currency peg and expand the money supply. This policy would be indicated to safeguard the domestic economy if currency mismatches do not pose a danger to domestic firms and banks. It is the policy that was advocated for Brazil in the midst of its 1999 crisis by Professor Jeff Sachs of Harvard, and it does appear that floating the currency in Brazil did not have the disastrous effects that it had in the Asian countries or in Mexico (where the currency mismatch was in the public sector's balance sheet).

iii. Expand the money supply, but impose controls on capital outflows as a temporary expedient to permit the central bank to continue to defend the value of the currency. This is an option that some observers have argued needs to be taken seriously, and it is the one controversially adopted in Malaysia in September 1998. The obvious doubts about it concern the possible distortions created, the potential loss of credibility, and the question of whether the controls can be made to stick. The jury is still out on the Malaysian experience.

The three previous lessons have one common theme: under high capital mobility, monetary policy is a single policy instrument, that at best can achieve either one out of two (domestic and external) objectives, in the intermediate case can achieve one objective, and in the worst of all cases can achieve neither objective. This has a clear policy message, important enough to enshrine as a separate lesson:

> Financial sector difficulties can severely constrain what monetary policy can achieve. Thus, policies to ensure a sound financial sector (that is, one with limited vulnerability to high domestic interest rates and real exchange rate depreciation) are important not only because they help to promote efficient

intermediation and to avoid financial crises, but also because they increase the effectiveness of monetary policy.

But even under the best of circumstances – with a healthy and well-functioning financial system – the "impossible trinity" of open-economy macroeconomics suggests that monetary policy will find itself having to choose among competing external (the exchange rate) and domestic (economic activity) objectives. One instrument cannot be used to achieve two objectives, so this means abandoning an objective or finding additional instruments. One way to "abandon" an objective is to make the need to achieve it less pressing. The constraint imposed by the external objective can be softened somewhat by holding large stocks of net international reserves or by maintaining large international credit lines. But how large do reserve stocks have to be? Another lesson from recent crises is the following:

> With high capital mobility, international reserve adequacy should not be measured with respect to traditional "flow" variables (e.g., months of import coverage), but rather by comparing $M2$ plus short-term government debt to reserves.

The reason is that the sustainability of the exchange rate depends on a comparison between the central bank's stock of liquid foreign-exchange-denominated assets and its liquid liabilities. The latter consist not just of the monetary base, but also of assets that can readily be converted into base, which in turn includes all the liabilities of financial institutions explicitly or implicitly insured by the government. When capital mobility is high, all of these claims can be presented to the central bank in short order (rather than gradually through the purchase of imports). Thus, reserve adequacy must be assessed by a comparison between the outstanding stocks of such claims and the means to satisfy them.

Holding large stocks of reserves can prolong the time during which an economy can pursue a domestic objective without having to give up an exchange rate peg. This allows more time for automatic adjustment mechanisms to take effect (e.g., for transitory shocks to play themselves out, or for domestic wage-price adjustments to take place) or for other adjustment policies to be deployed. Thus, the existence of large stocks of reserves makes it less likely that an exchange rate will eventually succumb to a speculative attack, which in turn makes it less likely that the currency will be attacked.

An alternative to easing the constraints imposed by an objective is to deploy additional instruments. Economic theory tells us that under perfect capital mobility monetary and exchange rate policy are not independent instruments, since either monetary policy must be at the service of the exchange rate (i.e., there is no monetary autonomy under a fixed exchange rate) or the exchange rate must adjust automatically to be consistent with the prevailing monetary policy, making the exchange rate a function of monetary policy (and thus preventing the two instruments from being deployed independently). Thus:

> The use of the exchange rate and monetary policy as independent instruments (in the short run) requires the presence of capital account restrictions. As "natural" barriers to capital movements have declined, monetary autonomy tends to decrease.

One interpretation of the recent crises, as mentioned above, is that central banks in the emerging economies that experienced crises (specifically in Mexico and Thailand) ignored this lesson and continued to pursue domestic objectives with monetary policy that were inconsistent with the fixed exchange rate. One way to explain their doing so is that they overestimated the degree of monetary autonomy they retained given the degree of integration their economies had achieved with world capital markets. A policy implication of this lesson is that to continue to exercise a degree of monetary autonomy comparable to what these economies had enjoyed in the past, it would have been necessary to replace the "natural" barriers that were weakened by technological and institutional developments by policy-induced ones, though the feasibility of this option remains problematic, as indicated previously.

It is worth noting that barriers to capital movements, if effective, by definition increase the costs of moving funds in and out of individual countries, and as such make these countries less vulnerable to speculative attacks. This suggests a final lesson for monetary policy, which combines elements of the two previous ones:

> A combination of large reserve stocks and barriers on capital movements appears to have been effective in resisting financial contagion, even when financial sector fragility and possible exchange rate overvaluation would have suggested vulnerability to speculative attacks.

This appears to have been a key lesson from the experience of China, which survived the Asian financial crisis in much better condition than many of its neighbors.

4. Fiscal Policy

Another way to match instruments to targets would be to use fiscal policy in a countercyclical fashion. Observers such as Guillermo Calvo have pointed out that countercyclical (i.e., tight) fiscal policy would have had desirable effects during the capital inflow period, because it would have reduced pressures for macroeconomic overheating and real exchange rate appreciation while permitting domestic interest rates to fall and building up the net worth of the public sector as a cushion to facilitate a less restrictive fiscal stance during future downturns. A key lesson from both the capital-inflow period as well as the recent crises, however, has been the following:

> Except for the effects of automatic stabilizers, countercyclical fiscal policies have not been easy to implement in capital-importing developing countries.

> During the good times of the capital-inflow period fiscal tightening appears to be politically difficult, while during crisis times, tight fiscal policies are often advocated to facilitate the adjustment of the current account and promote capital inflows through market confidence.

The term "are often advocated" is used advisedly above. While the desirability of fiscal tightening during the inflow period has not been controversial (though its feasibility has been questioned), the appropriate role of fiscal policy during crises has been. Particularly when the cause of the crisis was not actual or prospective fiscal insolvency, it is hard to defend discretionary fiscal tightening, especially in the midst of a severe crisis-induced recession. Two possibilities exist. The first arises when the fiscal implications of banking system restructuring imperil the solvency of the public sector. In that case a fiscal adjustment (in present-value terms) will be required to avoid triggering wholesale capital flight caused by prospective taxation or confiscation of assets. The second is when currency mismatches threaten the viability of firms and banks. In that case, fiscal tightening may be indicated to minimize the overshooting of the real exchange rate required to adjust balance of payments flows.

The second lesson regarding fiscal policy is less dramatic:

> High-interest long-term debt may ultimately be cheaper than low-interest short-term debt.

This issue arose for the public sector in the case of Mexico, and with reference to private debt in the case of the Asian countries. The problem, of course, is that short-maturity debt increases the liquidity of the liability side of the balance sheet, increasing the vulnerability of the public sector – or of the economy – to liquidity crises.

II. LESSONS THAT WE HAVE *NOT* LEARNED

As mentioned previously, the lessons listed above would probably command reasonably wide, though certainly not universal, agreement. Other lessons have also been drawn from the recent crises which, if valid, would have important implications for domestic macroeconomic management. These "lessons," however, are much more controversial than the previous set. Because there are many controversies surrounding the recent crises, there are a large number of such "lessons" to draw from. The listing below is selective, emphasizing only a few that appear to be among the most important.

1. Structural Reforms

An important component of the IMF-supported adjustment programs in response to crises in Indonesia, Korea, and Thailand was a broad package of structural reforms, intended to address problems not just in the financial sector, but also in the areas of corporate governance and in the real sector more broadly. These "real" reforms have proven to be quite controversial. The question is whether they should have been pursued in the midst of the crises. Thus, we can express our first controversial "lesson" as:

> Crises present an opportunity to undertake needed (i.e., productive) structural changes.

The argument in favor of this proposition is that crises may tend to disrupt political equilibria that sustain harmful structural policies in place. Thus, the occasion of a crisis may provide an opportunity to implement needed and long-lasting changes that would have been politically impossible to carry out during normal times. The controversy around this "lesson" concerns the fact that even if they are needed and appropriate, structural reforms are usually politically sensitive and difficult to implement. Conditioning balance of payments assistance (i.e., liquidity support) on the implementation of such reforms therefore creates uncertainty about whether that assistance will be forthcoming to crisis countries. The result may be to undermine confidence in the resources underpinning the macroeconomic adjustment program designed to extract the country from the crisis, thereby weakening the program and possibly aggravating the crisis.

2. Exchange Rate Regimes

As we discussed in Chapter 18, many observers have drawn sweeping conclusions from the crises of the nineties about what types of exchange rate regimes remain feasible for emerging economies that maintain open capital accounts. Specifically, they have concluded that:

> Given high capital mobility, developing countries must choose between extreme exchange rate regimes: either fixed exchange rates or dollarization/ currency boards.

Many economists have taken this view. As we saw in Chapter 18, it depends on the observation that in a situation of high capital mobility, any fixed exchange rate is subject to speculative attack, and the suspicion that in such circumstances most countries will not find it desirable to incur the costs associated with a sustained high-interest rate defense. Since we have already examined this argument in the previous chapter, there is no need to explore it further here.

3. Sources of Currency Mismatches

As we saw in Chapter 18, currency mismatches in the balance sheets of domestic firms and financial institutions can trigger speculative attacks. We also discussed earlier in this chapter how currency mismatches can complicate monetary management during crises. The question is why such currency mismatches arise. One "lesson" that has been drawn about the source of such mismatches from recent experience is the following:

> Officially determined exchange rate encourages currency mismatches in the balance sheets of domestic agents.

The argument in support of this view is that when the exchange rate is fixed, domestic agents tend to discount exchange rate risk. Consequently, when domestic interest rates exceed foreign ones, domestic agents tend to borrow in foreign currency, even if their assets are denominated in domestic currency, thus incurring exchange rate risk.

However, there are several problems with this story. First, higher interest rates on domestic-currency loans than on foreign-currency loans presumably reflect a perception of exchange rate risk among domestic lenders. It is unclear why there should be an asymmetry in perceived exchange rate risk between domestic lenders and borrowers. Second, if a fixed exchange rate really lowers the perception of exchange rate risk among all market participants, it is not clear why loans extended by foreign lenders to domestic borrowers would tend to be denominated systematically in foreign exchange. Presumably a credibly fixed exchange rate would lower exchange rate risk for both parties in the transaction, leaving indeterminate the currency of denomination of the loan. Finally, it is not at all clear that the mere announcement of a fixed exchange rate indeed reduces perceived exchange rate risk. As we saw earlier in this chapter, even countries that have buttressed their fixed exchange rates with the institutional apparatus associated with "hard" pegs (e.g., currency boards) have not been immune from the perception of currency risk. A more credible explanation for the emergence of currency mismatches probably has to rely on a moral hazard argument, in other words domestic borrowers are willing to assume exchange rate risk because they believe that in the event of a large depreciation of the domestic currency they will receive financial support from the government. But the factors giving rise to currency mismatches remain to be clearly identified.

4. Monetary and Fiscal Responses to Crises

A final controversial "lesson" concerns the appropriate monetary and fiscal response to the types of crises that some emerging economies have undergone in the nineties – specifically to crises featuring potential financial sector insolvency associated with currency mismatches in balance sheets:

> Responses to crises should feature tighter monetary and fiscal policies.

As we have seen, the argument for fiscal tightness can take two forms:

a. If the financial sector is prospectively insolvent, the public sector will have large contingent liabilities associated with the cost of recapitalizing domestic financial institutions. Since such liabilities may threaten the solvency of the public sector itself, tighter fiscal policies (in the form of a larger adjusted primary surplus, as in Chapter 6) are required to safeguard the solvency of the public sector.

b. Even if the public sector's solvency is not prospectively at risk, tighter fiscal policies will facilitate the adjustment in the current account of the balance of payments required by the drying up of capital inflows, thus reducing the required adjustment in the exchange rate (as in the liquidity-crisis model of Chapter 20).

The counter argument is that tightening fiscal policy in the context of a crisis, when the government's solvency is not at risk, is to cause fiscal policy to behave pro-cyclically, thereby aggravating the severity of the recession associated with the crisis. The jury is still out on this issue. It is easy to see that the outcome should depend on a host of characteristics that may vary from one country to another (e.g., on the composition of the fiscal contraction, the impact of fiscal policy on aggregate demand, the sensitivity of the current account to the exchange rate, the extent of currency mismatches in domestic balance sheets, and so on).

With respect to monetary policy, the argument for tight money is that it is required to defend the exchange rate, and thus minimize the damage to balance sheets from currency mismatches. The counterargument is that tight money will be ineffective in protecting the currency, because the damage that high domestic interest rates can do to the real economy under circumstances of financial fragility may actually repel capital flows, rather than attract them. This remains an unsettled issue, which is the subject of current research.

III. CONCLUSION

Based on the lessons that we have reviewed in this chapter, what can we say about the likely components of desirable domestic macroeconomic management in emerging economies in the context of an increasingly integrated world? A successful strategy would seem to entail the following:

a. First and foremost, the crises of the nineties in developing countries (and the Southern Cone crises of the early eighties) suggest strongly that the financial system can be the Achilles' heel of domestic macroeconomic management. Thus, structural policies to maintain a healthy financial system without severe currency mismatches and with substantial net worth, minimizing its vulnerability to exchange rate depreciation and high interest rates, should be high on the policy agenda. This is good for its own sake, but also helps to reserve the flexibility of monetary policy.

b. Structural policies that would tend to promote wage-price flexibility would be a useful complement. But what such policies are, and how successful they can be, are difficult questions to answer. We do not currently know enough about the causes of nominal wage-price rigidities to say much about these issues.

c. For countries that choose to maintain an officially determined exchange rate, the maintenance of a large stock of net international reserves – or an equivalent arrangement to provide liquid foreign currency assets in a pinch – would seem to be desirable. This reduces the urgency of having to continuously achieve external balance objectives. Side benefits are likely to be to reduce currency risk premia and the incidence of speculative attacks.

d. Even for such countries, it would seem desirable for exchange rate policy to allow some flexibility within a band, with a central parity that tracks the equilibrium real exchange rate. The difficulty, of course, is whether we can know what this is. Specifically, can we know when fundamentals change permanently and how large their empirical effect on the equilibrium real exchange rate should be? Chapter 16 suggested that this remains at present more of an art than a science.

e. Fiscal flexibility is a highly desirable goal in a financially integrated world, to provide an additional stabilization instrument to achieve internal balance. But the amount of fiscal flexibility that countries can realistically achieve should probably not be overestimated.

Finally, to end this book on a positive note, it is worth noting that the lessons reviewed in this chapter can indeed be learned. The case of Chile provides an example. The crises in Mexico and Thailand during the 1990s had as a precursor the Chilean crisis of 1982, and while Mexico and Thailand do not seem to have learned the lessons of the earlier Chilean crisis, Chile itself seems to have done so.

The management of capital inflows in Chile during the 1990s provides an interesting contrast with that of Mexico and Thailand. Like Mexico and Thailand, Chile entered the most recent capital inflow episode in a solid fiscal position. Because of lessons learned from its earlier financial crisis, however, Chile also entered the most recent episode with a liberalized, but secure and well-regulated, financial system. Its exchange rate policy was explicitly geared to the maintenance of a competitive real exchange rate, and the authorities managed the exchange rate flexibly to avoid misalignment, including revaluing the rate when necessary, a measure that signaled their intention to track the equilibrium rate.[4] These policies together precluded the emergence of the exchange market pressures that confronted Mexico and Thailand.

Perhaps more importantly, Chile also took measures to protect itself from vulnerability to a liquidity crisis, a situation which, as the model of Section I indicated, could have emerged independently of a prior exchange rate crisis and could itself have triggered such a crisis (of the self-fulfilling variety). Chile did so by explicitly targeting both its current account deficit through the use of exchange rate and aggregate demand policies, as well as the composition of its external debt through

---

[4] Though no developing country – including Chile – appears to have found the key to flexible countercyclical fiscal management, Chile was among those countries (as Thailand had been earlier) that explicitly attempted to use fiscal policy in a discretionary fashion as a tool to combat the overheating pressures emanating from inflows.

policies such as exchange rate variability within a wide band and the imposition of capital account restrictions designed to affect the structure of external debt.

However, no matter how appropriate its policies, no small country that is well integrated into the international real and financial economy can insulate itself from international economic upheavals on the scale of those caused by the Asian financial crisis, and Chile is not an exception to this rule. Transmission of the crisis to Chile, however, was primarily through real rather than financial channels. Overall, the country has weathered the period of volatile capital flows following its reintegration into the world financial economy remarkably well. The lessons of the broad capital-inflow experience, as well as the less fortunate later lessons from the experiences of Mexico and Thailand, suggest that Chile's successful performance has not been accidental.

References

Agenor, Pierre-Richard, and Peter J. Montiel (1999). *Development Macroeconomics, Second Edition* (Princeton: Princeton University Press).

Alba, Pedro, Amar Bhattacharya, Stijn Claessens, Swati Ghosh, and Leonardo Hernandez (1998). "Volatility and Contagion in a Financially-Integrated World: Lessons From East Asia's Recent Experience" (mimeo, World Bank, September).

Alesina, Alberto, Alessandro Prati, and Guido Tabellini (1990). "Public Confidence and Debt Management: A Model and a Case Study of Italy," in R. Dornbusch and M. Draghi, eds., *Public Debt Management: Theory and History* (Cambridge: Cambridge University Press), pp. 94–117.

Anand, Ritu, and Sweder Van Wijnbergen (1989). "Inflation and the Financing of Government Expenditure: An Introductory Analysis with an Application to Turkey." *World Bank Economic Review* (January), pp. 17–38.

Aryeetey, Ernest (1992). "The Relationship Between the Formal and Informal Sectors of the Financial Market in Ghana." African Economic Research Consortium Research Paper 10 (October).

Bacchetta, Philippe, and Eric van Wincoop (1998). "Does Exchange Rate Stability Increase Trade and Capital Flows?" National Bureau of Economic Research Working Paper 6704 (August).

Bagehot, Walter (1999). *Lombard Street* (New York: John Wiley & Sons).

Balino, Tomas, and V. Sundararajan (1991). *Banking Crises: Cases and Issues* (Washington, D.C.: International Monetary Fund).

Barro, Robert J. (1994). "Economic Growth and Convergence." International Center for Economic Growth Occasional Paper 46.

–––––– (1996). "Inflation and Growth." Federal Reserve Bank of St. Louis *Review* 78, no. 3 (May/June).

Barro, Robert J., and David B. Gordon (1983). "Rules, Discretion, and Reputation in a Model of Monetary Policy." *Journal of Monetary Economics* 12, pp. 101–21.

Bartolini, Leonardo, and Allan Drazen (1995). "Capital Account Liberalization as a Signal" (mimeo, International Monetary Fund, April).

Bosworth, Barry, and Susan Collins (1996). "Economic Growth in East Asia: Accumulation Versus Assimilation." *Brookings Papers on Economic Activity 2*.

Bruno, Michael, and William Easterly (1995). "Inflation Crises and Long-Run Growth" (mimeo, World Bank, June).

Calvo, Guillermo (1988). "Servicing the Public Debt: The Role of Expectations." *American Economic Review* 78, pp. 647–61.

–––––– (1991). "The Perils of Sterilization." International Monetary Fund *Staff Papers*, 38, no. 4 (December), pp. 921–26.

———— (1996). "Capital Flows and Macroeconomic Management: Tequila Lessons" (mimeo, International Monetary Fund).

Calvo, Guillermo, Leonardo Leiderman, and Carmen Reinhart (1993). "Capital Inflows to Latin America: The Role of External Factors." International Monetary Fund *Staff Papers* (March), pp. 108–51.

Calvo, Guillermo, and Enrique G. Mendoza (1996). "Reflections on Mexico's Balance of Payments Crisis: A Chronicle of a Death Foretold." *Journal of International Economics* 41 (November), pp. 235–64.

Cardenas, Mauricio S., and Felipe Barrera (1993). "Efectos Macroeconomicos de los Capitales Extranjeros: El Caso Colombiano." Interamerican Development Bank Working Paper 147 (June).

Cardoso, Eliana, and Ilan Goldfajn (1997). "Capital Flows to Brazil: The Endogeneity of Capital Controls." International Monetary Fund Working Paper WP/97/115 (September).

Carroll, Chris, and David N. Weil (1993). "Saving and Growth: A Reinterpretation." National Bureau of Economic Research Working Paper 4470 (September).

Chamley, Christophe, and Patrick Honohan (1990). "Taxation of Financial Intermediation: Measurement Principles and Applications to Five African Countries." World Bank WPS 421 (May).

Chipeta, C., and M.L.C. Mkandawire (1992). "Links Between the Informal and Formal/Semi-Formal Financial Sectors in Malawi." African Economic Research Consortium Research Paper 14 (November).

Chinn, Menzie (1998). "Before the Fall: Were East Asian Currencies Overvalued?" National Bureau of Economic Research Working Paper 6491 (April).

Chuhan, Punam, Stijn Claessens, and Nlandu Mamingi (1993). "Equity and Bond Flows to Latin America and Asia: The Role of Global and Country Factors." World Bank, IECIF Policy Research Working Paper 1160 (July).

Corbo, Vittorio, and Patricio Rojas (1995). "Exchange Rate Volatility, Investment, and Growth: Some New Evidence" (mimeo, World Bank).

Cukierman, Alex, Steven B. Webb, and Bilin Neyapti (1992). "Measuring Central Bank Independence and Its Effect on Policy Outcomes." *World Bank Economic Review* 6, no. 3, pp. 353–98.

———— (1994). "Measuring Central Bank Independence and Its Effect on Policy Outcomes." International Center for Economic Growth Occasional Paper 58.

Dayal-Gulati, Anuradha, and Christian Thimann (1997). Saving in Southeast Asia and Latin America Compared: Searching for Policy Lessons." IMF Working Paper WP/97/110 (September).

De Gregorio, Jose, and Pablo Guidotti (1996). "Financial Development and Economic Growth," in A. Solimano, ed., *Road Maps to Prosperity: Essays on Growth and Development* (Ann Arbor: University of Michigan Press), pp. 237–66.

Demigurc-Kunt, Asli, and Enrica Detragiache (1998). "The Determinants of Banking Crises in Developing and Developed Countries, IMF *Staff Papers* 45, no. 1 (March), pp. 81–109.

———— (2000). "Does Deposit Insurance Increase Banking Sector Stability?" IMF Working Paper WP/00/3 (January).

Diaz-Alejandro, Carlos (1985). "Good-Bye Financial Repression, Hello Financial Crash." *Journal of Development Economics* 19, pp. 1–24.

Dooley, Michael P. (1994). "Are Recent Capital Inflows to Developing Countries a Vote for or Against Economic Policy Reforms?" University of California, Santa Cruz Working Paper 295 (May).

———— (1995). "A Survey of Academic Literature on Controls over International Capital Transactions." NBER Working Paper 5352 (November).

———— (1997). "A Model of Crises in Emerging Markets." National Bureau of Economic Research Working Paper 6300 (December).

Dooley, Michael, Eduardo Fernandez-Arias, and Kenneth Kletzer (1994). "Is the Debt Crisis History? Recent Pivate Capital Inflows to Developing Countries." National Bureau of Economic Research Working Paper 4792 (July).

Dornbusch, Rudiger, and Alejandro Werner (1994). "Mexico: Stabilization, Reform, and No Growth." *Brookings Papers on Economic Activity* 1, pp. 253–98.

Drees, Burkhard, and Ceyla Pazarbasioglu (1995). "The Nordic Banking Crisis: Pitfalls in Financial Liberalization?" International Monetary Fund Working Paper WP/95/61 (June).

Easterly, William (2000). *The Quest for Growth* (Cambridge: MIT Press).

Easterly, William, and Klaus Schmidt-Hebbel (1994). "Fiscal Adjustment and Macroeconomic Performance: A Synthesis," in W. Easterly and K. Schmidt-Hebbel, *Public Sector Deficits and Macroeconomic Performance* (Oxford: Oxford University Press), pp. 15–78.

Edwards, Sebastian (1998). "Capital Flows, Real Exchange Rates, and Capital Controls: Some Latin American Experiences." National Bureau of Economic Research Working Paper 6800 (November).

Eichengreen, Barry, Andrew K. Rose, and Charles Wyplosz (1995). "Exchange Market Mayhem: The Antecedents and Aftermath of Speculative Attacks." *Economic Policy* 21 (October), pp. 249–312.

Fernald, John, Hali Edison, and Prakash Loungani (1998). "Was China the First Domino? Assessing Links Between China and the Rest of Emerging Asia." Board of Governors of the Federal Reserve System, International Finance Discussion Paper No. 604 (March).

Fernandez-Arias, Eduardo (1994). "The New Wave of Private Capital Inflows: Push or Pull?" World Bank, IECIF Policy Research Working Paper 1312 (June).

Fischer, Bernhard, and Helmut Reisen (1993). *Financial Opening: Why, How, When*, International Center for Economic Growth (San Francisco: ICS Press).

Fischer, Stanley (1993). "Does Macroeconomic Policy Matter? Evidence from Developing Countries." International Center for Economic Growth Occasional Paper 27.

———— (1993). "The Role of Macroeconomic Factors in Growth." *Journal of Monetary Economics*, pp. 485–512.

Frankel, Jeffrey A., and Andrew K. Rose (1996). "Currency Crises in Emerging Markets: Empirical Indicators." National Bureau of Economic Research Working Paper 5437 (January).

Frankel, Jeffrey A., and Shang-Jin Wei (1994). "Yen Bloc or Dollar Bloc? Exchange Rate Policies of the East Asian Economies," in T. Ito and A. Krueger, eds., *Macroeconomic Linkages: Savings, Exchange Rates, and Capital Flows* (Chicago: University of Chicago Press), pp. 295–329.

Galbis, Vicente (1993). "High Real Interest Rates Under Financial Liberalization: Is There a Problem?" International Monetary Fund Working Paper WP/93/7 (January).

Gavin, Michael, and Ricardo Hausmann (1996). "The Roots of Banking Crises: The Macroeconomic Context," in R. Hausmann and L. Rojas-Suarez, eds., *Banking Crises in Latin America* (Washington D.C.: Inter-American Development Bank).

Gertler, Mark, and Andrew Rose (1991). "Finance, Growth, and Public Policy." World Bank Policy Research Working Paper WPS 814 (December).

Ghosh, Atish R., Anne-Marie Gulde, Jonathan Ostry, and Holger Wolf (1997). "Does the Nominal Exchange Regime Matter?" National Bureau of Economic Research Working Paper 5874 (January).

Giavazzi, Francesco, and Marco Pagano (1990). "Confidence Crises and Public Debt Management," in R. Dornbusch and M. Draghi, eds., *Public Debt Management: Theory and History* (Cambridge: Cambridge University Press), pp. 125–42.

Giovannini, Alberto, and Martha de Melo (1993). "Government Revenue From Financial Repression." *American Economic Review* (September), pp. 953–63.

Goldfajn, Ilan, and Rodrigo Valdes (1999). "The Aftermath of Appreciations." *Quarterly Journal of Economics* 114 (February), pp. 229–62.

Gooptu, Sudarshan (1994). "Are Portfolio Flows to Emerging Markets Complementary or Competitive?" World Bank Policy Research Paper 1360 (September).

Grilli, Vittorio, and Gian Maria Milesi-Ferretti (1995). "Economic Effects and Structural Determinants of Capital Controls." International Monetary Fund *Staff Papers* 42, no. 3 (September), pp. 517–51.

Guidotti, Pablo, and Moammar Kumar (1991). "Domestic Public Debt of the Externally Indebted Countries." Occasional Paper 80, IMF (June).

Hadjimichael, Michael, Thomas Rumbaugh, and Eric Verreydt (1992). "The Gambia: Economic Adjustment in a Small Open Economy." International Monetary Fund Occasional Paper 100 (October).

Haque, Nadeem, and Peter J. Montiel (1999). "Long-Run Real Exchange Rate Changes in Developing Countries: Simulations From An Econometric Model," in L. Hinkle and P. Montiel, eds., *Exchange Rate Misalignment: Concepts and Measurement for Developing Countries* (Oxford: Oxford University Press).

Hernandez, Leonardo, and Heinz Rudolph (1994). "Domestic Factors, Sustainability, and Soft Landing in the New Wave of Private Capital Inflows" (mimeo, World Bank, November).

Hinkle, Lawrence, and Peter J. Montiel, eds. (1999). *Exchange Rate Misalignment: Concepts and Measurement for Developing Countries* (Oxford: Oxford University Press).

Hutchinson, Michael, and Kathleen McDill (1999). "Are All Banking Crises Alike? The Japanese Experience In International Comparison." National Bureau of Economic Research *Working Paper* 7253 (July).

Hyuha, M., M. O. Ndanshau, and J. P. Kipokola (1993). "Scope, Structure, and Policy Implications of Informal Financial Markets in Tanzania." African Economic Research Consortium *Research Paper* 18 (April).

Ikhide, S. I. (1992). "Financial Deepening, Credit Availability, and the Efficiency of Investment: Evidence from Selected African Countries." UN Economic Commission for Africa, Development Research Paper No. 2 (October).

Kaminsky, Graciela L., and Carmen M. Reinhart (1998). "On Crises, Contagion, and Confusion" (mimeo, University of Maryland).

——— (1999). "The Twin Crises: The Causes of Banking and Balance-of-Payments Problems." *American Economic Review* 89, pp. 473–500.

Kapur, Ishan, Michael Hadjimichael, Paul Hilbers, Jerald Schiff, and Philippe Szymczak (1991). "Ghana: Adjustment and Growth, 1983–91." International Monetary Fund Occasional Paper 86 (September).

King, Robert G., and Ross Levine (1992). "Financial Intermediation and Economic Development" (mimeo, World Bank, June).

——— (1993). "Finance, Entrepreneurship, and Growth: Theory and Evidence." *Journal of Monetary Economics* 32, pp. 513–42.

Krugman, Paul (1979). "A Model of Balance of Payments Crises." *Journal of Money, Credit, and Banking* (August), pp. 311–25.

——— (1993). "Target Zones and Exchange Rate Dynamics," in P. Krugman, ed., *Currencies and Crises* (Cambridge: MIT Press), pp. 77–89.

Laban, Raul, and Felipe Larrain (1993). "Can a Liberalization of Capital Outflows Increase Net Capital Inflows?" Department of Economics, Pontifica Universidad Catolica de Chile (June).

Le Fort, Guillermo V., and Carlos Budnevich (1996). "Capital Account Regulations and Macroeconomic Policy: Two Latin American Experiences." *Studies on International Monetary and Financial Issues for the Group of Twenty-Four, Report to the Group of Twenty-Four* (mimeo, The Group of Twenty-Four, March).

Levine, Ross (1992). "Financial Structure and Economic Development." World Bank Policy Research Working Paper WPS 849 (February).

——— (1996). "Financial Development and Economic Growth: Views and Agenda." World Bank Policy Research Working Paper 1678 (October).

Levine, Ross, and David Renelt (1992). "A Sensitivity Analysis of Cross-Country Growth Regressions." *American Economic Review* 82 (September), pp. 942–63.

Loayza, Norman, and J. Humberto Lopez (1997). "Misalignment and Fundamentals: Equilibrium Exchange Rates in Seven Latin American Countries" (mimeo, World Bank).

Mathieson, Donald J., and Liliana Rojas-Suarez (1993). "Liberalization of the Capital Account: Experiences and Issues." International Monetary Fund Occasional Paper 103 (March).

McKinnon, Ronald I. (1992). *The Order of Economic Liberalization* (Baltimore: Johns Hopkins University Press).

Mishkin, Frederic S. (1989). "Asymmetric Information and Financial Crises: A Historical Perspective," in R. Hubbard, ed., *Financial Markets and Financial Crises* (Chicago: University of Chicago Press), pp. 69–108.

Montiel, Peter J. (1992). "Fiscal Aspects of Developing-Country Debt Problems and DDSR Operations." Unpublished, World Bank (August).

———— (1996). "Financial Policies and Economic Growth: Theory, Evidence, and Country-Specific Experience from Sub-Saharan Africa." *Journal of African Economies, Part I,* 5, no. 3, pp. 65–98.

———— (1999). "Determinants of the Long-Run Equilibrium Real Exchange Rate: An Analytical Model," in L. Hinkle and P. Montiel, eds., *Exchange Rate Misalignment: Concepts and Measurement for Developing Countries* (Oxford: Oxford University Press).

Montiel, Peter J., and Carmen M. Reinhart (1999). "Do Capital Controls and Macroeconomic Policies Influence the Volume and Composition of Capital Flows? Evidence from the 1990s" (mimeo, Williams College).

Mussa, Michael (1986a). "Nominal Exchange Rate Regimes and the Behavior of Real Exchange Rates: Evidence and Implications," in K. Brunner and A. Meltzer, eds., *Real Business Cycles, Real Exchange Rates, and Actual Policies* (Amsterdam: North Holland).

———— (1986b). "The Effects of Commercial, Fiscal, Monetary, and Exchange Rate Policies on the Real Exchange Rate," in S. Edwards and L. Ahmed, eds., *Economic Adjustment and Exchange Rates in Developing Countries* (Chicago: University of Chicago Press), pp. 43–88.

Nissanke, Machiko (1991). "Mobilizing Domestic Resources for African Development and Diversification: Structural Impediments to Financial Intermediation," in A. Chibber and S. Fischer, eds., *Economic Reform in Sub-Saharan Africa* (Washington, D.C.: World Bank).

Ostry, Jonathan (1991). "Trade Liberalization in Developing Countries, Initial Trade Distortions, and Imported Intermediate Inputs." IMF *Staff Papers* 38 (September), pp. 447–80.

Page, John (1994). "The East Asian Miracle: Four Lessons for Development Policy," in S. Fischer and J. Rotenberg, eds., *NBER Macroeconomics Annual 1994* (Cambridge: MIT Press), pp. 219–68.

Patrick, Hugh T. (1994). "Comparisons, Contrasts, and Implications," Chapter 8 in Yung Chul Park and Hugh T. Patrick, *The Financial Development of Japan, Korea, and Taiwan: Growth, Repression, and Liberalization* (Oxford: Oxford University Press).

Patrick, Hugh T., and Yung Chul Park (1994). *The Financial Development of Japan, Korea, and Taiwan: Growth, Repression, and Liberalization* (Oxford: Oxford University Press), pp. xii, 384.

Quirk, Peter J., and Owen Evans (1995). "Capital Account Convertibility: Review of Experience and Implications for IMF Policies." International Monetary Fund Occasional Paper 131.

Radelet, Steven, and Jeffrey Sachs (1998). "The Onset of the East Asian Financial Crisis." National Bureau of Economic Research Working Paper 6680 (August).

Razin, Ofair, and Susan M. Collins (1997). "Real Exchange Rate Misalignments and Growth." National Bureau of Economic Research *Working Paper* 6174 (September).

Reinhart, Carmen M., and Steven Dunaway (1996). "Dealing with Capital Inflows: Are There Any Lessons?" UNU-WIDER Research for Action Working Paper 28.

Rodrik, Dani (1997). "TFPG Controversies, Institutions, and Economic Performance in East Asia." NBER Working Paper 5914 (February).

Roubini, N., and X. Sala-i-Martin (1992). "A Growth Model of Inflation, Tax Evasion, and Financial Repression." NBER WP 4062 (May).

Roubini, N., and X. Sala-i-Martin (1992). "Financial Repression and Economic Growth," *Journal of Development Economics* 39, pp. 5–30.

Sachs, Jefferey, Aaron Tornell, and Andres Velasco (1996). "Financial Crises in Emerging Markets: The Lessons from 1995." (mimeo, Harvard University, March).

Sarel, Michael (1997). "Growth in East Asia: What We Can and Cannot Infer." International Monetary Fund *Economic Issues* 1 (May).

Schadler, Susan, Maria Carkovic, Adam Bennett, and Robert Khan (1993). *Recent Experience with Surges in Capital Inflows.* International Monetary Fund Occasional Paper 108 (Washington, D.C.: International Monetary Fund).

Serven, Luis, and Andres Solimano (1993). "Economic Adjustment and Investment Performance in Developing Countries: The Experience of the Eighties," in L. Serven and A. Solimano, eds., *Striving for Growth After Adjustment: The Role of Capital Formation* (Washington, D.C.: World Bank), pp. 147–79.

Singh, Ajit (1995). "How Did East Asia Grow So Fast? Slow Progress Toward an Analytical Consensus." UNCTAD Working Paper No. 97 (February).

Steiner, Roberto (1995). "The Mexican Crisis: Why Did It Happen and What Can We Learn?" (mimeo, World Bank, March).

Tanboon, Surach (1998). "An Analysis of the Thai Currency in Retrospect." Unpublished, Williams College (May).

Taylor, Mark P., and Lucio Sarno (1997). "Capital Flows to Developing Countries: Long- and Short-Run Determinants." *World Bank Economic Review* 11 (September), pp. 451–70.

Thomas, Vinod, John Nash, and Associates (1991). *Best Practices in Trade Policy Reform* (London: Oxford University Press).

Tseng, Warda, and Robert Corber (1991). "Financial Liberalization, Money Demand, and Monetary Policy in Asian Countries." International Monetary Fund Occasional Paper no. 84 (March).

Turtelboom, Bart (1991). "Interest Rate Liberalization: Some Lessons From Africa." International Monetary Fund Working Paper WP/91/121 (December).

Valdes-Prieto, Salvador, and Marcelo Soto (1996). "New Selective Capital Controls in Chile: Are They Effective?" (mimeo, World Bank).

Vegh, Carlos (1992). "Stopping High Inflation." International Monetary Fund *Staff Papers* (September), pp. 626–95.

Velasco, Andres (1987). "Financial Crises and Balance of Payments Crises." *Journal of Development Economics* 27 (October), pp. 263–83.

Villanueva, Delano, and Abbas Mirakhor (1990). "Strategies for Financial Reforms." International Monetary Fund *Staff Papers* (September), pp. 509–36.

Vittas, Dimitri, and Yoon Je Cho (1995). "Credit Policies: Lessons from East Asia." World Bank Policy Research Working Paper 1458 (May).

Warner, Andrew M. (1992). "Did the Debt Crisis Cause the Investment Crisis?" *Quarterly Journal of Economics* (November), pp. 1161–86.

——— (1997). "Mexico's 1994 Exchange Rate Crisis Interpreted in Light of the Nontraded Model." National Bureau of Economic Research Working Paper 6165 (September).

Werner, Alejandro M. (1995). "The Currency Risk Premia in Mexico: A Closer Look at Interest Rate Differentials" (mimeo, International Monetary Fund, August).

Williamson, John (1991). "On Liberalizing the Capital Account," in R. O'Brien, ed., *Finance and the International Economy* (Oxford: Oxford University Press).

World Bank (1993). *The East Asian Miracle: Economic Growth and Public Policy* (New York: Oxford University Press).

——— (1994). *Adjustment in Africa: Reforms, Results, and the Road Ahead* (New York: Oxford University Press).

——— (1995). *Bureaucrats in Business: The Economics and Politics of Government Ownership* (New York: Oxford University Press).

——— (1997). *Private Capital Flows to Developing Countries: The Road to Financial Integration* (New York: Oxford University Press).

Index

adaptive expectations, and inflation stabilization, 138–9

adjusted primary deficit and surplus, 110, 112

adjustments. *See* financial reform; fiscal adjustment; macroeconomic adjustment process

adverse selection, and financial intermediation, 195

Africa. *See* Sub-Saharan Africa

agency costs, and financial intermediation, 196

aggregate demand, and domestic goods market, 29–34, 35

aggregate domestic financial wealth, 47–8

aggregate economic activity, and financial intermediation, 205–11

aggregate expenditure, and domestic goods market, 30

aggregate production function: and domestic goods market, 24, 28–9; and link between short-run macroeconomic performance and long-term economic growth, 4–7

Alba, Pedro, 395

Alesina, Alberto, 377–8

amortization payments, by public sector, 111–12

Anand, Ritu, 219n2

announcements, of exchange rates by central bank, 344–6

anticipated shocks, and goods and labor markets, 36–8

Argentina: and bank crises, 255–6; and capital inflows, 283, 301; and credibility of high interest rates, 403; and currency board, 164, 352, 353, 416–17; and debt crisis of 1980s,

154n7; and exchange rate management, 360–1; and financial integration, 407; and financial reform, 255–6, 273; and inflation stabilization, 144; and privatization, 181–2; and seignorage revenue, 122n9

Aryeetey, Ernest, 212

Asia, and "miracle" economies: and capital inflows, 283, 284, 301, 418; and currency crises, 366; and emergence of China as major exporter, 388, 393, 397; and financial integration, 407; and financial reform, 274–6; and financial repression, 226–37; and fragility of financial system, 384, 394–5; and monetary policy in Japan, 389. *See also specific countries*

asset demands, and balance sheets, 43–8

asset markets, and equilibrium of financial markets, 55–65, 66–7

asset pooling, and banks, 199

asset-price bubbles, and stock market, 205, 250. *See also* bubble factors

asset supplies, and equilibrium of financial markets, 48–54

asymmetric information, and financial transactions, 194–5. *See also* information content

Austria, and hyperinflation, 143

automatic stabilizer, and macroeconomic shocks, 350

balance sheets, and equilibrium of financial markets, 43–8, 66–7

Balassa-Samuelson effects, 393n16

Baliño, Tomas, 255–6

band width, and exchange rate management, 370–2, 373, 385